The Palace Square in St. Petersburg has come to represent revolutionary struggle in Russia because of events that took place there in 1825, 1905, and 1917. The Alexander Column and the Triumphal Arch celebrate victories of the War of 1812.

The
Great Ideas
Today

1994

Encyclopædia Britannica, Inc.

CHICAGO
AUCKLAND • LONDON • MADRID • MANILA • PARIS
ROME • SEOUL • SYDNEY • TOKYO • TORONTO

Library of Congress Number: 61-65561
International Standard Book Number: 0-85229-603-7
International Standard Serial Number: 0072-7288

A NOTE ON REFERENCE STYLE

In the following pages, passages in *Great Books of the Western World* are referred to by the initials "*GBWW*," followed by a roman numeral (indicating the first edition of 1952 [I] or the second edition of 1990 [II]) with volume and page number. Thus, "*GBWW* I: 5, 100; II: 4, 112" refers to a passage from Sophocles' *Oedipus the King,* which is on page 100 in Volume 5 of the first edition, and on page 112 in Volume 4 of the second edition. Sometimes only one reference will be given, since the contents of the first and second editions differ. Also note that passages quoted in an article may differ from the translation of that passage in either the first or second edition, since newer translations of some works are included in the second edition.

Gateway to the Great Books is referred to by the initials "*GGB*," followed by volume and page number. Thus, "*GGB* 10, 39–57" refers to pages 39 through 57 of Volume 10 of *Gateway to the Great Books,* which is James's essay, "The Will to Believe."

The Great Ideas Today is referred to by the initials "*GIT*," followed by the year and page number. Thus, "*GIT* 1968, 210" refers to page 210 of the 1968 edition of *The Great Ideas Today.*

Contents

Preface

The articles in this year's issue of *The Great Ideas Today* fall into our usual categories. There are discussions of the arts and sciences in Part One, reconsiderations of great books and ideas in Part Two, and a number of special features in Part Three; while Part Four, as is customary, is given over to reprints that will serve as "Additions to the Great Books Library."

Yet we discern, at least in the first three of these sections, a critical tone, a sense of taking issue, or a report that others have taken issue with the subjects at hand, which has not been present, or if present not nearly so marked, in previous volumes. The criticism is in no sense personal, nor is it concerned with the worth of anything under discussion. What is of concern is its truth, and whether that has been rightly grasped. The impression we are left with in these articles is that something is wrong with the current understanding of things, or perhaps with the understanding in which they were first conceived, and that we ought to be aware of the fact and reflect on it. Thus, our contributors are raising questions, trying to make us think, to consider their reservations carefully, and trying to wake us up.

Certainly, that is Evelyn Fox Keller's objective in the account she gives of developmental biology in Part One. Known for her writings on the significance of gender in science, she writes here of the role of the embryo in the formation of the organism, as distinct from the gene that was once thought to be wholly determinative, with everything programmed from the moment of conception. Is there not some familiar echo heard in this discussion? News has come of the death of Erik Erikson, the psychologist who did so much for our understanding of the ego as a thing subject to growth, not fixed from the beginning of life. Here again, a subject thought to be settled has had to be reopened. Not so, however, in religious matters, it appears. George Anastaplo's report on the Parliament of the World's Religions held at Chicago in 1993 indicates that in the century since the first such gathering the idea of God had disappeared from its program, though every euphemism was tried, and though the lack of such a presence, or any stated belief in it, was an embarrassment.

There are problems of a different sort, Otto Bird suggests, in Lucretius's *De Rerum Natura* (On the Nature of Things) of which he writes about in Part Two of our volume. Lucretius argues that because death is inevitable it ought not to be feared, still less hated, as men do, but he does not see that this attitude is a reflection of the passion for life and the wish for some purpose that distinguishes human existence. The poem is in some way unsatisfactory because of that. Not as grave is the concern of Jon Elster in the discussion of Tocqueville's *Democracy in America* that follows, but once again defects are found in a great book, while its virtues are carefully noted. And not a book in doubt, but a subject is the concern of Deal Hudson in his essay that follows the idea of human nature and what has happened to it in recent years—what has happened being a number of challenges in the name of gender, ethnicity, and so forth, which are hard to reconcile with—for example—Jefferson's words in the Declaration of Independence, and which indicate that the idea of human nature itself has ceased to function in our public discourse.

Part Three contains special features, of which the first is Thomas K. Simpson's essay on Leon Trotsky's *The History of the Russian Revolution*, a work devoted to events of the year 1917 in what became, for more than seventy years, the Soviet Union. That entity has disappeared and the revolution that created it is now despised—indeed the idea of revolution itself is in disrepute—but Mr. Simpson reminds us what it contained at the time and suggests that sooner or later we shall find ourselves in need of its aims and obliged to remember its hope of a rational society. Meanwhile we have problems with our own civil structure, dominated as it is by the legal profession, where a low standard of truth prevails in trial situations, William Braithwaite tells us, with important social and moral consequences.

Last in the third section of the book is a brief essay by Robert H. Kohn, the winner of the contest offered last year under the heading of "A Philosophical Problem to be Solved." Mr. Kohn's entry was judged the best of about thirty that were received, and we print his piece with great pleasure.

Part Four contains all or part of three important books which are classics of their kind. One of them is Ralph Waldo Emerson's *English Traits,* a memorable account of what the British were like in their Victorian heyday and an indication that America had in this case its own Tocqueville. Next is a selection—the last chapter and Conclusion—of Trotsky's *History,* where the Bolshevik (the word means "majority") Party, its antagonists having all collapsed, bloodlessly takes over the government in Petrograd (St. Petersburg) on Oct. 26th, 1917. And last will be found *The Pilgrim's Progress,* by John Bunyan, or more exactly the portion of it in which Bunyan tells us his dream of conversion and salvation by a Christian God. A second portion, written later, imagines the progress of his wife and children, and we think of printing that portion next year, both parts being too much for one issue of our book.

We cannot close without adding our regret at the death of Maurice Cranston, of London University, our frequent contributor, on Nov. 5, 1993. Mr. Cranston was an editor's dream in that not a syllable or a comma of what he submitted ever had to be changed. He was also an impeccable scholar and accomplished writer whose biography of Jean-Jacques Rousseau is a work of art—and, not least, he was a courteous and generous friend. He added much to the quality of *The Great Ideas Today* over the years. We shall miss him.

PART ONE

Current Developments in the Arts and Sciences

Language and Science: Genetics, Embryology, and the Discourse of Gene Action

Evelyn Fox Keller

Evelyn Fox Keller received her doctorate in theoretical physics from Harvard University with a dissertation in molecular biology, and subsequently became interested in questions concerning the history, philosophy, and sociology of science. Currently, she is a professor in the Program in Science, Technology, and Society at the Massachusetts Institute of Technology.

Professor Keller's books include *A Feeling for the Organism: The Life and Work of Barbara McClintock* (second edition, 1993), which has been translated into Spanish, French, Dutch, Italian, and Japanese. She is also the author of *Secrets of Life, Secrets of Death* (1992). A previous article by Professor Keller entitled "Gender and Science: 1990" appeared in *The Great Ideas Today,* 1990. She has written many articles in theoretical physics, molecular and mathematical biology, feminist theory, history of twentieth-century biology, and the philosophy of evolutionary biology.

She has received numerous awards and fellowships, including the Radcliffe Graduate Medal, a MacArthur Fellowship, and an Honorary Degree from the University of Amsterdam.

A belief long-standing among geneticists (and one which has acquired increased currency in recent years for the public at large) is that genes are the primary agents of life: They are the fundamental units of biological analysis; they "cause" the development of biological traits; and the ultimate goal of biological science is the understanding of how they "act." Such confidence in the power and agency of genes—codified in what I call "the discourse of gene action"—has been of immense importance to the history of genetics, and most recently, to the launching of the Human Genome Initiative. But what does it mean to attribute (or for that matter, to deny) causal power to genes? To what extent does this way of talking reflect a set of "natural facts," and to what extent does it reflect the facts of a particular disciplinary culture? And is it just a "way of talking?" Is it not also a way of thinking, a way of seeing, and a way of doing science? These are some of the questions I want to consider in the context of the history of two major areas of twentieth century life science: genetics and embryology. [1]

I. Introduction

Historians of biology routinely note that for nineteenth century biologists, the term *heredity* referred to both the "transmission of potentialities during reproduction *and* [the] development of those potentialities into specific adult traits" (Allen, 1986:114). The question that compelled their interests above all others was, as August Weismann put it in 1883, "How is a single germ cell capable of reproducing the entire body with all its detail?" [2]

At the turn of the century, however, a crucial change began to occur. In 1900, Gregor Mendel was rediscovered; in 1902, Mendelian "factors" were tied to chromosomal structures; the term *genetics* was coined in 1905 and *gene* in 1909. In 1915, Thomas Hunt Morgan published *The Mechanism of Mendelian Heredity;* in 1916, the first Genetics journal was founded, clearly marking the fact that a new discipline was off and running. For the new geneticists, the distinction between "genotype" and "phenotype" (originally introduced by Johannsen in 1911) provided a useful lexicon for distinguishing the problem of hereditary transmission from that of embryonic development (*see* Allen,

Thomas Hunt Morgan

1986:127–28; *also* Sapp, 1987:49). Indeed, the emergence of genetics coincided with the redefinition of the term *heredity* to refer exclusively to transmission: what had previously been seen as two aspects of a single subject (transmission and development) came to be regarded (at least by Americans) as distinct concerns. By the early decades of the twentieth century, the study of transmission had become the province of genetics, while that of development—now split off from genetics—continued as the province of embryology.

There evolved two separate disciplines with two different sets of concerns. In a passage from his book of 1926, *The Theory of the Gene*, Morgan described their relationship as follows:

> Between the characters, that furnish the data for the theory, and the postulated genes, to which the characters are referred, lies the whole field of embryonic development. The theory of the gene, as here formulated, states nothing with respect to the way in which the genes are connected with the end-product or character. The absence of information relating to this interval does not mean that the process of embryonic development is not of interest for genetics . . . but the fact remains that the sorting out of the characters in successive generations

can be explained at present without reference to the way in which the gene affects the developmental process. (p. 26)

Elsewhere, the same year, he cautioned that

> The confusion that is met with sometimes in the literature has resulted from a failure to keep apart the phenomenon of heredity, that deals with the transmission of the hereditary units, and the phenomena of embryonic development that take place almost exclusively by changes in the cytoplasm. (1926b:490)

Genetics, it must be remembered, was still a relatively new discipline struggling to establish itself against the established hegemony of embryology and physiology. The "phenomena of embryonic development," and their concurrent "changes in the cytoplasm," continued as powerful draws on the attention and interest of most biologists. Just two years earlier, in 1924, the German embryologist Hans Spemann and his graduate student Hilde Mangold (née Proscholdt) had published their classic paper on the "organiser," [3] thereby sparking a tremendous spurt of interest in the causal dynamics of embryonic development. Certainly,

R. A. Brink

genetics provided a powerful methodology for tracking the transmission of differences among existing organisms, but it could not answer the question of how a single germ cell might produce an organism—the pursuit of that question continued as the province of embryology.

Yet when the gene was still merely an abstract concept and the necessity of nuclear-cytoplasmic interactions clearly understood, geneticists of Morgan's school tended to take it for granted that these hypothetical particles, the genes, must somehow lie at the root of development. If Morgan gave the impression of being ecumenical, granting to embryology a separate but equal disciplinary status, and a separate but equal object of study (the cytoplasm), at other times he was quite clear about the proper epistemological ordering of the two disciplines. Though he well recognized that geneticists could say nothing about what genes are, or how they were subsequently connected to the formation of adult characters or traits, and little about how they interacted with the cytoplasm of the fertilized egg (the specifically maternal contribution), he nonetheless wrote in 1924, "[I]t is clear that whatever the cytoplasm contributes to development is almost entirely under the influence of the genes carried by the chromosome, and therefore may in a sense be said to be indifferent. . . ." [4] Others went even further. In an attempt to clarify Morgan's position, the geneticist R. A. Brink explained:

> The Mendelian theory postulates discrete, self-perpetuating, stable bodies—the genes—resident in the chromosomes, as the hereditary materials. *This means, of course, that the genes are the primary internal agents controlling development.* (my italics)

Brink described the great advantage of genetics over other approaches as follows:

> [W]ith the primary internal mechanism resolved into definite units which may be combined in various groups. . . . The hereditary complex need no longer serve merely as the passive object in physiological experimentation but may itself be varied in a precise fashion. . . . We are now in a favorable position to get at the dynamic properties of the hereditary mechanism by means of an analysis of the action of its separate elements. This, it seems to us, is the signal contribution which genetics makes to our outlook upon the problems of developmental physiology. (1927:280–82)

To Morgan's student, Hermann Joseph Muller, the most remarkable characteristic of the gene is that it possesses the property he called "specific autocatalysis" (by which he meant self-replication). "Still more remarkable," he wrote, "the gene can mutate without losing its specific autocatalytic power." Largely for this reason, he entitled his own 1926 paper "The Gene as the Basis of Life" (it is said that he refused to change his title to "The Gene as *a* Basis for Life"). There he concluded:

Hermann Joseph Muller

the great bulk . . . of the protoplasm [is], after all, only a by-product, originally, of the action of the gene material; its "function" (its survival-value) lies only in its fostering the genes, and the primary secrets common to all life lie further back, in the gene material itself. [5]

Today it may be hard to see what could be controversial in such claims. The attribution of agency, autonomy, and causal primacy to genes has become so familiar as to seem obvious, even self-evident. What I want to do, however, is attempt to dislodge that familiarity— by citing these arguments in their historical context, using the now somewhat quaint language in which they were first posed—to enable you to see them as novel, and thereby, to see something of the process by which they acquired their familiarity and ring of truth.

II. Language in action

It is well known that, by the mid-1920s, the taming of *Drosophila* and corn as model organisms for tracking the transmission of hereditary traits lent genetics a rigor and productivity that other disciplines could scarcely match. But the first generation of geneticists—Morgan and his school—did more than develop the techniques and practice of genetics as a rival to embryology; they also forged a way of talking about genes—about their role and meaning in reproduction, growth, and development. When Muller identified the gene as *the* basis of life, he was claiming for it both ontological and temporal priority. First the gene, then the remaining protoplasm (i.e., the cytoplasm), appearing as a "by-product" whose only function is that of facilitating environment, to "foster" the gene. First the gene, then life, or rather, with the gene comes life. The concept of gene invoked here is Janus faced: it is part physicist's atom and part Platonic soul; at one and the same time, fundamental building block and animating force. Only the "action" of genes can initiate the complex manifold of processes comprising a living organism.

But what exactly is it that genes *do*? This of course neither Muller, Brink, nor Morgan could say. The notion of "gene action" may even have been facilitated by the very absence of knowledge of what a gene is, in the sense that not knowing what a gene may have made it easier to attribute to it any, even miraculous, properties. But even though these early geneticists could tell us nothing about the nature of the presumed source of all subsequent growth and development, or could give no scientific account of "gene action," they offered future generations of geneticists something equally valuable.

Scientists usually assume that only their data and theories matter for scientific progress, that how they talk about these data and theories does not matter, that it is irrelevant to their actual work. But here, in introducing this particular way of talking, the first generation of American geneticists provided a conceptual framework that was of critical importance for the future course of biological research. To capture both its rhetorical and conceptual force, I will call this way of talking the "discourse of gene action"—a discourse that was, for genetics, undeniably productive. It enabled geneticists to get on with their work without worrying about their lack of information about the nature of this "action"; to a considerable degree, it even obscured the need for such information (throughout the interwar period, American geneticists routinely invoked the notion of "gene action" as if its meaning was self-evident). At the same time, the attribution of agency, autonomy, and causal responsibility to genes lent primacy both to the object of geneticists' concern and to the discipline of genetics—in their own eyes and in the eyes of others. They were dealing with *the* basis of life. If, as Brink wrote, the hereditary complex is elevated from a "passive object" to a locus of primary activity, the student of that hereditary complex is, by the same move, also elevated to primary activity.

I suggest that the "discourse of gene action" provides the specific hallmark (or trademark) of the American school of Morganian genetics, especially of its approach to development. If its first use was to bracket the question of development, later, in the mid-thirties, when a number of American geneticists did turn their attention to development, it helped define the approach they then took. That is, it framed the questions that could or could not be meaningfully asked, the organisms they chose to study, experiments that did or did not make sense to do, the explanations that were or were not acceptable. In this sense it served cognitive as well as political functions. Ian Hacking has suggested that every scientific discipline has its own "style of reasoning," and that this "style of reasoning" constitutes the epistemological context of that science. In other words, within its framework it creates the very possibility of truth and falsehood and therefore determines what counts as objective (Hacking, 1982). My notion of "discourse" is close to Hacking's notion of "style."

Needless to say, this way of talking about the relation between genes and development—a way that recasts the dynamics of development as a consequence of "gene action"—was markedly less congenial than Morgan's formulation had been to most embryologists. It offered the student of development not a separate domain of inquiry (as Morgan's remarks implied), but rather, a promissory note for inclusion, or, more accurately, for incorporation. As early as 1924, Spemann, Morgan's most important counterpart, wrote:

> The previous progress [of genetics] has been amazing, and it is not
> from a feeling of futile labours but rather from being aware of their
> paramount powers of appropriation that geneticists now are on the
> look-out for new connexions. They have cast their eye on us, on
> Entwicklungsmechanik . . . [6]

A decade later, in his presidential address to the American Association for the Advancement of Science, Ross Harrison sounded a similar warning:

> Now that . . . the "Wanderlust" of geneticists is beginning to urge
> them in our direction, it may not be inappropriate to point out a danger
> in this threatened invasion.
> The prestige of success enjoyed by the gene theory might easily
> become a hindrance to the understanding of development by directing
> out attention solely to the genome. . . . Already we have theories that
> refer the processes of development to genic action and regard the whole
> performance as no more than the realization of the potencies of the
> genes. Such theories are altogether too one-sided. [7]

Embryologists had good grounds for concern. Not only was the status of their discipline under threat, so too was the status of their question: how *does* a germ cell develop into a multicellular organism? If the genetic content of all cells in an organism is the same, then how is

9

one to make sense of the emergence of the manifest differences among all the cells that make up a complex organism? To the embryologists, it seemed self-evident that this problem of differentiation, so near the heart of their own concerns, was simply incompatible with the notion that the gene was the exclusive locus of action. [8] As Morgan himself subsequently admitted (speaking now as an embryologist):

> The implication in most genetic interpretation is that all the genes are acting all the time in the same way. This would leave unexplained why some cells of the embryo develop in one way, some in another, if the genes are the only agents in the results. (1934:9)

Few, if any, geneticists heeded Morgan's warning. (Morgan did not heed it himself.) Instead, those interested in the relation between genes and development found another route: they changed the subject. More precisely, they transformed the embryologist's question into a different one. Alfred H. Sturtevant spelled out how to do this. Sturtevant opened his paper on "the developmental effects of genes" at the 1932 International Congress of Genetics by observing:

> "One of the central problems of biology is that of differentiation— how does an egg develop into a complex many-celled organism? This is, of course, the traditional major problem of embryology; but it also appears in genetics in the form of the question, "How do genes produce their effects?" (1932:304)

To address this question, he examined the correlation of eye pigment with gonad constitution in *Drosophila* gynandromorphs, and concluded:

> It is clear that in most cases there is a chain of reactions between the direct activity of a gene and the end-product that the geneticist deals with as a character. . . .[T]he type of experiment that I have described may be considered as a beginning in the analysis of certain chains of reactions into their individual links. (1932:307)

I do not want to underestimate the importance of Sturtevant's suggestion that it was possible to use spontaneously occurring mosaics in *Drosophila* for the study of development, especially since *Drosophila* had, until then, been thought to be beyond the reach of embryology. [9] My point is merely to underscore the linear format in which he posed the problem (a gene "produces its effect" through a "chain of reactions," or "direct activity" that produces the end-product, its character). Contrast this formulation with, for example, that of Richard Goldschmidt, the leading figure in German physiological genetics, who had also been studying cases of intersexuality in insects (mostly moths) for some time, and who was also concerned with the nature of "gene action." Many differences in style are conspicuous (to an American reader, Goldschmidt was typically grandiose, leaning always toward overarching

Alfred H. Sturtevant

generalization). [10] However, the difference I want to point out is more subtle: Goldschmidt's emphasis was on *systems* of coordinated reactions of particular velocities ("Development ought to be disentangled into a series of coordinated reactions of definite velocities."[1932:345]) His search was precisely for the dynamic properties of such systems ("Zusammenspiel der Reaktionen"). "Gene action" meant, to him, that genes were both catalysts and catalyzed, actors and "reacting substances" (1932:343). In his book of 1927, he had advocated a "scheme of 'substrate-induced' differential gene activation" where "gene activation" ("Genaktivierung"), he argued, is effected by the appearance of an appropriate substrate (from Sander, 1985:368–69). [11]

To American geneticists, however, Sturtevant's rephrasing of the problem—and his recommendation to geneticists of the task of analyzing the "chains of reactions into their individual links"—had an immense appeal; certainly it seemed clearer than Goldschmidt's formulations. As they no doubt intuited, Sturtevant's rephrasing accomplished a great deal. Once the problem of development is translated into the question of "how genes produce their effects," the task is immediately and almost miraculously simplified. No longer need one get bogged down in the complex dynamics of eggs and multicellular organisms; it ought to suffice to study single-celled organisms where one should have a better chance of analyzing "chains of reaction." George W. Beadle and Edward L. Tatum chose *Neurospora*, a single-celled organism that can be cultured *in vitro*, and their choice paid off handsomely. In 1940 they proposed their explanation of how genes produce their effects in a form that came to be known as the "one gene-one enzyme" hypothesis. Beadle and Tatum provided a particular kind of answer to the question of how a gene produces its effects, namely, it catalyzes a specific chemical reaction, or, more colloquially, "It makes an enzyme." At last the mysterious notion of "gene action" seemed to have real content. With the "one gene-one enzyme" hypothesis, developmental genetics could henceforth be understood as the biochemistry of gene action.

Together, the turn to *Neurospora* and to the biochemistry of gene action proved to be of decisive importance to the future development of genetics. It provided critical encouragement for the development of bacterial genetics, and eventually, of molecular biology. The rest of the story is well known. In 1953, with the definitive identification of DNA as the genetic material, James Watson and Francis Crick struck gold. Simple hydrogen bonding turned out to provide the secret of how genes reproduce themselves, and nucleic acid sequences, of how they make enzymes. As Watson and Crick discreetly wrote:

> In a long molecule many different permutations are possible, and it therefore seems likely that the precise sequence of the bases is the code which carries the genetical information. (1953:965)

All one needed to know was the code, and soon that was forthcoming as well.

Geneticists and molecular biologists were euphoric: there, surely, must be the answer! DNA carries the genetical information (or program), and genes "produce their effects" by providing the "instructions" for protein synthesis. DNA makes RNA, RNA makes proteins, and proteins make us. It was without a doubt one of the greatest milestones in the history of science. But still one might ask (though few people did at the time), what kind of answer is this? What in fact do "information," "program," "instruction," or even the verb "makes," actually mean?

Watson and Crick have gotten a lot of credit for their work, and deservedly so, but one contribution has, I fear, been overlooked: the introduction of the "information" metaphor into the repertoire of biological discourse was a stroke of genius. The story of this metaphor—its uses and implications—is an immensely rich one. In brief, just a few years earlier, the mathematician Claude E. Shannon had proposed a precise quantitative measure of the complexity of linear codes. He called this measure "information"—by design independent of meaning or function—and by the early fifties, "information theory" had become a popular subject in the world of communications systems. It seemed to hold enormous promise for the analysis of all sorts of complex systems, even of biological systems. Indeed, the fact that DNA seemed to function as a linear code made the use of this notion of information for genetics appear natural. It was recognized, however, as early as 1952 that the technical definition of information simply could not serve for biological information. (It would, for example, assign the same amount of "information" to the DNA of a functioning organism as to a mutant form, however disabling that mutation was.) The notion of "genetical information" that Watson and Crick invoked was thus not literal, but metaphoric. But it was an extremely powerful metaphor. While it permitted no quantitative measure, it authorized the expectation, anticipated in the notion of "gene action," that biological information does not increase in the course of development: it is already fully contained in the genome.

By this authorization, and even more, by the subsequent melding of "information" with "program" and "instruction," the concept of gene action was vastly fortified. It was exactly what Erwin Schrödinger had anticipated in his widely read work, *What is Life?*, which said that the chromosome structures "are law-code and executive power—or, to use another simile, they are architect's plan and builder's craft—in one" (1944:23).

Classical embryologists would surely not have been happy with this turn of events—their questions, their organisms (even the lowly *Drosophila* had come to be seen as too complex, too messy), and they themselves had been left behind—but a new generation of biologists

13

had little cause to look back. The first generation of molecular biologists could not answer the question of how an egg turns into an organism (could say nothing about how a gene comes to make the particular enzymes that are needed for the development of a many-celled organism, in the right amounts, at the right time, and in the right place), but they had a powerful new rhetorical resource for managing such questions. They could talk instead about "development" in the abstract and the genetic programs or instructions that are needed to guide it. In his presidential address to the British Association for the Advancement of Science in 1965, Sir Peter Medawar offered something of a retrospective eulogy to embryology:

> Wise after the event, we can now see that embryology simply did not have, and could not have created, the background of genetical reasoning which would have made it possible to formulate a theory of development. . . . Embryonic development . . . [must] be an unfolding of pre-existing capabilities, an acting-out of genetically encoded instructions. (1965:1329)

Twenty years later, the progression from Watson and Crick to the Human Genome Initiative, as Watson himself has so often reminded us, appeared straightforward and logical. If all of development is merely an unfolding of preexisting instructions encoded in the nucleotide se-

James Watson (left) and Francis Crick

important function of all these models will be to stimulate the growth of just those intuitions about interactive and emergent phenomena that past discourses have so helped to stymie. I have no doubt that the effect will be a transformation in the way we think about biological systems that will make the changes we have already begun to witness look like mere harbingers.

For a historian of science, however, this story provokes other questions. Put simply, they are twofold: first, what lent the discourse of gene action such persuasiveness for so many years, and second, why is it now giving way? (Or relatedly we might ask, why did embryology languish for so many years, and what has permitted its return today?) These are different versions of the same questions just because of the extent to which the fate of embryology has historically been so intimately linked to talk of gene action. Posed either way, they are far more difficult to answer than naive empiricism might suggest. The simplistic answers might go like this: embryology languished because it was bad and unproductive science; we talked about gene action because we didn't know better; indeed, developmental phenomena are so difficult to study that real progress was impossible until the advent of techniques of recombinant DNA that were brought on by molecular biology. All of these claims might be true, and may still be only part of the story. What they leave out is the entire issue of motivation.

Relatedly, they also ignore the awkward fact that the first experimental studies to spark the interest of molecular biologists in the early development of higher organisms relied solely on classical techniques that were labor intensive to be sure, but that had long been available. I think especially of the studies of "maternal (or cytoplasmic) effect" mutants and of cytoplasmic rescue in *Drosophila* first undertaken by Alan Garen and others in the early seventies, and carried to such dramatic fruition a few years later by Christianne Nusslein-Volhard and her colleagues. [13] What these studies did was to establish the critical role played by the cytoplasmic structure of the egg prior to fertilization, i.e., *before* time zero. The most conspicuous question is, why were these efforts undertaken in the seventies, and not before?

Time and space preclude my going into the details, but they reveal, as Garen and others confirm, that no technical impasse prevented these studies being done years, if not decades, earlier. [14] Maternal effect mutants—even in *Drosophila*—had been accumulating since the early part of the century; and the most crucial technical instrument, the micromanipulator, had also been well developed and was in wide use by the thirties. Of course, it might be argued that *Drosophila* was an exceedingly difficult organism to study embryologically (and it surely was), but even this ostensible impasse had been largely overcome by the early fifties—again, by the application of long available technique. What was missing, both to the study of *Drosophila* embryology and to the more specific examination of maternal effects, was the motivation to invest the necessary effort. And once again nomenclature is relevant. Since 1930, geneticists had argued for the term "delayed inheritance" as a more accurate description of these mutants. [15] What relabeling "maternal effects" as "delayed inheritance" achieved was to reinforce the understanding of phenotypic expression, however late, as pure outcome—i.e., as merely epiphenomenal and hence lacking causal weight of its own. More generally, the belief—prevalent among geneticists at least since the mid-twenties—that the genetic message of the zygote "produces" the organism, that the cytoplasm is merely a passive substrate, could not but sap the motivation needed to undertake such undeniably difficult experiments. [16] The question therefore becomes, what overcame that assumption?

If, as I have been arguing, the ways in which we talk about scientific objects are not simply determined by empirical evidence, but rather, actively influence the kind of evidence we seek (and hence are more likely to find), then other factors must be considered if we are to understand the strength and persistence of the discourse of gene action. Let me, in the remainder of this essay, very schematically indicate what some of these other factors were, at least as they operated between the two world wars.

IV. A metaphor in context

In the 1930s, the Swiss embryologist Oscar Schotte liked to illustrate the relations between embryology and genetics with a sketch of two views of the cell: as perceived by the embryologist, the nucleus is very small, but as perceived by the geneticist, it virtually fills the entire cell. [17] In this sketch the nucleus and cytoplasm are employed as tropes for the two disciplines—each lends to their object of study a size in direct proportion to their perceived self-importance. In like fashion the two disciplines lent to each object—nucleus and cytoplasm—their own self-attributes of agency, autonomy, and power. As L. C. Dunn put it, "Genetics had to be a bit pushy in order to get itself established." [18]

In addition, the nucleus and cytoplasm also came to stand as tropes for national importance, agency, and power, with the former as the domain in which American genetics had come to stake its unique strengths, associated with American interests (and prowess), and the latter, with European and especially German interests and prowess. German biologists were often explicit about what they saw as the attempt by American geneticists to appropriate the entire field. In 1927, V. Haecker described the field between genetics and development as the "no-man's land" of somatogenesis—"a border field which by us has been tilled for quite some time . . . The Americans have taken no notice of this." Goldschmidt registered a similar complaint, attributing American indifference to "the rise of a school of geneticists (especially in America) to whom biological knowledge apart from Mendelism did not deem necessary, whereby they were entirely content with knowing the work of the schools most closely akin to their own approach" (translation by Sander, 1985:389). [19]

This tension showed some signs of abating as memories of World War I faded in the late twenties and early thirties, only to resurface with Hitler's rise to power. Spemann's fierce (Bismarckian) nationalism was recalled, as were his occasional references to the experimental superiority of the hair of Aryan babies, or to the special intuitive gifts of German scientists. [20] Even Goldschmidt was suspect, though himself a Jew obliged to emigrate in 1936. [21] On August 23, 1939, the Seventh International Congress of Genetics convened in Edinburgh. [22] Goldschmidt did not attend, but 42 of his colleagues from Germany did. The minutes from the meeting read as follows:

> For a day and a half the congress was able to immerse itself in its
> own enjoyable affairs. It even danced. But on the evening of the 24th
> its serenity was shattered. War, that outmoded futility of irrational
> immaturity, the antithesis of everything we represented, was about to
> overwhelm us. Britishers in Germany had been advised to leave for
> home. The German delegation, therefore, had no choice but to do
> likewise. . . . We had met as geneticists sharing the same interests and
> enthusiasms: suddenly we were required to behave as nationals with
> fiercely conflicting views (1939:57).

The war took its toll on everyone; when it was over, German biology needed to be rebuilt virtually from scratch.

Finally, there is another metaphoric reference of nucleus and cytoplasm, surely the most conspicuous of all, and that is to be found in sexual reproduction. By tradition as well as by biological experience, at least until World War II, nucleus and cytoplasm are also tropes for male and female.

Until the emergence of bacterial genetics in the mid 1940s, all research in genetics and embryology, both in Europe and the U.S., focused on organisms that pass through embryonic stages of development, and for these organisms a persistent asymmetry is evident in male and female contributions to fertilization: the female gamete, the egg, is vastly larger than the male gamete, the sperm. The difference is the cytoplasm, deriving from the maternal parent (a no-man's land indeed); by contrast, the sperm cell is almost pure nucleus. It is thus hardly surprising to find that, in the conventional discourse about nucleus and cytoplasm, cytoplasm is routinely taken to be synonymous with egg. Furthermore—by an all too familiar twist of logic—the nucleus was often taken as a stand-in for sperm. Boveri argued for the need to recognize at least some function for the cytoplasm on the grounds of "the absurdity of the idea that it would be possible to bring a sperm to develop by means of an artificial culture medium" (published posthumously in 1918 [p. 466]), and translated in Baltzer, 1967:83–4). [23]

Many of the debates about the relative importance of nucleus and cytoplasm in inheritance thus inevitably reflect older debates about the relative importance (or activity) of maternal and paternal contributions to reproduction, where the overwhelming historical tendency has been to attribute activity and motive force to the male contribution, while relegating the female contributions to the role of passive, facilitating environment. In Platonic terms the egg represented the body, and the nucleus the activating soul. (In a related vein, Edmund Beecher Wilson's remarks about Morgan's early passion for embryology may also be worth noting: "It is in fact an open secret that even now he sometimes escapes from the austere heights where *Drosophila* has its home in order to indulge in the illicit pleasures of the egg and its development.") [24] I suggest that in these associations surely lies part of the background both for the force of the assumption of gene action and perhaps even to its gradual fading away from the status of self-evident truth. More specifically, I suggest that such associations bore quite directly on the historic discounting of "maternal effects." [25]

V. Conclusion

Change, of course, did not come overnight. While embryology was no longer a thriving research enterprise after the war, the memory of that disciplinary struggle took time to abate. It also took time—roughly two decades—for German biology to rebuild. Lastly, it took the women's movement to change our ideas about gender, and perhaps the hiatus of bacterial genetics (where no one had to think about male and female contributions) for these changes to creep into biology. By the time that the study of higher organisms began to reemerge in the seventies, the entire world had changed, and so did the ways that seem natural to talk. Embryology was no longer a rival, Germany had become a friend, and gender equity was all the rage. There were of course also other changes, which I have not talked about—most notably perhaps, the emergence of a discourse of feedback, and of bodies as cyborgs, both associated with the extraordinary developments in systems analysis and computer science. Last but hardly least were the equally extraordinary developments internal to molecular biology, especially the techniques of recombinant DNA. Concurrent with the changes in the way we talked and thought, these developments soon effected dramatic changes in what could be done in the lab. Over the last decade, the world of technical feasibility has changed beyond recognition. These very different

I never saw you in the sun or shade,
Lady, remove your veil
After you knew the wish that makes me pale
By which all other wills from my heart fade.

While I was hiding the fair thoughts I bore,
That have undone my mind in this desire,
I saw compassion shine upon your face;
But when Love made you conscious of my fire
The blond hair became veiled and was no more,
The loving look closed in itself its grace.
What I most longed for finds its hiding-place
In you; the veil rules me,
Which to my death, hot or cold though it be,
Covers your eyes' sweet light as with a shade.

—Petrarch [1]

Religious differences have often fueled long and bitter conflicts all over the world. Our Age of Enlightenment, beginning perhaps in the seventeenth century, has attempted to dampen down such conflicts by promoting commerce, encouraging skepticism, and having recourse to interfaith accommodations. Nevertheless, the beneficial effects of religious discipline continue to be desired: moral and social effects that depend on religion being taken seriously.

The first half of this article, describing for the most part what I happened to observe of the 1993 convocation of the Parliament of the World's Religions, presents an assembly dedicated, for the sake of universal peace, to the advancement of toleration and cooperation across a broad range of religious and other diversity. The second half of this article, examining the principal statement issued in the name of that assembly, assesses both modern interfaith thought and the prospects of reconciliation grounded in such thought. [2]

Both a general enlightenment grounded in modern science and an array of religious faiths continue to enlist the allegiance of multitudes. Whether current accommodations can truly be both global and effective depends, in part, upon whether people can know the whole in such a way as to permit them to act sensibly in many different circumstances.

I

Chicago's Palmer House was occupied in August 1993 by delegates to the second Parliament of the World's Religions, many of them in colorful costumes that we usually see only in pictures. At times the colors, noises, incense, and culinary odors turned the corridors of the Palmer House into "instant Asia," a rather exhilarating place. The concluding public event of the Parliament was a well-received talk by an amiable Dalai Lama in Grant Park the evening of September 4. [3]

The Parliament of the World's Religions brought together more than eight thousand participants for five hundred meetings between August 28 and September 5. The participants, representing more than one hundred and twenty-five faiths, came from fifty-six countries, with the largest contingents from India and the United States.

The 1993 Parliament followed, by a century, the first such convention of the world's religions in September 1893, also held in Chicago. The 1893 effort (a Pentecost of sorts) extended over seventeen days and resulted in voluminous publications. That Parliament, with four hundred delegates from forty-one religious traditions and denominations and with thousands in its audiences, was one of the splendors of the great 1893 Columbian Exposition. [4]

Critical to the 1893 meeting of religious leaders had been an emphasis upon religious unity and brotherhood. Each religious group participating in that Parliament was permitted to display itself. The use of the term *parliament* presupposed the equality of the constituent members, a presupposition that evidently troubled many Christians in this country who did not want to surrender their faith's ancient claim to preeminence among the world's religions. By 1993 there was far less need for foreign, especially Asian, groups to introduce themselves to the West. The 1893 Parliament had been far more intriguing in that many of the foreign sects represented in Chicago that year were barely known in the United States. Those sects now have large permanent outposts in Chicago as elsewhere in this country. (African groups were not adequately represented at either Parliament.)

We can sense, upon comparing the 1893 and the 1993 Parliaments, the intellectual and social movements there had been during the intervening century among the members of the principal world religions. The influence upon everyone today of great wars, of profound economic and technological changes, is evident in how religious, as well as other, subjects have come to be discussed in the late twentieth century. The accepted verities of earlier times are no longer relied upon to the extent that they once were.

Another difference between the 1893 and the 1993 Parliaments in Chicago was that the earlier proceedings appeared to be more religious or spiritual in tone than the later, even as their scholarship was more

Chicago's mayor, Richard Daley, welcomes the Dalai Lama upon his arrival to the city. The Dalai Lama's eagerly awaited speech was the final public event of the Parliament.

serious. Related to this difference is the fact that respectable divinity schools in Chicago had little to do with the 1993 Parliament convening in their own city. For this and other reasons, there may have been more of a carnival atmosphere during the 1993 proceedings (with its determined celebration of diversity), even though the 1893 proceedings had been conducted as part of a spectacular world's fair.

II

One difficulty in arranging any convocation of the world's religions is with the very phrase, *the world's religions*. That term tends to lump together a variety of ways of organized worship, implicitly playing down (if not even negating) the specialness that most, if not all, of these associations see in themselves. To lump them together may be to distort them somewhat: they tend thereby to be seen from the outside. They can even be spoken of as "lifestyles."

34

Pictured here are participants of the 1893 Parliament of the World's Religions. *"That Parliament, with four hundred delegates from forty-one religious traditions and denominations and with thousands in its audience, was one of the splendors of the great 1893 Columbian Exposition."*

What we call a religion may not have originally been considered as *a religion*—that is, as an instance of a species—but rather it was often considered as *the* way of life of a people. An indication of the many fundamental differences there are here may be seen in this part of a protest submitted (on August 31, 1993) to the Council for the Parliament on behalf of some of the Buddhist participants in the Parliament:

> We cannot help but feel that the 1993 Parliament of the World's Religions is being held for the worshippers of Almighty and Creator God and efforts are being made towards "achieving oneness under God."

This protest included the following recommendation, a recommendation which suggests how even the most ancient sects have been influenced in our time by modern social science:

> Language and communication skills are important elements in bringing about agreement and cooperation. We must train ourselves to be sensitive to each other and learn to use language that is inclusive

and all embracing. We suggest we use "Great Being" or "power of the transcendent" or "Higher Spiritual Authority" instead of God in reference to the ultimate spiritual reality. We are open to other suggestions and discussions on this matter. [5]

The reference here to "the transcendent" can remind us of the influence of Ralph Waldo Emerson, an early Western student of Eastern texts and perhaps the first prominent American prophet of "interfaith dialogue." Consider, for example, Emerson's remarks about the relation between God and nature in his 1841 essay, "The Over-Soul":

> These questions which we lust to ask about the future are a confession of sin. God has no answer for them. No answer in words can reply to a question of things. It is not in an arbitrary "decree of God," but in the nature of man, that a veil shuts down on the facts of to-morrow: for the soul will not have us read any other cipher but that of cause and effect. By this veil which curtains events it instructs the children of men to live in to-day. The only mode of obtaining an answer to these questions of the senses is to forego all low curiosity, and, accepting the tide of being which floats us into the secret of nature, work and live, work and live, and all unawares the advancing soul has built and forged for itself a new condition, and the question and the answer are one.

It remains an important question whether the transcendent, or interfaith, approach seen in Emerson and his successors can ever help anyone to see and "feel" any traditional religion as the truly faithful do.

The long-fashionable interfaith approach to the world's religions does reflect a tendency to see each of them from the outside. However attractive such an approach can be, it should be recognized that particularity and immediacy are essential to an association if it is to be taken seriously by its members generation after generation—if it is to have the richness which promotes the deep attachments that can mean so much for people. [6]

Another way of putting the typical true believer's reservations about the interfaith approach to religion is to observe that that approach may be too rationalistic. Still another way of putting it is to observe that it is not vigorous enough, which may be related to a general slackening of spirit. It is a web of particulars that usually binds together most people through bad times as well as good, however sympathetic they may like to be toward what is happening "everywhere else" in the world.

The interfaith approach tends to collapse or at least to disregard differences that individual partisans naturally take seriously—differences between "us" and "them," between "the truly divine" and "all the other projections of the divine," between a world in which divinity is seen to act in human affairs and a world in which no such action is ever discerned.

III

Particularity and intense allegiances lead to variety, energy, and serious alternatives. No doubt, this variety can be traced, at least in part, to different climes and circumstances.

No doubt, also, a major impetus for the interfaith movement in recent centuries has been the history of violence and atrocities in large part attributable to religious differences separating peoples. Bosnia and its neighbors immediately come to mind today, and then Northern Ireland, the Middle East, Cyprus, India, Tibet, and several parts of the former Soviet Union.

So deep-rooted are these differences that it was surprising that there were so few expressions of hostility among the delegates in Chicago during this 1993 Parliament. (There *were* Hindu protests in response to Kashmir-related and Sikh grievances.) Perhaps this reflects that spirit in this country which still tends to contain the political conflicts arising between differing religious associations.

The sectarian outbursts we do observe from time to time, even in this country, remind us of political differences around the world which are grounded in long-standing religious differences. One suspects that the religions which are important in the lives of peoples may themselves really be peculiarly sensitive aspects of the political life of the communities involved.

IV

The religious practices of one people can be difficult for others to accept. Take, for example, one of the most "philosophical" of the religions of mankind, Zoroasterism (or the Parsi faith), which comes out of ancient Persia and India. [7] The adherents of that faith, who were ably represented at the 1993 Parliament, come to view as preeminently rationalistic.

Somewhat philosophical in appearance, but likely to be troubling to outsiders, is that seeming disregard (if not disrespect) for the body seen in the traditional Zoroastrian practice of leaving the corpses of their dead for the vultures to eat, a practice evidently still followed by them in Bombay. Herodotus long ago observed that differences in burial practices can be disturbing from one people to another.

The Zoroastrians explained to me, at one of their panels, that this ancient practice respected the cycle of nature, even as it pointed up the transitory character of the body for the human being. This practice was likened to what some American Indian tribes did with their dead and even to what animals do. [8]

A Hindu who was present defended the ancient Zoroastrian practice

Shown here at the opening of the 1993 Parliament are members of the Zoroastrian faith.

by also likening it to the prompt cremation (within twenty-four hours of death) called for in India. The Zoroastrians I talked with (some of whom are now settled, as prosperous businessmen, in Chicago suburbs) seemed to be eager to emphasize that cremation is pretty much the practice resorted to by most Zoroastrians outside of India today.

V

People, in explaining their own, can usually be trusted to appreciate whatever merits it may have, especially since they are not likely to see their own as others do. When one hears their explanations—which are usually so self-assured that they may not sound defensive—one recognizes, as Aristotle did, that all human beings aim by their actions at some good. [9] It is the good they have aimed at which permits a people to explain calmly, and even to justify, what can be most shocking to others.

If an association is long-established, it is almost certain that it will be able to justify its ways as good and moral. Such justification is routine. I have even heard career gangsters on trial quoted as speaking thus, perhaps not insincerely, about their violent way of life. I am reminded here of another remark by Emerson in his "Over-Soul" essay:

> We grant that human life is mean, but how did we find out that it
> was mean? What is the ground of this uneasiness of ours; of this old
> discontent? What is the universal sense of want and ignorance, but the
> fine innuendo by which the great soul makes its enormous claim?

There seems to be a common set of criteria about morality and the common good, recognizable down to our day, that can be drawn upon for such justifications. How those criteria are expressed may well depend upon the spirit and vocabulary of the time. Today, for example, *nature* is made much of in fashioning explanations: one could hear nature referred to again and again by partisans of one religion after another at the 1993 Parliament, even though the traditions out of which such partisans come never had the Western idea of nature as part of their understanding until modern times. But then, the need as well as the opportunity to provide the kinds of explanations they now provide may also be a modern development.

The often superficial use today of *nature* for this purpose may be traced back to, among others, Emerson, who is hardly superficial himself. The idea of nature may cut against the grain of the fundamental tenets of some, if not all, of the ancient faiths: nature suggests that there is a principle of rest and motion, accounting for how things are, which is independent of any superintending intelligence. There seems to be something Emersonian also in the Declaration of a Global Ethic that was prepared for the 1993 Parliament of the World's Religions.

Certainly *not* in the spirit of that interfaith Declaration, which is determinedly modernist in its accents, were such striking sights, on view at the Palmer House, as the heavy (however voluntary) veiling by which some Muslim women were distinguished and the abject (however joyful) veneration shown by some Hindus to their holy men and holy women.

Other unusual things were on display, of course, including the shaving of heads of men and women by some sects and the never-cut hair of other sectarians. But the heavily-veiled Muslim woman may have been the most troublesome, especially when observed in a Western setting. (That setting included, at the Parliament, the presence of most Muslim women dressed in the Western style.) One could—upon seeing what appeared to be a humble young woman shrouded in black cloth, with only her eyes, eyebrows, and hands (taking notes) showing—even get the impression of someone who had been buried alive. [10]

However many times the Westerner sees such veiling (which can cover the entire head), it can be hard to get used to. And yet I have heard a heavily-veiled woman explain to a gathering of graduate students, for hours at a time, the salutary purposes served by this practice. Some women can even wax enthusiastic about it, acclaiming it as a form of liberation from the pressures routinely exerted upon them by the typical male response to feminine beauty. Plausible opinions about human nature are drawn upon in such explanations.

The desire and ability of one people after another to have recourse to widely-accepted moral criteria in justifying their distinctive practices can be reassuring. This suggests that something more or less natural *is* available for everyone to apprehend and draw upon. It is this commonality in moral impulse that interfaith movements attempt to put to use worldwide.

Here is how Emerson, in his "Over-Soul" essay, saw the commonality at work in "religious" experience:

> A thrill passes through all men at the reception of new truth, or at
> the performance of a great action, which comes out of the heart of
> nature. . . . The character and duration of this enthusiasm varies with
> the state of the individual, from an exstasy and trance and prophetic
> inspiration,—which is its rarer appearance, to the faintest glow of
> virtuous emotion, in which form it warms, like our household fires,
> all the families and associations of men, and makes society possible. A
> certain tendency to insanity has always attended the opening of the
> religious sense in men, as if "blasted with excess of light." The trances
> of Socrates; the "union" of Plotinus; the vision of Porphyry; the
> conversion of Paul; the aurora of Behmen; the convulsions of George
> Fox and his Quakers; the illuminations of Swedenborg, are of this
> kind. What was in the case of these remarkable persons a ravishment,
> has, in innumerable instances in common life, been exhibited in less
> striking manner.

Whether a Socrates can be adequately dealt with, or understood, in these terms is an underlying question posed by this article. [11]

The general recourse by interfaith-minded peoples to moral criteria can be troubling as well as reassuring. This reminds us of the problems faced in attempting to reconcile contending "tribes" who are firmly grounded in their respective ways. Invariably, in the panels I attended at the Parliament, the members of a sect defended their own practices, confident in the soundness of the way they had always done things. This was evident also in the materials I collected from dozens of other organizations represented at the Palmer House. The most that the typical association did by way of accommodation was to try to "understand" the others, which usually consisted in translating what others say or do into its own terms. One could find something natural in this as well, just as there is something natural in the troublesome impulses or passions that nature can nevertheless guide us in checking or transforming.

The difficulties with others' ways of life can be readily noticed. But it should also be noticed that *they* do not usually regard them as difficulties. This should alert us to the difficulties that our own ways may really have.

VI

Even more fundamental differences than those between religions, and the practices of different religions, can be those between religious and nonreligious (if not antireligious) associations. This too can raise questions about what *religion* truly means. [12]

Such differences were dramatized by the withdrawal from the 1993 Parliament by the Chicago representatives of the Eastern Orthodox Church, primarily because of the leeway allowed during the meetings to avowed witches and neopagans. The trouble evidently began for these Greek-Americans with some of the invocations pronounced during the opening ceremonies, if not before. The prospect of a Grant Park moon-worshiping ceremony midway through the Parliament contributed to the decision of these Eastern Orthodox delegates to withdraw. Evangelical and other fundamentalist Christians, as well as Southern Baptists, Christian Scientists, and Orthodox Jews (with their reservations about interfaith dialogue), stayed clear of this enterprise altogether, as had their counterparts in 1893. Roman Catholic representatives, led by the Archbishop of the Chicago diocese, remained obviously uncomfortable participants throughout. Mainline Protestantism was not as prominent in 1993 as it had been in 1893.

One of the problems for the conventionally pious in the 1993 Parliament was the apparent "craziness" (as some put it) of various participants, including a few perhaps who could be considered to be spoofing

41

A neopagan woman dances during a ceremony at the 1993 Parliament.

much of what was going on at the Palmer House. Nor did the presence of voodoo, UFO enthusiasts, and perhaps of Satanists, help matters. But much of this was marginal, compared to what was implied by the neopagans and witches: they stood for an earthy passion, as exhibited in well-executed songs and dances I observed one morning in the Empire Room at the Palmer House. One could get a hint from their cavorting (including the dancing of a sensuous woman dressed in dazzling white) what the lure had been both of the bacchanals that appealed to the ancient Greeks and of the Canaanite and other practices into which the Israelites repeatedly strayed. Although abominations may naturally follow from such practices, they can entice us at their outset because of the all-too-human passions they draw upon and exploit.

The question remains as to what the community may properly do to promote restraint and to curb hedonism, whether or not that hedonism is legitimated by something called religion. Related questions may be posed as to whether any sect should ever have the final say in a civilized community about how children are treated medically and educated. [13]

VII

The sensuous woman, dressed in close-fitting white, can seem to many an effective refutation of the veiled woman, dressed in loose-fitting black. But do not all healthy communities of any size, if they are to endure, depend on veils? Each community has vital matters or relations that are likely to be kept from public view. That which is veiled is, in a sense, taken for granted, perhaps even cherished: it is not likely to be open to thorough examination by everyone. Precisely what is to be veiled, and how, may depend upon the particularities (including the fortuitous circumstances) to which I have referred.

Among the things to be veiled by communities may be the unverifiable stories that lie at their foundations. Chance may be critical here, especially as to what has been established and how. Chance may also have helped determine what I was personally able to observe during my own Palmer House visits. Even so, it was striking for me to notice, as I went from one group to another, how much was made by most groups of charismatic founders.

Interfaith movements find it difficult, if not impossible, to treat the revered founders of various faiths with anything like the veneration that their partisans like to display. We have noticed that an interfaith approach tends to blur or to transcend the differences between sects— but at the risk of draining from sectarians their vitality. Whatever may happen to a few people with exceptional talents, this devitalization of received doctrines and practices can undermine a community's dedication to the moral virtues and to civic duties. [14]

On the other hand, the vitality offered, and to some extent delivered, by earthbound movements (such as the neopagans and witches on display at the Palmer House) may naturally lead to the arousal of more and more expectations that lead in turn to suicidal desperation. Veils may even help protect us from being led astray by beauties that are only apparent or, at least, are far more limited in time or in effect than they seem to be.

In short, it would be imprudent to insist that neither the woman in black nor the woman in white has anything worthwhile to offer us. But it might also be imprudent to rely upon either of these exotic women to provide authoritative guidance about what we should take from the likes of them and their partisans, especially as we strive for mutual understanding and an enduring world peace.

We can well be reminded here of questions that are addressed by the most thoughtful. Some of those questions have always been dealt with, one way or another, by the religions of the world. However much one may have to approach those religions as an outsider, one may still be helped thereby to get to know oneself better.

That is, we should strive to see nature in her wondrous complexity, including how natural impulses take a variety of forms in different situations. There is something natural both in concealing and in uncovering what nature offers. In all this the human being of a philosophical inclination must take care not to seem cavalier about the moral and related religious concerns of his fellow citizens, however likely it may be that those concerns have been shaped by chance circumstances.

VIII

The most serious part of the 1993 Parliament, aside perhaps from the concluding address in Grant Park by the Dalai Lama, was intended to be the Declaration of a Global Ethic signed by two hundred and fifty religious leaders from around the world. This document, the original draft of which had been prepared before the Parliament convened, was reviewed by the leaders of participating groups during the Parliament. [15]

The Declaration opens with a description of the present deplorable condition of humankind and invokes "ancient guidelines for human behavior which are found in the teachings of the religions of the world and which are the condition for a sustainable world order." The signers identify themselves as "women and men who have embraced the precepts and practices of the world's religions." At the same time they "condemn aggression and hatred in the name of religion." They "commit" themselves to "a culture of nonviolence, respect, justice, and peace." (p. 11, col. 1)

Two participants of the 1993 Parliament sign the Declaration of a Global Ethic. By the conclusion of the Parliament, the Declaration had been signed by approximately two hundred and fifty religious leaders from around the world.

The Declaration is then devoted to "The Principles of a Global Ethic":

    I.   No new global order without a new global ethic!

    II.   A fundamental demand: Every human being must be treated humanely.

    III.   Irrevocable directives

        1.   Commitment to a Culture of Nonviolence and Respect for Life

        2.   Commitment to a Culture of Solidarity and a Just Economic Order

        3.   Commitment to a Culture of Tolerance and a Life of Truthfulness

        4.   Commitment to a Culture of Equal Rights and Partnership Between Men and Women.

    IV.   A Transformation of Consciousness!

It is also instructive to notice what is *not* to be found in this Declaration. There is no reference to the 1893 Parliament of the World's Religions which had inspired the 1993 Parliament. There are no quotations from, or even references to, religious authorities such as the Bible, except for drawing upon old prohibitions which are now cast in positive terms. [16] There are nowhere any names of persons, whether religious founders, theologians, or philosophers. Care is taken, it seems, lest it appear that any particular religion or any part of the world is displayed as authoritative (even though the Declaration is decidedly Western in tone). This is in marked contrast to the 1893 Parliament where, for example, the Lord's Prayer of Christendom was repeatedly heard, including at the end of the final plenary session when that prayer was recited under the guidance of the most eminent Chicago rabbi of that day. [17]

In short, we can see in the 1993 Declaration what, in matters of interfaith interests, is the effect of working primarily from what is generally shared by all, or almost all, of the participants.

IX

One of the things generally shared can be said to be the only document explicitly identified in the 1993 Declaration (p. 11, col. 3):

> We are convinced of the fundamental unity of the human family on
> Earth. We recall the 1948 Universal Declaration of Human Rights of
> the United Nations. What is formally proclaimed [there] on the level of
> rights, we wish to confirm and deepen here from the perspective of an

a Global Ethic is to notice that no high level of political philosophy
is drawn upon there. The problems, as well as the possibilities, of
statecraft are not noticed, including those problems which may oblige
the conscientious statesman to be more receptive to the necessity of
deception and the use of veils, for the sake of the common good, than
the Declaration seems to be. [23]

XII

Insensitivity to the possibilities of politics carries over into how organized religion is treated in the Declaration. May this naturally follow if

it should not be recognized that the typical religion is, at least in part, a form of political organization?

There are, in the Declaration, the repeated invocations of ancient religions to which I have referred. It is assumed that those ancient religions have much in common, especially when they prescribe how human beings should live. But may not the same be said about well-established political arrangements?

However much the ancient religions do have in common, they can also serve (we have noticed) as the underlying causes of the deadly enmities which are deplored in the Declaration. Those fundamental differences are recognized only intermittently in the Declaration, and then with the expectation that they can be transformed, virtually by acts of will, into no more than minor disturbances. It does not seem to be sufficiently appreciated that the divergent ways of lives to which great multitudes owe allegiance are rooted, in effect, in divergent and passionate opinions about the very nature of things.

What are the sources of the great ancient religions of the human race? Most of them invoke divine revelation in some form. Prophecy, it has been suggested, is the political name for political science. [24] Others can speak of revelation as a form of poetry, a divinely inspired poetry perhaps, however much poetry itself depends upon a kind of deception. We can be reminded by these observations that little is said about the arts in the Declaration of a Global Ethic.

It is significant that religious leaders of stature could be persuaded to subscribe to a declaration which ignored, if it did not tacitly repudiate, much that is associated with traditional doctrine and worship. This kind of consensus, in these circumstances, seems to be possible (barring an apparently unprecedented divine intervention that moves everyone, or almost everyone, at once) only if the primary concern should be with salvation in this world. [25]

Another way of putting these observations is to suggest that there is little if anything distinctively religious about the concerns and solutions expressed in the Declaration, however sincere and even high-minded those concerns no doubt are. That which had been distinctively religious in the ancient faiths which are repeatedly referred to in the Declaration has given way, at least on this occasion and perhaps even generally among the more sophisticated religionists today, to the prevailing modern mode of thinking—and a recognition of this can make study of the Declaration particularly instructive.

XIII

The leading minds of the Parliament of the World's Religions emphasized, as modernists, human beings and the Earth. (Earth, which is referred to, usually in capital letters, a score of times in the Declaration of a Global Ethic, seems to have taken the place of God. It is appropriate that environmental groups and earth-worshiping societies should have been publicized as much as they were during the 1993 Parliament.) The fashionable tilt in the proceedings could be seen in the Declaration's determined uses of "women and men," with only a few uses of "men and women."

Intermediate institutions, religious as well as secular, are played down. There is instead an emphasis upon extremes: the individual and the worldwide. It is as if all mankind is to be regarded as working out its thought and way of life together. But, it can be argued, it is in the intermediate that human beings truly live—in the intermediate political and religious associations which make much of particulars (and hence of errors, as well as of intimate and otherwise fulfilling relations).

The "universal" orientation of the Declaration testifies to what worldwide struggles, commerce, music, communications and entertainment (including highly-publicized sporting events) have done to us all in the twentieth century. Among the consequences of the remarkable technology to which we have become accustomed is the subversion both of humanity and of community. Another consequence of these developments is that a kind of sociology has replaced old-fashioned theology and philosophy, with the conscientious social worker replacing both the prophet and the politician as a reliable guide to right action.

If any "philosophical" position informs the Declaration, it is probably that of Existentialism mixed with Marxism. Decades of loose talk, not least in the Academy, are reflected here, most tellingly revealed perhaps in the repeated recourse in the Declaration to the "authentically human." (Other revealing usages are *commitment* and *values*.) *Authenticity* has found its way into the theological vocabulary of our time in large part through the influence of Heidegger, another thinker whose remarkable attributes did not include a sound understanding of politics. He, too, thought he could either overcome politics or do without it— but he succeeded only in being used, sadly misused in his self-centered naiveté, by politicians out of the gutter. [26]

A repudiation of Heidegger's political masters and their cruel intensification of partisan politics does not require repudiation of politics altogether, just as a repudiation of such a diabolical institution as the Inquisition does not require repudiation of religion altogether. The genuinely (as distinguished from the authentically?) human depends for most people upon some political/religious order. By far the most attractive feature of the 1993 Parliament of the World's Religions was not the argument made on behalf of a global consciousness but rather the character of the colorful representatives on exhibit from around the world. Those personable men and women, ever so dedicated and for the most part good-natured and high-minded, emanated from ways

53

The conclusion of the 1993 Parliament was a public event in a downtown Chicago park. "By far the most attractive feature of the 1993 Parliament of the World's Religions was not the argument made on behalf of a global consciousness but rather the character of the colorful representatives on exhibit from around the world. Those personable men and women, ever so dedicated and for the most part good-natured and high-minded, emanated from ways of life that have for centuries (if not for millennia) been much more substantial than any way of life likely to be tailored to the principles drawn upon in their Declaration of a Global Ethic."

PART TWO

Reconsiderations of Great Books and Ideas

Science and Religion
in the Work of Lucretius

Otto Bird

Otto Bird was executive editor of *The Great Ideas Today* from 1964 to 1970 and its consulting editor until 1988. Since 1981 he has contributed pieces of his own to "Reconsiderations of Great Books and Ideas."

His connection with the *Great Books of the Western World* set goes back to 1947, when for three years he worked as associate editor of *The Syntopicon*. Trained as a philosopher with particular interest in logic and medieval thought, he became subsequently a member of the faculty at the University of Notre Dame, where he founded and directed the general program of liberal studies from 1959 to 1963, and where he was university professor from 1970 until his retirement in 1976.

In addition to essays and reviews, Mr. Bird has written *Syllogistic Logic and its Extensions* (1964), *The Idea of Justice* (1967), and *Cultures in Conflict: An Essay in the Philosophy of the Humanities* (1976). He was also a major contributor to the *Propædia,* or *Outline of Knowledge,* of the fifteenth edition of the *Encyclopædia Britannica.* In 1991, Mr. Bird published his autobiography, *Seeking a Center: My Life as a "Great Bookie."*

Lucretius, the Roman poet of pagan antiquity, holds a large and important place in the history of ideas as well as in that of literature. As a poet, he was the greatest master of Latin epic verse until the advent of Virgil. As a scientist, he provided the fullest exposition of ancient atomism that we possess, since the works of the Greek founders of the theory, Epicurus and Democritus, are extant only in fragments. As a moralist, he upheld an ideal of the good life grounded upon science that denounced religion as a vicious influence. In this last respect he staked out a position that constitutes one of the paradigmatic theories regarding the relation between science and religion. It is this position, and not the atomic theory as such, that provides the principal subject of this essay.

But before we turn to that, and by way of an introduction, something must be said of the poetry. For Lucretius was a great poet, a master maker of verbal music. Unfortunately, that music achieves its full beauty only in the Latin in which it was composed. Since that prosody differs so greatly from English prosody, one needs an understanding of the elements that compose it. For this, a minimal groundwork suffices to obtain some appreciation of its beauty.

The musical basis of the poetry is supplied by rhythm: the measured motion of the sounding syllables. That is as true of English verse as it is of Latin. But Latin, like Greek in its classical form, employs a different measure from that of English and other modern languages. It uses a measure that is based on quantity instead of on accent. An example shows the difference. Consider the opening line of "An Elegy Written in a Country Church Yard" by Thomas Gray. Speak it slowly and naturally and mark the syllables on which the accent falls, thus:

The cúrfew tólls the knéll of párting dáy

The marked syllables are accented or stressed by being spoken more forcefully; the other syllables less so. As a result, the accented ones are also longer in duration. It is the accent, the stress, that makes them long and the others—by comparison—short.

In the quantitative verse of ancient Latin there is also a division between long and short syllables, but it rests on a different basis. It is not the accent but the intrinsic quantity of different vowel-and-consonant combinations that determines a long or short syllable. Take the first line of Lucretius and mark a long syllable with — and a short with ◡

Aeneadum genetrix, hominum divomque voluptas

There are a number of fairly complex rules for determining whether a syllable is long or short. Diphthongs, for example, are said to be long by nature, as *tenebrae, laudo.* Single vowels are sometimes naturally long, sometimes short. But these rules need not detain us, since in poetry the meter or verse pattern establishes what the arrangement of longs and shorts will be. Hence, once the basic rhythm is detected, the verse can be pronounced accordingly. But this is so only in general or on the whole. Much of the actual beauty of the verse depends upon the way in which a line agrees with or departs from the quantity of the syllable and the stress accent of a word; sometimes the two coincide, other times they do not.

A given rhythm is constituted by the buildup of long and short syllables. Thus, in Lucretius as in Virgil, the basic unit is that of the homeric epic verse: the dactyl, consisting of a long plus two shorts: $-\smile\smile$, where two shorts count as the equivalent of a long. The movement of the verse is determined by the number of such feet in a line. The epic or heroic line consists of six dactyls and hence is named the dactylic hexameter:

$$-\smile\smile \;\; -\smile\smile \;\; -\smile\smile \;\; -\smile\smile \;\; -\smile\smile \;\; -\smile\smile$$
$$1 \qquad 2 \qquad 3 \qquad 4 \qquad 5 \qquad 6$$

The dactyl establishes the basis of the rhythm within any given line but because a long equals two shorts, two longs (a spondee) can be substituted for a dactyl. The opening foot is usually a dactyl; the final one is often a spondee and may even end on a single short syllable. Word division occurs not only at the end of each line, but also with a pause (caesura) in the middle of the third foot. A final vowel of a word, or a vowel plus *m,* is suppressed or elided before another vowel (or *h*) of the next word.

Observing these few directions we are prepared to speak the verses of Lucretius and hear their music.

Aeneadum genetrix, hominum divomque voluptas
alma Venus, caeli subter labentia signa
quae mare navigerum, quae terras frugiferentis
concelebras, per te quoniam genus omne animantum
concipitur visitque exortum lumina solis:

te, dea, te fugiunt venti, te nubila caeli
adventumque tuum, tibi suavis daedala tellus
summittit flores, tibi rident aequora ponti
placatumque nitet diffuso lumine caelum.

Mother of the Aeneadae, darling of men and gods, increase-giving
Venus, who beneath the gliding signs of heaven fillest with thy presence
the ship-carrying sea, the corn-bearing lands, since through thee every

be produced from nothing, and what is begotten cannot be recalled to nothing, first-beginnings must be of an imperishable body" (Bk. I, ll. 540–45; *GBWW* I: 12, 7; II: 11, 8).

Sense experience is basic for Lucretius, as has already been noted several times. But among the senses one of them is primary, and the others secondary; one of them reaches to the nature of things, whereas the others are the psychological response that we make to the data provided by that primary one. This fundamental one is the sense of touch, by which we perceive the corporeal: what is tangible is material. Atoms compose the things of the world that ultimately produce the tangible. In themselves, atoms are devoid of color, heat, sound, taste, smell, or feelings of pain or pleasure, as Lucretius argues at length in his discussion of sensation (Bk. II, ll. 730–990; *GBWW* I: 12, 24–27; II: 11, 24–27). But those are secondary qualities. This distinction between primary and secondary qualities is another feature that Lucretius shares with the makers of modern physical theory.

So too is his optimistic belief in progress, the conviction that, provided science is given its way, the life of humankind will become better and happier than it has been in the past. How this improved state of affairs may eventuate will become clear when we consider how science can overcome the evils that prevent its fulfillment.

The idea of religion

Religion for Lucretius consists essentially in three beliefs: belief that the gods exist, that they influence the course of the world's events, and that by worship of them the pains that they can inflict, especially upon the soul after death, can be averted. Of these three beliefs he maintains that only the first of them is true; the other two are not only false but also greatly evil in their effect upon human life.

In accounting for the rise of religion, Lucretius explains how men came to believe in the existence of gods. Their belief began with divine sightings:

> the races of mortal men would see in waking mind glorious forms, would
> see them in sleep of yet more marvellous size of body. To these then
> they would attribute sense, because they seemed to move their limbs
> and to utter lofty words suitable to their glorious aspect and surpassing
> powers. And they would give them life everlasting, because their face
> would ever appear before them and their form abide; yes and yet
> without all this, because they would not believe that beings possessed of
> such powers could lightly be overcome by any force. And they would
> believe them to be pre-eminent in bliss, because none of them was ever
> troubled with the fear of death.
>
> (Bk. V, ll. 1169–81; *GBWW* I: 12, 76; II: 11, 73)

To this belief about the gods Lucretius himself would not object, and says much the same himself. Yet, to this true belief there was added a false inference about the power of the gods over the events of this world:

> Again they [men] would see the system of heaven and the different
> seasons of the years come round in regular succession, and could not
> find out by what causes this was done; therefore they would seek a
> refuge in handing over all things to the gods and supposing all things
> to be guided by their nod. And they placed in heaven the abodes and
> realms of the gods, because night and moon are seen to roll through
> heaven, moon, day, and night and night's austere constellations and
> night-wandering meteors of the sky and flying bodies of flame, clouds,
> sun, rains, snow, winds, lightnings, hail, and rapid rumblings and loud
> threatful thunderclaps.
>
> (Bk. V, ll. 1182–93; *GBWW* I: 12, 76; II: 11, 73)

In this latter belief about the power of the gods there is much error, according to Lucretius, and he aims to correct it by setting forth the truth about such beings. The gods, he says, are immortal and in this are like the indestructible atoms and the void. They dwell in unshakable peace, entirely free from any concern about our world, and hence from exercising any influence over it. In fact they dwell wholly apart from our world:

> This too you may not possibly believe, that the holy seats of the gods
> exist in any parts of the world: the fine nature of the gods far withdrawn
> from our senses is hardly seen by the thought of the mind; and since it
> has ever eluded the touch and stroke of the hands, it must touch nothing
> which is tangible for us. . . . And therefore their seats as well must be
> unlike our seats, fine, even as their bodies are fine.
>
> (Bk. V, ll. 146–54; *GBWW* I: 12, 63; II: 11, 61)

The abodes in which they dwell are tranquil since

> neither winds do shake nor clouds drench with rains nor snow
> congealed by sharp frosts harms with hoary fall: an ever cloudless ether
> o'ercanopies them, and they laugh with light shed largely round. Nature
> too supplies all their wants and nothing ever impairs their peace of mind.
>
> (Bk. III, ll. 18–24; *GBWW* I: 12, 30; II: 11, 30)

Dwelling in eternal tranquillity apart from the world and from concern with humankind, the gods are entirely indifferent, and it is folly to believe that they either made it or govern it (Bk. V, ll. 155–65; *GBWW* I: 12, 63; II: 11, 60–61). It is likewise folly to believe that prayers and worship can influence the gods to act in any way whatever. Nor does true piety lie in such action:

> No act it is of piety to be often seen with veiled head to turn to a stone
> and approach every altar and fall prostrate on the ground and spread

If man would but recognize the weight that lies upon his mind and oppresses with its heaviness, then on knowing its cause he would not act in the senseless way he does, ignorant of what he wants and seeking ever to change his place as if he could drop his burden. One leaves his great house because it bores him and then suddenly returns since he feels no better away. He drives his horses precipitately to the country house as though to extinguish a fire, but no sooner arrives then he yawns, falls into a deep sleep of oblivion, or else makes haste to get back to the city. He is obviously sick.

But what is the cause of his disease? He is fleeing from himself in any way he can. Yet, it still clings to him, since he cannot get away from himself, and he hates himself since he knows not the cause of his sickness. If he could see that well, he would put all things aside and study first to know the nature of things (*naturam primum studeat cognoscere rerum*). For the question in doubt is not his state for one hour, as the restless, hurrying man seems to think, but his state for all eternity, which is the time for mortals to pass that remains after death (Bk. III, ll. 1053–75; *GBWW* I: 12, 43–44; II: 11, 42–43).

This restless weariness of mankind betrays a diseased condition. The symptoms are unmistakable. But what is its cause? "What is this great evil lust of life [*vitai cupido*] that with such force makes us restless [*trepidare*] amid doubts and dangers" (Bk. III, ll. 1076–77; *GBWW* I: 12, 44; II: 11, 43). Lucretius now includes himself in the question, as though acknowledging that he too experiences the same suffering.

He admits that we have a never changing thirst for life, and that we crave what we do not have. Yet, he maintains that if we look rationally and dispassionately at our situation, we would admit the folly and futility of such an attitude and resign ourselves. The end of life is certain, and death cannot be avoided. We are ever involved in the same pursuits, and no new pleasure can be obtained by living on; we do not know what fortune may bring us or what exit we will have. Moreover, by continuing to live we cannot remove one whit from the time we will be dead or make any less the time after death. Even though you may live as many generations as you wish, death will remain nonetheless eternal. Nor will he be any less who ends his life with today's light than he who went down many months and years before (Bk. III, ll. 1076–94; *GBWW* I: 12, 44; II: 11, 43).

Such is the case that Lucretius advances to repel if not to overcome the fear of death. Strong as it is, it is still not without ambiguities. Perhaps I should not be indignant about dying, it is true considering that better than me have died. Yet, if good king Ancus and the philosopher Epicurus are still remembered, their names at least have lived on for thousands of years. And that constitutes a kind of immortality. It suffices at least to justify the dangers of battle, as the Trojan hero Sarpedon explains to his friend Glaukos:

> Man, supposing you and I, escaping this battle, would be able to live
> on forever, ageless, immortal, so neither would I myself go on fighting
> in the foremost nor would I urge you into the fighting where men win
> glory. But now, seeing that the spirits of death stand close about us in
> their thousands, no man can turn aside nor escape them, let us go on
> and win glory for ourselves, or yield it to others.
>
> (Bk. XII, ll. 322–28; *GBWW* I: 4, 85; II: 3, 145)

In the restlessness that besets human beings, Lucretius recognizes a
sign of ambiguity in them, being as they are of two minds about themselves and their lot. But he attributes this to a weakness that results from
erroneous thinking. Other writers of his age think differently. Yet, to
St. Augustine such restlessness provides evidence of a divine vocation,
since our heart is restless (*inquietum*) until it rests in God (Bk. I, l. 1;
GBWW I: 18, 1; II: 16, 1). Marcus Aurelius agrees with Lucretius that
there is no immortality, but unlike the poet he believes that the gods
can influence human life and even expresses regret that they have not
given man an unending life:

> How can it be that the gods after having arranged all things well and
> benevolently for mankind, have overlooked this alone, that some men
> and very good men . . . when they have once died should never exist
> again, but should be completely extinguished?
>
> (Bk. XII, l. 5; *GBWW* I: 12, 307–8; II: 11, 291)

For the Christian, of course, on the witness of Jesus Christ in the Gospel
eternal life has been promised to those who believe in Him.

Perhaps the strongest opposition to the teaching of Lucretius on this
subject is offered by Plato. Both contrast the short span of mortal life
with the endlessness of eternity. But whereas for Lucretius it is the
mistaken desire for immortality that sets the problem, for Plato it is
rather his mortality. "The whole period of three score years and ten is
surely but a little thing in comparison with eternity?" Socrates declares,
and then asks: "And should an immortal being seriously think of this
little space rather than of the whole?" (Bk. X, l. 608; *GBWW* I: 7, 434;
II: 6, 434). His account then ends by offering a myth to explain why an
immortal soul should have to suffer the indignity of a mortal bodily life.

Plato, like St. Thomas Aquinas, bases his confidence in immortality
upon the existence in human nature of an immaterial principle. Many
thinkers like Lucretius find their proof unconvincing. But how convincing is Lucretius's attack upon what strikes him as the great and evil lust
men have for life (*mala tanta vitai cupido*)? Is this a satisfactory view of
the matter? To be indifferent to death is to be indifferent to life, and
that demeans and devalues the goodness of life and our estimation of it.
It is through living that we exist as human beings, whose desire for life,
for being, has properly, it may be argued, some horror of not-being,
of nothingness.

The idea of happiness

In his attempt to change the way death is regarded Lucretius has a double purpose. He writes not only to set forth the way things are, but also to demolish what he considers a major obstacle to achieving a happy life. The idea he holds of happiness precludes the fear of death because of its effect upon the way that human beings pursue their lives. It renders the achievement of happiness impossible.

Lucretius freely acknowledges in gratitude and praise that Epicurus is his guide in this matter. It was Epicurus who

> cleansed men's breasts with truth-telling precepts and fixed a limit to
> lust and fear [*cuppedinis atque timoris*] and explained what was the chief
> good [*bonum summum*] which we all strive to reach, and pointed out
> the road along which by a short cross-track we might arrive at it in a
> straightforward course.   (Bk. VI, ll. 24–27; *GBWW* I: 12, 80; II: 11, 77)

This chief good, according to Epicurus, consists in a calm, peaceful, undisturbed mind, or *ataraxia*. This means, as stated in a text quoted by his ancient biographer, Diogenes Laertius (*Lives of Eminent Philosophers,* Bk. X, sec. 82), "being released from all these troubles and cherishing a continual remembrance of the highest and most important truths." Lucretius is confident that Epicurus has taught those truths which make possible the achievement of this enviable state. "Nothing is sweeter," the poet declares, "than to possess well fortified and serene temples built up by the teachings of the wise from which you can look down upon others and see them wandering about seeking the path of life" (Bk. II, ll. 7–10; *GBWW* I: 12, 15; II: 11, 15). He castigates the minds and hearts of those who fail to see that "nature craves for itself only that pain be removed apart from the body and that the mind enjoy a joyful sense apart from fear and care" (Bk. II, ll. 16–19; *GBWW* I: 12, 15; II: 11, 15).

But to reach such a state the mind and heart must be purged of the sources of care. After the fear of death Lucretius locates the other cause, equal if not greater in power, in the unbridled passion of sexual love.

The infatuation of sexual love

The discussion of love occurs as the final section of the account of sensation, thinking, sleep, and dreams in Book IV. The analysis of love is carried out by consideration of the following subjects:

Its physical genital cause
The characteristics of passionate love
Its evil consequences

Its prevention and cure
The reproductive purposes
Problems regarding reproduction
Why one person is loved rather than another
(Bk. IV, ll. 1037–1287; *GBWW* I: 12, 57–61; II: 11, 55–58).

From this list of subjects it appears at once that the only kind of love that Lucretius considers is genital sexual love. That reproduction receives separate discussion also indicates, as we will see, that the object under attack as evil is not the reproductive drive as such, but unbridled sexual infatuation. The praise given to Venus as the mother of generation in the invocation suffices to make that distinction.

The source and rise of the disorderly passion is physical. It lies in the generation of human seed in the mature body which then gather in one place (*partis genitalis*), incited by the desire (*libido*) for ejection. The act of love that ensues is compared to a battle:

> the body seeks that object from which the mind is wounded by love; for all as a rule fall towards their wound and the blood spirts out in that direction whence comes the stroke by which we are struck; and if he is at close quarters, the red stream covers the foe. Thus then [*sic igitur*] he who gets a hurt from the weapons of Venus, (whether he is being attacked by a young boy with effeminate limbs or a woman hurling love at him with all her body,) inclines to the quarter whence he is wounded, and yearns to unite [*coire*] with it (and project fluid [*umor*] from body to body;) for a mute desire [*cupido*] gives a presage of the pleasure.
> (Bk. IV, ll. 1047–55; *GBWW* I: 12, 57; II: 11, 55 [except for my translations in parentheses])

"This," Lucretius declares, "is our Venus"; hence too the name of *amor,* Lucretius claiming it comes from *umor;* "hence that drop of the sweetness of Venus that trickled into the heart" (Bk. IV, ll. 1058–60; *GBWW* I: 12, 57–58; II: 11, 55). But then Lucretius immediately adds: "Then follows frigid care," and with this a catalogue of the evils of this love.

It is a torment whether its object is present or absent. For if absent there remain still images of it and the sweet name. The passion is a sore, a pain, a madness (*furor*), that worsens as it is fed daily, "the one thing of which the more we have the more the breast burns with dreadful desire" (Bk. IV, ll. 1089–90; *GBWW* I: 12, 58; II: 11, 56).

Bad in itself, the passion leads on to yet further evils. Its victim consumes his strength in its labor, spends his life at the call of another, wastes any wealth that he has on presents for its object, lets his duties slide and loses his good name, and yet feels bitter in his conscious mind at living in slothfulness and perishing in brothels (Bk. IV, ll. 1121–36; *GBWW* I: 12, 58–59; II: 11, 56).

Whether happy or unhappy the infatuation of love brings so many evils that it is better avoided entirely. There are precautions to take in order to prevent it or at least cure it before becoming deadly: flee from its images, scare away whatever feeds the love, turn your mind to another and spend your passion upon that body rather than turning it entirely upon the love of one (Bk. IV, ll. 1063–66; *GBWW* I: 12, 58; II: 11, 55). If infatuated, try to see through the delusions you have of the beloved, ceasing to overlook faults of mind and body. Learn to recognize the inanities of the lovesick. Remember there are always others besides that one, that you got along without her before, and that however beautiful she is still the same as others (Bk. IV, ll. 1141–74; *GBWW* I: 12, 59; II: 11, 56–57).

To avoid or cure the infatuation Lucretius recommends "wandering with the lights-of-love of Venus" (Bk. IV, l. 1071; *GBWW* I: 12, 58; II: 11, 55). In his time sacred prostitution, male as well as female, was rife. However, Lucretius was sure that it was not sacred. No divine powers deprive anyone of genital force (Bk. IV, l. 1233; *GBWW* I: 12, 60; II: 11, 58), any more than they bestow it; nor is it due to divine influence or arrows of Venus that even a woman of uncomely shape is loved (Bk. IV, l. 1278; *GBWW* I: 12, 60–61; II: 11).

From his attack upon it and the bitter satiric picture he gives of sexual love as an infatuation, it is clear that Lucretius considers it a serious disease. In this he is followed by a long line of doctors of medicine in the Middle Ages, Moslem as well as Christian. Robert Burton (1577–1640) quotes extensively from them in his *Anatomy of Melancholy*. The lover's disease was supposed to be caused by an excess of black bile (Greek: *melas + chole*).

It is the unrestrained excessive disturbance of the passion that Lucretius attacks as evil. In this respect the sexual infatuation resembles the fear of death. They are alike in that each of them gives rise to worry and restlessness and the consequent destruction of the calm and peace of mind needed for knowing and considering the way things are. Both make impossible the achievement of a happy life. The fear of death is said to be rooted, as we have seen, in an innate desire to preserve life. Sexual infatuation has its source in the reproductive instinct, and can thus be viewed also as a craving to continue life.

Lucretius is not opposed to reproduction as such. Indeed, he states explicitly that one may have children without the excessive passion: "Nor does he lack the fruit of Venus who shuns love, but takes rather the advantage without pain; for certainly a purer pleasure comes to the healthy than to the wretched" (Bk. IV, ll. 1073–76; *GBWW* I: 12, 58; II: 11, 55). Thus he is not opposed to having a family, the reproductive purpose underlying sexuality. It is the excessive passion that may accompany its expression that he abhors. In it, as in the fear of death, there is an unhealthy and exaggerated craving for life.

Science and religion

Lucretius in his poem has a passionate concern and objective, but it is a passion not of sex but of knowledge: to know the way things are so as to grasp the truth about them. He is supremely confident that the science of Epicurus and the atomists has already discovered many truths and is progressing toward still more. Much still remains to be known, and when this is so, Lucretius provides the option of several possible explanations. Thus, for example, he writes that variations in the light of the moon from light to dark may come about from either (1) changes in light reflected from the sun relative to its different positions, or (2) obstructions of its own light caused by another moving body, or (3) revolving and showing at one time its bright side and at another its dark (Bk. V, ll. 705–30; *GBWW* I: 12, 70; II: 11, 67–68). However, although one cannot be certain which of these is the truth, Lucretius remains unshakably sure that the gods provide no true explanation themselves.

This poem on the nature of things has as its overriding objective the desacralization of the entire world, human as well as nonhuman. No theological or religious explanation is anything but false. That much can be shown either by refuting the explanation offered by religion or by providing a superior explanation based upon science. The fear of death that arises from religious beliefs is attacked as being without any rational basis, and the infatuation of sex, far from being a work of the gods Venus and Cupid, is diagnosed as a physical and psychological malady. In the fifth book Lucretius continues his work of demolition by considering the stars and other heavenly phenomena, the rise and eventual disappearance of the earth, the origin of living things, including man, the invention of language and the development of the arts and society. All of these matters are clearly taken to be of great interest in themselves, and they are presented as such. Yet, we as readers are never allowed to forget the ulterior purpose: "to prevent us from thinking that they have come about on account [*ratione*] of the gods" (Bk. V, l. 81; *GBWW* I: 12, 62; II: 11, 60).

In his effort to destroy belief in the influence of the pagan gods Lucretius bears comparison with the work of St. Augustine in the *City of God*. Both the saint and the poet attack the pagan religion of Rome and seek to eradicate its power over the beliefs and actions of humankind. They do so, of course, for entirely opposite reasons: Lucretius to establish the truth of science, Augustine the truth of Christianity.

Since Lucretius is determined to know the truth about things, the position he takes regarding the relation of science and religion depends upon his opinion of truth in religion. To understand this general question one needs to consider its truth-possibilities or the different ways in which religious belief may bear upon the truth. Here there are three possibilities depending upon the kind of truth that is involved, as

Mortimer Adler has shown in his recent book *Truth in Religion* (1990). Truth may be either descriptive, prescriptive, or poetic. A statement or belief that accords with the way things actually are in fact constitutes a descriptive or theoretical truth. A statement or belief that declares how one should act and conduct his life has a prescriptive or practical truth. A statement or belief that expresses an imaginative exploration of probabilities and possibilities has poetic truth. This last kind is the truth to be found in poems, novels, dramas; for that reason, when these are concerned only with probabilities and possibilities there is no incompatibility between the various expressions, however different they may be. In this respect, of not being subject to contradiction, poetic truth differs radically from both descriptive and prescriptive truth. The claim asserted by Lucretius that everything is made out of indestructible, indivisible material particles can be contradicted and has been in contemporary quantum physics. The same holds true for prescriptive statements. That we ought to fear death and the gods can be contradicted and has been by Lucretius.

On the issue of truth in religion, all three possibilities have representatives in today's controversy over religious belief, as Adler has shown in the book just cited. The claim that all religions, indeed all myths, are compatible with one another is the position taken by Joseph Campbell in *The Inner Reaches of Outer Space,* subtitled *Metaphor as Myth and as Religion* (1986). As indicated by the title, since religion is identified with metaphor, it contains only poetic truth and neither theoretic nor practical truth.

The view that emphasizes the prescriptive or practical truth of religion, and minimizes if it does not ignore any factual or theoretical truth is represented by Hans Küng in his book *Theology for the Third Millennium: An Ecumenical View* (1988).

The position that religion contains factual truth as well as truths that are prescriptive and poetic is that of the orthodox, whether Christian, Jew, or Muslim.

Where then does Lucretius stand on the issue of truth in religion and hence too on the relation of science and religion? He refuses to allow that religion, at least as he knows it as practised in pagan Rome, has any kind of truth. It lays claim to descriptive truth, as in its assertion of the existence of the gods, the immortality of the soul, divine power over the world, both human and nonhuman, the efficacy of prayer and worship of the gods. But with the exception of the existence of the gods, which Lucretius accepts, none of the rest has any truth at all, he says. Religion lays claim to prescriptive truth in declaring how one should live and act. Yet, even that can be refuted, he claims, inasmuch as its commands can be shown to result in evil consequences and a wretched life for man. Some measure of poetic truth Lucretius is willing to grant to religion, but only on the condition that its myths be interpreted as metaphors of evils in this present life, as shown by his interpretations of the mythical accounts of punishment in the afterlife.

Lucretius is a great poet with an epic reach. Yet, his remarks about poetry in his poem emphasize its ability to charm and persuade rather than to know. It is thus that he explains why he is expressing his doctrine in verse at the end of Book I, ll. 921–50 (*GBWW* I: 12, 12; II: 11, 13, and repeated with small changes at the beginning of Book IV). He knows, he says, that his doctrine is dark and obscure, and he wants to make it clearer. Thus, treating of great matters, his songs are so lucid that all is touched with the Muses's grace. But also, he is following the practice of physicians who beguile children into taking bitter medicine by coating the rim of the cup with honey so that they may regain health; since his doctrine seems bitter and people shrink from it, he expounds it in sweet-speaking Pierian song and, as it were, touches it with the Muses's sweet honey so as to hold the mind with his verses while showing forth the entire nature of things.

On the issue of science and religion, Lucretius takes a clear and pure position. His is the earliest representation of that which came to be known centuries later as Deism. This allows that the divine exists, but denies that it has any power over the events of the cosmos or the actions of mankind. Lucretius is also the first to declare war between science and religion and to hail the triumphal progress of science a millennium and a half before that was to begin. His hatred of religion and opposition to it is complete; he grants it nothing; all of it is false and evil in its effects. In this he differs from Freud, who holds that religion is an illusion, not an error but a wish fulfillment; and Freud knows that wishes may sometimes become realized, although he does not believe that this is possible for the wishes fostered by religion.

Conclusion

To conclude this study we ought to consider also how successful Lucretius is in achieving his purpose. Theoretically, he wants and seeks to know and provide rational explanations of the nature of things, of how they are and how they came to be as they are. As is clear from his enthusiastic praise of his master, the Greek philosopher Epicurus, he exulted in the knowledge he had acquired and was proud and pleased to teach it to others. Measured by the achievement of modern science, the physical explanation that he offers is still at a primitive stage. To some extent Lucretius seems to have been well aware of that fact, since he expresses confidence that scientific explanation was certain to continue and provide better and truer explanations.

But beyond his theoretical aim, of equal and even greater importance for Lucretius, is the practical end he hoped to accomplish. Science for him is not an end in itself. Its knowledge is to be put to use to make possible a happier life for mankind. It is to do so by clearing away the major obstructions. These consist for Lucretius in the belief and practice of religion, and especially in the baneful influence it exerts to encourage the fear of death and the infatuation of sexual love. This being so, the success or failure of achieving his practical objective is to be measured by the extent to which he succeeds in refuting if not destroying religion, the fear of death, and sexual infatuation.

On all three topics Lucretius is especially strong in describing the evils they inspire and in attacking them as greatly harmful to the pursuit of the good life. His refutation of them is entirely negative. They are wholly evil. Thus his argument is weakened and exposed to criticism by its total neglect of any good that can be found in the fear of death, sexual love, or religion.

Consider his account of the fear of death. There is no analysis of fear itself. Instead it centers upon the objects of punishment that may occur after death as taught by religious belief. Yet, once fear in itself is considered, it appears that there is more to say. Thus Aristotle in his discussion of fear in the *Rhetoric* (Bk. II, chap. 5; *GBWW* I: 9, 628–29; II: 8, 628–29) defines it as the imagination of an evil in the future that is either destructive or painful (Bk. II, chap. 5, l. 1382a21; *GBWW* I: 9, 628–29; II: 8, 628–29). Not all evils, but only some of them, inspire fear. Stupidity and ignorance are evils, yet are not fearful like those involving great loss or pain. Also, the evil must be in the future, since a present evil is an object of sorrow rather than of fear, though to be feared the object must not lie too far in the future, since, as Aristotle notes, "we all know we shall die, but we are not troubled thereby, because death is not close at hand" (Bk. II, chap. 5, l. 1382a25; *GBWW* I: 9, 628; II: 8, 628). Yet, Aristotle notes elsewhere that "death is the most terrible of all things" (Bk. III, chap. 6, l. 1115a26; *GBWW* I: 9, 361; II: 8, 361). Hence it is not that death is not a great evil, but rather that it does not become an object of fear unless it is imminent.

Aquinas follows Aristotle in his account of fear, but adds the note that it arises from love. Since evil is the privation of good, the evil that arouses fear involves the loss of some good. In the case of death the loss is not only that of life, but also of being itself. Hence Aquinas claims that the fear of death is natural inasmuch as there is a "natural desire of being" (Ques. 41, art. 3; *GBWW* I: 19, 800; II: 17, 800).

In the light of these observations it becomes clear where Lucretius is defective in his account of the fear of death. It is not that this fear is mistaken when it is based on a false belief in a bodily punishment after death. It is also true that death is not in every case regarded as an evil. Otherwise suicide would not be desired and pursued as a release from the evils of life. What Lucretius fails to note is that the pain of sense, as in bodily punishment, is not the only kind of pain. There is also the pain of loss, the grief that one feels on the loss of a loved one. Since there is a love of life and of being, the loss of it in death is an object of fear.

So too in his criticism of love, the argument of Lucretius is weak by defect in its neglect of all except extreme sexual passion. The only other love he appears to admit is that of friendship, such as is expressed in his regard for his patron Memmius. Yet, pagan antiquity possessed a far deeper and higher conception of love in the theory that Plato expressed through the words of Socrates in the *Symposium* (ll. 199–212 [*GBWW* I: 7, 161–68; II: 6, 161–68]). His encomium of love in this dialogue recognizes that it begins in sexual love of one person for another, but need not stop there. It can go on to recognize and love all physical beauty and thus come to love the beauty of the soul even more. That beauty can then be found and loved as it occurs in conduct and occupations, leading next to the beauty of the sciences so as to reach that of science in general, until at the height of the ladder it achieves a vision of beauty itself, a beauty that is eternal, perfect, and unique. Thus, Plato sees, as Lucretius does not, that love even at the lowest sexual degree possesses a transcendent power that can lead a person out of and beyond himself. The poem of Lucretius makes manifest his love of philosophy, the love of wisdom, and yet his theory of love can provide no reason for it.

On the subject of religion Lucretius again is completely one-sided in holding an entirely negative view of it. The polytheistic pagan religion he opposes contained many evil practices, especially for a Christian such as Augustine exposed in his *City of God.* Yet, there is more to be said even for that pagan religion than Lucretius allows. Virgil said it only a generation later in his *Georgics.* In words that allude to the claims that Lucretius makes, Virgil adds an addendum that constitutes a criticism, thus:

> Happy, [*felix*] who had the skill to understand
> Nature's hid causes, and beneath his feet
> All terrors cast, and death's relentless doom,
> And the loud roar of greedy Acheron.
> Blest too is he who knows the rural gods,
> Pan, old Silvanus, and the sister-nymphs!
> (Bk. II, ll. 490–94; *GBWW* I: 13, 65; II: 12, 51])

The Latin of the text makes clearer the difference between Virgil and Lucretius. Virgil agrees with Lucretius that the scientific man is *felix,* happy, because he has been able (*potuit*) to *rerum cognoscere causas* (to know the causes of things) which is the claim of Lucretius. The religious man like Virgil, but unlike Lucretius, is *fortunatus,* blessed, but blessed by fortune. Here a contrast is drawn between what a person can do (*potuit*) by his own powers and that which comes to a person from without, as a good from Fortuna. The verbs for knowledge also differ.

For the former, it is *cognoscere,* to know by inquiry and investigation; for the latter it is *noscere,* to know by personal acquaintance. That of the former disdains all fear, inexorable fate, and the roar of the greedy river of death, Acheron. The knowledge of the latter lies in acquaintance with the gods of woods and woodland, Pan and old Silvanus, and the sister nymphs of fountains, rivers, and trees. It does not diminish what it knows, but gathers and delights in it. Thus, in effect, Virgil criticizes and reproves Lucretius for his failure to see and recognize that there is a good in religious reflection.

In all three cases Lucretius fails by defect in successfully exposing and completely refuting as evil the three principal objects of his moral rage—religion, the fear of death, and sexual love. It is a great poem, but as with other great works, its limits too, are great.

References

Adler, Mortimer J. *Truth in Religion: The Plurality of Religions and the Unity of Truth.* New York: Macmillan Publishing Company, 1990.

Aristotle. *Nichomachean Ethics.* Translated by W. D. Ross.

Aristotle. *Rhetoric.* Translated by W. Rhys Roberts.

Burton, Robert. *The Anatomy of Melancholy.* London: J. M. Dent & Sons, 1932.

Diogenes Laërtius. *Lives of Eminent Philosophers.* Translated by R. D. Hicks. London: William Heinemann Ltd., 1931.

Freud, Sigmund. *The Future of an Illusion.* Translated by W. D. Robson-Scott. Garden City, N.Y.: Doubleday & Company, Inc., 1964.

Homer. *The Iliad and the Odyssey.* Translated by Richmond Lattimore.

Lucretius. *De rerum natura.* Latin text edited by W. H. D. Rouse. London: William Heinemann Ltd., 1931.

Lucretius. *On the Nature of Things.* Translated by H. A. J. Munro.

Marcus Aurelius. *The Meditations.* Translated by George Long.

Plato. *The Republic.* Translated by Benjamin Jowett.

Plato. *Symposium.* Translated by Benjamin Jowett.

Salem, Jean. *La Mort n'est Rien pour Nous: Lucrèce et l'éthique.* Paris: Librairie philosophique, J. Vrin, 1990.

Schrijvers, P. H. *Horror ac Divina Voluptas; Études sur la poétique et la poésie de Lucrèce.* Amsterdam: A. M. Hakkert, 1970.

Segal, Charles. *Lucretius on Death and Anxiety: Poetry and Philosophy in De rerum natura.* Princeton, N.J.: Princeton University Press, 1990.

Virgil. *Georgics.* Translated by James Rhodes.

West, David. *The Imagery and Poetry of Lucretius.* Edinburgh: Edinburgh University Press, 1969.

Whitehead, Alfred North. *Adventures of Ideas.* Cambridge: Cambridge University Press, 1935.

The Psychology of Tocqueville's Democracy in America

Jon Elster

Jon Elster is the Edward L. Ryerson Distinguished Service Professor of Political Science, Philosophy and the College at the University of Chicago. He divides his time between Chicago, Oslo, Norway, and France. He describes himself as a "methodological individualist," and his various writings have made substantial contributions to contemporary economics and political theory from the perspective of a social scientist.

His numerous books include *Ulysses and the Sirens* (1979), *Sour Grapes* (1983), *Making Sense of Marx* (1985), *The Cement of Society* (1989), *Local Justice* (1992), and *Political Psychology* (1993). An article by Professor Elster entitled "Egonomics: The Economics of Personal Conflict" appeared in last year's issue of *The Great Ideas Today*. He is currently writing on the process of constitution-making in Eastern Europe, and is preparing a book on the political thought of Alexis de Tocqueville.

I. Introduction

Alexis de Tocqueville's *Democracy in America* is perhaps the most famous book ever written about the United States. [1] It has also been taken to contain brilliant anticipations of the development of mass democracy in the twentieth century. I believe that the reasons why the book is still very much worthwhile reading today have little to do with this reputation. [2] It is probably among the half dozen most important books in *social* theory of the nineteenth century, but it is not a great work of *political* science. Compared for instance to the writings of J. S. Mill on liberty, utilitarianism, and democracy, *Democracy in America* has little to offer by way of systematic political analysis. In fact, I shall claim that it does not offer systematic analyses of any kind. In his later writings, notably *The Old Regime and the French Revolution,* Tocqueville showed that he was capable of constructing a consistent argument. *Democracy in America,* however, is very much a young man's first book: exuberant, penetrating, and largely incoherent. In the reader—at least in this reader—it generates both intellectual excitement and mental frustration to the highest degrees.

The work has too many facets for one article to do it anything like full justice. Rather than treating many aspects in what would inevitably be a brief and schematic manner, I have chosen to discuss one particular set of arguments in a more systematic way—Tocqueville's analyses of individual psychology under conditions of equality and democracy. To be sure, the reason he was concerned with individual desires and beliefs was that he intended to use them as the basic building blocks in larger historical and social analyses. In the following, I shall inevitably have to make some reference to these macro-sociological implications, but for the most part the focus will be resolutely at the micro level. I believe that many of his psychological discussions are as brilliantly path-breaking as anything else found in his work, and very much worthwhile discussing for their own sake.

I shall proceed as follows. Section II locates the work in the historical environment, both within the narrow context in which it was written and in the broader perspective of mid-nineteenth-century social thought. In Section III I sketch the methodological framework for my interpretations. Section IV focuses on "the psychology of democracy," with special emphasis on how equality generates selfishness, shortsightedness, and irreligiosity, and on the role of freedom in counteracting these tendencies. Here, I also consider Tocqueville's views on dogmatism, skepticism, conformism, and other modes of belief formation. Section V offers a brief conclusion.

II. The historical context

Tocqueville came from an aristocratic family and retained many of the values of his class. He knew, though, that aristocracy and hierarchy were being replaced by democracy and equality in an irresistible and irreversible historical process. Moreover, to some extent, or in some part of himself, that was a development he welcomed. Although the Introduction to the book remains agnostic on this point, [3] the last chapter of the second volume reluctantly concludes that democracy, all things considered, is a good thing: "It is natural to suppose that not the particular prosperity of the few, but the greater well-being of all, is most pleasing in the sight of the Creator and Preserver of men. What seems to me decay is thus in His eyes progress; what pains me is acceptable to Him. Equality may be less elevated, but it is more just, and in its justice lies its greatness and beauty" (p. 382).

This is hardly unreserved praise. Over and over in the book we find Tocqueville deploring the mediocrity and pettiness of democratic societies, comparing them unfavorably to the splendors of the past. In democracies men do more things, but each thing is less well done (p. 127). Or again, "if in your view the main object of government is not to achieve the greatest strength or glory for the nation as a whole but to provide for every individual therein the utmost well-being . . . then it is good to make conditions equal and to establish a democratic government" (ibid.). The dilemma resembles that put by G. A. Cohen in a discussion of Marx's philosophy of history: should one use, as the criterion for judging historical development, the self-realization of Mankind or that of individual human beings? [4] Marx with no reservations, and Tocqueville with a great many, opted for the second alternative. I shall return to the comparison between Marx and Tocqueville in several places below. Here, I want to observe that Tocqueville's main concern was elsewhere. Although he did believe that the progress of social equality was irresistible and irreversible, he thought it could go together with one of two political systems: freedom or despotism. Much of *Democracy in America* deals with the conditions under which men might choose freedom and resist the insidious encroachments of despotism. The triumph of equality over hierarchy, the substitution of the mediocre happiness of the many for the glory of the few: these were given facts, to be deplored or welcomed, but not to be opposed. But if we ask which of the political correlates of equality

Alexis de Tocqueville

would be realized, the answer is that "our fate is in our hands" (p. 3). In Tocqueville, fatalism with regard to social development goes together with a belief in agency as far as political institutions are concerned.

Tocqueville's own circle was not only aristocratic but reactionary. Although Tocqueville decided to swear allegiance to the quasi-liberal regime that came to power in July 1830, many of his friends did not and reproached him when he did. Moreover, he felt that were he to continue as magistrate under Louis-Philippe, the need to remove suspicions about his loyalty would force him to show more zeal for the new regime than would be honorable. By leaving the country for the United States, he could get out of his predicament: escape the political turmoil without resigning from his post, and then return when the dust had settled. [5] It remained only to find a pretext for leaving: he announced that he would study the penitentiary systems of the United States. With his friend Gustave de Beaumont he arrived in New York on May 11, 1831, and left from the same city to go back to France on Feb. 20, 1832.

One can read *Democracy in America* as an appeal by Tocqueville to his reactionary friends, intended to break down their antidemocratic and antiegalitarian prejudices. [6] In this perspective, the book contains three messages to them. First, they were simply wasting their time in trying to fight social equality: it is inevitable, irresistible, and irreversible. Privilege and hierarchy can never be restored. Second, equality and democracy are by no means as bad as the critics think they are. Many of the alleged nefarious effects of democratic institutions evaporate before a careful causal analysis. And third, the critics are wrong in believing that the political consequences of equality are necessarily dangerous. Instead of leading to universal leveling under an omnipotent despot, it can support the self-government of free citizens.

To support these three messages Tocqueville constantly invokes the American example. Writing about America for French readers, Tocqueville could well have used a phrase that Marx applied to England when writing for his German readers: "*De te fabula narratur.* . . . The country that is more developed . . . only shows, to the less developed, the image of its own future." [7] By observing American society the French will be able to grasp the causal mechanisms that lie behind the inevitable progress of equality and accept that "sooner or later we, like the Americans, will attain almost complete equality of conditions" (p. 6).

To expose the causal fallacies of the critics of democracy, one of Tocqueville's strategies is to point out that democratic institutions and habits have much less malign effects when they are widely diffused and have existed for a long time, as is the case in the United States, than when they are less pervasive or recently established. The most general application of this strategy is to warn against confusing the effects of equality with the effects of equalization. "One must be careful not to confuse the fact of equality with the revolution which succeeds in introducing it into the state of society and into the laws. In that lies the reason for almost all the phenomena which cause our surprise" (p. 373). For instance, "While equality favors sound morals, the social upheaval leading to it has a very damaging influence on them" (p. 322). [8]

Finally, Tocqueville could point to the United States to pacify those who believed that equality would inevitably lead to a leveling form of despotism. Following Montesquieu, [9] Tocqueville and his contemporaries assumed that in countries with a strong executive one needed a system of "intermediate powers" that could act as a buffer between the executive and the citizens and prevent the emergence of despotism. When applied to the history of France, this idea yields the following scenario. [10] The main achievement of the French Revolution was the destruction of feudal privilege rather than of the omnipotent central administration. Although the king was beheaded, his administration survived and in fact became stronger than ever, once the destruction of the nobility had removed the only force capable of opposing it. The argument looks compelling: a strong central power without the counterforce of hierarchy must lead to despotism.

Tocqueville observes, however, that the reasoning rests on the faulty premise that the nobility is the only social force that can serve as an

Following the July Revolution of 1830, Louis-Philipe (above) ruled France until his abdication in 1848. Tocqueville and Gustave de Beaumont toured the United States during the first months of his reign.

intermediate power. The Americans, he points out, have developed two *functional equivalents of nobility:* local self-government and political associations. Concerning the first, he writes that "It is . . . fair to say that in an aristocracy the people are always defended from the excesses of despotism, for there are always organized forces ready to resist a despot. A democracy *without provincial institutions* has no guarantee against such ills" (p. 47; italics added). Concerning the second, he asserts that "no countries need associations more—to prevent either despotism of parties or the arbitrary rule of a prince—than those with a democratic social state. In aristocratic nations secondary bodies form natural associations which hold abuses of power in check. In countries where such associations do not exist, if private people did not artificially and temporarily create something like them, I see no other dike to hold back tyranny of whatever sort" (p. 98). [11]

After this sketch of the place of *Democracy in America* in its immediate historical context, I turn to a larger issue, that of the place of the work and its author in nineteenth-century social thought, a period spanned by Hegel at one end and Spencer at the other. I believe it is fair to say that

91

lacking in such factual components. Even when the second volume has a chapter heading referring to "America" and "the Americans," the substance of the analysis may not be related to that country at all. For instance, the chapter titled "Why there are so many men of ambition in the United States but so few lofty ambitions" contains not a single reference to America and seems, in fact, to deal mainly with France. Tocqueville is certainly aware of the fact that many features of American democracy are unique to that country. In fact, he sometimes suggests that democracy itself, especially when organized on a federal basis, may not be able to survive elsewhere. Democracies in general tend to be inefficient in the short run, and federal systems especially so; hence they will usually be vulnerable to the predatory behavior of their neighbors. The American Union has the good luck, however, to be geographically situated so that "it has no great wars to fear" (p. 86) and hence can afford "to make retrievable mistakes" (p. 120). For democracy to survive in a European nation, "it would be necessary for republics to be established in all the others at the same time" (p. 116).

Also, Tocqueville understood very well that the abundant availability of free land imparted qualities to American democracy that could not be found elsewhere. Citing the fact that in 1830 thirty-six members of Congress were born in Connecticut, although only five were there as its representatives, he adds that "if those thirty-one had stayed in Connecticut, in all probability they would have remained humble laborers, not rich landowners, and would have passed their lives in obscurity, not able to venture on a political career, and instead of becoming useful legislators, they would have been dangerous citizens" (p. 147). Free land, in effect, provides a safety valve for American democracy.

Geographic conditions belong to the general category of "circumstances," given facts that cannot be affected by human action. These also include what Tocqueville refers to as "the point of departure," discussed at some length in the second chapter of the first volume. He argues that the Americans, especially in New England, were uniquely fortunate in starting from conditions of social and political equality. In particular, they had the good luck of building their political institutions from the bottom up rather than from the top down: "the local community was organized before the county, the county before the state, and the state before the Union" (p. 19). If local autonomy is not established from the beginning, it will be difficult to do so later. "A very civilized society find it hard to tolerate attempts at freedom in a local community; it is disgusted by its numerous blunders and is apt to despair of success before the experiment is finished" (p. 29). [21] Although European governments may deplore the lack of municipal spirit, they are also afraid of sharing their power with strong municipalities.

These given circumstances form one of the four major explanatory categories of *Democracy in America,* the other being laws, mores, and the social state (see p. 83 for a succinct statement). Tocqueville's explicit definition of "mores" (*moeurs*) is "the sum of the moral and intellectual dispositions of men in society" (p. 160 n). In the language I shall use below, mores are defined by the distribution of beliefs and desires in society. The idea of a social state is more complex. Roughly speaking, the social state of aristocracies is one of hierarchy and inequality, that of democracies one of equality. However, when Tocqueville refers to equality as the "democratic social state," the concept is not coextensive with political democracy. On the one hand, England was a political democracy that did not build on a democratic social state; on the other hand, we have already seen that the state of equality may well obtain under despotic regimes. In fact, when Tocqueville uses the phrase "democratic society" without further qualification, he tends to mean "societies based on equality." When he wants to refer to political democracy, i.e., the practice of collective self-government, he tends to use "freedom." In *Democracy in America,* that term does not mean independence from arbitrary political intervention nor the mere possession of political rights; rather it means the regular participation by the individual in political affairs, political debates, and political associations. [22] He scorns "the external forms of freedom" that amount to voting every few years and then retreating into an apolitical private life: "under this system the citizens quit their state of dependence just long enough to choose their masters and then fall back into it" (p. 376).

The concept of equality in *Democracy in America* is used with three main connotations. First, it includes the absence of legal privileges of any kind. For reasons to be explained shortly, this meaning of the term will be ignored here. Second, it includes a relatively flat distribution of income, wealth, and education. Third, it includes the idea of high de facto rates of social mobility. It is important to note that the absence of legal obstacles to social mobility is not in itself enough to ensure high mobility rates, any more than the possession of political rights will guarantee that they are widely and energetically exercised. To be sure, from a normative point of view rights may be valuable even if one chooses not to use them. [23] Even from an explanatory point of view, the possession of unexercised rights can have a stabilizing effect. [24] But this is not what concerned Tocqueville. He wanted to trace the effects on intellectual, social, and political life of a regular and energetic *exercise* of the right to participation in collective self-government and to the pursuit of happiness. Moreover, he wanted to explore the causal relations between those two practices: do political participation and economic self-betterment go hand in hand, or does the latter undermine the former? The answer, we shall see, is quite complex.

The explicit definition of a democratic social state is as follows: it obtains "when there are no longer any castes or classes in the community and all its members are nearly equal in education and in property"

(p. 358 n). The definition combines all three components of equality distinguished above. The flat distribution of wealth and education at any given point in time is explicitly asserted. The absence of caste clearly means that there is no legal privilege. In Tocqueville's somewhat idiosyncratic language, the absence of class implies high rates of mobility. For him, when the turnover among groups is very high, they do not form classes. Although the passages that support this interpretation (pp. 227–28, 300, 310, 342, 347 n) are somewhat ambiguous and not always consistent with each other, their overall thrust is quite clear. [25] For Tocqueville the existence of classes is incompatible both with very low rates of mobility (which transform them into castes) and with very high rates (which leave only a flux of individuals).

Some passages in *Democracy in America* could be summarized in the saying, "From rages to riches and to rags again in three generations" (e.g., pp. 24, 244, 295). Other passages stress in more general terms the extreme fluidity of the American social scene, be it because of economic, occupational, or geographic mobility. Moreover, American politics is in a state of similar flux, due mainly to the very short tenure of office. "After one brief moment of power, officials are lost again amid the ever-changing crowd" (p. 106); a democratic government "changes its mind often and its agents even more frequently" (p. 109). Or again, because "elections quickly follow one another, they keep society in feverish activity, with endless mutability in public affairs" (pp. 103–4). I believe, in fact, that mobility—a high metabolism in all spheres of social life—rather than equality in the literal sense is the main explanatory variable of *Democracy in America*. "It is not that in the United States, as everywhere, there are no rich; indeed I know no other country where love of money has such a grip on men's hearts or where stronger scorn is expressed for the theory of permanent quality of property. But wealth circulates there with incredible rapidity, and experience shows that two successive generations seldom enjoy its favors" (p. 25). This being said, there are many causal claims that clearly appeal to equality in the literal sense. In the following, I reserve "equality" for this literal reading, using "mobility" when the context makes it clear that this is what Tocqueville had in mind.

Tocqueville did not have a very clear understanding of the relations among the four main variables: circumstances, laws, mores, and social state. There is, to be sure, a subsection entitled "The laws contribute more to the maintenance of the democratic republic in the United States than do the physical circumstances of the country, and mores do more than the laws" (p. 159). Later he asserts that mores are supremely important (and not just more important than laws): "The importance of mores is a universal truth to which study and experience continually bring us back. I find it occupies the central position in my thoughts; all my ideas come back to it in the end" (p. 161). Now, saying that

A is more important than B could mean several things. It could mean that A offers an explanation of B, typically through being a cause of B, or it could mean that A explains more phenomena or more important phenomena than B, or contributes more powerfully to the explanation of the phenomena jointly caused by A and B. Whichever of these ways we choose to understand it, the idea that mores are more important than laws is incompatible with a number of other passages.

Tocqueville mentions that "More than once in the course of this work I have tried to point out the prodigious influence which, I believe, the social state exercises over laws and mores" (p. 172). Or consider the opening sentence of the second volume: "The Americans have a democratic social order which naturally suggested to them certain laws and certain political mores." [26] But if laws and mores are both the effects of a common cause, one can hardly claim that mores are fundamental. One may still claim, perhaps, that mores are more important than laws. That claim, however, is hard to reconcile with passages in which laws are said to shape the mores. Such is the case with the legal institution of slavery, which "explains the mores and the social state of the South" (p. 15: translation slightly modified). By giving priority to laws over the social state, this statement contradicts the two passages cited at the beginning of this paragraph. Another assertion of this priority comes in the important discussion of the effect of inheritance laws: "I am surprised that ancient and modern writers have not attributed greater importance to the laws of inheritance and their effect on the progress of human affairs. They are, it is true, civil laws, but they should head the list of all political institutions, for they have an unbelievable influence on the social state of peoples" (p. 23).

In these passages, then, we have seen Tocqueville asserting (1) the priority of mores over all other causes, (2) the priority of mores over laws, (3) the priority of the social state over laws and mores, (4) the priority of laws over mores, and (5) the priority of laws over the social state. He even claims that "When, after careful study of the history of America, we turn with equal care to political and social state there, we find ourselves deeply convinced of this truth, that there is not an opinion, custom, or law, nor, one might add, an event, which the point of departure will not easily explain" (p. 14). Geography, in fact, is the only variable that is not singled out in some passage as being *the* most important one. [27] To explain this confusion, two factors may be adduced.

First, there is the general tendency in Tocqueville, more fully documented and discussed below, to exaggeration, hyperbole, and lack of regard for consistency. He seems to have been capable to equal degrees of total concentration on the specific argument at hand, and then total oblivion of that argument when he turns to another matter which similarly calls for his full concentration. In the crucible of his thought the current object comes to dominate everything else, so that its importance is magnified out of proportion only to be forgotten and contradicted a few chapters or even pages later. This account is admittedly speculative, but I think something like it is called for if Tocqueville's inconsistencies are not to remain a total mystery.

Second, and more specifically, the cited passages show us Tocqueville groping after the idea of *circular causality*. I believe that *Democracy in America* was intended as an analysis of a society in a (relatively) stable equilibrium, whose characteristic feature is that the various elements that go into it support and maintain each other mutually. In equilibrium, there is no point in asking which element is most important; nor is there any logical problem involved in asserting that A causes B and that B causes A. For an illustration, consider the most general description of the economic process: the announcements of prices induce producers and consumers to make decisions that cause a new set of prices to be announced. In equilibrium, the two sets of prices are the same. We can say, with equal truth, that the announcements cause the decisions or that the decisions cause the announcements. What we cannot say is that one set of events is more important than the other.

Let me illustrate this idea with two examples from *Democracy in America*. A striking case of an apparent inconsistency occurs in the discussion of slavery. On the one hand, Tocqueville asserts that the slave "finds his joy and pride in a servile imitation of his oppressors" (p. 166). Slavery, in other words, causes servility. On the other hand, we find him comparing the two oppressed races in America in the following terms: "The Negro would like to mingle with the European and he cannot. The Indian might to some extent succeed in that, but he scorns to attempt it. The servility of the former delivers him into slavery; the pride of the latter leads him to death" (pp. 167–68). Servility, in other words, causes slavery. Charitably interpreted, the two passages need not contradict each other. We can read them simply as saying that slavery generates mental attitudes in the slaves that tend to stabilize the institution of slavery: a circular relation between laws and mores.

A second example is taken from Tocqueville's discussion of the relation between political and civil associations. In the published text, the main emphasis is on the idea that the habit of association generated in political life spills over into civil life: "politics spread a general habit and taste for association" (p. 279). Before the discussion of that link, however, there is a brief remark to the effect that "civil associations pave the way for political ones" (ibid.), suggesting the opposite causal connection. In the recently published drafts to this chapter we find an illuminating discussion of this duality:

> This chapter absolutely needs to be redrafted completely. The
> development is hampered and awkward and several of the ideas it

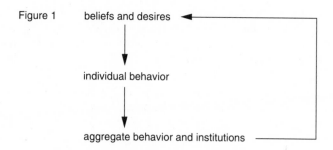

Figure 1

contains are contestable. One might say that I have proved that civil
associations arise from political associations, but that is false even by
my own account, as I say that in countries where political associations
are *forbidden,* civil associations are *rare. The first goal* of the chapter is
to show that civil associations are always weak, indolent, limited and
inept when political associations do not exist. Civil associations do not
arise from political associations any more than the latter arise from civil
associations. They develop each other mutually. In a country where
political associations are numerous, civil associations will be so too, and
similarly men who are already in the habit of associating with each other
in civil life have a great aptitude for associating in politics. [28]

If Tocqueville had explored this insight more systematically, he might
have dispelled much confusion both from his own mind and from his
readers'. I believe, however, that there is an easy remedy for this defect,
viz., to substitute a single statement of circular causality whenever we
encounter two apparently inconsistent statements of unilateral causality
in opposite directions.

We are now in a position to describe Tocqueville's method more
fully. Generally speaking, the methodology of the social sciences can be
summarized in figure 1 above (arrows stand for causal relations).

Individual human actions have their causal origin in the agent's beliefs and desires. [29] Large-scale patterns such as equality and mobility
are the aggregate outcome of such actions. Institutions, too, can be
understood in terms of individual behavior and individual expectations
about such behavior. Finally, individual psychology, including beliefs
and desires, are heavily shaped by the social environment. This scheme
is entirely general and does not presuppose a social system in equilib-

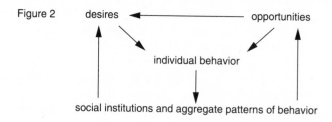

Figure 2

rium. It might well be the case, that is, that the beliefs and desires that are molded by the social environment differ from those that generated the actions that constituted that environment in the first place. Tocqueville's analyses in *The Old Regime and the French Revolution*, for instance, fall in this category. That work is an analysis of long-term change, not, as *Democracy in America*, a study of an equilibrium.

The general scheme set out in figure 1 can be spelled out more fully in a way that captures the specifics of Tocqueville's approach (see figure 2).

One difference between figure 1 and figure 2 is mainly expositional. The beliefs that enter among the determinants of action include, prominently, the agent's beliefs about the opportunities that he faces. Those beliefs, in turn, are in general roughly correlated with the actual opportunities. In this respect, figure 2 is just a simplified version of figure 1. [30] A new element is the inclusion of a causal link between opportunities and desires, exemplified in the idea that slavery induces servility. Also new is the idea that the social environment can act both on desires for action and on opportunities for action. For instance, "while the law allows the American people to do everything, there are things which religion prevents them from imagining and forbids them to dare" (p. 153). Given the claim, cited above, that religion arises naturally in a regime of political freedom, we can conclude that the very same political institutions that give people the opportunity to behave in a disorderly fashion also remove from them any desire to do so. This is a general theme of *Democracy in America:* the dangers of democracy are cured by democracy itself; the regime secretes the poison and its antidote at the same time. [31]

In other cases, the effects of the social and political environment work in tandem, by removing both the desire and the opportunity to act in a certain way. [32] We can call this the "not only" pattern, a famous example being the following: "Thus the law of inheritance not only makes it difficult for families to retain the same domains intact, but takes away their wish to try to do so" (p. 24). Another famous example concerns the impact of slavery on slaveowners. In the first place, slavery is unprofitable, compared to free labor. But "the influence of slavery extends even further, penetrating the master's soul and giving a particular turn to his ideas and tastes" (p. 182). Because work is associated with slavery, the Southern whites scorn "not only work itself but also enterprises in which work is necessary to success" (ibid.). They lack both the opportunities and the desire to get rich: "Slavery . . . not only prevents the white men from making their fortunes but even diverts them from wishing to do so" (ibid.).

A final example with the same structure occurs in Tocqueville's discussion of the fate of an occupied country under a democratic regime. Because individual citizens in a democracy are powerless and isolated, "none of them can either defend himself or offer a rallying point to others" (p. 359). Moreover, they do not really have an interest in defending their country: "each citizen has but a small share of political power, and often none at all; on the other hand, all are independent and have property to lose; as a result, they are much less afraid of conquest and much more afraid of war than the inhabitants of an aristocratic land" (ibid.). Hence he concludes, "not only will the population be unable to continue the war, but, I fear, they will not even want to try" (ibid.).

A more disturbing constellation occurs when the social and political environment generates a specific desire while at the same time blocking the opportunity to satisfy it. A key passage is the following: "The same equality which allows each man to entertain vast hopes makes each man by himself weak. His power is limited on every side, though his longings may wander where they will. . . . This constant strife between the desires inspired by equality and the means it supplies to satisfy them harasses and wearies the mind" (p. 289). Similarly, Tocqueville asserts that in democratic armies "the desire for promotion is greater and the opportunities for it are fewer than elsewhere" (p. 350).

When aspirations outreach opportunities, the ensuing frustration may yield one of three consequences. The individual may drive himself at an ever more frenzied pace to improve his conditions: this is the main argument of *Democracy in America* (*see* notably pp. 248–49). Or individuals may join forces to overthrow the regime that is perceived as responsible for the blocking of opportunities: this is a central argument in *The Old Regime and the French Revolution*. Or, finally, individuals may after a while come to reduce their aspiration level to their objective opportunities, as in the "sour grapes" syndrome. [33] (This effect is captured in the arrow from opportunities to desires in figure 2 above. [34]) Thus, under the old regime the people unthinkingly accepted their rulers, feeling "neither repugnance nor degradation in submitting to their severities, which seemed inevitable ills sent by God" (p. 3). He also asserts that a main contrast between the inhabitants of the Old World and those of the New World is that "the former do not give a moment's thought to the ills they endure, whereas the latter never stop thinking of the good things they have not got" (p. 288).

Thus in both of Tocqueville's major works much of the causal story hinges on two opposing causal mechanisms. On the one hand, there is a tendency for desires to go beyond the means available for satisfying them. On the other hand, there is a tendency for desires to adjust to the means at hand. If the latter mechanism corresponds to the "sour grapes" syndrome, the former reflects the idea of "forbidden fruit" or "the grass is always greener." [35] Roughly speaking, Tocqueville claims that the former mechanism dominates under conditions of high inequality and low mobility, whereas the latter comes to the forefront in the opposite state of affairs. Moreover, he claims that the frustration caused by excessive aspirations can lead either to collective or to individ-

their class, for in societies with high rates of activity and mobility there are no collective memory and no classes. Nor can they look to other individuals, since no one is any better than others. Hence they must turn inward, to themselves.

In the second chapter he begins by observing that by necessity men must always take some things on trust, since "if man had to prove for himself all the truths of which he makes use every day, he would never come to an end of it" (p. 230). He goes on to eliminate religion and superior individuals as sources of intellectual authority in democratic societies, leaving nothing but public opinion. Finally, he turns the argument around by asserting that public opinion, rather than being a "salutary bondage" (p. 230) that enables the individuals to make up their own mind on all important subjects, has become "mistress of the world" (p. 230). Rather than each man being "narrowly shut up in himself" (p. 227), he tends to "place almost unlimited confidence in the judgment of the public" (p. 231). Rather than turning inward, they look outward, to their fellow citizens. Nothing at all remains, it would seem, of the argument from the first chapter.

Another strange pair of passages is found in the discussion of the driving passions of the Americans. First, they are said to strive only for petty material pleasures: "Among them love of comfort appears as a tenacious, exclusive, and universal passion, but always a restrained one. There is no question of building vast palaces, of conquering or excelling nature, or sucking the world dry to satisfy one man's greed. It is more a question of adding a few acres to one's fields, planting an orchard, enlarging a house, making life ever easier and more comfortable, keeping irritations away, and satisfying one's slightest needs without trouble and almost without expense" (p. 286). A few pages later, however, they are portrayed as being restless and driven by the desire for novelty: "An American will build a house in which to pass his old age and sell it before the roof is on; he will plant a garden and rent it just as the trees are coming into bearing; he will clear a field and leave others to reap the harvest; he will take up a profession and leave it, settle in one place and soon go off elsewhere with his changing desires" (p. 288). Now, it can hardly be an accident that the very same examples—building a house, planting an orchard, clearing a field—occur in both passages. But it is also very hard to see how they can describe the same character and the same attitudes. The search for comfort and the search for novelty tend to pull individuals in opposite directions. [40]

Considered in themselves, Tocqueville's inconsistencies are obviously deplorable. I believe, however, that they may be rendered more innocuous if we emphasize that most of time he is pointing to (partial) *mechanisms* rather than proposing a (general) *theory*. A theory of democracy which asserted that democratic citizens are both independent and conformist would obviously be in bad trouble. It is quite another thing, however, to assert that in democracies one can observe both mechanisms that tend to make citizens more independent than elsewhere, and mechanisms that tend to make them less independent. It would clearly be more satisfactory if one could go on from that point and state the conditions under which the one or the other result will obtain. [41] Yet I believe that even the more limited achievement of identifying the range of mechanisms has considerable value.

IV. The psychology of democracy

I have already mentioned a number of ways in which the institutions of democracy shape individual desires and beliefs. I now want to develop this theme in a somewhat more systematic manner.

Societies depend, for their stable and continued existence, on some minimum of non-selfishness and foresight in their members. [42] In one place, Tocqueville notes that selfishness is "like rust in society" (p. 143). Similarly, as we shall see, he was very much concerned with the negative effects of myopic or shortsighted behavior, guided by immediate pleasure rather than by long-term prudential concerns. He was naturally led to ask, therefore, how the social state and institutions of democratic societies might work to promote the values of non-selfishness and foresight. In this connection he also insisted on the importance of religion as an intermediate variable.

Tocqueville does not claim that equality favors egoism. He does assert, however, that it favors two closely related attitudes: envy and individualism. Envy, in a way, is worse than selfishness. Whereas a selfish person doesn't care whether others have much or little, an envious person cares very much if they have more than he does, and he would if necessary be willing to give up some of what he has in order to drag others down to his level. [43] According to Tocqueville, envy is "the democratic sentiment." It expresses "a debased taste for equality," as distinct from the "legitimate passion for equality which rouses in all men a desire to be strong and respected" (p. 28). Envy is cited as the cause of the low salaries of officials in America, and as one explanation of the fact that the American voters rarely choose the best candidates. The anticipation of envy causes the rich to hide their wealth and to abstain from conferring benefits on the poor. Because of envy, military service in democracies has to be universal and compulsory: "it is the inequality of a burden, not its weight, which usually provokes resistance" (p. 353). Finally, envy induces a kind of self-poisoning of the mind. For democratic citizens "to attribute [another's] rise to his talents or his virtues is inconvenient, for it means admitting that they are less virtuous or capable than he. They therefore regard some of his vices as the main cause thereof" (p. 114).

(p. 234). And he claims to have "shown elsewhere by what secret means equality makes the passion for physical pleasures and an exclusive interest in immediate delights predominate in the human heart" (p. 341). I do not think he has shown any such link, however. What he does offer is a subtly different argument, to the effect that mobility (rather than equality) causes uncertainty about the future (rather than a tendency to disregard known benefits that the future might bring). [49]

His fundamental idea is not that democratic citizens are myopic but that their desires are constantly changing: "Social instability favors the natural instability of desires. Amid all these perpetual fluctuations of fate the present looms large and hides the future, so that men do not want to think beyond tomorrow" (p. 295). Or again, "Add to this taste for prosperity a social state in which neither law nor custom holds anyone in one place, and that is a great further stimulus to this restlessness of temper. One will then find people continually changing paths for fear of missing the shortest cut leading to happiness" (pp. 288–89). This vision of democracy does not exclude that each successive desire can have a remote temporal horizon, with the citizens pursuing distant— but constantly changing—aims at each particular moment. This idea would be an application to desires of an argument that Tocqueville uses elsewhere in connection with beliefs: "for a long time [freedom of the press] does not disturb [the] habit of firm belief without reflection, but it does daily change the object of their implicit belief. The human mind continues to discern only one point at a time on the whole intellectual horizon, but that point is constantly changing" (p. 96).

We might ask whether this paradoxical state of affairs could continue to operate in a state of equilibrium. Would people not eventually *recognize* the fluctuations in their beliefs and desires? According to Tocqueville, this is indeed what happens with beliefs: "soon almost the whole range of new ideas has been canvassed. Experience plunges mankind into universal doubt and distrust" (p. 96). Similarly, with respect to desires: democratic citizens "are afraid of themselves, dreading that, their taste having changed, they will come to regret not being able to drop what once had formed the object of their lust. And they are right to feel this fear, for in ages of democracy all things are unstable, but the most unstable of all is the human heart" (p. 313). Even though one should not confound myopic desires and short-lived desires, the *anticipated* instability of desires might give rise to myopic behaviors. Why work for future benefits when experience teaches us that we may well no longer want them when we get them? Similarly, why create something durable when we know that it will soon be obsolete? "I once met an American sailor and asked him why his country's ships are made so that they will not last long. He answered offhand that the art of navigation was making such quick progress that even the best of boats would be almost useless if it lasted more than a few years" (p. 241).

Tocqueville argues that myopia, induced by equality, also causes people to prefer equality over freedom. [50] On the one hand, "they see that the troubles they fear are distant and console themselves that they will only fall on future generations, for which the present generation hardly cares. The ills which liberty brings may be immediate; all can see them and all, more or less, feel them. The ills produced by extreme equality only become apparent little by little" (p. 270). On the other hand, "The good things that freedom brings are seen only as time passes, and it is always easy to mistake the cause that brought them about. The advantages of equality are felt immediately, and it is daily apparent where they come from" (ibid.). [51] Hence democratic citizens will often be tempted to welcome despotism, which offers all the benefits of equality and none of the turbulence of freedom.

In these two passages two claims are being made. First, democratic citizens are subject to what one might call a "motivational deficit," in according insufficient weight to future consequences of present actions. Second, they are also subject to a "cognitive deficit," due to their inability to understand what these consequences are. Elsewhere, Tocqueville asserts this cognitive deficit as a general feature of democracies: "it is this clear perception of the future, based on judgment and experience, which must often be lacking in a democracy" (p. 115). There he also offers a more charitable explanation of the motivational deficit: "The people not only see less clearly than the upper classes what can be hoped or feared for the future, but they also suffer the ills of the present in quite another way" (ibid.). The poor cannot *afford* to sacrifice short-term benefits for greater long-term gains, for if they did they might not survive to enjoy the latter.

The motivational deficit appears in the explanation of a number of other phenomena. Tocqueville claims that the impatience or indolence of democratic citizens causes them to have a predilection for general ideas, which hold out the promise of a shortcut to knowledge (p. 234). The same impatience acts as a break on great ambitions. On the one hand, equality tends to slow down political careers: "In a democratic society, as elsewhere, there are only a few great fortunes to be made. As the careers leading thereto are open without discrimination to every citizen, each man's progress is bound to be slow" (p. 340). On the other hand, equality tends to make men more reluctant to take on "a multitude of little intermediate obstacles, all of which have to be negotiated slowly, between them and the great object of their ultimate desires. The very anticipation of this prospect tires ambition and discourages it" (ibid.). Note that the argument falls into the "not only" pattern set out above: equality tends both to delay the realization of political ambition and to make men less willing to defer gratification.

To explain how democratic societies may overcome myopia Tocqueville offers a fairly complex argument. One claim is that myopia is neutralized by religions, which "instill a general habit of behaving with the future in view. In this respect they work as much in favor of happiness in this world as of felicity in the next" (p. 294). There is, in other words, a spillover effect from religion to secular decision making. [52] To the extent that religions have a natural affinity with democracy, this offers another instance of democracy producing the antidote for its own disease. Assume, however, that democracy is introduced in a society in which men have lost their religious faith. In that case, the rulers should design the political system so that steady effort is rewarded: "It is at all times important that the rulers of nations should act with the future in view. But this is even more necessary in ages of democracy and skepticism than in any others. By giving such a lead, the chief men in democracies not only bring prosperity in public affairs but also teach individuals by their example to conduct their private affairs properly. They must especially strive to banish chance, as much as possible, from the world of politics. . . . One must hope that all promotion will be seen as the reward of effort, so that no high position should be too easily acquired and men of ambition should be obliged to plan well ahead before they reach their goal" (p. 295). [53] Once habits of foresight have been acquired in secular matters, a reverse spillover effect may reintroduce religion: "in accustoming the citizens to think of the future in this world, they will gradually be led without noticing it themselves towards religious belief" (ibid.).

The two ills of democracies—selfishness (in the specific forms of envy and individualism) and myopia—are related, in the sense that a remedy to the latter will also help overcome the former. In his discussion of enlightened self-interest, or "self-interest properly understood," Tocqueville argues that concern for the future can mimic, as it were, concern for others. "American moralists do not pretend that one must sacrifice himself for his fellows because it is a fine thing to do so. But they boldly assert that such sacrifice is as necessary for the man who makes it as for the beneficiaries" (p. 282). He goes on to cite Montaigne, "If I did not follow the straight road for the sake of its straightness, I should follow it having found by experience that, all things considered, it is the happiest and the most convenient" (ibid.). He could also have quoted Descartes, who wrote that "God has arranged the order of things in such a way, and bound men together in such a close society, that even if everyone acted only out of concern for himself and had no charity for others, he would still do all that he could do for them, provided that he used his prudence." [54]

All things considered, religion appears as the most powerful remedy for the psychological pathologies produced by equality and mobility. By counteracting myopia, it also indirectly works against individualism. By enjoining citizens to care for their fellowmen, religion also works directly against that attitude and presumably, although Tocqueville does not mention this, against envy. To be sure, Tocqueville also mentions other counteracting forces, notably conventions of mutual assistance and the establishment of political systems which teach the citizens that "nothing of lasting value is achieved without trouble" (p. 295). I believe, however, that in the overall argument of the book these definitely take second place to religion. I now turn, therefore, to a more systematic discussion of Tocqueville's views on religion.

All the founders of sociology—Marx, Weber, Émile Durkheim— examined the relation between religion and society. For the present purposes, I belive that Marx yields the most relevant comparison. Both Marx and Tocqueville wanted to answer three questions. First, what are the causes that lead to the establishment of religion? Second, what are the causes that lead to the establishment of one specific religion rather than another, e.g., to Protestantism rather than to Catholicism? Third, what are the social consequences of religion? As noted above, a functionalist explanation would explain the establishment of religion in terms of its socially useful consequences, but neither Tocqueville nor Marx committed this fallacy. Rather, they tried to show that when individuals, for reasons of their own, adopt religion, they also benefit society or, in Marx's case, the rule of the capitalist class. Moreover, in their choice of explanatory variables, Marx and Tocqueville adopted the same general approach. To explain why there is religion at all, they appealed to the interests or needs of the individual. To explain the content of religion, or why religion A rather than B is adopted, they appealed to some elective affinity or cognitive "harmony" between the given social structure and religious dogma. The details, inevitably, differ. In particular, where Marx emphasized the place of the individual in *capitalism* in order to explain his religious beliefs, Tocqueville focuses on his place in *democracy*. Their analyses of the social consequences of religion differ in similar respects.

At the most general level, Tocqueville believed that men always and everywhere have a deep need for religion. Man's "natural disgust for existence and an immense longing to exist . . . drive his soul toward contemplation of the next world. . . . Incredulity is an accident; faith is the only permanent state of mankind" (p. 155). Statements like these are as difficult to prove as to refute. Tocqueville has more specific, and more interesting, things to say about the source of religious belief in different societies. In aristocratic societies, "the poor are driven to dwell in imagination on the next world; it is closed in by the wretchedness of the actual world but escapes therefrom and seeks for joys beyond" (p. 285; *see also* p. 292). This is close to Marx's argument that religion is the "opium of the people," a (self-administered) drug that dulls the feeling of misery that would otherwise obtain. [55] In democratic societies, as we have seen, religion serves a very different function for the individual, that of fulfilling his need for authority. Whereas the

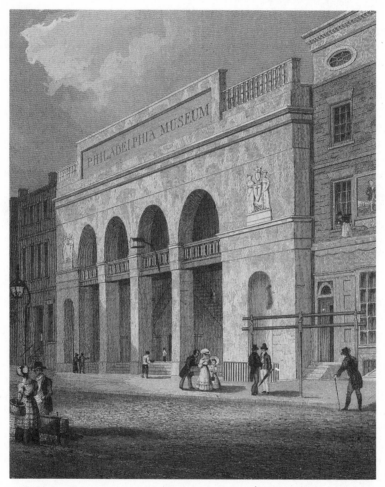

Street scenes during the 1830s in Boston (opposite page, top), New York City (opposite page, bottom), and Philadelphia (above), around the time of Tocqueville's visit.

poor in aristocratic societies used religion as a substitute for happiness on earth, the citizens of democracies use religious faith as a substitute for political obedience. Religion alleviates the burden of misery in the one case, the burden of freedom in the other. [56] By contraposition, the individual would not need religion in an affluent society organized on despotic lines, at least not beyond the need caused by the general "disgust for existence and longing to exist."

Whereas freedom predisposes men toward religion, equality turns them away from it. Tocqueville notes that "standards of equality give men a sort of instinctive incredulity about the supernatural" (p. 230). If an egalitarian society should nevertheless adopt a religion, it is more likely to be Catholicism than Protestantism. "Our contemporaries are naturally little disposed to belief, but once they accept religion at all, there is a hidden instinct within them which unconsciously urges them toward Catholicism. Many of the doctrines and customs of the Roman Church astonish them, but they feel a secret admiration for its discipline, and its extraordinary unity attracts them" (p. 239). The relationship also works in the other direction: "Catholicism may dispose the faithful to obedience, but it does not prepare them for inequality" (p. 150). Although "the priest is raised above the faithful; all below him are equal" (ibid.).

The general principle behind such arguments is that "The spirit of man, left to follow its bent, will regulate political society and the City of God in uniform fashion; it will, if I dare put it so, seek to *harmonize* earth with heaven" (ibid.). An illustration is that "Christianity itself has in some degree been affected by the influence of social and political conditions on religious beliefs" (p. 237). For instance, to the fragmentation of society after the fall of the Roman Empire there corresponded a fragmentation of religion: "Unable to subdivide the Deity, they could at least multiply and aggrandize His agents beyond measure. For most Christians the worship of angels and saints became an almost idolatrous cult" (ibid.). Later on, he observes that the opposite tendency is at work in democracies: "Even when equality does not bring religions crashing down, it simplifies them and turns attention away from secondary beings to concentrate it chiefly on the Supreme Being" (p. 259). That statement, however, stands in a puzzling relation to the proposition that equality favors Catholicism, which is precisely the religion that multiplies secondary beings.

While Catholicism favors equality, "Protestantism in general orients men much less toward equality than toward independence" (p. 150), i.e., toward freedom. Under certain circumstances, Catholics, too, might be favorably disposed toward freedom. "Most of the Catholics are poor, and unless all citizens govern, they will never attain to the government themselves. The Catholics are in a minority, and it is important for them that all rights should be respected so that they can be sure to enjoy their own in freedom. For these two reasons they are led, perhaps in spite of themselves, toward political doctrines which, maybe, they would adopt with less zeal were they rich and predominant" (p. 151). Note that this connection is extrinsic, not intrinsic, to Catholic dogma. It is also much more straightforward and plausible than the other purported links that I have cited, and less vulnerable to the strictures I am about to set out.

In my opinion, Tocqueville's efforts to demonstrate an intrinsic connection between social structure and religious dogma are arbitrary and unconvincing. They rely on what might be called "the first law of pseudoscience": everything is a little bit like everything else. [57] There will always be some similarities or resemblances between a complex social structure and a complex system of religious dogma, but to cite them as evidence for the claim that the specific form of religion is due to an impulse to harmonize heaven and earth is entirely speculative. There are so many different ways of harmonizing heaven and earth and, in choosing religion, so many more important reasons than the desire for harmony, that it is more plausible to think that the harmony comes after the event, to consolidate a choice that has already been made or imposed on other grounds. Could not one equally well say, for instance, that Catholicism, with its hierarchy of angels and saints, is especially well suited to an aristocratic society that is based on hierarchy? Or that Protestantism, by doing away with all intermediaries between men and God, places them on an equal footing that predisposes them toward democracy? In this respect, too, Tocqueville anticipates Marx, whose arguments about a natural affinity between capitalism and Protestantism are entirely arbitrary and, in fact, incoherent. [58]

Tocqueville has a number of things to say about the social consequences of religion. He notes that societies based on freedom derive particular benefits from religion, and that when sincere believers in democracy and liberty "attack religious beliefs, they obey the dictates of their passions, not their interests. Despotism may be able to do without faith, but freedom cannot. . . . How could society escape destruction if, when political ties are relaxed, moral ties are not tightened?" (p. 154). Note that this is a sociological statement, not a psychological one. The argument, discussed above, that the individual cannot support too much freedom is quite unrelated to the idea that free societies would break asunder if they did not have religion to glue them together. Moreover, to repeat, these cementing effects of religion are not cited as an explanation of its presence. Religion may be needed as an antidote to social anarchy, but it is produced as an antidote to individual restlessness.

Furthermore, "the great usefulness of religions is even more apparent among egalitarian peoples than elsewhere" (p. 236), for reasons that I have already canvassed. However, there is no invisible hand that tends to bring about religion in the egalitarian societies that need it, analogous to the mechanism by which the social need for religion in free societies is satisfied by the spontaneous tendency of individuals in these societies to embrace religion. Equality, therefore, needs freedom to generate the antidote for individualism and myopia.

Tocqueville insists that from the social point of view, what matters "is not that all citizens should profess the true religion but that they should profess religion" (p. 152). [59] The usefulness of religion, he says, is not necessarily linked to its deterrent effect, i.e., the fear of eternal damnation as sanction for immoral behavior. The mere "belief in an immaterial and immortal principle . . . has fine effects even when it is not united to a conception of rewards and punishments" (p. 293). As an amusing (and inaccurate) illustration of this proposition he cites the doctrine of metempsychosis, claiming (in slight paraphrase) that if a man believes he might turn into a pig in his next life he is less likely to behave like a pig in the present one (ibid.). [60]

I conclude by some comments on Tocqueville's views of *modes of belief* (including religious beliefs) in democratic societies. The main varieties are those of dogmatism, skepticism, and conformism. In addition, a select few may be able to go beyond these attitudes and attain a firm belief which is founded on deliberation rather than on instinct, prejudice, or social pressure.

Tocqueville claims that one can "distinguish three distinct and often successive states of human understanding" (p. 96). The first two stages have already been alluded to above. Initially, men believe firmly and blindly; they may change their opinion, but only to adopt another one in the same unreflective mode. Once they understand this process, however, they adopt an attitude of "universal doubt and distrust" (ibid.). They may choose an opinion and stick to it, "not because they are sure it is good but because they are not sure that there is a better one" (ibid.). To illustrate, Tocqueville notes that "in ages of religious fervor men sometimes changed their beliefs, whereas in skeptical centuries each man held obstinately to his own faith" (ibid.). "Only a few persevering people," however, will go beyond the second state and "attain to that deliberate and self-justified type of conviction born of knowledge and springing up in the very midst of doubt" (ibid.).

Prior to this discussion Tocqueville has staged a confrontation between two three-stage theories of belief development. On the one hand, there is the view just set out, which we may think of as the Hegel-Tocqueville conception of belief formation. First, there is naive and dogmatic belief, Hegel's "thesis." Next, there is doubt and skepticism, Hegel's "antithesis." Finally, there is mature and reflective belief, Hegel's "synthesis." On the other hand, there is the view that Tocqueville imputes to an unidentified "great man," who is alleged to have said that "ignorance lies at both ends of knowledge" (pp. 95–96). On this view, the first stage is one of naive ignorance; then there is the pretension to knowledge; and finally the recognition that the search for knowledge is in vain. We may refer to this as the Montaigne-Pascal view of belief formation, since it is asserted by both of these thinkers, either of whom may have been the "great man" Tocqueville had in mind. Montaigne's formulation, which no doubt influenced Pascal's, is the most pregnant: "It may be plausibly asserted that there is an infant-school ignorance which precedes knowledge and another doctoral ignorance which comes after it." [61]

Tocqueville does not offer any arguments against this conception but simply asserts his own: "Perhaps it would have been truer to say that deep convictions lie at the two ends, with doubt in the middle" (p. 96). At this level of abstraction and generality, it is obviously impossible to say which view is correct; it will all depend on the context. Speaking for myself, though, I believe that in matters such as those discussed by Tocqueville, the Montaigne-Pascal view is more nearly correct. It is not that we cannot know anything about societies: rather, it is that our knowledge will take the form of insight into *mechanisms* rather than statements of general *theories*. [62] To be sure, Tocqueville thought it possible to attain general and theoretical knowledge about societies. Without that belief, he might not have had the motivation to sustain the arduous mental efforts that enabled him to identify so many interesting mechanisms. [63]

Tocqueville's analyses of conformism in democratic societies are complex and ultimately, I believe, unsatisfactory. One basic argument is that both the social state of equality and political democracy independently of each other induce the individual to align his opinions with those of the majority. In the first place, "the same quality which makes [the citizen of a democracy] independent of each separate citizen leaves him isolated and defenseless in the face of the majority. So in democracies public opinion . . . uses no persuasion to forward its beliefs, but by some mighty pressure of the mind of all upon the intelligence of each it imposes its ideas and makes them penetrate men's very soul" (p. 231). In the second place, "American political laws give the majority the sovereign right to rule society, and that considerably increases the dominion it has anyhow over men's mind. For nothing comes more natural to man than to recognize the superior wisdom of his oppressor" (ibid.). The implication is that the first mechanism would operate even in a society in which all men were equal under an omnipotent despot. Tocqueville does not ask, however, whether in that case the second mechanism would not set up a rival source of authority.

Elsewhere we receive the impression that the pressure of the majority mainly constrains the outward expression of opinion, without reaching into the soul. "In America the majority has enclosed thought within a formidable fence. A writer is free inside that area, but woe to the man who goes beyond it. Not that he stands in fear of an *auto-da-fé*, but he must face all kinds of unpleasantness and everyday persecution"

and exuberance of thought displayed in this work. If I may allow myself an autobiographical aside, only two other books have generated in me the almost intolerable state of intellectual excitement that I experienced on first reading *Democracy in America*. One was Thomas Schelling's *The Strategy of Conflict*, the other Paul Veyne's *Le pain et le cirque*. What these writers have in common is a combination of exceptional imaginativeness and an attention to detail that enable them to find "infinity in a grain of sand and eternity in an hour." Anyone can construct a great system, but only a very few can take an everyday event and explain it in a way that suddenly opens a large vista on a whole set of related phenomena. To take an example at random among literally hundreds of others, I may cite Tocqueville's comments on marriages in a democracy.

He starts with the following observation: "Our ancestors conceived a singular opinion with regard to marriage. As they had noticed that the few love matches which took place in their days almost always ended in tragedy, they came to the firm conclusion that in such matters it was very dangerous to rely on one's own heart. They thought that chance saw clearer than choice" (p. 321). He then proceeds to give a number of arguments to question the logic of this inference. First, he observes that in this case as in many others, the ills of democracy can be cured by more democracy. "A democratic education is necessary to protect women against the dangers with which the institutions and mores of democracy surround them" (p. 318). If women in democracies were uneducated, love marriages would be disastrous—as they are in effect when they occur in aristocracies. Since, however, the education of women is itself an endogenous effect of democracy, this danger does not arise. Also, in democracies women have the "time to know" (p. 321) their future husbands, whereas in aristocracies women are kept so cloistered that they have no occasion to form an opinion about them. The fact that marrying for love is disastrous in societies that allow women neither the ability nor the opportunity to judge does not entitle us to infer that the same effect will be produced in democracies.

Tocqueville shows that the inference rests on a further fallacy. Suppose that in an aristocratic society two young, well-educated, and well-acquainted people make a love match. By going against the current they will tend to encounter the hostility of their friends and relatives, a situation that "soon wears down their courage and embitters their heart" (ibid.). In a society in which this practice was general, this effect would not arise. Finally, he points to another mechanism that explains why we cannot generalize from exceptional cases to the general case. For a man to marry for love in societies in which this practice is uncommon he must have "something of violence and adventure in his character, and people of this type, whatever direction they take, seldom achieve happiness or virtue" (p. 322). And one might add that a marriage of *two* people of this disposition is even less likely to be happy.

Thus in the space of slightly more than one page and with no fanfare at all, Tocqueville builds a tight, complex, and compelling causal argument that most other writers would have set out at great length and with great pride, had they had the wits to invent it. I believe that the extraordinary quality of *focus* displayed in this analysis and in many others is closely related to Tocqueville's almost obsessional preoccupation with individual psychology. He wanted to understand not only what made people tick but also the origins of their desires, passions, and beliefs; to understand, for instance, *why* those who marry for love in aristocratic societies tend to be unhappy. In this essay I have only been able to sample a small number of his insights, even within my self-imposed limitations. It is certainly no substitute for reading Tocqueville in the original. I have tried, though, to offer an interpretative scheme that may help orient the reader in the bewildering richness of his thought.

---

1. All page references are to vol. 44 of the second edition of *Great Books of the Western World.*

2. Much of this essay draws on chaps. 3 and 4 of John Elster, *Political Psychology* (Cambridge: Cambridge University Press, 1993). In those chapters, as well as in the present essay, I am heavily indebted to a long-standing collaboration with Stephen Holmes. After we first discussed Tocqueville some fifteen years ago, we have co-taught several courses on his work at the University of Chicago, with the intention of eventually writing a book that will cover not only *Democracy in America* but also his *Recollections* and *The Old Regime and the French Revolution.*

3. "I have not . . . claimed to judge whether the progress of the social revolution, which I consider irresistible, is profitable or prejudicial for mankind" (p. 6).

4. G. A. Cohen, "Marx's Dialectic of Labour," *Philosophy and Public Affairs* 3 (1974), pp. 235–61.

5. *See* the unpublished letter cited in André Jardin, *Alexis de Tocqueville* (Paris: Hachette, 1984), p. 89.

6. I am much indebted to Stephen Holmes for urging this perspective on me.

7. *Capital,* vol. 1 (New York: International Publishers, 1967), pp. 8–9.

8. For other applications of the strategy, *see* Elster, "Patterns of Causal Analysis in Tocqueville's *Democracy in America,*" *Rationality and Society* 3 (1991), pp. 277–97.

9. *De l'esprit des lois,* II. 4 (*GBWW* I: 38, 7–8; II: 35, 7–8).

10. The following argument reproduces a key idea in Tocqueville's *The Old Regime and the French Revolution* (New York: Doubleday Anchor Books, 1955), esp. pp. 19 ff., 60, 167 ff., 202, 209 ff. In this work (published in 1856) Tocqueville seems to be less optimistic with regard to the chance that France might adopt one of the functional equivalents of nobility that he had observed in the United States.

11. In the chapter from which this passage is excerpted, the danger said to be counteracted by political associations is the tyranny of the majority. In the second volume, political associations are praised mainly as a counterweight to the omnipotent central administration (p. 378). The difference reflects the fact that in the first volume Tocqueville is mainly concerned with democracy in its American form, whereas in the second volume he ranges more widely and often seems to refer to conditions in France rather than in the United States.

12. The seminal work is probably Raymond Aron, *Les Étapes de la Pensée Sociologique* (Paris: Gallimard, 1967).

13. For an overview, *see* H. O. Pappé, "Mill and Tocqueville," *Journal of the History of Ideas* 25 (1964), pp. 217–34.

14. Tocqueville's analyses are found in his *Recollections* (New Brunswick, N.J.: Transaction Books, 1987). Marx discusses the February revolution in *The Class Struggles in France,* in Karl Marx and Frederick Engels, *Collected Works,* vol. 10 (London: Lawrence

52. We may observe, as a curiosity, that Tocqueville also claims that when a religion makes the fatal mistake of forming an alliance with a secular government, "it makes the same mistake as any man might; it sacrifices the future for the present" (p. 155). Either the spillover effect is incomplete, or those who enter into such alliances are not true believers.

53. The argument of the preceding paragraph was that when promotion requires steady effort, the myopia of democratic citizens will wean them from lofty ambitions. Here he claims that the knowledge that steady effort will be rewarded will wean them from their myopia. Obviously, some additional premises—not provided by Tocqueville— are needed to make sense of the argument.

54. Letter to Princess Elisabeth of Bohemia, Oct. 6, 1645.

55. Marx, "Contribution to the Critique of Hegel's Philosophy of Law—Introduction," in Marx and Engels, *Collected Works*, vol. 3 (London: Lawrence and Wishart, 1975), p. 175.

56. Tocqueville's argument differs, however, from the theory of "fear of freedom" advanced by Erich Fromm. He claims that "Luther's attitude towards secular authority was closely related to his religious teachings. In making the individual feel worthless and insignificant as far as his own merits are concerned, in making him feel like a powerless tool in the hands of God, he deprived man of the self-confidence and of the feeling of human dignity which is the premise for any firm stand against oppressing secular authorities," *Fear of Freedom* (London: Routledge, 1960), p. 71. In the terminology used here, Fromm postulates a spillover effect from religious obedience to political obedience, whereas Tocqueville claimed to find a compensation effect linking political freedom and religious obedience.

57. The number and complexity of causal chains in *Democracy in America* is such that one sometimes also receives the impression that Tocqueville was under the way of what might be called the second law of pseudoscience: everything is causally related to everything else.

58. Elster, *Making Sense of Marx*, pp. 506–8.

59. It would also be in his spirit, or so I believe, to say that democracies are more stable if the citizens do not all profess the *same* religion.

60. The illustration is inaccurate, because Hinduism does in fact assert that the body chosen for your reincarnation in the next life depends on your behavior in the current one and that, moreover, the successive incarnations shape your chances of finally attaining Nirvana.

61. *Essays* I.54 (*GBWW* I: 25, 150; II: 23, 191); also Pascal, *Les Pensées* 117 (*GBWW* I: 33, 194; II: 30, 194).

62. For defenses of this view, *see* Paul Veyne, *Writing History* (Middletown, Conn.: Wesleyan University Press, 1984); Raymond Boudon, *Theories of Social Change* (Oxford: Blackwell, 1986); and the Introduction to my *Political Psychology*.

63. For discussion of the view that some amount of self-delusion is necessary for achievement *see* L. B. Alloy and L. Y. Abrahamson, "Depressive realism," in L. B. Alloy ed., *Cognitive Processes in Depression* (New York: Guildford Press, 1988), pp. 223–65.

64. A similar analysis is offered in *The Old Regime and the French Revolution*, p. 155. Modern psychologists refer to this phenomenon as "pluralistic ignorance"; *see*, for instance, D. T. Miller and Cathy McFarland, "When social comparison goes awry: The case of pluralistic ignorance," in Jerry Suls and T. A. Wills, eds., *Social Comparison Theory* (Hillsdale, N.J.: Lawrence Erlbaum, 1991), pp. 287–316.

Human Nature, Gender, and Ethnicity (Part One)

Deal W. Hudson

Deal W. Hudson has been an associate professor of philosophy at Fordham University in New York City since 1989. He has also been a visiting professor at New York University for the past three years. He received degrees from the University of Texas at Austin and Princeton Theological Seminary before earning his doctorate from the Institute of the Liberal Arts at Emory University in Atlanta. Professor Hudson previously taught for nine years at Mercer University in Atlanta, where he was chair of the philosophy department.

He has published extensively in the areas of contemporary Thomism, especially the work of Jacques Maritain, and theories of happiness. He was coeditor of *Understanding Maritain: Philosopher and Friend* (1988), *The Future of Thomism* (1992), and is the editor of *Sigrid Undset On Saints and Sinners* (1994). He is also editing a 900-page *Encyclopædia of Thomism*, and is writing a major work on the subject of happiness called *Happiness and the Limits of Satisfaction*. A previous article by Professor Hudson entitled "Contemporary Views of Happiness" was published in *The Great Ideas Today*, 1992. In addition, he recently wrote an introduction to the reprinted edition of Mortimer Adler's *The Difference of Man and the Difference It Makes* (1993). Professor Hudson was recently named the first Adler Fellow at the Aspen Institute of Humanistic Studies (1992) and returned as a Fellow in 1993–94.

A time will come when people will give up in practise those values about
which they no longer have any intellectual conviction. . . . There are
a certain number of moral tenets—about the dignity of the human
person, human rights, human equality, freedom, law, mutual respect and
tolerance, the unity of mankind and the ideal of peace among men—
on which democracy presupposes common consent; without a general,
firm, and reasoned-out conviction concerning such tenets, democracy
cannot survive.

(Jacques Maritain, *On the Use of Philosophy*) [1]

A nswers to the question "what is human nature?" have immediate
practical consequences. One only has to lend an ear to contro-
versies in ethics, politics, and public policy to hear the various sides
appealing to ideals of "humanity," "humanness," and, lately, "personhood." Rarely, however, do participants in these debates step back to
consider what is substantive about these appeals.

The general lack of philosophical accountability in public discourse is
partly to blame. For its part, the public is shy about demanding explanations for terms they are used to taking for granted. Political leaders,
it seems, prefer the safety of terms and phrases that can be "spun" in
various ways to please their audience. Meanwhile, people fail to notice
that the meanings of their "great ideas" have fundamentally changed.

However, historical events often intervene to reveal the extent of
these changes. The famous Scopes "monkey trial," for example, focused
public attention on the view of human nature posed by evolutionary
theory. The notoriety given to the debates between Clarence Darrow
and William Jennings Bryan revealed a deep division in the public
opinion about the relation of human beings to the lower animals. A
consensus about human nature was breaking apart. In its wake, the
adherents of Darwin, along with those of Marx and Freud, would join
the intellectual mainstream, alongside those holding fast to the witness
of Genesis and those who sought a synthesis of science and religion.

At present, the "culture wars" and debates over "political correct-
ness" attest to more disagreement about what human beings have in
common. While there has been more than enough media attention
given to this dispute on college campuses and in art museums, not much
has been said about its conspicuous appearance in international politics.

In June 1993, representatives of 161 countries attended a United Nations World Conference on Human Rights in Vienna. Its aim was to assess progress in human rights since the 1948 Universal Declaration of Human Rights. The conference faced a pointed challenge from countries that have begun to espouse cultural relativism as a principle to protect their customs from Western interference. Two months prior to the meeting, thirty-four Arab and Asian governments issued the Bangkok Declaration stating that the notion of human rights is relative to the cultural, religious, and historical diversity of nations, and that the Western powers should not use human rights "as an instrument of political pressures." [2]

During the conference representatives from countries such as China, Syria, Indonesia, and Iran invoked an inalienable "right to development" without interference. The Universal Declaration, they argued, as formulated by industrialized countries, reflects the values of colonialism. [3] The ensuing debate was described as a "battleground" between the universalists and the relativists who recognize human rights according to the standards and practices of the particular culture and tradition. [4]

In spite of the controversy a consensus was reached and the final document affirmed the universalist position: "Human rights and fundamental freedoms are the birthright of all human beings. . . . All human rights are universal, indivisible and interdependent and interrelated." [5] It went further than previous documents in emphasizing the rights of women, children, ethnic minorities, and the disabled. And it specified that the "right to development" can never justify the infringement of human rights: "the human person is the central subject of development." [6] It is significant, however, that the language of the document did not solely address human beings *qua* human but highlighted the rights of marginalized groups.

That Western nations found themselves defending a universal view of human nature is somewhat ironic. The debate itself has been generated by scholars in the West who have been calling for a reassessment of the idea of human nature, particularly in regard to gender and ethnicity. As it will be shown, the reasons behind this call for reassessment are in large part historical and political: the idea of a universal human nature has been associated with injustice, with the exclusion and domination of people who fail to measure up to a fully "human" standard. In sum, the idea of human nature has been employed as an instrument of power and coercion by those who are politically dominant.

The same argument can be heard in the resistance of some Third World nations to the idea of universal human rights; they see it as another means by which Western nations can interfere with their sovereign states. Whether or not an idea becomes intrinsically unsound by being put to an unjust use is an assumption to be considered later.

Needless to say, such a challenge, regardless of its historical justification, adds another obstacle to international cooperation and increases our awareness of social fragmentation.

Mortimer J. Adler, a longtime defender of a universal human nature, criticizes ethnocentrism as the sign of an "inveterate attachment to locality." [7] In his view, ethnocentrism, and much of feminism as well, exacerbates the divisions between people by placing too much emphasis on the *difference* between them resulting from nurture, thereby ignoring the *identity* of their basic human needs. He thinks it crucial that we continue to affirm our common humanity, especially in the light of even greater needs for international cooperation.

Adler's understanding of human nature has its roots deeply embedded in thinkers like Aristotle, Aquinas, Locke, and Maritain. His view is similar, if not identical, to the one expressed in both the 1948 and 1993 human rights documents. The possibility of peace and cooperation among nations depends on some degree of theoretical agreement about human beings. This requires that we agree to consider them, first of all, in terms of their natural endowments rather than their conventional attainments. Attention to human nature will disclose the basic goods we all seek rather than the natural differences in how we seek them.

To make the point obvious, the fact that one nation speaks English and another Arabic creates practical problems in cooperation but evinces the shared capacity for language. Or, take the difference in courtesy between Japanese and Americans. The customs are different, but both express a basic human good: the justice of showing respect toward strangers as well as friends. Shared capacities and shared goods underlie the entire gamut of cultural diversity. There is no need to posit differences in nature as long as one knows what a nature is and how to find it.

Indeed, one could talk about the difference between the "nature" of the Muslim society versus the "nature" of the American society as long as it is remembered that patterns of nurture are being classified, not the nature of the human beings living within them. As will be seen, this distinction between the "first nature" represented by the human species and the "second nature" represented by our individual and collective actualizations of first nature is often overlooked in the contemporary discussion. [8]

From Adler's Aristotelian viewpoint, the contemporary discussion of human nature, gender, and ethnicity takes place largely at the level of second nature. The long tradition of epistemological skepticism is partly responsible for this; philosophers since the time of Locke have grown increasingly doubtful about our ability to know the essences of natural substances. This skepticism, having become common among academic theorists in the humanities, focuses their attention on the social factors determining the characteristics of second natures, whether it be gender roles, ethnic traits, or class values. Knowing the second nature of a thing has become the special province of the social sciences and given them their contemporary authority.

However, much of what is said about human nature by both feminists and ethnocentrists has important implications for an understanding of first nature. As will be seen, the sex-gender distinction upon which so much of feminist theory is based de-emphasizes the *homo* aspect of human nature in favor of the *sapiens*. The attempt to place gender identity beyond the reach of sexual determinations has serious implications for a hylomorphic theory of human nature. Theorists of ethnicity tend, rather, to de-emphasize the distinctiveness of human intelligence—they see patterns of intelligent activity, both thinking and doing, as determined by the material conditions of existence. Their historicism implies a denial of immateriality in the intellect and the corresponding ability of thought to transcend concrete circumstance.

Whatever confusion may inhabit the world of theorists, it is inevitable that the concept of nature will be employed analogously in everyday speech. A "nature" is a discernible pattern, a predictable set of characteristics, found in a group of things. One can contrast the nature of men with the nature of women without ever addressing human nature as such. The discussion can turn to the nature of urban men in contrast to rural men, or rich to poor, or Southern to Northern. Though we qualify such generalizations, they are commonplace.

We talk daily about the natures of things, as the human mind habitually searches for patterns of intelligibility in experience. Most of what we say lacks scientific rigor, unless we are trained in the methodology of the appropriate science. But nearly all of this talk about nature takes place over a kind of metaphysical void created by the continued skepticism over knowing the natural quiddity of things.

Adler views our age as involved in another great inconsistency— the growth of cultural relativism parallels a growing reliance upon and confidence in the transcultural character of math, natural science, and technology. At the very moment when the "electronic superhighway" makes available an unprecedented international exchange of ideas and information, that exchange may be branded one more instrument of domination, a new form of colonialism exported by a society too befouled by practices of exclusion and exploitation to be trusted.

These critics are passionate in their condemnation of injustice. Yet, if the principles of the Bangkok Declaration were to be realized, the net effect would allow injustice as long as it is committed within a nation's borders. Even minimum political standards would no longer be applicable across cultures. Clearly this destroys the possibility of basing ethics and politics on a shared human nature, a first nature. It also confines the intelligibility of moral claims to the level of local customs. Nations, in effect, become immune from external scrutiny.

(Opposite page, top) Rigoberta Menchú, winner of the 1992 Nobel Prize for Peace, smiles while accepting applause from the audience at the 1993 United World Conference on Human Rights, which was held in Vienna. (Opposite page, bottom) Representatives of some of the 161 countries that participated in the conference display posters in support of human rights. (Above) Demonstrators against the Bosnian war struggle with policemen at the entrance to the building where the conference took place.

What happens to the original charge of historical injustice? Western nations, at present, will not defend those practices on an ethnocentric basis; they still feel compelled by the ideals embodied in the Universal Declaration. The proponents of "cultural rights," however, employ universalism to condemn other countries and ethnocentrism to justify their own.

Adler's call for consistency in this matter, a call back to canons of universality and rationality, is not likely to be heeded any time soon. The political critique of universal challenge is gathering momentum. This challenge will be examined in two parts: Part One will discuss the classical view of human nature, the feminist rereading of Western philosophies of human nature, and feminist theory; Part Two will analyze the empirical findings regarding gender differences and will outline the various claims and counterclaims about ethnocentrism and multiculturalism.

1. The classical view of human nature

Man with dog closes a gap in the universe.

(C. S. Lewis, *The Four Loves*) [9]

There is no single classical understanding of human nature. The ideal, for example, contained in the *Declaration of Independence,* that "all men are created equal," is the product of many intellectual and religious traditions. Neither Plato nor Aristotle would have agreed with the principle of human equality, but their view that a good life must satisfy the natural aspirations of human nature informs the Founding vision. The notion of equality, as it has finally emerged to include both women and minorities, was influenced by the religious teaching that all souls are equal in the order of salvation. The medievals were more directly attuned to the problem of eternal than temporal happiness, but they helped unawares in the realization of universal equality and human rights.

But both ancients and medievals agreed explicitly about one fact: that human beings are distinguished from other animals, including higher primates, by the nature of their distinctive intelligence, thus classifying human beings as belonging to the species *homo sapiens,* or thinking man. Differences of opinion still remain over the important question of whether this difference of intelligence is one of kind or degree. As will be seen later, this unsolved issue underlies much of the present controversy.

The classical view depicts human nature as belonging to a common species, or essence, and as possessing the natural powers belonging to that species. Definitions begin by placing the thing in its proximate genus, then differentiating it from other members of that genus by determining its specific difference. Human beings are in the genus of animal, but the fact of a distinctive intellectual power affects even those powers shared with other animals. For example, when smelling the sweetness of a rose, human beings are capable of classifying the smell as "sweet" and reflexively distinguishing it from other kinds of sweetness. In logical terms, human intelligence supplies the *differentia* of the species within the genus, but it is a difference that is not limited to mental activity but flows throughout an individual's being. As Aquinas said, "the whole human soul is in the whole body, and again, in every part." [10]

Individuals belong to a species by virtue of their essence, but they are individuated by matter. That is, the only reason for there being different human beings is the fact of their bodies. Matter is also the substratum of change; we change as we grow older, but we remain what we are—beings with a stable identity. Matter is always determined by a substantial form which determines it in a particular way, limiting and defining its immediate potentialities. Put in another way, while a human essence can belong to many individuals, the matter belonging to living persons can only belong to one of them, at least as long as they live.

The term *nature* has many meanings, and at least two of them are relevant here. To talk about "human nature" is to discuss what potentialities are common to all individuals in the species, regardless of their gender or their culture. In other words, how it is possible for a given being to act: can it fly? swim? bear children? think conceptually? Second, these potentialities are not chosen but are given. Nature stands for what is given, not made, not artificial. An individual being does not choose to be what it is; it does not decide to exist. In the case of human beings, who can reflect upon their existence, they are faced with the fact that they have an existence they did not request—they both have a nature and they belong to nature. Existentialist thinkers portray this metaphysical point by dramatizing the radical contingency of existence, the experience of being placed in existence without having requested it.

Thus the contrast of "nature" with "nurture" can be understood as analogous to the contrast of natural with artificial, or natural with conventional, and so on. [11] The natural, in short, is that which cannot be altered by either our doing or our making. While nurture fosters habits, modification of instincts, knowledge, etc., it cannot change the basic needs and potentialities specified by human nature. Nurtural differences correspond to what was termed earlier "second nature."

It is the intellectual power of human beings that makes culture and civilization possible, but it is nurture that creates and extends a particular form of civilization. The often startling contrast between differing societies and their patterns of nurture is due to the unique freedom human beings have in actualizing their nature. As Adler comments, this is the reason that human societies do not resemble beehives. [12] The freedom of our rational human nature bestows variability and diversity between and within societies, across history, and around the globe. But the freedom implicit in nurture does not destroy or alter the fundamental needs of human nature, which explains the patterns of common value discernible across cultures.

Given the fact of human freedom, some deviations from a cross-cultural norm, such as those cultural anthropologists discuss, should be expected. As Aristotle said in his *Nicomachean Ethics* (I, 3, 1094^{b}13–14 [*GBWW* I: 9, 339; II: 8, 339]), we should only expect the degree of intelligibility appropriate to a given subject matter. If we are right to say that human beings are two-legged beings free to pursue happiness in their own way, then we should be less surprised if they chose cannibalism than if they sprouted wings and flew off. Human nature, in this sense, accounts for the transcultural intelligibility and predictability of human behavior.

If one seeks to give an account of why human potentialities are actualized in differing ways, then we are led to contrast nature not only with artifice but also with chance of luck, as an incidental cause of things. Where a given child is born into poverty or wealth, into a Buddhist or a Muslim family, is a matter of chance. As that child grows into an adult, his or her language, values, and customs will reflect the chance of birth. There is no science of chance; the causal effects of chance are restricted by an essence only in the broadest fashion. Given human freedom, chance can play an even larger role in human development than in animals. But chance is the opposite of nature, at least in a world without divine governance. And even though chance events are necessarily involved in actualization of human potentialities, it is important to keep the order of nature distinct from the various causal factors that influence its actualization.

To summarize, the classical definition of human nature is *essentialist*—human beings are animals whose specific difference is the rational soul. Humans share certain powers with other animals but possess the distinct power of an abstracting reason capable of seizing the intelligibility in things. This additional power need not be considered dualistically, as another substance being added to the body. In the Aristotelian tradition, to which Adler belongs, a human being is a hylomorphic unity of body and soul. The body depends upon the essence and exists in virtue of the human soul which is its form. Though the soul determines the body and makes it human, they are in substantial unity: the whole person thinks and feels. It is not the mind that thinks, the nose that smells, or the hand that throws the baseball. The whole person is implicitly involved in each act.

But the superiority of human nature—and the reason why other animals are called "lower"—is found in an immaterial activity of thinking: the mind is capable of freeing itself from the limitations of matter through the process of abstracting universal forms and judging their existence or nonexistence. Adler insists that this mode of thinking represents a difference in kind rather than degree from nonhuman animal intelligence. Most "animalists," as Adler calls them, minimize the difference on the grounds that conceptual thinking is the product of larger brain size alone. Adler counters by arguing that not only does conceptual thinking represent a difference in kind but a radical difference, since even if lower animals had larger brains they would still not possess the immaterial element necessary to human thinking. The ability to think conceptually is not explained by brain weight but by immateriality, which alone can account for the intellect's ability to abstract the universal from the determinations of the sensible.

This is not to say that the intellect operates without sensible input, but to say that its three characteristic operations take from sensation far more than is "seen" in the perception of the sensible. The three acts of the intellect—abstraction of quiddities from sensible data, judgments of existence or nonexistence of these quiddities, further reflection on judgments—each of these operations provides knowledge that is not supplied by perception, that is, by the presence of the sensible singular alone.

Thus, animals who possess only perceptual, not conceptual, thought are not capable of either forming or reflecting upon conceptual abstractions. They obviously form generalizations based upon perceptual experience, as, for example, when Fido senses that his owner has arrived home. Fido will bark and dash for his empty bowl but will never reflect upon either the concept of ownership or hunger. Since Fido expects to be fed, he almost invariably wags his tail. Human beings are less predictable, and a father coming home from work may prefer to greet the dog for precisely that reason.

Conceptual thought provides human beings with a certain freedom from instinctual life, yet it also provides an opportunity for reflection and correction. A grumpy family can be called to account. Concepts enable them to understand the virtue of love, to recognize that loving acts are of a certain kind. Even more importantly, concepts allow the human mind to reflect upon these objects of thought while they are out of sight, so to speak, not sensibly present, and even when, like love itself, they are intrinsically imperceptible. [13]

The practical implications of this paradigm are clear: a common nature establishes the foundation for understanding human moral and political life. As Adler writes, "Nothing else but the sameness of human nature at all times and places, from the beginning of *Homo sapiens* 45,000 years ago, can provide the basis for a set of moral values that should be universally accepted." [14] Success in the moral and political spheres, the very happiness of the individual and the state, is judged on the basis of human beings coming to completion and growing into wholeness *according to the intrinsic teleologies of their nature*. Without a common rational nature, and our ability to apprehend it, any measure of human goodness will necessarily be the product of convention, leaving countries without any external, common standard by which to judge the success of political practices.

Aristotle also said that human beings are by their nature *zoon politikon* (*Politics*, I, 2, 1253ᵃ [*GBWW* I: 9, 446; II: 8, 446]), meaning that we by necessity seek our well-being in community. The state, which is naturally prior to the individual, is composed of families, villages, and cities. Life apart from such communities belongs only to villains, outcasts, or gods. We fulfill our nature only when we act politically, when fully appropriating not only our citizenship in the city but also in the most intimate associations which undergird it. Thus political action is not merely a means to the end of happiness but constitutive of a self-sufficient happiness; it is, one might say, human rationality expressed socially.

What does human rationality do? Basically it serves to direct individuals and society toward its ordinate end represented by *eudaimonia* or happiness. But in order to accomplish that, it must free itself somewhat from the effect of various determinisms, particularly the passions and instincts. This distinction provides Aristotle a criterion for establishing a hierarchy in the political order: freemen, freewomen, and slaves. Natural slaves, lacking the capacity for rational action, exist within households and depend upon the virtuous direction of their masters (*Politics*, I, 5, 1254ᵇ15–25 [*GBWW* I: 9, 448; II: 8, 448]). Women are given some direction over slaves, but since they have less of the rational principle than men do, they ultimately depend upon male guidance.

The universal view of human nature is now increasingly under attack. Postmoderns reject it as a hierarchical and essentialist perspective in service of powerful and oppressive interests. Aristotle's application of his intelligence principle to devise the natural slave and inferior woman exemplifies their concern. The postmodern view, of course, tends to be extremely localized—factors of gender, race, sexuality, wealth, and class create "rationality," thus denying even the possibility of a correspondence of the mind with reality. A leading postmodernist, Richard Rorty, argues that "there is nothing deep down inside us except what we have put there ourselves, no criterion that we have not created in the course of creating a practice, no standard of rationality that is not an appeal to such a criterion, no rigorous argumentation that is not obedience to our own conventions." [15]

Rorty and other practitioners of postmodernism, like Jacques Derrida and Michel Foucault, bring the legacy of radical existentialism and its monadic individualism to its logical conclusion. In its most extreme version, a localized human nature is the sovereign individual considered as the source of all meaning and value.

Yet the call from Nietzsche to "create oneself" is only part of the postmodern's inspiration. The other derives from another familiar source—the Marxist critique of ideas as masking economic interests. What is tricky about coming to grips with the postmodern views of human nature is the combination of these influences: while they purport to free human beings from any common teleology, they do so in the name of justice and service to the oppressed.

Whereas once upon a time it would have been considered axiomatic that an acknowledged "common good" grounded in the basic facts about human nature was considered necessary to have a conception of justice at all, this assumption is now viewed as one more temptation to exclude and to oppress in the name of a societal good as defined by those who benefit from that conception.

Derrida, for example, finds the roots of Heidegger's attachment to Nazism in his attempt to portray the dignity of human existence vis-à-vis an overarching or "totalizing" account of Being. Derrida regards Heidegger's retrieval of metaphysics as the clue to understanding his attraction to fascism—the case of Heidegger reveals the will-to-domination behind all hierarchical systems of reality. One commentator on this charge suggests that "the predicament in which we. find ourselves at the end of the twentieth century: is it possible to have *any* theory of human nature that does not become an intolerable chain on human freedom? In short, do all metaphysics and humanisms inevitably lead to what we may call for shorthand totalitarianism?" [16] Once again we are reminded of how important it is to understand the quarrel between ancients and moderns, specifically over whether or not human beings are free to create their own final end, without delusion.

Both feminists and ethnocentrists renounce the essentialist account of human nature for the same reason. If the charge of "totalitarianism" is not explicitly used, the accusations of "oppression" and "exclusion" are commonly heard. These critics deserve a fair hearing regardless of one's allegiance to the classical traditions. They cannot be dismissed lightly. There is no doubt that the language and concepts of traditional anthropology have been employed not only to exclude but also to eliminate ethnic groups who are found to be "subhuman" or "unnatural." Need one mention the history of Jewish persecution, or the treatment of Native Americans, or the African-American? And, sadly, it appears the politics of "racial cleansing" is far from over.

As has been suggested, wherever the idea of human nature implies a normative view of "humanness" there arises the possibility of oppression. A question that must be faced is whether or not this is accidental, whether or not individual freedom is necessarily threatened by a normative, universal account of human nature. It should be stressed that this dilemma is not merely the product of academic debate but has become the substance of judicial review.

For example, in the 1992 Supreme Court decision *Planned Parenthood of S. E. Pennsylvania v. Casey,* the joint opinion states: "At the heart of liberty is the right to define one's own concept of existence, of meaning, of the universe, of the mystery of human life. Beliefs about these matters could not define the attributes of personhood were they formed under compulsion of the State." Only a court whose justices had become sensitized to the issues raised above could deliver such an opinion.

Adler recognizes that different human communities and societies—whether differentiated along ethnic, religious, or class lines—are capable of actualizing their human potentialities in differing ways. The "babel" of different languages itself attests to this diversity. But those who are invested in the celebration of cultural diversity, as well as the protection of individual beliefs, can blind themselves to the more important point—that these languages themselves are unique to the human species and bespeak a uniquely human potential differing in *kind* rather than *degree* from other animals. Once attention has returned to the remarkable *sameness* of human potentialities, the issue of diversity will seem superficial by comparison. [17] But at the present time, the twin ideas of "cultural rights" espoused by the Bangkok Declaration and a philosophical liberty, which asserts the freedom to define one's existence without direction from the State, continue to gain greater support, while the idea of a universal human nature with inherent rights to the basic goods of life continues to lose credibility.

2. The feminist critique of Western philosophers

> The "male bias," if we can call it that, of past philosophical thought about Reason goes deeper than that. It is not a question simply of the applicability to women of neutrally specified ideals of rationality, but rather of the genderization of the ideals themselves. An exclusion or transcending of the feminine is built into past ideals of Reason as the sovereign human character trait.
>
> (Genevieve Lloyd, *The Man of Reason: "Male" and "Female" in Western Philosophy*) [18]

The ancient paradigm: Plato and Aristotle

The feminist rereading of the Western tradition is central to the current reassessment of human nature. While this survey could have begun with the portrayal of the natural slave and the barbarian in ancient thought, feminist scholarship is way ahead in its treatment of the Western classics. But as the later discussion of ethnocentrists shows, their rendering will very likely run in parallel lines to what follows.

Those who are skeptical about the probity of the feminist critique may be swayed by the sheer mass of evidence showing a consistent denigration of woman in Western thought. Textual studies vindicate the feminist protest. Feminist historians uncover the way in which our knowledge has been shaped by the viewpoint of the male knower by applying "standpoint epistemology" to the history of ideas. [19] To accomplish this, feminist research has brought texts to light that have been largely ignored in traditional scholarship. Feminists have allowed the great philosophers to speak for themselves in previously unheard ways. Thus in the overview which follows the discussion of primary texts has been included along with those of feminist commentators.

It will be seen that the arguments against the essentialist view are based upon the use to which these definitions have been put to exclude and dominate specific groups of people on the basis of their gender. Concepts associated with the pattern of subordination—terms like *nature, rationality,* and *hierarchy*—have become particularly objectionable to most feminist critics. Comments such as the following are typical: "It is questionable whether the concept of human nature means anything. People's 'nature' can be described only by looking at the things we do. To try to abstract or reify a human essence from the ways in which different groups of people have grappled with the issues of survival . . . is a dubious enterprise, because what one labels as 'natural' depends on one's experience and viewpoint." [20] Multiculturalists and ethnocentrists, as will be seen later, have similar objections.

The worst offenders appear to have been the Greeks. Those who revere the Greek tradition for its advocacy, albeit in differing forms, of philosophical and scientific reasoning will perhaps be surprised to find that an integral part of this legacy is a portrayal of the female as inferior to the male. This inferiority follows from consistent association of rational knowledge with masculinity and nature with femininity. The function of reason is to transform, to order, and to control natural forces. Femaleness must be left behind so that masculine reason can proceed in its conquest of the natural. [21]

It is no accident, feminist scholars argue, that the philosophical warrant for this subordination of the female to the male reflects the patriarchal structure of Greek society. "Once rationality is defined as what is not emotional and emotionality established as the characteristic of women, once rationality is seen as a characteristic of mind, not body, and a slave is understood as what is only a body, there could be no discussion of the institutions of slavery or sexism." [22]

Much of what feminist scholars find in their rereading is a consistent pattern of symbolic associations in which male and female are taken to represent opposite sides of dualities. As Lloyd says, the importance of the "symbolic association" cannot be underestimated since it remains consistent for centuries to come, generating further metaphors of dominance of men over women, master over slave, reason over body. [23] The Pythagorean table of opposites dramatically illustrates this with its associations of femaleness with badness, multiplicity, darkness, and motion, and maleness with unity, goodness, and light (Aristotle, *Metaphysics*, I, 5, 986ª22–35 [*GBWW* I: 8, 504; II: 7, 504]). These dualisms are not benign—they imply values. The philosophical tradition, in this sense, perpetuates the view of Hesiod's *Theogony* that the first generation of humans was exclusively men and that women were created later as a punishment because of Prometheus' theft of fire.

The theme of female existence as punishment is found in Plato. His creation account in the *Timaeus* (41 [*GBWW* I: 7, 452; II: 6, 452]) portrays the birth of all human souls as equal and masculine in their primordial state. Woman comes into existence in later births as punishment for the inability of man to rule his passions. The failure to squelch unruly passions destines a man to become a woman, the soul's next incarnation. If as a woman the same soul continues in its passionate ways, it becomes a lower animal, one which resembles the acquired evil. Thus, a woman's existence is viewed by Plato as secondary, as representing a lack of control, a punishment for being too sensual. Woman is man in his decline toward the animals. It should be no surprise that Plato remarks that the best punishment for a cowardly soldier would be to be changed into a woman (*Laws*, 944d–945a [*GBWW* I: 7, 786; II: 6, 786]).

The deprecation of the body, and of "nature" in general, has become a constant theme in feminism. Since Plato sets up reason against the influence of the passions, based upon his tripartite hierarchy of powers, feminists have become wary of hierarchies. In Plato's *Phaedo* (*GBWW* I: 7, 220–51; II: 6, 220–51), the body is represented as an obstacle to wisdom and to a happy death. Plato later came to see the nonrational elements within the soul itself, but still construes knowledge in terms of a process of dominance, an abstraction from matter culminating in an ecstatic contemplation. [24] Perhaps his view is best summarized in the *Symposium* (211c–e [*GBWW* I: 7, 167; II: 6, 167]), where Socrates describes the need to transcend the physical love of the body for the sake of an immaterial wisdom and beauty.

The political implications of Plato's association of reason with ruling and overcoming the body are seen in his tripartite division of the ideal state—a theory of natural classes which reflects the divisions of the soul. Individuals should perform the function in society for which they are best suited by nature. Here the concepts of nature and hierarchy create an unquestioned barrier to protect the power of a leisured patriarchy. To call such an arrangement "natural" is to place it beyond criticism.

Plato can be defended against the feminist critique on the grounds that he allows women to be part of the guardian class in his ideal state whether as philosophers or soldiers (*Republic*, 457a–b [*GBWW* I: 7, 360; II: 6, 360]). Obviously if women are suitable as rulers and soldiers then they must be capable of rational self-rule. But this opportunity for women does not go without qualification: Plato considers men as more gifted; they learn more easily because of a more ordinate disposition toward the body (*Republic*, 455b–c [*GBWW* I: 7, 359; II: 6, 359]). Thus within each class women would be less naturally gifted than men. And the guardian women themselves would have a job that guardian men would not; they would have to bear children, children who would be taken away from them. Nancy Tuana comments that this evinces the need for the state to gain power over the private sphere of the woman, who is a constant threat to the state, especially the female "lust of procreation." Reason must rule over appetite, and women serve as guardians only insofar as they are capable of being like men. [25]

Turning to Aristotle, feminist historians note a greater appreciation of the senses and the body but an overall worsening in the portrayal of women. Aristotle's hylomorphic theory closely integrates body and soul, while his theory of knowledge makes all knowing begin in the senses and its encounter with concrete things. Yet it is precisely this scientific bent that leads Aristotle to give a biological account of female inferiority. His view of female and male procreation has probably elicited more feminist scholarship than any other single text, with the exception of the Bible.

With the additional authority of biological science, Aristotle provides for his time a more convincing case than Plato for the superiority of males. However crude the argument, based upon the need for "vital heat" in the perfection of animal life, appears now (*Generation of Animals*, I, 19, 726^{b}30–33 [*GBWW* I: 9, 267; II: 8, 267]), it had long and pervasive influence. Vital heat, derived somehow from the stars, accounts for the presence of an immaterial form, the rational soul, in matter. Weaker things have less heat, and women generate less heat in their discharge than men, as seen in a comparison of female and male semen. Male semen, like female menstruation, is derived from blood but is transformed by an infusion of heat that turns it white. This lack of heat results in woman's being smaller, weaker, more delicate, less able to provide the active portion of conception. The male contributes the human form, the more perfect power, which actuates a substance, while the female provides the matter, the principle of individuation. It follows that sickly people are more likely to conceive females, and the most intelligent will have the hottest blood (*Generation of Animals*, II, 6, 744^{a}29–30 [*GBWW* I: 9, 285; II: 8, 285]).

An embryo becomes female when the "first principle cannot through lack of heat bring the matter into proper form" (*Generation of Animals*, IV, 1, 766^{a}17–21 [*GBWW* I: 9, 307; II: 8, 307]). The proper form of human nature, then, is always derived from the male. Nature always seeks perfection; therefore, women are a deviation from the best outcome. The female is a defective male or, as Aristotle calls her, "a mutilated male" (*Generation of Animals*, II, 3, 737^{b}25–30 [*GBWW* I: 9,

278; II: 8, 278]). Once again, the female is seen as the privation of the male, the man in decline toward the beast.

It has been argued against the feminist interpretation of these passages that Aristotle in his own time was a progressive. In ascribing a principle of generation to both male and female, he was arguing for the sharing of conception between male and female, an "elevation of the women's role," since such a view was unknown in the previous materialist accounts of Hippocrates. [26]

Whatever Aristotle actually meant, powerful symbolic associations remain in place: male is active, female passive. Active form is male, passive matter is female. No reasons are given by Aristotle for assigning form to men and matter to women in conception. Women are likewise assigned the character traits appropriate to human beings who are more bodies than mind—being more easily subject to the passions, they are compassionate, sentimental, jealous, argumentative, wrathful, despondent, despairing, shameless (*History of Animals,* IX, 1, 608^{b}9–13 [*GBWW* I: 9, 133–34; II: 8, 133–34]).

The social and moral implications are fairly clear. Man is by nature the superior ruler, and woman, having an obvious disadvantage in the realm of practical wisdom, should not be relied upon to rule (*Politics,* I, 5, 1254^{b}6–14 [*GBWW* I: 9, 448; II: 8, 448]). Women therefore are naturally subordinate to men, just as the mind should rule body, and the master his slave. A woman can become virtuous under a man's tutelage and should be kept at work in the household. This male-dominated household, being the most primitive of Aristotle's "natural" political associations, establishes the norm of "gendered" hierarchy for the polis. "Nature tossed them [women] a dash of reason—enough to make them members of the same species as male citizens—but clearly not the kind of reason found in the souls of their natural rulers." [27]

As with Plato, there are relevant qualifications in Aristotle—not all men will be smarter than all women; free women are better than male slaves, who have no deliberative ability at all (*Politics,* I, 13, 1260^{a}12–14 [*GBWW* I: 9, 454; II: 8, 454]). These points may soften criticism but hardly seem to qualify his basic position. Tuana concludes that Aristotle's position cannot be corrected simply by correcting his faulty biology: "For Aristotle's tenet of woman's inferiority, his association of woman and the female with incapacity, passivity, and matter, is a fundamental part of his metaphysics. Although Aristotle might indeed have been 'influenced by the misogyny of his time,' he inscribed this misogyny into the very heart of his philosophy." [28]

*The impact of religious traditions: Philo, Augustine,
Abelard and Héloïse, Aquinas*

In their attempt to uncover the reasons for the continued subordination of women, feminist scholars have combed patristic and medieval texts.

Perhaps it is ironic that texts ignored for so long in the mainstream of the academy, except by specialists, should now be in the spotlight. For years a small group of medievalists have been attempting to highlight the importance of the medieval synthesis of ancient philosophy and the three great religions of the West. Now that attention is forthcoming from a new generation of medievalists trained in the tenets of feminism, the results are hardly appreciative of the use made of ancient wisdom by the religious writers. Feminist historians argue that the impact of this development has been to give religious sanction to Greek misogyny.

This historical ratification is extremely important for those who receive their idea of human nature in part from a revealed wisdom. Natural subordination, although somewhat amended, is again corroborated in the Western tradition. No longer do females lack just intellect; now they are found lacking in the very image of God. The relation between Greek *nous* and the religious understanding of *imago dei* are close, given their relation to divine substance, but there is no doubt that placing Eve at a lower rung of the created order than man, however subtle, exacerbated the problem of subordination.

An additional factor is the nature of God "Himself"—the God of Christianity, Judaism, and Islam addressed in the masculine form. Feminist theologians are now drawing on this revisionist history to correct what they see as unnecessary exclusion of feminine language about God. Those shaped by their religious convictions, they say, are going to be shaped by their way of speaking about divinity, and by the symbols associated with divine being. Feminist theologians insist that there is no reason that God should not be addressed as "She Who Is," and that this new religious language can become integral to "the reform of patriarchal civil and ecclesial structures and the intellectual systems that support them in order to release all human beings for more just designs of living with each other and the earth." [29]

Feminists like Elizabeth Johnson seek a new alignment of revealed knowledge with classical wisdom. But it is clear that major figures in the theological traditions, such as Augustine, Abelard, Aquinas, and the Jewish theologian Philo, forge a synthesis of sorts between pagan wisdom and Scripture that does little to alleviate the problem of subordination. Feminists point out that key passages in both the Old and New Testaments, while suggesting some aspects of equality in the order of salvation, still elevate men over women in the natural sphere.

Particularly important are the passages presenting woman as being created after man, specifically from his rib (Gen. 2:21); woman as first falling prey to the temptation of the serpent (Gen. 3:4–6); man as the image and glory of God, woman as the glory of man, needing to cover their heads in church (1 Cor. 11:4–12) and remain silent (1 Tim. 2:12). Needless to say, these arguments play a prominent role in the present controversy in various religious communions over a female priesthood.

145

Those who think the use of the masculine gender in speaking about God is incidental should consider the example of the Jewish theologian, Philo of Alexandria (b. 15–10 B.C.—d. 45–50 A.D.), the pioneer of allegorical interpretation. He comments directly on why wisdom and virtue is referred to as feminine: "For that which comes after God, even it were chiefest of all other things occupies a second place, and therefore was termed feminine to express its contrast with the Maker of the Universe who is masculine and its affinity to everything else. For preeminence always pertains to the masculine and the feminine always comes short and is lesser than it." [30] During the medieval period the masculine sex of Christ was of as much interest as it is to feminist scholarship today, except that the theologians of that time were defending it. [31]

Philo also uses his allegorical method in *Questions and Answers on Genesis* to portray woman as symbolizing the lure of sense perception and, therefore, the source of the Fall. Eve, created out of the rib of Adam during his sleep, is a "half-measure" of the man; she needs the man to be a whole. When mind becomes a slave to sense, the man cleaves to the woman, the superior to the inferior. Thus, the serpent first spoke to Eve because she was more liable to be deceived. Adam, however, is mentioned first when they hid themselves from God, after eating the fruit, because "It was the more imperfect and ignoble element, the female, that made a beginning of transgression and lawlessness, while the male made the beginning of reverence and modesty and all good, since he was better and more perfect." [32]

Philo is one of the clearest examples of the binarism objected to by feminists. He uses the traditional oppositions and characteristics of male rationality and female physicality, male activity and female passivity, to posit a hierarchy of man over woman before God. The male element in the soul clings to God, while the female element seeks to possess what is perishable. Women symbolize the material world that drags down human nature. Moral progress requires the male virtue of triumphing over the world, the flesh, and satanic temptation. Salvation requires a giving up of female gender and changing into male! Philo, for example, praises Sarah when she stops menstruating and begins to resemble the male sex. [33]

Augustine's relation to women is more complicated than Philo's, both personally and theoretically. He opposed the tradition that saw women as inferior in their original nature and refused to interpret Eve's existence as if it symbolized the Fall. He also rejects Philo's view that men alone possess a rational soul. God, he argues, creates this soul to male and female alike. Thus women as well as men are created in the image of God, where there is no sex distinction. Again, this represents an advance over Philo, since women do not have to give up their sex for salvation (*Confessions,* 12.23 [*GBWW* I: 18, 107; II: 16, 135]).

But in spite of his upgrading the figure of Eve, women remain in an ambivalent position in respect to reason. Augustine does not deprive woman of reason, but he must find other ways to make sense of her subordination in both Genesis and the letters of Saint Paul. The symbolic significance of their bodily differences is that woman should be made subject to the man "in the same way that the appetite for action is made subject" to the mind (*Confessions*, 13.32 [*GBWW* I: 18, 123–24; II: 16, 157]). Woman represents the will's entanglements with the world and the turn of reason toward the body (*On the Trinity*, 12.7). Eve did not actually cause the Fall, but the serpent found it easier to seduce her than Adam because the woman was naturally weaker, not because she was without reason altogether.

Augustine recognizes a weakened moral capacity in woman, but he considers them equal in the order of salvation. The Greek philosophers found women wanting in their capacity for wisdom and earthly happiness, but theologians found little scriptural warrant for extending that subordination into eternity. But a heavenly equality does not require an earthly counterpart. Equal as they may be in heaven, where the inequality of the sexes will be erased, woman remains subordinate on earth. Woman serves the needs of the man and, it might be said, of the species. Before the Fall men and women were sexually different but spiritually equal; woman was subordinated morally as a result of the Fall—the fault of the woman making a master of her husband.

These attitudes toward women, scholars point out, are reflected in Augustine's personal life. He never recognized the real love he had for his mistress, who was probably from a lower class and lacked an education. After his conversion Augustine never cultivated a group of ascetic women friends as did Jerome and Ambrose. As Peter Brown writes, "Augustine moved in a monochrome, all-male world. . . . He would never visit a woman unchaperoned, and did not allow even his own female relatives to enter the bishop's palace." [34]

Still, Augustine argues against the Manichean disparagement of the body and sexuality: sexual organs are given by God, sexual intercourse is a good and could have been enjoyed by Adam and Eve in paradise. He was once challenged to explain, if sexuality is good, why purification was required after intercourse, nocturnal emissions, and menstrual periods. His answer draws upon the old Pythagorean binarism still much in evidence in the fifth century A.D.—purification is necessary after intercourse because male semen represents a "material shapelessness" and menstruation a "formless flow," either of which create the need to reassert order over the chaos. [35]

Order, control, reason, these are the controlling themes in Augustine's treatment of woman and sexuality. But he did not attribute all disorder to sexual desire, as some early Patristic writers did in explaining the Fall as sexual in origin. Rather, the origin of sin is disobedience against God, or simple pride. But the Fall was felt first and foremost in the sexual organs. Once reason loses its control over the body, women suffer pain in childbirth, since they cannot command the birth canal to open and allow the child to descend without pain.

Even though the Fall did not occur because of sex, original sin is passed on through the sexual act. Children are born sinful because it is impossible to have sexual intercourse without lust after the Fall. Augustine describes intercourse as an act of lust disturbing the whole man and causing the total extinction of mental alertness (*The City of God,* 14.16 [*GBWW* I: 18, 390; II: 16, 447–48]).

The inability to control lust is exemplified by the male erection and by Eve's need to cover her nakedness. It has been said that Augustine vindicated sexuality but not its passion: "Augustine would seem to be placed in the unusual position of maintaining that sex is good but erections are bad." [36] Indeed, Augustine argues that sex before the Fall would have been possible without full erections. In his literal commentary on the book of Genesis he writes, "Why, therefore, may we not assume that the first couple before they sinned could have given a command to their genital organs for the purpose of procreation as they did to the other members which the soul is accustomed to move . . . without any trouble and without any craving for pleasure." [37] After all, lustless sex in paradise would have kept all women virgins and the children would have resembled Jesus.

Augustine's description of Edenic marriage as "a faithful partnership based upon love and mutual respect" pointed the way to the appreciation of the unitive aspect of marriage, in addition to the procreative (*The City of God,* 14.26 [*GBWW* I: 18, 395–96; II: 16, 454]). Augustine is the first to call the sexless union of Joseph and Mary a marriage: a bonding of the mind is more intimate than that of the body. He tends to emphasize the good use of sexuality as the distinctive mark of marriage. But he was bound by the traditional estimate of woman's secondary status—a man should, therefore, take care in the presence of a woman, even when she is his wife.

The role of Augustine, as the most influential of the Patristic writers, is crucial to understanding the subsequent history of attitudes toward gender roles, marriage, sexuality, and the body. Some of his progressive steps, though, such as the closer identification of woman with the *imago dei,* went largely unnoticed in doctrinal development. The refusal to recognize woman as being created fully in the image of God was still commonly taught in the twelfth century, as seen in Gratian's *Decretum* (A.D. 1146), and even later. [38]

Another religious figure who has achieved ambivalent status among feminist historians is the twelfth-century theologian Peter Abelard. It is not surprising that feminists are interested in Abelard, whose affair with his much younger student Héloïse, and subsequent castration by

"[Abelard's] *affair with his much younger student Héloïse, and subsequent castration by her furious uncle, is one of the most celebrated romances in history,*" Abelard and Héloïse, miniature portrait by Jean de Meun, 14th century.

her furious uncle, is one of the most celebrated romances in history. Rather surprisingly, Abelard is rarely accused of sexual harassment, probably because the letters attest to Héloïse's intense passion for him, which outlasted the castration. In spite of his illicit relationship, he is viewed by one leading feminist historian as espousing an "evangelical feminism." [39]

The evidence is found in the seventh of his celebrated *Letters of Abelard and Héloïse*, the one written to her concerning the Benedictine rule for woman monastics. Here he twice urges Héloïse to "consider the dignity of women," a phrase evidently unique in the twelfth century. His explicit admiration for the heroines of the Bible—Deborah, Judith, Esther, the female Christian martyrs—is unprecedented. They exemplify the courage of genuine sanctity; about them he writes, "the rams fled while the ewes remained."

That this was not a slip of the pen is supported by his musical masterpiece, a *Planctus* on the subject of Jephthah's Daughter—her courage is celebrated as the essence of woman's dignity. [40] Unlike another well-known instructor of a younger woman, Abelard wonders aloud why men cannot be more like women. This *Planctus* contains a dramatic presentation of woman's fate; women at last are considered as subjects of their own experience, not measured in relationship to a man.

Abelard repeatedly emphasizes that divine grace has consistently honored and dignified feminine weakness over masculine strength, and even that the grace of Christ has always been more abundant to women. For this reason, as well as the example of Phoebe in the *Letter to the Romans* (16.1–2), he defends the legitimacy of a female diaconate.

Abelard was far from consistent in his praise of women. Woman, he thinks, does not possess the *imago dei* but a *similitudo dei*. He reaches this conclusion by employing once again an allegorical interpretation associating men with *ratio* and women with *sensualitas,* making women less able to govern their passions, and reinforcing the entire social structure surrounding this distinction. [41] He writes to Héloïse about the Devil, "what then can the weaker sex do against him? Who but women have his seductive ways so much to fear? It was a woman he first seduced, and through her her husband too, and so made captive all their descendants." [42]

The relationship between Abelard and Héloïse has also provided an opportunity to comment on the nature of philosophy itself as it has been shaped by a purely masculine voice. [43] Héloïse, as interpreted by Andrea Nye, offers a distinctive philosophical viewpoint that ought to emerge on its own merit. Abelard, in the wake of his shameful castration, falls back upon his talent at Aristotelian demonstration to avoid Héloïse's criticism of his failure to love. Héloïse contends that the castration is irrelevant—he ought to have continued loving. Abelard, in response, depreciates erotic love as nothing more than lust; a monastic

love for God is spiritually preferable. Héloïse does not sound like the victim of sexual harassment; she refuses to be ashamed of their past and her passion. Their attitudes reflect a different metaphysics, a different approach to moral issues. For him, rational consent is virtue severed from the body; for her, love overcomes the old Greek and Christian dualism of flesh and spirit.

Héloïse is seen as a gifted woman who refuses intellectual domination, however much she may have desired personal domination. She symbolizes the overthrow of male rationality and the denial of the passions, in short, all the old binarisms and essentialisms. Héloïse uses the "flowing quality of the female tongue" to reunite what the masculine intellect divides: "Might philosophers finally admit what Saint Paul and Abelard denied, that a woman can be the teacher of a man?" [44] Through the effort of this new scholarship, other medieval women, many of them mystics, are emerging as important figures: Hildegard von Bingen, Mechthild von Magdeburg, Beatrice of Nazareth, Hadewijch of Antwerp, Marguerite of Porete, Hrosvitha of Gandersheim, Elisabeth of Schonau, and Margery Kempe.

Aquinas has been called by his feminist critics "the man who should have known better." [45] Why? Aquinas, they contend, starts to correct the traditional deficiencies, such as the Augustinian dualism regarding the nature of bodily existence, but stops short. Aquinas is more androcentric and less misogynist than the Patristic writers but still suffers from the excessive intellectualism that marred Aristotle. [46] Aquinas is an "innovator" who appears interested in overcoming the natural subordination of women but never took the revolutionary steps necessary to complete this task. [47]

As an innovator, he explicitly qualifies the Pythagoreans binarism that associates the male with all that is good and female with evil (*Summa Contra Gentiles*, III 9.3). He speculates that in Paradise equal numbers of male and female children would have been born. He credits God, rather than the male, with the infusion of the rational soul into the fetus. He introduces a new notion of degree in perfection to explain male-female differences in the *imago dei*, which overcomes some of the sex polarization. [48] Marriage and sexual intercourse, he teaches, were a part of God's original purpose and do not result from original sin (*Summa Theologica*, I Q.98.a.2 [*GBWW* I: 19, 517–19; II: 17, 517–19]). And beyond its procreative purpose, sacramental marriage, Aquinas suggests, provides men and women a bond of genuine mutuality and friendship.

But Aquinas, as a theologian, must conform his understanding of men and woman to the testimony of Scripture, as he interprets it. Like Augustine, he teaches that both man and woman are equally *imago dei*, but following Pauline teaching he adds an important qualification: "for man is the beginning and end of the woman" (*Summa Theologica*,

I Q.93.a.4 [*GBWW* I: 19, 494–95; II: 17, 494–95]). His argument for subordination does not result from a defect in her intellectual nature but from her biological function. Although she is an intellectual being, a woman's purpose is mainly generative, which is said in spite of the fact that Aquinas sometimes talks about both sexes being necessary to the perfection of human nature. Women are used to show how the imperfect or defective can serve providentially the good of the whole:

> Thus, it is clear that the generation of a female is apart from the
> intention of a particular nature, that is, of the power which is in this
> semen which, as much as possible, tends to a perfect [male] result of
> conception; but it is in accord with the intention of the universal nature,
> that is, of the power of the universal agent for the generation of inferior
> beings, that a female be generated; for without a female the generation
> of a number of animals could not be accomplished. Similarly, corruption,
> decrease, and every defect pertain to the intention of the universal
> nature. . . . (*Summa Contra Gentiles,* III 94.11)

The reproductive role of the male does not exhaust his purpose, nor does it earn him association with the defective. Woman, however, because of her biology is "symbolically located outside the actual manifestations of Reason within human life." [49]

Once again, this closer identification with biological nature lends justification to woman's lesser authority in the household, where the subjection of women is necessary to the ordering of family life, since man has the greater order of reason and women have less control of their passions. Aquinas assumes that sex drive is stronger in the female. This weakness made Eve easier to seduce because she really believed she could be God (*Summa Theologica,* II-II Q.163.a.4). For Adam's part, his loyalty to Eve makes him less accountable for his fall. Eve's punishment for succumbing to the serpent is an aggravation of her natural subordination, requiring obedience to her husband.

As in Augustine, there is an equivalence in the order of salvation— the resurrected state is devoid of sexual distinction. In the beatified state of intellection, animal operations cease and woman loses her distinctive function to bear children. In regard to Christ, who opens the gates of heaven, Aquinas says, he became man because the male sex is more perfect and strong, but "lest the female sex should be despised, it was fitting that He should take flesh of woman" (*Summa Theologica,* III Q.31.a.4).

From a historical perspective, most of what is innovative in Aquinas is overshadowed by what is derivative. As one feminist historian comments, "It is significant that nowhere does Thomas discuss in an extended and complete fashion the inferior and subordinate nature of the female, simply because he assumes this state of affairs and therefore makes little effort to prove what all perceive as given." [50]

Aquinas may depend on Augustine, but his tone is more dispassion-ate. Some have said that his portrayal of woman reflects a renewal of Aristotelian attention to biology, and that the rediscovery of Aristotle in the thirteenth century exacerbated the depiction of women in the High Middle Ages. But biological descriptions of woman had been common to medieval literature since the seventh century:

> From Isidore on, anatomical description in the Middle Ages was strictly teleological. The description of woman's anatomy therefore focused on her primary function: everything about her—even the weakness that made her subservient to man—was directed toward one end, procreation. Consequently, woman's theological detractors could dispense with any consideration of her psychology. She was seen as a body undisciplined by mind, a creature ruled by her internal, and particularly her sexual organs—a disturbing force of nature. Because she was the instrument of human continuity, woman was to the core a creature of Nature, of that active force that brought the universe into being and preserved its order. . . . Woman's affinity with matter . . . could hardly fail to incur the disapproval of clergymen whose vocation it was to sever the ties that bound them to the material world. [51]

So it is impossible to assign individual blame, since very major stream of influence in the Middle Ages, from Plato and Aristotle, and the Neo-Platonism of Philo and Augustine, to the Arab Aristotelianism taught to Aquinas at Naples and Paris, was inscribed with a consistent portrait of woman as naturally subordinate to man. The tension set up between the supernatural equality of the sexes and their natural inequality produced some gestures in the direction of greater parity, but, overall, the medieval synthesis of religion and philosophy produced mixed results. In the medieval period, as Elisabeth Gössman tells us, "everything that was important for the soul, heaven, eternity, etc., was never refused to women. But everything that is important for social and political life and a persons' relation in the world, was regarded as 'only male.' " [52]

The modern twist: Rousseau, Hegel, Kierkegaard, Nietzsche

The representation of women in the Renaissance is not appreciably dif-ferent from the portrait of the late Middle Ages. [53] The modernist hostility to Aristotelian science and scholastic metaphysics did little to change the ideas of woman in the Enlightenment and beyond. Those who expect to find in later modernity the solution to the ills imposed by ancients and medievals will be disappointed. It is clear that the detrimental associations of woman with private life, the passions, and the body continue well into the twentieth century. However, the same philosophers who uphold these associations will supply the philosophical tools that feminists employ to release the image of woman from its sub-ordination. Some of these tools—individual rights, autonomy, historical consciousness—have become problematic for feminist theory in giving a positive account of gender to replace the one they want to destroy.

Rousseau, for example, calls for a return to nature in order to discover the pre-social dignity of the individual. He uses the feminine to symbolize this ideal of nature, and, one might expect, a corresponding appreciation of women in his philosophy. In *Emile*, Rousseau does contend that men and women are each equal to one another in spite of their differing characteristics. But when Rousseau gives his description of these differences, all the old stereotypes are present: women are passive, submissive, docile, made to be subjugated; their purpose is essentially to serve the interests of men, a purpose their proper education will confirm. In other words, while he grants that woman have genuine intelligence, it should be put to use in accord with a woman's proper function, that is, to be desirable to a man and contribute to his happiness. [54]

Rousseau also attempts to redress the aridity of Cartesian rationalism with a greater appreciation of emotion and intuitive reasoning. This provides him with an opportunity for elevating women to the status of full-fledged rationality. But women are still judged deficient: they are not disposed toward the natural sciences, such as physics, since they are unable to deal with abstractions and speculative issues in any form of thinking. [55] "This asymmetry in the relation of civilized women and men to rationality is further highlighted by the fact that woman's realm of competence does not have knowledge as its end, but rather the satisfaction of the needs of man." [56]

This judgment, reflecting the Greek view about a woman's inability to control her passion, has political motivation. Woman is by nature unable to accompany man beyond family life, beyond the state of nature, into the civilized community marked by rational action and consciously chosen values. For Rousseau, women choose their actions based upon instinct and taste—they never evolve beyond being children, while men become adults. [57] This natural inequality of gender roles serves the interests of the state and general will. The natural attachment between child and parent disposes both to be good citizens of the state. Since women tend to put the needs of their children ahead of the state, their participation in public life can only be disruptive. Men alone can discern and serve the needs of the general will which transcends those of the individual family. In Rousseau's world, women are subordinated not primarily to enable male contemplation, or to preserve the species, but to support the state.

Hegel also explores the difference and complementarity between men and women in the context of a political philosophy. Women are excluded from public life once again for reasons of their nature— woman's existence is naturally within the family. But the family has a crucial role—it is the first ethical relation in which people learn how to live in community and are prepared, if they are male, for participation in civil society and the state. Women play their role in the coming-to-be of Hegel's spirit by a devotion to the family itself, not to their particular husbands. [58] Thus, the woman's place is fixed within the family, and its ethical or universal significance is institutional rather than personal.

Men, through their participation in the state, achieve a self-conscious knowledge of the universal. As Hegel sees exemplified in the tragedy of *Antigone* (*GBWW* I: 5, 131–42; II: 4, 159–74), woman is relegated to an immediate and intuitive relation to spirit, unable to transcend the limitations of family life. She necessarily becomes the unwitting enemy of the higher communities—she is destined to be the "everlasting irony [in this life] of the community." [59] By this Hegel means that women play a necessary role in preparing men for a reality which they themselves cannot experience.

The family life controlled by the mother is to be transcended by all her sons. The male's self-conscious participation in larger political life takes him into the public world. Family life becomes an impediment; it drags men back to a lower form of rational life represented by the woman and her children. Regardless of the political progress that men may achieve in history, the family, as depicted in Hegel, never changes, because it is the domain of woman. Tuana comments that Hegel's woman is bound by her condition. "Unable to enter civil society, she cannot develop her individuality. Since it is through civil society that man comes to understand and participate fully in ethical life, only man fully participates in spirit. The family life precludes woman from developing full rationality or achieving true freedom." [60]

Rousseau and Hegel justify a continued subordination of women for reasons consonant with the principles of their political philosophy. Their view of the female duty to family life fits with their emphasis on the activity of male rationality in ordering the state. But if marriage and the family necessarily represent something retrograde for men, then they are bound to be regarded with dread by men who are devoted to serving higher ends. Both Kierkegaard and Nietzsche manifest just such an anxiety about marriage in particular and woman in general. They no longer couch their justification in political terms; they are preoccupied with protecting the authentic self against "the herd." Involvement with women, for each of them, represents a submission to the process of leveling or assimilation to bourgeois norms. [61] Woman and marriage come to symbolize the loss of selfhood.

Kierkegaard, who wrote at length under a pseudonym about the breaking of his engagement to Regine Olsen, regarded marriage as an impediment to his religious growth. Women, he writes in his journal, are naturally weak. They lack the inwardness to suffer through the demands of the Christian faith—they are always embroiled in the realm of the immediate. [62] To live in the immediate means living without dissatisfactions, without the awareness of contradictions in existence. This is just another way of saying that women are weaker because they lack the strength to persist in a morally strenuous cause.

Kierkegaard, like the medievals, sees men and women as equal before God, but in this life their natural differences prove harmful for men. Marriage especially represents a danger to man, since family life should be the exception rather than the rule for a Christian. The example of Martin Luther, a monk who married a cloistered nun, infected Christendom with worldliness. Any outward expression or institutional involvement places the passion of religious faith at risk. The sociality of marriage forces a man and a woman to enter bourgeois life and demeans the man spiritually by jeopardizing his absolute concentration on God.

Nietzsche, on an analogy with Kierkegaard, thinks women are an obstacle to his vocation—philosophy. Being a philosopher required him "to fly alone" and avoid marriage: he asks, "Every animal . . . instinctively strives for an optimum of favorable conditions under which it can expend all its strength and achieve its maximal feeling of power. . . . Thus the philosopher abhors marriage, together with what might persuade to it—marriage being a great hindrance and a calamity on his path to optimums. What great philosopher hitherto has been married?" [63]

Marriage debases the man by requiring him to combine his desires and goals with another person. (It is well known that Nietzsche despised Socrates, who was married but complained about his wife.) True power requires absolute autonomy which women cannot abide. Marriage is intrinsically debasing because it leads to a loss of power and solitude. Nietzsche's attitude, like that of Kierkegaard, looks back through Hegel and Rousseau, with their fear of family life, to Aristotelian intellectualism. The main difference, however, is that Aristotle welcomes a household of women and natural slaves who complete the practical tasks while the man attends to his contemplation. Aristotle, in this sense, considers community a necessary part of the contemplative ideal. That the mere presence of a woman becomes an impediment to the rational and spiritual activity shows how exacerbated, rather than improved, the situation had become in the nineteenth century.

The image of woman in these writers, like many others of their day, is a miniature of society as antagonist. Woman is the distillation of the corrupt habits that create a Public—sensuality, cowardice, superficiality. They are the emblem of the leveling process whereby gifted men are castrated by the masses. Marriage only subjects a man to the same process on a more intimate scale. The masculine intellect, once again, seeks to protect itself from female nature, from the woman's body.

The emerging feminist consensus on the history of ideas is that rationality has been conceived as an overcoming, a transcending, of the feminine. It is not enough to simply reassert the female side of reasoning—that is, emotion, intuition, love—since such a strategy simply reaffirms the old binarism. Neither is it simply a matter of insisting that women be allowed to participate in the public square. Attention to the portrayal of women reveals a consistent interweaving of female subordination throughout the paradigm shifts of Western culture, from Greek intellectualism to medieval spirituality, Enlightenment liberalism, and existentialism.

The issue, for Lloyd and others, is one of allowing women's experience to shape our understanding of reason and rationality, but without repeating the same mistake of gendering reason: she asks, can we get to a reason which knows no sex? [64] As a goal of feminist scholarship, this is the one which possibly most appeals to the traditionally minded, since it assumes the ability of eradicating most of the bias from our understanding of rationality. Another leading feminist historian, Nancy Tuana, cautions against any universalizing tendencies on the assumption that factors of "race, class, and culture not be erased." [65] This dispute as to whether feminist theory ought to pursue the ideal of a common nature or a particularized feminine ideal . . . between the universal and the local . . . runs throughout the contemporary debate on human nature.

3. Feminist theory

> The adult white male can no longer be taken to represent all of
> humanity. (Alison Jaggar, *Feminist Politics and Human Nature*) [66]

Feminist theory begins with the distinction between sex and gender. This distinction is treated as the first principle of feminist thinking, yet is rarely discussed directly. Like any first principle, the sex-gender distinction lays the groundwork for the whole spectrum of feminist thought. And even though it apparently is considered too accepted an idea to be discussed at length, its significance arises again and again as feminists advance toward more radical positions.

Simply put, sex is biology, the facticity of the body and especially its reproductive capacities. The idea of gender, feminine or masculine, it is argued, does not necessarily follow from the female or male body. Gender is a socially constructed role, which affects everything from consciousness of one's self and others to our behavioral and moral demands and expectations.

Among feminist writers, some call for a total divorce between considerations of sex and gender, while others realize that it is unrealistic, perhaps angelistic, to ignore the impact of sexual difference on gender roles. There are even a few who seem to employ the old patriarchal strategy of using the natural to proclaim themselves superior.

However, the sex-gender distinction contains a crucial assumption in the argument against essentialism: it removes biological considerations from any normative appraisal of second natures. It assumes that bodily inclinations are devoid of moral significance. In other words, male and female gender differences can be considered apart from sexual differences. Obviously this goes against the grain of Aristotle's hylomorphism. The human being as thinker is being opposed to the human being as animal. The realm of freedom is being pitted against necessity. The sex-gender distinction also limits the overall intelligibility of human nature, since it raises doubts about a principle that could unify body and soul. The feminist critique of essentialism is implicit in the sex-distinction, since these essences provide things with an order to their being, ensuring that they will act in intelligible patterns.

The problem with essentialism, according to feminists, is its epistemological naiveté and optimism. Essentialist theories, beginning with Plato and Aristotle, posit an ontological realm standing free of cultural influence and historical change. In fact, such factors are considered an impediment to knowing things in themselves—the ideal of knowledge is ahistorical, the mind has to be freed from the material surfaces of things in order to abstract their essence. Unless, of course, history itself is the object of knowledge; then contingent factors become relevant. But at the foundation of essentialism is a hierarchy, or degrees, of knowledge, beginning with physics, or matter in motion, rising to mathematics and finally to metaphysics, the knowing of being *qua* being.

This trajectory in knowing, away from the diversity of the material world, toward the immateriality of common being, may be considered as the contemplative ideal of knowledge for its own sake, but for many feminists it represents the masculine mind at its worst. Metaphysical contemplation leaves women behind at every level—it requires a turning from the body, which women are less able to do, and freedom from practical household affairs, such as raising children, which women and natural slaves are expected to do while the men study.

Such general comments are far too general to do justice to the panorama of feminist theory. For the sake of the present survey we can adopt a typology of feminism and human nature that distinguishes between liberal feminism, traditional Marxist feminism, radical feminism, and socialist feminism. [67] The differences between the basic types of feminist theory are diminished, according to Jaggar, by the fact that the goal of feminism is political—the end of woman's subordination and the achievement of liberation. But the question of women's liberation is best treated in relation to human nature, since traditional theories of human nature are being directly challenged by much of feminist theory.

One could guess that the goals of liberal feminism are what the majority of people immediately support in the feminist movement. In its demand for equal rights, both political and economic, liberal theory does not pose any radical challenge to traditional essentialist views of human nature—in fact, it relies upon them. There is no suggestion of a differing male and female essence, or an ability to construct an essence. The liberal appeal to universal human rights, such as that of Mary Wollstonecraft (*A Vindication of the Rights of Woman,* 1792), is based upon the same principles as is the American Founding. The problem is not one of human ends: it is an issue of procedural justice, securing for women those same human rights that men enjoy.

Wollstonecraft employs a universalist view to eradicate the traditional prejudice against women's intellectual and moral capacities. She rightly saw that the so-called natural differences between male and female capacities denied women not only an education but also political rights. Wollstonecraft is, perhaps, the model of liberal feminists since she simply demands that women receive the same opportunities for self-development and political involvement as men.

From the perspective of other feminist theorists, liberalism does not get to the root of the problem, since it does not address the issue of the freedom in choice of ends. In other words, Wollstonecraft employs the very essentialist model of human nature many feminists want to demolish. Liberalism, from this perspective, makes reason instrumental for the sake of a fixed, universal end, rather than a creative choice of the values an individual desires.

Like Adler, liberal feminists understand the difference between in-dividuals and groups as potentiality actualized to a greater or lesser degree. Basically this group calls for a gender-blind approach to solving the issue of subordination and oppression. Many feminists consider the use of liberal principles as naive, believing it relies upon a view of the individual transcending societal influences that do not exist historically. As the feminist legal scholar Catherine A. MacKinnon writes,

> Under sex law equality, then, to be human still means, in substance, to
> be a man. To be a person, an abstract individual with abstract rights,
> may be a bourgeois concept, but its content is male. . . . This may be in
> part why men persistently confuse procedural or abstract equality with
> substantive equality: for them, they are the same. Neither includes those
> rights women as women most need and never have had. All this appears
> rational and neutral in law because social reality is constructed from the
> same point of view. [68]

The liberal notion of rationality as that of an autonomous agent, free of the influences of one's time and place, is an illusion. In short, there is no level playing surface. Liberals lack a "hermeneutic of suspicion" that would enable them to see behind the surface of these accepted, stated needs and recognize the structure of male bias in this tradition. Wherever there is a consistent pattern of value in favor of the mind over body, intellect skills over practical, and a division of labor, men have been in control.

Liberal feminists only address the issue of biological difference to the extent that it should not be used against them in the marketplace. They have nothing against women staying at home with children . . . this, after all, is another aspect of individual choice . . . but the old prejudices against the weakness and irrationality of the feminine nature have to be overthrown in order to achieve economic and political parity.

Feminists who make use of traditional Marxism, that is, the texts of Engels and Marx, think that class division more than any other factor is the key to understanding women's oppression. Thus it is impossible to conceive of the human individual outside of historical and particularly economic context—the interrelation of biological, social, and physical factors, mediated by human labor or praxis. When women are studied in terms of the labor they perform, one can see how their subordination serves the interests of capital. The dominant forms of labor provide the characteristics of the human types; thus, human nature is necessarily constructed historically. If one can take control of history one can take control of human nature. As Marx himself wrote, "all history is nothing but a continuous transformation of human nature." [69] Such a strong denial of any and all natural stabilities is appealing to many feminists, whose project they consider just as revolutionary as that of Marx himself.

On the other hand, Marx and Engels did think that some division of labor was natural. Viewing the sexual act as paradigmatic, they considered the female work in the household, and for the private domain in general, to be natural. As a result, they advocated an abolition of gender distinctions in the marketplace and, like the liberals, proposed an androgynous ideal of equality.

That revolutionaries use the sexual relationship to justify retaining the status quo in the household underscores the need to destroy the ideal of normative heterosexuality. This alternative never occurred to Marx or Engels: "They waver," says Alison Jaggar, "between the radical ideal of full female participation in every area of life and the assumption that, while women's biology may allow for considerable participation, the complete achievement of this goal is impossible." [70]

Radical feminism confidently pursues this goal, but with more attention to the role which biological differences play in sustaining subordination. Each of the four types of radical feminism which can be delineated go well beyond the liberal appeal for equal rights and the Marxist preoccupation with the economic pressures of class divisions.

The first group sees the woman's biology—physical weakness and vulnerability to rape—as the source of male dominance. Men have not chosen to create dominance, nature has done it for them; but nature can be overthrown by technology. They advocate taking full advantage of the new methods of contraception and conception freeing women from the determination of their biology and their age. Men, too, should be reengineered in the process. Men, equipped by technology with the means to lactate, are envisioned suckling young babies.

Rather than lamenting the vulnerability of women to men, the second group of radical feminists celebrates those capacities integral to women's biology. Just as men cannot help being men, and this is seen as their basic problem, women cannot help possessing those qualities which, if made powerful, would correct the social and ecological problems created by patriarchy. Men are so subject to the dominance of their reasoning that they necessarily lack the closeness to nature and the nurturing power inherent in the female, whose privileged relationship with her body and its passions disposes her to a superior care for "otherness."

Carol Gilligan thinks that women may have an approach to morality that has generated a movement called "the ethics of care." [71] In her investigation of Kohlberg's hierarchy of moral development, and its invariable stages of moral growth, she found that females tested lower because male responses created the standard by which women were judged. Gilligan found two different voices of moral reasoning: male abstract principles of justice and female personal relationships, although she is doubtful about whether this disposition is essentially gendered.

Other feminists in this group have posited the existence of an earlier, female-dominated civilization that at some point in primordial history was overthrown by patriarchy. A good example of this approach is the work of Carolyn Merchant, who links mechanization of the world picture to the demise of the older, feminine-nurturant vision of the world as a loving provider—harmonious cooperation with the environment, the holistic approach to understanding nature. [72]

The other two identifiable groups within radical feminism attempt to eradicate, rather than inflate, male-female differences by ignoring biology altogether. Some early feminist theorists, representing the third group, advanced an ideal of androgyny in which all distinction between sex roles disappeared. Biology need not dictate the destiny of either men or woman; social roles can be constructed at will without any regard for the determinisms of the body. In addition, as long as sex roles are part of popular parlance they will be used to advance the dominance of men over women.

A more extreme version of this approach is taken by members of the fourth group, who challenge more than the gendering of sex roles but sexual distinction itself. Monique Wittig, for example, argues that the category of woman is artificial, that women have been "programmed to produce children," and the very notion of a distinctive female body is socially created: "We have been compelled in our bodies and in our minds to correspond, feature by feature, with the *idea* of nature that has been established for us." [73] The intent here seems to be more than sex-gender distinction but the obliteration of sex as a biological fact.

Socialist feminism attempts to combine the insights of Marxist analysis with that of the radical feminists. In accounting for woman's subordination it takes into account the panorama of social practices that influence the consciousness of and consciousness about women. Not simply class, but gender, race, ethnicity, age, and national background are also seen to contribute to this construction. This analysis avoids the universalist and biological determinism emphasized by radical feminists but shares their concern for reinterpreting the private along with the public sphere of life.

In delving into the arena of private, inner life of women, socialist feminism can employ a version of Freudian psychoanalysis, shorn of biological determinism, with its emphasis on infantile development. Women are not, therefore, necessarily different from men; their difference stems from the social relations and circumstances—where they live, what exists to live on—that construct their inner lives as well as their public roles and expectations.

The political objective of socialist feminism is to take conscious control of these changes in the social construction of human nature. By changing the social relations, you change the nature. Socialist feminism claims all of the following:

> that our "inner" lives, as well as our bodies and behavior, are structured
> by gender; that this gender-structuring is not innate but is socially
> imposed; that the specific characteristics that are imposed are related
> systematically to the historically prevailing system of organizing social
> production; that the gender-structuring of our "inner" lives occurs when
> we are very young and is reinforced throughout our lives in a variety of
> different spheres; and that these relatively rigid masculine and feminine
> character structures are a very important element in maintaining male
> dominance. [74]

Since much of feminist theory attempts to replace a patriarchal account of human purpose, it is illustrative to look at Mary Daly's treatment of human happiness. In terms of the typology, Daly is a radical of the third kind, one who venerates feminine gender as paradigm of morality, politics, and spirituality. Her *Pure Lust* is particularly advantageous in this regard since she explicitly treats this theme against the background of Greek and medieval eudaemonism. (She also serves up some marvelous samples of the "subversive parody" feminists often employ.)

Eudaemonism can be characterized as a view of happiness, or human flourishing, that identifies it with the subjective appropriation of the final or total good for all human lives. Nature, thus, serves as a norm and guide to the happy life. Feminists, in general, are critical of eudaemonists for their unwillingness to acknowledge different ways of achieving happiness. The appeal to nature, they say, is at its root politicized. Male power pays homage to some values and regards others as either lesser in degree, subhuman, or unnatural. What is actually the social custom of a male-dominated society has been accepted as the model of true happiness, the *summum bonum* of human life, just another spin-off of essentialism. This is not to say that feminists are rejecting happiness as the end of life. They can be said to be finding in the desire for happiness a motivation for their critique of the patriarchal habits blocking their pursuit.

Of course, eudaemonism comes in various forms—Platonic, Aristotelian, Epicurean, Stoic, Thomist—but Daly sees them all as suffering from the same basic failing: they reflect a *phallocentric* viewpoint concerning the human nature and its fulfillment. This is illustrated by the gradual evolution of eudaemonism from the philosophical contemplation of Aristotle to the Beatific vision of the high Middle Ages. This transposition helps to justify the misery of woman by teaching that happiness is not possible in this life. In Aquinas' account of heaven, for example, the eternally happy soul is portrayed in a completely passive posture before God. "One could see this doctrine of happiness, then, as a confession and legitimation of male impotence. It is by no means a woman-originated doctrine. Women do not experience a need for a supernaturally stimulated eternal erection." [75]

Daly proposes a view of women's happiness that overcomes the "metapatterning" left behind by centuries of male domination. She agrees that there is a kind of teleology operating within all human beings, but as such it is a principle of change and adaptation with no fixed end. In other words, it is a teleology without a telos, or an "anti-telos"—because there are no fixed ends in Daly's cosmos. [76]

This is especially true of human beings: "The traditional concept of 'species,' especially of 'the human species' does not adequately encompass the differently oriented lives supposedly contained therein." [77] Her version of Aristotelian teleology ignores any imaginable charge of incoherence as it posits an endlessness in which women are free to imagine any identity. Since the old philosophical concept of species is obsolete, and the human essence can be changed at will, masculine metapatterning can be overturned: "the Spirited Searcher may speak of the soul not as that which confines an individual with a 'species,' but rather as a principle of uniqueness/diversity." [78]

Earlier it was suggested that the sex-gender distinction could lead to a kind of philosophical angelism. This is the condition, sometimes attributed to Descartes, of treating human beings as if they had no body, no material limitations to their nature. Daly confirms this suspicion. She remarks, without any hint of exaggeration, that women should aspire to the kind of angelic being Aquinas describes—each angel having its own species. This way woman can remain as far apart as possible from the male. Who, after all, she argues, would want to be associated with a murderous species like the male? The ancient pattern of association, so derogatory toward the male, has been entirely reversed, as surely Daly is aware.

Daly calls women to self-creation but in self-consciously outrageous style. When Nietzsche remarks that the best way to kill is with laughter, Daly, like many other feminists, is listening. She does not explain how "to transform from one species to another" [79]—she does not think she has to. Her call to affirm a kind of ultimate creativity does not operate in the universe of Aristotelian logic and demonstration. The old rhetorical rules, like the old stable Aristotelian essence, do not apply to "metamorphosing" women.

Daly duplicates at the level of spirit what some radical feminists propose to do with the aid of technology—to remake the human being. It is no surprise that they should be accused of angelism, that is, the forgetfulness of the body: "Feminists and cultural relativists seem to think men are composed of a material body and a nonmaterial soul, and that this soul is free to manipulate its body like a puppet, design cultures, and redefine even itself, all without regard for that inert shell they call the body," writes Thomas Fleming. [80]

Other critics question the feminist emphasis on passion and power over reason. They argue that this leads to contradiction and instability in the feminist project. Feminism begins by overturning essentialism but finds itself caught in a trap of its own making. Without any tools for providing its own position with an account of ends and desires, feminism is left with what Daryl McGowan Tress calls "raw opposition," an end in itself, a "permanent instability without foundation of any kind." [81]

Another obstacle for the more radical proponents of feminist theory is the findings of the empirical research on gender differences. As will be seen in Part II, many of the differences between women and men that feminists consider purely nurtural are in fact rooted in biological nature. This research reminds us that to study human nature is not only to consider the consequences of the rational differences but also the as yet unavoidable consequences of our animal nature.

---

1. Jacques Maritain, *On the Use of Philosophy* (Princeton, N.J.: Princeton University Press, 1961), p. 12.

2. "Universality of Rights Is Defined by U.S.; Protest Over Dalai Lama Mars Vienna Talks," *The Washington Post*, June 15, 1993, Sec. 1, p. A15.

3. "Differing Views on Human Rights Threaten Forum," *The New York Times*, June 6, 1993, Sec. 1, p. 14. The 1948 Declaration was signed by 55 member countries with eight countries of the Soviet bloc and South Africa abstaining. Since then 18 Third World countries have incorporated the Declaration into their constitutions.

4. "U.S. Rejects Notion That Human Rights Vary With Culture," *The New York Times*, July 15, 1993, Sec. A, p. 1.

5. *World Conference On Human Rights: The Vienna Declaration and Programme of Action, June 1993* (New York: United Nations Department of Public Information, 1993), pp. 28–30.

6. Ibid., p. 31.

7. Mortimer J. Adler, *Haves Without Have-Nots: Essays for the 21st Century On Democracy and Socialism* (New York: Macmillan, 1991), p. 263.

8. *See* Saint Thomas Aquinas, *Summa Theologica*, I-II Q.32.a.2, on custom as "second nature" (*GBWW* I: 19, 175–79; II: 17, 175–79).

9. C. S. Lewis, *The Four Loves* (New York: Harcourt Brace Jovanovich, 1960), p. 79.

10. Saint Thomas Aquinas, *Summa Theologica*, I Q.89.a.2 (*GBWW* I: 19, 475; II: 17, 475).

11. Mortimer J. Adler, *The Great Ideas* (New York: Macmillan, 1993), pp. 560–68.

12. Ibid., p. 560.

13. Adler, *Intellect: Mind Over Matter* (New York: Macmillan, 1990), p. 35.

14. *Haves Without Have-Nots*, p. 230.

15. Richard Rorty, *Consequences of Pragmatism* (Minneapolis: University of Minnesota Press, 1981), p. xlii.

16. Robert Royal, "Human Nature and Unnatural Humanisms" in *From Twilight to Dawn: The Cultural Vision of Jacques Maritain*, ed. Peter A. Redpath (Notre Dame, Ind.: University of Notre Dame Press, 1990), p. 175.

17. Adler's classic work on this subject has been reprinted with a new introduction by the present author: *The Difference of Man and the Difference It Makes* (New York: Fordham University Press, 1993); *see* p. 234.

18. Genevieve Lloyd, *The Men of Reason: "Male" and "Female" in Western Philosophy* (Minneapolis: University of Minnesota Press, 1984), p. 37.

19. Sandra G. Harding, *The Science Question in Feminism* (Ithaca, N.Y.: Cornell University Press, 1986).

20. Ruth Hubbard, "The Political Nature of 'Human Nature,' " in *Theoretical Perspectives on Sexual Difference*, ed. Deborah L. Rhode (New Haven, Conn.: Yale University Press, 1990), pp. 70–71.

21. Ibid., p. 72.

22. Andrea Nye, *Words of Power: A Feminist Reading of the History of Logic* (New York: Routledge, 1990), p. 50.

23. Lloyd, p. 4.

24. Ibid., p. 7.

25. Nancy Tuana, *Woman and the History of Philosophy* (New York: Paragon House, 1992), p. 22.

26. Daryl McGowan Tress, "The Metaphysical Science of Aristotle's Generation of Animals and Its Feminist Critics, *Review of Metaphysics* 46 (December 1992), pp. 319–20.

27. Elizabeth V. Spelman, *Inessential Woman: Problems of Exclusion in Feminist Thought* (Boston: Beacon Press, 1988), p. 45.

28. Tuana, p. 30.

29. Elizabeth A. Johnson, *She Who Is: The Mystery of God in Feminist Theological Discourse* (New York: Crossroad, 1992), p. 9.

30. Philo, "On Flight and Finding" in *Philo* V, trans. F. H. Colson (Cambridge: Harvard University Press, 1934), p. 51.

31. Joan Gibson, "Could Christ Have Been Born a Woman?: A Medieval Debate," *Journal of Feminist Studies in Religion* 8 (Spring 1992), pp. 65–82.

32. Philo, *Questions and Answers on Genesis*, trans. Ralph Marcus (Cambridge: Harvard University Press, 1953), p. 37.

33. Dorothy Sly, *Philo's Perception of Women*, (Atlanta, Ga.: Scholar's Press, 1990), pp. 84–89.

34. Peter Brown, *The Body and Society: Men, Women and Sexual Renunciation in Early Christianity* (New York: Columbia University Press, 1988), p. 396.

35. Joyce E. Salisbury, *Church Fathers, Independent Virgins* (New York: Verso, 1991), p. 41.

36. Salisbury, p. 45.

37. Saint Augustine, *The Literal Meaning of Genesis*, 9.10, trans. John Hammond Taylor, S. J. (New York: Newman Press, 1982), p. 81.

38. Kari Elisabeth Børresen, "God's Image, Is Woman Excluded?" in *Image of God and Gender in the Judaeo-Christian Tradition*, ed. Kari Elisabeth Børresen (Oslo: Solum Forlag/Humanities Press, USA, 1991), p. 208.

39. Mary Martin McLaughlin, "Peter Abelard and the Dignity of Women: Twelfth Century <<Feminism>> in Theory and Practice," in *Pierre Abélard, Pierre le Vénérable, Les courants philosophiques, littéraires et artistiques en Occident au milieu du XIIe siècle* (Paris: Éditions du Centre National de la Recherche Scientifique, 1975), p. 304.

40. Mary M. McLaughlin, "Abelard as Autobiographer: The Motives and Meaning of His Story of Calamities," *Speculum* 42 (1967), p. 312.

41. Elisabeth Gössman, "The Image of the Human Being According to Scholastic Theology and the Reaction of Contemporary Women," *Ultimate Reality & Meaning* 11 (1988), pp. 187–88.

42. *The Letters of Abelard and Heloise,* trans. Betty Radice (New York: Penguin, 1974), p. 206.

43. Andrea Nye, "A Woman's Thought or a Man's Discipline? The Letters of Abelard and Heloise," *Hypatia* 7 (Summer 1992), p. 1.

44. Ibid., p. 17.

45. *Women and Religion: A Feminist Sourcebook of Christian Thought,* eds. Elizabeth Clark and Herbert Richardson (New York: Harper and Row, 1977), p. 78.

46. Eleanor Commo McLaughlin, "Equality of Souls, Inequality of Sexes: Woman in Medieval Theology," *Religion and Sexism: Images of Woman in the Jewish and Christian Traditions,* ed. Rosemary Radford Ruether (New York: Simon and Schuster, 1974), p. 216.

47. Kari Elisabeth Børresen, *Subordination and Equivalence: The Nature and Role of Woman in Augustine and Thomas Aquinas,* trans. Charles H. Talbot (Washington, D.C.: University Press of America, 1981), p. 143.

48. Prudence Allen, R.S.M., *The Concept of Woman:* The Aristotelian Revolution, 750 B.C.–A.C. 1250 (Montreal: Eden Press, 1985), p. 385.

49. Lloyd, p. 36.

50. Eleanor Commo McLaughlin, p. 218.

51. Claude Thomasset, "The Nature of Woman," in *A History of Women in the West, Vol. II: Silences of the Middle Ages* (Cambridge: Harvard University Press, 1992), pp. 43–44.

52. Gössman, pp. 189–90.

53. Ian MacLean, *The Renaissance Notion of Woman: A Study of the Fortunes of Scholasticism and Medical Science in European Intellectual Life* (Cambridge: Cambridge University Press, 1980).

54. *See* J. J. Rousseau, *Emile,* trans. Allan Bloom (New York: Basic Books, Inc., 1979), pp. 57–59, and comment by Susan Moller Okin, *Women in Western Political Thought* (Princeton, N.J.: Princeton University Press, 1979), p. 130.

55. Rousseau, p. 385.

56. Tuana, p. 49.

57. Rousseau, p. 211.

58. Tuana, p. 100.

59. G. W. F. Hegel, *The Phenomenology of Spirit,* trans. A. V. Miller (Oxford: Clarendon Press, 1977), par. 475, p. 288.

60. Tuana, p. 106.

61. The comments on Kierkegaard and Nietzsche draw upon the author's unpublished dissertation: Deal W. Hudson, "Three Responses to Romanticism: Baudelaire, Nietzsche and Kierkegaard," Diss. Emory University 1978, pp. 145–59.

62. *Soren Kierkegaard's Journals and Papers,* vol. 4, trans. and ed. Howard V. Hong and Edna H. Hong (Bloomington: Indiana University Press, 1975), 4998–5008.

63. *Genealogy of Morals,* Sec. 3.7 in *The Basic Writings of Nietzsche,* trans. and ed. Walter Kaufman (New York: Random House, Inc., 1968).

64. Lloyd, p. 107.

65. Tuana, p. 121.

66. Alison Jagger, *Feminist Politics and Human Nature* (New York: Rowman & Littlefield, 1988), p. 22.

67. Ibid., passim.

68. Catherine A. MacKinnon, "Legal Perspectives on Sexual Difference," in *Theoretical Perspectives on Sexual Difference,* ed. Deborah L. Rhode (New Haven, Conn.: Yale University Press, 1990), pp. 223–24.

69. Karl Marx, *The Poverty of Philosophy* (New York: International Publishers Co., Inc., 1963), p. 147.

70. Jaggar, p. 69.

71. Carol Gilligan, *In a Different Voice* (Cambridge: Harvard University Press, 1982); Gilligan later revised her findings to call the voice of care "different" rather than exclusively female.

72. Carolyn Merchant, *The Death of Nature: Women, Ecology, and the Scientific Revolution* (San Francisco: Harper and Row, 1980). *See also* Val Plumwood, "Women, Humanity and Nature," in *Socialism, Feminism and Philosophy: A Radical Philosophy Reader,* eds. Sean Sayers and Peter Osborne (New York: Routledge, 1990), pp. 211–34.

73. Jaggar, pp. 98–99.

74. Jaggar, p. 127.

75. Mary Daly, *Pure Lust: Elemental Feminist Philosophy* (Boston: Beacon Press, 1984), p. 339.

76. Ibid., p. 352.

77. Ibid., p. 351.

78. Ibid., p. 352.

79. Ibid., p. 353.

80. Thomas Fleming, *The Politics of Human Nature* (New Brunswick, N.J.: Transaction, Inc., 1988), p. 79.

81. Daryl McGowan Tress, "Feminist Theory and Its Discontents," *Interpretation* 18 (Winter 1990–91), p. 306.

PART THREE

Special Features

Trotsky's The History of the Russian Revolution

Thomas K. Simpson

Thomas K. Simpson, pictured here in front of Leon Trotsky's former office in New York City, is a frequent contributor to *The Great Ideas Today*. Until 1990 he was a tutor at St. John's College in Annapolis, Maryland, and Santa Fe, New Mexico. Under a grant from the National Endowment for the Humanities, he has prepared an edition, scheduled for publication by Rutgers University Press, of three papers on the electromagnetic field by James Clerk Maxwell designed to make Maxwell's text accessible to readers without special training in mathematics. Other projects include his current role as president of a small corporation, Paraspectives™, Inc., which holds a patent application on a commercially interesting technology for placing the human eye directly into non-Euclidean spaces, making possible four-dimensional Cartesian graphing in a wide variety of applications.

Mr. Simpson's education was at the Virginia Polytechnic Institute, at St. John's College, at Wesleyan University, and at The Johns Hopkins University, where he earned a doctorate in the history of science and technology. He currently resides in Saratoga Springs, New York.

I. Introduction

In general, books are meant to dwell on shelves: they are to be taken down, read, perhaps enter the life of society, but then return to their places within the accumulating library of the literature of a civilization; anything which won't accept such a place presents a problem. Such an irregular entity is Trotsky's *The History of the Russian Revolution*. [1] Few shelves have made room for it—in the West, its message has on the whole been unwelcome, the very name of its author carrying pejorative overtones, while in the Soviet Union under Stalin, Trotsky was identified as a prime enemy: the *History* was written from a position of exile, and was unmentionable in Russia. Thus excluded by both camps, the work has found relatively few readers.

Indeed, the *History* tends to elbow its way off a shelf, even when admitted. It is in an important sense an agitational instrument, and, like radioactive material, even after the passage of two-thirds of a century, may remain active and suggest special handling. Like Socrates, it is reasonably considered for banishment as a threat to established order. It quite deliberately challenges our concept of "history" itself. It does not set out to present a simply "objective" account of the events of 1917, written from a comfortable speculative distance or politically neutral standpoint. Quite the contrary, it forthrightly occupies a specific, revolutionary political position. As we shall see, Trotsky calls attention to this situation, and carefully develops the claim that history, to be true, must be subjective. This is a proposition one might entertain more comfortably if the "subject" in question were only the author. Here, however, the intended "subject" is the reader as well—the book is directed as if *ad hominem* to every reader who picks it up, for the revolution it describes is seen as only having begun in Russia in 1917. Trotsky delivers the revolution to our doorsteps.

Perhaps with the collapse of the Soviet Union and efforts, current as this is being written, to complete the erasure of socialism from the world's agenda Trotsky's material may now be regarded as sufficiently deactivated to revert from agitation to speculation, and thereby to gain a wider readership. If so, many people will be surprised to discover what they have been missing. Trotsky combines a disarming sense for the human detail with the skills of a novelist and a penetrating wit which might stand comparison with Swift or Twain. Trotsky writes fact as fiction—not, certainly, in the sense that he invents his material, but rather, having searched out an intensively documented archival record, he tells its story in the mode of the living event. He falls very naturally at times into the interesting mode grammarians call the "vivid present." As we shall see, that is close to his point—the past in Trotsky's hands will not take its place behind us, but rather tends to loom in advance: history presents itself as prospective and oncoming.

My purpose in the present essay is very limited. Since I can hardly expect that the reader has already encountered this work, my effort will be to provide a simple introduction to the book itself, and an invitation, for I feel confident many readers will find a reading of Trotsky's *History* highly rewarding. There is a difficulty, admittedly. If we are in this way to read the book on its own terms, we must be prepared to lend something to the enterprise, for it is written from the far side of a formidable dialectical watershed. Its stance is that of confident effort to achieve a radically new social order, the vision of a rational society, fully implementing democracy and lying beyond war and the nation-state—the very opposite, we might note, of Stalinism, but far, too, from the principles of our capitalistic society, which Trotsky will call "bourgeois." Few readers will in fact share Trotsky's viewpoint, yet much may be learned by entering for a season into the spirit of this work. I suggest, then, that it be read in the manner in which disbelievers often read the Bible with great profit in courses on our Western heritage—"as literature." Any who happen to be converted in the process do so at their own risk: the management takes no responsibility.

It is an intriguing fact that although Trotsky wrote this history with a strong sense of vividness and presence, he was not, in fact, in Russia at the time of the February uprising, and was unable to reach Petrograd until May. [2] A brief review of Trotsky's life prior to the revolution may be useful to readers for whom his name has come to refer to a political camp, rather than to a person. Leon Trotsky, born Lev Davidovich Bronstein in the Ukraine in 1879, had been exiled to Siberia for revolutionary activity as a youth; he escaped and played a dramatic role in the failed revolution of 1905. Arrested again in 1906, and once again escaping from exile, he spent many years in Europe as a correspondent, writer, and revolutionary theorist. At the point in 1917 at which the events described in the *History* begin, Trotsky was in the United States, living with his family in the Bronx, and working on St. Mark's Place in Manhattan at the office of Nikolay Bukharin's Russian emigre newspaper, *Novy Mir* ("The New World"). Trotsky and his family left for Russia as soon as possible upon learning of an insurrection which had occurred in Petrograd in February, but his passage was interrupted by his arrest by the British naval police and imprisonment in Canada. They did not actually arrive in Petrograd until May 4, 1917. It tells us much about Trotsky to learn that during his detainment in

Canada, he proceeded to educate some 800 German prisoners of war in the principles of revolutionary politics. "The camp resounded with his speeches, and life in it turned into a 'perpetual meeting.' " We should know, as well, that by the time in 1930 in which this *History* was being written, Trotsky had successfully led the Red Army in a desperate defense of the revolution in a Civil War, and had subsequently been exiled by Stalin. The *History* is thus written from a position of exile, on the small Turkish island of Prinkipo. [3]

II. Trotsky's theory of history

Underlying the *History* is a theory of history, and behind Trotsky's theory of history lies his study of Marx. Beyond Marx in turn lies Hegel, and the concept of the historical dialectic. It is important to Trotsky that these theoretical foundations be secure:

> The question of a correct philosophical doctrine, that is, a correct
> method of thought, is of decisive significance to a revolutionary party
> just as a good machine shop is of decisive significance to production. [4]

As appropriate, we will be making connections with these philosophical foundations as the discussion of the *History* proceeds.

Trotsky writes with the skill and manner of a novelist: specifically, his *History* reminds the present writer in many respects of a strikingly parallel epic, Tolstoy's *War and Peace*. [5] At the very outset of Trotsky's discussion of the task of the materialist historian—more exactly, that of the historian of a revolution, who is working in the mode of dialectical materialism—Trotsky makes a claim which comes very close to asserting that *style* is of the essence in materialist history:

> . . . The fundamental thing is the narrative. In the facts themselves the
> reader ought to find sufficient support for the inferences. [II:iii]
>
> The history of a revolution, like every other history, ought first of all
> to tell what happened and how. That, however, is little enough. *From
> the very telling* it ought to become clear why it happened thus and not
> otherwise. Events can neither be regarded as a series of adventures,
> nor strung on the thread of some preconceived moral. They must obey
> their own laws. The discovery of these laws is the author's task. [I:xvii]
> (emphasis mine) [6]

A demand is thus placed on the *narrative*—what Aristotle calls the MYTHOS, the *plot*—of an altogether exceptional sort.

The notion that plot has its logic is not new. Readers of the *Great Books of the Western World* may well turn to the *Poetics,* for Aristotle, too, sees the excellence of poetics in plot, and of plot in its obedience to truth. It is for this reason that the *Poetics* stands at the pinnacle of

Aristotle's logical works, and that Aristotle can speak quite earnestly of fiction as truer than history. [7] Trotsky is thus not breaking new ground in claiming that narrative has its logic, or that a story well told will make its truth manifest to reason—though in our age of scientific objectivity, it may seem strange to claim for history any criterion beyond conscientious adherence to the data alone.

The logic of the plot in the *Poetics* is, however, very different from the logic of narrative that Trotsky has in view. Aristotle speaks of the subject matter of discourse as the "what," and the manner of the telling as the "how." It is that "how" which corresponds to the term "style." In turn, the question of style is inherently geared to the nature of the object: style must be "appropriate" to its object. [8] The Aristotelian narrative and that of Trotsky will require radically different styles because they address radically different worlds. The modern "objective" historian, by contrast, means to presuppose no world at all, and thus to write in the style of detached and academic disinterest—although we may suspect that to claim to presuppose "no world," and to write such a neutered history founded only in research and nourished only upon footnotes, is the work of a school of thought which itself belongs to a certain kind of world.

The "method of dialectical materialism," then, which governs Trotsky's work as historian, is geared in the scene confronting him, to the world of exploitation which Marx described, in which the underlying fact is that of class and class interest. The conflict of class interest in turn becomes the energy source which gives life and motion, and at the same time discipline, to Trotsky's narrative:

> For us the fundamental forces of the historic process are classes; political parties rest upon them; ideas and slogans emerge as the small change of objective interests. The whole course of the investigation proceeds from the objective to the subjective, from the social to the individual, from the fundamental to the incidental. [II:v]

One might suppose that this would leave small room for subjectivity, or small concern for the individual. Surprisingly, Trotsky draws the very opposite conclusion. Though these objective forces are real, they lie very deep and work their ways into the events of historic narrative through the mediation of the human psyche. It is by this route that Trotsky's dialectical materialism arrives at a central concern for the process of development of *consciousness*.

> In a society that is seized by revolution classes are in conflict. It is perfectly clear, however, that the changes introduced between the beginning and the end of a revolution in the economic bases of the society and its social substratum of classes, are not sufficient to explain the course of the revolution itself, which can overthrow in a short

interval age-old institutions, create new ones, and again overthrow them. The dynamic of revolutionary events is *directly* determined by swift, intense and passionate changes in the psychology of classes which have already formed themselves before the revolution. [I:xvii–xviii]

The emphasis on the term "directly" is Trotsky's own, and points to a special task for historical narrative. For it is the narrative, the story, which first of all concerns the domain of the direct, the observable detail which unfolds before our eyes. [9] By Trotsky's account, this realm of consciousness does not merely mediate mechanically, but has its own dialectical laws, not at all mechanical, which are themselves "directly" determinative of the events. If the narrative is to carry an inherently convincing logic, this must be a logic in this domain of conscious awareness:

> The swift changes of mass views and moods in an epoch of revolution thus derive, not from the flexibility and mobility of man's mind, but just the opposite, from its deep conservatism. The chronic lag of ideas and relations behind new objective conditions, right up to the moment when the latter crash over people in the form of a catastrophe, is what creates in a period of revolution that leaping movement of ideas and passions which seems to the police mind a mere result of the activities of "demagogues." [I:xviii]

We see now the canvas upon which the historian who works in the mode of dialectical materialism must paint—not just the facts of underlying economic and social relations, nor just the detail of the revolutionary events, but above all, developments in the domain of human awareness, awakening from the sleep of unquestioning acceptance of the familiar as if it were permanent and necessary, and breaking through to that "leaping movement" of the mind which is prepared to conceive things in an entirely new light. In fact, that "leaping movement" is precisely that moment we speak of in other contexts as the achievement of a dialectical insight—the radical shift from one view of things to another entirely different—while the institutions which we take as "given once for all" are those consistent with the first principles of a system whose assumptions have not been subjected to dialectical questioning. Socrates' truly threatening role in Athens, which quite understandably led to his execution, was to question at their foundations the principles upon which the existing order stood.

Only under very special conditions will that leap occur, the three-fold cycle of dialectic: first a thrust forward of the human spirit, then the disillusionment of a suffered negation, and finally an act of true learning, a passage to a recognition in which an old world is shattered, to yield to a new. The deep motions of the human psyche—mind and spirit—are in this view of the essence of the historic process; it is these which the narrative must catch and regenerate, and if it does, readers will grasp and endorse, by resonance of their own psyches, the human truth the story bears. Objective privation is not alone or directly the cause of the process:

> In reality the mere existence of privations is not enough to cause an insurrection; if it were, the masses would always be in revolt. It is necessary that the bankruptcy of the social regime, being conclusively revealed, should make these privations intolerable, and that new conditions and new ideas should open the prospect of a revolutionary way out. [II:vii]

Trotsky will see in Russia an underlying *objective* factor in the sheer fact of deprivation and suffering. The bankruptcy of the tzarist regime, its inability to solve such objective questions, is itself a further objective factor. But these are not enough; Trotsky has listed here three consequent *subjective* factors which turn objective suffering into that act of mind and body which constitutes revolt: the bankruptcy must be "conclusively revealed" and thus become an object of sharp awareness; only in that context do the sufferings become "intolerable." Still, intolerable conditions do not themselves open a path to action. There must arise "new ideas." He is describing the threefold dialectic, culminating in a birth. A cause is born, and insurrection becomes a matter of conditions and timing. Yet even, as we shall see, the intimate detail of that timing—on which all is to be wagered—is itself crucial, and develops through a

Two portraits of Trotsky: from his French passport during World War I (left), and with his wife, Natalia, and son, Leon Sedov, in their first exile in Alma-Ata, Kazakhstan (right).

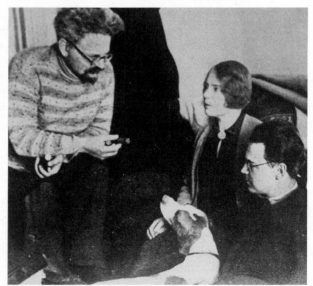

further, embedded dialectical learning process. Our narrative will thus be dealing with the most vital, aware, and committed human actions. The *History* is fully as *dialectical* as Plato's dialogues or Kierkegaard's crisis of the believing soul, both of which pass—though in very different ways—through these same phases. But can this be *materialism*? It may be "materialist" in Marx's use of the term, referring both to concrete physical realities and specific social relationships. Trotsky reminds us:

> Let us not forget that revolutions are accomplished through people, although they be nameless. Materialism does not ignore the feeling, thinking and acting man, but explains him. What else is the task of the historian? [II:vii]

Evidently the "explanation" Trotsky has in mind here, so far as it concerns the immediate work of the historian, is not "materialist" in the conventional sense, but points rather to the operation of the force of very real conditions upon the consciousness and actions of equally real people.

The logic of events that is to be the essence of the narrative will belong to the realm of the human mind, and will be seen in a class perspective. A class society is a society of *two* minds—the bourgeois mind and the mind of the vast majority of the people, the "masses." Each will be complex, but when it is a case of popular revolution, the mind which leads in breaking through old principles and forming new ones—the innovative mind in which the dialectical process arises—will

Trotsky is shown at work in Prinkipo in 1931 where he organized the opposition to Stalin and wrote the *History*. The headline reads, *"Lenin Lives in the Work of the Opposition."*

be that of the people. Real dialectical progress is here seen not as the work of conventional philosophers or statesmen, but of those closest to the suffering and contradictions of society, as new concepts form out of crises of human yearning and strife.

Are the *people* in fact capable of such original, leading thought? Formal representative democracy doubts it, and in granting the vote entrusts the people only with the judgment to hand such matters over to their own selection of competent persons. As we know, the founders of the United States of America avoided pure democracy, prudently instituting a constitutional republic of representative government in its stead. By contrast, the revolution which Trotsky describes is a dialectical revolt against such a limiting premise:

> The most indubitable feature of a revolution is the direct interference of the masses in historic events. In ordinary times the state, be it monarchical or democratic, elevates itself above the nation, and history is made by specialists in that line of business—kings, ministers, bureaucrats, parliamentarians, journalists. But at those crucial moments when the old order becomes no longer endurable to the masses, they break over the barriers excluding them from the political arena, sweep aside their traditional representatives, and create by their own interference the initial groundwork for a new régime. . . . The history of a revolution is for us first of all a history of the forcible entrance of the masses into the realm of rulership over their own destiny. [I:xvii]

Direct rulership by the masses over their own destiny would be democracy in the full, unqualified sense. [10]

We begin to see the nature of the historian's problem in the context of dialectical materialism. The consciousness under study, whose narrative it is to be, is that of the people; objective class forces move this from below. But how can all this be brought under observation? How can such phenomena be captured in narrative? These are processes which occur among millions of people—factory workers, peasantry, soldiers, and sailors—the task of telling their story demands new arts from the narrator. We are on the track of a new regime of *style*.

> The difficulties which stand in the way of studying the changes of mass consciousness in a revolutionary epoch are quite obvious. The oppressed classes make history in the factories, in the barracks, in the villages, on the streets of the cities. Moreover, they are least of all accustomed to write things down. Periods of high tension in social passions leave little room for contemplation and reflection. All the muses—even the plebeian muse of journalism, in spite of her sturdy hips—have hard sledding in times of revolution. . . . For better or worse, a revolutionary party bases its tactics upon a calculation of the changes of mass consciousness. . . . If it can be made by a revolutionary leader in the whirlpool of the struggle, why not by the historian afterwards? [I:xix]

A metal fabrication factory in St. Petersburg at the end of the nineteenth century suggests the scale and manner of Russian factory organization from the earliest introduction of modern manufacture. Trotsky speaks of workers "half-liberated" from serfdom.

the lessons of 1905, and of the harsh years between, are important components of the picture which is to unfold: indeed he sees here the unity of a threefold dialectical passage, from the initiative of 1905, through the years of negation, to the resulting new initiative of 1917.

Trotsky speaks of Russia as an instance of "the law of combined development," according to which backward societies, as they begin to introduce certain modern methods, live in mixed states, in multiple worlds. This is a dialectical "law"; though it operates powerfully, its consequences may be quite different in response to different circumstances. It appears in the enormity of the Russian factories and the corresponding huge aggregations of capital which appear in a nation still only "half-liberated" from serfdom. [I:6] It appears again in the military arena in World War I, where, as he says, an enormous army of peasants had "no correspondence to modern military technique":

> In the matter of military supplies and finances, Russia at war suddenly finds herself in slavish dependence upon her allies. This is merely a

military expression of her general dependence upon advanced capitalist countries. . . . The lack of munitions, the small number of factories for their production, the sparseness of railroad lines for their transportation, soon translated the backwardness of Russia into the familiar language of defeat—which served to remind the Russian national liberals that their ancestors had not accomplished the bourgeois revolution and that the descendants, therefore, owed a debt to history. [I:18]

About 15 million men had been mobilized, of whom some 5.5 million had been killed, wounded, or captured; and conditions on the fronts had become unbearable. [17] From the point of view of the Russian bourgeoisie, the military command, and the palace, the widespread disruptions and desertions which resulted, were measured in terms of patriotism and loyalty, and seen as failures of moral will on the part of the soldiers. But as we shall see throughout the *History*, Trotsky is alert to voices from below, indicators of forces at work among the people which higher authority and the press do not reflect. For Trotsky, discourse is a class question, and he invites us to recognize it as such by counter-poising voices from the two camps. He quotes an outcry from a group of government ministers:

> Poor Russia! Even her army, which in past ages filled the world with the thunder of its victories. . . . Even her army turns out to consist only of cowards and deserters. [I:19]

By contrast, he quotes a soldier, known to us only as Pireiko:

> Everyone, to the last man, was interested in nothing but peace . . . Who should win and what kind of peace it would be, that was of small interest to the army. It wanted peace at any cost, for it was weary of war. [I:21]

He adds reference to a book by an "observant woman, Feodorchenko, serving as sister of mercy" who "listened to the conversations of soldiers, almost to their thoughts, and cleverly wrote them down on scattered slips of paper . . . ":

> The little book thus produced, *The People at War*, permits us to look in that laboratory where bombs, barbed-wire entanglements, suffocating gases, and the baseness of those in power, had been fashioning for long months the consciousness of several million Russian peasants, and where along with human bones age-old prejudices were cracking. [I:21]

Trotsky uses a great many such lenses, focusing from above and below, in a relentless effort to get a fuller picture of the actual state of affairs, and a closer look at the motions of consciousness among the masses. Crossed lights are thrown by reports from observant intellectuals, and even at times, from notes of agents of the secret police or, as in the following, the director of police:

. . . the weariness of war. . . . observed everywhere, and the longing for
a swift peace, regardless of the conditions upon which it is concluded.
[I:23]

Trotsky examines with interest a wave of profiteering which was
going on in the capital, Petrograd. After reviewing statistics from various companies on a surge in incomes, he draws a vivid picture of the
accompanying social behavior:

The lack of bread and fuel in the capital did not prevent the court
jeweler Faberget from boasting that he had never before done such a
flourishing business. Lady-in-waiting Vyrubova says that in no other
season were such gowns to be seen as in the winter of 1915–16, and
never were so many diamonds purchased. The night clubs were brimfull
of heroes of the rear. . . . Nobody had any fear of spending too much. A
continual shower of gold fell from above. [I:25]

Evidently the situation which in 1912–13, Trotsky tells us, had already become objectively revolutionary had thereafter been immensely
aggravated by the war. Indeed, the enormous Russian army, gathered
under the conditions of a "world war" which itself reflected the powers of modern capitalism, matched revealingly the industrial armies of
workers gathered in great factories, who constituted the new proletariat in Petrograd (until 1914, and now again, St. Petersburg). The
peasantry, from whose ranks the army was largely recruited, was thus
being welded in the barracks into a body increasingly conscious of its
interests as a class, and ready to communicate with its counterparts in
the factories of the urban centers.

IV. The "February days"

Over a period of five days in February of 1917, an insurrection took
place in Russia—first of all, in Petrograd—which no one had foreseen,
but which nonetheless overthrew the monarchy and succeeded in placing power in the hands of the workers, soldiers, and peasants. It began
on International Women's Day, February 23, a day for which, under
the grinding adversities of the war, little had been planned. "It had not
occurred to anyone," Trotsky begins, "that it might become the first
day of the revolution." [I:101]

It was the women who took the first step on the path which was
destined to bring down the tzar and overturn the state. Here indeed is
a telling instance of Trotsky's principle that revolutions move "from the
objective to the subjective," for the most immediate demand, closest to
the concerns of the women, was the demand for bread. The beginning
was woman's courage. No strikes had been planned, yet:

УПРАВ.ПЕТРОГР.УѢЗДН.ПОЛИЦ.НАЧАЛЬН.

ДА ЗДРАВСТВУЕТЪ

ДА ЗДРАВСТВУЕТЪ
СОЦІАЛИЗМЪ
РАБ.ОБ.МАСТ. ... СТИТ.

Всенародный праздникъ 1-го Мая
18-го Апрѣля 1917 г. въ Петроградѣ.   Дворцовая площадь.

The mass demonstration of May Day 1917 proved to be a fragile moment for the "all-national festival" (from a postcard of the time). The standard of the soldiers on the left reads, *"Long Live the Democratic Republic!"* while that of the workers reads, *"Long Live Socialism!"*

> . . . . in spite of all directives, the women textile workers in several
> factories went on strike, and sent delegates to the metal workers with an
> appeal for support. [I:101]

As one might trace a great river to its source in the hope of knowing it better, and in the process indeed learn something of the watershed of which it is ultimately the expression, here is the first step of the revolution which five days later had overthrown the tzar and ushered in a epoch of history which runs to our own doorstep today.

These women did not *intend* to overthrow the tzar and the state—that is, they had no plan, no "idea" of doing so. Yet the logic of their act, as it unfolded, proved to contain in itself just that consequence. To get closer to the act itself, from his distance as revolutionary in exile, Trotsky turns to the memoirs of a participant witness, a certain Kayurov, introduced simply as "one of the leaders in the workers' district." We perceive that he is a Bolshevik, with a leading role in the Vyborg Bolshevik Committee. Kayurov writes:

> With reluctance . . . the Bolsheviks agreed to this [the women's call for
> a mass strike], and they were followed by the workers—Mensheviks

and Social Revolutionaries. But once there is a mass strike, one must call everybody into the streets and take the lead. . . . The idea of going into the streets had long been ripening among the workers; only at that moment nobody imagined where it would lead. (I:101) [18]

Here in operation is the very spirit of the logic of Hegel; it is what Marx calls *praxis*. [19] It moves from the unconscious to the conscious in the way Trotsky sees as paradigm for the entire *History*. Yet in that initial act inheres in fact a high sense of purpose. If an end is simply foreknown, one begins with a blueprint; reasoning in an orderly manner from blueprints belongs to the mode we might call "calculative" reason. Here we have the reverse; the process is spirited and illumined by strong intent, but the implications—though dialectically already entailed—are not, cannot be humanly predicted or anticipated in any way. Calculation does not suffice; reason must work in a higher, intuitive mode. Trotsky comments:

> . . . no one, positively no one—we can assert this categorically upon the basis of all the data—then thought that February 23 was to mark the beginning of a decisive drive against absolutism. [I:102]

Workers leave the famous Putilov factory in Vyborg District following the proclamation of a general strike in February 1917. Later, in July, Trotsky describes 80,000 Putilov workers making their way by night to present their demands to the Soviet Executive Committee.

Revolutionary literature was distributed in Moscow during the first days of the events of February 1917. Trotsky described the demonstrations in Moscow as having lagged behind those of Petrograd by only a few days.

To Trotsky it is of the essence of the event—of, then, the revolution—that it was begun "from below":

> . . . being taken of their own accord by the most oppressed and downtrodden part of the proletariat—the women textile workers, among them no doubt many soldiers' wives. The overgrown bread-lines had provided the last stimulus. . . . A mass of women, not all of them workers, flocked to the municipal duma demanding bread. It was like demanding milk from a he-goat. (I:102) [20]

Red banners, Trotsky notes, appeared in various parts of the city, but no strikes or demonstrations began other than in the one district of Vyborg. The day, he adds, "passed successfully, with enthusiasm and without victims. But what it concealed in itself, no one had guessed even by nightfall. [I:102]

On the second day, many more participate, and the slogans, reflecting a growing awareness of latent implications of the event, shift from the immediate call for bread to denunciation of the war and the autocracy. About half, Trotsky estimates, of the industrial workers of the city were on strike on the second day. "Throughout the entire day," he tells us, "crowds of people poured from one part of the city to another." During that second day, a crucial development begins—again, Trotsky watches intently the vital signs of nascent consciousness. He again quotes Kayurov:

"The promenading crowd was sympathetically disposed toward us, and soldiers in some of the war-hospitals greeted us by waving whatever was at hand." [I:103]

To this testimony of a participant witness, Trotsky adds this reflection:

How many clearly realized what was being ushered in by this
sympathetic waving from sick soldiers to demonstrating workers? [I:103]

Again, Trotsky's focus is on the first increment, the indication of human impulse at work. [21] Evidently, the reaction of the soldiers to the demonstration, is critical, for before long they will yield their wills to the demonstrators and swing the balance of the event. Ultimately, whole military units will become participants in insurrection. Such a development is not a matter of chance—we have seen what the war means for these soldiers, how alienated they have become in spirit from the patriotic ideal which might place duty above these sympathies. Evidently, the sensitive writing of history depends on this ability to recognize in small symptoms, portents of developments to come. This is no matter of mechanical categorization, of "factual" reporting, but calls for an insight into the deeper process of which these are tokens. Here interpretation must incorporate a dialectical logic, giving recognition to such momentary oracles of unfolding consciousness. Such a token is ephemeral, a thing of a critical instant.

Trotsky, still drawing upon the report of Kayurov, brings to life such a moment of crisis. The workers of the Erikson factory have encountered a group of Cossacks at a narrow place:

Cutting their way with the breasts of their horses, the officers first
charged through the crowd. Behind them, filling the whole width of the
Prospect, galloped the Cossacks. Decisive moment! But the horsemen,
cautiously, in a long ribbon, rode through the corridor just made by
the officers. "Some of them smiled," Kayurov recalls, "and one of them
gave the workers a good wink." This wink was not without meaning.
The workers were emboldened with a friendly, not hostile, kind of
assurance, and slightly infected the Cossacks with it. The one who
winked found imitators. In spite of renewed efforts from the officers, the
Cossacks, without openly breaking discipline, failed to force the crowd to
disperse, but flowed through it in streams. [I:104]

Trotsky comments wryly:

The revolution does not choose its paths: it made its first steps toward
victory under the belly of a Cossack's horse. [I:105]

Here is Trotsky's microscope at work. [22] At this point of human detail we are witnessing a true crisis in the dialectic of events, that turning point which is the *aporia* of the Platonic dialogue, at which the old set of ideas dissolves, and nothing new has as yet been born to take its place. In terms of a tragic plot, this is the point of peripety. Old limits are being violated, the way has been opened for an idea of a new sort to take form. With a dawning awareness of personal autonomy, on the instant, the soldier meant to discipline the people elects to regard himself as their friend. Here again is a paradigm of *praxis:* the bold, precarious action and the hesitant birth of both a new thought and a new personal identity are inseparable. With many centers of initiative, all at the level of innovative and courageous individual actions, the event becomes *molecular.* Such history is best observed from the level of the street.

> A remarkable incident! And remarkable the eye of its narrator—an eye which took an impression of every bend in the process. No wonder, for the narrator was a leader; he was at the head of over two thousand men [the Erikson workers, in their encounter with the Cossacks]. The eye of a commander watching for enemy whips and bullets looks sharp. [I:105]

Eye to eye—the eye of the historian, looking for evidences of the nascent impulses which begin below and only gradually take explicit form, and the eye of the proletarian leader, giving crucial guidance to an insurrection which is running in advance of him, and does not yet have a plan.

V. The wanderings of the tzar's train

Over the course of five days, the insurrection moved from the first beginnings which we have watched, to complete victory over the tzar and an altogether startling seizure of power in Russia. We must send the reader to these chapters in the *History* for any sense of the delightfully seriocomic narrative in which the spirit of this bloodless revolution is captured. One vignette may serve to suggest the style, which steers always close to the human.

The tzar, who has been situated at military headquarters "not because he was needed, but in flight from the Petrograd disorders," has decided, at the far more resolute tzarina's prompting, to return to his residence near the city. The railroad workers, however, have something to say about this:

> His train went as far as the Visher station. The railroad workers would not let it go farther: "The bridge is damaged." Most likely this pretext was invented by the courtiers themselves in order to soften the situation.

Nicholas tried to make his way, or they tried to get him through, by way of Bologoe on the Nikolaevsk railroad; but here too the workers would not let the train pass. This was far more palpable than all the Petrograd telegrams. The tzar had broken away from headquarters, and could not make his way to the capital. With its simple railroad "pawns" the revolution had cried "check" to the king!

. . . While the train was wandering and finding no road, the tzarina was sending the tzar telegram after telegram, appealing to him to return as soon as possible. But her telegrams came back to her from the office with the inscription in blue pencil: "Whereabouts of the addressee unknown." The telegraph clerks were unable to locate the Russian tzar. . . .

The tzar—his location unknown—turns back to Pskov, to the headquarters of the northern front. . . . [I:82–3]

We see here the "molecular" principle in operation, as an effective instrument of the revolutionary process. In Pskov, where representatives of a new Provisional Government succeeded in finding him, the tzar abdicated; by March 8th, he had been placed under formal arrest.

VI. Spontaneity

A central issue arises concerning the question of leadership. "Who led the February insurrection?" A conceptual watershed divides two categories of answer. What we may call the standard account has two components: on the one hand, major, successful events such as the February insurrection are assumed to have leaders and to have been planned in advance, while on the other, the masses in Petrograd are regarded as a restless, aggrieved populace, without internal direction, and hence easily kindled to revolt and violence, and being led. The insurrection would then lack any inner meaning, and in this sense was called by most observers merely "spontaneous." [23]

This view is in virtually every respect the opposite of the dialectical view of causality held by Trotsky. The question of leadership of the February insurrection is thus of great interest to Trotsky, raising as it does issues fundamental to the entire *History*. The events of February become a laboratory in which this crucial question is put to test. Once again, Trotsky's distinctive instrument of historic analysis is the revealing incident, which in its detail becomes almost surreal, bearing as it does an intensity of meaning for the whole. Looking, so Trotsky puts it, ". . . . as through a keyhole into the laboratory of the revolutionary process." Trotsky reports a revealing incident:

On Friday, February 24, when nobody in the upper circles as yet expected a revolution in the near future, a tramcar in which the senator was riding turned off quite unexpectedly, with such a jar that the windows rattled and one was broken, from the Liteiny [Prospect] into a side street, and there stopped. The conductor told everybody to get off: "The car isn't going any farther." The passengers objected, scolded, but got off. "I can still see the face of that unanswering conductor: angrily resolute, a sort of wolf look." [I:149]

Trotsky's comment, drawing an inference we might not have anticipated from the unyielding steadiness of that gaze, is this:

That resolute conductor, in whom the liberal official could already catch a glimpse of the "wolf look," must have been dominated by a high sense of duty in order all by himself to stop a car containing officials on the streets of imperial Petersburg in time of war. It was just such conductors who stopped the car of the monarchy and with practically the same words—this car does not go any farther!—and who ushered out the bureaucracy . . . *The conductor on the Liteiny boulevard was a conscious factor of history. It had been necessary to educate him in advance.* [I:149 (emphasis mine)]

For Trotsky, the important conclusion is that we see at work a "high sense of duty"—an action not at all "spontaneous" as merely impulsive, but a *conscious* act. This means here, I suggest, an act which has been thought about, which is understood in context, and which is in the dialectical sense deliberate and intentional. The conductor does not intend to unseat the tzar, yet intent in a broader sense is a defining component of his act. It is for that reason, then, that Trotsky interprets the "wolf" look as the consequence of *education in advance.* This suggests leadership in a more interesting sense, implying not that the conductor had been commanded to stop the car, but rather that he had gained in advance certain convictions which lay behind his principled, autonomous intervention.

To the objective ingredients we discussed earlier, then, we must add the fact that the workers of St. Petersburg had grown aware of their situation through an extensive process of education. The long series of events from 1905 to 1917 had, as we have seen, laid a groundwork in consciousness—the earlier revolution with its brutal suppression, the development at that time of the *soviet* as a new, more directly representative form, the sufferings and defeats of the Russian experience in the war. But these events, however provocative, would not have been *educational* if conscious thought had not accompanied them.

It was necessary that throughout this mass [of workers] should be scattered workers who had thought over the experience of 1905, criticized the constitutional illusions of the liberals and Mensheviks, assimilated the perspectives of the revolution, meditated hundreds of times about the question of the army, watched attentively what was going on in its midst—workers capable of making revolutionary inferences from what they observed and communicating them to others. [I:150]

We have here a most interesting set of verbs which might well characterize any sound educational process. Teachers will recognize them as functions one would wish to promote in an intelligent classroom—clearly to be contrasted with conventional formal "education" in which the purpose is to pass on listable sets of facts, methods, or doctrines. These are verbs which characterize initiatives of the dialectical mind. We might well be reminded of the distinction Socrates makes between this dialectical education, and that parody of education which he describes as the process of pouring from one container into another.

We may not always recognize classrooms when we see them. Here, the school is that of the workers' praxis: the harsh experience in the Russian factories over a period of more than a decade. Trotsky describes these real schools of Petrograd in this way:

> In every factory, in each guild, in each company, in each tavern, in the military hospital, at the transfer stations, even in the depopulated villages, the molecular work of revolutionary thought was in progress. [I:151]

Trotsky, without apology, identifies this work of revolutionary thought as *propaganda:*

> . . . finally, it was necessary that there should be in the troops of the garrison itself progressive soldiers, seized, or at least touched, in the past by revolutionary propaganda. [I:150]

It is customary to speak of "propaganda" pejoratively, but the word has, as is well known, long usage in an honorable sense. Is not all intensely motivated, earnest teaching in some sense *propaganda* for the good as we understand it, and when sincere, among the most respectable of human endeavors? The ironic mask of ignorance cannot hide the fact that Socrates was always propagandist for dialectic and the illumination of the good.

Trotsky will give us, with our conventional ideas, no peace. Not only does he transfer the concept of education from those institutions and methods which have granted us our diplomas, to those masses whose lack of education we elaborately regret; as we have seen, he challenges as well our very concept of *science.* He says of that thought which was "drilling through the thick of the working class":

> . . . this thought was more scientific: not only because it was to a considerable degree fertilized with the methods of Marxism, but still more because it was ever nourishing itself on the *living experience of the masses* which were soon to take their place on the revolutionary arena.

> *Thoughts are scientific if they correspond to an objective process and make it possible to influence that process and guide it.* [I:151 (emphasis mine)]

Evidently, the model of the "laboratory" is for Trotsky more than metaphor. The social relations within which we live, the unfolding events in which we participate, are objective processes to which it is possible to bring thought into correspondence. We can, and must, be right about them; only if we are will we gain the ability to influence the development of events. These molecular teachers, Trotsky is seriously claiming, are being *scientific*. Perhaps the aspects of this suggestion most offensive to a conventional concept of science are those of *consciousness* and *caring*. We may be getting close to the center of Trotsky's challenge to our structure of thought. For he is describing a "thick" process of total involvement, thought motivated throughout by suffering and longing—suffering the horrors and pain of war, or the deprivation of bread for one's family; longing for peace and a better life. Science in this sense will not be *objective,* but strongly motivated, passionately caring—and if this is bias, then strongly biased as well. [24]

Completing his investigation of the question "Who led the February revolution?" Trotsky draws the conclusion:

> . . . in the working masses there was taking place an independent and deep process of growth, not only of hatred for the rulers, but of critical understanding of their impotence, an accumulation of experience and creative consciousness which the revolutionary insurrection and its victory only completed.
>
> To the question, Who led the February revolution? we can then answer definitely enough: Conscious and tempered workers educated for the most part by the party of Lenin. [I:152]

Lenin, we may remark, is for Trotsky the epitome of that scientist who is able accurately and insightfully to comprehend the nature of the unfolding social process, and thereby also to intervene in a way which verifies the accuracy of his comprehension.

VII. The arrival of Lenin

As Trotsky captures them, the events of 1917 follow an intricate, dialectical course, marked by acute contradictions. One central contradiction Trotsky calls the "February Paradox," in which the victors in the successful insurrection insist on handing governing power to the bourgeoisie, who in turn are able to impose what conditions they like by the simple threat of handing the power back again. The victors, the proletariat, simply cannot conceive themselves as governing—as we have seen, they are convinced this is something which must be done

The first members of the Provisional Government assemble in the State Council chamber. The Soviet, mistrusting its ability to rule, handed its February victory back to the existing Duma, insisting that it form this new body. A dysfunctional sharing of power resulted.

by the bourgeoisie, who are experienced at "this line of business." The paradox reflects, then, an acute contradiction between the fact of holding power and the absence of an adequate awareness of the possibility of exercising it. Refuge could be sought, sincerely enough, in a long-standing theory, well-founded in Marx and which Russian revolutionaries had learned from Lenin himself in an earlier era. It was understood that the proletarian revolution would emerge from a period of successful capitalism, itself founded on an initial revolt against monarchy. In this light, it appeared that the February revolution could usher in only the bourgeois, capitalist period, and that, since this itself was succeeding badly enough, the proletarian revolution remained remote. It took the arrival of Lenin from exile to challenge these old assumptions in their application to a new context, and bring the present contradiction into sharp focus.

Lenin, born Vladimir Ilich Ulyanov in Russia in 1870, like Trotsky had already endured a term of exile in Siberia prior to the revolution of 1905. He lived in Europe by choice after 1900, returned during the revolution, and lived in Europe as an exile from 1907 and 1917. Over the years he had written several major works, including *The Development of Capitalism in Russia* (1899), *What is to be Done?* (1902), and *Imperial-*

Soldiers and sailors, with a few civilians, men and women, gather to hear a speech in the Great Catherine Hall of Tauride Palace in 1917.

Speaking is Provisional Government president, Mikhail Rodzianko, whose chief talent was said by a contemporary to lie *"not in his mind, but his voice—an excellent bass."*

ism, the Highest Stage of Capitalism (1917). Through these, and through the publication *Iskra* ("The Spark"), his theories of the revolutionary process had become widely known. By insisting on a separate conference of the Bolshevik faction of the Social Democrats in 1912, Lenin became in effect the founder and leader of the Bolsheviks as a distinct party. He was living in Zurich at the time of the February insurrection in Petrograd, and it was from there that the "sealed train" in which he returned had departed.

Immediately on seizure of power in February, the soviet, an institution which had been an achievement of the 1905 revolution but thereafter annulled, had been revived. This remarkably democratic structure involved a hierarchical system of direct representation, beginning with soviets (councils) in factories, villages, and barracks. [25] These local soviets elected delegates chosen from their own membership to meet and vote at higher levels, until finally representation was achieved at the regional or national level. A central feature of this arrangement was that workers delegated from the factory floor, village, or barracks would themselves constitute the membership of the highest councils. Frequent local meetings and the process of recall made this in principle a highly democratic structure. Yet it was the executive committee of the Soviet which in February had passed power to a bourgeois Provisional Government, thereby instituting an inherently dysfunctional system of "dual power." [26] While the people had begun to realize that this system was not serving them well, the Soviet meant to represent them continued to yield power to the bourgeoisie. It is in this sense that Trotsky says the leadership lagged behind the masses. Lenin's arrival on April 3 threw a dramatic spotlight on this contradiction.

VIII. The Finland station

Although Trotsky was still far from the scene on the occasion of Lenin's arrival on his return from exile, we have already seen that this merely geographical impediment will not prevent our author from painting the event in all its world-historic vividness. [27] For it was indeed a moment on which history pivoted. He relies in part, as he will often, on the extensive *Notes* of the liberal N. N. Sukhanov. [28] Lenin had arrived through Germany—enemy territory in the intensity of wartime—by way of a "sealed train," destined to become legendary, which indeed no one had been permitted to leave or enter throughout the trip. Trotsky describes the arrangement as contrived by way of a "unique international treaty between the editorial staff of a revolutionary paper and the empire of the Hohenzollerns." [29]

The president of the Petrograd Soviet, Nikolay Chiedze, welcomed Lenin as he arrived from the north at the Finland station, located in the workers' own Vyborg district, and in a brief address, which took place in the "Tzar's Room," as Sukhanov tells us, very deliberately invited him to support the coalition government in continuing the war in defense of the revolution. [30] Nothing could have been further from the intentions of Lenin, for whom internationalism was a first principle. To invoke workers' support of a war which was not their own, in supposed defense of a revolution whose aims were the opposite of those of the war, had in fact no chance of Lenin's support. Sukhanov describes the reaction thus:

> . . . Lenin, it seemed, knew well how to deal with all that. He stood there looking as though what was happening did not concern him in the least, glanced from one side to the other, looked over the surrounding public, and even examined the ceiling of the "Tzar's Room" while rearranging his bouquet (which harmonized rather badly with his whole figure), and finally, having turned completely away from the delegates of the Executive Committee, "answered" thus: "Dear comrades, soldiers, sailors and workers, I am happy to greet in you the victorious Russian revolution, to greet you as the advance guard of the international proletarian army. . . . The hour is not far when, at the summons of our comrade Karl Liebknecht, the [German] people will turn their weapons against their capitalist exploiters. . . . The Russian revolution achieved by you has opened a new epoch. Long live the world-wide socialist revolution!" [I:296]

The contradiction here is indeed total. Rather than fight the Germans in the guise of enemies—who are after all, workers in uniform—in supposed defense of the "Russian" revolution, Lenin totally recasts the situation. They should rather join their German comrades, of whom Karl Liebknecht and Rosa Luxemburg are the leaders, in revolution against German capitalism, as the first step of a "new epoch" of revolution against capitalism everywhere. [31] There is no room in this for Russian patriotism; Lenin's response is thus in total contradiction to Chiedze's invitation to collaborate with the Provisional Government in the present war. This could well be construed as a rude rejection of the sincere efforts of the revolutionary leadership. Nevertheless, as Trotsky observes:

> . . . that clumsy revolution instantly and heartily took its leader into its bosom. The soldiers demanded that Lenin climb up on one of the armored cars, and he had to obey. The oncoming night made the procession especially impressive. The lights on the other armored cars being dimmed, the night was stabbed by the sharp beam from the projector of the machine on which Lenin rode. It sliced out from the darkness of the street sections of excited workers, soldiers, sailors—the same ones who had achieved the great revolution and then let the power slip through their fingers . . . [I:297]

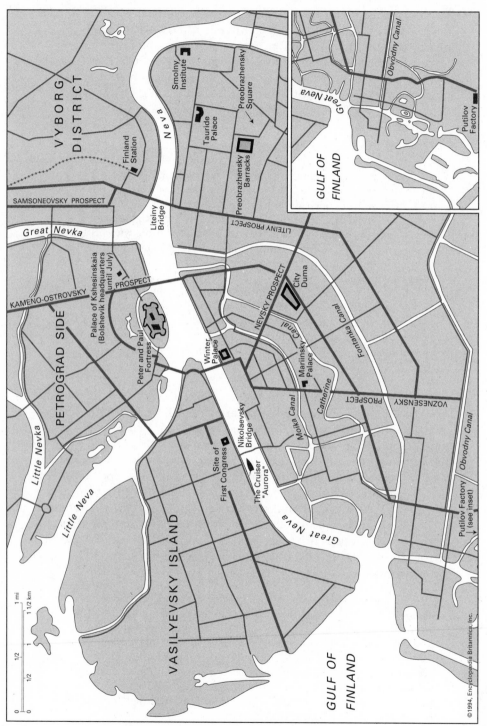

VYBORG DISTRICT

Smolny Institute

Preobrazhensky Square

Tauride Palace

Preobrazhensky Barracks

Neva

Finland Station

SAMSONEOVSKY PROSPECT

Liteiny Bridge

LITEINY PROSPECT

Great Nevka

KAMENO-OSTROVSKY PROSPECT

Palace of Kshesinskaia (Bolshevik headquarters until July)

PETROGRAD SIDE

Peter and Paul Fortress

Little Nevka

Little Neva

Winter Palace

City Duma

NEVSKY PROSPECT

Marinsky Palace

Catherine

Fontanka Canal

Moika Canal

VOZNESENSKY PROSPECT

Nikolaevsky Bridge

Site of First Congress

The Cruiser "Aurora"

Great Neva

VASILYEVSKY ISLAND

Putilov Factory (see inset)

Obvodny Canal

GULF OF FINLAND

GULF OF FINLAND

Great Neva

Obvodny Canal

Putilov Factory

1 mi

1 1/2 km

1/2

1

1/2

1

0

0

1/2

1/2

© 1994, Encyclopædia Britannica, Inc.

Petrograd in 1917.

Lenin was thus delivered in triumphal procession to Bolshevik head-quarters, established as it happened in the former palace of the court-favorite ballerina Kshesinskaia, an irony Trotsky is confident Lenin must especially have enjoyed. Sukhanov reports:

> I will never forget that thunderlike speech, startling and amazing . . . nobody there had expected anything of the kind. It seemed as if all the elements and the spirit of universal destruction had risen from their lairs . . . [I:298]

To this, Trotsky responds: "Not the elements were hovering in that banquet hall, but human thoughts—and they were not embarrassed by the elements, but were trying to understand in order to control them."

> We don't need any parliamentary republic. We don't need any bourgeois democracy. We don't need any government except the Soviet of workers', soldiers', and farmhands' deputies! [I:299]

The following day Lenin presented to the party his renowned *Theses of April 4th,* a hastily written, ringing account of the principles which his lecture had laid down. [32]

IX. The struggle for first principles

If Apollo is the god of orderly reason, the god of dialectic is Dionysus. Lenin appeared at the Finland station as Dionysus himself. Dionysus challenges all existing assumptions, and carries us to a world beyond. He is figured often enough in the Platonic dialogues, but most memorably when he comes in the guise of Alcibiades in the *Symposium,* inebriated, wreathed, and surrounded by the flute girls. All rules are shattered as Alcibiades captivates the company with an account of the real, hidden Socrates, and the splendors of dialectic. In a more sober vein, Plato elsewhere tells us of two contrasting orders: that of Cronos, and that of Zeus. Zeus has overthrown Cronos, and brought law to the affairs of mankind. But the old order, the Golden Age in which the world turned the other way, was prior, and superior to the realm of law. So *nous* is prior to *dianoia,* insight is above the law; for law if well-founded derives from a higher insight. [33]

Lenin comes to defy law in the form of one of the most deep-seated of obligations: that of patriotic defense of one's fatherland. At the very outset of the *Republic,* confronted with the well-earned complacency of the wealthy Cephalus, Socrates proposes a problem which breaks the law: the problem is that of a borrowed knife which, despite the formal obligation of debtor to creditor, should not be returned to an owner who has gone mad in the meantime. This is a piece of Dionysian stealth.

Three leaders of the 1917 revolution: Trotsky, Lenin, and Lev
Borisovich Kamenev. Kamenev later supported Trotsky's opposition
to Stalin, for which he was tried and executed in 1936.

It will lead before long to a set of outrageous, taboo-breaking Socratic
propositions, requiring that the women strip to exercise with the men,
that the guardians of the new polis have wives in common, that they
own no property and take delight in a communist order. Their styles
are different, but Socrates and Lenin alike are outrageous: both deeply
offend the good order of mind and all social decorum. Socrates' three
shocking *waves* in the *Republic* meet their match in Lenin's *April Theses.* [34] Both lift our sights from the world we know to a Golden Age;
the difference is that for Socrates the Golden Age lies in a mythic past,
while for Lenin it carries the urgency of an attainable future.

It seems to me not at all out of order to put Lenin's crashing propositions in such a mythic and philosophic context, for he is challenging
beliefs which go far beyond the ordinary calculus of party strategies
and tactics. Demagogues had no trouble branding Lenin with charges
of complicity with the enemy and subversion of the Russian state, for
those who play these easy tricks are working with something real and
very powerful: it is not easy to think beyond allegiance to one's native
land, to turn one's thought to a possible obligation which transcends
and violates the "interests" or "security" of one's nation. And Lenin,
following Marx and Engels demands just that. The real loyalty of the
worker is not to the state, the "agent of capital," but to humanity itself,
in the person of the international body of the workers of the world. [35]

Lenin was far from understood at the outset, but with the distribution of the *April Theses* Trotsky sees the beginning of an uneasy shift

in consciousness within the Bolshevik ranks. Lenin understood dialectics, which does not develop by easy stages; he had deliberately and in the end successfully applied shock therapy to the consciousness of the Bolshevik leadership. In this way the power of the negation—not unrelated in its ancient ancestry to the unwelcome sting of the Socratic refutation—dramatically entered the history of the Russian Revolution.

X. The dark period

Following the victory in the February insurrection, the compromise government led by Aleksandr Kerensky, based on the "paradox" by which the Soviet insisted upon passing formal power to the bourgeoisie, generated a scene of increasing frustration and ineffectiveness. [36] It

A demonstration is fired upon on the Nevsky Prospect on July 3rd, the beginning of the "July Days."

was, Trotsky says, "indecisiveness organized." Trotsky speaks of "the everlasting nervous obstinate meeting of innumerable masses seeking a way out and unwilling to be told there was none." In July, as part of a new wave of demonstrations, some eighty thousand workers of the vast Putilov plant in the Vyborg district made their way during the night to the Tauride Palace to present their demands to the executive committee of their own soviet. [37] Even as they awaited an answer to their petition, their government was anxiously awaiting the arrival of troops to disperse them. Trotsky finds in this scene an image of the depth the stage of negation and disillusionment has reached:

> The throng of workers, hungry and dead-tired, scattered about on the
> street and in the garden, a majority immediately stretching themselves
> out, thinking to wait there for an answer. The entire Putilov factory
> lying there on the ground at three o'clock in the morning around
> the Tauride Palace, where the democratic leaders were waiting for
> the arrival of troops from the front—that is one of the most startling
> pictures offered by the revolution on this summit of the pass between
> February and October. [II:29]

Trotsky sees one anecdote as speaking for the whole. Chernov, a minister in the coalition government, is preparing to address a crowd on behalf of the compromise government:

> Miliukov . . . relates how "a husky worker, shaking his fist in the face
> of the minister, shouted furiously: "Take the power, you son-of-a-bitch,
> when they give it to you." Even though nothing more than an anecdote,
> this expresses with crude accuracy the essence of the July situation.
> (II:40) [38]

Not without bloodshed, the workers were dispersed and the demonstration evaporated. A period of reaction ensued which marked for the workers the very depths of the year.

Groping for a way out which would ensure the future of the coalition government, Kerensky conceived the project of a Conference of all parties to take place in Moscow, at a comfortable distance from the disruptive workers' districts of Petrograd. In response, the Moscow workers greeted the conference with a highly effective general strike. Trotsky sees the Conference as an image of death; his imagery suggests Milton's vision of the conference in Hell, or Odysseus' visit to Hades:

> It created nothing and decided nothing. However, it has left to the
> historian an invaluable impression of the revolution—although a
> negative impression, one in which light appears as shadow, weakness

Aleksandr Fyodorovich Kerensky arrives in Moscow for the opening of the State Conference, which was described by Trotsky as "a kingdom of shades." At the same moment, workers in Moscow were greeting the conference with a general strike, tying up transport and services.

> parades as strength, greed as disinterestedness, treachery as the highest valor. . . . The impression . . . bore the character of a negative to the last detail: in this kingdom of half-buried shades, giving themselves out for "the living forces of the nation," the authentic people's leader could not possibly figure otherwise than as a political cadaver. [II:160–1]

A certain General Lavr Georgiyevich Kornilov, whom Kerensky had introduced to the Conference as the savior of Russia, was in truth preparing a counterrevolution intended to finish off Kerensky and his revolutionary government altogether. [39] By Trotsky's account, organized efforts of the workers in defense of the revolution in their own terms had much to do with bringing this rebellion from the right to a standstill:

> The conspiracy was conducted by those circles who were not accustomed to know how to do anything without the lower ranks, without labor forces, without cannon-fodder, without orderlies, servants, clerks, chauffeurs, messengers, cooks, laundresses, switchmen, telegraphers, stablemen, cab drivers. [II:227]

Once again, we find railroad movements faring no better than had those of the tzar:

General Lavr Kornilov was described by Trotsky as the hero of the conservative factions in the State Conference and the intended saviour of the Provisional government. In fact, shortly thereafter, he conducted an unsuccessful military coup against the same government.

In a mysterious way echelons would find themselves moving on the wrong roads. Regiments would arrive in the wrong division, artillery would be sent up a blind alley, staffs would get out of communication with their units. . . . Parts of the army of Krymov were in this way scattered about in the stations, sidings, and branch lines, of eight different railroads. [II:239]

The Kornilov rebellion, intended to give a final blow to the revolution, ended in complete defeat. And yet the structure of coalition government, seeking to compromise the many factions of the parliamentary parties, remained stuck essentially where it had been.

XI. The October insurrection

As we move through this brief overview of Trotsky's careful *History*, we are able here to look at only a few selected chapters to sense the overall story Trotsky is telling, and to get a better sense of the means he employs as narrator. It is indeed unfortunate that we must omit at this point discussion of one of the most significant and difficult sections of the work, in which Trotsky examines with care Lenin's role in prompting and guiding the discussion which led to the decision to mount an insurrection in October. It is at this juncture that dialectic bears most intensely on human life—the point at which a turn of thought must become an irreversible commitment to radically new action. Instead, we will have to go directly at this point to Trotsky's account of the insurrection itself.

As elsewhere in the *History*, we will find that here too it is the image of the human which comes through: formal efforts tend to disaster, while intuitive, "molecular" processes vindicate the power of the human spirit. The people's forces took shape as the Red Guard, a popular organization in a tradition familiar to the American historian; in another context, many of its methods would be identified as true "Yankee ingenuity." During the course of the year, the Red Guard as such took form only gradually, and its role shifted by stages. At first highly informal and defending only individual workplaces, it came in time to assume responsibility for the defense of the revolution as a whole—openly, following the Kornilov rebellion in August, which had made the threat of counterrevolution overt. Further yet, as its organization was taken in charge by the Military Revolutionary Committee of the soviets, while the center of gravity of the soviets in turn shifted toward the Bolsheviks, it began to conceive itself as, in Trotsky's words, "a future army of insurrection."

Its mode of operation was informal, democratic, and spirited:

> "Drill in the art of handling a rifle," says the worker Skorinko, "formerly carried on in flats and tenements, was now brought out into the light and air, into the parks, the boulevards." "The shops were turned into camps," says another worker, Rakitov.
> . . . "The worker would stand at his bench with knapsack on his back and rifle beside him." . . . After the whistle all would draw up in the court for drill. "Side by side with a bearded worker you would see a boy apprentice, and both of them attentively listening to the instructor . . . ."
> [III:186–87]

Of the problem of command, Trotsky remarks:

> The entire commanding staff was elective. There was no risk in this: all were volunteers here and knew each other well. [III:189]

Finally, when as we shall see the Bolsheviks become the majority party in the October Congress of the Soviets, the Red Guard fully emerges as the military force of the Soviets in bringing down the Provisional Government.

The proletarian revolution of October, despite this impressive, if irregular, armament, took place with remarkably little disturbance to the life of the capital. This is altogether in accord with Trotsky's sense of its essence: it is molecular, from below, leaving little trace in terms of the drama normally expected of historic events:

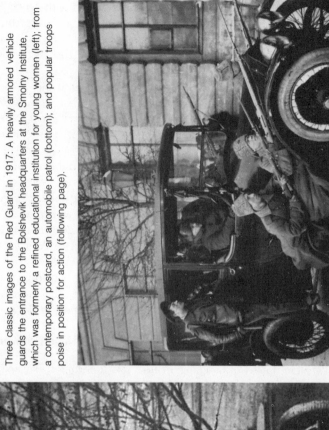

Three classic images of the Red Guard in 1917: A heavily armored vehicle guards the entrance to the Bolshevik headquarters at the Smolny Institute, which was formerly a refined educational institution for young women (left); from a contemporary postcard, an automobile patrol (bottom); and popular troops poise in position for action (following page).

The final act of the revolution seems, after all this, too brief, too dry, too business-like—somehow out of correspondence with the historic scope of the events. The reader experiences a kind of disappointment. He is like a mountain climber, who, thinking the main difficulties are still ahead, suddenly discovers that he is already on the summit or almost there. Where is the insurrection? There is no picture of the insurrection. The events do not form themselves into a picture. A series of small operations, calculated and prepared in advance, remain separated one from another both in space and time. A unity of thought and aim unites them, but they do not fuse in the struggle itself. There is no action of great masses. There are no dramatic encounters with the troops. There is nothing of all that which imaginations brought up upon the facts of history associate with the idea of insurrection. . . . The bourgeois classes had expected barricades, flaming conflagrations, looting, rivers of blood. In reality a silence reigned more terrible than all the thunders of the world. The social ground shifted noiselessly like a revolving stage, bringing forward the popular masses, carrying away to limbo the rulers of yesterday. [III:232–33]

He remarks, "At times it seems as though it was easier to capture Petrograd in the autumn of 1917 than to recount the process fourteen years later," [III:224]. Trotsky would have us see the motion thus generated so quietly but powerfully from below as of the essence of the operation of dialectical materialism. On the night in which the Winter Palace is being taken by the Red Guard, Trotsky observes, "The theaters and moving-picture houses were open. . . . Chaliapin had been incomparable in *Don Carlos*." When victory was announced, it was in terms of an event which was to remain to the end very nearly bloodless:

At 2:35 in the afternoon—the foreign journalists looked at their watches, the Russians were too busy—an emergency session of the Petrograd Soviet was opened with a report by Trotsky, who in the name of the Military Revolutionary Committee announced that the Provisional Government no longer existed. "They told us that an insurrection would drown the revolution in torrents of blood . . . . We do not know of a single casualty." There is no example in history of a revolutionary movement involving such gigantic masses being so bloodless. (III:238) [40]

Nonetheless, beneath the surface of Petrograd life, important events of a tense and complex nature had in fact been taking place, operations of the unique military arm of the masses. Those in command were by no means military men, and the plan which they developed for the capture of the Winter Palace, the seat of the Provisional Government, which was supposed to initiate the insurrection, proved far too complex. [41]

The leaders were many hours late with the concentration of forces, and the operations against the palace, not even begun during the night,

Cadets guard the chambers of the Winter Palace on the night of its fall. Purportedly, more injuries were sustained in Eisenstein's reenactment for his epic film, *October*, than in the actual capture!

A drawbridge opens over the Neva River with the Cathedral of St. Peter and St. Paul and the Fortress shown beyond. The raised drawbridge served to defend Petrograd from the worker's suburbs. The top image shows the interior of the Peter and Paul Fortress.

formed a special chapter of the revolution ending only on the night of the 26th—that is, a whole twenty-four hours late. The most brilliant victories are not achieved without duds. [III:219]

In this, again, Trotsky would have us read a moral. Those limited but practical objectives which were essential to the insurrection were carried out successfully and on schedule. Only by attempting to operate on a level which was too grand, too formally complete, did the insurrection get itself into a position in which it could not react to simple opportunities which in fact presented themselves unexpectedly in the unfolding course of events.

Although there were few set-pieces and nothing in the way of a genuine battle, a series of crucial, intensive actions were carried out during the night of the 25th. Railroad stations, municipal utilities, the State Bank, the Telegraph Station, and the Post Office were all systematically occupied. It is very close to the center of Trotsky's work to show how little these elementary processes accord with the classic notion of "history," which calls for formal actions, named commanders, and heroic sacrifice. Here we have nameless actions and courageous men who are no less heroic for remaining anonymous. Once again, Trotsky reflects on the nature of history in the face of this new kind of event:

> Meagre and colorless is the record of the episodes of that October night. It is like a police report. All the participants were shaking with a nervous fever. There was no time to observe and record and no one to do it. . . . Those workers, sailors, and soldiers who really inspired and lead the operation took their places soon after at the head of the first detachments of the Red Army, and the majority laid down their lives in the various theaters of the civil war. [III:224]

It is interesting to Trotsky to consider how very different these same men, some of them destined, as he knows, to give their lives in the service of the future Red Army, could appear to the bourgeois observer. To Kerensky, looking toward his political right flank, they could appear as "rabble"—"I choose my words deliberately: rabble." [III:216] Trotsky is interested as well in the view of the lawyer Nabokov, a keen observer whose view from the opposite perspective is often cited in the *History,* describing the intervention of the revolutionary guards into one of the chambers of government:

> "The impression created was appalling," testifies Nabokov. . . .
> "Ordinary, meaningless, obtuse, malicious physiognomies," writes the liberal patriot . . . of these Russian soldiers and sailors. (III:235) [42]

The capture of the Peter and Paul Fortress, an edifice familiar enough to many of the revolutionaries from its use as a political prison, is an epic in the plebeian style. [43] A certain "oratorical battle," in which recalcitrant troops stationed within the Fortress required persuasion to join the revolution, fared better than the military operation: it proved easier to capture the Fortress than to learn how to use it. [44] It had been agreed that the Fortress was to signal the moment at which the elaborate encirclement of the Winter Palace had been accomplished, upon which an artillery attack upon it would begin. The idea—in a familiar revolutionary tradition—was to raise a lantern on the flagpole, upon which the cruiser *Aurora,* whose crew had placed her in the service of the revolution, would fire a blank volley to frighten the Palace. If the government would not submit, a more serious attack would begin. Difficulties of the very human sort humor quickly ensued, however:

> . . . the too complicated solution of a simple problem threatened to lead to an opposite result. The difficulty of carrying this plan out is too obvious. They are to start off with a red lantern. It turns out that they have none on hand. They lose time hunting for it, and finally find it. However, it is not so simple to tie a lantern to a flagpole in such a way that it will be visible in all directions. Efforts are renewed and twice renewed with a dubious result, and meanwhile the precious time is slipping away. [III:262]

Greater difficulties, however, are faced by the two revolutionary commanders, Blagonravov and Antonov, in charge of the operation. [45] Field guns have been introduced into the Fortress, but there is a problem in finding anyone to fire them. The artillery men at the Fortress do not wish to get involved; they report that the guns are rusty and there is no gun-oil:

> Antonov dashes up on a cutter in a state of fury. Who is sabotaging the plan? Blagonravov tells him about the lantern, about the oil, about the ensign. They both start to go up to the cannon. Night, darkness, puddles in the court from the recent rains. . . . In the darkness Blagonravov loses the road. Splashing through the puddles, burning with impatience, stumbling and falling the mud, Antonov blunders after the commissar through the dark court. . . .
>
> The position of the guns was finally found. The artillery men were stubborn: Rust . . . compressors . . . oil. [III:262–63]

Trotsky divines an underlying reluctance of the men to bring the guns into action: "perhaps they would not be needed."

In the end, the artillery of the *Aurora* does play an important role, firing upon the Winter Palace and at the same time electrifying the imagination of Petrograd. But the artillery consists of blanks, which make an even more frightening sound than the firing of shells: ". . . the effect," Trotsky remarks, "was only acoustic."

The situation within the Winter Palace becomes one of desperation and gloom. However, at a point of low morale within the Palace, a piece of news arrives which gives new heart. The City Duma has been meeting in the face of this emergency elsewhere in Petrograd. News comes of a decision which has been reached by the Duma:

> Nothing can save the day now but a miracle. And suddenly into the despairing atmosphere of the Winter Palace there bursts—not, to be sure, a miracle, but the news of its approach. . . . They have just telephoned from the City Duma that the citizens are getting ready to march from there for the rescue of the government. "Tell everybody . . . that the people are coming." . . . Passing from mouth to mouth the news becomes more colorful and impressive. The public men, the merchantry, the people, with the clergy at their head, are marching this way to free the beleaguered palace. The people with the clergy! "That will be strikingly beautiful!" (III:266) [46]

Later, Trotsky returns to this popular miracle to ask, "But what had become of the people advancing with the clergy at their head . . . ?" He describes the decision at the Duma:

> The duma must march in a body to the Winter Palace in order to die there, if necessary, with the government. . . . Meanwhile the members decided, in the interest of history, to take a vote by roll call. After all, one cannot die too late—even though the death be glorious. Sixty-two members of the duma ratify the decision: yes, they are actually going to die under the ruins of the Winter Palace. [III:272–73]

Here is Trotsky's account of the unfolding of the glorious event:

> . . . the column finally sets out along the Nevsky. At the head of the column march the burgomaster, Schreider, and the minister Prokopovich. . . . The clergy were not present. The clergy had been created out of misty fragments of the history of the fatherland by the none too opulent imagination of the junkers. But the people also were absent. Their absence determined the character of the whole scheme. Three or four hundred "representatives" and not one man of those whom they represented! (III:273–74) [47]

The marchers find their way blocked by a party of armed sailors.

> Some one of the marchers suggested that they die right there on the spot. But in the decision adopted by a roll call vote in the duma this variant had not been foreseen. The minister Prokopovich clambered up on some sort of elevation and "waving his umbrella"—rains are frequent in the autumn in Petrograd—urged the demonstrators not to lead into temptation those dark and deceived people who might actually resort to arms . . . what can you do with armed ruffians who will not permit the leaders of the democracy to die a heroic death? [III:274]

The marchers agreed and abandoned the heroic project.

The cruiser ''Aurora,'' and members of her revolutionary crew.

The Winter Palace occupation was in the mode of a popular event:

> The palace is getting more and more like a sieve. . . . It is no longer
> quite clear who is surrendering to whom, who is disarming whom. The
> artillery continues to boom.
> Workers, sailors, soldiers are pushing up from outside in chains and
> groups. . . . The square pours into the court. The court pours into
> the palace, and floods up and down stairways and through corridors.
> [III:267–69]

Here, finally, is the account of the rather undramatic end of the government, as the victorious party enters the chambers of the government:

> "In front of the crowd and trying to hold back the onpressing ranks
> strode a rather small, unimpressive man. His clothes were in disorder,
> a wide-brimmed hat askew on his head, eyeglasses balanced uncertainly
> on his nose, but his little eyes gleamed with the joy of victory and spite
> against the conquered." In these annihilating strokes the conquered
> have described Antonov. It is not hard to believe that his clothes and his
> hat were in disorder: It is sufficient to remember the nocturnal journey
> through the puddles of the Peter and Paul fortress. The joy of victory
> might also doubtless have been read in his eyes; but hardly any spite
> against the conquered in those eyes. I announce to you, members of the
> Provisional Government, that you are under arrest—exclaimed Antonov
> in the name of the Military Revolutionary Committee. The clock then
> pointed to 2:10 in the morning of October 26. [III:270]

In this way a modest but dedicated leader, clothing awry, twenty-four hours late in the execution of his too-complicated plan, accepted the surrender of the government ministers, preserved order, and saved the vanquished from the vengeance of the crowd. Such is Trotsky's image of the appropriate hero of the proletarian revolution.

XII. The Congress of the Soviets [48]

The insurrection had been timed to coordinate with the Congress of the Soviets at which the people's elected representatives would be assembling from throughout Russia. The insurrection had been gauged to present the Congress with an accomplished fact, but as we have seen, missed by an awkward twenty-four hours. The result was that the opening day of the Congress coincided with a second day of the insurrection, that day in which the six-inch guns of the *Aurora* were carrying out their alarming acoustic attack on the Winter Palace. Since the fact that the shelling was purely fictitious was not at first known to the listeners, the result was for the Congress, as for all Petrograd, a peculiarly dramatic accompaniment to the affairs of the day. Trotsky introduces this culminating event of the *History* with these challenging words:

> In Smolny of the 25th of October the most democratic of all parliaments in the world's history was to meet. Who knows—perhaps also the most important. (III:302) [49]

He dwells on the contrast between this assemblage and an earlier, first Congress in June, which had been composed of the normal spectrum of political representatives and "compromisist intellectuals."

> The officers' chevrons, the eye-glasses and neckties of intellectuals to be seen at the first Congress had almost completely disappeared. A grey color prevailed uninterruptedly, in costumes and in faces. All had worn out their clothes during the war. Many of the city workers had provided themselves with soldiers' coats. The trench delegates were by no means a pretty picture. . . . The plebeian nation had for the first time sent up an honest representation made in its own image and not retouched. [III:302]

The opening of the Congress had been delayed as "the Bolshevik leaders wanted to finish with the Winter Palace first." There are many caucuses and meetings, as various factions attempt to locate their political positions in this new context. Lenin is present now, but

> "with his make-up still on, in wig and big spectacles, was sitting in a passage-way. . . . Lenin was in no hurry to appear publicly. He preferred to look round a little and gather the threads into his hands while remaining behind the scenes. [III:305–6]

A range of factions and parties are represented in this Congress, by no means of a single opinion. Trotsky describes the opening of the meeting:

> An unusual, dull, alarming rumble breaks into the noise of the meeting from outside. This is Peter and Paul Fortress ratifying the order of the day with artillery fire. A high tension current runs through the Congress, which now suddenly feels and realizes what it really is: the convention of a civil war. [III:306]

There are proposals for compromise with the government at the moment besieged within the Winter Palace. "Vain hope!" Trotsky comments. "A revolution never moves on diagonals." (III:307) [50] Right-wing members invite the delegates to join the members of the duma who have decided to march unarmed to die in the ruins of the Winter Palace, but are shouted down by the delegates with cries of "Deserters!" and "Enemies of the people!" Trotsky comments, "The unctuous orator has obviously mistaken his audience." Suddenly the Congress receives a welcome report:

> A sailor just arrived from the *Aurora* ironically announces that there *are* no ruins, since they are only firing blanks from the cruiser. "Proceed

with your business in peace," he says. The soul of the congress finds
rest in this admirable black-bearded sailor, incarnating the simple and
imperious will of the insurrection. [III:312]

With a report that the Twelfth Army and other segments of the armed
forces had come over to the support of the soviets, there is widespread
relief. "Pandemonium," says the American observer-participant John
Reed, "men weeping, embracing each other." (III:317) [51] A proclamation is at last read and ratified, bringing the all-night session to an
end at six o'clock in the morning:

> . . . this was not merely a proclamation. By its mere exposition of what
> had happened and what was proposed, this hastily written document laid
> down the foundations of a new state structure. "The authority of the
> compromisist Central Executive Committee is at an end. The Provisional
> Government is deposed. The Congress assumes the power. . . ." The
> soviet government proposes immediate peace. [III:317]

Complex political developments unfolded during the second day's
meeting of the Congress. Let us look at the occasion of Lenin's appearance before the assembly. The quotation is from John Reed's report:

> Lenin, whom the Congress has not yet seen, is given the floor for a
> report on peace. His appearance in the tribune evokes a tumultuous
> greeting. [III:323]

At the front, in a long, systematic campaign of calumny, soldiers had
begun to regard Lenin and Trotsky as German agents; now their delegates are getting their first direct look at Lenin himself:

> The trench delegates gaze with all their eyes at this mysterious being
> whom they had been taught to hate and whom they have learned
> without seeing him to love. "Now Lenin, gripping the edges of the
> reading-stand, let little winking eyes travel over the crowd as he stood
> there waiting, apparently oblivious to the long-rolling ovation, which
> lasted several minutes. When it finished, he said simply, 'We shall now
> proceed to construct the socialist order.' " [III:323–24]

His proposals are for the immediate cessation of the war, and the
achievement of a "just and democratic peace," one without "annexations," meaning those goals of territorial gain and imperialism in fact
built into the war aims of the warring nations. Trotsky reflects on
the significance of all that was occurring in this Congress; he sees a
conversion from earlier concerns with the mechanics of revolution, to
something deeper:

> Only now was its historic meaning becoming clear in action. The
> victorious insurrection had built under this congress of workers and

soldiers an indestructible foundation of power. The delegates were voting this time not for a resolution, not for a proclamation, but for a governmental act of immeasurable significance.

Listen, nations! The revolution offers you peace. It will be accused of violating treaties. But of this it is proud. . . . Pride surges up of its own accord. Eyes shine. All are on their feet. No one is smoking now. It seems as though no one breathes. The præsidium, the delegates, the guests, the sentries, join in a hymn of insurrection and brotherhood. [III:327]

Trotsky, greeted by the delegates, Reed reports, with "an immense crusading acclaim," spoke as well on behalf of peace:

In our proclamation on peace we address ourselves simultaneously to the governments and the peoples. That is a purely formal symmetry. Of course we do not think to influence the imperialist governments with our proclamations, although as long as they exist we cannot ignore them. We rest all our hope on the possibility that our revolution will unleash the European revolution. If the revolting peoples of Europe do not crush imperialism, then we will be crushed—that is indubitable. Either the Russian revolution will raise the whirlwind of struggle in the west, or the capitalists of all countries will crush our revolution. . . . " (III:340) [52]

The narrative of *The History of the Russian Revolution* concludes with the adjournment of this Congress, and the launching of Lenin's project, "to construct the socialist order."

XIII. Conclusion: the real revolution

At the outset of this discussion, we agreed to lend credence to Trotsky's view of the world, in order to make the *History* approachable as a work of literature. What we have found is that indeed the work is conceived as a single composition, a whole, in which thought and action cohere in the narrative to shed light on a unified world view. Not only a new structure of society and a complex of strategies and events, but a certain humor, a sense of humanity, a pervasive style—all belong together in this history which has become itself a window into something larger. Now that it comes time to collect back that debt of credence, we may do well to appraise what Trotsky's world view has entailed. The real revolution, the ultimate subject of the *History,* is not so much that sequence of events which occurred once in Russia, and now lies in the past, but a proposition about humanity which remains before us as a dialectical alternative, which may yet provide food for thought and action. It is this more fundamental, ongoing process which forms the foundation of what Trotsky called the *permanent revolution.* [53]

How can we move from a literal reading of the *History* to take the measure, overall, of this dialectical watershed, figured by Trotsky as "the pass between February and October"—that is, between the apparent revolution and the real one, between that which dismissed the tzar and introduced formal democracy, and that fully implemented democracy, the free and rational human society which was the elusive goal of October?

I propose that we look at a set of *paradoxes,* which seem to place the question before us. Each of these has appeared as a problem for thought at one point or another in the course of this essay; let us now attempt to gather them as facets of a single vision. Across this one watershed dividing two fundamentally distinct worlds, terms convert into their opposites, and in this juxtaposition of antithetical intentions, which the ancients used to call *antilogies* and which serve always to arrest thought, we may be able to survey the distance between one human terrain and the other. This would be the real revolution, the ultimate subject matter of Trotsky's book.

The particular becomes universal

We have seen as an element of Trotsky's theory of history, as well as of his style throughout the work, that the particular incident or image, the vignette, becomes the mode of access to the whole. We may think of the

Putilov workers assemble for the direct election of delegates from the factory to the soviet in 1918. In the soviet system, delegates thus chosen represent the workplace directly at the next level of the legislative process, in this case the Petrograd Soviet.

"wink" of the Cossack, the tzar's wandering train, the "wolf" look of the tramcar conductor, the black-bearded sailor from the *Aurora*—each of these is a telling particular, not, Trotsky would have us see, as symbol for a universal, but as a point of access to a whole which is not composed of universals. They tell of a different world, which we must enter by way of Hegel and Marx, whose unity is not in the fixity of forms but in a process which inheres in each individual, not in the universal but in each moment of life of the human spirit. We are not human by way of a fixed human nature, but rather through participation in a process of growth by which our very consciousness of what it is to be human, is evolving. It is the spark of a new moment in that evolution which Trotsky would have us see in his modest, but noble heroes. By analogy with Newton's mathematics of nascent motions, we catch the suggestion here of a literary calculus of evolving human consciousness.

Objectivity becomes subjectivity

The *History* is plunged, we might say, in subjectivity—and yet makes the serious claim that in this way, and this way only, it is enabled to be *scientific*. Has Trotsky made a case in the *History* for this striking point of view, even as an option for thought? He has claimed that his narrative will incorporate a logic which will speak for itself. We have experienced the coherence of the narrative, but have we seen through to a possible science? The tale has been told as a story of unfolding consciousness, not to be known by a camera-like recording mind, but by a correspondingly active, consciously aware, subjective intellect. We could take such a proposal seriously only if we believed that indeed, what is to be known as the object of science lies not merely in the physical world, but in the realm of social relationships, consciousness, and the human spirit. That is surely remote from the assumptions of most scientists operating on our side of the dialectical watershed.

"Democracy" versus "democracy"

When Trotsky claims that the Congress of the Soviets is the "most democratic of all parliaments in the world's history," we take umbrage, and rise to his challenge with images of 1776. The Russian Congress may have been something else, but we are confident we know well enough about democracy. Trotsky teases us a bit when he says:

> The plebeian nation had for the first time sent up an honest
> representation made in its own image and not retouched. [III:302]

And we suspect he is caricaturing us in the duma procession on the darkened Nevsky Prospect, from which "the people were absent." It may be that our practice of democracy tends to make of "politics," as he has said, a technical matter, carried out by "specialists in that line of business." Yet more fundamentally, Trotsky appears to be juxtaposing

A procession accompanies Lenin's casket in Moscow. After his death, Stalin took power while Trotsky gradually moved toward a "Left Opposition" position.

realism to formalism: we are formally democratic, and offer the right to vote, and freedoms of speech and thought, which Trotsky most of all will agree are priceless—but do we imagine implementing this formal right with genuinely equal opportunity? One side of this democratic watershed will then ask the other: is such envisioned material democracy really compatible with formal democracy? Has history now shown us that Trotsky's idea is inherently flawed: that the attempt to go beyond formal democracy toward a greater democracy of equal access and opportunity converts to dictatorship, and self destructs?

Materialism becomes the study of consciousness

If the question of democracy is elusive, that of materialism may be even more so. On which side of our dialectical watershed does materialism lie? Dialectical materialism lays claim to the term, and yet the *History* only verifies what has long been known of Marx, that the *matter* in question does not reduce to little-hard-bodies. Perhaps the term *concrete* comes closest to the mark. Or, juxtaposing the very material Moscow general strike to the formal histrionics of Kerensky's concurrent Moscow Conference, the question reduces to reality versus illusion. The real, the concrete, the material—these measure the actual, existential situation. Here life is found, and we have seen that in the Moscow dialectics, life exists in the streets, while the formal Conference becomes a chilling image of death. Thus materialism in the sense in which Trotsky intends it seems to lay claim to the very domain with which we would want to identify life and the human spirit.

Patriotism becomes internationalism

The most sensitive nerve is touched when Lenin proposes loyalty to the International as overriding patriotism to Russia or to any nation-state. Proposals to trespass upon what is perceived as loyalty to one's flag still activate the taboo of treason and invoke a sense of anathema yet capable of stirring the Furies of ancient tragedy. National security, the coin for which we may long have been selling our own democracy, speaks the final word in every discussion. By contrast, Trotsky and Lenin see a true world community already emerging, uniting the exploited workers of all countries through objective common interests, common grounds for struggle, and a new consciousness of a single humanity not bounded by the national and ethnic loyalties of a darker past. The October revolution asserted a new order of loyalty in direct contradiction to the patriotism which is our embedded tradition.

This last in our set of paradoxes, with its suggestion of anathema, reminds us of the seriousness of them all. If they are indeed aspects of one dialectical alternative—if we live in one world, and Trotsky is depicting another—then the energies unleashed by this last paradox may be coupled to the others as well. The first paradoxes entail violations

Lenin addresses troops in Sverdlov Square, Moscow, in May 1920. In the upper photograph, Trotsky and Kamenev are seen standing beside the podium. After their exile by Stalin, the official photograph was modified as shown below.

of law and rejection of rights of property, as dire in their consequences as the treason associated with the last. In the *History*, Trotsky has in effect walked us over this "pass," to survey forbidden terrain. A tzar has been deposed, property rights are dismissed, an elected government has been arrested, an anthem has been sung announcing loyalty, not to the state, but to the workers of the world. In the guise of this history of a few months in the life of one segment of modern humanity, we have studied what it would mean to convert the fundamental terms of which our entire world view is constructed.

We have seen Trotsky assert to the Congress that unless revolutions occur elsewhere in Europe, this one in Russia must surely fail; he was evidently prepared for the ruin which has now emerged. Indeed, the demise of the vision of Lenin and Trotsky occurred, not with the recent liquidation of the Soviet Union, but in the new regime's first decade. The dictatorship which had gripped the new society under Stalin by the time Trotsky writes his *History* already entailed the very opposite of the new era of freedom the revolution had intended. Whether it could have survived had Lenin not died in 1924 and circumstances been otherwise may be matter for speculation; we see that Trotsky himself found little prospect for success in a revolution confined to a single country.

The proposition Trotsky is making in *The History of the Russian Revolution*, however, goes beyond the case of Russia itself. As he states:

> The historic ascent of humanity, taken as a whole, may be summarized as a succession of victories of consciousness over blind forces—in nature, in society, in man himself. Critical and creative thought can boast its greatest victories up to now in the struggle with nature. The physico-chemical sciences have already reached a point where man is clearly about to become master of matter. But social relations are still forming in the manner of the coral islands. [III:347]

On such an extended time scale, it may be that the dialectical question Trotsky poses may remain a continuing topic on the world's agenda.

-----

1. Trotsky, Leon, *The History of the Russian Revolution* (New York: Pathfinder Press, 1980). Originally written during Trotsky's early exile in Prinkipo, Turkey, and published in London in 1932–33. It should be noted, as Trotsky himself particularly acknowledges, that we are indebted to Max Eastman for a highly readable English translation.

2. Dates in 1917 will be given here in the "old style" in use in Russia at the time; to find the date in the international calendar, add thirteen days. As Trotsky points out, if we did not make this concession to imperial Russia, what is known to history as the "February Revolution" would have happened in March, and the "October Revolution," in November!

3. Two principal accounts of Trotsky's life are his own autobiography, written during the same exile and originally published in 1930, *My Life* (New York: Pathfinder Press, 1970), and an extensive biography by Isaac Deutscher in three volumes separately titled. These are *The Prophet Armed* (New York: Vintage Books, 1965), *The Prophet Unarmed* (New York: Vintage Books, 1959), and *The Prophet Outcast* (Oxford: Oxford University Press, 1963). There are many other biographies, related personal memoirs, and studies

of Trotsky written from a striking variety of viewpoints. The account of Trotsky's experience in the Canadian prison camp is taken from Deutscher, *The Prophet Armed*, p. 247.

4. Trotsky, *In Defense of Marxism* (New York: Pathfinder Press, 1973), p. 74.

5. Tolstoy, Leo, *War and Peace* (*GBWW* I: 51; II: 51). Apart from the threefold epic form of Tolstoy's work, in which Russia's fate passes through the nemesis of the burning of Moscow so suggestive of the dark "July days" in Trotsky's account, I find strong stylistic resonances. For example, the theater is a realm of illusion and the absence of life for both (*GBWW* I: 51, 318; II: 51, 318), while Natasha's inexplicable dance is a vignette full of significance in ways to be discussed below in relation to Trotsky's style (*GBWW* I: 51, 289; II: 51, 289). Like Trotsky, Tolstoy through Pierre's eyes shows us the reality, as opposed to the formal account, of battle itself (*GBWW* I: 51, 150; II: 51, 150).

6. Reference to the *History* will be made to the Pathfinder edition cited earlier, by volume and page, as here (I:xvii) denotes volume I, page xvii.

7. For Aristotle's discussion of plot, or narrative, see (*GBWW* I: 9, 686; II: 8, 686). Literally, Aristotle's claim is that poetry is "something more philosophic and of graver import than history," since its statements are in the nature of universals.

8. Style, or diction, is discussed in the *Poetics* at (*GBWW* I: 9, 694; II: 8, 694), and more extensively in Book III of the *Rhetoric* (*GBWW* I: 9, 653; II: 8, 653). Concerning the criterion of *appropriateness*, see [Ibid., p. 659].

9. It can be argued that a new era of narrative was instituted by Cervantes in *The History of Don Quxiote de la Mancha*, with the introduction of a strict order of *verisimilitude*, a new realism in which the formal story is embedded in the harsh, material reality of the Spanish countryside. (*GBWW* I: 29; II: 27). In such "materialism" may lie the beginning of the modern novel.

10. Rousseau, *The Social Contract* (*GBWW* I: 38, 395; II: 38, 395).

11. A vivid account of Trotsky's own involvement in Petrograd during 1917 is found in the autobiography. See especially his account of an evening at the popular auditorium which became his special forum, the "Cirque Moderne," [Modern Circus] in *My Life*, 294–97.

12. Trotsky's verbal portraits of a number of revolutionary figures and compatriots are collected in *Portraits: Political and Personal* (New York: Pathfinder Press, 1977).

13. His words, which I take as an uncomplimentary reference to Plato's image of Socrates as dialectical midwife, are: "however this image may have been abused" [III:172].

14. The concept is developed by Max Wertheimer, in *Productive Thinking* (Chicago: University of Chicago Press, 1982).

15. In mathematics, dialectical progress is represented for example by Lobachevsky's unintended discovery of the possibility of an entirely new geometry. There is an interesting report that Lenin's father had been a student of Nikolay Ivanovich Lobachevsky, the mathematical revolutionary.

16. Trotsky's long view of dialectical history is summarized in the form of an amusing legend of a fox whose legs are "Hegelian," contained in a letter written to an American comrade who has dismissed dialectical philosophy as irrelevant: *In Defense of Marxism*, p. 84. The closing words of a "Testament" written by Trotsky a few months before his death in 1940 suggest the depths of this conviction:

I shall die a proletarian revolutionary, a Marxist, a dialectical materialist, and consequently an irreconcilable atheist. My faith in the communist future of mankind is not less ardent, indeed it is firmer today, than it was in the days of my youth. . . .

Natasha has just come up to the window from the courtyard and opened it wider so that the air may enter more freely into my room. I can see the bright green strip of grass beneath the wall, and sunlight everywhere. Life is beautiful. Let the future generations cleanse it of all evil, oppression, and violence, and enjoy it to the full. (Deutscher, *The Prophet Outcast*, p. 479)

17. Trotsky's account of the experiences of the Russian army in World War I is found in his chapter "Tzarist Russia in the War" [I:16 ff].

18. The "Vyborg Side" is an industrial district across the Neva River from the central portion of Petrograd (see map). There were located the immense Putilov locomotive and armament works.

The Bolshevik ("majority") party was so named from a split which occurred in the ranks of the Russian Social-Democratic Workers' Party at a conference in 1903; as opposed to the Menshevik ("minority") group, the Bolsheviks refused to compromise with more moderate socialist parties. For many years they had been led, from exile, by Lenin. At the beginning of 1917, Trotsky was not a member of the Bolshevik party, but led the Mezhrayontsi, a small group occupying a position between the two camps.

19. Simpson, [*GIT* 1987, p. 120].

20. The term *duma* translates as *council, parliament* or *assembly*. The state Duma was the Russian parliament, sharing powers with the State Council, while the powers of both were limited by the authority of the tzar, who appointed the ministers of government. The Duma had in fact defied an order of dissolution issued by the tzar in the previous September.

21. Newton is similarly interested, in the *Principia,* in comprehending a nascent motion through scrupulous examination of its first-beginnings. Simpson, "Science as Mystery: A Speculative Reading of Newton's *Principia*" [*GIT* 1992, pp. 127 ff]. The suggestion here is of a social calculus, counterpart of the formal mathematics of motion.

22. Significantly, Newton likewise uses a "microscope," the better to see the relationships in a nascent motion. [loc. cit., 132].

23. Thus, we may read in a respected publication, "The February Revolution of 1917 was spontaneous, leaderless, and fueled by deep resentment over . . . economic and social conditions . . ." [*EB* (15) 26: 991]. It is worth noting that the term *spontaneous* has virtually the opposite meaning in Marx, who uses it to denote the most significant, creative act of the free individual. Simpson, "Toward a Reading of *Capital,*" [*GIT* 1987, pp. 74–125].

24. On Marx, objectivity and dialectical science, see Simpson, "Toward a Reading of *Capital,*" (*GIT* 1987, p. 117).

25. Trotsky, who himself took a leading role in the first Soviet of Workers' Deputies in Petrograd in 1905, describes the soviet concept with conviction in his history of the 1905 revolution, *1905* (New York: Random House, 1971), pp. 109 ff.

26. Immediately upon the success of the uprising, both a Soviet of Workers' and Soldiers' Deputies and a Provisional Committee of members of the former Duma were formed. The latter, urged and supported by the Soviet, took on itself the management of state affairs, while the Soviet remained formally a private organization. Both looked to the convening of a future Constituent Assembly as the forum for the establishment of a constitutional government, with the result that the needed resolution of many crucial questions was postponed until that indeterminate time. A convenient documentary history of governmental affairs during 1917 is Robert V. Daniels, ed., *The Russian Revolution* (Englewood Cliffs, N.J.: Prentice-Hall, 1972).

27. As we have seen, Trotsky arrived in Petrograd on May 4. Promptly on the day following his arrival, he made a speech to the Petrograd Soviet, advocating "all power to the soviets," which created a sensation. Isaac Deutscher, *The Age of Permanent Revolution; a Trotsky Anthology* (New York: Dell Publishing Co., 1964), p. 96.

28. N. N. Sukhanov (pseudonym of N. N. Himmler), a Menshevik, played a remarkable role as intimate observer of the revolution, and published his memoirs in seven volumes of *Notes on the Revolution* (in Russian). An abridged English translation is Joel Carmichael (New York: Oxford University Press, 1955). He missed, however, one intimate observation, as his wife, who was a Bolshevik, contrived that he should be away from home on the night when Lenin and the Central Committee met at his apartment to resolve upon the October uprising! [III:146]. Excerpts from the *Notes,* in addition to those included throughout Trotsky's *History,* may be found at Daniels, op. cit., pp. 41 ff, and in Dimitri von Mohrenshildt, *The Russian Revolution of 1917: Contemporary Accounts* (New York: Oxford University Press, 1971), pp. 129 ff.

29. [I:294]

30. A fuller description is given by Edmund Wilson, *To the Finland Station* (New York: Farrar, Strauss and Giroux, 1972), pp. 533 ff.

31. Karl Liebknecht and Rosa Luxemburg were heroic revolutionary socialist leaders in Germany. They broke with the German Socialist Party by refusing to support the war, and were both imprisoned for their antiwar activities. During the year following the October revolution, workers' and soldiers' councils on the model of the Russian soviets were set up in major cities in Germany, and in November, 1918 (new style), a

general strike forced the dissolution of the German government and the abdication of the monarch. Germany at that point seemed close to following the lead of the Russian revolution. Liebknecht and Luxemburg were released from prison but in January, 1919, were rearrested by the supposedly socialist government, and were murdered while in custody. A joint portrait is given by Trotsky in *Portraits,* pp. 16 ff.

32. The "Theses" can be found in Daniels, op. cit., p. 23.

33. *Nous* and *dianoia* are terms used throughout the Platonic dialogues; the first may be thought of as "intellectual intuition," and the second, as "calculative reason" or "deduction" from given premises. On the eras of Cronos and Zeus, see Plato, *Statesman,* (*GBWW* I: 7, 588; II: 6, 588).

Trotsky has a word for each of us. Speaking of two categories of erstwhile followers who have dissented from his views, he says of one "You proceed as anti-Marxist," and says the other proceeds "as *Platonic* Marxists. Who is worse, it is not easy to determine." (The emphasis is Trotsky's) The latter "respects the principled politics of Marxism only when it has aged long enough for the archives." (*In Defense of Marxism,* p. 80.) Let us hope Plato's thought invoked here is liberated from such confinement!

34. The "three waves" begin with the joining of the activities of men and women, continue to the community of wives and children, and culminate in the greatest wave— that if the city is to be just, the philosopher must be king. Plato, *Republic,* (*GBWW* I: 7, 369; II: 6, 369).

35. The internationalist principle was represented by the Second (Socialist) International, uniting the worldwide socialist movement. It had been active since its founding in Paris in 1889, but was effectively destroyed by the divisions of the first World War.

In 1914, Trotsky had been the first of the Russian socialists to speak out against the war and call for a proletarian United States of Europe, in a pamphlet on the war and the International. This was published in the United States in 1918 as *The Bolshiviki and World Peace,* with an introduction by Lincoln Steffens, and is said to have influenced Wilson in the drafting of the "Fourteen Points." Isaac Deutscher, *The Age of Permanent Revolution,* p. 71. In 1915, a small group of socialists from eleven nations at war with one another assembled in Zimmerwald, Switzerland. Trotsky drafted their anti-war proclamation as the *Zimmerwald Manifesto* (Deutscher, op. cit., p. 80). Trotsky's own account of this effort, in which "half a century after the founding of the first International, it was still possible to seat all the internationalists in four coaches," is found in *My Life,* p. 249.

36. Aleksandr Fyodorovich Kerensky, born in Russia in 1881, as an eloquent politician of the moderate left had been a member of earlier dumas. He supported the war, and was first appointed Minister of War under the Provisional Government. Later, from July through October, he served as Prime Minister. The "June Offensive" which he launched on the eastern front proved an unmitigated disaster. Trotsky says he had "no theoretical preparation, no political schooling, no ability to think, no political will. . . . [and] that kind of eloquence which operates neither upon mind or will, but upon the nerves." [I:183]

37. In the Tauride Palace (see map), both the Soviet and the Provisional Government took form in February. [I:129–30] It was well situated to become the center of activity in February, being close to the center of military installations, and a short distance from the Vyborg district. Its name hides a mockery of its new revolutionary use, for it had been built in the eighteenth century for Grigory Aleksandrovich Potemkin, Catherine II's lover and conqueror of new territories for the Russian empire. He was named by her, "Prince of Tauris" (Tabriz, Iran), to honor such territorial greed.

38. Pavel Nikolayevich Milivkov, born in Moscow in 1859, was both an eminent historian and a leading political figure. As editor of *Rech* ("Speech") he was a leader of the Constitutional Democratic ("Kadet") Party, and was appointed Foreign Minister in the Provisional Government. Aiming for moderation, he supported continuation of the monarchy after the abdication of Nicholas, and strongly supported the war and the alliance with the Western Powers. Excerpts from his *Political Memoirs* are included in von Mohrenschildt, op. cit., pp. 88 ff.

39. Lavr Georgiyevich Kornilov, born in Western Siberia in 1870, served in the Russo-Japanese war in 1903–4, and was made a divisional commander in World War I. In an effort to restore order in the city, the Provisional Government had placed him in charge of the military district of Petrograd, where he became highly unpopular with the troops. In July, Kerensky appointed him commander-in-chief.

40. Trotsky had been elected president of the Petrograd Soviet in September. When the Soviet subsequently assumed responsibility for the defense of Petrograd against counterrevolution or possible German attack and a Military Revolutionary Committee was formed, Trotsky became *ex officio* its chairman. In this capacity, he effectively directed the insurrection. Deutscher, *The Prophet Armed,* p. 298.

41. The Winter Palace (see map) had been the principal residence of the tzar, and became the center of Kerensky's government.

42. V. D. Nabokov, father of the renowned author, was a leader of the Constitutional Democratic ("Kadet") party, played important roles in the Provisional Government, and wrote memoirs for which Trotsky expresses sincere respect, though from the far side of the dialectical watershed: "Nabokov . . . whose truthful memoirs seem at times to be the very diary of his party and of his class" [I:117].

43. Trotsky recalls his own early solitary confinement in the Peter and Paul Fortress in *My Life,* p. 189.

44. It was Trotsky who had been summoned urgently to persuade a body of troops assigned to the Fortress to come over to the revolution. The men were assembled in Trotsky's Cirque Moderne (note 11), and the mission proved eminently successful [III:215].

45. V. A. Antonov-Ovseenko as an officer in the tzar's army, had rebelled in 1905 and been sentenced to death. He escaped, and reappeared in Paris in 1915 as organizer of a new paper *Nashe Slovo* ("Our World") which, though published under severe censorship and financial adversity, gained great respect. Trotsky had worked with him on that paper. (Deutscher, *The Prophet Armed,* p. 221.) Excerpts from G. I. Blagonravov's account of events in the Peter and Paul Fortress during the attack on the Winter Palace are included in Daniels, op. cit., pp. 139 ff.

46. The building of the Petrograd Duma (see map) is not many blocks from the Winter Palace. It is described by Trotsky as a center for anti-Bolshevik activities [III:272].

47. Prokopovich had been appointed Minister of Trade and Industry in a more conservative Coalition Government formed in July. Trotsky characterizes him as "a writer without party and without personality" [II:125].

48. The full text of Trotsky's chapter on "The Congress of the Soviet Dictatorship," together with the Conclusion of his *History,* is reproduced elsewhere in this volume.

49. The Smolny Convent (see map), a school for "daughters of the nobility" with impressive eighteenth-century buildings and park, was taken over as Bolshevik headquarters following the party's expulsion from the Palace of Kshesinskaia. See Trotsky's dramatic account of the transformation of Smolny from the academic retreat of one class to the headquarters of another [III:202–3].

50. The "diagonal" Trotsky has in view is evidently the result of Newton's parallelogram of forces, the vector summation of two nonconcurrent forces (*GBWW* I: 34, 15; II: 32, 15). Metaphors from the sciences abound in Trotsky's writing (we have only to think of the recurrence of the fundamental image of the "molecular process"), revealing his early study and continuing interest in the physical sciences.

51. John Reed, born in Portland, Oregon in 1887, graduated from Harvard and soon after began writing for the Socialist newspaper, *The Masses.* He had reported, and encouraged, the Mexican revolution before becoming an eyewitness to that of 1917 in Russia, where he became an enthusiastic supporter and a friend of Lenin's. His vivid account of the 1917 revolution is *Ten Days that Shook the World* (New York: Vintage Books, 1960). Trotsky says that he "knew how to see and hear, and . . . has left an immortal book of chronicler's notes." [II:187] As leader of the Communist Labor Party in the United States, he was indicted for treason and escaped to the Soviet Union, where he died of typhus in 1920.

52. One aspect of the attack which was to follow is analyzed in Robert J. Maddox, *The Unknown War with Russia* (San Rafael, California: Presidio Press, 1977).

53. This difficult term admits interpretation at various levels, of which I am suggesting here only the most basic. As a practical proposition, it directly challenges the possibility of a bounded revolution, which would establish "socialism in one country," and emphasizes instead the worldwide as well as the ongoing character of the process. "Permanent" thus evidently means here *ongoing* or *unresting,* and *universal*—but of course not simply "perpetual." *See* Trotsky, *The Permanent Revolution* (New York: Pathfinder Press, 1969).

Why Lawyers Lie

William T. Braithwaite

William Braithwaite was educated at the Virginia Military Institute and the
law school at Washington and Lee University. In 1973 he joined the firm of
Mayer, Brown, and Platt in Chicago, where he was admitted to partnership
in 1978. He left the firm in 1979 to teach at the Loyola University of Law.
Currently he is associate professor of law at Loyola teaching Professional
Responsibility, Remedies, Argument and Law and Literature. He has also
taught at the University of Iowa Law School and Rosary College. His articles
include "On Legal Practice and Education at the Present Time" (*The Great
Ideas Today*, 1989), "Poetry and the Criminal Law" (1982), and "Why,
and How, Judges Should Study Poetry" (1988). He is co-editor of *Law and
Philosophy: The Practice of Theory* (1992), and is currently working on
*John Locke's The Reasonableness of Christianity (1695): Text, Notes, and
An Interpretation.*

Prologue

> ... there is such a distance between how one lives and how one
> should live that he who lets go that which is done for that which ought
> to be done learns his ruin rather than his preservation—for a man who
> wishes to profess the good in everything needs must fall among so many
> who are not good.
>
> Machiavelli, *The Prince* (1525)

> In your assumption that there may be a *fair* decision of the slavery
> question in Kansas, I plainly see you and I would differ about the
> Nebraska-law. I look upon that enactment not as a *law*, but as *violence*
> from the beginning. It was conceived in violence, passed in violence, is
> maintained in violence, and is being executed in violence.
>
> Abraham Lincoln to Joshua F. Speed, Aug. 24, 1855

Why do lawyers lie (some of them anyway—perhaps too many)?
Because, I propose, deep down they believe that law does not
displace war (because it cannot) but only imitates it—an opinion that is
not simply wrong. In their rule of law, accordingly, words are weapons,
due process means the rules of the game, and trials are rather like a
working-class soccer match—bloody and rough and tumble. In litigation
so conceived, lying is in effect, if not intention, a form of violence—
a way to get what you fear you might not if you eschewed chicane for
candor and civility. For lawyers (and their clients) who understand the
law and litigation this way, justice means to win, to keep what you have
or get more than you give, and winning is everything.

I

> Violence is characteristic of wild beasts, and violence is most manifest
> in war; wherefore the more diligently effort should be put forth that it
> be tempered with humanity, lest by imitating wild beasts too much we
> forget to be human.
>
> Hugo Grotius, *On the Law of War and Peace* (1625)

The legal profession's standards for telling the truth are found in
a system of law whose primary formal mode of resolving disputes,
the courtroom trial (or "adversary process"), is seen by some lawyers
as a demilitarized form of war. They think that what is fair for the

advocate to do in advancing or defending the client's cause in court is like whatever may be effectual for the commander to do when advancing his troops or defending in battle. In the professional talk of many lawyers, consequently, the military metaphor is commonplace: litigation strategy, bury the opponent with paper, trial tactics, attack the witness's credibility.

The analogy between war and litigation, a battle and a trial, is not peculiarly modern nor is it happenstance. It has such ancient historical antecedents, in fact, as to suggest its ultimate source may be in the very constitution of the human psyche. The Dutch jurist Hugo Grotius, one of the fathers of modern international law, wrote in 1625, for example:

> It is evident that the sources from which wars arise are as numerous
> as those from which lawsuits spring; for where judicial settlement fails,
> war begins. [1]

Or this, from *On War* (1833) by the Prussian general Carl von Clausewitz:

> War is not merely a political act, but also a political instrument, a
> continuation of political relations, a carrying out of the same by
> other means. [2]

Clausewitz's writings, well-known to military historians and generals studied in the art of war, advocate attacking all of the enemy's military forces, territory, property, and citizens, i.e., "total" war.

Some lawyers think the same way. They talk of "Rambo" litigation or say that their trial strategy is to "take no prisoners." "Your true purpose is to convict the guilty man who sits at the defense table," one prosecutor said in a lecture at the National College of District Attorneys, "and to go for the jugular as viciously and rapidly as possible. . . . You must never forget that your goal is total annihilation." [3]

Trials *were* battles, some of them at least, at an earlier time in the history of Anglo-American law. Trial by battle was introduced in England by the Normans after the conquest of 1066 and may have been known in Europe in the tenth century. It was used, in England, in both civil and some criminal cases. [4]

When the prosecutor of a criminal case was not the Crown but a private individual, the accuser and accused could fight one another in person; if the defendant lost but survived alive, he was promptly hanged, defeat having proved his guilt. In civil cases, the parties paid champions to fight for them. One historian's description makes this medieval institution seem remarkably familiar:

> We very soon find from the rolls [court records] that there was a
> professional band of champions who undertook business all over
> the country; courts would arrange the dates of battle so that the

Hugo Grotius

champions could fit in their engagements conveniently. Some very great landowners, such as the larger monasteries, were so constantly involved in litigation that they maintained their own full-time champions. The names of these champions constantly appear on the rolls, and we sometimes hear of a champion's "master" or manager, and of a champion who abandoned his client because the other side offered him a premium. [5]

The trial lawyer as hired gun seems to be nothing new.

Why have human beings always been at war against one another, often with arms, at other times with words? One ancient answer from Plato's *Laws* is that "nothing is really beneficial . . . unless one triumphs in war. For then all the good things of the defeated belong to the victors." Kleinias, the mature Cretan statesman who is speaking, then observes that when this argument is followed to its source, one finds

that all are enemies of all in public, and in private each is an enemy of himself. . . . [T]he first and best of all victories, [is] the victory of oneself

234

over oneself; and being defeated by oneself is the most shameful and at the same time the worst of all defeats. These things indicate that there is a war going on in us, ourselves against ourselves. [6]

Politics and psychology are mirror images: the struggle between reasonable men and willful men in the political life of the city reflects the struggle between reason and will (i.e., desire or appetite) in the self-governance of the soul of the individual. The city is man writ large, and each of the different kinds of regimes corresponds to a type of human soul.

Nearly twenty centuries after Plato, Hobbes (1588–1679) made the opinion that "all are enemies of all in public" the taproot of his theory of politics and jurisprudence. Hobbes is the first thinker in our epoch of modernity to construct a comprehensive political philosophy, and his thought contains the grounds of modern legal positivism, the reigning theory of American jurisprudence since at least 1938.

In his most famous work, *Leviathan* (1651), Hobbes postulated a "state of nature," a pre-political age when man was without law and government. Men then lived, he affirmed, "in that condition which is called Warre; and such a warre, as is of every man, against every man." [7] His earlier treatise, the seminal work of modern jurisprudence, *The Elements of Law* (1640), asserted the same postulate:

> Seeing then to the offensiveness of man's nature one to another, there is added a right of every man to every thing, whereby one man invadeth with right, and another with right resisteth; and men live thereby in perpetual diffidence, and study how to preoccupate each other; the estate of men in this natural liberty is the estate of war. [8]

Justice, then, in Hobbes's view, is simply the will of the stronger: "one man invadeth another *with right*, and another *with right* resisteth." This can only mean, since every man has a "right" to every thing, that whatever the thing may be that men happen to desire, it will belong rightfully to him who can soonest get it and only for so long as he can keep it, whether it be land, money, women, power, or a crown.

This was also the view of Hobbes's great forerunner, Machiavelli (1469–1527). In a passage that has since become famous, he wrote:

> You ought to know, then, that there are two kinds of fighting: one with the laws, the other with force. The first one is proper to man; the second to the beasts; but because the first proves many times to be insufficient, one needs must resort to the second. . . .
> Since a prince must of necessity know well how to use the beast, he ought of the beasts to pick the fox and the lion; for the lion cannot defend himself from snares, and the fox cannot defend himself from wolves. One needs, then, to be fox to know snares, and lion to terrify wolves. [9]

In this view of political life, words and swords are alternative means to the same end, each to be used or not used according to the occasion. To that antagonist for whom the only objects are victory and glory, it matters not whether the arena of conflict is the terrain of battle or thirty square feet in front of a jury. No moral problem arises, for the Machiavellian, in sending his ambassador, to whom he does not tell his plan, to meet with diplomats of another country to talk about peace (the fox) at the very hour his war planes are bombing that country's military bases in a massive surprise attack (the lion), as the Japanese government did on Dec. 7, 1941. Every experienced trial lawyer has seen the fox and the lion in litigation.

But suppose winning in the courtroom is not by nature the same as winning in battle. Suppose deliberating by argument toward justice is essentially different from contending by force toward victory. This I take to be Plato's position, implicit in the *Republic* as well as his other dialogues, and also Aristotle's, comprehensively developed in his *Ethics, Politics,* and *Rhetoric.*

Then the lawyer must be governed by different rules from those of the soldier or commander (or Machiavelli's prince). He cannot justify lying to an opponent in litigation simply because in the Persian Gulf War, General Norman Schwartzkopf fed tales to the media (which they seem to have believed) of a planned assault by sea, in order to conceal the actual strategy of a massive rapid troop, armor, and air attack across Iraq's southern desert, out-flanking Saddam Hussein's forces dug in on the Kuwaiti coastline.

In war, strategy and force are inseparable. The object of war is victory, victory is unlikely without strategy, and strategy requires both force and wiles. Lying is usually preferable to bloodshed when the choice is deception or many more casualties than would occur otherwise.

But is lying, which is in words the equivalent of force, innate in law and litigation? It is by necessity that the object of the general is victory, but victory is the lawyer's object only if he chooses to have it so (or permits the client to choose). Those lawyers will so choose who believe with Hobbes and Machiavelli that society is at bottom a war "of every man against every man"—or (softer word) a competition. The fashionable and influential "law and economics" school of jurisprudence, whose adherents think of society as a marketplace, now comes to light as in truth no more than a bourgeoisified Machiavellianism defanged of its ruthlessness.

Even if we were to grant that war and competition are innate in the human psyche (and therefore also in politics and law), do we know with equal certainty that goodwill, amity, and cooperation are not? Men, barbarian and civilized, have always made war, yes. Have not civilized men also always made peace, sought truth, pursued justice?

If so, it is as natural for the law to nurture what is noble in human

Nicolò Machiavelli

nature as to aim at no more than the domestication of what is brutish, by the replacement of war with trade. And justice is no less in accordance with nature than winning as the object of litigation. At the practical level, doing justice means that the lawyer tries his best to see that the client neither suffers wrong nor does any.

The axiom proposed here is that law is a reaching for what is highest, not simply an imitation of war, which can show man at his lowest. Lawyers should therefore be guided by the differences, not the similarities. Is the legal profession, by this standard, in good health ethically? I shall make a preliminary diagnosis using as a point of reference the question of when the lawyer must tell the truth. This general question will be exemplified by two specific ones that have exercised the legal profession a good deal in the last thirty years or so and which continue to vex law students, practitioners, scholars, and judges:

1. Does the lawyer in negotiations have a duty to tell the truth, or do the same moral standards apply there as in, say, dickering with a used-car salesman?

2. What should the lawyer do if the client insists he wants to testify, or has already testified, to what the lawyer knows is false?

II

The Athenians to the Melians:

> But out of those things which we both of us do really think, let us go through with that which is feasible; both you and we knowing, that in human disputation justice is then only agreed on when the necessity is equal; whereas they that have odds of power exact as much as they can, and the weak yield to such conditions as they can get.

The Melians to the Athenians:

> Well then, (seeing you put the point of profit in the place of justice), we hold it profitable for ourselves, not to overthrow a general profit to all men, which is this: that men in danger, if they plead reason and equity, nay, though somewhat without the strict compass of justice, yet it ought ever to do them good.
> Thucydides, *The Peloponnesian War* (*GBWW* I: 6, 505; II: 5, 505)

The national professional organization of lawyers is the American Bar Association (ABA), whose formal published standards of ethics are the Model Rules of Professional Conduct. [10] The Preamble states: "As negotiator, a lawyer seeks a result advantageous to the client but consistent with requirements of honest dealing with others." For some people, "honest dealing" means tell the truth; to the ABA, as we shall see, it means don't commit fraud.

The ethics of negotiating are important because bargaining for the client's interest is what most lawyers do most of the time. (Advocacy in the courtroom, though easily dramatized and more visible, is not the primary activity of most lawyers.) Some negotiations are aimed at settling disputes, including lawsuits; others at making deals, e.g., selling a business or dickering contract terms.

ABA Rule 4.1 covers both kinds of negotiations, deals and disputes, and makes no distinction between them in respect of the lawyer's ethical duty. It says:

> In the course of representing a client a lawyer shall not *knowingly:*
> (a) make a false statement of *material* fact or law to a third person; or
> (b) fail to disclose a *material* fact to a third person when disclosure is necessary to avoid assisting a criminal or fraudulent act by a client, unless disclosure is prohibited by Rule 1.6. ["Confidentiality of Information"]　　　　　　　　　　　　　　　(emphasis added)

"Knowingly" makes sense because usually a false statement is not morally blamed, even when harmful in its effects, if the speaker did not know, and through no fault of his own had not the means or opportunity to know, that the statement was in fact false.

"Material" makes sense because always telling the whole truth about everything—that is, everything you know the whole truth about—is neither desirable nor even possible for most people; besides, common social morality accepts certain evasions in small matters ("How do you like my new suit?"). In serious matters, however, practical morality is concerned mainly with untruths that are malevolent ("knowingly") and that make a real difference ("material"), i.e., true lies.

Rule 4.1 does not require the lawyer to tell the truth in negotiations. It is a prohibition, not a command: it does not say what the lawyer ought to do, or must do, but what he is forbidden to do. And although the Rule may seem to say that what it forbids is lying, the prohibition is not really that broad. It does not cover all lies, only some—those that amount to legal fraud. What 4.1 really means, then, is that while it is unethical for a lawyer to commit fraud in negotiations, he is not otherwise required to speak truthfully.

Fraud is a legal wrong, for which the law can award money as compensation to the defrauded party. It can be active or passive. Clause (a) of Rule 4.1 covers active fraud; clause (b), passive fraud.

Clause (a) forbids the lawyer in negotiations to "knowingly" make a "false statement" of a "material fact." A false statement of material fact, if made knowingly and reasonably relied on, is active fraud. Since a lawyer who affirms in negotiations something he knows is false usually intends the lie to be believed (and intends, as well, to profit by its being believed, or for his client to profit), the net effect of clause (a) is simply to prohibit active fraud.

As to clause (b), it is for practical purposes a dead letter. It forbids the lawyer to keep silent when silence would abet the client's crime or fraud. This language implies that the lawyer has a duty to speak when by doing so he can stop a fraud. But the lawyer is not obligated to speak, nor even permitted to, if another rule, 1.6, prohibits his doing so. And it does.

Rule 1.6 imposes on the lawyer an ethical duty to effect the attorney-client privilege, which is like the doctor-patient privilege. So that doctors and lawyers can put their expertise to best use for us, we have to tell them things we reveal to few, if any other people, but we expect they will keep our secrets to themselves except insofar as the performance of their services requires disclosure (to nurses and secretaries, for example). Rule 1.6 implements this justifiable expectation, in respect to lawyers.

The rule forbids the lawyer, unless the client consents, to reveal anything the client told him "relating to" the representation. (The exceptions are not material here.) But 1.6 does *not* allow, hence it forbids, a lawyer to reveal confidences in order to stop a fraud, either planned or in progress. Read together, 4.1(b) and 1.6 allow the lawyer to sit mum and poker-faced at the negotiating table while the client, with the lawyer's knowledge, lies through his teeth.

The net result is that 4.1(b) means practically nothing as far as fraud or lying is concerned. One commentator has said the exception for confidential information makes 4.1(b) a "meaningless semantic puzzle." [11] Two others find a "merry-go-round of inconsistencies" among 4.1(b), 1.6, and 1.2(d) (which forbids the lawyer to advise or abet crime or fraud). [12]

Reduced to its essential, Rule 4.1 as a whole says no more than that it is unethical for the lawyer intentionally to commit fraud in negotiations by actively lying. The lawyer's moral duty here is the same as the citizen's, no more, no less: obey the positive law. In negotiations, legal ethics mean law-abidingness, and that is all it means.

This standard is the same as in the Rules' predecessor, the Model Code of Professional Responsibility, [13] although in the course of writing the Rules, the ABA's drafting committee ("the Kutak Commission") proposed a different and higher standard—trustworthiness. But the proposal was withdrawn because of "the vehemence of the objections" to it. [14] (The ABA regards the Code, approved in 1969, as superseded by the Rules, approved in 1983.)

We can learn a good deal about what many lawyers—or those who are most vociferous in the councils of the profession—today believe is the real nature of their work, by pondering this official repudiation by the ABA of the idea that a lawyer in negotiations ought to be trustworthy.

The proposed standard was expressed in the Kutak Commission's

Jan. 30, 1980 Discussion Draft, Rules 4.2 and 4.3. The two Draft Rules differed from approved Rule 4.1 in several ways:

1. The title of 4.2 was "Fairness to Other Participants" [in negotiations], and the Rule actually imposed an affirmative duty to be fair, while 4.1, titled "Truthfulness in Statements to Others," in fact imposes no duty to tell the truth, only a duty not to cheat ("assist a fraudulent act"), which is a rather meaner obligation on the moral scale.

2. Clause (a) of 4.2 provided: "In conducting negotiations a lawyer shall be fair in dealing with other participants." The Commission's chief draftsman, Professor Geoffrey Hazard, says this language "certainly encompasses a concept of truthful representations" and "went well beyond the fraud standard" of the 1969 Code [15] (of the 1983 Rules, too, as finally approved).

3. Draft Rule 4.3, titled "Illegal, Fraudulent, or Unconscionable Transactions," said: "A lawyer shall not conclude an agreement, or assist a client in concluding an agreement, that the lawyer knows or reasonably should know . . . would work a fraud, or would be held unconscionable as a matter of law." This provision seems to mean that the lawyer must not cheat nor help the client do so. But proposed 4.3 fell between the cracks; it has no equivalent in the Rules as approved.

Why did the ABA reject the trustworthiness standard and instead simply reaffirm in the Rules the no-fraud standard of the Code? Professor Hazard, one of the several most thoughtful and well-informed authorities nationally on lawyers' ethics, gives this answer:

> The fundamental difficulty appears to stem from the lack of a firm professional consensus regarding the standard of openness that should govern lawyers' dealings with others and the lack of settled and homogeneous standards of technique in the practice of law. [16]

On its moral first principles, at least as to when the lawyer in negotiations should tell the truth, the profession is a house divided. "Lawyers, at least nationally, do not share a common conception of fairness in the process of negotiation," Hazard says; they have neither "the language to express [such] norms" nor "the institutional means" to put them into effect. [17]

The ABA may believe differently. It claims there is indeed something like "a common conception" about how lawyers may conduct themselves in negotiations. The second official Comment ("Statements of Fact") to Rule 4.1 says:

> This Rule refers to statements of fact. Whether a particular statement should be regarded as one of fact can depend on the circumstances. Under *generally accepted conventions* in negotiation, certain types of statements ordinarily are not taken as statements of material fact.
>
> (emphasis added)

Some actual statements of fact are thus not statements of fact under the Rules because they are not "taken" to be.

A statement of fact not taken as fact by the speaker sounds as if it could be an intended lie. (He does not take it as fact because he knows it isn't?) A statement of fact not taken as fact by the speaker but intended by him to be taken as fact by the hearer is what most people mean by a lie (saying what you do not believe yourself, in order to get something you fear you might not get if you told the truth). A statement of fact not taken as fact by either party is probably a lie that failed. (Why would the speaker make the statement if he did not intend the hearer to take it as fact?)

Are there indeed as the ABA claims, "generally accepted conventions" about telling the truth in negotiations? The evidence is not free from doubt. To begin with, the ethics of lawyers reflect the ethics of society, and there are many local and industry variations between the extremes, which Professor Hazard calls the "rural God-fearing standard" and "New York hardball." So it is hard to specify a practicable national standard, he concludes, one likely to be generally obeyed most of the time by either the negotiating parties or their lawyers. [18]

Moreover, the professional literature shows no agreement that there are generally accepted conventions.

Judge Alvin Rubin says flatly that lawyers must act "honestly and in good faith." People who deal with them should not need to act as they would if "trading for reputedly antique copper jugs in an oriental bazaar." [19] Professor Walter W. Steele agrees. He proposes a rule affirming that lawyers owe one another "total candor and total cooperation to the extent required to insure that the result is fair." [20] Harvard's Roger Fisher, well-known in his field as the senior author of *Getting to Yes: Negotiating Agreement Without Giving In,* is doubtful that lies in negotiation even work. He says they are "risky for clients, bad for lawyers, and bad for society." [21]

Professor Gerald B. Wetlaufer disagrees. He thinks lies work and are ineradicable but are morally wrong nonetheless ("highly effective" if "well-told"; "a permanent feature of advocacy"). [22] Professor Charles Craver says, "I've never been involved in legal negotiations where both sides didn't lie," but Wayne Brazil, a federal magistrate in Chicago, says, "My opinion is, no lying." [23] (Craver may be talking about what he thinks lawyers *actually* do, though, and Brazil about what he thinks they *ought* to do, or ought not to do.)

Judge Richard Neely (West Virginia Supreme Court) knows from experience that lies work. He tells how, while a lawyer, he represented a railroad brakeman who got tired of marriage and ran off with a woman who loved motorcycles as much as he did. The wife's divorce action, to which the husband had no real defense, came before a rural judge known for giving high alimony and child support awards. Yet a "rather modest" award was negotiated by Neely after the husband followed his advice to threaten to contest custody (the children were nine and twelve), which he did not really want and had virtually no chance of getting, but which the wife did not want to run any risk whatsoever of losing. [24]

Is this the kind of negotiation the Rule 4.1 Comment refers to (some statements of fact "ordinarily are not taken" as statements of fact)? The client and his lawyer say things they do not believe themselves (the father wants custody) in order to get what they likely could not get (lower alimony and child support) if they told the truth (custody is the last thing the father wanted). *They* do not "take" their statements as fact— they know better. But they hope the wife (emotionally vulnerable?) and her attorney (over-cautious or inexperienced?) will take them as fact.

The ABA can say negotiating like this is "generally accepted" if it wants to, but it looks like the family-law species of West Virginia hardball to me. I do not know whether most lawyers approve of such tactics. Certainly some do, perhaps even many. What would trouble a few whom I know is that in asking whether one should do this kind of thing because it is generally accepted (if it is), other questions that seem important get lost somehow. How much money does the wife really need? How much can the husband reasonably afford? Is it truly in the client's interest to help him shirk his duties as a father?

Has this father done right by his children? How are they going to feel about him five or ten years down the line? Is the lawyer doing right by the client if he does not try to make the client face up to what he is really doing? If the father is morally accountable for the care of his children, what is the lawyer morally accountable for when he helps play on the mother's natural fears in order to inveigle her acquiescence in the most niggardly possible contribution to the children's care?

What the ABA appears actually to have done in the Rule 4.1 Comment is endorse New York hardball by pronouncing it generally accepted. The idea of negotiations which animates the Comment is well-described by Professor James J. White in a much-cited article aptly titled, *Machiavelli and the Bar: Ethical Limitations on Lying in Negotiation.* "To conceal one's true position, to mislead an opponent about one's true settling point, is the essence of negotiation." [25]

White believes that the negotiator's job is a "paradox":

> On the one hand the negotiator must be fair and truthful; on the other he must mislead his opponent. Like the poker player, a negotiator hopes his opponent will overestimate the value of his hand. . . . The critical difference between those who are successful negotiators and those who are not lies in this capacity both to mislead and not to be misled. [26]

It is White's opinion, for example, that exaggerating the degree of pain your client experienced is "well within the range of puffing." Ronald

Rotunda responds, "If lawyers want to be like used car salesmen, this is a good place to start." [27]

III

> Alexander VI [father of Cesare Borgia; Pope, 1492–1503] never did anything else and he never thought about anything else but how to deceive men, and he always found a subject for his practice. And there never was a man who was more efficacious in asseverating, or with greater oaths affirmed a thing, who less observed [his faith]. Nevertheless, his deceptions always succeeded at his will, because he knew so well this part of the world.
>
> Machiavelli, *The Prince* (*GBWW* I: 23, 25; II: 21, 25)

> For I've been called the weaker speech among the thinkers here because of this very thing: that I was first to have it in mind to speak things opposed to these laws and to justice.
>
> Aristophanes, *Clouds* (*GBWW* I: 5, 505; II: 4, 713)

ABA Rule 1.6 forbids the lawyer to reveal what the client told him in confidence "relating to" the representation unless the client consents. (The exceptions are not material here.) But in the usual case, it is just on account of what the client told him that the lawyer knows (if he does know) what is true and what is not. So if the client testifies falsely, the lawyer can recognize the lie by reason of the confidence, but if he reveals the lie, he indirectly reveals the confidence, and this is just what 1.6 says he cannot do. This is the client perjury problem.

Should the plan or fact of perjury be a privileged confidence? Rule 1.6 does not answer this question, but Rule 3.3, "Candor Toward the Tribunal," seems to:

> (a) A lawyer *shall not* knowingly . . . (4) offer evidence that the lawyer knows to be false. If a lawyer has offered material evidence and comes to know of its falsity the lawyer *shall* take reasonable remedial measures.
>
> (emphasis added)

Beneath this express prohibition and command lie a number of perplexities. These arise from deep differences of opinion within the profession about the nature of the lawyer's job in a trial and what the proper object of the trial itself is. There is no open opposition to the axiom that client perjury is wrong; what the profession cannot agree about is how to prevent or remedy it.

In civil (non-criminal) cases, the lawyer can avoid the problem simply by not calling the client to testify. If the client insists on testifying, and falsely, the lawyer *must* withdraw from the representation. [28] If he learns of the perjury afterward, he must reveal it. [29] In criminal cases, however, there are four complications:

1. *The criminal defendant's right to testify.* The Supreme Court has said the defendant in a criminal case has a constitutional right to testify in his own defense and that this is such a right as cannot be given up or taken away or waived by his lawyer. [30] Thus the defense lawyer cannot avoid the perjury problem by refusing to call his client to testify, as the lawyer in a civil case can do (and do lawfully, because the civil defendant has no constitutional right to testify).

2. *The defendant's right to counsel.* The Sixth Amendment provides: "In all criminal prosecutions, the accused shall enjoy the right . . . to have the Assistance of Counsel for his defence." "Assistance" means "effective" assistance, the Supreme Court has said. [31] Is the lawyer "effective" if he fails or refuses to present the defendant's case the way he wants it presented? (Assume him to be sane, adult, and competent.)

3. *The right to a fair trial.* The Supreme Court has said the accused has a constitutional right to a "fair" trial, wherein it is the lawyer's duty "to advocate the defendant's cause," to be loyal to him, and to avoid conflicts of interest. [32]

If the client says he intends to testify falsely, and the lawyer, to prevent the perjury, threatens to reveal it if it occurs, has the lawyer breached his duty of loyalty? Does he have a conflict of interest? Rule 3.3 does not say; nor does any other ABA Rule.

4. *The privilege against self-incrimination.* The Fifth Amendment provides: "No person . . . shall be compelled in any criminal case to be a witness against himself." In *Fisher* v. *United States* (1976), [33] the Supreme Court ruled that documents privileged, by reason of this provision, against legally compelled disclosure while in the hands of the defendant did not lose their Fifth Amendment protection when given to his lawyer.

If *Fisher* were extended from what the client wrote to what he said to his lawyer, one effect could be that a disclosure of client perjury by the lawyer might be interpreted to violate the client's privilege against self-incrimination. [34]

Some of these complications were resolved by the Supreme Court in *Nix* v. *Whiteside* (1986), [35] decided two and a half years after the ABA approved its Model Rules.

Late one night in February 1977, in Cedar Rapids, Iowa, Emmanual Charles Whiteside stabbed and killed Calvin Love during a failed marijuana buy. He told his lawyer, Gary L. Robinson, that although he did not actually see a gun, he thought Love had one. Robinson told him, correctly, the law of self-defense required him to show at trial only that he himself had a reasonable belief Love had a gun, not that Love in fact did.

Shortly before trial, Whiteside told Robinson he would testify he saw a gun (or something "metallic") because otherwise "I'm dead." Robinson replied that he believed the proposed testimony was not true.

Of the 25 judges on five courts who heard the case, none seriously questioned Robinson's judgment on this point, or that he had a legally sufficient factual basis for it.

Robinson told Whiteside that if he did testify this way, he would withdraw as counsel, tell the judge Whiteside had lied, and "probably would be allowed to attempt to impeach that particular testimony." [36] Chastened by these threats, Whiteside did not testify as he had proposed.

At trial, the evidence showed that when Whiteside killed Love, three other persons were in the room; but no witness testified to having seen a gun, and no gun was found at the scene. Whiteside admitted he heard Love tell his girlfriend to get his "piece," which Whiteside understood meant his gun, showing that Love did not then believe himself to have a gun within reach and that Whiteside knew this. [37]

Robinson "tried to create a gun." He called defense witnesses who testified they had seen Love with a sawed-off shotgun on occasion. The prosecution stipulated Love had once been convicted of unlawful possession of a weapon. Robinson cross-examined the State's witnesses so as to imply that the police, who found no gun, had been hasty in their initial search and that Love's girlfriend had taken his gun away from his apartment (where the killing occurred) before a second, more thorough search. Whiteside testified that he "most certainly" thought Love had a gun. [38]

A jury found him guilty of second degree murder, and the court sentenced him to forty years. After judgment, through a different lawyer, he argued that he had not gotten a fair trial because Robinson's threats stopped him from presenting his defense as he wished. The trial judge rejected this argument, as did the Iowa Supreme Court and the U.S. District Court, where he sought federal court review of his state court conviction.

The U.S. Court of Appeals, Eighth Circuit, agreed with Whiteside, however, and reversed the lower court's judgment, only to be itself reversed by the U.S. Supreme Court. That neither Robinson's threats nor their effect denied Whiteside a fair trial or "Assistance of Counsel" all nine justices agreed (four dissented on secondary issues). Chief Justice Burger's majority opinion for himself and four others expressed these views:

1. The constitutional right to testify is not a right to testify falsely. [39]

2. The Sixth Amendment right to counsel does not include the right to a lawyer "who will cooperate with planned perjury." Hence Whiteside was not deprived of his right to a fair trial. [40]

3. The duty of confidentiality (ABA Rule 1.6) does not cover "announced plans to engage in future criminal conduct," i.e., proposed perjury. [41]

4. The duty of loyalty is limited to "legitimate, lawful conduct compatible with the very nature of a trial as a search for truth." Thus the

lawyer may not at trial present false evidence, otherwise violate the law, or help the client to do so. [42]

5. The only "conflict" of interest was the one Whiteside "imposed" on Robinson by his proposal to lie, and this "conflict" (Burger's quotation marks) did not make Robinson's representation constitutionally ineffective. [43]

Nix means that a lawyer's threat, when the defendant proposes perjury, to tell the judge if he actually does it, is not a means of prevention the Sixth Amendment prohibits. Under Rule 3.3, if perjury happens despite the lawyer's threats (or without his foreknowledge), he "shall" remedy it, "even if [to do so] requires disclosure of information otherwise protected by Rule 1.6." The ABA's Committee on Ethics and Professional Responsibility confirmed in its Formal Opinion 87-353 the year after *Nix* that the lawyer *must* reveal a criminal defendant's perjury to the court if the client fails to do so. In other words, if the threat does not work, the lawyer has a duty to carry it out.

The most extreme way to deal with client perjury would have been to relieve the lawyer of any duty to disclose it. This was first proposed, in 1966, and has since been championed, by Professor Monroe H. Freedman. He says, "An overwhelming proportion of trial lawyers agree," but notes that law teachers "generally disagree" and twits the professorate for "a career choice that removes them from service to clients." [44] But the ABA, whose members are not removed from service to clients, rejected Freedman's proposal when it approved the Model Rules in 1983, saying it makes the lawyer "a knowing instrument of perjury." [45]

Another proposal was to permit the accused to testify by narration rather than by answers to specific questions. Narration supposes a sufficient moral distinction between presenting testimony by that mode and the usual question-and-answer interrogation. The lawyer who asks specific questions, if he knows the client has lied about a material fact, is required to reveal the perjury because his questions elicited it and he is therefore taken to be an active and intending agent in the crime if he remains silent about it.

But the lawyer who uses narration, because he asks only one general question rather than many specific ones, is supposed not to be actively abetting, therefore is not an accomplice, so has no duty of disclosure ("Now, Mr. Whiteside, tell the court and jury everything you want them to hear about what happened the night you killed Calvin Love, and let me know, please, when you're done").

Is this distinction of any more weight than that between active and passive fraud? The law treats that distinction as in the facts only; because ordinarily without difference in effect or intention, it is also without difference in legal classification or consequences.

Is the intended effect of perjury likely to be different when the lawyer presents the defendant's testimony by narration instead of question-and-answer? Does the defendant aim at a different effect? He wants the lie to be believed in any event, does he not? What relieves the lawyer of moral accountability for helping do the wrong he knows is purposed and of which he deliberately decides to serve as the willing instrument?

Narration is ill-advised because the judge knows, even if a jury might not, what the irregular mode of testimony means, and the law (as it should) lets the judge take perjury by a defendant into account when fixing a sentence. [46] If the case is being heard by the judge alone, narration also increases the likelihood of conviction.

Despite its impracticability and moral ambiguity, narration was, before *Nix*, the solution favored by the ABA, whose policy-making body—the House of Delegates—endorsed in 1971. Up to 1986, when *Nix* was decided, four federal courts and five state courts (in Alaska, Florida, Illinois, Kansas, and South Carolina) had approved narration; California approved it in 1988. [47] Some commentators, both before and since *Nix*, have recommended it. [48]

In 1979, the ABA withdrew its approval, pending its House of Delegates' action on the then-proposed Model Rules of Professional Conduct. The Rules as finally approved, in 1983, rejected narration, and the Supreme Court's majority opinion in *Nix* ratifies the Rules on this point.

Narration in effect implements Professor Freedman's proposal to hold the lawyer blameless, under the profession's rules of ethics, for abetting and concealing perjury (a felony in most states). No one in the "intense debate"—the ABA's words—that has gone on about client perjury for nearly thirty years now, not even Freedman, has denied it is morally wrong to help your client lie under oath. The position taken (or assumed) by Freedman and the defenders of narration has been, rather, that the positive law, including the positive law of lawyers' ethics, commands it anyway.

To accept this opinion means to accept its implicit self-contradiction that one can by reason of the positive law have a moral duty to do a moral wrong. That the law cannot be always perfectly just, and so must at times let moral wrongs go by, permitting by not forbidding them, is something I believe most people sense the practical necessity for. Is it not a different matter, though, to say the law *requires* one to do a moral wrong, when everyone agrees (or concedes) it *is* truly wrong?

The profession at an earlier time did not, apparently, see the same difficulty with client perjury. Take the ABA's 1908 Canons of Professional Ethics, predecessor of the 1969 Code and 1983 Rules. The profession that declared these moral injunctions more than half a century ago was not evidently troubled by any notion that the lawyer in a criminal case has some duty to help the defendant lie if he wants to:

Canon 15: "The office of attorney does not permit, much less does it demand of him for any client, violation of law or any manner of fraud or chicane."

Canon 32: "The lawyer advances . . . the best interests of his client when he renders service or gives advice tending to impress upon the client and his undertaking exact compliance with the strictest principles of the moral law."

Canon 37 (added in 1928): "The announced intention of a client to commit a crime is not included within the confidences which [the lawyer] is bound to respect."

Or consider David Hoffman's "Fifty Resolutions in Regard to Professional Deportment" (1836), which are generally taken to be the earliest formal declaration of ethics for American lawyers (they had an indirect effect on the ABA's 1908 Canons):

> When employed to defend those charged with crimes of the deepest dye, and the evidence against them, whether legal, or moral, be such as to leave no just doubt of their guilt, I shall not hold myself privileged, much less obliged, to use my endeavors to arrest, or to impede the course of justice, by special resorts to ingenuity—to the artifices of eloquence—to appeals to the morbid and fleeting sympathies of weak juries. . . . Persons of atrocious character, who have violated the laws of God and man, are entitled to no such special exertions . . . indeed, to no intervention beyond securing to them a fair and dispassionate investigation of the *facts* of their cause, and the due application of the law: all that goes beyond this, either in manner or substance, is unprofessional, and proceeds, either from a mistaken view of the relation of client and counsel, or from some unworthy and selfish motive, which sets a higher value on professional display and success than on truth and justice, and the substantial interests of the community. [49]

Something has changed, it seems evident, in the way the profession understands itself. What was this change, and how did it come about?

IV

> As a law student he had done things which had before that seemed to him vile and at the time had made him feel disgusted with himself; but later on when he saw that such conduct was practised by people of high standing and not considered wrong by them, he came not exactly to regard those actions of his as all right but simply to forget them entirely or not be at all troubled by their recollection.
>
> Leo Tolstoy, "The Death of Ivan Ilyich"

Law works through words, and what we are examining is how lawyers use them: when and where do they understand themselves to have a professional duty to speak the truth? We have asked this question first with respect to an activity that takes place in private, negotiations, and then with respect to an activity that takes place in public, criminal trials, where we find the most troublesome form of the client perjury problem.

Whether the lawyer, supposing him to know the truth, or to have the duty, the means, and the opportunity to find it out, has also a duty always to tell it in negotiations and criminal trials, or not actively to conceal it, is a question that has elicited a diversity of opinions. These are ranged between two opposed conceptions of lawyers' ethics, the God-fearing standard and New York hardball. What lies beneath these conceptions? And what follows from them?

In the context of American law and the history of the profession's ethics, "God-fearing" means someone who takes seriously what is implied by "the laws of Nature and of Nature's God," words found in the first sentence of the Declaration of Independence. Massive differences there are, to be sure, between the God of the Bible, of revelation, and the God of Nature uncovered in Aristotle's *Physics* (in Greek, *phusis*, "nature"), the so-called Prime Mover, to say nothing of the less massive but still weighty differences between the God of Abraham and the God of the Gospels and St. Paul's Letters.

Yet in all these cases, "God" or "Nature" signifies that to which human beings can look up, a transcendent standard of right and wrong against which to measure both our own conduct and the positive law. The God-fearing lawyer "fears" God and Nature, looks up to them, because he sees that since man is not his own maker, he cannot be the measure of all things.

This kind of lawyer believes that it is in his own interest, and the client's, for the client to get what is due him, if possible. But in no event should he try to take, or should the lawyer help him try to take, what he has no rightful claim to. Better to suffer injustice than to commit it.

This lawyer sees words as tools for the work of establishing justice, the second of the six objects stated in the Preamble to the Constitution ("establish" means to make firm). Like tools, words have a proper purpose, determined by the work they are designed to do. And like any tool, speech should ordinarily be used for its proper work, even though it can in fact be bent to other tasks.

The purpose of speech, according to nature, is the nurture of reason, that unique human faculty which speech makes possible and is for the sake of. Reason has to be nurtured so that man may be better able to exercise the powers necessary to the pursuit of his curiosity. The most exalted objects of this curiosity are the order and the meaning of our world, however much of it is accessible to our senses or can through the cultivation of reason become accessible to our thought.

Because they typically arise from passion (specifically, fear), not from reason and thought, lies are in a sense unnatural. They are not the highest and best use of man's highest and best faculties. Lies are thus alien to that human excellence which is man's highest potentiality and which is left by "the laws of Nature and of Nature's God" to his choice, and his alone, whether it is to be realized.

Machiavelli, writing in 1525, and Grotius, a century later, agree that violence is the way of fighting proper to animals. They agree, too, that speech, and therefore law, are other ways of fighting, used only by man. But at this point there is a deep difference between the two thinkers, and this difference distinguishes, as well, the God-fearing and the hardball lawyer.

According to Grotius, the more we choose to fight like beasts, the more we will come to be like them. Our choice is to grasp for what is high in human nature or stoop to what is low. Grotius encourages us to reach up.

Machiavelli makes us look down. Supposing the generality of men to be sheep or wolves, he advises rulers to imitate the fox and the lion. Fighting with laws, he says (i.e., with speech properly used), "proves many times to be insignificant," making it necessary to resort to force. The rebuttal Grotius offers is implied in the title of his great work, *The Law of War and Peace,* signifying his belief (or hope), which many decent people today share, that even the use of force might be made subject to law.

For Machiavelli, the "law" of war is a redundancy, or a self-contradiction. Law *is* war, with the locale moved from battlefield to courtroom and legislative chamber, a contest of power using words as weapons in the manner of Alexander VI. Since truth in speech "proves many times to be insignificant," the weapon of choice must sometimes be lies.

By entitling his defense of lies in negotiation "Machiavelli and the Bar," Professor White candidly shows the fundamental orientation of the hardball lawyer. This lawyer believes, with Machiavelli, that right and wrong are measured by what people actually do, not by what the high-minded but naive suppose they ought to do. The most frankly skeptical of hardball lawyers agree with Hobbes that good and evil are no more than "names that signify our Appetites, and Aversions." [50]

The God-fearing lawyer's virtues are prudence and resourcefulness; the hardball lawyer's, cunning and opportunism. The former take their ethics from Aristotle and the Bible; the latter, from Machiavelli and Hobbes (and behind them, the sophists).

The God-fearing lawyer's heroes are Odysseus and Lincoln; the hardball lawyer's, John C. Calhoun and Roger Brooke Taney (see p. 254). Or Thomas Cromwell in Robert Bolt's "A Man for All Seasons": "You're absolutely right, it must be done by law. It's just a matter of finding the right law. Or making one." [51] The legislature is only an alternate terrain for the exercise of force.

The God-fearing lawyer does not deny that power is a necessity if law is to be effectual, but he believes that moral authority, not power,

Roger Brooke Taney

makes law what it truly is. Law without power may be a paper tiger, but law without moral authority is not even law. "Nazi law," a historical fact, is according to nature an oxymoron. Not all that is, is right.

For hardball lawyers, on the other hand, since law is subordinate to politics and actions in politics aim at either getting power or keeping it, power is more fundamental than either one. The actions, or motions, of politics follow the same laws as motions in physics: lighter bodies and weaker forces give way to the heavier and stronger.

Power is at once the elemental cause in nature and the elemental fact of political life. Not ancient physics (i.e., Aristotle's) but classical modern physics, shaped by Hobbes into the groundwork for modern political science, provides the conception of human nature implicit in the hardball lawyer's ideas of what law is: the only truth in law (and politics) is the truth that truth is defined by the strong.

We have now plumbed to its bottom, though certainly not in all its bearings, the observation by Professor Hazard that with respect to telling the truth in negotiations, lawyers today lack "a firm professional consensus," "a common conception of fairness." I would go further. I believe that this is also true with respect to virtually all the big questions of lawyers' ethics that have arisen during the past fifty years.

To the extent that the profession has been divided on these questions, the reason, I suggest, is that lawyers, in common with American society as a whole, have conflicting views of what law, politics, human nature, and the world itself are really like. Indeed, they have conflicting views even on how much, if anything, we can truly *know* of what the world is like. Our opinions about ethics are rooted in our beliefs, and these differ, about Nature and Nature's God.

Yet despite the deep philosophical differences, the weight and main tendency of the profession's present rules of ethics are pretty clearly tilted toward the hardball conception of the lawyer's work rather than the God-fearing standard. From a strictly historical point of view, this is a sea change, and one of no small proportions. How did this change come about? And what have been its effects?

According to Lincoln at Gettysburg, the American regime is founded on the belief, nobly and memorably expounded in the Declaration of Independence, that the basic rights of all men come not from positive (man-made) law but from "the laws of Nature and of Nature's God." One consequence of understanding law this way is that court decisions, strictly speaking, are not themselves law but only "evidence" of the law. This was the view expressed in Blackstone's *Commentaries on the Laws of England* (published 1765–69): "So that *the law,* and the *opinion of the judge* are not always convertible terms . . . ; since it sometimes may happen that the judge may *mistake* the law." [52]

Blackstone is the authority who more than any other, directly shaped the practical understanding of law held by the generation of the Found-

Joseph Story

ing Fathers. [53] His view of the law was expressed, approved, and applied by the U.S. Supreme Court, speaking through Justice Joseph Story, in *Swift* v. *Tyson* (1842). [54] The legal point was a narrow and technical question of the law of negotiable instruments (e.g., bank checks and promissory notes). But to decide it, the Court found it had first to affirm explicitly, following Blackstone, that court decisions are not "laws," because the judicial power is not a law-*making* power, only a power to *apply* the law so as to do justice in the particular case.

A corollary of this distinction between making laws and applying them is that in trying to do justice, judges must on occasion measure positive law (legislation) against some higher-than-human standard. For only in this way can it be determined whether the law in question is truly law, i.e., whether it is right, as applied to the facts of the case at hand. The Court in *Swift* assumes the judge's power and duty to do this.

This understanding of law, affirmed by Justice Story for the Court in *Swift*, was rejected by Chief Justice Taney for the Court in *Dred Scott* v. *Sandford* (1857). [55] Taney there found that the Constitution gave Congress no power to prohibit slavery in the territories eventually to become states. To this end, he resorted to a demonstrably false reading of the Declaration of Independence and a legalistic reading of the Constitution notable for its lack of moral and political imagination.

It is the Declaration's view, it was Lincoln's view, and it is the view of most decent Americans today that slavery as known in this country was, and is always, simply wrong and unjust. By saying, in *Dred Scott,* that Congress could not prohibit slavery, Taney was saying, in effect, that no one had legal authority to halt the spread of slavery, i.e., to stop an injustice. The reasons he gave were that the Constitution made slaves property and that property rights were, under the Constitution, unalienable.

Lincoln thought Taney's reading of the Constitution was wrong and said so publicly. [56] But whether right or wrong, Taney's view meant the supremacy of positive law (the Constitution) over "the laws of Nature and of Nature's God" invoked in the Declaration of Independence. It meant, in effect, a repudiation of any higher standard by which to judge whether human laws are just.

Taney did not say openly that he was rejecting a higher-law standard. This step was taken by the Supreme Court in 1938, in *Erie Railroad* v. *Tomkins,* [57] which overrules the *Swift* case. Speaking through Justice Brandeis, who quoted from and relied upon earlier opinions by Justice Oliver Wendell Holmes, the Court said it is "a fallacy" to assume that there is "a transcendental body of law." According to *Erie,* "law in the sense in which courts speak of it today does not exist without some definite power behind it."

This is the idea of law that today rules the legal profession and its standards of ethics. The profession's standards during this century have moved from "should," "should not" (the language of the 1908 Canons), to "shall," "shall not" (the language of the 1983 Rules). This is a movement from aspirations to commands; from moral judgment to procedural nicety. There has been a corresponding change in what lawyers understand to be their primary work, a movement from the higher to the lower, from the lawyer's political task, the administration of justice, to his private task, representing the interests of clients.

In 1908, the profession thought legal ethics meant honorable character. Today it means complying with the Rules. Obedience, not honor based on moral excellence, is now the lawyer's touchstone in ethics.

Another long-term effect of *Erie's* de-naturing of American jurisprudence has been the legalization of lawyers' ethics. The issues treated as moral in the 1908 Canons are assumed by the 1983 Rules to be legal. Questions of ethics have been transformed into questions of positive law, and a positive law largely enervated of explicit moral content and concerns.

A secondary consequence is the moral relativism lawyers now have in common with society as a whole. Among the concrete signs of this are abuses of the pre-trial discovery (fact-finding) process, "Rambo" litigation tactics, and a general decline in the level of civility among lawyers in their professional relations.

Oliver Wendell Holmes

In legal education, the long-term effect of *Erie's* positivism (which defines law as the say-so of those in power) has been the gradual disappearance of a serious interest in jurisprudence and the philosophical study of legal history. In the half-century since *Erie,* law teachers and law students have therefore become more and more cut off from the roots of the law and from the history of its practice as a profession. The practice is, in fact, no longer a profession in the true sense; it is a commercial enterprise, with all the good and bad this implies.

Modernity's standard of truth is that of modern natural science, but since political, legal, and moral issues cannot be counted and weighed, lawyers, in common with society, have come to believe there is no truth in such matters, nor even any better-informed and more reliable opinions. When my students see that many lawyers and judges regard law the way Machiavelli and Hobbes regarded politics, as a game of power, the moral relativism they imbibed before law school is reinforced. This attitude will breed in the coming generation more of the cynicism, greed, and weariness of soul we see in the profession today.

Law schools are now largely uncommitted to the study of serious books about the law. Most law teachers concern themselves with purveying the current positive law or coaching students in practical skills. This approach continues a trend that has been under way for some time. The result is a profession uncertain of its purpose. When a decent, competent, and conscientious law teacher like Monroe Freedman concludes that the law obliges him to argue publicly that aiding and abetting client perjury is not only not wrong, but is indeed a moral duty, then we ought to know there is something deeply awry.

That something, I believe, is the profession's understanding of Pontius Pilate's question to Jesus, what is truth? (John 18.38). For the founders of modernity and of our country, for the best lawyers of the past (e.g., Lincoln), this question was vital and serious. For many lawyers today, as for Pilate, it is only rhetorical. And this is why lawyers lie. As a profession, we no longer care enough about the truth.

Epilogue

Law, then, wishes to be the discovery of what is.

Plato, *Minos* (4th century B.C.)

We hold these truths to be self-evident . . .

The Declaration of Independence (1776).

We live under a Constitution but the Constitution is what the judges say it is.

Charles Evans Hughes (1907) [Chief Justice of the U.S. Supreme Court, 1930–41]

257

1. *On the Law of War and Peace,* Francis W. Kelsey, trans. (New York: Oceana Publications, Inc., reprinted 1964) p. 171.

2. John Bartlett, *Bartlett's Familiar Quotations,* 16th ed., (Boston: Little, Brown and Company, 1992), p. 393.

3. Maurice Nadjari, "Selection of the Jury (Voir Dire)," Lecture, University of Houston (Summer 1971), quoted in Marvin E. Frankel, *Partisan Justice* (1980), p. 32.

4. Theodore F. T. Plucknett, *A Concise History of the Common Law,* 5th ed. (Boston: Little, Brown and Company, 1956), pp. 116–17.

5. Id., p. 117.

6. 626b, d, e, *The Laws of Plato,* trans. Thomas L. Pangle (New York: Basic Books, Inc., 1980) [*GBWW* I: 7, 641; II: 6, 641].

7. Hobbes, *Leviathan,* Richard Tuck, ed. (Cambridge: The University Press, 1991) Chap. XIII (Hobbes' p. 62) [*GBWW* I: 23, 25; II: 21, 25] p. 88.

8. Hobbes, *The Elements of Law Natural and Politic,* Ferdinand Tönnies, ed., 2nd edition (M. M. Goldsmith, 1889), pp. 72–73.

9. *The Prince,* Leo Paul S. de Alvarez, trans. (Irving, Texas: University of Dallas Press, 1980), pp. 107–8.

10. American Bar Association, Center for Professional Responsibility, *Annotated Model Rules of Professional Conduct,* 2nd ed. (Chicago: American Bar Association, 1992), cited here as "Rule(s)."

11. Charles W. Wolfram, *Modern Legal Ethics* (St. Paul: West Publishing Co., 1986), pp. 724–25.

12. Geoffrey C. Hazard & W. William Hodes, *The Law of Lawyering,* 2nd ed., vol. 2, (Englewood Cliffs, N.J.: Prentice Hall Law and Business, 1990), p. 722.

13. The "net requirement of the Code of Professional Responsibility is that lawyers avoid fraudulent representations." Geoffrey C. Hazard, Jr. "The Lawyer's Obligation to be Trustworthy when Dealing with Opposing Parties," 33 *South Carolina Law Review* (1981), pp. 181, 190.

14. Id., p. 192.

15. Id., p. 191.

16. Id., p. 193.

17. Ibid.

18. Ibid.

19. "A Causerie on Lawyers' Ethics in Negotiation," 35 *Louisiana Law Review,* (1975) p. 589.

20. Walter W. Steele, Jr., "Deceptive Negotiating and High-Toned Morality," 39 *Vanderbilt Law Review,* (1986) pp.1387, 1403.

21. *Negotiation Journal* 1, 2, (1985), p. 106.

22. Gerald B. Wetlaufer, "The Ethics of Lying in Negotiations," 75 *Iowa Law Review* (1990), pp. 1219, 1272.

23. Lempert, "In Settlement Talks, Does Telling the Truth Have Its Limits?," 2 *Inside Litigation* 1 (1988).

24. Richard Neely, "The Primary Caretaker Parent Rule: Child Custody and the Dynamics of Greed," 3 *Yale Law and Policy Review,* (1984) pp. 168, 177–78.

25. James J. White, "Machiavelli and the Bar: Ethical Limitations on Lying in Negotiation," *American Bar Foundation Research Journal* (1980), pp. 926, 928.

26. Id., p. 927.

27. Lempert, p. 15.

28. Wolfram, n. 11, pp. 847, 860.

29. Hazard & Hodes, note 12, p. 548, vol. I.

30. *Harris* v. *New York,* 401 United States Reports [hereafter cited as 'U.S.'], (1971), p. 222.

31. *Strickland* v. *Washington,* 466 U.S., (1984), p. 668.

32. Id., p. 688.

33. 425 U.S., p. 391.

34. Monroe H. Freedman, "*Nix* v. *Whiteside:* Is Incrimination by Counsel Constitutional?," XII *Social Responsibility,* (Lexington, Va: Washington and Lee University, 1986), pp. 40–46.

35. 475 U.S., pp. 157–191.

36. Id., n. 7, pp. 172–73.

37. *State* v. *Whiteside,* 272 North Western Reporter, 2nd Series, (Iowa, 1978), p. 471.

38. *Nix,* n. 35, p. 178 (Opinion of Blackmun, J., concurring).

39. Id., pp. 164, 173.

40. Id., p. 173.

41. Id., p. 174.

42. Id., pp. 166, 171.

43. Id., p. 176.

44. Monroe H. Freedman, "Professional Responsibility of the Criminal Defense Lawyer: The Three Hardest Questions," 64 *Michigan Law Review,* (1966) pp. 1469, 1475–78; Freedman, *Understanding Lawyer's Ethics* (New York: Matthew Bender & Co., 1990), n. 1, p. 109.

45. Rules, n. 10, p. 331.

46. *U.S.* v. *Grayson,* 438 U.S., (1978), p. 41.

47. Rules, n. 10, pp. 340–41; *Nix,* n. 35, p. 170, n. 6; Norman Lefstein, "Client Perjury in Criminal Cases: Still in Search of an Answer," 1 *Georgetown Journal of Legal Ethics,* (1988), pp. 521, 543.

48. Lefstein, n. 47, p. 529.; n. 15, p. 523.

49. Resolution XV, David Hoffman, *A Course of Legal Study,*(Baltimore : published by Joseph Neal, 1836).

50. *Leviathan,* n. 7, p. 110.

51. (Vintage, 1962), pp. 42, 60.

52. Vol. I, p. 71 (Chicago: University of Chicago Press, 1979) [emphasis in original].

53. Stanley N. Katz, a prominent legal historian, calls the *Commentaries* "the most important legal treatise ever written in the English language . . . the dominant lawbook in England and America in the century after its publication." Id., p. iii.

54. 41 U.S., pp. 1–24 (1842).

55. 60 U.S., pp. 393–633.

56. Speech at Springfield, Illinois, June 26, 1857.

57. 304 U.S., pp. 64–92.

The Mystery of the Mind

The winner of the prize offered in last year's *GIT* for the best solution to the philosophical problem posed there, which was to explain, so far as possible, the evident inheritance by certain individuals of superior intellectual capacity, without asserting that the intellect itself is a material—i.e., genetically transmittable—entity, is Robert H. Kohn, of Scotts Valley, California. In fulfillment of the editor's promise, his essay is reprinted here, and he has been sent a set of *Great Books of the Western World*.

It is no disparagement of Mr. Kohn's effort to say that it is not entirely successful, in the editor's judgment, and that a certain mystery in the matter remains after he has said what he could say about it. The prize was awarded to him because he seemed to know best among those who submitted papers where the mystery begins, what we have to concede to it, and what (by virtue of what we know of hereditary mechanisms) we do not. That is as much as can be achieved, perhaps, at the present time, and with such knowledge as is available. It is not a solution or an answer in any final sense.

Other papers received—there were about thirty in all, of which half deserved serious consideration—illuminated partial aspects of the problem, and many of their authors showed, as he did, a gratifying familiarity with works in *GBWW*, which they used well. In any case, honorable mention should be made of Michael P. Allen, Roy P. Amatore, Dan Ferris, Alfred G. Holtum, Michael S. Talcott, and Max Weismann, and thanks are rendered to all who took the trouble to write something on the subject. Apologies are offered to readers in Australia whose copies of *GIT* arrived too late for them to meet the deadline for submissions.

Mind and Brain:
The Genius of Fortune

Robert H. Kohn

Robert Kohn is senior vice president and general counsel for Borland International, Inc., a leading developer of personal computer software. Mr. Kohn has been an avid reader of the *Great Books of the Western World* since his discovery of Mortimer Adler's *How to Read a Book* in 1974.

With his father Al Kohn, then vice president of licensing for Warner Brothers Music, Mr. Kohn has written *The Art of Music Licensing* (1992), a practical guide to granting licenses and obtaining permission to use copyrighted music. Father and son frequently lecture on the subject of licensing music and other copyrighted content for use in multimedia and new media information and entertainment products.

Prior to his association with Borland, Mr. Kohn was legal counsel for Candle Corporation, a leading developer of software for IBM mainframe computers, and for Ashton-Tate Corporation, a publisher of personal computer software. He is a graduate of Loyola Law School, Los Angeles, and has been a member of the California Bar since 1981. Born in New York City in 1957, Mr. Kohn now resides with his family in Pebble Beach, California.

Jesus, according to the Bible, [1] tells his followers a parable about a man who, before embarking on a long journey, called together his three servants and entrusted them with the greater part of his wealth. To the first servant, he gave five talents [2] of gold, to the second, two talents, and to the third, one talent. Upon his return several years later, he called upon his servants to deliver up the wealth which he had left to them. The first servant reported that he had made productive use of the five talents entrusted to him and thereupon returned ten talents to his master, who was so delighted with this good and faithful servant, he rewarded him. The second servant made a similar report and returned not only his original two talents, but an additional two which he had earned during his master's absence. The man was as delighted with this servant as he was with the first, and the second servant was similarly rewarded. The third servant reported that, because he had dug a hole in the ground and hid the one talent entrusted to him, he was only able to offer back to his master his one original talent. This report angered the man, who took the one talent from the servant, gave it to the first servant, and cast the slothful servant out of doors, where, according to Matthew, there was much gnashing of teeth.

T the *Parable of the Talents* is intended to warn even those with the meanest ability to use to the best advantage their God-given or natural "talents." We do commonly observe that some people appear to exercise more or less talent than others, and these differing degrees of talent among individuals vary from field to field—for example, some have a higher degree of talent in artistic creation, others in their power to solve problems in mathematics. Why is this so? Are these talents, as the parable may suggest, God-given, or is there some material explanation for varying degrees of artistic and intellectual abilities?

Our inquiry builds upon the *moderate immaterialistic* view of the relationship between the mind and body, a view articulated by Mortimer J. Adler in his book, *Intellect,* [3] and which may be summarized as follows: *The brain is a necessary, but not a sufficient condition of conceptual thought.* In other words, some immaterial substance (e.g., human soul, spirit, or intellect) is required for conceptual thought, but conceptual thought *depends upon* the operation of the material brain, without which we could not think conceptually. [4] Upon that, it is submitted that the difference in degree among humans in intellectual talent—a difference, when evident in one extreme, we call *gifted talent* or *genius*—has its basis in the *dependence* of conceptual thought upon the structure and operation of the material brain. Specifically, an intellectual talent springs from physical conditions in the brain that are disposed toward the exercise of that talent—the better those conditions, the better the talent is likely to be. The causes of these bodily dispositions are, paradoxically, both material and, in a sense, divine.

This inquiry will begin with a brief review of the ancient concept of the mind or soul of living things, including their rational and nonrational powers, followed by a brief discussion of the human potentialities, acquired habits and bodily dispositions that influence human behavior. Recent neuroscientific evidence is shown to be entirely consistent with the thinking of ancient and Middle Age philosophy. Finally, this essay concludes with some final thoughts on an important question raised by the consequences of the conclusion reached.

The mind—its nonrational and rational powers

Every living thing, believed Aristotle, possesses a soul and each soul has various kinds of powers. [5] Those animals that possess nutritive, sensitive, appetitive, imaginative, and "rememorative" powers use those powers to think *perceptually*—that is, using their senses they perceive real objects in the world, such as prey or predators, and by combining these senses with their other powers they are able to recognize similarities between a real object and a stored image remembered—a process which has been called *perceptual abstraction.* [6] To this perceptual abstraction the animal applies its appetitive powers to determine whether it should be attracted to the object or whether the object is to be avoided, and to act accordingly. The nature of an animal's appetitive power determines its behavior toward objects it perceives. Lower forms of animals, such as ants, bees, and other insects, have appetitive powers that are completely determined by *instinct,* an innate, preprogrammed pattern of behavior. Higher animals combine instinct with an ability to learn from experience. In both the lower and higher animals, "thinking" occurs merely on the perceptual level, using only the nutritive, sensitive, appetitive, imaginative, and rememorative powers, what the ancient Greeks would call the *nonrational* powers of the soul.

The souls of *human* animals, by contrast, consist of all of the foregoing *nonrational* powers, powers which are shared by many other animals, plus the *rational* powers, which only human souls possess. The rational, or higher, powers of the soul comprise the *cognitive* (i.e., the power of knowing or opining about real objects—things that are variable, such as things perceived by the senses), the *calculative* (i.e., the power to reason

263

or to make inferences), and the *conceptive* (i.e., the power to understand intelligible objects—things that are invariable, such as forms and ideas). These rational powers are used, together with our animalistic nonrational powers, to perform distinctly *human* thinking. The possession of these rational powers of the mind—which provides us with the ability to think *conceptually*, rather than just *perceptually*—is what distinguishes man from all other animals.

Potentiality

Perceptual experiences influence the appetitive behavior of all animals, but the appetitive behavior of all animals is not governed the same way. Although a nonhuman animal's appetitive power is governed by its instinct, the appetitive power of the *human* animal is governed by its rational powers. Humans have no instinct—no innate, preprogrammed patterns of behavior—to instruct the individual how to act. Instead, humans are endowed with what we call a *free will*, the potential to allow our rational powers to govern our appetitive desires, so that, even in the absence of a preprogrammed instinct to tell us what is really good for us, our reason may prompt a desire to perform those actions that are really good for us, including those actions which involve no physical pleasure to attract us or those for which we suffer some pain or discomfort.

The natural powers, or potentialities, of the human mind are the same in every human being, under all cultural conditions, at all times, and at all places. [7] Potentiality is like a tablet on which there is nothing actually written. [8] Thus, the *potential* to use our rational powers for our own good is something all humans have and have to the same degree—that is, every person is born with the same potential to use his or her cognitive, calculative, and conceptive powers. Nevertheless, there is a difference between *possessing* something and *using* it—as in the difference between *having the power* to think rationally and *actually exercising* the power. Accordingly, the degree to which a person's "talent" in the exercise of his or her rational powers varies from the talents of others derives not from our innately endowed, natural potentials, which all humans possess on an equal basis, but from something that affects each individual's *exercise* of his or her human potential. Thus, genius does not result from our equal powers or potentialities for rational thought—our immaterial, clean slate—but from something else.

Acquired habits

As noted, we use our rational powers to help govern the exercise of our appetitive powers—that is, we use our reason to govern our desires. [9] The proper governing of our desires is aided by the development of *virtues,* or good habits (and impeded by the development of *vices,* or bad habits). Habits are dispositions of our appetitive powers and are formed by the repetition of particular acts. Being formed by actions taken after we are alive, habits are not natural powers, but products of nurturing, and are influenced by such things as cultural conditions and the individual's social environment. Thus, a person may certainly acquire a "talent" through an acquired habit, such as taking piano lessons or practicing one's math drills.

It does not escape common observation, however, that certain individuals, though they may be the product of the same environment as others, such as a gifted child and his or her normal siblings, just seem better disposed than others to perform certain actions. Thus, mathematical, artistic, or other genius discovered in the very young cannot be explained solely by cultural conditions, social environment, or other factors that contribute to the development of good habits. In other words, genius does *not* appear to be an acquired habit.

Bodily dispositions

Genetic research has discovered that genius runs in families. Genes are physical causes. Thus, leaving aside acquired habits which may be employed to develop one's talents, the degrees to which the exercise of human talents vary from individual to individual appear to be physically, or materially, caused. If genius is materially determined, then it is not a product of the immaterial, natural powers of man. This is not to say that the exercise of genius is based in purely material operations: Genius involves the exercise of the immaterial powers of the mind; what is materially caused is the varying *degrees* to which individuals have the ability to exercise such immaterial powers.

Thus, there appears to be something *material* that underlies the virtuous exercise of human potential—some physical structure in our body, perhaps genetically determined, that is particularly conducive to the development of good habits or the exercise of what we call genius or gifted talent. Is this not what Aquinas suggested in his examination of the question, "*Whether one person can understand one and the same thing better than another can?*" [10] Experience shows, says Aquinas, that some understand more deeply than others, and in the following sentence, he suggests why this is so:

"[B]ecause some men have bodies of better disposition, their souls have a greater power of understanding."

Thus, the cause of superior intellectual talent appears to involve something else besides *natural powers,* or potentialities shared equally by all men, on the one hand, and *acquired habits,* the dispositions to act that we acquire by performing certain actions repeatedly, on the other. What's new here are dispositions that are neither natural nor acquired—dispositions that are in-born but *material* and which vary from individual to individual. We will call these, after Aquinas's suggestion, *bodily dispositions.*

Neuroscientific evidence

In pondering this material source of genius, it is useful to briefly review recent developments in neuroscience. Neuroscientists have been busily researching "the neural basis of mental phenomena." [11] These scientists estimate that a three to four pound human brain contains 100 billion nerve cells, called *neurons,* and believe that mental events can be correlated with patterns of nerve impulses in the brain. By studying how these neurons work, how they communicate with one another, how they are organized into local or distributed networks, and how the connections between neurons change with experience, these scientists believe that they can unlock the key to the "grand synthesis of mental life."

By research conducted through the observation of abnormalities in human sensory perception, combined with new tissue-staining techniques and the advent of the positron emission tomographer (i.e., a device which can measure increases in regional cerebral blood flow when people perform specific tasks), scientists have begun to discover that discrete areas of the brain specialize in certain sensory functions and work in parallel to accomplish particular tasks, such as vision. For example, the evidence suggests that the movement, color, and shape of an oncoming tennis ball are each processed in a different area of the brain. How this "parallel processing" works remains a mystery, but it is hoped that further research into the structure and composition of the brain will uncover some answers.

This research has already revealed a great diversity in the kinds of neurons found in the brain, including differences in their shape, molecular structure, and chemical composition. Some neurons have short axons, or tentacular arms, designed to communicate with neighboring neurons and others have long axons that project to other regions. At birth, the brain is only one-fourth of adult size. The brain grows in size because its neurons grow in size and the number of axons and extent of their connections increase. The development of neural connections within the brain as it grows can be compared with the process of stringing telephone lines between homes and between cities. [12] This massive "wiring" project is largely genetically determined, but genes seem to go only as far as sending the axons to the right "town." The hookups of axons to the right "addresses" is aided by molecular clues in the neurons, which can be influenced by external factors such as chemicals, hormones, and sensory stimulation. Thus, the specificity of synaptic connections that comes about during development of the brain is influenced not only by genetic factors, but also by a variety of other internal and external factors occurring during the growth of the brain while in the womb and during early childhood.

Brain structure and talent

Behavioral research is also beginning to reveal differences between individuals that cannot be explained by environmental or cultural factors. For example, recent evidence suggests that men and women differ in the way in which they solve perceptual problems: men tend to perform better than women on certain spatial tasks, and women tend to be better than men at rapidly identifying matching items. [13] Scientists are beginning to attribute these differences to the influence of sex hormones on the "wiring" or organization of the brain during its early stages of growth.

If factors such as genetic makeup, chemical balance, sex hormones, and sensory stimulation influence how the brain develops its specific structure, and if that structure plays a role in determining patterns of ability or talent in individuals, then was not Aquinas correct in his view that the souls of some men have a greater power of understanding, because of their "bodies of better disposition"? The evidence does seem to suggest that the structure and composition of the brain influences how well an individual is able to perform certain tasks, and this seems quite consistent with Aquinas's view of the matter as stated in the *Summa Theologica*:

> [O]ne may understand the same thing better than someone else, through having a greater power of understanding, just as a man may see a thing better with his bodily sight, whose power is greater, and whose sight is more perfect. [14]

Thus, it appears some may have a greater power of understanding than others by reason of a better disposition of the body. For example, actors, and those who are said to have "photographic memories," would seem to have brains disposed to the exercise of their rememorative powers, or potential to memorize, and recall on demand, lines of text, images, or other information. Of course, excellence in intellectual activities, such as art, acting, and calculating, can be created purely through the development of good habits, but no doubt, one who has the gift of bodily disposition toward a certain kind of intellectual activity would tend to out-perform those whose bodies are not similarly disposed toward that kind of activity.

Relationship between bodily dispositions and rational powers

Thus far, it has been suggested, if not reasonably established, that material conditions in the body affect our exercise of human potentialities. A key problem that must be addressed is whether material conditions in the body which affect intellectual thought do so by directly affecting our rational powers. For example, would a mathematical genius have a brain disposed to the superior exercise of his rational power of calculative thought, or do his superior calculative powers arise from conditions in the brain disposed to the exercise of some combination of nonrational powers, such as imaginative and rememorative? In other words, do material conditions in the body better dispose the mind for nutritive, sensitive, imaginative, and rememorative (nonrational) powers, which, being better disposed, aid the operation of the rational powers, or do material conditions in the body better dispose the rational powers directly?

Aquinas appears to have suggested that material conditions directly improve the exercise of *both* the nonrational and rational powers when he said that the effect of bodily dispositions applies to the intellect "in two ways": "First, as regards the *intellect itself* . . . [and] [s]econdly, this occurs in regard to the *lower powers* of which the intellect has need in its operation." [emphasis mine] Moreover, he says, "The intellect is that which most pertains to form in man." [15] What if neurological research suggested that even the understanding of form depends upon the material attributes of the brain? Consider the following passage:

> Blindsight patients are people who "see" but do not "understand."
> Because they are unaware of what they have seen, they have not
> acquired any knowledge. . . . [One such] patient has an extensive
> prestriate lesion [i.e., affecting the visual association cortex] from a
> stroke that has generally spared area V1 [i.e., the primary visual cortex].
> He can reproduce a sketch of St. Paul's Cathedral with greater skill
> than many normal people, although it takes him a great deal of time
> to do so. Yet this patient has no comprehension of what he has drawn.
> Because his V1 system is largely intact, he can identify the local elements
> of form, such as angles and simple shapes, and accurately copy the lines
> he sees and understands. The prestriate lesion, however, prevents him
> from integrating the lines into a complex whole and recognizing it as
> a building. [16]

It would appear that the patient's rational power of cognitive thought (i.e., the power of understanding real objects, things that are variable, such as things perceived by the senses) has been adversely affected by a material condition of the patient's brain. Of course, it could be said that this proves nothing—that a closer examination of the facts would reveal that merely perception, not rational understanding of invariable forms, is impeded by the patient's physical condition, in which case the answer may need await further neurological research.

Nevertheless, assuming that neuroscientific research has proven, or will soon prove, that our rational powers are directly affected by material conditions, does this suggest we must alter our assumption of the moderate immaterialistic view of the relationship between the mind and the brain? No. Intellect is only *potentially* the object of thought. [17] As Aristotle pointed out, potentiality is like that of the tablet on which there is nothing actually written. [18] In his work, *On the Soul,* the philosopher says,

> It was a good idea to call the soul the 'place of the forms,' though (1) this description holds only of the intellective soul, and (2) even this is the forms only *potentially, not actually.* [19] (emphasis mine)

We thus return to the important difference between possessing something and using it—between possessing our rational powers, which are merely potentialities, and the actual *exercise* of those powers. It is the *exercise* of our rational powers, not the mere *possession* of them, which depends upon the material brain as a necessary condition, and, as noted above, it is the actual exercise of our rational powers, not the mere possession of them potentially, which influences the degree to which an individual's talents vary from those of others. Nevertheless, because the immaterial potentiality—the empty tablet—remains a necessary condition of intellectual thought, a scientific finding that the recognition of forms, or any act of rational thinking, is influenced by the material condition of the brain is not inconsistent with the view that the possession of the necessary means of rational thought is purely immaterial. Accordingly, even if neuroscientific research successfully proves that our rational powers are directly affected by material conditions, the moderate immaterialistic view of the relationship between the mind and the brain stands unaffected.

The cause of superior intellectual power

The *material* cause [20] of a superior intellectual power (i.e., that out of which the superior power is made) is, as we have said, a physical structure of the body or brain well disposed to the exercise of that power. The exercise of intellectual power exhibits itself in a variety of talents and the particular talent is dependent on the particular structural and chemical composition of the brain. [21] The *formal cause* of superior intellectual power (i.e., that into which the power is made) is, of course, the product of the *exercise* of the power—the particular display of genius—in whatever form the variety of human genius may take.

The *efficient* cause of superior intellectual power (i.e., that by which the power is made) is, as noted, a confluence of nature and art: the internal genetic makeup of the individual and external material factors (some of which are man-made) that influence the structure, chemical composition, and operation of the brain during its early development. Yet, there appears to be an additional factor influencing the degree of intellectual talent in an individual, and that is chance, or Fortune. As noted, parents who have certain gene structures may combine to produce offspring with brains conducive to genius. The environment into which one is born is, or certainly appears to be, entirely determined by fortuity. Moreover, neuroscientists may well find that Fortune—a goddess they may prefer to call *randomness*—may even play a considerable role in the development of the brain, as the wiring of a billion neurons guided by "molecular clues"—like the development of a crystal into one of a seemingly infinite variety of structures—would appear to leave to chance a material role to play in the development of genius.

But is the notion that chance plays a role in superior intellectual power a reasonable one? "There is no incompatibility whatsoever," says Adler, "between the presence of chance, randomness, and contingency in the cosmos and God's creation of it (and presumably, gift to man of conceptual thought)." [22] The structure of all human brains is substantially similar, but as the film director Cecil B. DeMille once said, "God is in the details."

Final thoughts

Not every human develops the material bodily conditions that are well disposed to the exercise of human genius. However, if these conditions are material, as suggested, it would appear that man does have the capacity to create or modify those conditions, through genetic and pharmaceutical research. If neuroscience succeeds in understanding the structural and chemical composition of the brain and discovering techniques to artificially enhance the conditions that underlie human genius, then we will be forced to make a prescriptive judgment about whether we *should* use this knowledge to engineer genius in coming generations—the development of what marketers might call *designer kids*.

In considering that question, we would need look no further than to the *final cause* (i.e., the purpose) of superior intellectual power. Whether we determine that final cause to be the discovery of truth, the performance of virtuous acts, or just plain contemplation, it is clear that the improvement of our intellectual capabilities, essential to all three of these pursuits, would serve the end of intellectual power. Would we not be justified in improving human contemplation itself, what Aristotle called the highest form of activity, an activity which is appreciated for its own sake? [23]   As noted at the outset, the *Parable of the Talents* warns even those with the meanest ability to use to the best advantage their natural talents. If, therefore, through scientific inquiry we can find a way to improve our bodily dispositions to improve our powers of conceptual thought, it appears, from sources both reasonable and divine, that we should do so. But prudently.

> "What is a man,
> If his chief good and market of his time
> Be but to sleep and feed? a beast, no more.
> Sure, he that made us with such large discourse,
> Looking before and after, gave us not
> That capability and god-like reason
> To fust in us unused."

> Shakespeare, *Hamlet*
> (*GBWW* I: 27, 59; II: 25, 59)

---

1. Matt. 25: 14–30.

2. According to Dr. Samuel Johnson's *Dictionary*, "1. A talent signified so much weight or a sum of money, the value differing according to the differing ages and countries. . . . 2. Faculty, power, gift of nature. A metaphor borrowed from the talents mentioned in the holy writ." Samuel Johnson, LL.D, *A Dictionary of the English Language*, 8th Edition (London: J. Johnson, 1799).

3. *See* Mortimer J. Adler, *Intellect: Mind over Matter* (New York: Macmillan Publishing Co., 1990), pp. 41–53.

4. The concept of *thinking conceptually* encompasses all the rational powers described below.

5. *See*, generally, Aristotle, *On the Soul* (*GBWW* I: 8, 631–68; II: 7, 631–68) For example, Aristotle believed that plants have souls, the powers of which may be summarized as follows: the *nutritive* (i.e., the power to take in nutrition and grow), the *sensitive* (i.e., the power to use certain senses, such as touch, to perceive real objects in the world) and the *appetitive* (i.e., the power to desire, which compels them to seek nourishment, such as by facing the sun and sprouting roots in the direction of water). The souls of higher forms of life have those powers, plus some additional powers. Some animals, in addition to the sensitive power of touch shared by plants, possess the sensitive powers of sight, hearing, smell, and taste. Many animals which possess these additional senses also possess higher powers, such as the *imaginative* (i.e., the power to grasp images in the mind without the physical presence of image) and the *rememorative* (i.e., the power to store and recall images). The foregoing description of the nonrational powers, and that of the rational powers set forth in the text, are intended to differ in name only from the descriptions set forth in Adler's *Intellect*, merely for the purpose of simplifying the discussion.

6. Adler, *Intellect*, pp. 34, 36, 57–60.

7. Ibid., p. 136.

8. Aristotle, *On the Soul* (*GBWW* I: 8, 661–62; II: 7, 661–62).

9. Our desires are governed properly when we act upon *right desires*. *See* Mortimer J. Adler, *Desires, Right and Wrong* (New York: Macmillan Publishing Co., 1991).

10. Aquinas, *Summa Theologica* (*GBWW* I: 19, 459–60; II: 17, 459–60).

11. Gerald D. Fischbach, "Mind and Brain," 267 *Scientific American* (September 1992), p. 48.

12. Carla J. Shatz, "The Developing Brain," 267 *Scientific American* (September 1992), pp. 62–63.

13. Doreen Kimura, "Sex Differences and the Brain," 267 *Scientific American* (September 1992), p. 119.

14. Aquinas, *Summa Theologica* (*GBWW* I: 19, 460; II: 17, 460). *See also*, Aristotle, *On the Soul*, (*GBWW* I: 8, 642; II: 7, 642). If an eye were an animal, its soul would be vision.

Thus, just as vision is better with the better formed eye, the powers of the soul are better with a better formed brain.

15. Aquinas, *Summa Theologica* (*GBWW* I: 19, 459–60; II: 17, 459–60).

16. Semir Zeki, "The Visual Image in Mind and Brain," 267 *Scientific American* (September 1992), p. 74.

17. Aristotle, *On the Soul* (*GBWW* I: 8, 661–62; II: 7, 661–62).

18. Id.

19. Aristotle, *On the Soul* (*GBWW* I: 8, 661; II: 7, 661).

20. Aristotle's doctrine of the "four causes"—material, formal, efficient and final—may be found in Aristotle, *Metaphysics* (*see*, for example, Book I, chaps. 3–10) [*GBWW* I: 8, 501–11; II: 7, 501–11].

21. The disposition of some bodies toward the exercise of artistic talent and others toward talent in mathematics may be likened to the structure and composition of computer semiconductor chips: some chips are structured specifically for enhanced graphical capabilities, some for rapid numerical calculations.

22. Adler, "Natural Theology, Chance, and God" (*GIT* 1992, 298–99).

23. Aristotle, *Ethics* (*GBWW* I: 9, 430–32; II: 8, 430–32).

PART FOUR

Additions
to the
Great Books Library

English Traits

Ralph Waldo Emerson

Editor's Introduction

America was still new or something strange to European travelers of the nineteenth century, who wrote books describing what they found there—the life, the institutions, and the character of the people. Toqueville's *Democracy in America* (*GBWW* II: 44, discussed elsewhere in this issue of *GIT*) is no doubt the greatest of these works. Comparable in range was Lord Bryce's *The American Commonwealth* (1888). Of hated memory was *Domestic Manners of the Americans* (1832) by Frances Trollope, mother of the great English novelist, who based her unflattering report on an interval she had spent in frontier Cincinnati.

Few American accounts of Europe in those days were of comparable importance, unless we include the novels, say, of Henry James, which were not on purpose documentary. Books that were, inevitably revealed more about their provincial authors than they did about the "foreign" nations they described, based as mostly they were upon brief visits and intended for compatriots who had never been abroad. An exception was Ralph Waldo Emerson's *English Traits,* a book not about England itself but the British people, which was, and is, a classic of its kind.

Emerson ought not to have liked the English, least transcendent of all races, and indeed there was much about them that was alien to him. But he saw their virtues as well as their defects, and on balance he found that he respected them, masters of the world as in that century they seemed to be. They were as prodigious in his estimation as they were perverse, or at least limited—but even their limitations, indeed especially their limitations, were striking to him and mostly admirable. One senses the pleasure this gave him even when it seemed absurd.

He went abroad twice himself, notwithstanding his belief that "the wise man stays at home" looking to himself for inspiration, and both times he visited England. The first occasion was in 1832, when he was 29. He had just resigned from the Unitarian ministry for which his education had prepared him—resigned because, after reading new biblical criticism and being unable to accept the historicity of miracles, he found himself opposed to basic tenets of Christian doctrine and could only give sermons supporting private intuition of the moral law as the basis of a virtuous life, which neither required Christianity nor allowed it.

of coal in the island is also felt in modifying the general climate.

Factitious climate, factitious position. England resembles a ship in its shape, and if it were one, its best admiral could not have worked it or anchored it in a more judicious or effective position. Sir John Herschel said, "London is the center of the terrene globe." The shopkeeping nation, to use a shop word, has a *good stand.* The old Venetians pleased themselves with the flattery that Venice was in 45°, midway between the poles and the line; as if that were an imperial centrality. Long of old, the Greeks fancied Delphi the navel of the earth, in their favorite mode of fabling the earth to be an animal. The Jews believed Jerusalem to be the center. I have seen a kratometric chart designed to show that the city of Philadelphia was in the same thermic belt, and by inference in the same belt of empire, as the cities of Athens, Rome and London. It was drawn by a patriotic Philadelphian, and was examined with pleasure, under his showing, by the inhabitants of Chestnut Street. But when carried to Charleston, to New Orleans and to Boston, it somehow failed to convince the ingenious scholars of all those capitals.

But England is anchored at the side of Europe, and right in the heart of the modern world. The sea, which, according to Virgil's famous line, divided the poor Britons utterly from the world, proved to be the ring of marriage with all nations. It is not down in the books—it is written only in the geologic strata—that fortunate day when a wave of the German Ocean burst the old isthmus which joined Kent and Cornwall to France, and gave to this fragment of Europe its impregnable seawall, cutting off an island of eight hundred miles in length, with an irregular breadth reaching to three hundred miles; a territory large enough for independence, enriched with every seed of national power, so near that it can see the harvests of the continent, and so far that who would

cross the strait must be an expert mariner, ready for tempests. As America, Europe and Asia lie, these Britons have precisely the best commercial position in the whole planet, and are sure of a market for all the goods they can manufacture. And to make these advantages avail, the river Thames must dig its spacious outlet to the sea from the heart of the kingdom, giving road and landing to innumerable ships, and all the conveniency to trade that a people so skilful and sufficient in economizing waterfront by docks, warehouses and lighters required. When James the First declared his purpose of punishing London by removing his Court, the Lord Mayor replied that "in removing his royal presence from his lieges, they hoped he would leave them the Thames."

In the variety of surface, Britain is a miniature of Europe, having plain, forest, marsh, river, seashore; mines in Cornwall; caves in Matlock and Derbyshire; delicious landscape in Dovedale, delicious sea-view at Tor Bay, Highlands in Scotland, Snowdon in Wales, and in Westmoreland and Cumberland a pocket Switzerland, in which the lakes and mountains are on a sufficient scale to fill the eye and touch the imagination. It is a nation conveniently small. Fontenelle thought that nature had sometimes a little affectation; and there is such an artificial completeness in this nation of artificers as if there were a design from the beginning to elaborate a bigger Birmingham. Nature held counsel with herself and said, "My Romans are gone. To build my new empire, I will choose a rude race, all masculine, with brutish strength. I will not grudge a competition of the roughest males. Let buffalo gore buffalo, and the pasture to the strongest. For I have work that requires the best will and sinew. Sharp and temperate northern breezes shall blow, to keep that will alive and alert. The sea shall disjoin the people from others, and knit them to a fierce nationality. It shall give them markets on every side. Long time I will keep them on their feet, by

Editor's Introduction

America was still new or something strange to European travelers of the nineteenth century, who wrote books describing what they found there—the life, the institutions, and the character of the people. Toqueville's *Democracy in America* (*GBWW* II: 44, discussed elsewhere in this issue of *GIT*) is no doubt the greatest of these works. Comparable in range was Lord Bryce's *The American Commonwealth* (1888). Of hated memory was *Domestic Manners of the Americans* (1832) by Frances Trollope, mother of the great English novelist, who based her unflattering report on an interval she had spent in frontier Cincinnati.

Few American accounts of Europe in those days were of comparable importance, unless we include the novels, say, of Henry James, which were not on purpose documentary. Books that were, inevitably revealed more about their provincial authors than they did about the "foreign" nations they described, based as mostly they were upon brief visits and intended for compatriots who had never been abroad. An exception was Ralph Waldo Emerson's *English Traits,* a book not about England itself but the British people, which was, and is, a classic of its kind.

Emerson ought not to have liked the English, least transcendent of all races, and indeed there was much about them that was alien to him. But he saw their virtues as well as their defects, and on balance he found that he respected them, masters of the world as in that century they seemed to be. They were as prodigious in his estimation as they were perverse, or at least limited—but even their limitations, indeed especially their limitations, were striking to him and mostly admirable. One senses the pleasure this gave him even when it seemed absurd.

He went abroad twice himself, notwithstanding his belief that "the wise man stays at home" looking to himself for inspiration, and both times he visited England. The first occasion was in 1832, when he was 29. He had just resigned from the Unitarian ministry for which his education had prepared him—resigned because, after reading new biblical criticism and being unable to accept the historicity of miracles, he found himself opposed to basic tenets of Christian doctrine and could only give sermons supporting private intuition of the moral law as the basis of a virtuous life, which neither required Christianity nor allowed it.

In England he looked up chiefly literary figures, calling upon Samuel Taylor Coleridge, William Wordsworth, and Thomas Carlyle. He admired Coleridge for his belief in the imagination as the force by which we bring together our intuitions and our ideas about the material world, a notion Emerson himself was groping for. Wordsworth was of course the great English poet of the day and another apostle of the imagination. Carlyle was younger, Emerson's contemporary, a scorner of Christianity himself, and a champion of the heroic soul; the two men took to one another at once and remained epistolary friends for many years.

A second English visit came later, in 1847, when Emerson had become a celebrated figure in his own right. This time, instead of going to see famous men, they came to see him, or at least he had audiences (including Carlyle, who rarely listened to anyone) for the lectures he gave in London and elsewhere. He also had social engagements, went to dinner parties, and was otherwise feted and made over. It was the experience of this trip, combined with the knowledge gained by a lifetime of reading, that went into *English Traits,* a book that appeared only in 1856, eight years after he returned home. By then he had had an opportunity to think about the contrary feelings of attraction and repulsion he had for his subject—the conflict in his own mind between his belief in solitude and the self-sufficient life, on the one hand, and his honest recognition that the society of interesting men and women could be stimulating even if he disapproved of it. He saw that this was at odds with what he had expected. For it was the strength of character in the English, their be-damned-with-everyone-else independence, that attracted him, along with their vigor and certainty of mind—qualities he did not find in his own countrymen. And he felt that it ought to have been the other way around.

English Traits, which Carlyle called "a book by a real *man,* with eyes in his head; nobleness, vision, humor, and many other things, in the heart of him," is reprinted here in the main, but with one chapter, called "Literature" left out, it being mostly about books that have ceased to matter with the passing of the Victorian world.

English Traits

Land

Alfieri thought Italy and England the only countries worth living in; the former because there Nature vindicates her rights and triumphs over the evils inflicted by the governments; the latter because art conquers nature and transforms a rude, ungenial land into a paradise of comfort and plenty. England is a garden. Under an ash-colored sky, the fields have been combed and rolled till they appear to have been finished with a pencil instead of a plough. The solidity of the structures that compose the towns speaks the industry of ages. Nothing is left as it was made. Rivers, hills, valleys, the sea itself, feel the hand of a master. The long habitation of a powerful and ingenious race has turned every rood of land to its best use, has found all the capabilities, the arable soil, the quarriable rock, the highways, the byways, the fords, the navigable waters; and the new arts of intercourse meet you everywhere; so that England is a huge phalanstery, where all that man wants is provided within the precinct. Cushioned and comforted in every manner, the traveler rides as on a cannon-ball, high and low, over rivers and towns, through mountains in tunnels of three or four miles, at near twice the speed of our trains; and reads quietly the *Times* newspaper, which, by its immense correspondence and reporting seems to have machinized the rest of the world for his occasion.

The problem of the traveler landing at Liverpool is, Why England is England? What are the elements of that power which the English hold over other nations? If there be one test of national genius universally accepted, it is success; and if there be one successful country in the universe for the last millennium, that country is England.

A wise traveler will naturally choose to visit the best of actual nations; and an American has more reasons than another to draw him to Britain. In all that is done or begun by the Americans towards right thinking or practice, we are met by a civilization already settled and overpowering. The culture of the day, the thoughts and aims of men, are English thoughts and aims. A nation considerable for a thousand years since Egbert, it has, in the last centuries, obtained the ascendant, and stamped the knowledge, activity and power of mankind with its impress. Those who resist it do not feel it or obey it less. The Russian in his snows is aiming to be English. The Turk and Chinese also are making awkward efforts to be English. The practical common-sense of modern society, the utilitarian direction which labor, laws, opinion, religion take, is the natural genius of the British mind. The influence of France is a constituent of modern civility, but not enough opposed to the English for the most wholesome effect. The American is only the continuation of the English genius into new conditions, more or less propitious.

See what books fill our libraries. Every book we read, every biography, play, romance, in whatever form, is still English history and manners. So that a sensible Englishman once said to me, "As long as you do not grant us copyright, we shall have the teaching of you."

But we have the same difficulty in making a social or moral estimate of England,

277

that the sheriff finds in drawing a jury to try some cause which has agitated the whole community and on which everybody finds himself an interested party. Officers, jurors, judges have all taken sides. England has inoculated all nations with her civilization, intelligence and tastes; and to resist the tyranny and prepossession of the British element, a serious man must aid himself by comparing with it the civilizations of the farthest east and west, the old Greek, the Oriental, and, much more, the ideal standard; if only by means of the very impatience which English forms are sure to awaken in independent minds.

Besides, if we will visit London, the present time is the best time, as some signs portend that it has reached its highest point. It is observed that the English interest us a little less within a few years; and hence the impression that the British power has culminated, is in solstice, or already declining.

As soon as you enter England, which, with Wales, is no larger than the State of Georgia, this little land stretches by an illusion to the dimensions of an empire. The innumerable details, the crowded succession of towns, cities, cathedrals, castles and great and decorated estates, the number and power of the trades and guilds, the military strength and splendor, the multitudes of rich and of remarkable people, the servants and equipages—all these catching the eye and never allowing it to pause, hide all boundaries by the impression of magnificence and endless wealth.

I reply to all the urgencies that refer me to this and that object indispensably to be seen—Yes, to see England well needs a hundred years; for what they told me was the merit of Sir John Soane's Museum, in London—that it was well packed and well saved—is the merit of England; it is stuffed full, in all corners and crevices, with towns, towers, churches, villas, palaces, hospitals and charity-houses. In the history of art it is a long way from a cromlech to York minster; yet all the intermediate steps may still be traced in this all-preserving island.

The territory has a singular perfection. The climate is warmer by many degrees than it is entitled to by latitude. Neither hot nor cold, there is no hour in the whole year when one cannot work. Here is no winter, but such days as we have in Massachusetts in November, a temperature which makes no exhausting demand on human strength, but allows the attainment of the largest stature. Charles the Second said "It invited men abroad more days in the year and more hours in the day than another country." Then England has all the materials of a working country except wood. The constant rain—a rain with every tide, in some parts of the island—keeps its multitude of rivers full and brings agricultural production up to the highest point. It has plenty of water, of stone, of potter's clay, of coal, of salt and of iron. The land naturally abounds with game; immense heaths and downs are paved with quails, grouse and woodcock, and the shores are animated by water birds. The rivers and the surrounding sea spawn with fish; there are salmon for the rich and sprats and herrings for the poor. In the northern lochs, the herring are in innumerable shoals; at one season, the country people say, the lakes contain one part water and two parts fish.

The only drawback on this industrial conveniency is the darkness of its sky. The night and day are too nearly of a color. It strains the eyes to read and to write. Add the coal smoke. In the manufacturing towns, the fine soot or *blacks* darken the day, give white sheep the color of black sheep, discolor the human saliva, contaminate the air, poison many plants and corrode the monuments and buildings.

The London fog aggravates the distempers of the sky, and sometimes justifies the epigram on the climate by an English wit, "in a fine day, looking up a chimney; in a foul day, looking down one." A gentleman in Liverpool told me that he found he could do without a fire in his parlor about one day in the year. It is however pretended that the enormous consumption

"The constant rain—a rain with every tide, in some parts of the island—keeps its multitude of rivers full and brings agricultural production up to the highest point."

centuries of churching and civilizing have not been able to sweeten. Alfieri said "the crimes of Italy were the proof of the superiority of the stock"; and one may say of England that this watch moves on a splinter of adamant. The English uncultured are a brutal nation. The crimes recorded in their calendars leave nothing to be desired in the way of cold malignity. Dear to the English heart is a fair stand-up fight. The brutality of the manners in the lower class appears in the boxing, bear-baiting, cock-fighting, love of executions, and in the readiness for a set-to in the streets, delightful to the English of all classes. The costermongers of London streets hold cowardice in loathing—"we must work our fists well; we are all handy with our fists." The public schools are charged with being bear-gardens of brutal strength, and are liked by the people for that cause. The fagging is a trait of the same quality. Medwin, in the *Life of Shelley,* relates that at a military school they rolled up a young man in a snowball, and left him so in his room while the other cadets went to church—and crippled him for life. They have retained impressment, deck-flogging, army-flogging and school-flogging. Such is the ferocity of the army discipline that a soldier, sentenced to flogging, sometimes prays that his sentence may be commuted to death. Flogging, banished from the armies of Western Europe, remains here by the sanction of the Duke of Wellington. The right of the husband to sell the wife has been retained down to our times. The Jews have been the favorite victims of royal and popular persecution. Henry III mortgaged all the Jews in the kingdom to his brother the Earl of Cornwall, as security for money which he borrowed. The torture of criminals, and the rack for extorting evidence, were slowly disused. Of the criminal statutes, Sir Samuel Romilly said: "I have examined the codes of all nations, and ours is the worst, and worthy of the Anthropophagi." In the last session (1848), the House of Commons was listening to the details of flogging and torture practiced in the jails.

As soon as this land, thus geographically posted, got a hardy people into it, they could not help becoming the sailors and factors of the globe. From childhood, they dabbled in water, they swam like fishes, their playthings were boats. In the case of the ship-money, the judges delivered it for law, that "England being an island, the very midland shires therein are all to be accounted maritime"; and Fuller adds, "the genius even of landlocked counties driving the natives with a maritime dexterity." As early as the conquest it is remarked, in explanation of the wealth of England, that its merchants trade to all countries.

The English at the present day have great vigor of body and endurance. Other countrymen look slight and undersized beside them, and invalids. They are bigger men than the Americans. I suppose a hundred English taken at random out of the street would weigh a fourth more than so many Americans. Yet, I am told, the skeleton is not larger. They are round, ruddy, and handsome; at least the whole bust is well formed, and there is a tendency to stout and powerful frames. I remarked the stoutness on my first landing at Liverpool; porter, drayman, coachman, guard—what substantial, respectable, grandfatherly figures, with costume and manners to suit. The American has arrived at the old mansion-house and finds himself among uncles, aunts and grandsires. The pictures on the chimney tiles of his nursery were pictures of these people. Here they are in the identical costumes and air which so took him.

It is the fault of their forms that they grow stocky, and the women have that disadvantage—few tall, slender figures of flowing shape, but stunted and thickset persons. The French say that the English-women have two left hands. But in all ages they are a handsome race. The bronze monuments of crusaders lying cross-legged in the Temple Church at London, and those in Worcester and in Salisbury Cathedrals, which are seven hundred years old, are of the same type as the best youthful heads of men now in England—please by beauty of the same character, an expression blending good nature, valor and refinement, and mainly by that uncorrupt youth in the face of manhood, which is daily seen in the streets of London.

Both branches of the Scandinavian race are distinguished for beauty. The anecdote of the handsome captives which Saint Gregory found at Rome, A.D. 600, is matched by the testimony of the Norman chroniclers, five centuries later, who wondered at the beauty and long flowing hair of the young English captives. Meantime the *Heimskringla* has frequent occasion to speak of the personal beauty of its heroes. When it is considered what humanity, what resources of mental and moral power the traits of the blond race betoken, its accession to empire marks a new and finer epoch, wherein the old mineral force shall be subjugated at last by humanity and shall plough in its furrow henceforward. It is not a final race, once a crab always crab—but a race with a future.

On the English face are combined decision and nerve with the fair complexion, blue eyes and open and florid aspect. Hence the love of truth, hence the sensibility, the fine perception and poetic construction. The fair Saxon man, with open front and honest meaning, domestic, affectionate, is not the wood out of which cannibal, or inquisitor, or assassin is made, but he is molded for law, lawful trade, civility, marriage, the nurture of children, for colleges, churches, charities and colonies.

They are rather manly than warlike. When the war is over, the mask falls from the affectionate and domestic tastes, which make them women in kindness. This union of qualities is fabled in their national legend of *Beauty and the Beast*, or, long before, in the Greek legend of Hermaphrodite. The two sexes are co-present in the English mind. I apply to Britannia, queen of seas and colonies, the words in which her latest novelist portrays his heroine; "She is as mild as she is game, and as game as she is mild." The English delight in the antagonism which combines in one person the extremes of courage and tenderness. Nelson, dying at Trafalgar, sends his love to Lord Collingwood, and like an innocent schoolboy that goes to bed, says "Kiss me, Hardy," and turns to sleep. Lord Collingwood, his comrade, was of a nature the most affectionate and domestic. Admiral Rodney's figure approached to delicacy and effeminacy, and he declared himself very sensible to fear, which he surmounted only by considerations of honor and public duty. Clarendon says the Duke of Buckingham was so modest and gentle, that some courtiers attempted to put affronts on him, until they found that this modesty and effeminacy was only a mask for the most terrible determination. And Sir Edward Parry said of Sir John Franklin, that "if he found Wellington Sound open, he explored it; for he was a man who never turned his back on a danger, yet of that tenderness that he would not brush away a mosquito." Even for their highwaymen the same virtue is claimed, and Robin Hood comes described to us as *mitissimus proedonum;* the gentlest thief. But they know where their wardogs lie. Cromwell, Blake, Marlborough, Chatham, Nelson and Wellington are not to be trifled with, and the brutal strength which lies at the bottom of society, the animal ferocity of the quays and cockpits, the bullies of the costermongers of Shoreditch, Seven Dials and Spitalfields, they know how to wake up.

They have a vigorous health and last well into middle and old age. The old men are as red as roses, and still handsome. A clear skin, a peach-bloom complexion and good teeth are found all over the island. They use a plentiful and nutritious diet. The operative cannot subsist on water cresses. Beef, mutton, wheat-bread and malt-liquors are universal among the first-class laborers. Good feeding is a chief point of national pride among the vulgar, and in their caricatures they represent the Frenchman as a poor, starved body. It is curious that Tacitus found the English beer already in use among the Germans: "They make from barley or wheat a drink corrupted into some resemblance to wine." Lord Chief Justice Fortescue, in Henry VI's time, says "The inhabitants of England drink no water, unless at certain times on a religious score and by way of penance." The extremes of poverty and ascetic penance, it would seem, never reach cold water in England. Wood the antiquary, in describing the poverty and maceration of Father Lacey, an English Jesuit, does not deny him beer. He says: "His bed was under a thatching, and the way to it up a ladder; his fare was coarse; his drink, of a penny a gawn, or gallon."

They have more constitutional energy than any other people. They think, with Henri Quatre, that manly exercises are the foundation of that elevation of mind which gives one nature ascendant over another; or with the Arabs, that the days spent in the chase are not counted in the length of life. They box, run, shoot, ride, row, and sail from pole to pole. They eat and drink, and live jolly in the open air, putting a bar of solid sleep between day and day. They walk and ride as fast as they can, their head bent forward, as if urged on some pressing affair. The French say that Englishmen in the street always walk straight before them like mad dogs. Men and women walk with infatuation. As soon as he can handle a gun, hunting is the fine art of every Englishman of condition. They are the most voracious people of prey that ever existed. Every season turns out the aristocracy into the country to shoot and fish. The more vigorous run out of the island to America, to Asia, to Africa and Australia, to hunt with fury by gun, by trap, by harpoon, by lasso, with dog, with horse, with elephant or with dromedary, all the game that is in nature. These men have written the game-books of all countries, as Hawker, Scrope, Murray, Herbert, Maxwell, Cumming, and

a host of travelers. The people at home are addicted to boxing, running, leaping and rowing matches.

I suppose the dogs and horses must be thanked for the fact that the men have muscles almost as tough and supple as their own. If in every efficient man there is first a fine animal, in the English race it is of the best breed, a wealthy, juicy, broad-chested creature, steeped in ale and good cheer and a little overloaded by his flesh. Men of animal nature rely, like animals, on their instincts. The Englishman associates well with dogs and horses. His attachment to the horse arises from the courage and address required to manage it. The horse finds out who is afraid of it, and does not disguise its opinion. Their young boiling clerks and lusty collegians like the company of horses better than the company of professors. I suppose the horses are better company for them. The horse has more uses than Buffon noted. If you go into the streets, every driver in bus or dray is a bully, and if I wanted a good troop of soldiers, I should recruit among the stables. Add a certain degree of refinement to the vivacity of these riders, and you obtain the precise quality which makes the men and women of polite society formidable.

They come honestly by their horsemanship, with Hengst and Horsa for their Saxon founders. The other branch of their race had been Tartar nomads. The horse was all their wealth. The children were fed on mares' milk. The pastures of Tartary were still remembered by the tenacious practice of the Norsemen to eat horseflesh at religious feasts. In the Danish invasions the marauders seized upon horses where they landed, and were at once converted into a body of expert cavalry.

At one time this skill seems to have declined. Two centuries ago the English horse never performed any eminent service beyond the seas; and the reason assigned was that the genius of the English hath always more inclined them to foot-service, as pure and proper manhood, without any

"syllogisms do breed or rather are all the variety of man's life. They are the steps by which we walk in all our businesses. Man, as he is man, doth nothing else but weave such chains. Whatsoever he doth, swerving from this work, he doth as deficient from the nature of man: and, if he do aught beyond this, by breaking out into divers sorts of exterior actions, he findeth, nevertheless, in this linked sequel of simple discourses, the art, the cause, the rule, the bounds and the model of it."

There spoke the genius of the English people. There is a necessity on them to be logical. They would hardly greet the good that did not logically fall—as if it excluded their own merit, or shook their understandings. They are jealous of minds that have much facility of association, from an instinctive fear that the seeing many relations to their thought might impair this serial continuity and lucrative concentration. They are impatient of genius, or of minds addicted to contemplation, and cannot conceal their contempt for sallies of thought, however lawful, whose steps they cannot count by their wonted rule. Neither do they reckon better a syllogism that ends in syllogism. For they have a supreme eye to facts, and theirs is a logic that brings salt to soup, hammer to nail, oar to boat; the logic of cooks, carpenters and chemists, following the sequence of nature, and one on which words make no impression. Their mind is not dazzled by its own means, but locked and bolted to results. They love men who, like Samuel Johnson, a doctor in the schools, would jump out of his syllogism the instant his major proposition was in danger, to save that at all hazards. Their practical vision is spacious, and they can hold many threads without entangling them. All the steps they orderly take; but with the high logic of never confounding the minor and major proposition; keeping their eye on their aim, in all the complicity and delay incident to the several series of means they employ. There is room in their minds for this and that—a science of degrees. In the courts the independence of the judges and the loyalty of the suitors are equally excellent. In Parliament they have hit on that capital invention of freedom, a constitutional opposition. And when courts and parliament are both deaf, the plaintiff is not silenced. Calm, patient, his weapon of defence from year to year is the obstinate reproduction of the grievance, with calculations and estimates. But, meantime, he is drawing numbers and money to his opinion, resolved that if all remedy fails, right of revolution is at the bottom of his charterbox. They are bound to see their measure carried, and stick to it through ages of defeat.

Into this English logic, however, an infusion of justice enters, not so apparent in other races—a belief in the existence of two sides, and the resolution to see fair play. There is on every question an appeal from the assertion of the parties to the proof of what is asserted. They kiss the dust before a fact. Is it a machine, is it a charter, is it a boxer in the ring, is it a candidate on the hustings—the universe of Englishmen will suspend their judgment until the trial can be had. They are not to be led by a phrase, they want a working plan, a working machine, a working constitution, and will sit out the trial and abide by the issue and reject all preconceived theories. In politics they put blunt questions, which must be answered; Who is to pay the taxes? What will you do for trade? What for corn? What for the spinner?

This singular fairness and its results strike the French with surprise. Philip de Commines says, "Now, in my opinion, among all the sovereignties I know in the world, that in which the public good is best attended to, and the least violence exercised on the people, is that of England." Life is safe, and personal rights; and what is freedom without security? whilst, in France, "fraternity," "equality," and "indivisible unity" are names for assassination. Montesquieu said, "England is the freest country in the world. If a man in England had as many enemies as hairs on his head, no harm would happen to him."

Their self-respect, their faith in causation, and their realistic logic or coupling of means to ends, have given them the leadership of the modern world. Montesquieu said, "No people have true common sense but those who are born in England." This common sense is a preception of all the conditions of our earthly existence; of laws that can be stated, and of laws that cannot be stated, or that are learned only by practice, in which allowance for friction is made. They are impious in their skepticism of theory, and in high departments they are cramped and sterile. But the unconditional surrender to facts, and the choice of means to reach their ends, are as admirable as with ants and bees.

The bias of the nation is a passion for utility. They love the lever, the screw and pulley, the Flanders draught-horse, the waterfall, windmills, tidemills; the sea and the wind to bear their freight ships. More than the diamond Koh-i-noor, which glitters among their crown jewels, they prize that dull pebble which is wiser than a man, whose poles turn themselves to the poles of the world and whose axis is parallel to the axis of the world. Now, their toys are steam and galvanism. They are heavy at the fine arts, but adroit at the coarse; not good in jewelry or mosaics, but the best ironmasters, colliers, woolcombers and tanners in Europe. They apply themselves to agriculture, to draining, to resisting encroachments of sea, wind, traveling sands, cold and wet subsoil; to fishery, to manufacture of indispensable staples—salt, plumbago, leather, wool, glass, pottery and brick—to bees and silkworms—and by their steady combinations they succeed. A manufacturer sits down to dinner in a suit of clothes which was wool on a sheep's back at sunrise. You dine with a gentleman on venison, pheasant, quail, pigeons, poultry, mushrooms and pineapples, all the growth of his estate. They are neat husbands for ordering all their tools pertaining to house and field.

All are well kept. There is no want and no waste. They study use and fitness in their building, in the order of their dwellings and in their dress. The Frenchman invented the ruffle; the Englishman added the shirt. The Englishman wears a sensible coat buttoned to the chin, of rough but solid and lasting texture. If he is a lord, he dresses a little worse than a commoner. They have diffused the taste for plain substantial hats, shoes and coats through Europe. They think him the best-dressed man whose dress is so fit for his use that you cannot notice or remember to describe it.

They secure the essentials in their diet, in their arts and manufactures. Every article of cutlery shows, in its shape, thought and long experience of workmen. They put the expense in the right place, as, in their sea-steamers, in the solidity of the machinery and the strength of the boat. The admirable equipment of their arctic ships carries London to the pole. They build roads, aqueducts; warm and ventilate houses. And they have impressed their directness and practical habit on modern civilization.

In trade, the Englishman believes that nobody breaks who ought not to break; and that if he do not make trade everything, it will make him nothing; and acts on this belief. The spirit of system, attention to details, and the subordination of details, or the not driving things too finely (which is charged on the Germans), constitute that despatch of business which makes the mercantile power of England.

In war, the Englishman looks to his means. He is the opinion of Civilis, his German ancestor, whom Tacitus reports as holding that "the gods are on the side of the strongest"—a sentence which Bonaparte unconsciously translated, when he said that "he had noticed that Providence always favored the heaviest battalion." Their military science propounds that if

English men dining in a city coffee room: *"Each man walks, eats, drinks, shaves, dresses, gesticulates, and, in every manner, acts and suffers without reference to the bystanders, in his own fashion, only careful not to interfere with them or annoy them; not that he is trained to neglect the eyes of his neighbors—he is really occupied with his own affair and does not think of them."*

municable. In a company of strangers you would think him deaf; his eyes never wander from his table and newspaper. He is never betrayed into any curiosity or unbecoming emotion. They have all been trained in one severe school of manners, and never put off the harness. He does not give his hand. He does not let you meet his eye. It is almost an affront to look a man in the face without being introduced. In mixed or in select companies they do not introduce persons; so that a presentation is a circumstance as valid as a contract. Introductions are sacraments. He withholds his name. At the hotel, he is hardly willing to whisper it to the clerk at the book-office. If he give you his private address on a card, it is like an avowal of friendship; and his

bearing, on being introduced, is cold, even though he is seeking your acquaintance and is studying how he shall serve you.

It was an odd proof of this impressive energy, that in my lectures I hesitated to read and threw out for its impertinence many a disparaging phrase which I had been accustomed to spin, about poor, thin, unable mortals—so much had the fine physique and the personal vigor of this robust race worked on my imagination.

I happened to arrive in England at the moment of a commercial crisis. But it was evident that let who will fail, England will not. These people have sat here a thousand years, and here will continue to sit. They will not break up, or arrive at any desperate revolution, like their neighbors;

for they have as much energy, as much continence of character as they ever had. The power and possession which surround them are their own creation, and they exert the same commanding industry at this moment.

They are positive, methodical, cleanly and formal, loving routine and conventional ways; loving truth and religion, to be sure, but inexorable on points of form. All the world praises the comfort and private appointments of an English inn, and of English households. You are sure of neatness and of personal decorum. A Frenchman may possibly be clean; an Englishman is conscientiously clean. A certain order and complete propriety is found in his dress and in his belongings.

Born in a harsh and wet climate, which keeps him indoors whenever he is at rest, and being of an affectionate and loyal temper, he dearly loves his house. If he is rich, he buys a demesne and builds a hall; if he is in middle condition, he spares no expense on his house. Without, it is all planted; within, it is wainscoted, carved, curtained, hung with pictures and filled with good furniture. 'Tis a passion which survives all others, to deck and improve it. Hither he brings all that is rare and costly, and with the national tendency to sit fast in the same spot for many generations, it comes to be, in the course of time, a museum of heirlooms, gifts and trophies of the adventures and exploits of the family. He is very fond of silver plate, and though he have no gallery of portraits of his ancestors, he has of their punchbowls and porringers. Incredible amounts of plate are found in good houses, and the poorest have some spoon or saucepan, gift of a godmother, saved out of better times.

An English family consists of a few persons, who, from youth to age, are found revolving within a few feet of each other, as if tied by some invisible ligature, tense as that cartilage which we have seen attaching the two Siamese. England produces under favorable conditions of ease and culture the finest women in the world. And as the men are affectionate and true-hearted, the women inspire and refine them. Nothing can be more delicate without being fantastical, nothing more firm and based in nature and sentiment, than the courtship and mutual carriage of the sexes. The song of 1596 says, "the wife of every Englishman is counted blest." The sentiment of Imogen in *Cymbeline* is copied from English nature; and not less the Portia of Brutus, the Kate Percy and the Desdemona. The romance does not exceed the height of noble passion in Mrs. Lucy Hutchinson, or in Lady Russell, or even as one discerns through the plain prose of *Pepys's Diary*, the sacred habit of an English wife. Sir Samuel Romilly could not bear the death of his wife. Every class has its noble and tender examples.

Domesticity is the taproot which enables the nation to branch wide and high. The motive and end of their trade and empire is to guard the independence and privacy of their homes. Nothing so much marks their manners as the concentration on their household ties. This domesticity is carried into court and camp. Wellington governed India and Spain and his own troops, and fought battles, like a good family man, paid his debts, and though general of an army in Spain, could not stir abroad for fear of public creditors. This taste for house and parish merits has of course its doting and foolish side. Mr. Cobbett attributes the huge popularity of Perceval, prime minister in 1810, to the fact that he was wont to go to church every Sunday, with a large quarto gilt prayer book under one arm, his wife hanging on the other, and followed by a long brood of children.

They keep their old customs, costumes, and pomps, their wig and mace, sceptre and crown. The Middle Ages still lurk in the streets of London. The Knights of the Bath take oath to defend injured ladies; the gold-stick-in-waiting survives. They repeated the ceremonies of the eleventh century in the coronation of the present

Queen. A hereditary tenure is natural to them. Offices, farms, trades and traditions descend so. Their leases run for a hundred and a thousand years. Terms of service and partnership are lifelong, or are inherited. "Holdship has been with me," said Lord Eldon, "eight-and-twenty years, knows all my business and books." Antiquity of usage is sanction enough. Wordsworth says of the small freeholders of Westmoreland, "Many of these humble sons of the hills had a consciousness that the land which they tilled had for more than five hundred years been possessed by men of the same name and blood." The ship carpenter in the public yards, my lord's gardener and porter, have been there for more than a hundred years, grandfather, father, and son.

The English power resides also in their dislike of change. They have difficulty in bringing their reason to act, and on all occasions use their memory first. As soon as they have rid themselves of some grievance and settled the better practice, they make haste to fix it as a finality, and never wish to hear of alteration more.

Every Englishman is an embryonic chancellor: his instinct is to search for a precedent. The favorite phrase of their law is, "a custom whereof the memory of man runneth not back to the contrary." The barons say, *"Nolumus mutari"*; and the cockneys stifle the curiosity of the foreigner on the reason of any practice with "Lord, sir, it was always so." They hate innovation. Bacon told them, Time was the right reformer; Chatham, that "confidence was a plant of slow growth"; Canning, to "advance with the times"; and Wellington, that "habit was ten times nature." All their statesmen learn the irresistibility of the tide of custom, and have invented many fine phrases to cover this slowness of perception and prehensility of tail.

A seashell should be the crest of England, not only because it represents a power built on the waves, but also the hard finish of the men. The Englishman is finished like a cowry or a murex. After the spire and the spines are formed, or with the formation, a juice exudes and a hard enamel varnishes every part. The keeping of the proprieties is as indispensable as clean linen. No merit quite countervails the want of this, whilst this sometimes stands in lieu of all. " 'Tis in bad taste," is the most formidable word an Englishman can pronounce. But this japan costs them dear. There is a prose in certain Englishmen which exceeds in wooden deadness all rivalry with other countrymen. There is a knell in the conceit and externality of their voice, which seems to say, *Leave all hope behind.* In this Gibraltar of propriety, mediocrity gets intrenched and consolidated and founded in adamant. An Englishman of fashion is like one of those souvenirs, bound in gold vellum, enriched with delicate engravings on thick hot-pressed paper, fit for the hands of ladies and princes, but with nothing in it worth reading or remembering.

A severe decorum rules the court and the cottage. When Thalberg the pianist was one evening performing before the Queen at Windsor, in a private party, the Queen accompanied him with her voice. The circumstance took air, and all England shuddered from sea to sea. The indecorum was never repeated. Cold, repressive manners prevail. No enthusiasm is permitted except at the opera. They avoid everything marked. They require a tone of voice that excites no attention in the room. Sir Philip Sidney is one of the patron saints of England, of whom Wotton said, "His wit was the measure of congruity."

Pretension and vaporing are once for all distasteful. They keep to the other extreme of low tone in dress and manners. They avoid pretension and go right to the heart of the thing. They hate nonsense, sentimentalism and high-flown expression; they use a studied plainness. Even Brummell, their fop, was marked by the severest simplicity in dress. They value themselves on the absence of everything theatrical in the public business, and on conciseness and going to the point, in private affairs.

"Everyone dresses for dinner, in his own house, or in another man's. The guests are expected to arrive within half an hour of the time fixed by card of invitation, and nothing but death or mutilation is permitted to detain them."

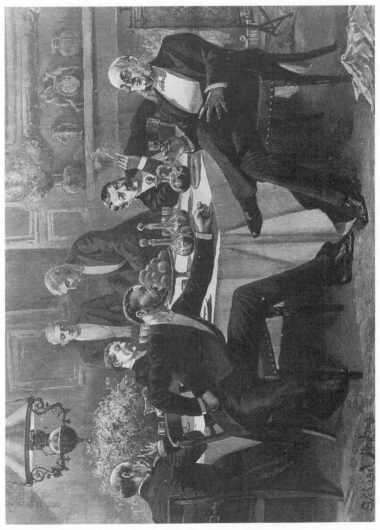

"The English dinner is precisely the model on which our own are constructed in the Atlantic cities. The company sit one or two hours before the ladies leave the table. The gentlemen remain over their wine an hour longer, and rejoin the ladies in the drawing room and take coffee."

In an aristocratical country like England, not the Trial by Jury, but the dinner, is the capital institution. It is the mode of doing honor to a stranger, to invite him to eat—and has been for many hundred years. "And they think," says the Venetian traveler of 1500, "no greater honor can be conferred or received, than to invite others to eat with them, or to be invited themselves, and they would sooner give five or six ducats to provide an entertainment for a person, than a groat to assist him in any distress." It is reserved to the end of the day, the family-hour being generally six, in London, and if any company is expected, one or two hours later. Everyone dresses for dinner, in his own house, or in another man's. The guests are expected to arrive within half an hour of the time fixed by card of invitation, and nothing but death or mutilation is permitted to detain them. The English dinner is precisely the model on which our own are constructed in the Atlantic cities. The company sit one or two hours before the ladies leave the table. The gentlemen remain over their wine an hour longer, and rejoin the ladies in the drawing room and take coffee. The dress-dinner generates a talent of table-talk which reaches great perfection: the stories are so good that one is sure they must have been often told before, to have got such happy turns. Hither come all manner of clever projects, bits of popular science, of practical invention, of miscellaneous humor; political, literary and personal news; railroads, horses, diamonds, agriculture, horticulture, pisciculture and wine.

English stories *bon-mots* and the recorded table-talk of their wits, are as good as the best of the French. In America, we are apt scholars, but have not yet attained the same perfection: for the range of nations from which London draws, and the steep contrasts of condition, create the picturesque in society, as broken country makes picturesque landscape: whilst our prevailing equality makes a prairie tameness: and secondly, because the usage of a dress-dinner every day at dark has a tendency to hive and produce to advantage everything good. Much attrition has worn every sentence into a bullet. Also one meets now and then with polished men who know everything, have tried everything, and can do everything, and are quite superior to letters and science. What could they not, if only they would?

Truth

The Teutonic tribes have a national singleness of heart, which contrasts with the Latin races. The German name has a proverbial significance of sincerity and honest meaning. The arts bear testimony to it. The faces of clergy and laity in old sculptures and illuminated missals are charged with earnest belief. Add to this hereditary rectitude the punctuality and precise dealing which commerce creates, and you have the English truth and credit. The government strictly performs its engagements. The subjects do not understand trifling on its part. When any breach of promise occurred, in the old days of prerogative, it was resented by the people as an intolerable grievance. And in modern times, any slipperiness in the government of political faith, or any repudiation or crookedness in matters of finance, would bring the whole nation to a committee of inquiry and reform. Private men keep their promises, never so trivial. Down goes the flying word on the tablets, and is indelible as *Domesday Book.*

Their practical power rests on their national sincerity. Veracity derives from instinct, and marks superiority in organization. Nature has endowed some animals with cunning, as a compensation for strength withheld; but it has provoked the malice of all others, as if avengers of public wrong. In the nobler kinds, where strength could be afforded, her races are loyal to truth, as truth is the foundation of the social state. Beasts that make no truce with man, do not break with each other. 'Tis said that the wolf, who makes a *cache* of his prey and brings his fellows with him to the spot, if, on digging, it is not found, is instantly and unresistingly torn in pieces. English veracity seems to result on a sounder animal structure, as if they could afford it. They are blunt in saying what they think, sparing of promises, and they require plain dealing of others. We will not have to do with a man in a mask. Let us know the truth. Draw a straight line, hit whom and where it will. Alfred, whom the affection of the nation makes the type of their race, is called by a writer at the Norman Conquest, the *truthspeaker; Alueredus veridicus.* Geoffrey of Monmouth says of King Aurelius, uncle of Arthur, that "above all things he hated a lie." The Northman Guttorm said to King Olaf, "It is royal work to fulfil royal words." The mottoes of their families are monitory proverbs, as, *Fare fac*—Say, do—of the Fairfaxes; *Say and seal,* of the House of Fiennes; *Vero nil verius,* of the DeVeres. To be king of their word is their pride. When they unmask cant, they say, "The English of this is," etc.; and to give the lie is the extreme insult. The phrase of the lowest of the people is "honor-bright," and their vulgar praise, "His word is as good as his bond." They hate shuffling and equivocation, and the cause is damaged in the public opinion, on which any paltering can be fixed. Even Lord Chesterfield, with his French breeding, when he came to define a gentleman, declared that truth made his distinction; and nothing ever spoken by him would find so hearty a suffrage from his nation. The Duke of Wellington, who had the best right to say so, advises the French General Kellermann that he may rely on the parole of an English officer. The English, of all classes, value themselves on this trait, as distinguishing them from the French, who, in the popular belief, are more polite than true. An Englishman understates, avoids the superlative, checks himself in compliments, alleging that in the French language one cannot speak without lying.

They love reality in wealth, power, hospitality, and do not easily learn to make a show, and take the world as it goes. They are not fond of ornaments, and if they wear them, they must be gems. They read gladly in old Fuller that a lady, in the reign of Elizabeth, "would have as patiently digested a lie, as the wearing of false stones or pendants of counterfeit pearl." They have the earth-hunger, or preference for property in land, which is said to mark the Teutonic nations. They build of stone: public and private buildings are massive and durable. In comparing their ships' houses and public offices with the American, it is commonly said that they spend a pound where we spend a dollar. Plain rich clothes, plain rich equipage, plain rich finish throughout their house and belongings mark the English truth.

They confide in each other—English believes in English. The French feel the superiority of this probity. The Englishman is not springing a trap for his admiration, but is honestly minding his business. The Frenchman is vain. Madame de Staël says that the English irritated Napoleon, mainly because they have found out how to unite success with honesty. She was not aware how wide an application her foreign readers would give to the remark. Wellington discovered the ruin of Bonaparte's affairs, by his own probity. He augured ill of the empire, as soon as he saw that it was mendacious and lived by war. If war do not bring in its sequel new trade, better agriculture and manufactures, but only games, fireworks and spectacles—no prosperity could support it; much less a nation decimated for conscripts and out of pocket, like France. So he drudged for years on his military works at Lisbon, and from this base at last extended his gigantic lines to Waterloo, believing in his countrymen and their syllogisms above all the *rhodomontade* of Europe.

At a St. George's festival, in Montreal, where I happened to be a guest since my return home, I observed that the chairman complimented his compatriots, by saying, "they confided that wherever they met an Englishman, they found a man who would speak the truth." And one cannot think this festival fruitless, if, all over the world, on the 23rd of April, wherever two or three English are found, they meet to encourage each other in the nationality of veracity.

In the power of saying rude truth, sometimes in the lion's mouth, no men surpass them. On the king's birthday, when each bishop was expected to offer the king a purse of gold, Latimer gave Henry VIII a copy of the *Vulgate,* with a mark at the passage, "Whoremongers and adulterers God will judge"; and they so honor stoutness in each other that the king passed it over. They are tenacious of their belief and cannot easily change their opinions to suit the hour. They are like ships with too much head on to come quickly about, nor will prosperity or even adversity be allowed to shake their habitual view of conduct. Whilst I was in London, M. Guizot arrived there on his escape from Paris, in February 1848. Many private friends called on him. His name was immediately proposed as an honorary member of the Athenaeum. M. Guizot was blackballed. Certainly they knew the distinction of his name. But the Englishman is not fickle. He had really made up his mind now for years as he read his newspaper, to hate and despise M. Guizot; and the altered position of the man as an illustrious exile and a guest in the country, makes no difference to him, as it would instantly to an American.

They require the same adherence, thorough conviction and reality, in public men. It is the want of character which makes the low reputation of the Irish members. "See them," they said, "one hundred and twenty-seven all voting like sheep, never proposing anything, and all but four voting the income tax," which was an ill-judged concession of the government, relieving Irish property from the burdens charged on English.

They have a horror of adventurers in or out of Parliament. The ruling passion of Englishmen in these days is a terror of humbug. In the same proportion they value honesty, stoutness, and adherence to your own. They like a man committed to his objects. They hate the French, as frivolous; they hate the Irish, as aimless; they hate the Germans, as professors. In February 1848, they said, Look, the French king and his party fell for want of a shot; they had not conscience to shoot, so entirely was the pith and heart of monarchy eaten out.

They attack their own politicians every day, on the same grounds, as adventurers. They love stoutness in standing for your right, in declining money or promotion that costs any concession. The barrister refuses the silk gown of Queen's Counsel, if his junior have it one day earlier. Lord Collingwood would not accept his medal for victory on 14th February, 1797, if he did not receive one for victory on 1st June, 1794; and the long withholden medal was accorded. When Castlereagh dissuaded Lord Wellington from going to the king's levee until the unpopular Cintra business had been explained, he replied, "You furnish me a reason for going. I will go to this, or I will never go to a king's levee." The radical mob at Oxford cried after the Tory Lord Eldon, "There's old Eldon; cheer him; he never ratted." They have given the parliamentary nickname of *Trimmers* to the time-servers, whom English character does not love.

They are very liable in their politics to extraordinary delusions; thus to believe what stands recorded in the gravest books, that the movement of 10th April, 1848, was urged or assisted by foreigners: which, to be sure, is paralleled by the democratic whimsy in this country which I have noticed to be shared by men sane on other points, that the English are at the bottom of the agitation of slavery, in American politics: and then again by the French popular legends on the subject of *perfidious*

Albion. But suspicion will make fools of nations as of citizens.

A slow temperament makes them less rapid and ready than other countrymen, and has given occasion to the observation that English wit comes afterwards—which the French denote as *esprit d'escalier.* This dulness makes their attachment to home and their adherence in all foreign countries to home habits. The Englishman who visits Mount Etna will carry his teakettle to the top. The old Italian author of the *Relation of England* (in 1500), says, "I have it on the best information, that, when the war is actually raging most furiously, they will seek for good eating and all their other comforts, without thinking what harm might befall them." Then their eyes seem to be set at the bottom of a tunnel, and they affirm the one small fact they know, with the best faith in the world that nothing else exists. And as their own belief in guineas is perfect, they readily, on all occasions, apply the pecuniary argument as final. Thus when the Rochester rappings began to be heard of in England, a man deposited £100 in a sealed box in the Dublin Bank, and then advertised in the newspapers to all somnambulists, mesmerizers and others, that whoever could tell him the number of his note should have the money. He let it lie there six months, the newspapers now and then, at his instance, stimulating the attention of the adepts; but none could ever tell him; and he said, "Now let me never be bothered more with this proven lie." It is told of a good Sir John that he heard a case stated by counsel, and made up his mind; then the counsel for the other side taking their turn to speak, he found himself so unsettled and perplexed that he exclaimed, "So help me God! I will never listen to evidence again." Any number of delightful examples of this English stolidity are the anecdotes of Europe. I knew a very worthy man—a magistrate, I believe he was, in the town of Derby—who went to the opera to see Malibran. In one scene, the heroine was to rush across a ruined bridge. Mr. B. arose and mildly yet firmly called the attention of the audience and the performers to the fact that, in his judgment, the bridge was unsafe! This English stolidity contrasts with French wit and tact. The French, it is commonly said, have greatly more influence in Europe than the English. What influence the English have is by brute force of wealth and power; that of the French by affinity and talent. The Italian is subtle, the Spaniard treacherous: tortures, it is said, could never wrest from an Egyptian the confession of a secret. None of these traits belong to the Englishman. His choler and conceit force everything out. Defoe, who knew his countrymen well, says of them—

In close intrigue, their faculty's but weak,
For generally whate'er they know, they speak,
And often their own counsels undermine
By mere infirmity without design;
From whence, the learned say, it doth proceed,
That English treasons never can succeed;
For they're so open-hearted, you may know
Their own most secret thoughts, and others'
  too.

Character

The English race are reputed morose. I do not know that they have sadder brows than their neighbors of northern climates. They are sad by comparison with the singing and dancing nations: not sadder, but slow and staid, as finding their joys at home. They, too, believe that where there is no enjoyment of life there can be no vigor and art in speech or thought; that your merry heart goes all the way, your sad one tires in a mile. This trait of gloom has been fixed on them by French travelers, who, from Froissart, Voltaire, Le Sage, Mirabeau, down to the lively journalists of the *feuilletons,* have spent their wit on the solemnity of their neighbors. The French say, gay conversation is unknown in their island. The Englishman finds no relief from reflection, except in reflection. When he wishes for amusement, he goes to work. His hilarity is like an attack of fever. Religion, the theater and the reading the books of his country all feed and increase his natural melancholy. The police does not interfere with public diversions. It thinks itself bound in duty to respect the pleasures and rare gayety of this inconsolable nation; and their well-known courage is entirely attributable to their disgust of life.

I suppose their gravity of demeanor and their few words have obtained this reputation. As compared with the Americans, I think them cheerful and contented. Young people in this country are much more prone to melancholy. The English have a mild aspect and a ringing cheerful voice. They are large-natured and not so easily amused as the southerners, and are among them as grown people among children, requiring war, or trade, or engineering, or science, instead of frivolous games. They are proud and private, and even if disposed to recreation, will avoid an open garden. They sported sadly; *ils s'amusaient tristement, selon la coutume de leur pays,* said Froissart; and I suppose never nation built their party walls so thick, or their garden fences so high. Meat and wine produce no effect on them. They are just as cold, quiet and composed, at the end, as at the beginning of dinner.

The reputation of taciturnity they have enjoyed for six or seven hundred years; and a kind of pride in bad public speaking is noted in the House of Commons, as if they were willing to show that they did not live by their tongues, or thought they spoke well enough if they had the tone of gentlemen. In mixed company they shut their mouths. A Yorkshire mill-owner told me he had ridden more than once all the way from London to Leeds, in the first-class carriage, with the same persons, and no word exchanged. The clubhouses were established to cultivate social habits, and it is rare that more than two eat together, and oftenest one eats alone. Was it then a stroke of humor in the serious Sweden-

borg, or was it only his pitiless logic, that made him shut up the English souls in a heaven by themselves?

They are contradictorily described as sour, splenetic and stubborn—and as mild, sweet and sensible. The truth is they have great range and variety of character. Commerce sends abroad multitudes of different classes. The choleric Welshman, the fervid Scot, the bilious resident in the East or West Indies, are wide of the perfect behavior of the educated and dignified man of family. So is the burly farmer; so is the country squire, with his narrow and violent life. In every inn is the Commercial-Room, in which "travelers," or bagmen who carry patterns and solicit orders for the manufacturers, are wont to be entertained. It easily happens that this class should characterize England to the foreigner, who meets them on the road and at every public house, whilst the gentry avoid the taverns, or seclude themselves whilst in them.

But these classes are the right English stock, and may fairly show the national qualities, before yet art and education have dealt with them. They are good lovers, good haters, slow but obstinate admirers, and in all things very much steeped in their temperament, like men hardly awaked from deep sleep, which they enjoy. Their habits and instincts cleave to nature. They are of the earth, earthy; and of the sea, as the sea-kinds, attached to it for what it yields them, and not from any sentiment. They are full of coarse strength, rude exercise, butcher's meat and sound sleep; and suspect any poetic insinuation or any hint for the conduct of life which reflects on this animal existence, as if somebody were fumbling at the umbilical cord and might stop their supplies. They doubt a man's sound judgment if he does not eat with appetite, and shake their heads if he is particularly chaste. Take them as they come, you shall find in the common people a surly indifference, sometimes gruffness and ill temper; and in minds of more power, magazines of inexhaustible war, challenging

The ruggedest hour that time and spite dare bring
To frown upon the enraged Northumberland.

They are headstrong believers and defenders of their opinion, and not less resolute in maintaining their whim and perversity. Hezekiah Woodward wrote a book against the Lord's Prayer. And one can believe that Burton, the Anatomist of Melancholy, having predicted from the stars the hour of his death, slipped the knot himself round his own neck, not to falsify his horoscope.

Their looks bespeak an invincible stoutness: they have extreme difficulty to run away, and will die game. Wellington said of the young coxcombs of the Life-Guards, delicately brought up, "But the puppies fight well"; and Nelson said of his sailors, "They really mind shot no more than peas." Of absolute stoutness no nation has more or better examples. They are good at storming redoubts, at boarding frigates, at dying in the last ditch, or any desperate service which has daylight and honor in it; but not, I think, at enduring the rack, or any passive obedience, like jumping off a castle roof at the word of a czar, being both vascular and highly organized, so as to be very sensible of pain; and intellectual, so as to see reason and glory in a matter.

Of that constitutional force which yields the supplies of the day, they have the more than enough; the excess which creates courage on fortitude, genius in poetry, invention in mechanics, enterprise in trade, magnificence in wealth, splendor in ceremonies, petulance and projects in youth. The young men have a rude health which runs into peccant humors. They drink brandy like water, cannot expend their quantities of waste strength on riding, hunting, swimming and fencing, and run into absurd frolics with the gravity of the Eumenides. They stoutly carry into every nook and corner of the earth their turbulent sense; leaving no lie uncontradicted; no pretension unexamined. They chew hasheesh; cut themselves with poisoned creases; swing their hammock in the boughs of the Bohon Upas; taste every poison; buy every secret; at Naples they put St. Januarius's blood in an alembic; they saw a hole into the head of the "winking Virgin," to know why she winks; measure with an English footrule every cell of the Inquisition, every Turkish caaba, every Holy of holies; translate and send to Bentley the arcanum bribed and bullied away from shuddering Brahmins; and measure their own strength by the terror they cause. These travelers are of every class, the best and the worst; and it may easily happen that those of rudest behavior are taken notice of and remembered. The Saxon melancholy in the vulgar rich and poor appears as gushes of ill-humor, which every check exasperates into sarcasm and vituperation. There are multitudes of rude young English who have the self-sufficiency and bluntness of their nation, and who, with their disdain of the rest of mankind and with this indigestion and choler, have made the English traveler a proverb for uncomfortable and offensive manners. It was no bad description of the Briton generically, what was said two hundred years ago of one particular Oxford scholar: "He was a very bold man, uttered anything that came into his mind, not only among his companions, but in public coffee-houses, and would often speak his mind of particular persons then accidentally present, without examining the company he was in; for which he was often reprimanded and several times threatened to be kicked and beaten."

The common Englishman is prone to forget a cardinal article in the bill of social rights, that every man has a right to his own ears. No man can claim to usurp more than a few cubic feet of the audibilities of a public room, or to put upon the company with the loud statement of his crotchets or personalities.

But it is in the deep traits of race that the fortunes of nations are written, and however derived—whether a happier tribe or mixture of tribes, the air, or what circumstance that mixed for them the golden mean of temperament—here exists the best stock in the world, broad-fronted, broad-bottomed, best for depth, range and equability; men of aplomb and reserves, great range and many moods, strong instincts, yet apt for culture; war-class as well as clerks; earls and tradesmen; wise minority, as well as foolish majority; abysmal temperament, hiding wells of wrath, and glooms on which no sunshine settles, alternated with a common sense and humanity which hold them fast to every piece of cheerful duty; making this temperament a sea to which all storms are superficial; a race to which their fortunes flow, as if they alone had the elastic organization at once fine and robust enough for dominion; as if the burly inexpressive, now mute and contumacious, now fierce and sharp-tongued dragon, which once made the island light with his fiery breath, had bequeathed his ferocity to his conqueror. They hide virtues under vices, or the semblance of them. It is the misshapen hairy Scandinavian troll again, who lifts the cart out of the mire, or "threshes the corn that ten day-laborers could not end," but it is done in the dark and with muttered maledictions. He is a churl with a soft place in his heart, whose speech is a brash of bitter waters, but who loves to help you at a pinch. He says no, and serves you, and your thanks disgust him. Here was lately a cross-grained miser, odd and ugly, resembling in countenance the portrait of Punch with the laugh left out; rich by his own industry; sulking in a lonely house; who never gave a dinner to any man and disdained all courtesies; yet as true a worshipper of beauty in form and color as ever existed, and profusely pouring over the cold mind of his countrymen creations of grace and truth, removing the reproach of sterility from English art, catching from their savage climate every fine hint, and importing into their galleries every tint and trait of sunnier cities and skies; making an era in painting; and when he saw that the splendor of one of his pictures in the Exhibition dimmed his rival's that hung next it, secretly took a brush and blackened his own.

They do not wear their heart in their sleeve for daws to peck at. They have that phlegm or staidness which it is a compliment to disturb. "Great men," said Aristotle, "are always of a nature originally melancholy." 'Tis the habit of a mind which attaches to abstractions with a passion which gives vast results. They dare to displease, they do not speak to expectation. They like the sayers of No, better than the sayers of Yes. Each of them has an opinion which he feels it becomes him to express all the more that it differs from yours. They are meditating opposition. This gravity is inseparable from minds of great resources.

There is an English hero superior to the French, the German, the Italian, or the Greek. When he is brought to the strife with fate, he sacrifices a richer material possession, and on more purely metaphysical grounds. He is there with his own consent, face to face with fortune, which he defies. On deliberate choice and from grounds of character, he has elected his part to live and die for, and dies with grandeur. This race has added new elements to humanity and has a deeper root in the world.

They have great range of scale, from ferocity to exquisite refinement. With larger scale, they have great retrieving power. After running each tendency to an extreme, they try another tack with equal heat. More intellectual than other races, when they live with other races they do not take their language, but bestow their own. They subsidize other nations, and are not subsidized. They proselyte, and are not proselyted. They assimilate other races to themselves, and are not assimilated. The English did not calculate the conquest of the Indies. It fell to their character. So they administer, in different parts of the world, the codes of every empire and race; in Canada, old French law; in the Mauritius, the Code Napoleon; in the West Indies, the edicts of the Spanish Cortes; in the East Indies, the Laws of Menu; in the Isle of Man, of the Scandinavian Thing; at the Cape of Good Hope, of the old Netherlands; and in the Ionian Islands, the Pandects of Justinian.

They are very conscious of their advantageous position in history. England is the lawgiver, the patron, the instructor, the ally. Compare the tone of the French and of the English press: the first querulous, captious, sensitive about English opinion; the English press never timorous about French opinion, but arrogant and contemptuous.

They are testy and headstrong through an excess of will and bias; churlish as men sometimes please to be who do not forget a debt, who ask no favors and who will do what they like with their own. With education and intercourse, these asperities wear off and leave the goodwill pure. If anatomy is reformed according to national tendencies, I suppose the spleen will hereafter be found in the Englishman, not found in the American, and differencing the one from the other. I anticipate another anatomical discovery, that this organ will be found to be cortical and caducous; that they are superficially morose, but at last tenderhearted, herein differing from Rome and the Latin nations. Nothing savage, nothing mean resides in the English heart. They are subject to panics of credulity and of rage, but the temper of the nation, however disturbed, settles itself soon and easily, as, in this temperate zone, the sky after whatever storms clears again, and serenity is its normal condition.

A saving stupidity masks and protects their perception, as the curtain of the eagle's eye. Our swifter Americans, when they first deal with English, pronounce them stupid; but, later, do them justice as people who wear well, or hide their strength. To understand the power of performance that is in their finest wits, in the patient Newton, or in the versatile transcendent poets, or in the Dugdales, Gibbons, Hallams, Eldons and Peels, one should see how English day-laborers hold out. High and low,

they are of an unctuous texture. There is an adipocere in their constitution, as if they had oil also for their mental wheels and could perform vast amounts of work without damaging themselves.

Even the scale of expense on which people live, and to which scholars and professional men conform, proves the tension of their muscle, when vast numbers are found who can each lift this enormous load. I might even add, their daily feasts argue a savage vigor of body.

No nation was ever so rich in able men; "Gentlemen," as Charles I said of Strafford, "whose abilities might make a prince rather afraid than ashamed in the greatest affairs of state"; men of such temper, that, like Baron Vere, "had one seen him returning from a victory, he would by his silence have suspected that he had lost the day; and, had he beheld him in a retreat, he would have collected him a conqueror by the cheerfulness of his spirit."

The following passage from the *Heimskringla* might almost stand as a portrait of the modern Englishman—"Haldor was very stout and strong and remarkably handsome in appearances. King Harold gave him this testimony, that he, among all his men, cared least about doubtful circumstances, whether they betokened danger or pleasure; for, whatever turned up, he was never in higher nor in lower spirits, never slept less nor more on account of them, nor ate nor drank but according to his custom. Haldor was not a man of many words, but short in conversation, told his opinion bluntly and was obstinate and hard: and this could not please the king, who had many clever people about him, zealous in his service. Haldor remained a short time with the king, and then came to Iceland, where he took up his abode in Hiardaholt and dwelt in that farm to a very advanced age."

The national temper, in the civil history, is not flashy or whiffling. The slow, deep English mass smolders with fire, which at last sets all its borders in flame. The wrath of London is not French wrath, but has a long memory, and, in its hottest heat, a register and rule.

Half their strength they put not forth. They are capable of a sublime resolution, and if hereafter the war of races, often predicted, and making itself a war of opinions also (a question of despotism and liberty coming from Eastern Europe), should menace the English civilization, these sea-kings may take once again to their floating castles and find a new home and a second millennium of power in their colonies.

The stability of England is the security of the modern world. If the English race were as mutable as the French, what reliance? But the English stand for liberty. The conservative, money-loving, lord-loving English are yet liberty-loving; and so freedom is safe: for they have more personal force than any other people. The nation always resist the immoral action of their government. They think humanely on the affairs of France, of Turkey, of Poland, of Hungary, of Schleswig Holstein, though overborne by the statecraft of the rulers at last.

Does the early history of each tribe show the permanent bias, which, though not less potent, is masked as the tribe spreads its activity into colonies, commerce, codes, arts, letters? The early history shows it, as the musician plays the air which he proceeds to conceal in a tempest of variations. In Alfred, in the Northmen, one may read the genius of the English society, namely that private life is the place of honor. Glory, a career, and ambition, words familiar to the longitude of Paris, are seldom heard in English speech. Nelson wrote from their hearts his homely telegraph, "England expects every man to do his duty."

For actual service, for the dignity of a profession, or to appease diseased or inflamed talent, the army and navy may be entered (the worst boys doing well in the navy); and the civil service in departments where serious official work is done; and they hold in esteem the barrister engaged in the severer studies of the law. But the calm, sound and most British Briton shrinks from public life as charlatanism, and respects an economy founded on agriculture, coal mines, manufactures or trade, which secures an independence through the creation of real values.

They wish neither to command nor obey, but to be kings in their own houses. They are intellectual and deeply enjoy literature; they like well to have the world served up to them in books, maps, models, and every mode of exact information, and, though not creators in art, they value its refinement. They are ready for leisure, can direct and fill their own day, nor need so much as others the constraint of a necessity. But the history of the nation discloses, at every turn, this original predilection for private independence, and however this inclination may have been disturbed by the bribes with which their vast colonial power has warped men out of orbit, the inclination endures, and forms and reforms the laws, letters, manners and occupations. They choose that welfare which is compatible with the commonwealth, knowing that such alone is stable; as wise merchants prefer investments in the three per cents.

Cockayne

The English are a nation of humorists. Individual right is pushed to the uttermost bound compatible with public order. Property is so perfect that it seems the craft of that race, and not to exist elsewhere. The king cannot step on an acre which the peasant refuses to sell. A testator endows a dog or a rookery, and Europe cannot interfere with his absurdity. Every individual has his particular way of living, which he pushes to folly, and the decided sympathy of his compatriots is engaged to back up Mr. Crump's whim by statutes and chancellors and horse-guards. There is no freak so ridiculous but some Englishman has attempted to immortalize by money and law.

British citizenship is as omnipotent as Roman was. Mr. Cockayne is very sensible of this. The pursy man means by freedom the right to do as he pleases, and does wrong in order to feel his freedom, and makes a conscience of persisting in it.

He is intensely patriotic, for his country is so small. His confidence in the power and performance of his nation makes him provokingly incurious about other nations. He dislikes foreigners. Swedenborg, who lived much in England, notes "the similitude of minds among the English, in consequence of which they contract familiarity with friends who are of that nation, and seldom with others; and they regard foreigners as one looking through a telescope from the top of a palace regards those who dwell or wander about out of the city." A much older traveler, the Venetian who wrote the *Relation of England,* in 1500, says—"The English are great lovers of themselves and of everything belonging to them. They think that there are no other men than themselves and no other world but England; and whenever they see a handsome foreigner, they say that he looks like an Englishman and it is a great pity he should not be an Englishman; and whenever they partake of any delicacy with a foreigner, they ask him whether such a thing is made in his country." When he adds epithets of praise, his climax is, "So English"; and when he wishes to pay you the highest compliment, he says, I should not know you from an Englishman. France is, by its natural contrast, a kind of blackboard on which English character draws its own traits in chalk. This arrogance habitually exhibits itself in allusions to the French. I suppose that all men of English blood in America, Europe, or Asia, have a secret feeling of joy that they are not French natives. Mr. Coleridge is said to have given public thanks to God, at the close of a lecture, that he had defended him from being able to utter a single sentence in the French language. I have found that Englishmen have such a good opinion of England, that the ordinary

phrases in all good society, of postponing or disparaging one's own things in talking with a stranger, are seriously mistaken by them for an insuppressible homage to the merits of their nation; and the New Yorker or Pennsylvanian who modestly laments the disadvantage of a new country, log huts and savages, is surprised by the instant and unfeigned commiseration of the whole company, who plainly account all the world out of England a heap of rubbish.

The same insular limitation pinches his foreign politics. He sticks to his traditions and usages, and, so help him God! he will force his island by-laws down the throat of great countries, like India, China, Canada, Australia, and not only so, but impose Wapping on the Congress of Vienna and trample down all nationalities with his taxed boots. Lord Chatham goes for liberty and no taxation without representation—for that is British law; but not a hobnail shall they dare make in America, but buy their nails in England—for that also is British law; and the fact that British commerce was to be re-created by the independence of America, took them all by surprise.

In short, I am afraid that English nature is so rank and aggressive as to be a little incompatible with every other. The world is not wide enough for two.

But beyond this nationality, it must be admitted, the island offers a daily worship to the old Norse god Brage, celebrated among our Scandinavian forefathers for his eloquence and majestic air. The English have a steady courage that fits them for great attempts and endurance: they have also a petty courage, through which every man delights in showing himself for what he is and in doing what he can; so that in all companies, each of them has too good an opinion of himself to imitate anybody. He hides no defect of his form, features, dress, connection, or birthplace, for he thinks every circumstance belonging to him comes recommended to you.

315

If one of them have a bald, or a red, or a green head, or bow legs, or a scar, or mark, or a paunch, or a squeaking or a raven voice, he has persuaded himself that there is something modish and becoming in it, and that it sits well on him.

But nature makes nothing in vain, and this little superfluity of self-regard in the English brain is one of the secrets of their power and history. It sets every man on being and doing what he really is and can. It takes away a dodging, skulking, secondary air, and encourages a frank and manly bearing, so that each man makes the most of himself and loses no opportunity for want of pushing. A man's personal defects will commonly have, with the rest of the world, precisely that importance which they have to himself. If he makes light of them, so will other men. We all find in these a convenient meter of character, since a little man would be ruined by the vexation. I remember a shrewd politician, in one of our western cities, told me that "he had known several successful statesmen made by their foible." And another, an ex-governor of Illinois, said to me, "If the man knew anything, he would sit in a corner and be modest; but he is such an ignorant peacock that he goes bustling up and down and hits on extraordinary discoveries."

There is also this benefit in brag, that the speaker is unconsciously expressing his own ideal. Humor him by all means, draw it all out and hold him to it. Their culture generally enables the traveled English to avoid any ridiculous extremes of this self-pleasing, and to give it an agreeable air. Then the natural disposition is fostered by the respect which they find entertained in the world for English ability. It was said of Louis XIV, that his gait and air were becoming enough in so great a monarch, yet would have been ridiculous in another man; so the prestige of the English name warrants a certain confident bearing, which a Frenchman or Belgian could not carry. At all events, they feel themselves at liberty

to assume the most extraordinary tone on the subject of English merits.

An English lady on the Rhine hearing a German speaking of her party as foreigners, exclaimed, "No, we are not foreigners; we are English; it is you that are foreigners." They tell you daily in London the story of the Frenchman and Englishman who quarreled. Both were unwilling to fight, but their companions put them up to it; at last it was agreed that they should fight alone, in the dark, and with pistols: the candles were put out, and the Englishman, to make sure not to hit anybody, fired up the chimney—and brought down the Frenchman. They have no curiosity about foreigners, and answer any information you may volunteer with "Oh, Oh!" until the informant makes up his mind that they shall die in their ignorance, for any help he will offer. There are really no limits to this conceit, though brighter men among them make painful efforts to be candid.

The habit of brag runs through all classes, from the *Times* newspaper through politicians and poets, through Wordsworth, Carlyle, Mill and Sydney Smith, down to the boys of Eton. In the gravest treatise on political economy, in a philosophical essay, in books of science, one is surprised by the most innocent exhibition of unflinching nationality. In a tract on Corn, a most amiable and accomplished gentleman writes thus—"Though Britain, according to Bishop Berkeley's idea, were surrounded by a wall of brass ten thousand cubits in height, still she would as far excel the rest of the globe in riches, as she now does both in this secondary quality and in the more important ones of freedom, virtue and science."

The English dislike the American structure of society, whilst yet trade, mills, public education and Chartism are doing what they can to create in England the same social condition. America is the paradise of the economists; is the favorable exception invariably quoted to the rules of ruin; but when he speaks directly of the Americans the islander forgets his philosophy and remembers his disparaging anecdotes.

But this childish patriotism costs something, like all narrowness. The English sway of their colonies has no root of kindness. They govern by their arts and ability; they are more just than kind; and whenever an abatement of their power is felt, they have not conciliated the affection on which to rely.

Coarse local distinctions, as those of nation, province, or town, are useful in the absence of real ones; but we must not insist on these accidental lines. Individual traits are always triumphing over national ones. There is no fence in metaphysics discriminating Greek, or English, or Spanish science. Æsop and Montaigne, Cervantes and Saadi are men of the world; and to wave our own flag at the dinner table or in the University is to carry the boisterous dulness of a fire-club into a polite circle. Nature and destiny are always on the watch for our follies. Nature trips us up when we strut; and there are curious examples in history on this very point of national pride.

George of Cappadocia, born at Epiphania in Cilicia, was a low parasite who got a lucrative contract to supply the army with bacon. A rogue and informer, he got rich and was forced to run from justice. He saved his money, embraced Arianism, collected a library, and got promoted by a faction to the episcopal throne of Alexandria. When Julian came, A.D. 361, George was dragged to prison; the prison was burst open by the mob and George was lynched, as he deserved. And this precious knave became, in good time, Saint George of England, patron of chivalry, emblem of victory and civility and the pride of the best blood of the modern world.

Strange, that the solid truth-speaking Briton should derive from an impostor. Strange, that the New World should have no better luck—that broad America must wear the name of a thief. Amerigo Vespucci, the pickledealer at Seville, who went out, in 1499, a subaltern with Hojeda, and whose highest naval rank was boatswain's mate in an expedition that never sailed, managed in this lying world to supplant Columbus and baptize half the earth with his own dishonest name. Thus nobody can throw stones. We are equally badly off in our founders; and the false pickledealer is an offset to the false baconseller.

Wealth

There is no country in which so absolute a homage is paid to wealth. In America there is a touch of shame when a man exhibits the evidences of large property, as if after all it needed apology. But the Englishman has pure pride in his wealth, and esteems it a final certificate. A coarse logic rules throughout all English souls—if you have merit, can you not show it by your good clothes and coach and horses? How can a man be a gentleman without a pipe of wine? Haydon says, "There is a fierce resolution to make every man live according to the means he possesses." There is a mixture of religion in it. They are under the Jewish law, and read with sonorous emphasis that their days shall be long in the land, they shall have sons and daughters, flocks and herds, wine and oil. In exact proportion is the reproach of poverty. They do not wish to be represented except by opulent men. An Englishman who has lost his fortune is said to have died of a broken heart. The last term of insult is, "a beggar." Nelson said, "The want of fortune is a crime which I can never get over." Sydney Smith said, "Poverty is infamous in England." And one of their recent writers speaks, in reference to a private and scholastic life, of "the grave moral deterioration which follows an empty exchequer." You shall find this sentiment, if not so frankly put, yet deeply implied in the novels and romances of the present century, and not only in these, but in biography and in the votes of public assemblies, in the tone of the preaching and in the table talk.

I was lately turning over Wood's *Athenæ Oxonienses,* and looking naturally for another standard in a chronicle of the scholars of Oxford for two hundred years. But I found the two disgraces in that, as in most English books, are, first, disloyalty to Church and State, and second, to be born poor, or to come to poverty. A natural fruit of England is the brutal political economy. Malthus finds no cover laid at nature's table for the laborer's son. In 1809, the majority in Parliament expressed itself by the language of Mr. Fuller in the House of Commons, "If you do not like the country, damn you, you can leave it." When Sir S. Romilly proposed his bill forbidding parish officers to bind children apprentices at a greater distance than forty miles from their home, Peel opposed, and Mr. Wortley said, "though, in the higher ranks, to cultivate family affections was a good thing, it was not so among the lower orders. Better take them away from those who might deprave them. And it was highly injurious to trade to stop binding to manufacturers, as it must raise the price of labor and of manufactured goods."

The respect for truth of facts in England is equaled only by the respect for wealth. It is at once the pride of art of the Saxon, as he is a wealth-maker, and his passion for independence. The Englishman believes that every man must take care of himself, and has himself to thank if he do not mend his condition. To pay their debts is their national point of honor. From the Exchequer and the East India House to the huckster's shop, everything prospers because it is solvent. The British armies are solvent and pay for what they take. The British empire is solvent; for in spite of the huge national debt, the valuation mounts. During the war from 1789 to 1815, whilst they complained that they were taxed within an inch of their lives, and by dint of enormous taxes were subsidizing all the continent against France, the English were growing rich every year faster than any people ever grew before. It is their maxim that the weight of taxes must be calculated, not by what is taken, but by what is left. Solvency is in the ideas and mechanism of an Englishman. The Crystal Palace is not considered honest until it pays; no matter how much convenience, beauty, or *éclat,* it must be self-supporting. They are contented with slower steamers, as long as they know that swifter boats lose money. They proceed logically by the double method of labor and thrift. Every household exhibits an exact economy, and nothing of that uncalculated headlong expenditure which families use in America. If they cannot pay, they do not buy; for they have no presumption of better fortunes next year, as our people have; and they say without shame, I cannot afford it. Gentlemen do not hesitate to ride in the second-class cars, or in the second cabin. An economist, or a man who can proportion his means and his ambition, or bring the year round with expenditure which expresses his character without embarrassing one day of his future, is already a master of life, and a freeman. Lord Burleigh writes to his son that "one ought never to devote more than two-thirds of his income to the ordinary expenses of life, since the extraordinary will be certain to absorb the other third."

The ambition to create value evokes every kind of ability; government becomes a manufacturing corporation, and every house a mill. The headlong bias to utility will let no talent lie in a napkin—if possible will teach spiders to weave silk stockings. An Englishman, while he eats and drinks no more or not much more than another man, labors three times as many hours in the course of a year as another European; or, his life as a workman is three lives. He works fast. Everything in England is at a quick pace. They have reinforced their own productivity by the creation of that marvelous machinery which differences this age from any other age.

It is a curious chapter in modern history, the growth of the machine shop. Six hundred years ago, Roger Bacon explained the precession of the equinoxes, the consequent necessity of the reform of the calendar; measured the length of the year; invented gunpowder; and announced (as if looking from his lofty cell, over five centuries, into ours), that "machines can be constructed to drive ships more rapidly than a whole galley of rowers could do; nor would they need anything but a pilot to steer them. Carriages also might be constructed to move with an incredible speed, without the aid of any animal. Finally, it would not be impossible to make machines which by means of a suit of wings should fly in the air in the manner of birds." But the secret slept with Bacon. The six hundred years have not yet fulfilled his words. Two centuries ago the sawing of timber was done by hand; the carriage wheels ran on wooden axles; the land was tilled by wooden ploughs. And it was to little purpose that they had pit-coal, or that looms were improved, unless Watt and Stephenson had taught them to work force pumps and power looms by steam. The great strides were all taken within the last hundred years. *The Life of Sir Robert Peel,* in his day the model Englishman, very properly has, for a frontispiece, a drawing of the spinning jenny, which wove the web of his fortunes. Hargreaves invented the spinning jenny, and died in a workhouse. Arkwright improved the invention, and the machine dispensed with the work of ninety-nine men; that is, one spinner could do as much work as one hundred had done before. The loom was improved further. But the men would sometimes strike for wages and combine against the masters, and, about 1829–30, much fear was felt lest the trade would be drawn away by these interruptions and the emigration of the spinners to Belgium and the United States. Iron and steel are very obedient. Whether it were not possible to make a spinner that would not rebel, nor mutter, nor scowl, nor strike for wages, nor emigrate? At the solicitation of the masters, after a mob and riot at Staley Bridge, Mr. Roberts of Manchester undertook to create this peaceful fellow, instead of the quarrelsome fellow God had made. After a few trials, he succeeded, and in 1830 procured a patent for his self-acting mule; a creation, the delight of mill-owners, and "destined," they said, "to restore order among the industrious classes"; a machine requiring only a child's hand to piece the broken yarns. As Arkwright had destroyed domestic spinning, so Roberts destroyed the factory spinner. The power of machinery in Great Britain, in mills, has been computed to be equal to 600,000,000 men, one man being able by the aid of steam to do the work which required two hundred and fifty men to accomplish fifty years ago. The production has been commensurate. England already had this laborious race, rich soil, water, wood, coal, iron and favorable climate. Eight hundred years ago commerce had made it rich, and it was recorded, "England is the richest of all the northern nations." The Norman historians recite that "in 1067, William carried with him into Normandy, from England, more gold and silver than had ever before been seen in Gaul." But when, to this labor and trade and these native resources was added this goblin of steam, with his myriad arms, never tired, working night and day everlastingly, the amassing of property has run out of all figures. It makes the motor of the last ninety years. The steampipe has added to her population and wealth the equivalent of four or five Englands. Forty thousand ships are entered in Lloyd's lists. The yield of wheat has gone on from 2,000,000 quarters in the time of the Stuarts, to 13,000,000 in 1854. A thousand million of pounds sterling are said to compose the floating money of commerce. In 1848, Lord John Russell stated that the people of this country had laid out £300,-000,000 of capital in railways, in the last four years. But a better measure than these sounding figures is the estimate that there is wealth enough in England to support the entire population in idleness for one year.

The wise, versatile, all-giving machinery makes chisels, roads, locomotives, telegraphs. Whitworth divides a bar to a millionth of an inch. Steam twines huge cannon into wreaths, as easily as it braids straw, and vies with the volcanic forces which twisted the strata. It can clothe shingle mountains with ship-oaks, make sword blades that will cut gun barrels in two. In Egypt, it can plant forests, and bring rain after three thousand years. Already it is ruddering the balloon, and the next war will be fought in the air. But another machine more potent in England than steam is the Bank. It votes an issue of bills, population is stimulated and cities rise; it refuses loans, and emigration empties the country; trade sinks; revolutions break out; kings are dethroned. By these new agents our social system is molded. By dint of steam and of money, war and commerce are changed. Nations have lost their old omnipotence; the patriotic tie does not hold. Nations are getting obsolete, we go and live where we will. Steam has enabled men to choose what law they will live under. Money makes place for them. The telegraph is a limp band that will hold the Fenris-wolf of war. For now that a telegraph line runs through France and Europe from London, every message it transmits makes stronger by one thread the band which war will have to cut.

The introduction of these elements gives new resources to existing proprietors. A sporting duke may fancy that the state depends on the House of Lords, but the engineer sees that every stroke of the steam-piston gives value to the duke's land, fills it with tenants; doubles, quadruples, centuples the duke's capital, and creates new measures and new necessities for the culture of his children. Of course it draws the nobility into the competition, as stockholders in the mine, the canal, the railway, in the application of steam to agriculture, and sometimes into trade. But it also introduces

large classes into the same competition; the old energy of the Norse race arms itself with these magnificent powers; new men prove an overmatch for the landowner, and the mill buys out the castle. Scandinavian Thor, who once forged his bolts in icy Hecla and built galleys by lonely fiords, in England has advanced with the times, has shorn his beard, enters Parliament, sits down at a desk in the India House and lends Miollnir to Birmingham for a steam-hammer.

The creation of wealth in England in the last ninety years is a main fact in modern history. The wealth of London determines prices all over the globe. All things precious, or useful, or amusing, or intoxicating, are sucked into this commerce and floated to London. Some English private fortunes reach, and some exceed a million of dollars a year. A hundred thousand palaces adorn the island. All that can feed the senses and passions, all that can succor the talent or arm the hands of the intelligent middle class, who never spare in what they buy for their own consumption; all that can aid science, gratify taste, or soothe comfort, is in open market. Whatever is excellent and beautiful in civil, rural, or ecclesiastic architecture, in fountain, garden, or grounds—the English noble crosses sea and land to see and to copy at home. The taste and science of thirty peaceful generations; the gardens which Evelyn planted; the temples and pleasure-houses which Inigo Jones and Christopher Wren built; the wood that Gibbons carved; the taste of foreign and domestic artists, Shenstone, Pope, Brown, Loudon, Paxton—are in the vast auction, and the hereditary principle heaps on the owner of today the benefit of ages of owners. The present possessors are to the full as absolute as any of their fathers in choosing and procuring what they like. This comfort and splendor, the breadth of lake and mountain, tillage, pasture and park, sumptuous castle and modern villa— all consist with perfect order. They have no revolutions; no horse guards dictating to the crown; no Parisian *poissardes* and

families. Their proverb is, that fifty miles from London, a family will last a hundred years; at a hundred miles, two hundred years; and so on; but I doubt that steam, the enemy of time as well as of space, will disturb these ancient rules. Sir Henry Wotton says of the first Duke of Buckingham, "He was born at Brookeby in Leicestershire, where his ancestors had chiefly continued about the space of four hundred years, rather without obscurity, than with any great lustre." Wraxall says that in 1781, Lord Surrey, afterwards Duke of Norfolk, told him that when the year 1783 should arrive, he meant to give a grand festival to all the descendants of the body of Jockey of Norfolk, to mark the day when the dukedom should have remained three hundred years in their house, since its creation by Richard III. Pepys tells us, in writing of an Earl Oxford, in 1666, that the honor had now remained in that name and blood six hundred years.

This long descent of families and this cleaving through ages to the same spot of ground, captivates the imagination. It has too a connection with the names of the towns and districts of the country.

The names are excellent—an atmosphere of legendary melody spread over the land. Older than all epics and histories which clothe a nation, this undershirt sits close to the body. What history too, and what stores of primitive and savage observation it infolds! Cambridge is the bridge of the Cam; Sheffield the field of the river Sheaf; Leicester the *castra,* or camp, of the Lear, or Leir (now Soar); Rochdale, of the Roch; Exeter or Excester, the *castra* of the Ex; Exmouth, Dartmouth, Sidmouth, Teignmouth, the mouths of the Ex, Dart, Sid and Teign rivers. Waltham is strong town; Radcliffe is red cliff; and so on—a sincerity and use in naming very striking to an American, whose country is whitewashed all over by unmeaning names, the cast-off clothes of the country from which its emigrants came; or named at a pinch from a psalm tune. But the English

are those "barbarians" of Jamblichus, who "are stable in their manners, and firmly continue to employ the same words, which also are dear to the gods."

'Tis an old sneer that the Irish peerage drew their names from playbooks. The English lords do not call their lands after their own names, but call themselves after their lands, as if the man represented the country that bred him; and they rightly wear the token of the glebe that gave them birth, suggesting that the tie is not cut, but that there in London—the crags of Argyle, the kail of Cornwall, the downs of Devon, the iron of Wales, the clays of Stafford are neither forgetting nor forgotten, but know the man who was born by them and who, like the long line of his fathers, has carried that crag, that shore, dale, fen, or woodland, in his blood and manners. It has, too, the advantage of suggesting responsibleness. A susceptible man could not wear a name which represented in a strict sense a city or a county of England, without hearing in it a challenge to duty and honor.

The predilection of the patricians for residence in the country, combined with the degree of liberty possessed by the peasant, makes the safety of the English hall. Mirabeau wrote prophetically from England, in 1784, "If revolution break out in France, I tremble for the aristocracy: their chateaux will be reduced to ashes and their blood spilt in torrents. The English tenant would defend his lord to the last extremity." The English go to their estates for grandeur. The French live at court, and exile themselves to their estates for economy. As they do not mean to live with their tenants, they do not conciliate them, but wring from them the last *sous.* Evelyn writes from Blois, in 1644: "The wolves are here in such numbers, that they often come and take children out of the streets; yet will not the Duke, who is sovereign here, permit them to be destroyed."

In evidence of the wealth amassed by ancient families, the traveler is shown the palaces in Piccadilly, Burlington House, Devonshire House, Lansdowne House in Berkshire Square, and lower down in the city, a few noble houses which still withstand in all their amplitude the encroachment of streets. The Duke of Bedford includes or included a mile square in the heart of London, where the British Museum, once Montague House, now stands, and the land occupied by Woburn Square, Bedford Square, Russell Square. The Marquis of Westminster built within a few years the series of squares called Belgravia. Stafford House is the noblest palace in London. Northumberland House holds its place by Charing Cross. Chesterfield House remains in Audley Street. Sion House and Holland House are in the suburbs. But most of the historical houses are masked or lost in the modern uses to which trade or charity has converted them. A multitude of town palaces contain inestimable galleries of art.

In the country, the size of private estates is more impressive. From Barnard Castle I rode on the highway twenty-three miles from High Force, a fall of the Tees, towards Darlington, past Raby Castle, through the estate of the Duke of Cleveland. The Marquis of Breadalbane rides out of his house a hundred miles in a straight line to the sea, on his own property. The Duke of Sutherland owns the county of Sutherland, stretching across Scotland from sea to sea. The Duke of Devonshire, besides his other estates, owns 96,000 acres in the County of Derby. The Duke of Richmond has 40,000 acres at Goodwood and 300,000 at Gordon Castle. The Duke of Norfolk's park in Sussex is fifteen miles in circuit. An agriculturist bought lately the island of Lewes, in Hebrides, containing 500,000 acres. The possessions of the Earl of Lonsdale gave him eight seats in Parliament. This is the Heptarchy again; and before the Reform of 1832, one hundred and fifty-four persons sent three hundred and seven members to Parliament. The boroughmongers governed England.

These large domains are growing larger. The great estates are absorbing the small freeholds. In 1786 the soil of England was owned by 250,000 corporations and proprietors; and in 1822, by 32,000. These broad estates find room in this narrow island. All over England, scattered at short intervals among shipyards, mills, mines and forges, are the paradises of the nobles, where the livelong repose and refinement are heightened by the contrast with the roar of industry and necessity, out of which you have stepped aside.

I was surprised to observe the very small attendance usually in the House of Lords. Out of 573 peers, on ordinary days only twenty or thirty. Where are they? I asked. "At home on their estates, devoured by *ennui*, or in the Alps, or up the Rhine, in the Harz Mountains, or in Egypt, or in India, on the Ghauts." But, with such interests at stake, how can these men afford to neglect them? "O," replied my friend, "why should they work for themselves, when every man in England works for them and will suffer before they come to harm?" The hardest radical instantly uncovers and changes his tone to a lord. It was remarked, on the 10th April, 1848 (the day of the Chartist demonstration), that the upper classes were for the first time actively interesting themselves in their own defence, and men of rank were sworn special constables with the rest. "Besides, why need they sit out the debate? Has not the Duke of Wellington, at this moment, their proxies—the proxies of fifty peers—in his pocket, to vote for them if there be an emergency?"

It is however true that the existence of the House of Peers as a branch of the government entitles them to fill half the Cabinet; and their weight of property and station gives them a virtual nomination of the other half; whilst they have their share in the subordinate offices, as a school of training. This monopoly of political power has given them their intellectual and social eminence in Europe. A few law lords and a few political lords take the brunt of public business. In the army, the nobility fill a large part of the high commissions, and give to these a tone of expense and splendor and also of exclusiveness. They have borne their full share of duty and danger in this service, and there are few noble families which have not paid, in some of their members, the debt of life or limb in the sacrifices of the Russian war. For the rest, the nobility have the lead in matters of state and of expense; in questions of taste, in social usages, in convivial and domestic hospitalities. In general, all that is required of them is to sit securely, to preside at public meetings, to countenance charities and to give the example of that decorum so dear to the British heart.

If one asks, in the critical spirit of the day, what service this class have rendered?—uses appear, or they would have perished long ago. Some of these are easily enumerated, others more subtle make a part of unconscious history. Their institution is one step in the progress of society. For a race yields a nobility in some form, however we name the lords, as surely as it yields women.

The English nobles are high-spirited, active, educated men, born to wealth and power, who have run through every country and kept in every country the best company, have seen every secret of art and nature, and, when men of any ability or ambition, have been consulted in the conduct of every important action. You cannot wield great agencies without lending yourself to them, and when it happens that the spirit of the earl meets his rank and duties, we have the best examples of behavior. Power of any kind readily appears in the manners; and beneficent power, *le talent de bien faire*, gives a majesty which cannot be concealed or resisted.

These people seem to gain as much as they lose by their position. They survey society as from the top of St. Paul's, and if they never hear plain truth from men, they see the best of everything, in every kind, and they see things so grouped and amassed as to infer easily the sum and genius, instead of tedious particularities. Their good behavior deserves all its fame, and they have that simplicity and that air of repose which are the finest ornament of greatness.

The upper classes have only birth, say the people here, and not thoughts. Yes, but they have manners, and it is wonderful how much talent runs into manners—nowhere and never so much as in England. They have the sense of superiority, the absence of all the ambitious effort which disgusts in the aspiring classes, a pure tone of thought and feeling, and the power to command, among their other luxuries, the presence of the most accomplished men in their festive meetings.

Loyalty is in the English a sub-religion. They wear the laws as ornaments, and walk by their faith in their painted May-Fair as if among the forms of gods. The economist of 1855 who asks, Of what use are the lords? may learn of Franklin to ask, Of what use is a baby? They have been a social church proper to inspire sentiments mutually honoring the lover and the loved. Politeness is the ritual of society, as prayers are of the church, a school of manners, and a gentle blessing to the age in which it grew. 'Tis a romance adorning English life with a larger horizon; a midway heaven, fulfilling to their sense their fairy tales and poetry. This, just as far as the breeding of the nobleman really made him brave, handsome, accomplished and great-hearted.

On general grounds, whatever tends to form manners or to finish men, has a great value. Every one who has tasted the delight of friendship will respect every social guard which our manners can establish, tending to secure from the intrusion of frivolous and distasteful people. The jealousy of every class to guard itself is a testimony to the reality they have found in life. When a man once knows that he has done justice to himself, let him dismiss all terrors of aristocracy as superstitions, so far as he is concerned. He who keeps the door of a mine, whether of cobalt, or mercury, or nickel, or plumbago, securely knows that the world cannot do without him. Everybody who is real is open and ready for that which is also real.

Besides, these are they who make England that strongbox and museum it is; who gather and protect works of art, dragged from amidst burning cities and revolutionary countries, and brought hither out of all the world. I look with respect at houses six, seven, eight hundred, or, like Warwick Castle, nine hundred years old. I pardoned high park-fences, when I saw that besides does and pheasants, these have preserved Arundel marbles, Townley galleries, Howard and Spenserian libraries, Warwick and Portland vases, Saxon manuscripts, monastic architectures, millennial trees and breeds of cattle elsewhere extinct. In these manors, after the frenzy of war and destruction subsides a little, the antiquary finds the frailest Roman jar or crumbling Egyptian mummy-case, without so much as a new layer of dust, keeping the series of history unbroken and waiting for its interpreter, who is sure to arrive. These lords are the treasurers and librarians of mankind, engaged by their pride and wealth to this function.

Yet there were other works for British dukes to do. George Loudon, Quintinye, Evelyn, had taught them to make gardens. Arthur Young, Bakewell and Mechi have made them agricultural. Scotland was a camp until the day of Culloden. The Dukes of Athol, Sutherland, Buccleugh and the Marquis of Breadalbane have introduced the rape-culture, the sheep-farm, wheat, drainage, the plantation of forests, the artificial replenishment of lakes and ponds with fish, the renting of game preserves. Against the cry of the old tenantry and the sympathetic cry of the English press, they have rooted out and planted anew, and now six millions of people live, and live better, on the same land that fed three millions.

The English barons, in every period, have been brave and great, after the estimate and opinion of their times. The grand old halls scattered up and down in England, are dumb vouchers to the state and broad hospitality of their ancient lords. Shakespeare's portraits of good Duke Humphrey, of Warwick, of Northumberland, of Talbot, were drawn in strict consonance with the traditions. A sketch of the Earl of Shrewsbury, from the pen of Queen Elizabeth's archbishop Parker; Lord Herbert of Cherbury's autobiography; the letters and essays of Sir Philip Sidney; the anecdotes preserved by the antiquaries Fuller and Collins; some glimpses at the interiors of noble houses, which we owe to Pepys and Evelyn; the details which Ben Jonson's masques (performed at Kenilworth, Althorpe, Belvoir and other noble houses), record or suggest; down to Aubrey's passages of the life of Hobbes in the house of the Earl of Devon, are favorable pictures of a romantic style of manners. Penshurst still shines for us, and its Christmas revels, "where logs not burn, but men." At Wilton House the "Arcadia" was written, amidst conversations with Fulke Greville, Lord Brooke, a man of no vulgar mind, as his own poems declare him. I must hold Ludlow Castle an honest house, for which Milton's "Comus" was written, and the company nobly bred which performed it with knowledge and sympathy. In the roll of nobles are found poets, philosophers, chemists, astronomers, also men of solid virtues and of lofty sentiments; often they have been the friends and patrons of genius and learning, and especially of the fine arts; and at this moment, almost every great house has its sumptuous picture gallery.

Of course there is another side to this gorgeous show. Every victory was the defeat of a party only less worthy. Castles are proud things, but 'tis safest to be outside of them. War is a foul game, and yet war is not the worst part of aristocratic history. In later times, when the baron, educated only for war, with his brains paralyzed by his stomach, found himself idle at home, he grew fat and wanton and a sorry brute. Grammont, Pepys and Evelyn show the kennels to which the king and court went in quest of pleasure. Prostitutes taken from the theaters were made duchesses, their bastards dukes and earls. "The young men sat uppermost, the old serious lords were out of favor." The discourse that the king's companions had with him was "poor and frothy." No man who valued his head might do what these potcompanions familiarly did with the king. In logical sequence of these dignified revels, Pepys can tell the beggarly shifts to which the king was reduced, who could not find paper at his council table, and "no handkerchers" in his wardrobe, "and but three bands to his neck," and the linendraper and the stationer were out of pocket and refusing to trust him, and the baker will not bring bread any longer. Meantime the English Channel was swept and London threatened by the Dutch fleet, manned too by English sailors, who, having been cheated of their pay for years by the king, enlisted with the enemy.

The Selwyn correspondence, in the reign of George III, discloses a rottenness in the aristocracy which threatened to decompose the state. The sycophancy and sale of votes and honor, for place and title; lewdness, gaming, smuggling, bribery and cheating; the sneer at the childish indiscretion of quarreling with ten thousand a year; the want of ideas; the splendor of the titles, and the apathy of the nation, are instructive, and make the reader pause and explore the firm bounds which confined these vices to a handful of rich men. In the reign of the Fourth George, things do not seem to have mended, and the rotten debauchee let down from a window by an inclined plane into his coach to take the air, was a scandal to Europe which the ill fame of his queen and of his family did nothing to retrieve.

Under the present reign the perfect decorum of the Court is thought to have put a check on the gross vices of the aristocracy; yet gaming, racing, drinking and mistresses bring them down, and the democrat can still gather scandals, if he will. Dismal anecdotes abound, verifying the gossip of the last generation, of dukes served by bailiffs, with all their plate in pawn; of great lords living by the showing of their houses, and of an old man wheeled in his chair from room to room, whilst his chambers are exhibited to the visitor for money; of ruined dukes and earls living in exile for debt. The historic names of the Buckinghams, Beauforts, Marlboroughs and Hertfords have gained no new lustre, and now and then darker scandals break out, ominous as the new chapters added under the Orleans dynasty to the *causes célèbres* in France. Even peers who are men of worth and public spirit are overtaken and embarrassed by their vast expense. The respectable Duke of Devonshire, willing to be the Mecænas and Lucullus of his island, is reported to have said that he cannot live at Chatsworth but one month in the year. Their many houses eat them up. They cannot sell them, because they are entailed. They will not let them, for pride's sake, but keep them empty, aired, and the grounds mown and dressed, at a cost of four or five thousand pounds a year. The spending is for a great part in servants, in many houses exceeding a hundred.

Most of them are only chargeable with idleness, which, because it squanders such vast power of benefit, has the mischief of crime. "They might be little Providences on earth," said my friend, "and they are, for the most part, jockeys and fops." Campbell says, "Acquaintance with the nobility, I could never keep up. It requires a life of idleness, dressing and attendance on their parties." I suppose too that a feeling of self-respect is driving cultivated men out of this society, as if the noble were slow to receive the lessons of the times and had not learned to disguise his pride of place. A man of wit, who is also one of the celebrities of wealth and fashion, confessed to his friend that he could not enter their houses without being made to feel that they were great lords, and he a low plebeian. With the tribe of *artistes,* including the musical tribe, the patrician morgue keeps no terms, but excludes them. When Julia Grisi and Mario sang at the houses of the Duke of Wellington and other grandees, a cord was stretched between the singer and the company.

When every noble was a soldier, they were carefully bred to great personal prowess. The education of a soldier is a simpler affair than that of an earl in the nineteenth century. And this was very seriously pursued; they were expert in every species of equitation, to the most dangerous practices, and this down to the accession of William of Orange. But graver men appear to have trained their sons for civil affairs. Elizabeth extended her thought to the future; and Sir Philip Sidney in his letter to his brother, and Milton and Evelyn, gave plain and hearty counsel. Already too the English noble and squire were preparing for the career of the country-gentleman and his peaceable expense. They went from city to city, learning receipts to make perfumes, sweet powders, pomanders, antidotes, gathering seeds, gems, coins and divers curiosities, preparing for a private life thereafter, in which they should take pleasure in these recreations.

All advantages given to absolve the young patrician from intellectual labor are of course mistaken. "In the university, noblemen are exempted from the public exercises for the degree, etc., by which they attain a degree called *honorary.* At the same time, the fees they have to pay for matriculation, and on all other occasions, are much higher." Fuller records "the observation of foreigners, that Englishmen, by making their children gentlemen before they are men, cause they are so seldom wise men." This cockering justifies Dr. Johnson's bitter apology for primogeniture, that "it makes but one fool in a family."

The revolution in society has reached this class. The great powers of industrial art have no exclusion of name or blood. The tools of our time, namely steam, ships, printing, money and popular education, belong to those who can handle them; and their effect has been that advantages once confined to men of family are now open to the whole middle class. The road that grandeur levels for his coach, toil can travel in his cart.

This is more manifest every day, but I think it is true throughout English history. English history, wisely read, is the vindication of the brain of that people. Here at last were climate and condition friendly to the working faculty. Who now will work and dare, shall rule. This is the charter, or the chartism, which fogs and seas and rains proclaimed—that intellect and personal force should make the law; that industry and administrative talent should administer; that work should wear the crown. I know that not this, but something else is pretended. The fiction with which the noble and the bystander equally please themselves is that the former is of unbroken descent from the Norman, and so has never worked for eight hundred years. All the families are new, but the name is old, and they have made a covenant with their memories not to disturb it. But the analysis of the peerage and gentry shows the rapid decay and extinction of old families, the continual recruiting of these from new blood. The doors, though ostentatiously guarded, are really open, and hence the power of the bribe. All the barriers to rank only whet the thirst and enhance the prize. "Now," said Nelson, when clearing for battle, "a peerage, or Westminster Abbey!" "I have no illusion left," said Sydney Smith, "but the Archbishop of Canterbury." "The lawyers," said Burke, "are only birds of passage in this House of Commons," and then added, with a new figure, "they have their best bower anchor in the House of Lords."

Another stride that has been taken appears in the perishing of heraldry. Whilst the privileges of nobility are passing to the middle class, the badge is discredited and the titles of lordship are getting musty and cumbersome. I wonder that sensible men have not been already impatient of them. They belong, with wigs, powder and scarlet coats, to an earlier age and may be advantageously consigned, with paint and tattoo, to the dignitaries of Australia and Polynesia.

A multitude of English, educated at the universities, bred into their society with manners, ability and the gifts of fortune, are every day confronting the peers on a footing of equality, and outstripping them, as often, in the race of honor and influence. That cultivated class is large and ever enlarging. It is computed that, with titles and without, there are seventy thousand of these people coming and going in London, who make up what is called high society. They cannot shut their eyes to the fact that an untitled nobility possess all the power without the inconveniences that belong to rank, and the rich Englishman goes over the world at the present day, drawing more than all the advantages which the strongest of his kings could command.

Universities

Of British universities, Cambridge has the most illustrious names on its list. At the present day too, it has the advantage of Oxford, counting in its *alumni* a greater number of distinguished scholars. I regret that I had but a single day wherein to see King's College Chapel, the beautiful lawns and gardens of the colleges, and a few of its gownsmen.

But I availed myself of some repeated invitations to Oxford, where I had introductions to Dr. Daubeny, Professor of Botany, and to the Regius Professor of Divinity, as well as to a valued friend, a Fellow of Oriel, and went thither on the last day of March, 1848. I was the guest of my friend in Oriel, was housed close upon that college, and I lived on college hospitalities.

My new friends showed me their cloisters, the Bodleian Library, the Randolph Gallery, Merton Hall and the rest. I saw several faithful, high-minded young men, some of them in the mood of making sacrifices for peace of mind—a topic, of course, on which I had no counsel to offer. Their affectionate and gregarious ways reminded me at once of the habits of *our* Cambridge men, though I imputed to these English an advantage in their secure and polished manners. The halls are rich with oaken wainscoting and ceiling. The pictures of the founders hang from the walls; the tables glitter with plate. A youth came forward to the upper table and pronounced the ancient form of grace before meals, which, I suppose, has been in use here for ages, *Benedictus benedicat; benedictur, benedicatur.*

It is a curious proof of the English use and wont, or of their good nature, that these young men are locked up every night at nine o'clock, and the porter at each hall is required to give the name of any belated student who is admitted after that hour. Still more descriptive is the fact that out of twelve hundred young men, comprising the most spirited of the aristocracy, a duel has never occurred.

Oxford is old, even in England, and conservative. Its foundations date from Alfred and even from Arthur, if, as is alleged, the Pheryllt of the Druids had a seminary here. In the reign of Edward I, it is pretended, here were thirty thousand students; and nineteen most noble foundations were then established. Chaucer found it as firm as if it had always stood; and it is, in British story, rich with great names, the school of the island and the link of England to the learned of Europe. Hither came Erasmus, with delight, in 1497. Albericus Gentilis, in 1580, was relieved and maintained by the university. Albert Alaskie, a noble Polonian, Prince of Sirad, who visited England to admire the wisdom of Queen Elizabeth, was entertained with stage plays in the Refectory of Christ-Church in 1583. Isaac Casaubon, coming from Henri Quatre of

(Top) Queen's College—founded 1340—is one of the many colleges and collegial institutions of Oxford University. "On every side, Oxford is redolent of age and authority. Its gates shut of themselves against modern innovation. It is still governed by the statues of Archbishop Laud." (Bottom) Interior of the Bodleian Library at Oxford University. "No candle or fire is ever lighted in the Bodleian. Its catalogue is the standard catalogue on the desk of every library in Oxford. In each several college they underscore in red ink on this catalogue the titles of books contained in the library of that college—the theory being that the Bodleian has all books."

France by invitation of James I, was admitted to Christ-Church, in July, 1613. I saw the Ashmolean Museum, whither Elias Ashmole in 1682 sent twelve cartloads of rarities. Here indeed was the Olympia of all Antony Wood's and Aubrey's games and heroes, and every inch of ground has its lustre. For Wood's *Athenæ Oxonienses,* or calendar of the writers of Oxford for two hundred years, is a lively record of English manners and merits, and as much a national monument as Purchas's Pilgrims or Hansard's Register. On every side, Oxford is redolent of age and authority. Its gates shut of themselves against modern innovation. It is still governed by the statutes of Archbishop Laud. The books in Merton Library are still chained to the wall. Here, on August 27, 1660, John Milton's *Pro Populo Anglicano Defensio* and *Iconoclastes* were committed to the flames. I saw the school court or quadrangle where, in 1683, the Convocation caused the *Leviathan* of Thomas Hobbes to be publicly burnt. I do not know whether this learned body have yet heard of the Declaration of American Independence, or whether the Ptolemaic astronomy does not still hold its ground against the novelties of Copernicus.

As many sons, almost so many benefactors. It is usual for a nobleman, or indeed for almost every wealthy student, on quitting college to leave behind him some article of plate; and gifts of all values, from a hall or a fellowship or a library, down to a picture or a spoon, are continually accruing, in the course of a century. My friend Doctor J. gave me the following anecdote. In Sir Thomas Lawrence's collection at London were the cartoons of Raphael and Michael Angelo. This inestimable prize was offered to Oxford University for seven thousand pounds. The offer was accepted, and the committee charged with the affair had collected three thousand pounds, when, among other friends, they called on Lord Eldon. Instead of a hundred pounds, he surprised them by putting down his name for three thousand pounds. They

told him they should now very easily raise the remainder. "No," he said, "your men have probably already contributed all they can spare; I can as well give the rest": and he withdrew his cheque for three thousand, and wrote four thousand pounds. I saw the whole collection in April, 1848.

In the Bodleian Library, Dr. Bandinel showed me the manuscript Plato, of the date of A.D. 896, brought by Dr. Clarke from Egypt; a manuscript Virgil of the same century; the first Bible printed at Mentz (I believe in 1450); and a duplicate of the same, which had been deficient in about twenty leaves at the end. But one day, being in Venice, he bought a room full of books and manuscripts—every scrap and fragment—for four thousand louis d'ors, and had the doors locked and sealed by the consul. On proceeding afterwards to examine his purchase, he found the twenty deficient pages of his Mentz Bible, in perfect order; brought them to Oxford with the rest of his purchase, and placed them in the volume; but has too much awe for the Providence that appears in bibliography also, to suffer the reunited parts to be rebound. The oldest building here is two hundred years younger than the frail manuscript brought by Dr. Clarke from Egypt. No candle or fire is ever lighted in the Bodleian. Its catalogue is the standard catalogue on the desk of every library in Oxford. In each several college they underscore in red ink on this catalogue the titles of books contained in the library of that college—the theory being that the Bodleian has all books. This rich library spent during the last year (1847), for the purchase of books, £1,668.

The logical English train a scholar as they train an engineer. Oxford is a Greek factory, as Wilton mills weave carpet and Sheffield grinds steel. They know the use of a tutor, as they know the use of a horse; and they draw the greatest amount of benefit out of both. The reading men are kept, by hard walking, hard riding and measured eating and drinking, at the top of their condition, and two days before the examination, do no work, but lounge, ride, or run, to be fresh on the college doomsday. Seven years' residence is the theoretic period for a master's degree. In point of fact, it has long been three years' residence, and four years more of standing. This "three years" is about twenty-one months in all.

"The whole expense," says Professor Sewel, "of ordinary college tuition at Oxford, is about sixteen guineas a year." But this plausible statement may deceive a reader unacquainted with the fact that the principal teaching relied on is private tuition. And the expenses of private tuition are reckoned at from £50 to £70 a year, or $1,000 for the whole course of three years and a half. At Cambridge, $750 a year is economical, and $1,500 not extravagant.

The number of students and of residents, the dignity of the authorities, the value of the foundations, the history and the architecture, the known sympathy of entire Britain in what is done there, justify a dedication to study in the undergraduate such as cannot easily be in America, where his college is half suspected by the Freshman to be insignificant in the scale beside trade and politics. Oxford is a little aristocracy in itself, numerous and dignified enough to rank with other estates in the realm; and where fame and secular promotion are to be had for study, and in a direction which has the unanimous respect of all cultivated nations.

This aristocracy, of course, repairs its own losses; fills places, as they fall vacant, from the body of students. The number of fellowships at Oxford is 540, averaging £200 a year, with lodging and diet at the college. If a young American, loving learning and hindered by poverty, were offered a home, a table, the walks and the library in one of these academical palaces, and a thousand dollars a year, as long as he chose to remain a bachelor, he would dance for joy. Yet these young men thus happily placed, and paid to read, are im-

patient of their few checks, and many of them preparing to resign their fellowships. They shuddered at the prospect of dying a Fellow, and they pointed out to me a paralytic old man, who was assisted into the hall. As the number of undergraduates at Oxford is only about 1,200 or 1,300, and many of these are never competitors, the chance of a fellowship is very great. The income of the nineteen colleges is conjectured at £150,000 a year.

The effect of this drill is the radical knowledge of Greek and Latin and of mathematics, and the solidity and taste of English criticism. Whatever luck there may be in this or that award, an Eton captain can write Latin longs and shorts, can turn the Court-Guide into hexameters, and it is certain that a Senior Classic can quote correctly from the *Corpus Poetarum* and is critically learned in all the humanities. Greek erudition exists on the Isis and Cam, whether the Maud man or the Brasenose man be properly ranked or not; the atmosphere is loaded with Greek learning; the whole river has reached a certain height, and kills all that growth of weeds which this Castalian water kills. The English nature takes culture kindly. So Milton thought. It refines the Norseman. Access to the Greek mind lifts his standard of taste. He has enough to think of, and, unless of an impulsive nature, is indisposed from writing or speaking, by the fulness of his mind and the new severity of his taste. The great silent crowd of thoroughbred Grecians always known to be around him, the English writer cannot ignore. They prune his orations and point his pen. Hence the style and tone of English journalism. The men have learned accuracy and comprehension, logic, and pace, or speed of working. They have bottom, endurance, wind. When born with good constitutions, they make those eupeptic studying-mills, the cast-iron men, the *dura ilia*, whose powers of performance compare with ours as the steam-hammer with the music box—Cokes, Mansfields, Seldens and Bentleys, and when it happens that a superior brain puts a rider on this admirable horse, we obtain those masters of the world who combine the highest energy in affairs with a supreme culture.

It is contended by those who have been bred at Eton, Harrow, Rugby and Westminster, that the public sentiment within each of those schools is high-toned and manly; that, in their playgrounds, courage is universally admired, meanness despised, manly feelings and generous conduct are encouraged: that an unwritten code of honor deals to the spoiled child of rank and to the child of upstart wealth, an even-handed justice, purges their nonsense out of both and does all that can be done to make them gentlemen.

Again, at the universities, it is urged that all goes to form what England values as the flower of its national life—a well-educated gentleman. The German Huber, in describing to his countrymen the attributes of an English gentleman, frankly admits that "in Germany, we have nothing of the kind. A gentleman must possess a political character, an independent and public position, or at least the right of assuming it. He must have average opulence, either of his own, or in his family. He should also have bodily activity and strength, unattainable by our sedentary life in public offices. The race of English gentlemen presents an appearance of manly vigor and form not elsewhere to be found among an equal number of persons. No other nation produces the stock. And in England, it has deteriorated. The university is a decided presumption in any man's favor. And so eminent are the members that a glance at the calendars will show that in all the world one cannot be in better company than on the books of one of the larger Oxford or Cambridge colleges."

These seminaries are finishing schools for the upper classes, and not for the poor. The useful is exploded. The definition of a public school is "a school which excludes all that could fit a man for standing behind a counter."

No doubt, the foundations have been perverted. Oxford, which equals in wealth several of the smaller European states, shuts up the lectureships which were made "public for all men thereunto to have concourse"; misspends the revenues bestowed for such youths "as should be most meet for towardness, poverty and painfulness"; there is gross favoritism; many chairs and many fellowships are made beds of ease; and it is likely that the university will know how to resist and make inoperative the terrors of parliamentary inquiry; no doubt their learning is grown obsolete—but Oxford also has its merits, and I found here also proof of the national fidelity and thoroughness. Such knowledge as they prize they possess and impart. Whether in course or by indirection, whether by a cramming tutor or by examiners with prizes and foundation scholarships, education, according to the English notion of it, is arrived at. I looked over the Examination Papers of the year 1848, for the various scholarships and fellowships, the Lusby, the Hertford, the Dean-Ireland and the University (copies of which were kindly given me by a Greek professor), containing the tasks which many competitors had victoriously performed, and I believed they would prove too severe tests for the candidates for a Bachelor's degree in Yale or Harvard. And in general, here was proof of a more searching study in the appointed directions, and the knowledge pretended to be conveyed was conveyed. Oxford sends out yearly twenty or thirty very able men and three or four hundred well-educated men.

The diet and rough exercise secure a certain amount of old Norse power. A fop will fight, and in exigent circumstances will play the manly part. In seeing these youths I believed I saw already an advantage in vigor and color and general habit, over their contemporaries in the American colleges. No doubt much of the power and brilliancy of the reading-men is merely constitutional or hygienic. With a hardier habit and resolute gymnastics, with five miles more walking, or five ounces less eating, or with a saddle and gallop of twenty miles a day, with skating and rowing-matches, the American would arrive at as robust exegesis and cheery and hilarious tone. I should readily concede these advantages, which it would be easy to acquire, if I did not find also that they read better than we, and write better.

English wealth falling on their school and university training, makes a systematic reading of the best authors, and to the end of a knowledge how the things whereof they treat really stand: whilst pamphleteer or journalist, reading for an argument for a party, or reading to write, or at all events for some by-end imposed on them, must read meanly and fragmentarily. Charles I said that he understood English law as well as a gentleman ought to understand it.

Then they have access to books; the rich libraries collected at every one of many thousands of houses, give an advantage not to be attained by a youth in this country, when one thinks how much more and better may be learned by a scholar who, immediately on hearing of a book, can consult it, than by one who is on the quest, for years, and reads inferior books because he cannot find the best.

Again, the great number of cultivated men keep each other up to a high standard. The habit of meeting well-read and knowing men teaches the art of omission and selection.

Universities are of course hostile to geniuses, which seeing and using ways of their own, discredit the routine: as churches and monasteries persecute youthful saints. Yet we all send our sons to college, and though he be a genius, the youth must take his chance. The university must be retrospective. The gale that gives direction to the vanes on all its towers blows out of antiquity. Oxford is a library, and the professors must be librarians. And I should as soon think of quarreling with the janitor for not magnifying his office by hostile sallies into the street, like the Governor of Kertch or

Kinburn, as of quarreling with the professors for not admiring the young neologists who pluck the beards of Euclid and Aristotle, or for not attempting themselves to fill their vacant shelves as original writers.

It is easy to carp at colleges, and the college, if we will wait for it, will have its own turn. Genius exists there also, but will not answer a call of a committee of the House of Commons. It is rare, precarious, eccentric and darkling. England is the land of mixture and surprise, and when you have settled it that the universities are moribund, out comes a poetic influence from the heart of Oxford, to mold the opinions of cities, to build their houses as simply as birds their nests, to give veracity to art and charm mankind, as an appeal to moral order always must. But besides this restorative genius, the best poetry of England of this age, in the old forms, comes from two graduates of Cambridge.

Religion

No people at the present day can be explained by their national religion. They do not feel responsible for it; it lies far outside of them. Their loyalty to truth and their labor and expenditure rest on real foundations, and not on a national church. And English life, it is evident, does not grow out of the Athanasian creed, or the Articles, or the Eucharist. It is with religion as with marriage. A youth marries in haste; afterwards, when his mind is opened to the reason of the conduct of life, he is asked what he thinks of the institution of marriage and of the right relations of the sexes? "I should have much to say," he might reply, "if the question were open, but I have a wife and children, and all question is closed for me." In the barbarous days of a nation, some *cultus* is formed or imported; altars are built, tithes are paid, priests ordained. The education and expenditure of the country take that direction, and when wealth, refinement, great men, and ties to the world supervene, its pru-dent men say, Why fight against Fate, or lift these absurdities which are now mountainous? Better find some niche or crevice in this mountain of stone which religious ages have quarried and carved, wherein to bestow yourself, than attempt anything ridiculously and dangerously above your strength, like removing it.

In seeing old castles and cathedrals, I sometimes say, as today in front of Dundee Church tower, which is eight hundred years old, "This was built by another and a better race than any that now look on it." And plainly there has been great power of sentiment at work in this island, of which these buildings are the proofs; as volcanic basalts show the work of fire which has been extinguished for ages. England felt the full heat of the Christianity which fermented Europe, and drew, like the chemistry of fire, a firm line between barbarism and culture. The power of the religious sentiment put an end to human sacrifices, checked appetite, inspired the crusades, inspired resistance to tyrants, inspired self-respect, set bounds to serfdom and slavery, founded liberty, created the religious architecture—York, Newstead, Westminster, Fountains Abbey, Ripon, Beverley and Dundee—works to which the key is lost, with the sentiment which created them; inspired the English Bible, the liturgy, the monkish histories, the chronicle of Richard of Devizes. The priest translated the *Vulgate,* and translated the sanctities of old hagiology into English virtues on English ground. It was a certain affirmative or aggressive state of the Caucasian races. Man awoke refreshed by the sleep of ages. The violence of the northern savages exasperated Christianity into power. It lived by the love of the people. Bishop Wilfrid manumitted two hundred and fifty serfs, whom he found attached to the soil. The clergy obtained respite from labor for the boor on the Sabbath and on church festivals. "The lord who compelled his boor to labor between sunset on Saturday and sunset on Sunday, forfeited

him altogether." The priest came out of the people and sympathized with his class. The church was the mediator, check and democratic principle, in Europe. Latimer, Wicliffe, Arundel, Cobham, Antony Parsons, Sir Harry Vane, George Fox, Penn, Bunyan are the democrats, as well as the saints of their times. The Catholic Church, thrown on this toiling, serious people, has made in fourteen centuries a massive system, close-fitted to the manners and genius of the country, at once domestical and stately. In the long time, it has blended with everything in heaven above and the earth beneath. It moves through a zodiac of feasts and fasts, names every day of the year, every town and market and headland and monument, and has coupled itself with the almanac, that no court can be held, no field ploughed, no horse shod, without some leave from the church. All maxims of prudence or shop or farm are fixed and dated by the church. Hence its strength in the agricultural districts. The distribution of land into parishes enforces a church sanction to every civil privilege; and the gradation of the clergy—prelates for the rich and curates for the poor—with the fact that a classical education has been secured to the clergyman, makes them "the link which unites the sequestered peasantry with the intellectual advancement of the age."

The English Church has many certificates to show of humble effective service in humanizing the people, in cheering and refining men, feeding, healing and educating. It has the zeal of martyrs and confessors; the noblest books; a sublime architecture; a ritual marked by the same secular merits, nothing cheap or purchasable.

From this slow-grown church important reactions proceed; much for culture, much for giving a direction to the nation's affection and will today. The carved and pictured chapel—its entire surface animated with image and emblem—made the parish church a sort of book and Bible to the people's eye.

Then, when the Saxon instinct had secured a service in the vernacular tongue, it was the tutor and university of the people. In York minster, on the day of the enthronization of the new archbishop, I heard the service of evening prayer read and chanted in the choir. It was strange to hear the pretty pastoral of the betrothal of Rebecca and Isaac, in the morning of the world, read with circumstantiality in York minster, on the 13th January, 1848, to the decorous English audience, just fresh from the *Times* newspaper and their wine, and listening with all the devotion of national pride. That was binding old and new to some purpose. The reverence for the Scriptures is an element of civilization, for thus has the history of the world been preserved and is preserved. Here in England every day a chapter of Genesis, and a leader in the *Times*.

Another part of the same service on this occasion was not insignificant. Handel's coronation anthem "God save the King," was played by Dr. Camidge on the organ, with sublime effect. The minster and the music were made for each other. It was a hint of the part the church plays as a political engine. From his infancy, every Englishman is accustomed to hear daily prayers for the queen, for the royal family and the Parliament, by name; and this lifelong consecration cannot be without influence on his opinions.

The universities also are parcel of the ecclesiastical system, and their first design is to form the clergy. Thus the clergy for a thousand years have been the scholars of the nation.

The national temperament deeply enjoys the unbroken order and tradition of its church; the liturgy, ceremony, architecture; the sober grace, the good company, the connection with the throne and with history, which adorn it. And whilst it endears itself thus to men of more taste than activity, the stability of the English nation is passionately enlisted to its support, from its inextricable connection with the cause of public order, with politics and with funds.

Good churches are not built by bad men; at least there must be probity and enthusiasm somewhere in the society. These minsters were neither built nor filled by atheists. No church has had more learned, industrious or devoted men; plenty of "clerks and bishops, who, out of their gowns, would turn their backs on no man." Their architecture still glows with faith in immortality. Heats and genial periods arrive in history, or, shall we say, plenitudes of Divine Presence, by which high tides are caused in the human spirit, and great virtues and talents appear, as in the eleventh, twelfth, thirteenth, and again in the sixteenth and seventeenth centuries, when the nation was full of genius and piety.

But the age of the Wicliffes, Cobhams, Arundels, Beckets; of the Latimers, Mores, Cranmers; of the Taylors, Leightons, Herberts; of the Sherlocks and Butlers, is gone. Silent revolutions in opinion have made it impossible that men like these should return, or find a place in their once sacred stalls. The spirit that dwelt in this church has glided away to animate other activities, and they who come to the old shrines find apes and players rustling the old garments.

The religion of England is part of good breeding. When you see on the continent the well-dressed Englishman come into his ambassador's chapel and put his face for silent prayer into his smooth-brushed hat, you cannot help feeling how much national pride prays with him, and the religion of a gentleman. So far is he from attaching any meaning to the words, that he believes himself to have done almost the generous thing, and that it is very condescending in him to pray to God. A great duke said on the occasion of a victory, in the House of Lords, that he thought the Almighty God had not been well used by them, and that it would become their magnanimity, after so great successes, to take order that a proper acknowledgment be made. It is the church of the gentry, but it is not the church of the poor. The operatives do not own it, and gentlemen lately testified in the House of Commons that in their lives they never saw a poor man in a ragged coat inside a church.

The torpidity on the side of religion of the vigorous English understanding shows how much wit and folly can agree in one brain. Their religion is a quotation; their church is a doll; and any examination is interdicted with screams of terror. In good company you expect them to laugh at the fanaticism of the vulgar; but they do not; they are the vulgar.

The English, in common perhaps with Christendom in the nineteenth century, do not respect power, but only performance; value ideas only for an economic result. Wellington esteems a saint only as far as he can be an army chaplain: "Mr. Briscoll, by his admirable conduct and good sense, got the better of Methodism, which had appeared among the soldiers and once among the officers." They value a philosopher as they value an apothecary who brings bark or a drench; and inspiration is only some blowpipe, or a finer mechanical aid.

I suspect that there is in an Englishman's brain a valve that can be closed at pleasure, as an engineer shuts off steam. The most sensible and well-informed men possess the power of thinking just so far as the bishop in religious matters, and as the chancellor of the exchequer in politics. They talk with courage and logic, and show you magnificent results, but the same men who have brought free trade or geology to their present standing, look grave and lofty and shut down their valve as soon as the conversation approaches the English Church. After that, you talk with a box turtle.

The action of the university, both in what is taught and in the spirit of the place, is directed more on producing an English gentleman, than a saint or a psychologist. It ripens a bishop, and extrudes a philosopher. I do not know that there is more

cabalism in the Anglican than in other churches, but the Anglican clergy are identified with the aristocracy. They say here, that if you talk with a clergyman, you are sure to find him well-bred, informed and candid: he entertains your thought or your project with sympathy and praise. But if a second clergyman come in, the sympathy is at an end: two together are inaccessible to your thought, and whenever it comes to action, the clergyman invariably sides with his church.

The Anglican Church is marked by the grace and good sense of its forms, by the manly grace of its clergy. The gospel it preaches is "By taste are ye saved." It keeps the old structures in repair, spends a world of money in music and building, and in buying Pugin and architectural literature. It has a general good name for amenity and mildness. It is not in ordinary a persecuting church; it is not inquisitorial, not even inquisitive; is perfectly well-bred, and can shut its eyes on all proper occasions. If you let it alone, it will let you alone. But its instinct is hostile to all change in politics, literature, or social arts. The church has not been the founder of the London University, of the Mechanics' Institutes, of the Free School, of whatever aims at diffusion of knowledge. The Platonists of Oxford are as bitter against this heresy, as Thomas Taylor.

The doctrine of the Old Testament is the religion of England. The first leaf of the New Testament it does not open. It believes in a Providence which does not treat with levity a pound sterling. They are neither transcendentalists nor Christians. They put up no Socratic prayer, much less any saintly prayer for the queen's mind; ask neither for light nor right, but say bluntly, "Grant her in health and wealth long to live." And one traces this Jewish prayer in all English private history, from the prayers of King Richard, in Richard of Devizes' *Chronicle,* to those in the diaries of Sir Samuel Romilly and of Haydon the painter. "Abroad with my wife," writes

Pepys piously, "the first time that ever I rode in my own coach; which do make my heart rejoice and praise God, and pray him to bless it to me, and continue it." The bill for the naturalization of the Jews (in 1753) was resisted by petitions from all parts of the kingdom, and by petition from the city of London, reprobating this bill, as "tending extremely to the dishonor of the Christian religion, and extremely injurious to the interests and commerce of the kingdom in general, and of the city of London in particular."

But they have not been able to congeal humanity by act of Parliament. "The heavens journey still and sojourn not," and arts, wars, discoveries and opinion go onward at their own pace. The new age has new desires, new enemies, new trades, new charities, and reads the Scriptures with new eyes. The chatter of French politics, the steam whistle, the hum of the mill and the noise of embarking emigrants had quite put most of the old legends out of mind; so that when you came to read the liturgy to a modern congregation, it was almost absurd in its unfitness, and suggested a masquerade of old costumes.

No chemist has prospered in the attempt to crystallize a religion. It is endogenous, like the skin and other vital organs. A new statement every day. The prophet and apostle knew this, and the nonconformist confutes the conformists, by quoting the texts they must allow. It is the condition of a religion to require religion for its expositor. Prophet and apostle can only be rightly understood by prophet and apostle. The statesman knows that the religious element will not fail, any more than the supply of fibrine and chyle; but it is in its nature constructive, and will organize such a church as its wants. The wise legislator will spend on temples, schools, libraries, colleges, but will shun the enriching of priests. If in any manner he can leave the election and paying of the priest to the people, he will do well. Like the Quakers, he may resist the separation of a class of priests, and

create opportunity and expectation in the society to run to meet natural endowment in this kind. But when wealth accrues to a chaplaincy, a bishopric, or rectorship, it requires moneyed men for its stewards, who will give it another direction than to the mystics of their day. Of course, money will do after its kind, and will steadily work to unspiritualize and unchurch the people to whom it was bequeathed. The class certain to be excluded from all preferment are the religious—and driven to other churches; which is nature's *vis medicatrix*.

The curates are ill-paid, and the prelates are overpaid. This abuse draws into the church the children of the nobility and other unfit persons who have a taste for expense. Thus a bishop is only a surpliced merchant. Through his lawn I can see the bright buttons of the shopman's coat glitter. A wealth like that of Durham makes almost a premium on felony. Brougham, in a speech in the House of Commons on the Irish elective franchise, said, "How will the reverend bishops of the other house be able to express their due abhorrence of the crime of perjury, who solemnly declare in the presence of God that when they are called upon to accept a living, perhaps of £4,000 a year, at that very instant they are moved by the Holy Ghost to accept the office and administration thereof, and for no other reason whatever?" The modes of initiation are more damaging than customhouse oaths. The bishop is elected by the dean and prebends of the cathedral. The queen sends these gentlemen a *congé d'élire*, or leave to elect; but also sends them the name of the person whom they are to elect. They go into the cathedral, chant and pray and beseech the Holy Ghost to assist them in their choice; and, after these invocations, invariably find that the dictates of the Holy Ghost agree with the recommendations of the Queen.

But you must pay for conformity. All goes well as long as you run with conformists. But you, who are an honest man in other particulars, know that there is alive somewhere a man whose honesty reaches to this point also that he shall not kneel to false gods, and on the day when you meet him, you sink into the class of counterfeits. Besides, this succumbing has grave penalties. If you take in a lie, you must take in all that belongs to it. England accepts this ornamented national church, and it glazes the eyes, bloats the flesh, gives the voice a stertorous clang, and clouds the understanding of the receivers.

The English Church, undermined by German criticism, had nothing left but tradition; and was led logically back to Romanism. But that was an element which only hot heads could breathe: in view of the educated class, generally, it was not a fact to front the sun; and the alienation of such men from the church became complete.

Nature, to be sure, had her remedy. Religious persons are driven out of the Established Church into sects, which instantly rise to credit and hold the Establishment in check. Nature has sharper remedies, also. The English, abhorring change in all things, abhorring it most in matters of religion, cling to the last rag of form, and are dreadfully given to cant. The English (and I wish it were confined to them, but 'tis a taint in the Anglo-Saxon blood in both hemispheres)—the English and the Americans cant beyond all other nations. The French relinquish all that industry to them. What is so odious as the polite bows to God, in our books and newspapers? The popular press is flagitious in the exact measure of its sanctimony, and the religion of the day is a theatrical Sinai, where the thunders are supplied by the property-man. The fanaticism and hypocrisy create satire. *Punch* finds an inexhaustible material. Dickens writes novels on Exeter-Hall humanity. Thackeray exposes the heartless high life. Nature revenges herself more summarily by the heathenism of the lower classes. Lord Shaftesbury calls the poor thieves together and reads sermons to them, and they call it "gas." George

Borrow summons the Gypsies to hear his discourse on the Hebrews in Egypt, and reads to them the Apostles' Creed in Romany. "When I had concluded," he says, "I looked around me. The features of the assembly were twisted, and the eyes of all turned upon me with a frightful squint: not an individual present but squinted; the genteel Pepa, the good-humored Chicharona, the Cosdami, all squinted; the Gypsy jockey squinted worst of all."

The Church at this moment is much to be pitied. She has nothing left but possession. If a bishop meets an intelligent gentleman and reads fatal interrogations in his eyes, he has no resource but to take wine with him. False position introduces cant, perjury, simony and ever a lower class of mind and character into the clergy: and, when the hierarchy is afraid of science and education, afraid of piety, afraid of tradition and afraid of theology, there is nothing left but to quit a church which is no longer one.

But the religion of England—is it the Established Church? no; is it the sects? no; they are only perpetuations of some private man's dissent, and are to the Established Church as cabs are to a coach, cheaper and more convenient, but really the same thing. Where dwells the religion? Tell me first where dwells electricity, or motion, or thought, or gesture. They do not dwell or stay at all. Electricity cannot be made fast, mortared up and ended, like London Monument or the Tower, so that you shall know where to find it, and keep it fixed, as the English do with their things, forevermore; it is passing, glancing, gesticular; it is a traveler, a newness, a surprise, a secret, which perplexes them and puts them out. Yet, if religion be the doing of all good, and for its sake the suffering of all evil, *souffrir de tout le monde, et ne faire souffrir personne,* that divine secret has existed in England from the days of Alfred to those of Romilly, of Clarkson and of Florence Nightingale, and in thousands who have no fame.

Result

England is the best of actual nations. It is no ideal framework, it is an old pile built in different ages, with repairs, additions and makeshifts; but you see the poor best you have got. London is the epitome of our times, and the Rome of today. Broad-fronted, broad-bottomed Teutons, they stand in solid phalanx four-square to the points of compass; they constitute the modern world, they have earned their vantage ground and held it through ages of adverse possession. They are well marked and differing from other leading races. England is tenderhearted. Rome was not. England is not so public in its bias; private life is its place of honor. Truth in private life, untruth in public, marks these home-loving men. Their political conduct is not decided by general views, but by internal intrigues and personal and family interest. They cannot readily see beyond England. The history of Rome and Greece, when written by their scholars, degenerates into English party pamphlets. They cannot see beyond England, nor in England can they transcend the interests of the governing classes. "English principles" mean a primary regard to the interests of property. England, Scotland and Ireland combine to check the colonies. England and Scotland combine to check Irish manufactures and trade. England rallies at home to check Scotland. In England, the strong classes check the weaker. In the home population of near thirty millions, there are but one million voters. The Church punishes dissent, punishes education. Down to a late day, marriages performed by dissenters were illegal. A bitter class-legislation gives power to those who are rich enough to buy a law. The game-laws are a proverb of oppression. Pauperism incrusts and clogs the state, and in hard times becomes hideous. In bad seasons, the porridge was diluted. Multitudes lived miserably by shellfish and sea-ware. In cities, the children are trained to beg, until they shall be old enough to rob. Men and women were convicted of poisoning scores of children for burial fees. In Irish districts, men deteriorated in size and shape, the nose sunk, the gums were exposed, with diminished brain and brutal form. During the Australian emigration, multitudes were rejected by the commissioners as being too emaciated for useful colonists. During the Russian war, few of those that offered as recruits were found up to the medical standard, though it had been reduced.

The foreign policy of England, though ambitious and lavish of money, has not often been generous or just. It has a principal regard to the interest of trade, checked however by the aristocratic bias of the ambassador, which usually puts him in sympathy with the continental Courts. It sanctioned the partition of Poland, it betrayed Genoa, Sicily, Parga, Greece, Turkey, Rome and Hungary.

Some public regards they have. They have abolished slavery in the West Indies and put an end to human sacrifices in the East. At home they have a certain statute hospitality. England keeps open doors, as a trading country must, to all nations. It is one of their fixed ideas, and wrathfully supported by their laws in unbroken sequence for a thousand years. In *Magna Charta* it was ordained that all "merchants shall have safe and secure conduct to go out and come into England, and to stay there, and to pass as well by land as by water, to buy and sell by the ancient allowed customs, without any evil toll, except in time of war, or when they shall be of any nation at war with us." It is a statute and obliged hospitality and peremptorily maintained. But this shop-rule had one magnificent effect. It extends its cold unalterable courtesy to political exiles of every opinion, and is a fact which might give additional light to that portion of the planet seen from the farthest star. But this perfunctory hospitality puts no sweetness into their unaccommodating manners, no check on that puissant nationality which makes their existence incompatible with all that is not English.

What we must say about a nation is a superficial dealing with symptoms. We cannot go deep enough into the biography of the spirit who never throws himself entire into one hero, but delegates his energy in parts or spasms to vicious and defective individuals. But the wealth of the source is seen in the plenitude of English nature. What variety of power and talent; what facility and plenteousness of knighthood, lordship, ladyship, royalty, loyalty; what a proud chivalry is indicated in *Collins's Peerage*, through eight hundred years! What dignity resting on what reality and stoutness! What courage in war, what sinew in labor, what cunning workmen, what inventors and engineers, what seamen and pilots, what clerks and scholars! No one man and no few men can represent them. It is a people of myriad personalities. Their many-headedness is owing to the advantageous position of the middle class, who are always the source of letters and science. Hence the vast plenty of their esthetic production. As they are many-headed, so they are many-nationed: their colonization annexes archipelagoes and continents, and their speech seems destined to be the universal language of men. I have noted the reserve of power in the English temperament. In the island, they never let out all the length of all the reins, there is no Berserker rage, no abandonment or ecstasy of will or intellect, like that of the Arabs in the time of Mahomet, or like that which intoxicated France in 1789. But who would see the uncoiling of that tremendous spring, the explosion of their well-husbanded forces, must follow the swarms which pouring now for two hundred years from the British islands, have sailed and rode and traded and planted—through all climates, mainly following the belt of empire, the temperate zones, carrying the Saxon seed, with its instinct for liberty and law, for arts and for thought—acquiring under some skies a more electric energy than the native air allows—to the conquest of the globe. Their colonial policy, obeying the necessities of a vast empire, has become liberal. Canada and Australia have been contented with substantial independence. They are expiating the wrongs of India by benefits; first, in works for the irrigation of the peninsula, and roads, and telegraphs; and secondly, in the instruction of the people, to qualify them for self-government, when the British power shall be finally called home.

Their mind is in a state of arrested development—a divine cripple like Vulcan; a blind *savant* like Huber and Sanderson. They do not occupy themselves on matters of general and lasting import, but on a corporeal civilization, on goods that perish in the using. But they read with good intent, and what they learn they incarnate. The English mind turns every abstraction it can receive into a portable utensil, or a working institution. Such is their tenacity and such their practical turn, that they hold all they gain. Hence we say that only the English race can be trusted with freedom—freedom which is double-edged and dangerous to any but the wise and robust. The English designate the kingdoms emulous of free institutions, as the sentimental nations. Their culture is not an outside varnish, but is thorough and secular in families and the race. They are oppressive with their temperament, and all the more that they are refined. I have sometimes seen them walk with my countrymen when I was forced to allow them every advantage, and their companions seemed bags of bones.

There is cramp limitation in their habit of thought, sleepy routine, and a tortoise's instinct to hold hard to the ground with his claws, lest he should be thrown on his back. There is a drag of inertia which resists reform in every shape—law-reform, army-reform, extension of suffrage, Jewish franchise, Catholic emancipation—the abolition of slavery, of impressment, penal code and entails. They praise this drag, under the formula that it is the excellence of the British constitution that no law can anticipate the public opinion. These poor tortoises must hold hard, for they feel no wings sprouting at their shoulders. Yet somewhat divine warms at their heart and waits a happier hour. It hides in their sturdy will. "Will," said the old philosophy, "is the measure of power," and personality is the token of this race. *Quid vult valde vult.* What they do they do with a will. You cannot account for their success by their Christianity, commerce, charter, common law, Parliament, or letters, but by the contumacious sharp-tongued energy of English *naturel,* with a poise impossible to disturb, which makes all these its instruments. They are slow and reticent, and are like a dull good horse which lets every nag pass him, but with whip and spur will run down every racer in the field. They are right in their feeling, though wrong in their speculation.

The feudal system survives in the steep inequality of property and privilege, in the limited franchise, in the social barriers which confine patronage and promotion to a caste, and still more in the submissive ideas pervading these people. The fagging of the schools is repeated in the social classes. An Englishman shows no mercy to those below him in the social scale, as he looks for none from those above him; any forbearance from his superiors surprises him, and they suffer in his good opinion. But the feudal system can be seen with less pain on large historical grounds. It was pleaded in mitigation of the rotten borough, that it worked well, that substantial justice was done. Fox, Burke, Pitt, Erskine, Wilberforce, Sheridan, Romilly, or whatever national man, were by this means sent to Parliament, when their return by large constituencies would have been doubtful. So now we say that the right measures of England are the men it bred; that it has yielded more able men in five hundred years than any other nation; and, though we must not play Providence and balance the chances of producing ten great men against the comfort of ten thousand mean men, yet retrospectively, we may strike the balance and prefer one Alfred, one Shakespeare, one Milton, one Sidney, one Raleigh, one Wellington, to a million foolish democrats.

The American system is more democratic, more humane; yet the American people do not yield better or more able men, or more inventions or books or benefits than the English. Congress is not wiser or better than Parliament. France has abolished its suffocating old *régime,* but is not recently marked by any more wisdom or virtue.

The power of performance has not been exceeded—the creation of value. The English have given importance to individuals, a principal end and fruit of every society. Every man is allowed and encouraged to be what he is and is guarded in the indulgence of his whim. "Magna Charta," said Rushworth, "is such a fellow that he will have no sovereign." By this general activity and by this sacredness of individuals, they have in seven hundred years evolved the principles of freedom. It is the land of patriots, martyrs, sages and bards, and if the ocean out of which it emerged should wash it away, it will be remembered as an island famous for immortal laws, for the announcements of original right which make the stone tables of liberty.

From The History of
the Russian Revolution

Leon Trotsky

Editor's Introduction

Three men are recognized everywhere as having established the Communist Revolution in Russia. Lenin, the acknowledged leader of the movement at its beginning, died not many years after it arrived and has since become a kind of frozen relic of the event—literally, in the embalmed figure that lies entombed outside the Kremlin wall in Moscow, otherwise in the countless effigies that once adorned every public building and every public room in the former Soviet Union. Joseph Stalin, who succeeded him, has gained mythical proportions as a monster of cruelty and power who returns to our consciousness with every mention of his name. Only the third founder, Leon Trotsky, has almost disappeared from our perceptions since his death in 1940. And yet, as Mr. Simpson's article elsewhere in this issue of *The Great Ideas Today* makes clear, he was the most commanding figure of them all at the time (though he deferred to Lenin), as he was the most brilliant thinker, the ablest administrator, and the most compelling orator.

Can Trotsky be—should he be—restored to our awareness? It seems worthwhile to try, considering the importance he had, and considering that he was the apostle of the idea of revolution, which has not many protagonists at present. Trotsky, who was profoundly serious, thought it the most important idea in the world. Why did he think that? What did it mean to him? The answers to these questions are suggested by Mr. Simpson's article and evident in the concluding chapter from *The History of the Russian Revolution,* a book Trotsky composed like Thucydides from exile, which is reprinted here.

Born in 1879 in what is now Ukraine, Trotsky was drawn to Marxism and Socialism at an early age. Arrested in 1898 for illegal activities, he was sentenced to four years in Siberia, from where he escaped to London. There he joined Russian Social-Democrats working on a revolutionary paper edited by Lenin. Returning to St. Petersburg, Trotsky organized the workers' movement there during the revolutionary uprising of 1905, of which he was the guiding spirit. After a second exile to Siberia, he again escaped and spent the years leading up to World War I in Vienna, where he became a war correspondent. He moved variously to Switzerland, France, Spain, and the United States. In New York City he joined Nikolay Bukharin, who was editor of the Leninist newspaper *Novy Mir* ("The New World"). With the outbreak of the Russian Revolution in February 1917, he made his way to Petrograd, assumed leadership of a left-wing faction, and was arrested in August by the liberal Social-Democratic government of Aleksandr Kerensky. In September, on his release, he joined the Bolsheviks, who rejected compromise with Kerensky. Trotsky became at once a leading Bolshevik figure, though he never challenged Lenin's leadership of that party.

Of his activities during the climactic month of October 1917, and his own view of them, Mr. Simpson gives an account in his article. After the Bolshevik triumph, Trotsky was called upon to create an army capable of defending the country against counterrevolutionary forces aided by no fewer than thirteen foreign countries determined to overthrow the Communist government. In this he was brilliantly successful, and by 1920 his forces had defeated its many enemies.

Turning himself to economic matters after the war, Trotsky tried to reduce the centralization which it had made necessary. When Lenin became ill in 1922, there began a struggle for succession which eventually pitted Trotsky against Stalin, who rejected the principle of world revolution in which Trotsky believed. Stalin preferred to settle for "Socialism in one country," which Trotsky thought doomed to failure as well as certain to revive autocratic tendencies. After Lenin's death in 1924, however, Stalin won out, and over the next few years Trotsky was removed from the various positions of power that he held. In 1929 he was finally forced to leave the Soviet Union. Subsequently he lived in Turkey, where this *History* was written, moving in turn to France, Germany, Norway, and finally, Mexico. There his life came to an end, when, still regarded by Stalin as a threat because of his writings and his international reputation, he was murdered by a Soviet agent.

The *History*, which runs to many pages, nevertheless covers only the months between February and October 1917, ending with this chapter in which the Bolshevik (i.e., "Majority") Party gains power. Of Trotsky's numerous other writings the most important is probably *Results and Prospects* (1906), composed in jail after the failed revolution of 1905, which sets forth the theory of permanent revolution by which he is best known, and of which Mr. Simpson's article gives a brief description.

Chapter X. The Congress of the Soviet Dictatorship

In Smolny on the 25th of October the most democratic of all parliaments in the world's history was to meet. Who knows—perhaps also the most important.

Having got free of the influence of compromisist intellectuals, the local soviets had sent up for the most part workers and soldiers. The majority of them were people without big names, but who had proved themselves in action and won lasting confidence in their own localities. From the active army it was almost exclusively rank-and-file soldiers who had run the blockade of army committees and headquarters and come here as delegates. A majority of them had begun to live a political life with the revolution. They had been formed by an experience of eight months. They knew little, but knew it well. The outward appearance of the Congress proclaimed its make-up. The officers' chevrons, the eyeglasses and neckties of intellectuals to be seen at the first Congress had almost completely disappeared. A grey color prevailed uninterruptedly, in costumes and in faces. All had worn out their clothes during the war. Many of the city workers had provided themselves with soldiers' coats. The trench delegates were by no means a pretty picture: long unshaven, in old torn trench-coats, with heavy *papakhi** on their disheveled hair, often with cotton sticking out through a hole, with coarse, weather-beaten faces, heavy cracked hands, fingers yellowed with tobacco, buttons torn off, belts hanging loose, and long unoiled boots wrinkled and rusty. The plebeian nation had for the first time sent up an honest representation made in its own image and not retouched.

The statistics of this Congress which assembled during the hours of insurrection are very incomplete. At the moment of opening there were 650 delegates with votes. 390 fell to the lot of the Bolsheviks—by no means all members of the party, but they were of the flesh and blood of the masses, and the masses had no roads left but the Bolshevik road. Many of the delegates who had brought doubts with them were maturing fast in the red-hot atmosphere of Petrograd.

How completely had the Mensheviks and Social Revolutionaries squandered the political capital of the February revolution! At the June Congress of Soviets the Compromisers had a majority of 600 votes out of the whole number of 832 delegates. Now the Compromisist opposition of all shades made up less than a quarter of the Congress. The Mensheviks, with the national group adhering to them, amounted to only 80 members—about half of them "Lefts." Out of 159 Social Revolutionaries—according to other reports, 190—about three-fifths were Lefts, and moreover the Right continued to melt fast during the very sitting of the Congress. Toward the end the total number of delegates, according to several lists, reached 900. But this figure, while including a number of advisory members, does not on the other hand include all those with votes. The registration was carried on intermittently; documents have been lost;

_____
*Tall fur hats.

A group of Red Guards stand at the entrance to the Smolny Institute in Petrograd,
October 1917. Formerly a state-supported school for well-bred young women, the

Institute became the headquarters for the Bolsheviks during the Russian Revolution of 1917.

the information about party affiliations was incomplete. In any case the dominant position of the Bolsheviks in the Congress remains indubitable.

A straw-vote taken among the delegates revealed that 505 soviets stood for the transfer of all power to the soviets; 86 for a government of the "democracy"; 55 for a coalition; 21 for a coalition, but without the Kadets. Although eloquent even in this form, these figures give an exaggerated idea of the remains of the Compromisers' influence. Those for democracy and coalition were soviets from the more backward districts and least important points.

From early in the morning of the 25th, caucuses of the factions were held in Smolny. Only those attended the Bolshevik caucus who were free from fighting duties. The opening of the Congress was delayed: the Bolshevik leaders wanted to finish with the Winter Palace first. But the opposing factions, too, were in no hurry. They themselves had to decide what to do, and that was not easy. Hours passed. Subfactions were disputing within the factions. The split among the Social Revolutionaries took place after a resolution to withdraw from the Congress had been rejected by 92 votes against 60. It was only late in the evening that the Right and Left Social Revolutionaries began to sit in different rooms. At 8 o'clock the Mensheviks demanded a new delay: they had too many opinions. Night came on. The operations at the Winter Palace were dragging out. But it became impossible to wait longer. It was necessary to say some clear word to the aroused and watchful nation.

The revolution had taught the art of filling space. Delegates, guests, guards, jammed into the commencement hall of the noble maidens, making room for more and more. Warnings of the danger of the floor's collapsing had no effect, nor did appeals to smoke a little less. All crowded closer and smoked twice as much. John Reed with difficulty fought his way through the noisy crowd around the doors. The hall was not heated, but the air was heavy and hot.

Jamming the entries and the side exits, sitting on all the window sills, the delegates now patiently await the president's gong. Tseretelli, Cheidze, Chernov—none of them is on the platform. Only leaders of the second rank have come to their funeral. A short man in the uniform of a military doctor opens the session at 10:40 in the evening in the name of the Executive Committee. The Congress, he says, assembles in such "exceptional circumstances" that he, Dan, obeying the directions of the Central Executive Committee, will refrain from making a political speech. His party friends are now indeed under fire in the Winter Palace "while loyally fulfilling their duty as ministers." The last thing these delegates are expecting is a blessing from the Central Executive Committee. They look up at the platform with hostility. If those people still exist politically, what have they got to do with us and our business?

In the name of the Bolsheviks a Moscow delegate, Avanessov, moves that the praesidium be elected upon a proportional basis: 14 Bolsheviks, 7 Social Revolutionaries, 3 Mensheviks and 1 Internationalist. The Right immediately declines to enter the praesidium. Martov's group sits tight for the time being; it has not decided. Seven votes go over to the Left Social Revolutionaries. The Congress watches these introductory conflicts with a scowl.

Avanessov announces the Bolshevik candidates for the praesidium: Lenin, Trotsky, Zinoviev, Kamenev, Rykov, Nogin, Skliansky, Krylenko, Antonov-Ovseënko, Riazanov, Muranov, Lunacharsky, Kollontai, Stuchka. "The praesidium," writes Sukhanov, "consisted of the principal Bolshevik leaders and six (in reality seven) Left Social Revolutionaries." Zinoviev and Kamenev were included in the praesidium as authoritative party names in spite of their active opposition to the insurrection; Rykov and Nogin as representatives of the

Moscow Soviet; Lunacharsky and Kollontai as popular agitators of that period; Riazanov as a representative of the trade unions; Muranov as an old worker-Bolshevik who had carried himself courageously during the trial of the deputies of the State Duma; Stuchka as head of the Lettish organization; Krylenko and Skliansky as representatives of the army; Antonov-Ovseënko as a leader of the Petrograd battles. The absence of Sverdlov's name is obviously explained by the fact that he himself drew up the list, and in the confusion nobody corrected it. It is characteristic of the party morals of the time that the whole headquarters of the opponents of the insurrection turned up in the praesidium: Zinoviev, Kamenev, Nogin, Rykov, Lunacharsky, Riazanov. Of the Left Social Revolutionaries only the little fragile and courageous Spiridonova, who had served long years at hard labor for assassinating the subduer of the Tombovsk peasants, enjoyed an all-Russian renown. The Left Social Revolutionaries had no other "names." The Rights, on the other hand, had now little or nothing but names left.

The Congress greeted its praesidium with enthusiasm. While the factions had been assembling and conferring, Lenin with his make-up still on, in wig and big spectacles, was sitting in the passage-way in the company of two or three Bolsheviks. On the way to a meeting of their faction Dan and Skobelev stopped still opposite the table where the conspirators were sitting, stared at Lenin, and obviously recognized him. Time, then, to take the make-up off. But Lenin was in no hurry to appear publicly. He preferred to look round a little and gather the threads into his hands while remaining behind the scenes. In his recollections of Lenin published in 1924, Trotsky writes: "The first session of the Second Congress of Soviets was sitting in Smolny. Lenin did not appear there. He remained in one of the rooms of Smolny in which, as I remember, there was for some reason no furniture, or almost none. Later

somebody spread blankets on the floor and put two cushions on them. Vladimir Ilych and I took a rest there lying side by side. But in just a few minutes I was called: 'Dan is talking and you must answer him.'* Returning after my reply, I again lay down beside Vladimir Ilych, who of course had no thought of going to sleep. Was that indeed possible? Every five or ten minutes somebody would run in from the assembly hall to tell us what was going on."

The president's chair is occupied by Kamenev, one of those phlegmatic types designed by nature herself for the office of chairman. There are three questions, he announces, on the order of the day: organization of a government; war and peace; convocation of the Constituent Assembly. An unusual, dull, alarming rumble breaks into the noise of the meeting from outside. This is Peter and Paul Fortress ratifying the order of the day with artillery fire. A high tension current runs through the Congress, which now suddenly feels and realizes what it really is: the convention of a civil war.

Lozovsky, an opponent of the insurrection, demanded a report from the Petrograd Soviet. But the Military Revolutionary Committee was a little behind hand. Replying artillery testified that the report was not ready. The insurrection was in full swing. The Bolshevik leaders were continually withdrawing to the rooms of the Military Revolutionary Committee to receive communications or give orders. Echoes of the fighting would burst up through the assembly like tongues of flame. When votes were taken hands would be raised among bristling bayonets. A blue-grey acrid tobacco smoke hid the beautiful white columns and chandeliers.

The verbal battles of the two camps were extraordinarily impressive against a background of cannon-shots. Martov demanded the floor. The moment when the

---

*Evidently the name here should be Martov, to whom Trotsky did make a reply.

balance is still oscillating is his moment—this inventive statesman of eternal waverings. With his hoarse tubercular voice Martov makes instant rejoinder to the metallic voice of the guns: "We must put a stop to military action on both sides. . . . The question, of power is beginning to be decided by conspiratorial methods. All the revolutionary parties have been placed before a *fait accompli*. . . . A civil war threatens us with an explosion of counter-revolution. A peaceful solution of the crisis can be obtained by creating a government which will be recognized by the whole democracy." A considerable portion of the Congress applauds. Sukhanov remarks ironically: "Evidently many and many a Bolshevik, not having absorbed the spirit of the teachings of Lenin and Trotsky, would have been glad to take just that course." The Left Social Revolutionaries and a group of United Internationalists support the proposal of peace negotiations. The right wing, and perhaps also the close associates of Martov, are confident that the Bolsheviks will reject this proposal. They are wrong. The Bolsheviks send Lunacharsky to the tribune, the most peace-loving, the most velvety of their orators. "The Bolshevik faction," he says, "has absolutely nothing against Martov's proposal." The enemy are astonished. "Lenin and Trotsky in thus giving way a little to their own masses," comments Sukhanov, "are at the same time cutting the ground from under the Right Wing." Martov's proposal is adopted unanimously. "If the Mensheviks and Social Revolutionaries withdraw now," runs the comment in Martov's group, "they will bury themselves." It is possible to hope, therefore, that the Congress "will take the correct road of creating a united democratic front." Vain hope! A revolution never moves on diagonals.

The Right Wing immediately violates the just approved initiation of peace negotiations. The Menshevik Kharash, a delegate from the 12th Army with a captain's stars on his shoulders, makes a statement:

"These political hypocrites propose that we decide the question of power. Meanwhile it is being decided behind our backs. . . . Those blows at the Winter Palace are driving nails in the coffin of the party which has undertaken such an adventure. . . ." The captain's challenge is answered by the Congress with a grumble of indignation.

Lieutenant Kuchin who had spoken at the State Conference in Moscow in the name of the front, tries here also to wield the authority of the army organizations: "This Congress is untimely and even unauthorized." "In whose name do you speak?" shout the tattered trench-coats, their credentials written all over them in the mud of the trenches. Kuchin carefully enumerates eleven armies. But here this deceives nobody. At the front as at the rear the generals of compromisism are without soldiers. The group from the front, continues the Menshevik lieutenant, "declines to assume any responsibility for the consequences of this adventure." That means a complete break with the revolution. "Henceforth the arena of struggle is transferred to the localities." That means fusion with the counter-revolution against the soviets. And so the conclusion: "The front group . . . withdraws from this Congress."

One after another the representatives of the Right mount the tribune. They have lost the parishes and churches, but they still hold the belfries, and they hasten for the last time to pound the cracking bells. These socialists and democrats, having made a compromise by hook and crook with the imperialist bourgeoisie, today flatly refuse to compromise with the people in revolt. Their political calculations are laid bare. The Bolsheviks will collapse in a few days, they are thinking, we must separate ourselves from them as quickly as possible, even help to overthrow them, and thus to the best of our ability insure ourselves and our future.

In the name of the Right Menshevik faction, Khinchuk, a former president of the Moscow soviet and a future soviet ambassador in Berlin, reads a declaration: "The military conspiracy of the Bolsheviks . . . will plunge the country into civil dissension, demolish the Constituent Assembly, threaten us with a military catastrophe, and lead to the triumph of the counter-revolution." The sole way out: "Open negotiations with the Provisional Government for the formation of a power resting on all layers of the democracy." Having learned nothing, these people propose to the Congress to cross off the insurrection and return to Kerensky. Through the uproar, bellowing, and even hissing, the words of the representative of the Right Social Revolutionaries are hardly distinguishable. The declaration of his party announces "the impossibility of work in collaboration" with the Bolsheviks, and declares the very Congress of Soviets, although convoked and opened by the compromisist Central Executive Committee, to be without authority.

This demonstration of the Right Wing does not cow anybody, but causes alarm and irritation. The majority of the delegates are too sick and tired of these bragging and narrow-minded leaders who fed them first with phrases and then with measures of repression. Can it be that the Dans, Khinchuks and Kuchins still expect to instruct and command us? A Lettish soldier, Peterson, with a tubercular flush on his cheeks and burning hatred in his eyes, denounces Kharash and Kuchin as impostors. "The revolution has had enough gab! We want action! The power should be in our hands. Let the impostors leave the Congress—the army is through with them!" This voice tense with passion relieves the mind of the Congress, which has received nothing so far but insults. Other front-line soldiers rush to the support of Peterson. "These Kuchins represent the opinions of little gangs who have been sitting in the army committees since April. The army long ago demanded new elections." "Those who live in the trenches are impatiently awaiting the transfer of power to the soviets."

But the Rights still hold the belfries. A representative of the Bund declares that "all that has happened in Petrograd is a misfortune," and invites the delegates to join the members of the duma who have decided to march unarmed to the Winter Palace in order to die with the government." "Gibes were to be heard in the general uproar," writes Sukhanov, "some coarse and some poisonous." The unctuous orator has obviously mistaken his audience. "Enough from you!" "Deserters!" shout the delegates, guests, Red Guards and sentries at the door to the withdrawing delegates. "Join Kornilov!" "Enemies of the people!"

The withdrawal of the Rights did not leave any vacant space. Evidently the rank-and-file delegates had refused to join the officers and junkers for a struggle against the workers and soldiers. Only about 70 delegates—that is, a little more than half of the Right Wing faction—went out. The waverers took their place with the intermediate groups who had decided not to leave the Congress. Whereas before the opening of the Congress the Social Revolutionaries of all tendencies had numbered not over 190 men, during the next few hours the number of Left Social Revolutionaries alone rose to 180. They were joined by all those who had not yet decided to join the Bolsheviks although ready to support them.

The Mensheviks and Social Revolutionaries were quite ready to remain in a Provisional Government or some sort of a Pre-Parliament under any circumstances. Can one after all break with cultured society? But the soviets—that is only the people. The soviets are all right while you can use them to get a compromise with the bourgeoisie, but can one possibly think of tolerating soviets which have suddenly imagined themselves masters of the country? "The Bolsheviks were left alone," wrote the Social Revolutionary, Zenzinov, subsequently, "and from that moment they began to rely only upon crude physical force." Moral Principle undoubtedly slammed the door along with Dan and Gotz. Moral Principle will march in a procession of 300 men with two lanterns to the Winter Palace, only to run into the crude physical force of the Bolsheviks and—back down.

The motion adopted by the Congress in favor of peace negotiations was left hanging in the air. If the Rights had admitted the possibility of compromising with a victorious proletariat, they would have been in no hurry to break with the Congress. Martov could not have failed to understand this. Nevertheless he clung to the idea of a compromise—the thing upon which his whole policy always stands or falls. "We must put a stop to the bloodshed . . ." he begins again. "Those are only rumors!" voices call out. "It is not only rumors that we hear," he answers, "If you come to the windows you will hear cannon shots." This is undeniable. When the Congress quiets down, shots are audible without going to the windows.

Martov's declaration, hostile through and through to the Bolsheviks, and lifeless in its arguments, condemns the revolution as "accomplished by the Bolshevik party alone by the method of a purely military plot," and demands that the Congress suspend its labors until an agreement has been reached with all the socialist parties. To try to find the resultant of a parallelogram of forces in a revolution is worse than trying to catch your own shadow!

At that moment there appeared in the Congress the Bolshevik faction of the city duma, those who had refused to seek a problematic death under the walls of the Winter Palace. They were led by Joffé, subsequently the first soviet ambassador at Berlin. The Congress again crowded up, giving its friends a joyful welcome.

But it was necessary to put up a resistance to Martov. This task fell to Trotsky. "Now since the exodus of the Rights,"—concedes Sukhanov—"his position is as strong as Martov's is weak." The opponents stand side by side in the tribune, hemmed in on all sides by a solid ring of excited delegates. "What has taken place," says Trotsky, "is an insurrection, not a conspiracy. An insurrection of the popular masses needs no justification. We have tempered and hardened the revolutionary energy of the Petersburg workers and soldiers. We have openly forged the will of the masses to insurrection, and not conspiracy. . . . Our insurrection has conquered, and now you propose to us: Renounce your victory; make a compromise. With whom? I ask: With whom ought we to make a compromise? With that pitiful handful who just went out? . . . Haven't we seen them through and through. There is no longer anybody in Russia who is for them. Are the millions of workers and peasants represented in this congress, whom they are ready now as always to turn over for a price to the mercies of the bourgeoisie, are they to enter a compromise with these men? No, a compromise is no good here. To those who have gone out, and to all who make like proposals, we must say, 'You are pitiful isolated individuals; you are bankrupts; your rôle is played out. Go where you belong from now on—into the rubbish-can of history!' "

"Then we will go!"—cries Martov without awaiting the vote of the Congress. "Martov in anger and affectation," regrets Sukhanov, "began to make his way from the tribune towards the door. And I began to gather together my faction for a conference in the form of an emergency session. . . ." It was not wholly a matter of affectation. The Hamlet of democratic socialism, Martov would make a step forward when the revolution fell back as in July; but now when the revolution was ready for a tiger's leap, Martov would fall back. The withdrawal of the Rights had deprived him of the possibility of parliamentary maneuvering, and that put him instantly out of his element. He hastened to abandon the Congress and break with the insurrection. Sukhanov replied as best he could. The faction split almost in half: Martov won by 14 votes against 12.

Trotsky introduced a resolution—an act of indictment against the Compromisers: They prepared the ruinous offensive of June 18th; they supported the government of treason to the people; they screened the deception of the peasants on the land question; they carried out the disarming of the workers; they were responsible for the purposeless dragging out of the war; they permitted the bourgeoisie to deepen the economic ruin of the country; having lost the confidence of the masses, they resisted the calling of a soviet congress; and finally, finding themselves in a minority, they broke with the soviets.

Here again the order of the day is suspended for a declaration. Really the patience of the Bolshevik praesidium has no bounds. The president of the executive committee of the peasant soviet has come to summon the peasants to abandon this "untimely" congress, and go to the Winter Palace "to die with those who were sent there to do our will." This summons to die in the ruins of the Winter Palace is getting pretty tiresome in its monotony. A sailor just arrived from the *Aurora* ironically announces that there *are* no ruins, since they are only firing blanks from the cruiser. "Proceed with your business in peace," he says. The soul of the Congress finds rest in this admirable black-bearded sailor, incarnating the simple and imperious will of the insurrection. Martov with his mosaic of thoughts and feelings belongs to another world. That is why he breaks with the Congress.

Still another special declaration—this time half friendly. "The Right Social Revolutionaries," says Kamkov "have gone out, but we, the Lefts, have remained." The Congress welcomes those who have remained. However, even they consider it necessary to achieve a united revolutionary front, and come out against Trotsky's sharp resolution shutting the doors against a compromise with the moderate democracy.

Here too the Bolsheviks make a concession. Nobody ever saw them before, it seems, in such a yielding mood. No wonder: they are the masters of the situation and they have no need to insist upon the forms of words. Again Lunacharsky takes the tribune. "The weight of the task which has fallen upon us is not subject to any doubt," he says. A union of all the genuinely revolutionary elements of the democracy is necessary. But have we, the Bolsheviks, taken any steps whatever to repel the other groups? Did we not adopt Martov's proposal unanimously? For this we have been answered with accusations and threats. Is it not obvious that those who have left the Congress "are ceasing even their compromisist work and openly going over to the camp of the Kornilovists?"

The Bolsheviks did not insist upon an immediate vote on Trotsky's resolution. They did not want to hinder the attempts to reach an agreement on a soviet basis. The method of teaching by object-lesson can be successfully applied even to the accompaniment of artillery! As before with the adoption of Martov's proposal, so now the concession to Kamkov only revealed the impotence of these conciliatory labor pains. However, in distinction from the Left Mensheviks, the Left Social Revolutionaries did not quit the Congress: They were feeling too directly the pressure of the villages in revolt.

A mutual feeling-out has taken place. The primary positions have been occupied. There comes a pause in the evolution of the Congress. Shall we adopt the basic decrees and create a soviet government? It is impossible: the old government is still sitting there in the semi-darkness of a chamber in the Winter Palace, the only lamp on the table carefully barricaded with newspapers. Shortly after two o'clock in the morning the praesidium declares a half-hour recess.

The red marshals employed the short delay accorded to them with complete success. A new wind was blowing in the atmosphere of the Congress when its sitting was renewed. Kamenev read from the tribune a telephonogram just received from Antonov. The Winter Palace has been captured by the troops of the Revolutionary Military Committee; with the exception of Kerensky the whole Provisional Government with the dictator Kishkin at its head is under arrest. Although everybody had already learned the news as it passed from mouth to mouth, this official communication crashed in heavier than a cannon salute. The leap over the abyss dividing the revolutionary class from power has been made. Driven out of the Palace of Kshesinskaia in July, the Bolsheviks have now entered the Winter Palace as rulers. There is no other power now in Russia but the power of the soviets. A complex tangle of feelings breaks loose in applause and shouting: triumph, hope, but also anxiety. Then come new and more confident bursts of applause. The deed is done. Even

the most favorable correlation of forces contains concealed surprises, but the victory becomes indubitable when the enemy's staff is made prisoner.

Kamenev impressively reads the list of those arrested. The better known names bring hostile or ironic exclamations from the Congress. Especially bitter is the greeting of Tereshchenko who has guided the foreign destinies of Russia. And Kerensky? Kerensky? It has become known that at ten o'clock this morning he was orating without great success to the garrison of Gatchina. "Where he went from there is not exactly known; rumor says to the front."

The fellow-travelers of the revolution feel bad. They foresee that now the stride of the Bolsheviks will become more firm. Somebody from the Left Social Revolutionaries objects to the arrest of the socialist ministers. A representative of the United Internationalists offers a warning—

A room in the Winter Palace after the October 25, 1917 invasion by Bolshevik-led workers and sailors. This ended the provisional government formed by the Duma in February 1917, and established power for the Bolsheviks.

"lest the Minister of Agriculture, Maslov, turn up in the same cell in which he sat under the monarchy." He is answered by Trotsky, who was imprisoned during the ministry of Maslov in the same "Kresty" as under Nicholas: "Political arrest is not a matter of vengeance; it is dictated . . . by considerations of expediency. The government . . . should be indicted and tried, first of all for its indubitable connection with Kornilov. . . . The socialist ministers will be placed only under house arrest." It would have been simpler and more accurate to say that the seizure of the old government was dictated by the demands of the still unfinished struggle. It was a question of the political beheading of the hostile camp, and not of punishment for past sins.

But this parliamentary query as to the arrests was immediately crowded out by another infinitely more important episode. The third Bicycle Battalion sent by Kerensky against Petrograd had come over to the side of the revolutionary people! This too favorable news seemed unbelievable, but that was exactly what had happened. This selected military unit, the first to be chosen out from the whole active army, adhered to the insurrection before ever reaching the capital. If there had been a shade of restraint in its joy at the arrest of the ministers, the Congress was now seized with unalloyed and irrepressible rapture.

The Bolshevik commissar of Tzarskoe Selo together with a delegate from the bicycle battalion ascended the tribune: They had both just arrived to make a report to the Congress: "The garrison of Tzarskoe Selo is defending the approaches to Petrograd." The defensists withdrew from the soviet. "All the work rested upon us alone." Learning of the approach of the bicycle men, the soviet of Tzarskoe Selo prepared to resist, but the alarm happily turned out to be false. "Among the bicycle men are no enemies of the Congress of Soviets." Another battalion will soon arrive at Tzarskoe, and a friendly greeting is already in preparation there. The Congress drinks down this report in great gulps.

The representative of the bicycle men is greeted with a storm, a whirlwind, a cyclone. This Third Battalion, he reports, was suddenly sent from the southwestern front to the north under telegraphic orders "for the defense of Petrograd." The bicycle men advanced "with eyes blindfolded," only confusedly guessing what was up. At Peredolsk they ran into an echelon of the Fifth Bicycle Battalion, also moving on the capital. At a joint meeting held right there at the station, it became clear that "among all the bicyclers there is not one man to be found who would consent to take action against his brothers." It was jointly decided not to submit to the government.

"I tell you concretely," says the bicycle soldier, "we will not give the power to a government at the head of which stand the bourgeoisie and the landlords!" That word "concretely," introduced by the revolution into the everyday language of the people, sounded fine at this meeting!

How many hours was it since they were threatening the Congress from that same tribune with punishments from the front? Now the front itself had spoken its "concrete" word. Suppose the army committees do sabotage the Congress. Suppose the rank-and-file soldier mass only succeeds in getting its delegates there rather as an exception. Suppose in many regiments and divisions they have not yet learned to distinguish a Bolshevik from a Social Revolutionary. Never mind! The voice from Peredolsk is the authentic, unmistakable, irrefutable voice of the army. From this verdict there is no appeal. The Bolsheviks, and they only, had understood in time that the soldier-cook of the bicycle battalion infinitely better represented the front than all the Kharashes and Kuchins with their wilted credentials. A portentous change occurred here in the mood of the delegates. "They began to feel," writes Sukhanov, "that things were going to go smoothly and well, that the horrors promised on the right would not after all be so terrible, and that the leaders might be correct in everything else too."

The unhappy Mensheviks selected this moment to draw attention to themselves. They had not yet, it seems, withdrawn. They had been considering in their faction what to do. Out of a desire to bring after him the wavering groups, Kapelinsky, who had been appointed to inform the Congress of the decision adopted, finally spoke aloud the most candid reason for breaking with the Bolsheviks: "Remember that the troops are riding towards Petrograd; we are threatened with catastrophe." "What! Are you still here?"—the question was shouted from all corners of the hall. "Why, you went out once!" The Mensheviks moved in a tiny group towards the entrance, accompanied by scornful farewells. "We went out," grieves Sukhanov, "completely untying the hands of the Bolsheviks, turning over to them the whole arena of the revolution." It would have made little difference if they had stayed. In any case they went to the bottom. The waves of events closed ruthlessly over their heads.

It was time for the Congress to address a manifesto to the people, but the session continued to consist only of special declarations. Events simply refused to fit into the order of the day. At 5:17 in the morning Krylenko, staggering tired, made his way to the tribune with a telegram in his hand: The Twelfth Army sends greetings to the Congress and informs it of the creation of a military revolutionary committee which has undertaken to stand guard on the northern front. Attempts of the government to get armed help have broken against the resistance of the army. The commander-in-chief of the northern front, General Cheremissov, has submitted to the Committee. The commissar of the Provisional Government, Voitinsky, has resigned, and awaits a substitute. Delegations from the echelons moved against Petrograd have one after another announced to the Military Revolutionary Committee their solidarity with the Petrograd garrison. "Pandemonium," says Reed, "men weeping, embracing each other."

Lunacharsky at last got a chance to read a proclamation addressed to the workers, soldiers and peasants. But this was not merely a proclamation. By its mere exposition of what had happened and what was proposed, this hastily written document laid down the foundations of a new state structure. "The authority of the compromisist Central Executive Committee is at an end. The Provisional Government is deposed. The Congress assumes the power. . . ." The soviet government proposes immediate peace. It will transfer the land to the peasant, democratize the army, establish control over production, promptly summon the Constituent Assembly, guarantee the right of the nations of Russia to self-determination. "The Congress resolves: That all power in the localities goes over to the soviets." Every phrase as it is read turns into a salvo of applause. "Soldiers! Be on your guard! Railroad workers! Stop all echelons sent by Kerensky against Petrograd! . . . The fate of the revolution and the fate of the democratic peace is in your hands!"

Hearing the land mentioned, the peasants pricked up their ears. According to its constitution the Congress represented only soviets of workers and soldiers; but there were delegates present from individual peasant soviets. They now demanded that they be mentioned in the document. They were immediately given a right to vote. The representative of the Petrograd peasant soviet signed the proclamation "with both hands and both feet." A member of Avksentiev's Executive Committee, Berezin, silent until now, stated that out of 68 peasant soviets replying to a telegraphic questionnaire, one-half had expressed themselves for a soviet government, the other half for the transfer of power to the Constituent Assembly. If this was the mood of the provincial soviets, half composed of governmental functionaries, could there be any doubt that a future peasant congress would support the soviet power?

While solidifying the rank-and-file delegates, the proclamation frightened and even repelled some of the fellow-travelers by its irrevocableness. Small factions and remnants again filed through the tribune. For the third time a group of Mensheviks, obviously the most leftward now, broke away from the Congress. They withdrew, it seems, only in order to be in a position to save the Bolsheviks: "Otherwise you will destroy yourselves and us and the revolution." The president of the Polish Socialist Party, Lapinsky, although he remained at the Congress in order to "defend his point of view to the end," gave essential adherence to the declaration of Martov: "The Bolsheviks will not be able to wield the power which they are assuming." The United Jewish Workers Party abstained from the vote—likewise the United Internationalists. How much, though, did all these "uniteds" amount to altogether? The proclamation was adopted by all votes against two, with 12 abstaining! The delegates had hardly strength left to applaud.

The session finally came to an end at about six o'clock. A gray and cold autumn morning was dawning over the city. The hot spots of the campfires were fading out in the gradually lightening streets. The graying faces of the soldiers and the workers with rifles were concentrated and unusual. If there were astrologers in Petrograd, they must have observed portentous signs in the heavens.

The capital awoke under a new power. The everyday people, the functionaries, the intellectuals, cut off from the arena of events, rushed for the papers early to find out to which shore the wave had tossed during the night. But it was not easy to make out what had happened. To be sure, the papers reported the seizure by conspirators of the Winter Palace and the ministers, but only as a passing episode. Kerensky has gone to headquarters; the fate of the government will be decided by the front. Reports of the Soviet Congress reproduce only the declarations of the Right Wing, enumerate those who withdrew, and expose the impotence of those who remained. The political editorials, written before the seizure of the Winter Palace, exude a cloudless optimism.

The rumors of the street do not wholly coincide with the tone of the newspapers. Whatever you say, the ministers are after all locked up in the fortress. Reinforcements from Kerensky are not yet in sight. Functionaries and officers confer anxiously. Journalists and lawyers ring each other up. Editors try to collect their thoughts. The drawing-room oracles say: We must surround the usurpers with a blockade of universal contempt. Storekeepers don't know whether to do business or refrain. The new authorities give orders to do business. The restaurants open; the tramcars move; the banks languish with evil forebodings; the seismograph of the Stock Exchange describes a convulsive curve. Of course the Bolsheviks will not hold out long, but they may do damage before they tumble.

The reactionary French journalist, Claude Anet, wrote on this day: "The victors are singing a song of victory. And quite rightly too. Among all these blabbers they alone acted. . . . Today they are reaping the harvest. Bravo! Fine work." The Mensheviks estimated the situation quite otherwise. "Twenty-four hours have passed since the 'victory' of the Bolsheviks," wrote Dan's paper, "and the historic fates have already begun to take their cruel revenge. . . . Around them is an emptiness created by themselves . . . They are isolated from all . . . The entire clerical and technical machinery refuses to serve them . . . They . . . are sliding at the very moment of their triumph into the abyss."

The liberal and compromisist circles, encouraged by the sabotage of the functionaries and their own light-mindedness, believed strangely in their own impunity. They spoke and wrote of the Bolsheviks in the language of the July Days. "Hirelings of Wilhelm"—"the pockets of the Red Guard full of German marks"—"German officers in command of the insurrection." . . . The new government had to show these people a firm hand before they began to believe in it. The more unbridled papers were detained already on the night of the 26th. Some others were confiscated on the following day. The socialist press for the time being was spared: It was necessary to give the Left Social Revolutionaries, and also some elements of the Bolshevik party, a chance to convince themselves of the groundlessness of the hope for coalition with the official democracy.

The Bolsheviks developed their victory amid sabotage and chaos. A provisional military headquarters, organized during the night, undertook the defense of Petrograd in case of an attack from Kerensky. Military telephone men were sent to the central exchange where a strike had begun. It was proposed to the armies that they create their own military revolutionary committees. Gangs of agitators and organizers, freed by the victory, were sent to the front and to the provinces. The Central organ of the party wrote: "The Petrograd Soviet has acted; it is the turn of the other soviets."

News came during the day which especially disturbed the soldiers. Kornilov had escaped. As a matter of fact, the lofty captive, who had been living in Bykhov, guarded by Tekintsi, loyal to him, and kept in touch with all events by Kerensky's headquarters, decided on the 26th that things were taking a serious turn, and without the slightest hindrance from anybody abandoned his pretended prison. The connections between Kerensky and Kornilov were thus again obviously confirmed in the eyes of the masses. The Military Revolutionary Committee summoned the soldiers and the revolutionary officers by telegram

to capture both former commanders-in-chief and deliver them in Petrograd.

As had the Tauride Palace in February, so now Smolny became the focal point for all functions of the capital and the state. Here all the ruling institutions had their seat. Here orders were issued, and hither people came to get them. Hence a demand went out for weapons, and hither came rifles and revolvers confiscated from the enemy. Arrested people were brought in here from all ends of the city. The injured began to flow in seeking justice. The bourgeois public and its frightened cab-drivers made a great yoke-shaped detour to avoid the Smolny region.

The automobile is a far more genuine sign of present-day sovereignty than the orb and sceptre. Under the régime of dual power the automobiles had been divided between the government, the Central Executive Committee and private owners. Now all confiscated motors were dragged into the camp of the insurrection. The Smolny district looked like a gigantic military garage. The best of automobiles smoked in those days from the low-grade gas. Motorcycles chugged impatiently and threateningly in the semi-darkness. Armored cars shrieked their sirens. Smolny seemed like a factory, a railroad and power station of the revolution.

A steady flood of people poured along the sidewalks of the adjoining streets. Bonfires were burning at the outer and inner gates. By their wavering light armed workers and soldiers were belligerently inspecting passes. A number of armored cars stood shaking with the action of their own motors in the court. Nothing wanted to stop moving, machines or people. At each entrance stood machine guns abundantly supplied with cartridge-belts. The endless, weakly lighted, gloomy corridors echoed with the tramping of feet, with exclamations and shouts. The arriving and departing poured up and down the broad staircase. And this solid human lava would be cut through by impatient and imperative individuals, Smolny workers, couriers, commissars, a mandate or an order lifted high in their hand, a rifle on a cord slung over their shoulder, or a portfolio under their arm.

The Military Revolutionary Committee never stopped working for an instant. It received delegates, couriers, volunteer informers, devoted friends, and scoundrels. It sent commissars to all corners of the town, set innumerable seals upon orders and commands and credentials—all this in the midst of intersecting inquiries, urgent communications, the ringing of telephone bells and the rattle of weapons. People utterly exhausted of their force, long without sleep or eating, unshaven, in dirty linen, with inflamed eyes, would shout in hoarse voices, gesticulate fantastically, and if they did not fall half dead on the floor, it seemed only thanks to the surrounding chaos which whirled them about and carried them away again on its unharnessed wings.

Adventurers, crooks, the worst off-scouring of the old régime, would sniff about and try to get a pass to Smolny. Some of them succeeded. They knew some little secret of administration: Who has the key to the diplomatic correspondence, how to write an order on the treasury, where to get gasoline or a typewriter, and especially where the best court wines are kept. They did not all find their cell or bullet immediately.

Never since the creation of the world have so many orders been issued—by word of mouth, by pencil, by typewriter, by wire, one following after the other—thousands and myriads of orders, not always issued by those having the right, and rarely to those capable of carrying them out. But just here lay the miracle—that in this crazy whirlpool there turned out to be an inner meaning. People managed to understand each other. The most important and necessary things got done. Replacing the old web of administration, the first threads of the new were strung. The revolution grew in strength.

During that day, the Central Committee of the Bolsheviks was at work in Smolny. It was deciding the problem of the new government of Russia. No minutes were kept—or they have not been preserved. Nobody was bothering about future historians, although a lot of trouble was being prepared for them right there. The evening session of the Congress was to create a cabinet of ministers. M-i-n-i-s-t-e-r-s? What a sadly compromised word! It stinks of the high bureaucratic career, the crowning of some parliamentary ambition. It was decided to call the government the Soviet of Peoples Commissars: that at least had a fresher sound. Since the negotiations for a coalition of the "entire democracy" had come to nothing, the question of the party and personal staff of the government was simplified. The Left Social Revolutionaries minced and objected. Having just broken with the party of Kerensky, they themselves hardly knew what they wanted to do. The Central Committee adopted the motion of Lenin as the only thinkable one: to form a government of Bolsheviks only.

Martov knocked at the door of this session in the capacity of intercessor for the arrested socialist ministers. Not so long ago he had been interceding with the socialist ministers for the imprisoned Bolsheviks. The wheel had made quite a sizeable turn. Through one of its members sent out to Martov for negotiations—most probably Kamenev—the Central Committee confirmed the statement that the socialist ministers would be transferred to house arrest. Apparently they had been forgotten in the rush of business, or perhaps had themselves declined privileges, adhering even in the Trubetzkoy Bastion to the principle of ministerial solidarity.

The Congress opened its session at nine o'clock in the evening. "The picture on the whole was but little different from yesterday—fewer weapons, less of a jam." Sukhanov, now no longer a delegate, was able to find himself a free seat as one of the public. This session was to decide the questions of peace, land and government. Only three questions: end the war, give the land to the people, establish a socialist dictatorship. Kamenev began with a report of the work done by the praesidium during the day: the death penalty at the front introduced by Kerensky abolished; complete freedom of agitation restored; orders given for the liberation of soldiers imprisoned for political convictions, and members of land committees; all the commissars of the Provisional Government removed from office; orders given to arrest and deliver Kerensky and Kornilov. The Congress approved and ratified these measures.

Again some remnants of remnants took the floor, to the impatient disapproval of the hall. One group announced that they were withdrawing "at the moment of the victory of the insurrection and not at the moment of its defeat." Others bragged of the fact that they had decided to remain. A representative of the Donetz miners urged immediate measures to prevent Kaledin from cutting the north off from coal. Some time must pass, however, before the revolution learns to take measures of such scope. Finally it becomes possible to take up the first point on the order of the day.

Lenin, whom the Congress has not yet seen, is given the floor for a report on peace. His appearance in the tribune evokes a tumultuous greeting. The trench delegates gaze with all their eyes at this mysterious being whom they had been taught to hate and whom they have learned without seeing him to love. "Now Lenin, gripping the edges of the reading-stand, let little winking eyes travel over the crowd as he stood there waiting, apparently oblivious to the long-rolling ovation, which lasted several minutes. When it finished, he said simply, 'We shall now proceed to construct the socialist order.' "

The minutes of the Congress are not preserved. The parliamentary stenographers, invited in to record the debates, had abandoned Smolny along with the Mensheviks and Social Revolutionaries. That was one of the first episodes in the campaign of sabotage. The secretarial notes have been lost without a trace in the abyss of events. There remain only the hasty and tendential newspaper reports, written to the tune of the artillery or the grinding of teeth in the political struggle. Lenin's speeches have suffered especially. Owing to his swift delivery and the complicated construction of his sentences, they are not easily recorded even in more favorable conditions. That initial statement which John Reed puts in the mouth of Lenin does not appear in any of the newspaper accounts. But it is wholly in the spirit of the orator. Reed could not have made it up. Just in that way Lenin must surely have begun his speech at the Congress of Soviets—simply, without unction, with inflexible confidence: "We shall now proceed to construct the socialist order."

But for this it was first of all necessary to end the war. From his exile in Switzerland Lenin had thrown out the slogan: Convert the imperialist war into a civil war. Now it was time to convert the victorious civil war into peace. The speaker began immediately by reading the draft of a declaration to be published by the government still to be elected. The text had not been distributed, technical equipment being still very weak. The Congress drank in every word of the document as pronounced.

"The workers' and peasants' government created by the revolution of October 24–25, and resting upon the soviets of workers', soldiers' and peasants' deputies, proposes to all the warring peoples and their governments to open immediate negotiations for a just, democratic peace." Just conditions exclude annexations and indemnities. By annexations is to be understood the forceful accession of alien peoples or the retention of them against their will, either in Europe or in remote lands over the seas. "Herewith the government declares that it by no means considers the above indicated conditions of peace ultimative—that is, it agrees to examine any other conditions," demanding only the quickest possible opening of negotiations and the absence of any secrecy in their conduct. On its part the soviet government abolishes secret diplomacy and undertakes to publish the secret treaties concluded before October 25, 1917. Everything in these treaties directed toward the accruing of profit and privilege to the Russian landlords and capitalists, and the oppression of other peoples by the Great Russians, "the government declares unconditionally and immediately annulled." In order to enter upon negotiations, it is proposed to conclude an immediate armistice, for not less than three months at least. The workers' and peasants' government addresses its proposals simultaneously to "the governments and peoples of all warring countries . . . especially the conscious workers of the three most advanced countries," England, France and Germany, confident that it is they who will "help us successfully carry through the business of peace and therewith the business of liberating the toilers and the exploited masses of the population from all slavery and all exploitation."

Lenin limited himself to brief comments on the text of the declaration. "We cannot ignore the governments, for then the possibility of concluding peace will be delayed . . . , but we have no right not to appeal at the same time to the people. The people and the governments are everywhere at variance, and we ought to help the people interfere in the matter of war and peace." "We will, of course, defend in all possible ways our program of peace without annexations or indemnities," but we ought not to present our conditions in the form of an ultimatum, as that will make it easier for the governments to refuse to negotiate. We will consider also every other proposal. "*Consider* does not mean that we will accept it."

The manifesto issued by the Compromisers on March 14th proposed to the workers of other countries to overthrow the bankers in the name of peace; however the Compromisers themselves not only did not demand the overthrow of their own bankers, but entered into a league with them. "Now we have overthrown the government of the bankers." That gives us a right to summon the other peoples to do the same. We have every hope of victory. "It must be remembered that we live not in the depths of Africa, but in Europe where everything can become quickly known." The guarantee of victory Lenin sees, as always, in converting the national into an international revolution. "The workers' movement will get the upper hand and lay down the road to peace and socialism."

The Left Social Revolutionaries sent up a representative to present their adherence to the declaration. Its "spirit and meaning are close and understandable to us." The United Internationalists were for the declaration, but only on condition that it be issued by a government of the entire democracy. Lapinsky, speaking for the Polish Left Mensheviks, welcomed "the healthy proletarian realism" of the document. Dzerzhinsky for the social democracy of Poland and Lithuania, Stuchka for the social democracy of Latvia, Kapsukass for the Lithuanian social democracy, adhered to the declaration without qualification. The only objection was offered by the Bolshevik, Eremeev, who demanded that the peace conditions be given the character of an ultimatum—otherwise "they may think that we are weak, that we are afraid."

Lenin decisively, even fiercely, objected to the ultimative presentation of the conditions: In that way, he said, we will only "make it possible for our enemies to conceal the whole truth from the people, to hide the truth behind our irreconcilability." You say that "our not presenting an ultimatum will show our impotence." It is time to have done with bourgeois falsities in politics. "We need not be afraid of telling the truth about our weariness. . . ." The future disagreements of Brest Litovsk gleam out for a moment already in this episode.

Kamenev asked all who were for the proclamation to raise their delegates' cards. "One delegate," writes Reed "dared to raise his hand against, but the sudden sharp outburst around him brought it swiftly down." The appeal to the peoples and governments was adopted unanimously. The deed was done! And it impressed all the participants by its close and immediate magnitude.

Sukhanov, an attentive although also prejudiced observer, noticed more than once at that first session the listlessness of the Congress. Undoubtedly the delegates—like all the people, indeed—were tired of meetings, congresses, speeches, resolutions, tired of the whole business of marking time. They had no confidence that this Congress would be able and know how to carry the thing through to the end. Will not the gigantic size of the task and the insuperable opposition compel them to back down this time too? An influx of confidence had come with the news of the capture of the Winter Palace, and afterward with the coming over of the bicycle men to the insurrection. But both these facts still had to do with the mechanics of insurrection. Only now was its historic meaning becoming clear in action. The victorious insurrection had built under this Congress of workers and soldiers an indestructible foundation of power. The delegates were voting this time not for a resolution, not for a proclamation, but for a governmental act of immeasurable significance.

Listen, nations! The revolution offers you peace. It will be accused of violating treaties. But of this it is proud. To break up the leagues of bloody predation is the greatest historic service. The Bolsheviks have dared to do it. They alone have dared. Pride surges up of its own accord. Eyes shine. All are on their feet. No one is smoking now. It seems as though no one breathes. The praesidium, the delegates, the guests, the sentries, join in a hymn of insurrection and brotherhood. "Suddenly, by common impulse,"—the story will soon be told by John Reed, observer and participant, chronicler and poet of the insurrection—"we found ourselves on our feet, mumbling together into the smooth lifting unison of the Internationale. A grizzled old soldier was sobbing like a child. Alexandra Kollontai rapidly winked the tears back. The immense sound rolled through the hall, burst windows and doors and soared into the quiet sky." Did it go altogether into the sky? Did it not go also to the autumn trenches, that hatch-work upon unhappy, crucified Europe, to her devastated cities and villages, to her mothers and wives in mourning? *"Arise ye prisoners of starvation! Arise ye wretched of the earth!"* The words of the song were freed of all qualifications. They fused with the decree of the government, and hence resounded with the force of a direct act. Everyone felt greater and more important in that hour. The heart of the revolution enlarged to the width of the whole world. "We will achieve emancipation. . . . " The spirit of independence, of initiative, of daring, those joyous feelings of which the oppressed in ordinary conditions are deprived—the revolution had brought them now. " . . . with our own hand!" The omnipotent hand of those millions who had overthrown the monarchy and the bourgeoisie would now strangle the war. The Red Guard from the Vyborg district, the gray soldier with his scar, the old revolutionist who had served his years at hard labor, the young black-bearded sailor from the *Aurora*—all vowed to carry through to the end this "last and deciding fight." "We will build our own new world!" We will build! In that word eagerly spoken from the heart was included already the future years of the civil war and the coming five-year periods of labor and privation. "Who was nothing shall be all!" All! If the actualities of the past have often been turned into song, why shall not a song be turned into the actuality of the future? Those trench-coats no longer seemed the costumes of galley-slaves. The

Lenin ". . . the short, sturdy figure . . . with his extraordinary head, his high cheekbones and simple features . . . and with that gaze of his small, slightly Mongol eyes which looked straight through everything."

papakhi with their holes and torn cotton took a new aspect above those gleaming eyes. "The race of man shall rise again!" Is it possible to believe that it will not rise from the misery and humiliation, the blood and filth of this war?

"The whole praesidium, with Lenin at its head, stood and sang with excited enraptured faces and shining eyes." Thus testifies a sceptic, gazing with heavy feelings upon an alien triumph. "How much I wanted to join it," confesses Sukhanov, "to fuse in one feeling and mood with that mass and its leaders! But I could not." The last sound of the anthem died away, but the Congress remained standing, a fused human mass enchanted by the greatness of that which they had experienced. And the eyes of many rested on the short, sturdy figure of the man in the tribune with his extraordinary head, his high cheekbones and simple features, altered now by the shaved beard, and with that gaze of his small, slightly Mongol eyes which looked straight through everything. For four months he had been absent. His very name had almost separated itself from any living image. But no. He was not a myth. There he stood among his own—how many now of "his own"!—holding the sheets of a message of peace to the peoples of the world in his hand. Even those nearest, those who knew well his place in the party, for the first time fully realized what he meant to the revolution, to the people, to the peoples. It was he who had taught them; it was he who had brought them up. Somebody's voice from the depth of the hall shouted a word of greeting to the leader. The hall seemed only to have awaited the signal. Long live Lenin! The anxieties endured, the doubts overcome, pride of initiative, triumph of victory, gigantic hopes—all poured out together in one volcanic eruption of gratitude and rapture. The sceptical observer dryly remarks: "Undoubted enthusiasm of mood . . . They greeted Lenin, shouted hurrah, threw their caps in the air. They sang the Funeral March in memory of the victims of the war—and again applause, shouts, throwing of caps in the air."

What the Congress experienced during those minutes was experienced on the next day, although less compactly, by the whole country. "It must be said," writes Stankevich, in his memoirs, "that the bold gesture of the Bolsheviks, their ability to step over the barbed-wire entanglements which had for four years divided us from the neighboring peoples, created of itself an enormous impression." Baron Budberg expresses himself more crudely but no less succinctly in his diary: "The new government of Comrade Lenin went off with a decree for immediate peace. . . . This was now an act of genius for bringing the soldier masses to his side: I saw this in the mood of several regiments which I made the rounds of today; the telegram of Lenin on an immediate three months' armistice and then peace, created a colossal impression everywhere, and evoked stormy joy. We have now lost the last chance of saving the front." By saving the front which they had ruined, those men had long ceased to mean anything but saving their own social positions.

If the revolution had had the determination to step over the barbed-wire entanglements in March and April, it might still have soldered the army together for a time—provided the army was at the same time reduced to a half or a third its size—and thus created for its foreign policy a position of exceptional force. But the hour of courageous action struck only in October, when to save even a part of the army for even a short period was unthinkable. The new government had to load upon itself the debt, not only for the war of tzarism, but also for the spendthrift light-mindedness of the Provisional Government. In this dreadful, and for all other parties hopeless, situation, only Bolshevism could lead the country out on an open road—having uncovered through the October revolution inexhaustible resources of national energy.

Lenin is again in the tribune—this time

with the little sheets of a decree on land. He begins with an indictment of the overthrown government and the compromisist parties, who by dragging out the land question have brought the country to a peasant revolt. "Their talk about pogroms and anarchy in the country rings false with cowardly deceit. Where and when have pogroms and anarchy been caused by reasonable measures?" The draft of the decree has not been multigraphed for distribution. The speaker has the sole rough draft in his hands, and it is written so badly— Sukhanov remembers—"that Lenin stumbles in the reading, gets mixed up, and finally stops entirely. Somebody from the crowd jammed around the tribune comes to his help. Lenin eagerly yields his place and the undecipherable paper." These rough spots did not, however, in the eyes of that plebeian parliament diminish by an iota the grandeur of what was taking place.

The essence of the decree is contained in two lines of the first point: "The landlord's property in the land is annulled immediately and without any indemnity whatever. The landlord, appanage, monastery and church estates with all their goods and chattels are given in charge of the town land committees and county soviets of peasant deputies until the Constituent Assembly. The confiscated property is placed as a national possession under the protection of the local soviets. The land of the rank-and-file peasants and rank-and-file Cossacks is protected against confiscation. The whole decree does not come to more than thirty lines. It smashes the Gordian knot with a hammer. To the fundamental text certain broader instructions are adjoined, borrowed wholly from the peasants themselves. In *Izvestia of the Peasant Soviet* there had been printed on August 19th a summary of 242 instructions given by the electors to their representatives at the First Congress of Peasant Deputies. Notwithstanding that it was the Social Revolutionaries who prepared these collated instructions, Lenin did not hesitate to at-

tach the document in its entirety to his decree "for guidance in carrying out the great land transformation."

The collated instructions read: "The right to private property in the land is annulled forever." "The right to use the land is accorded to all citizens . . . desiring to cultivate it with their own labor." "Hired labor is not permitted." "The use of the land must be equalized—that is, the land is to be divided among the toilers according to local conditions on the basis of standards either of labor or consumption."

Under a continuation of the bourgeois régime, to say nothing of a coalition with the landlords, these Social Revolutionary instructions remained a lifeless Utopia, where they did not become a conscious lie. Even under the rule of the proletariat, they did not become realizable in all their sections. But the destiny of the instructions radically changed with a change in the attitude toward them of the governmental power. The workers' state gave the peasants a period in which to try out their self-contradictory program in action.

"The peasants want to keep their small properties," wrote Lenin in August, "standardize them on a basis of equality, and periodically re-equalize them. Let them do it. No reasonable socialist will break with the peasant poor on that ground. If the lands are confiscated, that means that the rule of the banks is undermined—if the equipment is confiscated, that means that the rule of capital is undermined. The rest . . . with a transfer of political power to the proletariat . . . will be suggested by practice."

A great many people, and not only enemies but friends, have failed to understand this far-sighted, and to a certain extent pedagogical, approach of the Bolshevik party to the peasantry and its agrarian program. The equal distribution of the land—objected Rosa Luxemburg for example—has nothing in common with socialism. The Bolsheviks, it goes without saying, had no illusion upon this point. On the contrary, the very construction of the decree bears witness to the critical vigilance of the legislator. Whereas the collated instructions say that all the land, both that of the landlords and the peasants, "is converted into national property," the basic decree does not commit itself at all as to the new form of property in the land. Even a none too pedantic jurist would be horrified at the fact that the nationalization of the land, a new social principle of world-historic importance, is inaugurated in the form of a list of instructions adjoined to a basic law. But there was no editorial slovenliness here. Lenin wanted as little as possible to tie the hands of the party and the soviet power *a priori* in a still unexplored historic realm. Here again he united unexampled audacity with the greatest caution. It still remained to determine in experience how the peasants themselves would understand the conversion of the land into "the property of the whole people." Having made so long a dash forward, it was necessary to fortify the positions also in case a retreat should become necessary. The distribution of the landlord's land among the peasants, while not in itself a guarantee against bourgeois counter-revolution, made impossible in any case a feudal-monarchic restoration.

It would be possible to speak of socialist perspectives only after the establishment and successful preservation of the proletarian power. And this power could preserve itself only by giving determined co-operation to the peasant in carrying out his revolution. If the distribution of the land would strengthen the socialist government politically, it was then wholly justified as an immediate measure. The peasant had to be taken as the revolution found him. Only a new régime could re-educate him—and not at once, but in the course of a generation, with the help of new technique and a new organization of industry. The decree together with the instructions meant that the dictatorship of the proletariat assumed an obligation not only to take an attentive attitude toward the interests of the land

laborer, but also to be patient of his illusions as a petty proprietor. It was clear in advance that there would be a number of stages and turning-points in the agrarian revolution. The collated instructions were anything but the last word. They represented merely a starting-point which the workers agreed to occupy while helping the peasants to realize their progressive demands, and warning them against false steps.

"We must not ignore," said Lenin in his speech, "the resolutions of the lower ranks of the people, even though we are not in agreement with them. . . . We must give full freedom to the creative capacity of the popular masses. The essence of the thing is that the peasantry should have full confidence that there are no more landlords in the country, and let the peasants themselves decide all questions and build their own life." Opportunism? No, it was revolutionary realism.

Before even the applause was over, a Right Social Revolutionary, Pianykh, arrived from the Peasants' Executive Committee and took the floor with a furious protest on the subject of the socialist ministers being under arrest. "During the last days," cried the orator pounding the table as though beside himself, "a thing is on foot which has never happened in any revolution. Our comrades, members of the Executive Committee, Maslov and Salazkin, are locked up in prison. We demand their immediate release!" "If one hair falls from their heads . . . " threatened another messenger in a military coat. To the Congress they both seemed like visitors from another world.

At the moment of the insurrection there were about 800 men in prison in Dvinsk, charged with Bolshevism, in Minsk about 6,000, in Kiev 535—for the most part soldiers. And how many members of the peasant committees were under lock and key in various parts of the country! Finally a good share of the delegates to this very Congress, beginning with the praesidium, had passed through the prisons of Kerensky since July. No wonder the indignation of the friends of the Provisional Government could not pluck at any heart-strings in this assembly. To complete their bad-luck a certain delegate, unknown to anybody, a peasant from Tver, with long hair and a big sheepskin coat, rose in his place, and having bowed politely to all four points of the compass, adjured the Congress in the name of his electors not to hesitate at arresting Avksentiev's executive committee as a whole: "Those are not peasants' deputies, but Kadets. . . . Their place is in prison." So they stood facing each other, these two figures: The Social Revolutionary Pianykh, experienced parliamentarian, favorite of ministers, hater of Bolsheviks, and the nameless peasant from Tver who had brought Lenin a hearty salute from his electors. Two social strata, two revolutions: Pianykh was speaking in the name of February, the Tver peasant was fighting for October. The Congress gave the delegate in a sheepskin coat a veritable ovation. The emissaries of the Executive Committee went away swearing.

"The resolution of Lenin is greeted by the Social Revolutionary faction as a triumph of their ideas," announces Kalegaev, but in view of the extraordinary importance of the question we must take it up in caucus. A Maximilist, representative of the extreme left wing of the disintegrated Social Revolutionary party, demands an immediate vote: "We ought to give honor to a party which on the very first day and without any blabber brings such a measure to life." Lenin insisted that the intermission should be at any rate as short as possible. "News so important to Russia should be in print by morning. No filibustering!" The decree on land was not only, indeed, the foundation of the new régime, but also a weapon of the revolution, which had still to conquer the country. It is not surprising that Reed records at that moment an imperative shout breaking through the noise of the hall: "Fifteen agitators wanted in room 17 at once! To go to the front!" At one o'clock in the morning a delegate from the Russian troops in Macedonia enters a complaint that the Petersburg governments one after the other have forgotten them. Support for peace and land from the soldiers in Macedonia is assured! Here is a new test of the mood of the army—this time from a far corner of southeastern Europe. And here Kamenev announces: The Tenth Bicycle Battalion, summoned by the government from the front, entered Petrograd this morning, and like its predecessors has adhered to the Congress of Soviets. The warm applause testifies that no amount of these confirmations of its power will seem excessive to the Congress.

After the adoption, unanimously and without debate, of a resolution declaring it an affair of honor of the local soviets not to permit Jewish or any other pogroms on the part of the criminal element, a vote is taken on the draft of the land law. With one vote opposed and eight abstaining, the Congress adopts with a new burst of enthusiasm the decree putting an end to serfdom, the very foundation stone of the old Russian culture. Henceforth the agrarian revolution is legalized, and therewith the revolution of the proletariat acquires a mighty basis.

A last problem remains: the creation of a government. Kamenev reads a proposal drawn up by the Central Committee of the Bolsheviks. The management of the various branches of the state life is allotted to commissions who are to carry into action the program announced by the Congress of Soviets "in close union with the mass organizations of working men and women, sailors, soldiers, peasants and clerical employees." The governmental power is concentrated in the hands of a collegium composed of the presidents of these commissions, to be called the Soviet of Peoples Commissars. Control over the activities of the government is vested in the Congress of Soviets and its Central Executive Committee.

Seven members of the Central Committee of the Bolshevik party were nominated to the first Council of Peoples Commissars: Lenin as head of the government, without portfolio; Rykov as Peoples' Commissar of the Interior; Miliutin as head of the Department of Agriculture; Nogin as chief of Commerce and Industry; Trotsky as head of the Department of Foreign Affairs; Lomov of Justice; Stalin, president of a Commission on the Affairs of the Nationalities; Military and naval affairs were allotted to a committee consisting of Antonov-Ovseënko, Krylenko and Dybenko; the head of the Commissariat of Labor is to be Shliapnikov; the chief of the Department of education, Lunacharsky; the heavy and ungrateful task of Minister of Provisions is laid upon Theodorovich; the Posts and Telegraph upon the worker, Glebov; the position of Peoples Commissar of Communications is not yet allotted, the door being left open here for an agreement with the organizations of the railroad workers.

All fifteen candidates, four workers and eleven intellectuals have behind them years of imprisonment, exile and emigrant life. Five of them had been imprisoned even under the régime of the democratic republic. The future prime-minister had only the day before emerged from the democratic underground. Kamenev and Zinoviev did not enter the Council of Peoples Commissars. The former was selected for president of the new Central Executive Committee, the latter for editor of the official organ of the soviets. "As Kamenev read the list of Commissars," writes Reed, there were "bursts of applause after each name, Lenin's and Trotsky's especially." Sukhanov adds also that of Lunacharsky.

A long speech against the proposed staff of the government was made by a representative of the United Internationalists, Avilov, once a Bolshevik, literateur from Gorky's paper. He conscientiously enumerated the difficulties standing before the revolution in the sphere of domestic and foreign politics. We must "clearly realize . . . whither we are going. . . . Before the new government stand all the old questions: of bread and of peace. If it does not solve these problems it will be overthrown." There is little grain in the country; it is in the hands of the well-to-do peasants; there is nothing to give in exchange for grain; industry is on the decline; fuel and raw material are lacking. To collect the grain by force is a difficult, long and dangerous task. It is necessary, therefore, to create a government which will have the sympathy not only of the poor but also of the well-to-do peasantry. For this a coalition is necessary.

"It will be still harder to obtain peace." The governments of the Entente will not answer the proposal of the Congress for an immediate armistice. Even without that the Allied ambassadors are planning to leave. The new government will be isolated; its peace initiative will be left hanging in the air. The popular masses of the warring countries are still far from revolution. The consequences may be two: either extermination of the revolution by the troops of the Hohenzollern or a separate peace. The peace terms in both cases can only be the worst possible for Russia. These difficulties can be met only by "a majority of the people." The unfortunate thing is the split in the democracy: the left half wants to create a purely Bolshevik government in Smolny, and the right half is organizing in the city duma a Committee of Public Safety. To save the revolution it is necessary to form a government from both groups.

A representative of the Left Social Revolutionaries, Karelin, spoke to the same effect. It is impossible to carry out the program adopted without those parties which have withdrawn from the Congress. To be sure "the Bolsheviks are not to blame for their withdrawal." But the program of the Congress ought to unite the entire democracy. "We do not want to take the road of isolating the Bolsheviks, for we understand that with the fate of the Bolsheviks is bound up the fate of the whole revolution. Their ruin will be the ruin of the revolution. If they, the Left Social Revolutionaries, have nevertheless declined the invitation to enter the government, their purpose is a good one: to keep their hands free for mediation between the Bolsheviks and the parties which have abandoned the Congress. In such mediations . . . the Left Social Revolutionaries see their principal task at the present moment." The Left Social Revolutionaries will support the work of the new government in solving urgent problems. At the same time they vote against the proposed government.—In a word the young party has got mixed up as badly as it knows how.

"Trotsky rose to defend a government of Bolsheviks only," writes Sukhanov, himself wholly in sympathy with Avilov and having inspired Karelin behind the scenes. "He was very clear, sharp, and in much absolutely right. But he refused to understand in what consisted the center of the argument of his opponents. . . . " The center of the argument consisted of an ideal diagonal. In March they had tried to draw it between the bourgeoisie and the compromisist soviets. Now Sukhanov dreamed of a diagonal between the compromisist democracy and the dictatorship of the proletariat. But revolutions do not develop along diagonals.

"They have tried to frighten us more than once with a possible isolation of the Left Wing," said Trotsky. "Some days back when the question of insurrection was first openly raised, they told us that we were headed for destruction. And in reality if you judged the grouping of forces by the political press, then insurrection threatened us with inevitable ruin. Against us stood not only the counter-revolutionary bands, but also the defensists of all varieties. The Left Social Revolutionaries, only one wing of them, courageously worked with us in the Military Revolutionary Committee. The rest occupied a position of watchful neutrality. And nevertheless even

with these unfavorable circumstances and when it seemed that we were abandoned by all, the insurrection triumphed. . . .

"If the real forces were actually against us, how could it happen that we won the victory almost without bloodshed. No, it is not we who are isolated, but the government and the so-called democrats. With their wavering, their compromisism, they have erased themselves from the ranks of the authentic democracy. Our great superiority as a party lies in the fact that we have formed a coalition with the class forces, creating a union of the workers, soldiers and poorest peasants.

"Political groupings disappear, but the fundamental interests of the classes remain. That party conquers which is able to feel out and satisfy the fundamental demands of a class. . . . We pride ourselves upon the coalition of our garrison, chiefly composed of peasants, with the working class. This coalition has been tried by fire. The Petrograd garrison and proletariat went hand in hand into that great struggle which is the classic example in the history of revolutions among all peoples.

"Avilov has spoken of the vast difficulties which stand before us. To remove those difficulties he proposes that we form a coalition. But he makes no attempt to lay bare his formula and tell us what coalition. A coalition of groups, or classes, or simply a coalition of newspapers? . . .

"They tell us the split in the democracy is a misunderstanding. When Kerensky is sending shock troops against us, when with the consent of the Central Executive Committee we are deprived of the telephone at the most critical moment of our struggle with the bourgeoisie, when they deal us blow after blow—is it possible to talk of misunderstanding?

"Avilov says to us: There is little bread, we must have a coalition with the defensists. Do you imagine that this coalition will increase the quantity of bread? The problem of bread is the problem of a program of action. The struggle with economic col-

The last Russian emperor, Nicholas II (1895–1917), and his wife Alexandra, in court robes.

(Left) Nicholas II and his family in Tobolsk, Siberia after being arrested. During the spring of 1918 they were moved to Yekaterinburg, in the Urals. During the night of July 16/17 Nicholas, Alexandra, and their five children were executed, with Lenin's approval, in the cellar of the house where they had been held. (Bottom) The head of a statue of Alexander III (father of Nicholas II) lies on the ground in Moscow, representing the end of the last ruling dynasty of Russia.

lapse demands a definite system from below, and not political groupings on top.

"Avilov speaks of a union with the peasantry: But again of what peasantry is he talking? Today and right here, a representative of the peasants of Tver province demanded the arrest of Avksentiev. We must choose between this Tver peasant and Avksentiev who has filled the prisons with members of the peasant committees. A coalition with the kulak elements of the peasantry we firmly reject in the name of a coalition of the working class and the poorer peasant. We are with the Tver peasants against Avksentiev. We are with them to the end and inseparably.

"Whoever now chases the shadow of coalition is totally cutting himself off from life. The Left Social Revolutionaries will lose support among the masses to the extent that they venture to oppose our party. Every group which opposes the party of the proletariat, with whom the village poor have united, cuts himself off from the revolution.

"Openly and before the face of the whole people we raised the banner of insurrection. The political formula of this insurrection was: All power to the soviets—through the Congress of Soviets. They tell us: You did not await the Congress with your uprising. We thought of waiting, but Kerensky would not wait. The counter-revolutionists were not dreaming. We as a party considered this our task: to make it genuinely possible for the Congress of Soviets to seize the power. If the Congress had been surrounded with junkers, how could it have seized the power? In order to achieve this task, a party was needed which would wrench the power from the hands of the counter-revolution and say to you: 'Here is the power and you've got to take it!' (Stormy and prolonged applause.)

"Notwithstanding that the defensists of all shades stopped at nothing in their struggle against us, we did not throw them out. We proposed to the Congress as a whole to take the power. How utterly you distort the perspective, when after all that has happened you talk from this tribune of our irreconcilability. When a party surrounded with a cloud of gunpowder smoke, comes up to them and says, 'Let us take the power together!' they run to the city duma and unite there with open counter-revolutionists! They are traitors to the revolution with whom we will never unite!

"For the struggle for peace, says Avilov, we must have a coalition with the Compromisers. At the same time he acknowledges that the Allies do not want to make peace. . . . The Allied imperialists laughed, says Avilov, at the oleomargarine delegate Skobelev. Nevertheless if you form a block with the oleomargarine democrats, the cause of peace is assured!

"There are two roads in the struggle for peace. One road is to oppose to the Allied and enemy governments the moral and material force of revolution. The other is a bloc with Skobelev, which means a bloc with Tereshchenko and complete subjection to Allied imperialism. In our proclamation on peace we address ourselves simultaneously to the governments and the peoples. That is a purely formal symmetry. Of course we do not think to influence the imperialist governments with our proclamations, although as long as they exist we cannot ignore them. We rest all our hope on the possibility that our revolution will unleash the European revolution. If the revolting peoples of Europe do not crush imperialism, then we will be crushed—that is indubitable. Either the Russian revolution will raise the whirlwind of struggle in the west, or the capitalists of all countries will crush our revolution. . . . "

"There is a third road," says a voice from the benches.

"The third road," answers Trotsky, "is the road of the Central Executive Committee—on the one hand sending delegates to the west European workers, and on the other forming a union with the Kishkins and Konovalovs. That is a road of lies and hypocrisy which we will never enter.

"Of course we do not say that only the day of insurrection of the European workers will be the day that the peace treaty is signed. This also is possible: that the bourgeoisie, frightened by an approaching insurrection of the oppressed, will hasten to make peace. The dates are not set. The concrete forms cannot be foretold. It is important and it is necessary to define the method of struggle, a method identical in principle both in foreign and domestic politics. A union of the oppressed here and everywhere—that is our road."

The delegates of the Congress, says John Reed, "greeted him with an immense crusading acclaim, kindling to the daring of it, with the thought of championing mankind." At any rate it could not have entered the mind of any Bolshevik at that time to protest against placing the fate of the Soviet Republic, in an official speech in the name of the Bolshevik party, in direct dependence upon the development of the international revolution.

The dramatic law of this Congress was that each significant act was concluded, or even interrupted, by a short intermission during which a figure from the other camp would suddenly appear upon the stage and voice a protest, or a threat, or present an ultimatum. A representative of the Vikzhel, the executive committee of the railroad workers' union, now demanded the floor immediately and on the instant. He must needs throw a bomb into the assembly before the vote was taken on the question of power. The speaker—in whose face Reed saw implacable hostility—began with an accusation. His organization, "the strongest in Russia" had not been invited to the Congress. . . . "It was the Central Executive Committee that did not invite you," was shouted at him from all sides. But he continued: And be it known that the original decision of the Vikzhel to support the Congress of Soviets has been revoked. The speaker hastened to read an ultimatum already distributed by telegraph throughout the country: The Vikzhel condemns the seizure of power by one party; the government ought to be responsible before the "entire revolutionary democracy"; until the creation of a democratic government only the Vikzhel will control the railroad lines. The speaker adds that counter-revolutionary troops will not be admitted to Petrograd; but in general the movements of troops will henceforth take place only at the direction of the old Central Executive Committee. In case of repressions directed against the railroad workers, the Vikzhel will deprive Petrograd of food.

The Congress bristled under the blow. The chiefs of the railroad union were trying to converse with the representatives of the people as one government with another! When the workers, soldiers, and peasants take the administration of the state into their hands, the Vikzhel presumes to give commands to the workers, soldiers, and peasants! It wants to change into petty cash the overthrown system of dual power. In thus attempting to rely not upon its numbers, but upon the exceptional significance of railroads in the economy and culture of the country, these democrats of the Vikzhel exposed the whole frailty of the criterion of formal democracy upon the fundamental issues of a social struggle. Truly revolution has a genius for education!

At any rate the moment for this blow was not badly chosen by the Compromisers. The faces of the praesidium were troubled. Fortunately the Vikzhel was by no means unconditional boss on the railroads. In the local districts the railroad workers were members of the city soviets. Even here at the Congress the ultimatum of the Vikzhel met resistance. "The whole mass of the railroad workers of our district," said the delegate from Tashkent, "have expressed themselves in favor of the transfer of power to the soviets." Another delegate from railroad workers declared the Vikzhel a "political corpse." That doubtless was exaggerated. Relying upon the rather numerous upper layers of railroad clerks, the Vikzhel had preserved more life force than the other higher-up organizations of the Compromisers. But it belonged indubitably to the same type as the army committees or the Central Executive Committee. Its star was swiftly falling. The workers were everywhere distinguishing themselves from the clerical employees; the lower clerks were opposing themselves to the higher. The impudent ultimatum of the Vikzhel would undoubtedly hasten these processes. No, the station masters can't hold back the locomotive of the October revolution!

"There can be no questioning the legal rights of this Congress," declared Kamenev with authority. "The quorum of the Congress was established not by us, but by the old Central Executive Committee. . . . The Congress is the highest organ of the worker and soldier masses." A simple return to the order of the day!

The Council of Peoples Commissars was ratified by an overwhelming majority. Avilov's resolution, according to the excessively generous estimate of Sukhanov, got 150 votes, chiefly Left Social Revolutionaries. The Congress then unanimously confirmed the membership of the new Central Executive Committee: out of 101 members—62 Bolsheviks, 29 Left Social Revolutionaries. The Central Executive Committee was to complete itself in the future with representatives of the peasant soviets and the reelected army organizations. The factions who had abandoned the Congress were granted the right to send their delegates to the Central Executive Committee on the basis of proportional representation.

The agenda of the Congress was completed! The soviet government was created. It had its program. The work could begin. And there was no lack of it. At 5:15 in the morning Kamenev closed the Constituent Congress of the soviet régime. To the stations! Home! To the front! To the factories and barracks! To the mines and the far-off villages! In the decrees of the Soviet, the delegates will carry the leaven of the proletarian revolution to all corners of the country.

On that morning the central organ of the Bolshevik party, again under the old name *Pravda,* wrote: "They wanted us to take the power alone, so that we alone should have to contend with the terrible difficulties confronting the country. . . . So be it! We take the power alone, relying upon the voice of the country and counting upon the friendly help of the European proletariat. But having taken the power, we will deal with the enemies of revolution and its saboteurs with an iron hand. They dreamed of a dictatorship of Kornilov. . . . We will give them the dictatorship of the proletariat. . . . "

Conclusion

A remarkable consecutiveness of stages is to be observed in the development of the Russian revolution—and this for the very reason that it was an authentic popular revolution, setting in motion tens of millions. Events succeeded each other as though obeying laws of gravitation. The correlation of forces was twice verified at every stage: first the masses would demonstrate the might of their assault, then the possessing classes, attempting revenge, would reveal only the more clearly their isolation.

In February the workers and soldiers of Petrograd rose in insurrection—not only against the patriotic will of all the educated classes, but also contrary to the reckonings of the revolutionary organizations. The masses demonstrated that they were inconquerable. Had they themselves been aware of this, they would have become the government. But there was not yet a strong and authoritative revolutionary party at their head. The power fell into the hands of the petty-bourgeois democracy tinted with a protective socialist coloration. The Mensheviks and Social Revolutionaries could make no other use of the confidence of the masses but to summon to the helm the liberal bourgeoisie, who in their turn could only place the power slipped to them by the Compromisers at the service of the interests of the Entente.

In the April days the indignation of the regiments and factories—again without the summons of any party—brought them out on the streets of Petrograd to resist the imperialist policy of the government wished on them by the Compromisers. This armed demonstration attained an appearance of success. Miliukov, the leader of Russian imperialism, was removed from the government. The Compromisers entered the government, superficially as plenipotentiaries of the people, in reality as call-boys of the bourgeoisie.

Without having decided one of the problems which had evoked the revolution, the coalition government violated in June the *de facto* armistice that had been established on the front, throwing the troops into an offensive. By this act the February régime, already characterized by the declining trust of the masses in the Compromisers, dealt itself a fatal blow. The period opened of direct preparation for a second revolution.

At the beginning of July the government, having all the possessing and educated classes behind it, was prosecuting every revolutionary manifestation whatever as treason to the fatherland and aid to the enemy. The official mass organizations—the soviets, the social-patriotic parties—were struggling against a coming-out with all their power. The Bolsheviks for tactical reasons were trying to restrain the workers and soldiers from coming into the streets. Nevertheless the masses came out. The movement proved unrestrainable and universal. The government was nowhere to be seen. The Compromisers hid. The workers and soldiers proved masters of the situation in the capital. Their offensive went to pieces, however, owing to the inadequate readiness of the provinces and the front.

At the end of August all the organs and institutions of the possessing classes stood for a counter-revolutionary overturn: the diplomats of the Entente, the banks, the leagues of landed proprietors and industri-

alists, the Kadet party, the staffs, the officers, the big press. The organizer of the overturn was no other than the supreme commander-in-chief with the officer-apparatus of an army of millions to rely on. Military detachments specially selected from all fronts were thrown against Petrograd under pretense of strategic considerations and by secret agreement with the head of the government.

In the capital everything, it seemed, was prepared for the success of the enterprise: the workers had been disarmed by the authorities with the help of the Compromisers; the Bolsheviks were under a steady rain of blows; the more revolutionary regiments had been removed from the city; hundreds of specially selected officers were concentrated in shock brigades—with the officer schools and Cossack detachments they should constitute an impressive force. And what happened? The plot, patronized it would seem by the gods themselves, barely came in contact with the revolutionary people when it scattered in dust.

These two movements, at the beginning of July and the end of August, relate to each other as a theorem and its converse. The July days demonstrated the might of the self-dependent movement of the masses. The August days laid bare the complete impotence of the ruling groups. This correlation signalized the inevitability of a new conflict. The provinces and the front were meanwhile drawing closer to the capital. This predetermined the October victory.

"The ease with which Lenin and Trotsky overthrew the last coalition government of Kerensky," wrote the Kadet, Nabokov, "revealed its inward impotence. The degree of this impotence was an amazement at that time even to well-informed people." Nabokov himself seems hardly aware that it was a question of his impotence, that of his class, of his social structure.

Just as from the armed demonstration of July the curve rises to the October insurrection, so the movement of Kornilov seems a dress-rehearsal of the counter-revolutionary campaign undertaken by Kerensky in the last days of October. The sole military force against the Bolsheviks found at the front by the democratic commander-in-chief after his flight under cover of the little American flag, was that same Third Cavalry Corps which two months before had been designated by Kornilov for the overthrow of Kerensky himself. The commander of the corps was still the Cossack General, Krasnov, militant monarchist placed in this post by Kornilov. A more appropriate commander for the defense of democracy was not to be found.

Moreover nothing was left of the corps but its name. It had been reduced to a few Cossack squadrons, who after an unsuccessful attempt to take the offensive against the Reds near Petrograd, fraternized with the revolutionary sailors and turned Krasnov over to the Bolsheviks. Kerensky was obliged to take flight—both from the Cossacks and the sailors. Thus eight months after the overthrow of the monarchy the workers stood at the head of the country. And they stood firmly.

"Who would believe," wrote one of the Russian generals, Zalessky, expressing his indignation at this, "that the janitor or watchman of the court building would suddenly become Chief Justice of the Court of Appeals? Or the hospital orderly, manager of the hospital; the barber a big functionary; yesterday's ensign, the commander-in-chief; yesterday's lackey or common laborer, burgomaster; yesterday's train oiler, chief of division or station superintendent; yesterday's locksmith, head of the factory?"

"Who would believe it?" They had to believe it. It was impossible not to believe it, when ensigns routed the generals, when burgomasters from the ranks of common labor put down the resistance of yesterday's lords, train oilers regulated transport, and locksmiths as directors revived industry.

The chief task of a political régime, according to an English aphorism, is to put the right people in the right positions. How does the experiment of 1917 look from this point of view? During the first two months Russia was ruled, through right of monarchic succession, by a man inadequately endowed by nature who believed in saints' mummies and submitted to Rasputin. During the next eight months the liberals and democrats attempted from their governmental high places to prove to the people that the revolution had been accomplished in order that all should remain as before. No wonder those people passed over the country like wavering shadows leaving no trace. From the 25th of October the man at the head of Russia was Lenin, the greatest figure in Russian political history. He was surrounded by a staff of assistants who, as their most spiteful enemies acknowledge, knew what they wanted and how to fight for their aims. Which of these three systems, in the given concrete conditions, proved capable of putting the right people in the right positions?

The historic ascent of humanity, taken as a whole, may be summarized as a succession of victories of consciousness over blind forces—in nature, in society, in man himself. Critical and creative thought can boast of its greatest victories up to now in the struggle with nature. The physico-chemical sciences have already reached a point where man is clearly about to become master of matter. But social relations are still forming in the manner of the coral islands. Parliamentarism illumined only the surface of society, and even that with a rather artificial light. In comparison with monarchy and other heirlooms from the cannibals and cave-dwellers, democracy is of course a great conquest, but it leaves the blind play of forces in the social relations of men untouched. It was against this deeper sphere of the unconscious that the October revolution was the first to raise its hand. The soviet system wishes to bring aim and plan into the very basis of society, where up to now only accumulated consequences have reigned.

Enemies are gleeful that fifteen years after the revolution the soviet country is still but little like a kingdom of universal well-being. Such an argument, if not really to be explained as due to a blinding hostility, could only be dictated by an excessive worship of the magic power of socialist methods. Capitalism required a hundred years to elevate science and technique to the heights and plunge humanity into the hell of war and crisis. To socialism its enemies allow only fifteen years to create and furnish a terrestrial paradise. We took no such obligation upon ourselves. We never set these dates. The process of vast transformations must be measured by an adequate scale.

But the misfortunes which have overwhelmed living people? The fire and bloodshed of the civil war? Do the consequences of a revolution justify in general the sacrifices it involves. The question is teleological and therefore fruitless. It would be as well to ask in face of the difficulties and griefs of personal existence: Is it worth while to be born? Melancholy reflections have not so far, however, prevented people from bearing or being born. Even in the present epoch of intolerable misfortune only a small percentage of the population of our planet resorts to suicide. But the people are seeking the way out of their unbearable difficulties in revolution.

Is it not remarkable that those who talk most indignantly about the victims of social revolutions are usually the very ones who, if not directly responsible for the victims of the world war, prepared and glorified them, or at least accepted them? It is our turn to ask: Did the war justify itself? What has it given us? What has it taught?

It will hardly pay now to pause upon the assertions of injured Russian proprietors that the revolution led to the cultural decline of the country. The aristocratic culture overthrown by the October revolution was in the last analysis only a superficial imitation of higher western models. Remaining inaccessible to the Russian people, it added nothing essential to the treasure-store of humanity. The October revolution laid the foundation of a new culture taking everybody into consideration, and for that very reason immediately acquiring international significance. Even supposing for a moment that owing to unfavorable circumstances and hostile blows the soviet régime should be temporarily overthrown, the inexpungable impress of the October revolution would nevertheless remain upon the whole future development of mankind.

The language of the civilized nations has clearly marked off two epochs in the development of Russia. Where the aristocratic culture introduced into world parlance such barbarisms as *tzar, pogrom, knout,* October has internationalized such words as *Bolshevik, soviet* and *piatiletka*. This alone justifies the proletarian revolution, if you imagine that it needs justification.

The Pilgrim's Progress

John Bunyan

Editor's Introduction

The Pilgrim's Progress is one of two great allegories of salvation—great not only in their quality as literature, but as documents of religious faith—which have established themselves in the consciousness of the Christian world. The other such account is Dante's *Divine Comedy*. The *Comedy* is the greater work if we consider the range of its vision, which includes the world of the damned as well as the orders of heaven and the ineffable Godhead itself, and which incorporates science and philosophy with religion. John Bunyan, who had no comparable learning, confines himself for the most part to what Dante takes up in Purgatory, where the sinful soul rids itself of its defects and prepares to enter Paradise. But Bunyan depicts, as Dante does not, the trials of ordinary human beings in this progression, which he dreams of as occurring in this life, and the persons we see undertaking it are such as we can easily recognize. It is not surprising that his were household words for as long as their subject seemed to be important. Nor do they lack all power even now in their imagery, their acute perception, and their dogged seriousness of purpose.

Bunyan was born in 1628, the son of a brazier, or tinker, in the English Midlands, who attended grammar school in the region among, as he said, "a multitude of poor plowmen's children." This was his only formal education. Although his parents were not Puritans but members of the "national church," there was much popular literature around depicting Puritan lives, as there were books of medieval romance and also the King James translation of the Bible, recently published, which influenced Bunyan's prose so markedly.

As a boy, Bunyan tells us, he had terrifying dreams of sin and damnation, although there is no evidence that he was like the black soul he imagined himself to be. He had overcome these by the time he was mustered into arms on the Parliamentary side in the Civil War of 1642–47. There he encountered religious sects such as the Quakers, whose rejection of any authority except the individual conscience he thought pernicious, and which he never accepted, as his Christian does not.

Married about 1648 to a pious woman by whom he had four children, he underwent a crisis of the soul between 1650 and 1655 that caused him to give up all the country diversions and village sports in which he had participated to concentrate upon his inner life, undergoing intervals of spiritual despair—accompanied by a desire to blaspheme—which he recounts in his autobiography, *Grace Abounding* (1666). He recovered from these only by reading devotional texts that encouraged him to believe in spiritual progress and divine grace. This culminated in his conversion, when he was taken into the Separatist Church at Bedford (1655). There he became a lay preacher, chiefly against the Quakers, opposed as he was to their belief in the sufficiency of inner light for salvation.

The Restoration of the monarchy in 1660 brought suppression to the Puritans. Bunyan, who would not give up his Nonconformist ways, was imprisoned and remained so—despite occasional liberties and without having undergone any trial—for the next twelve years. Besides the autobiography, which he wrote in an effort to sustain his spiritual life during this interval, he probably wrote much or all of the First Part of *The Pilgrim's Progress,* though this was not published until 1678, four years after his release under a Royal Declaration of Indulgence.

The Pilgrim's Progress was at once a popular success throughout the English-speaking world, and its scenes and characters—Vanity Fair, the Valley of the Shadow of Death, the Slough of Despond, the Delectable Mountains—became in due course staples of the English imagination, from which they were evicted only by the adoption of state-supported education in the nineteenth century.

Bunyan wrote other books as well, including *The Life and Death of Mr. Badman* (1680), *The Holy War* (1682), and *A Book for Boys and Girls* containing poems and pictures (1686). Eventually offered an official position by James II, who sought Puritan support against the Anglican Establishment, Bunyan sensibly refused it as being contrary to the whole tenor of his life. He died at London in 1688 and was buried in Bunhill Fields, the famous Nonconformist graveyard where George Fox, Daniel Defoe, and William Blake lie also, and where his grave was the object of many an American pilgrimage in the nineteenth century, when the descendants of the Puritans took tourist trips to "the old home" that England was in their imaginations, which had been formed by no one more completely than the author of *The Pilgrim's Progress.*

The
Pilgrim's Progress
from
This World
to
That Which Is to Come

_____

Delivered Under the Similitude
of a Dream
Wherein Is Discovered
the Manner of His Setting Out,
His Dangerous Journey,
and
Safe Arrival at the Desired
Country

_____

by John Bunyan

"I have used similitudes." Hosea 12:10

The Author's Apology
for His Book

When at the first I took my pen in hand
Thus for to write, I did not understand
That I at all should make a little book
In such a mode; nay, I had undertook
To make another, which when almost done,
Before I was aware, I this begun.

    And thus it was: I, writing of the way
And race of saints in this our gospel day,
Fell suddenly into an allegory
About their journey and the way to glory,
In more than twenty things, which I set down;
This done, I twenty more had in my crown,
And they again began to multiply,
Like sparks that from the coals of fire do fly.
Nay then, thought I, if that you breed so fast,
I'll put you by yourselves, lest you at last
Should prove *ad infinitum,* and eat out
The book that I already am about.

    Well, so I did; but yet I did not think
To show to all the world my pen and ink
In such a mode; I only thought to make
I knew not what; nor did I undertake
Thereby to please my neighbour; no, not I,
I did it my own self to gratify.

    Neither did I but vacant seasons spend
In this my scribble; nor did I intend
But to divert myself in doing this,
From worser thoughts, which make me do amiss.

    Thus I set pen to paper with delight,
And quickly had my thoughts in black and white.
For having now my method by the end,
Still as I pulled, it came; and so I penned
It down until it came at last to be,
For length and breadth, the bigness which you see.

    Well, when I had thus put my ends together,
I showed them others, that I might see whether
They would condemn them or them justify.
And some said, "Let them live"; some, "Let them die."
Some said, "John, print it"; others said, "Not so."
Some said, "It might do good"; others said, "No."

    Now was I in a straight, and did not see
Which was the best thing to be done by me.
At last I thought, "Since you are thus divided,
I print it will," and so the case decided.

For, thought I, some, I see, would have it done,
Though others in that channel do not run;
To prove then who advised for the best,
Thus I thought fit to put it to the test.

I further thought if now I did deny
Those that would have it, thus to gratify,
I did not know but hinder them I might
Of that which would to them be great delight.

For those that were not for its coming forth
I said to them, "Offend you I am loth;
Yet since your brethren pleased with it be,
Forbear to judge till you do further see.

"If that thou wilt not read, let it alone;
Some love the meat, some love to pick the bone."
Yea, that I might them better palliate,
I did too with them thus expostulate:

"May I not write in such a style as this?
In such a method, too, and yet not miss
My end, thy good? Why may it not be done?
Some love the meat, some love to pick the bone."
Yea, dark or bright, if they their silver drops.
Cause to descend, the earth, by yielding crops,
Gives praise to both, and carpeth not at either,
But treasures up the fruit they yield together.
Yea, so commixes both, that in her fruit
None can distinguish this from that. They suit
Her well when hungry, but if she be full,
She spews out both and makes their blessings null.

"You see the ways the fisherman doth take
To catch the fish, what engines doth he make?
Behold! how he engageth all his wits,
Also his snares, lines, angles, hooks and nets.
Yet fish there be that neither hook nor line
Nor snare nor net nor engine can make thine;
They must be groped for and be tickled, too,
Or they will not be catch'd whate're you do.

"How doth the fowler seek to catch his game?
By divers means, all which one cannot name:
His gun, his nets, his lime-twigs, light and bell;
He creeps, he goes, he stands; yea, who can tell
Of all his postures? Yet there's none of these
Will make him master of what fowls he please.
Yea, he must pipe, and whistle to catch *this*;
Yet if he does so, *that* bird he will miss.

"If that a pearl may in a toad's head dwell,
And may be found too in an oyster shell;
If things that promise nothing do contain
What better is than gold; who will disdain,
(That have an inkling of it) there to look

387

That they may find it? Now my little book,
(Though void of all those paintings that may make
It with this or the other man to take)
Is not without those things that do excel
What do in brave, but empty, notions dwell.
    "Well, yet I am not fully satisfied,
That this your book will stand, when soundly tried."
    "Why, what's the matter?" "It is dark." "What though?"
"But it is feigned." "What of that? I trow
Some men by feigning words as dark as mine
Make truth to spangle and its rays to shine."
    "But they want solidness." "Speak, man, thy mind."
"They drowned the weak; metaphors make us blind."
    Solidity indeed becomes the pen
Of him that writeth things divine to men;
But must I needs want solidness, because
By metaphors I speak; were not God's laws,
His Gospel laws, in olden time held forth
By types, shadows and metaphors? Yet loth
Will any sober man be to find fault
With them, lest he be found for to assault
The highest wisdom. No, he rather stoops
And seeks to find out what by pins and loops,
By calves and sheep, by heifers and by rams,
By birds and herbs, and by the blood of lambs,
God speaketh to him; and happy is he
That finds the light and grace that in them be.
    Be not too forward, therefore, to conclude
That I want solidness, that I am rude;
All things solid in show not solid be;
All things in parables despise not we,
Lest things most hurtful lightly we receive,
And things that good are of our souls bereave.
    My dark and cloudy words they do but hold
The truth, as cabinets inclose the gold.
    The prophets used much by metaphors
To set forth truth; yea, who so considers
Christ, his apostles too, shall plainly see
That truths to this day in such mantles be.
    Am I afraid to say that holy writ,
Which for its style and phrase puts down all wit,
Is everywhere so full of all these things
(dark figures, allegories) yet there springs
From that same book that lustre and those rays
Of light that turns our darkest nights to days?
    Come, let my carper to his life now look,
And find there darker lines than in my book
He findeth any. Yea, and let him know
That in his best things there are worse lines, too.

May we but stand before impartial men;
To his poor one I durst adventure ten,
That they will take my meaning in these lines
Far better then his lies in silver shrines.
Come, truth, although in swaddling clouts,* I find
Informs the judgement, rectifies the mind,
Pleases the understanding, makes the will
Submit; the memory too it doth fill
With what doth our imagination please;
Likewise it tends our troubles to appease.

    Sound words, I know, Timothy is to use,
And old wives' fables he is to refuse;
But yet grave Paul him nowhere doth forbid
The use of parables, in which lay hid
That gold, those pearls, and precious stones that were
Worth digging for, and that with greatest care.

    Let me add one word more, O man of God!
Art thou offended? Dost thou wish I had
Put forth my matter in another dress,
Or that I had in things been more express?
Three things let me propound; then I submit
To those that are my betters (as is fit).

    1. I find not that I am denied the use
Of this my method, so I no abuse
Put on the words, things, readers, or be rude
In handling figure, or similitude,
In application; but, all that I may,
Seek the advance of truth, this or that way.
Denied did I say? Nay, I have leave
(Example, too, and that from them that have
God better pleased by their words or ways
Than any man that breatheth nowadays)
Thus to express my mind, thus to declare
Things unto thee that excellentest are.

    2. I find that men (as high as trees) will write
Dialogue-wise, yet no man doth them slight
For writing so. Indeed, if they abuse
Truth, cursed be they and the craft they use
To that intent; but yet let truth be free
To make her sallies upon thee and me,
Which way it pleases God; for who knows how
Better than he that taught us first to plow
To guide our mind and pens for his design?
And he makes base things usher in divine.

    3. I find that holy writ in many places
Hath semblance with this method, where the cases
Doth call for one thing to set forth another.

---

*Swaddling clothes.

Use it I may then, and yet nothing smother
Truth's golden beams; nay, by this method may
Make it cast forth its rays as light as day.
  And now, before I do put up my pen,
I'll show the profit of my book, and then
Commit both thee and it unto that hand
That pulls the strong down and makes weak ones stand.
  This book it chalketh out before thine eyes
The man that seeks the everlasting prize;
It shows you whence he comes, whither he goes,
What he leaves undone, also what he does;
It also shows you how he runs and runs
Till he unto the gate of glory comes.
  It shows, too, who sets out for life amain,
As if the lasting crown they would attain.
Here also you may see the reason why
They lose their labour and like fools do die.
  This book will make a traveller of thee,
If by its counsel thou wilt ruled be;
It will direct thee to the Holy Land,
If thou wilt its directions understand.
Yea, it will make the slothful active be,
The blind, also, delightful things to see.
  Art thou for something rare and profitable?
Wouldest thou see a truth within a fable?
Art thou forgetful? Wouldest thou remember
From New Year's Day to the last of December?
Then read my fancies; they will stick like burrs,
And may be to the helpless comforters.
  This book is writ in such a dialect,
As may the minds of listless men affect.
It seems a novelty, and yet contains
Nothing but sound and honest gospel strains.
  Wouldst thou divert thyself from melancholy?
Wouldst thou be pleasant, yet be far from folly?
Wouldst thou read riddles, and their explanation,
Or else be drowned in thy contemplation?
Dost thou love picking meat? Or wouldst thou see
A man i' th' clouds and hear him speak to thee?
Wouldst thou be in a dream and yet not sleep?
Or wouldst thou in a moment laugh and weep?
Wouldst thou lose thyself and catch no harm?
And find thyself again without a charm?
Wouldst read thyself and read thou knowest not what
And yet know whether thou art blest or not,
By reading the same lines? O then come hither,
And lay my book, thy head and heart together.

The Pilgrim's Progress:
In the Similitude
of a Dream

As I walked through the wilderness of this world, I lighted on a certain place where was a den, and I laid me down in that place to sleep, and as I slept I dreamed a dream. I dreamed, and behold I saw a man clothed with rags, [Isaiah 64:6] standing in a certain place, with his face from his own house, a book in his hand, and a great burden upon his back. [Psalms 38:4] I looked, and saw him open the book, and read therein; and as he read he wept and trembled, and not being able longer to contain, he brake out with a lamentable cry, saying, "What shall I do?" [Acts 16:30–31]

In this plight therefore he went home and refrained himself as long as he could that his wife and children should not perceive his distress; but he could not be silent long, because that his trouble increased. Wherefore at length he brake his mind to his wife and children; and thus he began to talk to them, "O my dear wife," said he, "and you, the children of my bowels, I your dear friend am in myself undone, by reason of a burden that lieth hard upon me; moreover, I am for certain informed that this our city will be burned with fire from heaven, in which fearful overthrow both myself, with thee, my wife, and you, my sweet babes, shall miserably come to ruin; except (the which, yet I see not) some way of escape can be found, whereby we may be delivered." At this his relations were sore amazed; not for that they be-lieved that what he said to them was true, but because they thought that some frenzy distemper had got into his head; therefore, it drawing towards night, and they hoping that sleep might settle his brains, with all haste they got him to bed. But the night was as troublesome to him as the day; wherefore instead of sleeping, he spent it in sighs and tears. So when the morning was come, they would know how he did, and he told them worse and worse. He also set to talking to them again, but they began to be hardened. They also thought to drive away his distemper by harsh and surly carriages* to him: sometimes they would deride; sometimes they would chide; and sometimes they would quite neglect him. Wherefore he began to retire himself to his chamber to pray for and pity them, and also to condole his own misery; he would also walk solitarily in the fields, sometimes reading, and sometimes praying, and thus for some days he spent his time.

Now, I saw upon a time when he was walking in the fields that he was (as he was wont) reading in his book and greatly distressed in his mind; and as he read, he burst out, as he had done before, crying, "What shall I do to be saved?"

I saw also that he looked this way and that way, as if he would run; yet he stood still, because, as I perceived, he could not

---

*Conduct, behaviour.

tell which way to go. I looked then and saw a man named Evangelist coming to him and asked, "Wherefore dost thou cry?" He answered, "Sir, I perceive, by the book in my hand, that I am condemned to die and after that to come to judgement; and I find that I am not willing to do the first, nor able to do the second."

Then said Evangelist, "Why not willing to die since this life is attended with so many evils?" The man answered, "Because I fear that this burden that is upon my back will sink me lower than the grave, and I shall fall into Tophet.* And, sir, if I be not fit to go to prison, I am not fit (I am sure) to go to judgement and from thence to execution; and the thoughts of these things make me cry."

Then said Evangelist, "If this be thy condition, why standest thou still?" He answered, "Because I know not whither to go." Then he gave him a parchment roll, and there was written within, "Fly from the wrath to come." [Matthew 3:7]

The man therefore read it, and look-ing upon Evangelist very carefully, said, "Whither must I fly?" Then said Evangelist, pointing with his finger over a very wide field, "Do you see yonder wicket-gate?" [Matthew 7:13, 14] The man said, "No." Then said the other, "Do you see yonder shining light?" [Psalms 119:105, 2 Peter 1:19] He said, "I think I do." Then said Evangelist, "Keep that light in your eye, and go up directly thereto; so shalt thou see the gate, at which when thou knockest, it shall be told thee what thou shalt do."

So I saw in my dream that the man be-gan to run. Now he had not run far from his own door, but his wife and children perceiving it, began to cry after him to return. But the man put his fingers in his ears and ran on crying, "Life, life, eternal life." So he looked not behind him, but fled towards the middle of the plain. [Genesis 19:17]

The neighbours also came out to see

---

*Cf. Isaiah 30:33.

392

him run, and as he ran, some mocked, others threatened, and some cried after him to return. Now among those that did so, there were two that were resolved to fetch him back by force. The name of the one was Obstinate and the name of the other Pliable. Now by this time the man was got a good distance from them; but, however, they were resolved to pursue him, which they did and in little time they overtook him. Then said the man, "Neighbours, wherefore are you come?" They said, "To persuade you to go back with us." But he said, "That can by no means be. You dwell," said he, "in the City of Destruction [Isaiah 19:18] (the place also where I was born). I see it to be so, and dying there, sooner or later, you will sink lower than the grave, into a place that burns with fire and brimstone. Be content, good neighbours, and go along with me."

"What!" said Obstinate, "and leave our friends and our comforts behind us!"

"Yes," said Christian (for that was his name), "because, that all which you shall forsake is not worthy to be compared with a little of that that I am seeking to enjoy, and if you will go along with me, and hold it, you shall fare as I myself; for there where I go is enough and to spare. Come away and prove my words."

OBST. "What are the things you seek, since you leave all the world to find them?"

CHR. "I seek an 'inheritance, incorruptible, undefiled, and that fadeth not away,' [I Peter 1:4] and it is laid up in Heaven, and fast there, to be bestowed at the time appointed on them that diligently seek it. Read it so, if you will, in my book."

OBST. "Tush," said Obstinate, "away with your book; will you go back with us or no?"

CHR. "No, not I," said the other, "because I have laid my hand to the plow." [Luke: 9:62]

OBST. "Come, then, neighbour Pliable, let us turn again, and go home without him; there is a company of these crazed-headed coxcombs, that when they take a fancy by the end are wiser in their own eyes than seven men that can render a reason." [Proverbs 26:16]

PLI. Then said Pliable, "Don't revile; if what the good Christian says is true, the things he looks after are better than ours; my heart inclines to go with my neighbour."

OBST. "What! more fools still? Be ruled by me and go back; who knows whither such a brain-sick fellow will lead you? Go back, go back, and be wise."

CHR. "Come with me, neighbour Pliable; there are such things to be had which I spoke of and many more glories besides; if you believe not me, read here in this book, and for the truth of what is expressed therein, behold all is confirmed by the blood of him that made it."

PLI. "Well, neighbour Obstinate," said Pliable, "I begin to come to a point; I intend to go along with this good man and to cast in my lot with him. But, my good companion, do you know the way to this desired place?"

CHR. "I am directed by a man whose name is Evangelist to speed me to a little gate that is before us, where we shall receive instruction about the way."

PLI. "Come then, good neighbour, let us be going." Then they went both together.

OBST. "And I will go back to my place," said Obstinate. "I will be no companion of such misled fantastical fellows."

Now I saw in my dream that when Obstinate was gone back, Christian and Pliable went talking over the plain, and thus they began their discourse.

CHR. "Come, neighbour Pliable, how do you do? I am glad you are persuaded to go along with me, and had even Obstinate himself but felt what I have felt of the powers and terrors of what is yet unseen, he would not thus lightly have given us the back."

PLI. "Come, neighbour Christian, since there is none but us two here, tell me now further, what the things are and how to be enjoyed, whither we are going."

CHR. "I can better conceive of them with my mind than speak of them with my tongue. But yet since you are desirous to know, I will read of them in my book."

PLI. "And do you think that the words of your book are certainly true?"

CHR. "Yes, verily, for it was made by him that cannot lie." [Titus 1:2]

PLI. "Well said; what things are they?"

CHR. "There is an endless kingdom to be inhabited and everlasting life to be given us, that we may inhabit that kingdom forever."

PLI. "Well said, and what else?"

CHR. "There are crowns of glory to be given us, and garments that will make us shine like the sun in the firmament of heaven."

PLI. "This is excellent, and what else?"

CHR. "There shall be no more crying, nor sorrow; for He that is owner of the place will wipe all tears from our eyes." [Revelation 21:4]

PLI. "And what company shall we have there?"

CHR. "There we shall be with seraphims and cherubims, creatures that will dazzle your eyes to look on them. There also you shall meet with thousands and ten thousands that have gone before us to that place; none of them are hurtful, but loving and holy, every one walking in the sight of God, and standing in his presence with acceptance forever. In a word, there we shall see the elders with their golden crowns. There we shall see the holy virgins with their golden harps. [Revelation 5:11, 4:4, 14:1–5] There we shall see men that by the world were cut in pieces, burned in flames, eaten of beasts, drowned in the seas, for the love that they bare to the Lord of the place, all well and clothed with immortality, as with a garment."

PLI. "The hearing of this is enough to ravish one's heart; but are these things to be enjoyed? How shall we get to be sharers hereof?"

CHR. "The Lord, the governor of that country, hath recorded that in this book,

the substance of which is: if we be truly willing to have it, he will bestow it upon us freely."

PLI. "Well, my good companion, glad am I to hear of these things. Come on, let us mend our pace."

CHR. "I cannot go so fast as I would, by reason of this burden that is upon my back."

Now I saw in my dream, that just as they had ended this talk, they drew near to a very miry slough that was in the midst of the plain, and they, being heedless, did both fall suddenly into the bog. The name of the slough was Despond. Here therefore they wallowed for a time, being grievously bedaubed with the dirt; and Christian, because of the burden that was on his back, began to sink in the mire.

PLI. Then said Pliable, "Ah, neighbour Christian, where are you now?"

CHR. "Truly," said Christian, "I do not know."

PLI. At that Pliable began to be offended; and angrily said to his fellow, "Is this the happiness you have told me all this while of? If we have such ill speed at our first setting out, what may we expect, 'twixt this and our journey's end? May I get out again with my life, you shall possess the brave country alone for me."* And with that he gave a desperate struggle or two and got out of the mire, on that side of the slough which was next to his own house. So away he went, and Christian saw him no more.

Wherefore Christian was left to tumble in the slough of Despond alone; but still he endeavoured to struggle to that side of the slough that was still further from his own house and next to the wicket-gate; the which he did, but could not get out, because of the burden that was upon his back. But I beheld in my dream that a man came to him, whose name was Help, and asked him what he did there?

CHR. "Sir," said Christian, "I was bid go

---

*Bunyan adds the note, "It is not enough to be pliable."

this way by a man called Evangelist, who directed me also to yonder gate, that I might escape the wrath to come. And as I was going thither, I fell in here."

HELP. "But why did you not look for the steps?"

CHR. "Fear followed me so hard, that I fled the next way and fell in."

HELP. "Then," said he, "give me thy hand." So he gave him his hand, and he drew him out, and set him upon sound ground, and bid him go on his way. [Psalms 40:2]

Then I stepped to him that plucked him out and said, "Sir, wherefore, since over this place is the way from the City of Destruction to yonder gate, is it that this plot is not mended that poor travellers might go thither with more security?" And he said unto me, "This miry slough is such a place as cannot be mended. It is the descent whither the scum and filth that attends conviction for sin doth continually run, and therefore is it called the Slough of Despond; for still as the sinner is awakened about his lost condition, there ariseth in his soul many fears, and doubts, and discouraging apprehensions, which all of them get together, and settle in this place. And this is the reason of the badness of this ground.

"It is not the pleasure of the King that this place should remain so bad; his labourers also have, by the direction of His Majesty's surveyors, been for above this sixteen hundred years employed about this patch of ground, if perhaps it might have been mended. Yea, and to my knowledge," saith he, "here hath been swallowed up at least twenty thousand cart-loads, yea millions of wholesome instructions that have at all seasons been brought from all places of the King's dominions, and they that can tell say they are the best materials to make good ground of the place. If so be it might have been mended, but it is the Slough of Despond still and so will be when they have done what they can.

"True, there are, by the direction of the law-giver, certain good and substantial steps, placed even through the very midst of this Slough; but at such time as this place doth much spew out its filth, as it doth against change of weather, these steps are hardly seen; or if they be, men, through the dizziness of their heads, step besides, and then they are bemired to purpose, notwithstanding the steps be there; but the ground is good when they are once got in at the gate."

Now I saw in my dream that by this time Pliable was got home to his house again. So his neighbours came to visit him, and some of them called him wise man for coming back, and some called him fool for hazarding himself with Christian; others again did mock at his cowardliness, saying, "Surely since you began to venture, I would not have been so base to have given out for a few difficulties." So Pliable sat sneaking among them. But at last he got more confidence, and then they all turned their tales and began to deride poor Christian behind his back. And thus much concerning Pliable.

Now as Christian was walking solitary by himself, he espied one afar off come crossing over the field to meet him; and their hap was to meet just as they were crossing the way of each other. The gentleman's name was Mr. Worldly Wiseman; he dwelt in the town of Carnal Policy, a very great town, and also hard by from whence Christian came. This man then meeting with Christian, and having some inkling of him, for Christian's setting forth from the City of Destruction was much noised abroad, not only in the town where he dwelt, but also it began to be the towntalk in some other places, Master Worldly Wiseman therefore, having some guess of him, by beholding his laborious going, by observing his sighs and groans, and the like, began thus to enter into some talk with Christian.

WORLD. "How now, good fellow, whither away after this burdened manner?"

CHR. "A burdened manner, indeed, as

ever I think poor creature had. And whereas you ask me, 'Whither away,' I tell you, sir, I am going to yonder wicket-gate before me; for there, as I am informed, I shall be put into a way to be rid of my heavy burden."

WORLD. "Hast thou a wife and children?"

CHR. "Yes, but I am so laden with this burden that I cannot take that pleasure in them as formerly; methinks, I am as if I had none." [I Corinthians 7:29]

WORLD. "Wilt thou hearken to me, if I give thee counsel?"

CHR. "If it be good, I will, for I stand in need of good counsel."

WORLD. "I would advise thee then that thou with all speed get thyself rid of thy burden; for thou wilt never be settled in thy mind till then, nor canst thou enjoy the benefits of the blessing which God hath bestowed upon thee till then."

CHR. "That is that which I seek for, even to be rid of this heavy burden; but get it off myself I cannot, nor is there a man in our country that can take it off my shoulders; therefore am I going this way, as I told you, that I may be rid of my burden."

WORLD. "Who bid thee go this way to be rid of thy burden?"

CHR. "A man that appeared to me to be a very great and honourable person; his name, as I remember, is Evangelist."

WORLD. "I beshrew him for his counsel; there is not a more dangerous and troublesome way in the world than is that unto which he hath directed thee; and that thou shalt find, if thou wilt be ruled by his counsel. Thou hast met with something (as I perceive) already; for I see the dirt of the Slough of Despond is upon thee; but that slough is the beginning of the sorrows that do attend those that go on in that way. Hear me, I am older than thou! Thou art like to meet with in the way which thou goest wearisomeness, painfulness, hunger, perils, nakedness, sword, lions, dragons, darkness, and in a word, death, and what not? These things are certainly true, having been confirmed by many testimonies.

And why should a man so carelessly cast away himself by giving heed to a stranger?"

CHR. "Why, sir, this burden upon my back is more terrible to me than are all these things which you have mentioned. Nay, methinks I care not what I meet with in the way, so be I can also meet with deliverance from my burden."

WORLD. "How camest thou by thy burden at first?"

CHR. "By reading this book in my hand."

WORLD. "I thought so; and it happened unto thee as to other weak men, who, meddling with things too high for them, do suddenly fall into thy distractions; which distractions do not only unman men, as thine, I perceive, has done thee, but they run them upon desperate ventures, to obtain they know not what."

CHR. "I know what I would obtain; it is ease for my heavy burden."

WORLD. "But why wilt thou seek for ease this way, seeing so many dangers attend it, especially since, hadst thou but patience to hear me, I could direct thee to the obtaining of what thou desirest, without the dangers that thou in this way wilt run thyself into; yea, and the remedy is at hand. Besides, I will add, that instead of those dangers thou shalt meet with much safety, friendship, and content."

CHR. "Pray, sir, open this secret to me."

WORLD. "Why in yonder village (the village is named Morality) there dwells a gentleman whose name is Legality, a very judicious man (and a man of a very good name) that has skill to help men off with such burdens as thine are from their shoulders; yea, to my knowledge he hath done a great deal of good this way. Ay, and besides, he hath skill to cure those that are somewhat crazed in their wits with their burdens. To him, as I said, thou mayest go, and be helped presently. His house is not quite a mile from this place; and if he should not be at home himself, he hath a pretty young man to his son, whose name is Civility, that can do it (to speak on) as well as the old gentleman himself. There, I say, thou mayest be eased of thy burden, and if thou art not minded to go back to thy former habitations, as indeed I would not wish thee, thou mayest send for thy wife and children to thee to this village, where there are houses now stand empty, one of which thou mayest have at reasonable rates. Provision is there also cheap and good; and that which will make thy life the more happy is, to be sure; there thou shalt live by honest neighbours, in credit and good fashion.''

Now was Christian somewhat at a stand, but presently he concluded, if this be true which this gentleman hath said, my wisest course is to take his advice; and with that he thus farther spoke.

CHR. "Sir, which is my way to this honest man's house?"

WORLD. "Do you see yonder high hill?"

CHR. "Yes, very well."

WORLD. "By that hill you must go, and the first house you come at is his."

So Christian turned out of his way to go to Mr. Legality's house for help; but behold, when he was got now hard by the hill, it seemed so high, and also that side of it that was next the wayside did hang so much over that Christian was afraid to venture further, lest the hill should fall on his head. Wherefore there he stood still, and wotted not what to do. Also his burden, now, seemed heavier to him than while he was in his way. There came also flashes of fire out of the hill that made Christian afraid that he should be burned; [Exodus 19:16, 18] here therefore he sweat, and did quake for fear. [Hebrews 12:21] And now he began to be sorry that he had taken Mr. Worldly Wiseman's counsel; and with that he saw Evangelist coming to meet him, at the sight also of whom he began to blush for shame. So Evangelist drew nearer, and nearer, and coming up to him, he looked upon him with a severe and dreadful countenance, and thus began to reason with Christian.

EVAN. "What doest thou here?" said he,

at which word Christian knew not what to answer; wherefore, at present, he stood speechless before him. Then said Evangelist farther, "Art not thou the man that I found crying, without the walls of the City of Destruction?"

CHR. "Yes, dear sir, I am the man."

EVAN. "Did not I direct thee the way to the little wicket-gate?"

CHR. "Yes, dear sir," said Christian.

EVAN. "How is it then that thou art so quickly turned aside, for thou art now out of the way?"

CHR. "I met with a gentleman so soon as I had got over the Slough of Despond, who persuaded me that I might in the village before me find a man that could take off my burden."

EVAN. "What was he?"

CHR. "He looked like a gentleman, and talked much to me, and got me at last to yield; so I came hither. But when I beheld this hill, and how it hangs over the way, I suddenly made a stand, lest it should fall on my head."

EVAN. "What said that gentleman to you?"

CHR. "Why, he asked me whither I was going, and I told him."

EVAN. "And what said he then?"

CHR. "He asked me if I had a family, and I told him; but, said I, I am so laden with the burden that is on my back, that I cannot take pleasure in them as formerly."

EVAN. "And what said he then?"

CHR. "He bid me with speed get rid of my burden, and I told him 'twas ease that I sought. And said I, I am therefore going to yonder gate to receive further direction how I may get to the place of deliverance. So he said that he would show me a better way, and short, not so attended with difficulties, as the way, sir, that you set me; which way, said he, will direct you to a gentleman's house that hath skill to take off these burdens. So I believed him, and turned out of that way into this, if haply I might be soon eased of my burden; but when I came to this place, and beheld things as they are, I stopped for fear (as I said) of danger, but I now know not what to do."

EVAN. "Then," said Evangelist, "stand still a little that I may show thee the words of God." So he stood trembling. Then said Evangelist, "See that ye refuse not him that speaketh; for if they escaped not who refused him that spake on earth, much more shall not we escape, if we turn away from him that speaketh from Heaven." [Hebrews 12:25] He said moreover, "Now the just shall live by faith; but if any man draws back, my soul shall have no pleasure in him." [Hebrews 10:38] He also did thus apply them, "Thou art the man that art running into this misery, thou has began to reject the counsel of the Most High, and to draw back thy foot from the way of peace, even almost to the hazarding of thy perdition."

Then Christian fell down at his foot as dead, crying, "Woe is me, for I am undone." [Isaiah 6:5] At the sight of which Evangelist caught him by the right hand, saying, "All manner of sin and blasphemies shall be forgiven unto men; [Matthew 12:31; Mark 3:28] be not faithless, but believing." [John 20:27] Then did Christian again a little revive, and stood up trembling, as at first, before Evangelist.

Then Evangelist proceeded, saying, "Give more earnest heed to the things that I shall tell thee of. I will now show thee who it was that deluded thee, and who 'twas also to whom he sent thee. The man that met thee is one Worldly Wiseman, and rightly is he so called; partly, because he favoureth only the doctrine of this world (therefore he always goes to the town of Morality to church) and partly because he loveth that doctrine best, for it saveth him from the cross; and because he is of this carnal temper, therefore he seeketh to prevent my ways, though right. Now there are three things in this man's counsel that thou must utterly abhor.

1. His turning thee out of the way.

2. His labouring to render the cross odious to thee.

3. And his setting thy feet in that way that leadeth unto the administration of death.

"First, thou must abhor his turning thee out of the way, yea, and thine own consenting thereto; because this is to reject the counsel of God, for the sake of the counsel of a Worldly Wiseman. The Lord says, 'Strive to enter in at the strait gate,' [Luke 13:24] the gate to which I sent thee; for 'strait is the gate that leadeth unto life, and few there be that find it. [Matthew 7:13, 14] From this little wicket-gate, and from the way thereto hath this wicked man turned thee, to the bringing of thee almost to destruction; hate therefore his turning thee out of the way, and abhor thyself for hearkening to him.

"Secondly, thou must abhor his labouring to render the cross odious unto thee; for thou art to prefer it before the treasures in Egypt; [Hebrews 11:26] besides, the King of Glory hath told thee that he that 'will save his life shall lose it,' [Mark 8:35] and he that comes after him, 'and hates not his father and mother, and wife, and children, and brethren, and sisters, yea, and his own life also, he cannot be my disciple.' [Luke 14:26] I say, therefore, for a man to labour to persuade thee that that shall be thy death, without which, the truth hath said, thou canst not have eternal life, this doctrine thou must abhor.

"Thirdly, thou must hate his setting of thy feet in the way that leadeth to the ministration of death. And for this thou must consider to whom he sent thee and also how unable that person was to deliver thee from thy burden.

"He to whom thou wast sent for ease, being by name Legality, is the son of the bondwoman [Galatians 4:21–31] which now is, and is in bondage with her children, and is in a mystery, this Mount Sinai, which thou hast feared will fall on thy head. Now if she with her children are in bondage, how canst thou expect by them to be made free? This Legality therefore is not able to set thee free from thy burden. No man was as yet ever rid of his burden by him, no, nor ever is like to be; ye cannot be justified by the works of the law, for by the deeds of the law no man living can be rid of his burden. Therefore Mr. Worldly Wiseman is an alien, and Mr. Legality a cheat; and for his son Civility, notwithstanding his simpering looks, he is but an hypocrite, and cannot help thee. Believe me, there is nothing in all this noise that thou hast heard of this sottish man, but a design to beguile thee of thy salvation, by turning thee from the way in which I had set thee." After this Evangelist called aloud to the heavens for confirmation of what he had said; and with that there came words and fire out of the mountain under which poor Christian stood, that made the hair of his flesh stand. The words were thus pronounced, "As many as are of the works of the law are under the curse: for it is written, Cursed is everyone that continueth not in all things which are written in the book of the law to do them." [Galatians 3:10]

Now Christian looked for nothing but death, and began to cry out lamentably, even cursing the time in which he met with Mr. Worldly Wiseman, still calling himself a thousand fools for hearkening to his counsel; he also was greatly ashamed to think that this gentleman's arguments, flowing only from the flesh, should have that prevalency with him as to cause him to forsake the right way. This done, he applied himself again to Evangelist in words and sense as follows.

CHR. "Sir, what think you? Is there hope? May I now go back and go up to the wicket-gate? Shall I not be abandoned for this, and sent back from thence ashamed? I am sorry I have hearkened to this man's counsel, but may my sin be forgiven."

EVAN. Then said Evangelist to him, "Thy sin is very great, for by it thou hast committed two evils; thou hast forsaken the way that is good, to tread in forbidden paths. Yet will the man at the gate receive thee, for he has good will for men. Only," said he, "take heed that thou turn not aside again, lest thou perish from the way when his wrath is kindled but a little." [Psalms 2:12] Then did Christian address himself to go back, and Evangelist, after he had kissed him, gave him one smile, and bid him Godspeed; so he went on with haste; neither spake he to any man by the way; nor, if any man asked him, would he vouchsafe them an answer. He went like one that was all the while treading on forbidden ground, and could by no means think himself safe till again he was got into the way which he left to follow Mr. Worldly Wiseman's counsel; so in process of time Christian got up to the gate. Now over the gate there was written, "Knock and it shall be opened unto you." [Matthew 7:8] He knocked therefore, more than once or twice, saying,

May I now enter here? Will he within
Open to sorry me, though I have been
An undeserving rebel? Then shall I,
Not fail to sing his lasting praise on high.

At last there came a grave person to the gate, named Good Will, who asked who was there, and whence he came, and what he would have?

CHR. "Here is a poor burdened sinner. I come from the City of Destruction, but am going to Mount Zion, that I may be delivered from the wrath to come; I would therefore, sir, since I am informed that by this gate is the way thither, know if you are willing to let me in."

GOOD WILL. "I am willing with all my heart," said he; and with that he opened the gate.

So when Christian was stepping in, the other gave him a pull. Then said Christian, "What means that?" The other told him, "A little distance from this gate, there is erected a strong castle, of which Beelzebub is the captain; from thence both he and them that are with him shoot arrows

at those that come up to this gate; if happily they may die before they can enter in." Then said Christian, "I rejoice and tremble." So when he was got in, the man of the gate asked him, "Who directed him thither?"

CHR. "Evangelist bid me come hither and knock, as I did; and he said, that you, sir, would tell me what I must do."

GOOD WILL. "An open door is set before thee, and no man can shut it." [Revelation 3:8]

CHR. "Now I begin to reap the benefits of my hazards."

GOOD WILL. "But how is it that you came alone?"

CHR. "Because none of my neighbours saw their danger as I saw mine."

GOOD WILL. "Did any of them know of your coming?"

CHR. "Yes, my wife and children saw me at the first, and called after me to turn again. Also some of my neighbours stood crying, and calling after me to return; but I put my fingers in mine ears, and so came on my way."

GOOD WILL. "But did none of them follow you to persuade you to go back?"

CHR. "Yes, both Obstinate and Pliable. But when they saw that they could not prevail, Obstinate went railing back, but Pliable came with me a little way."

GOOD WILL. "But why did he not come through?"

CHR. "We indeed came both together, until we came at the Slough of Despond, into the which we also suddenly fell. And then was my neighbour Pliable discouraged, and would not adventure further. Wherefore getting out again, on that side next to his own house, he told me I should possess the brave country alone for him. So he went his way, and I came mine, he after Obstinate, and I to this gate."

GOOD WILL. Then said Good Will, "Alas, poor man, is the celestial glory of so small esteem with him that he counteth it not worth running the hazards of a few difficulties to obtain it?"

CHR. "Truly," said Christian, "I have said the truth of Pliable, and if I should also say all the truth of myself, it will appear there is no betterment 'twixt him and myself. 'Tis true, he went back to his own house, but I also turned aside to go in the way of death, being persuaded thereto by the carnal arguments of one Mr. Worldly Wiseman."

GOOD WILL. "Oh, did he light upon you! What, he would have had you a sought* for ease at the hands of Mr. Legality; they are both of them a very cheat. But did you take his counsel?"

CHR. "Yes, as far as I durst; I went to find out Mr. Legality, until I thought that the mountain that stands by his house would have fallen upon my head; wherefore there I was forced to stop."

GOOD WILL. "That mountain has been the death of many, and will be the death of many more; 'tis well you escaped being by it dashed in pieces."

CHR. "Why, truly I do not know what had become of me there had not Evangelist happily met me again as I was musing in the midst of my dumps; but 'twas God's mercy that he came to me again, for else I had never come hither. But now I am come, such a one as I am, more fit indeed for death by that mountain than thus to stand talking with my Lord. But, oh, what a favour is this to me, that yet I am admitted entrance here."

GOOD WILL. "We make no objections against any, notwithstanding all that they have done before they come hither; they in no wise are cast out; [John 6:37] and therefore, good Christian, come a little way with me, and I will teach thee about the way thou must go. Look before thee; dost thou see this narrow way? That is the way thou must go. It was cast up by the patriarchs, prophets, Christ, and his apostles, and it is as straight as a rule can make it. This is the way thou must go."

CHR. "But," said Christian, "is there no turning nor windings, by which a stranger may lose the way?"

GOOD WILL. "Yes, there are many ways but down upon this; and they are crooked and wide. But thus thou mayst distinguish the right from the wrong, that only being straight and narrow. [Matthew 7:13-14]

Then I saw in my dream that Christian asked him further if he could not help him off with his burden that was upon his back, for as yet he had not got rid thereof, nor could he by any means get it off without help.

He told him, "As to the burden, be content to bear it, until thou comest to the place of deliverance; for there it will fall from thy back itself."

Then Christian began to gird up his loins and to address himself to his journey. So the other told him that by that he was gone some distance from the gate, he would come at the house of the Interpreter, at whose door he should knock; and he would show him excellent things. Then Christian took his leave of his friend, and he again bid him Godspeed.

Then he went on, till he came at the house of the Interpreter, where he knocked over, and over. At last one came to the door, and asked who was there.

CHR. "Sir, here is a traveller, who was bid by an acquaintance of the good man of this house to call here for my profit. I would therefore speak with the master of

---

*Colloquial for "have sought."

the house." So he called for the master of the house, who after a little time came to Christian, and asked him what he would have?

CHR. "Sir," said Christian, "I am a man that am come from the City of Destruction, and am going to the Mount Zion, and I was told by the man that stands at the gate, at the head of this way, that if I called here, you would show me excellent things, such as would be an help to me in my journey."

INTER. Then said the Interpreter, "Come in, I will show thee that which will be profitable to thee." So he commanded his man to light the candle, and bid Christian follow him; so he had him into a private room and bid his man open the door; the which when he had done, Christian saw a picture of a very grave person hang up against the wall, and this was the fashion of it. It had eyes lifted up to heaven, the best of books in its hand; the law of truth was written upon its lips; the world was behind its back; it stood as if it pleaded with men, and a crown of gold did hang over its head.

CHR. Then said Christian, "What means this?"

INTER. "The man whose picture this is is one of a thousand; he can beget children, travel* in birth with children, and nurse them himself when they are born. And whereas thou seest him with his eyes lift up to heaven, the best of books in his hand, and the law of truth writ on his lips, it is to show thee that his work is to know and unfold dark things to sinners, even as also thou seest him stand as if he pleaded with men. And whereas thou seest the world as cast behind him, and that a crown hangs over his head, that is to show thee that slighting and despising the things that are present, for the love that he hath to his Master's service, he is sure in the world that comes next to have glory for his reward. Now," said the Interpreter, "I have showed thee this picture first, because the man whose picture this is is the only man

whom the Lord of the place whither thou art going hath authorized to be thy guide in all difficult places thou mayest meet with in the way; wherefore take good heed to what I have showed thee, and bear well in thy mind what thou hast seen; lest, in thy journey, thou meet with some that pretend to lead thee right, but their way goes down to death."

Then he took him by the hand, and led him into a very large parlour that was full of dust, because never swept; the which, after he had reviewed a little while, the Interpreter called for a man to sweep. Now when he began to sweep, the dust began so abundantly to fly about, that Christian had almost therewith been choked. Then said the Interpreter to a damsel that stood by, "Bring hither water, and sprinkle the room," which when she had done was swept and cleansed with pleasure.

CHR. Then said Christian, "What means this?"

INTER. The Interpreter answered, "This parlour is the heart of a man that was never sanctified by the sweet grace of the Gospel. The dust is his original sin and inward corruptions that have defiled the whole man. He that began to sweep at first is the law; but she that brought water, and did sprinkle it, is the Gospel. Now, whereas thou sawest that so soon as the first began to sweep, the dust did so fly about that the room by him could not be cleansed, but that thou wast almost choked therewith, this is to show thee that the law, instead of cleansing the heart (by its working) from sin, doth revive, put strength into, and increase it in the soul, even as it doth discover and forbid it, for it doth not give power to subdue.

"Again, as thou sawest the damsel sprinkle the room with water, upon which it was cleansed with pleasure. This is to show thee that when the Gospel comes in the sweet and precious influences thereof to the heart, then, I say, even as thou sawest

---

*Suggesting.

the damsel lay the dust by sprinkling the floor with water, so is sin vanquished and subdued, and the soul made clean, through the faith of it, and consequently fit for the King of Glory to inhabit."

I saw moreover in my dream that the Interpreter took him by the hand, and had him into a little room, where sat two little children, each one in his chair. The name of the eldest was Passion, and of the other, Patience; Passion seemed to be much discontent, but Patience was very quiet. Then Christian asked, "What is the reason of the discontent of Passion?" The Interpreter answered, "The governor of them would have him stay for his best things till the beginning of the next year; but he will have all now. But Patience is willing to wait."

Then I saw that one came to Passion, and brought him a bag of treasure, and poured it down at his feet; the which he took up, and rejoiced therein, and withal, laughed Patience to scorn. But I beheld but a while, and he had lavished all away, and had nothing left him but rags.

CHR. Then said Christian to the Interpreter, "Expound this matter more fully to me."

INTER. So he said, "These two lads are figures: Passion, of the men of this world; and Patience, of the men of that which is to come. For as here thou seest, Passion will have all now, this year, that is to say, in this world. So are the men of this world; they must have all their good things now; they cannot stay till next year, that is, until the next world, for their portion of good. That proverb, a bird in the hand is worth two in the bush, is of more authority with them than are all the divine testimonies of the good of the world to come. But as thou sawest, that he had quickly lavished all away, and had presently left him nothing but rags. So will it be with all such men at the end of this world."

CHR. Then said Christian, "Now I see that Patience has the best wisdom and that upon many accounts: 1. Because he stays for the best things. 2. And also because he

will have the glory of his, when the other hath nothing but rags."

INTER. Nay, you may add another, to wit, the glory of the next world will never wear out, but these are suddenly gone. Therefore Passion had not so much reason to laugh at Patience, because he had his good things first, as Patience will have to laugh at Passion, because he had his best things last; for first must give place to last, because last must have his time to come, but last gives place to nothing, for there is not another to succeed. He therefore that hath his portion first must needs have a time to spend it; but he that has his portion last must have it lastingly. Therefore it is said of Dives, "In thy life thou receivedst thy good things, and likewise Lazarus evil things: but now he is comforted, and thou art tormented." [Luke 16:25]

CHR. "Then I perceive 'tis not best to covet things that are now, but to wait for things to come."

INTER. "You say the truth, 'for the things that are seen are temporal; but the things that are not seen are eternal.' [2 Corinthians 4:18] But though this be so, yet since things present and our fleshly appetite are such near neighbours one to another, and again because things to come and carnal sense are such strangers one to another, therefore it is that the first of these so suddenly fall into amity and that distance is so continued between the second."

Then I saw in my dream that the Interpreter took Christian by the hand, and led him into a place, where was a fire burning against a wall, and one standing by it always, casting much water upon it to quench it. Yet did the fire burn higher and hotter.

Then said Christian, "What means this?"

The Interpreter answered, "This fire is the work of grace that is wrought in the heart; he that casts water upon it to extinguish and put it out is the Devil; but in that thou seest the fire, notwithstanding, burn higher and hotter, thou shalt also see the reason of that." So he had him about to the back side of the wall, where he saw a man with a vessel of oil in his hand of the which he did also continually cast, but secretly, into the fire. Then said Christian, "What means this?" The Interpreter answered, 'This is Christ, who continually with the oil of his grace maintains the work already begun in the heart, by the means of which, notwithstanding what the Devil can do, the souls of his people prove gracious still. And in that thou sawest that the man stood behind the wall to maintain the fire; this is to teach thee that it is hard for the tempted to see how this work of grace is maintained in the soul."

I saw also that the Interpreter took him again by the hand, and led him into a pleasant place, where was builded a stately palace, beautiful to behold; at the sight of which Christian was greatly delighted; he saw also upon the top thereof certain persons walked, who were clothed all in gold. Then said Christian, "May we go in thither?" Then the Interpreter took him, and led him up toward the door of the palace; and behold, at the door, stood a great company of men, as desirous to go in, but durst not. There also sat a man, at a little distance from the door, at a table side with a book, and his inkhorn before him, to take the name of him that should enter therein. He saw also that in the doorway stood many men in armour to keep it, being resolved to do to the man that would enter what hurt and mischief they could. Now was Christian somewhat in a muse; at last, when every man started back for fear of the armed men, Christian saw a man of a very stout countenance come up to the man that sat there to write, saying, "Set down my name, sir." The which when he had done, he saw the man draw his sword, and put an helmet upon his head, and rush toward the door upon the armed men, who laid upon him with deadly force; but the man, not at all discouraged, fell to cutting and hacking most fiercely; so after he had received and given many wounds to those that attempted to keep him out, he cut

his way through them all, and pressed forward into the palace; at which there was a pleasant voice heard from those that were within, even of the three that walked upon the top of the palace, saying,

Come in, come in;
Eternal glory thou shalt win.

So he went in and was clothed with such garments as they. Then Christian smiled and said, "I think verily I know the meaning of this.

"Now," said Christian, "let me go hence." "Nay, stay," said the Interpreter, "till I have showed thee a little more, and after that, thou shalt go on thy way." So he took him by the hand again and led him into a very dark room, where there sat a man in an iron cage.

Now the man to look on seemed very sad. He sat with his eyes looking down to the ground, his hands folded together, and he sighed as if he would break his heart. Then said Christian, "What means this?" At which the Interpreter bid him talk with the man.

CHR. Then said Christian to the man, "What art thou?" The man answered, "I am what I was not once."

CHR. "What wast thou once?"

MAN. The man said, "I was once a fair and flourishing professor,* both in mine own eyes and also in the eyes of others. I once was, as I thought, fair for the Celestial City, and had then even joy at the thoughts that I should get thither."

CHR. "Well, but what art thou now?"

MAN. "I am now a man of despair and am shut up in it, as in this iron cage. I cannot get out. O, now I cannot."

CHR. "But how camest thou in this condition?"

MAN. "I left off to watch, and be sober. I laid the reins upon the neck of my lusts. I sinned against the light of the word, and

---

*One who professes beliefs or opinions.

the goodness of God. I have grieved the Spirit, and he is gone. I tempted the Devil, and he is come to me. I have provoked God to anger, and he has left me. I have so hardened my heart, that I cannot repent."

Then said Christian to the Interpreter, "But is there no hopes for such a man as this?" "Ask him," said the Interpreter.

CHR. Then said Christian, "Is there no hope but you must be kept in this iron cage of despair?"

MAN. "No, none at all."

CHR. "Why? The Son of the Blessed is very pitiful."*

MAN. "I have crucified him to myself afresh; I have despised his person; I have despised his righteousness; I have counted his blood an unholy thing, I have 'done despite to the Spirit of grace.' [Hebrews 10:29] Therefore I have shut myself out of all the promises, and there now remains to me nothing but threatenings, dreadful threatenings, fearful threatenings of certain judgement and fiery indignation, which shall devour me as an adversary."

CHR. "For what did you bring yourself into this condition?"

MAN. "For the lusts, pleasures, and profits of this world; in the enjoyment of which I did then promise myself much delight. But now even every one of those things also bite me and gnaw me like a burning worm."

CHR. "But canst thou not now repent and turn?"

MAN. "God hath denied me repentance; his Word gives me no encouragement to believe; yea, himself hath shut me up in this iron cage, nor can all the men in the world let me out. O eternity! eternity! how shall I grapple with the misery that I must meet with in eternity?"

INTER. Then said the Interpreter to Christian, "Let this man's misery be remembered by thee and be an everlasting caution to thee."

CHR. "Well," said Christian, "this is fearful; God help me to watch and be sober and to pray that I may shun the cause of this man's misery. Sir, is it not time for me to go on my way now?"

INTER. "Tarry till I shall show thee one thing more, and then thou shalt go on thy way."

So he took Christian by the hand again and led him into a chamber, where there was one arising out of bed; and as he put on his raiment, he shook and trembled. Then said Christian, "Why doth this man thus tremble?" The Interpreter then bid him tell to Christian the reason of his so doing. So he began, and said, "This night as I was in my sleep, I dreamed, and behold the heavens grew exceeding black; also it thundered and lightened in most fearful wise, that it put me into an agony. So I looked up in my dream, and saw the clouds rack at an unusual rate, upon which I heard a great sound of a trumpet, and saw also a man sit upon a cloud, attended with the thousands of heaven; they were all in flaming fire; also the heavens was on a burning flame. I heard then a voice, saying, 'Arise, ye dead, and come to judgement'; and with that the rocks rent, the graves opened, and the dead that were therein came forth; some of them were exceeding glad, and looked upward; and some sought to hide themselves under the mountains. Then I saw the man that sat upon the cloud open the book, and bid the world draw near. Yet there was by reason of a fiery flame that issued out and came from before him a convenient distance betwixt him and them, as betwixt the judge and the prisoners at the bar. I heard it also proclaimed to them that attended on the man that sat on the cloud, 'Gather together the tares, the chaff, and stubble, and cast them into the burning lake,' and with that the bottomless pit opened, just whereabout I stood, out of the mouth of which there came in an abundant manner smoke, and coals of fire, with hideous noises. It was also said to the same persons, 'Gather my wheat into my garner.' [Luke

---

*Compassionate.

3:17; Matthew 3:12] And with that I saw many catched up and carried away into the clouds, but I was left behind. I also sought to hide myself, but I could not, for the man that sat upon the cloud still kept his eye upon me. My sins also came into mind, and my conscience did accuse me on every side. Upon this I awaked from my sleep."*

CHR. "But what was it that made you so afraid of this sight?"

MAN. "Why, I thought that the day of judgement was come, and that I was not ready for it. But this frighted me most, that the angels gathered up several, and left me behind; also the pit of hell opened her mouth just where I stood. My conscience too within afflicted me; and as I thought, the judge had always his eye upon me, showing indignation in his countenance."

Then said the Interpreter to Christian, "Hast thou considered all these things?"

CHR. "Yes, and they put me in hope and fear."

INTER. "Well, keep all things so in thy mind, that they may be as a goad in thy sides to prick thee forward in the way thou must go." Then Christian began to gird up his loins, and to address himself to his journey. Then said the Interpreter, "The Comforter be always with thee, good Christian, to guide thee in the way that leads to the City."

So Christian went on his way, saying,

Here I have seen things rare, and profitable;
Things pleasant, dreadful, things to make me
    stable
In what I have began to take in hand.
Then let me think on them, and understand
Wherefore they showed me was, and let me be
Thankful, O good Interpreter, to thee.

Now I saw in my dream that the highway up which Christian was to go was fenced on either side with a wall, and that wall is called Salvation. Up this way therefore did burdened Christian run, but not with-out great difficulty, because of the load on his back.

He ran thus till he came at a place somewhat ascending, and upon that place stood a cross, and a little below in the bottom, a sepulchre. So I saw in my dream that just as Christian came up with the cross, his burden loosed from off his shoulders, and fell from off his back, and began to tumble, and so continued to do, till it came to the mouth of the sepulchre where it fell in, and I saw it no more.

Then was Christian glad and lightsome, and said with a merry heart, "He hath given me rest, by his sorrow, and life, by his death." Then he stood still awhile to look and wonder, for it was very surprising to him that the sight of the cross should thus ease him of his burden. He looked therefore, and looked again, even till the springs that were in his head sent the waters down his cheeks. Now as he stood looking and weeping, behold three Shining Ones came to him, and saluted him, with "Peace be to thee." So the first said to him, "Thy sins be forgiven." [Mark 2:5] The second stripped him of his rags, and clothed him with change of raiment. [Zechariah 3:3–5] The third also set a mark in his forehead, and gave him a roll with a seal upon it, which he bid him look on as he ran, and that he should give it in at the Celestial Gate. So they went their way. Then Christian gave three leaps for joy, and went on singing.

Thus far did I come laden with my sin,
Nor could ought ease the grief that I was in,
Till I came hither. What a place is this!
Must here be the beginning of my bliss?
Must here the burden fall from off my back?
Must here the strings that bound it to me
    crack?
Blest cross! Blest sepulchre! Blest rather be
The Man that there was put to shame for me.

---

*This passage echoes many in the Bible, including 1 Corinthians 15, 1 Thessalonians 4, Jude, 2 Thessalonians 1, Revelation 14, 20, Isaiah 26, Daniel 7, Malachi 3, 4, and Matthew 3.

I saw then in my dream that he went on thus, even until he came at a bottom, where he saw, a little out of the way, three men fast asleep, with fetters upon their heels. The name of the one was Simple, another Sloth, and the third Presumption.

Christian then seeing them lie in this case went to them, if peradventure he might awake them. And cried, "You are like them that sleep on the top of a mast, [Proverbs 23:34] for the Dead Sea is under you, a gulf that hath no bottom. Awake, therefore, and come away; be willing also, and I will help you off with your irons." He also told them, "If he that goeth about like a roaring lion comes by, you will certainly become a prey to his teeth." [I Peter 5:8] With that they looked upon him and began to reply in this sort: Simple said, "I see no danger"; Sloth said, "Yet a little more sleep"; and Presumption said, "Every fat* must stand upon his own bottom; what is the answer else that I should give thee?" And so they lay down to sleep again, and Christian went on his way.

Yet was he troubled to think that men in that danger should so little esteem the kindness of him that so freely offered to help them, both by awakening of them, counselling of them, and proffering to help them off with their irons. And as he was troubled thereabout, he espied two men come tumbling over the wall, on the left hand of the narrow way; and they made up a pace to him. The name of the one was Formalist, and the name of the other Hypocrisy. So, as I said, they drew up unto him, who thus entered with them into discourse.

CHR. "Gentlemen, whence came you, and whither do you go?"

FORM. and HYP. "We were born in the Land of Vainglory, and are going for praise to Mount Zion."

CHR. "Why came you not in at the gate which standeth at the beginning of the way? Know you not that it is written that he cometh not in by the door, but climbeth up some other way, the same is a thief and a robber." [John 10:1]

FORM. and HYP. They said that to go to the gate for entrance was by all their countrymen counted too far about, and that therefore their usual way was to make a short cut of it and to climb over the wall as they had done.

CHR. "But will it not be counted a trespass against the Lord of the city whither we are bound, thus to violate his revealed will?"

FORM. and HYP. They told him that as for that, he needed not to trouble his head thereabouts; for what they did they had custom for, and could produce, if need were, testimony that would witness it for more than a thousand years.

CHR. "But," said Christian, "will your practice stand a trial at law?"

FORM. and HYP. They told him that custom, it being of so long a standing, as above a thousand years, would doubtless now be admitted as a thing legal, by any impartial judge. "And besides," said they, "so be we get into the way, what matter which way we get in; if we are in, we are in. Thou art but in the way, who, as we perceive, came in at the gate; and we are also in the way that came tumbling over the wall. Wherein now is thy condition better than ours?"

CHR. "I walk by the rule of my Master; you walk by the rude working of your fancies. You are counted thieves already by the Lord of the way; therefore I doubt you will not be found true men at the end of the way. You come in by yourselves without his direction, and shall go out by yourselves without his mercy."

To this they made him but little answer; only they bid him look to himself. Then I saw that they went on every man in his way, without much conference one with another; save that these two men told Christian that, as to laws and ordinances, they doubted not, but they should as conscientiously do them as he. Therefore said they, "We see not wherein thou differest from us, but by the coat that is on thy

———
*A cask or barrel.

back, which was, as we trow, given thee by some of thy neighbours to hide the shame of thy nakedness."

CHR. "By laws and ordinances you will not be saved, since you came not in by the door. And as for this coat that is on my back, it was given me by the Lord of the place whither I go, and that, as you say, to cover my nakedness with. And I take it as a token of his kindness to me, for I had nothing but rags before; and besides, thus I comfort myself as I go. Surely, think I, when I come to the gate of the city, the Lord thereof will know me for good, since I have his coat on my back; a coat that he gave me freely in the day that he stripped me of my rags. I have moreover a mark in my forehead, of which perhaps you have taken no notice, which one of my Lord's most intimate associates fixed there in the day that my burden fell off my shoulders. I will tell you, moreover, that I had then given me a roll sealed to comfort me by reading, as I go in the way. I was also bid to give it in at the Celestial Gate, in token of my certain going in after it; all which things I doubt you want,* and want them, because you came not in at the gate."

To these things they gave him no answer, only they looked upon each other and laughed. Then I saw that they went on all, save that Christian kept before, who had no more talk but with himself, and that sometimes sighingly, and sometimes comfortably. Also he would be often reading in the roll that one of the Shining Ones gave him, by which he was refreshed.

I believe then that they all went on till they came to the foot of an hill, at the bottom of which was a spring. There was also in the same place two other ways besides that which came straight from the gate; one turned to the left hand, and the other to the right, at the bottom of the hill; but the narrow way lay right up the hill (and the name of the going up the side of the hill is called Difficulty). Christian now went to the spring and drank thereof to refresh himself, and then began to go up the hill, saying,

This hill, though high, I covet to ascend;
The difficulty will not me offend,
For I perceive the way to life lies here.
Come, pluck up, heart; let's neither faint nor
*   fear.*
Better, though difficult, the right way to go,
Than wrong, though easy, where the end is
*   woe.*

The other two also came to the foot of the hill. But when they saw that the hill was steep and high and that there was two other ways to go, and supposing also that these two ways might meet again with that up which Christian went, on the other side of the hill, therefore they were resolved to go in those ways. Now the name of one of those ways was Danger, and the name of the other Destruction. So the one took the way which is called Danger, which led him into a great wood; and the other took directly up the way to Destruction, which led him into a wide field full of dark mountains, where he stumbled and fell, and rose no more.

I looked then after Christian to see him go up the hill, where I perceived he fell from running to going,† and from going to clambering upon his hands and his knees, because of the steepness of the place. Now about the midway to the top of the hill was a pleasant arbour, made by the Lord of the hill, for the refreshing of weary travellers. Thither therefore Christian got, where also he sat down to rest him. Then he pulled his roll out of his bosom, and read therein to his comfort; he also now began afresh to take a review of the coat or garment that was given him as he stood by the cross. Thus pleasing himself awhile, he at last fell into a slumber, and thence into a fast sleep, which detained him in

---

*Fear you lack.
†Walking.

that place until it was almost night, and in his sleep his roll fell out of his hand. Now as he was sleeping, there came one to him and awaked him, saying "Go to the ant, thou sluggard; consider her ways, and be wise." [Proverbs 6:6] And with that Christian suddenly started up, and sped him on his way, and went apace till he came to the top of the hill.

Now when he was got up to the top of the hill, there came two men running against him amain; the name of the one was Timorous, and the name of the other Mistrust. To whom Christian said, "Sirs, what's the matter you run the wrong way?" Timorous answered that they were going to the City of Zion, and had go up that difficult place. "But," said he, "the further we go, the more danger we meet with, wherefore we turned, and are going back again."

"Yes," said Mistrust, "for just before us lie a couple of lions in the way, whether sleeping or waking we know not, and we could not think, if we came within reach, but they would presently pull us in pieces."

CHR. Then said Christian, "You make me afraid, but whither shall I fly to be safe? If I go back to mine own country, that is prepared for fire and brimstone; and I shall certainly perish there. If I can get to the Celestial City, I am sure to be in safety there. I must venture: to go back is nothing but death, to go forward is fear of death, and life everlasting beyond it. I will yet go forward." So Mistrust and Timorous ran down the hill; and Christian went on his way. But thinking again of what he heard from the men, he felt in his bosom for his roll, that he might read therein and be comforted; but he felt, and found it not. Then was Christian in great distress, and knew not what to do, for he wanted that which used to relieve him, and that which should have been his pass into the Celestial City. Here therefore he began to be much perplexed, and knew not what to do; at last he bethought himself that he had slept

in the arbour that is on the side of the hill, and falling down upon his knees, he asked God forgiveness for that his foolish fact,* and then went back to look for his roll. But all the way he went back, who can sufficiently set forth the sorrow of Christian's heart? Sometimes he sighed, sometimes he wept, and often times he chid himself for being so foolish to fall asleep in that place which was erected only for a little refreshment from his weariness. Thus therefore he went back, carefully looking on this side and on that, all the way as he went, if happily he might find his roll that had been his comfort so many times in his journey. He went thus till he came again within sight of the arbour, where he sat and slept, but that sight renewed his sorrow the more, by bringing again, even afresh, his evil of sleeping unto his mind. Thus therefore he now went on, bewailing his sinful sleep, saying, "O wretched man that I am, [Romans 7:24] that I should sleep in the day time! That I should sleep in the midst of difficulty! That I should so indulge the flesh, as to use that rest for ease to my flesh, which the Lord of the hill hath erected only for the relief of the spirits of pilgrims! How many steps have I took in vain! (Thus it happened to Israel for their sin. They were sent back again by the way of the Red Sea.) And I am made to tread those steps with sorrow, which I might have trod with delight, had it not been for this sinful sleep. How far might I have been on my way by this time! I am made to tread those steps thrice over, which I needed not to have trod but once. Yea, now also I am like to be benighted, for the day is almost spent. O that I had not slept!" Now by this time he was come to the arbour again, where for a while he sat down and wept, but at last (as Christian would have it) looking sorrowfully down under the settle, there he espied his roll, the which he with trembling and haste catched up, and put it into

*Act performed, deed.

his bosom; but who can tell how joyful this man was when he had gotten his roll again! For this roll was the assurance of his life and acceptance at the desired haven. Therefore he laid it up in his bosom, gave thanks to God for directing his eye to the place where it lay, and with joy and tears betook himself again to his journey. But, oh, how nimbly now did he go up the rest of the hill! Yet before he got up, the sun went down upon Christian; and this made him again recall the vanity of his sleeping to his remembrance, and thus he again began to condole with himself. "Ah, thou sinful sleep! How for thy sake am I like to be benighted in my journey! I must walk without the sun, darkness must cover the path of my feet, and I must hear the noise of doleful creatures, because of my sinful sleep!" Now also he remembered the story that Mistrust and Timorous told him of, how they were frighted with the sight of the lions. Then said Christian to himself again, "These beasts range in the night for their prey, and if they should meet with me in the dark, how should I shift them? How should I escape being by them torn in pieces?" Thus he went on his way, but while he was thus bewailing his unhappy miscarriage, he lift up his eyes, and behold there was a very stately palace before him, the name whereof was Beautiful, and it stood just by the highway side.

So I saw in my dream that he made haste and went forward, that if possible he might get lodging there. Now before he had gone far, he entered into a very narrow passage, which was about a furlong off of the Porter's lodge, and looking very narrowly before him as he went, he espied two lions in the way. Now, thought he, I see the dangers that Mistrust and Timorous were driven back by. (The lions were chained, but he saw not the chains.) Then he was afraid, and thought also himself to go back after them, for he thought nothing but death was before him. But the Porter at the lodge, whose name is Watchful, perceiving that Christian made a halt, as if he would go back, cried unto him saying, "Is thy strength so small? Fear not the lions, for they are chained, and are placed there for trial of faith where it is, and for discovery of those that have none. Keep in the midst of the path, and no hurt shall come unto thee."

Then I saw that he went on, trembling for fear of the lions, but taking good heed to the directions of the Porter; he heard them roar, but they did him no harm. Then he clapped his hands, and went on till he came and stood before the gate where the Porter was. Then said Christian to the Porter, "Sir, what house is this? And may I lodge here tonight?" The Porter answered, "This house was built by the Lord of the hill, and he built it for the relief and security of pilgrims." The Porter also asked whence he was, and whither he was going.

CHR. "I am come from the City of Destruction, and am going to Mount Zion; but because the sun is now set, I desire, if I may, to lodge here tonight."

POR. "What is your name?"

CHR. "My name is now Christian; but my name at the first was Graceless. I came of the race of Japheth, whom God will persuade to dwell in the tents of Shem."

POR. "But how doth it happen that you come so late the sun is set?"

CHR. "I had been here sooner, but that wretched man that I am! I slept in the arbour that stands on the hill side; nay, I had, notwithstanding that, been here much sooner, but that in my sleep I lost my evidence, and came without it to the brow of the hill; and then feeling for it, and finding it not, I was forced, with sorrow of heart, to go back to the place where I slept my sleep, where I found it, and now I am come."

POR. "Well, I will call out one of the virgins of this place, who will, if she likes your talk, bring you in to the rest of the family, according to the rules of the house." So Watchful the Porter rang a bell; at the sound of which came out at the door of the house a grave and beautiful damsel, named Discretion, and asked why she was called.

The Porter answered, "This man is in a journey from the City of Destruction to Mount Zion, but being weary, and be-nighted, he asked me if he might lodge here tonight; so I told him I would call for thee, who, after discourse had with him, mayest do as seemeth thee good, even according to the law of the house."

Then she asked him whence he was, and whither he was going, and he told her. She asked him also how he got into the way and he told her. Then she asked him what he had seen and met with in the way, and he told her; and last, she asked his name. So he said, "It is Christian; and I have so much the more a desire to lodge here tonight, because, by what I perceive, this place was built by the Lord of the hill for the relief and security of pilgrims." So she smiled, but the water stood in her eyes. And after a little pause, she said, "I will call forth two or three more of the family." So she ran to the door, and called out Prudence, Piety and Charity, who, after a little more discourse with him, had him in to the family; and many of them meeting him at the threshold of the house, said, "Come in, thou blessed of the Lord; this house was built by the Lord of the hill, on purpose to entertain such pilgrims in." Then he bowed his head, and followed them into the house. So when he was come in, and set down, they gave him something to drink, and consented together that until supper was ready, some one or two of them should have some particular discourse with Christian, for the best improvement of time; and they appointed Piety and Prudence and Charity to discourse with him; and thus they began.

PIETY. "Come, good Christian, since we have been so loving to you, to receive you in to our house this night, let us, if perhaps we may better ourselves thereby, talk with you of all things that have happened to you in your pilgrimage."

CHR. "With a very good will, and I am glad that you are so well disposed."

PIETY. "What moved you at first to betake yourself to a pilgrim's life?"

CHR. "I was driven out of my native country by a dreadful sound that was in mine ears: to wit, that unavoidable destruction did attend me, if I abode in that place where I was."

PIETY. "But how did it happen that you came out of your country this way?"

CHR. "It was as God would have it; for when I was under the fears of destruction, I did not know whither to go; but by chance there came a man, even to me (as I was trembling and weeping) whose name is Evangelist, and he directed me to the wicket-gate, which else I should never have found, and so set me into the way that hath led me directly to this house."

PIETY. "But did you not come by the house of the Interpreter?"

CHR. "Yes, and did see such things there, the remembrance of which will stick by me as long as I live, especially three things: to wit, how Christ, in despite of Satan, maintains his work of grace in the heart; how the man had sinned himself quite out of hopes of God's mercy; and also the dream of him that thought in his sleep the Day of Judgement was come."

PIETY. "Why? Did you hear him tell his dream?"

CHR. "Yes, and a dreadful one it was, I thought. It made my heart ache as he was telling of it, but yet I am glad I heard it."

PIETY. "Was that all that you saw at the house of the Interpreter?"

CHR. "No, he took me and had me where he showed me a stately palace, and how the people were clad in gold that were in it; and how there came a venturous man, and cut his way through the armed men that stood in the door to keep him out; and how he was bid to come in, and win eternal glory. Methought those things did ravish my heart; I could have stayed at that good man's house a twelve-month, but that I knew I had further to go."

411

PIETY. "And what saw you else in the way?"

CHR. "Saw! Why, I went but a little further, and I saw one, as I thought in my mind, hang bleeding upon the tree; and the very sight of him made my burden fall off my back (for I groaned under a weary burden) but then it fell down from off me. 'Twas a strange thing to me, for I never saw such a thing before. Yea, and while I stood looking up (for then I could not forbear looking) three Shining Ones came to me. One of them testified that my sins were forgiven me; another stripped me of my rags, and gave me this broidered coat which you see; and the third set the mark which you see in my forehead, and gave me this sealed roll." (And with that he plucked it out of his bosom.)

PIETY. "But you saw more than this, did you not?"

CHR. "The things that I have told you were the best. Yet some other matters I saw, as namely I saw three men, Simple, Sloth, and Presumption, lie asleep a little out of the way as I came, with irons upon their heels. But do you think I could awake them? I also saw Formalist and Hypocrisy come tumbling over the wall to go, as they pretended, to Zion, but they were quickly lost, even as I myself did tell them, but they would not believe. But, above all, I found it hard work, to get up this hill, and as hard to come by the lions' mouths; and truly if it had not been for the good man, the Porter that stands at the gate, I do not know, but that after all, I might have gone back again. But now I thank God I am here, and I thank you for receiving of me."

Then Prudence thought good to ask him a few questions and desired his answer to them.

PRU. "Do you not think sometimes of the country from whence you came?"

CHR. "Yes, but with much shame and detestation. Truly, if I had been mindful of that country from whence I came out, I might have had opportunity to have re-turned; but now I desire a better country, that is, an heavenly. [Hebrews 11:15–16]

PRU. "Do you not yet bear away with you some of the things that then you were conversant withal?"

CHR. "Yes, but greatly against my will, especially my inward and carnal cogitations, with which all my countrymen, as well as myself, were delighted; but now all those things are my grief, and might I but choose mine own things, I would choose never to think of those things more; but when I would be doing of that which is best, that which is worst is with me."

PRU. "Do you not find sometimes as if those things were vanquished, which at other times are your perplexity?"

CHR. "Yes, but that is but seldom; but they are to me golden hours, in which such things happens to me."

PRU. "Can you remember by what means you find your annoyances at times as if they were vanquished?"

CHR. "Yes, when I think what I saw at the cross, that will do it; and when I look upon my broidered coat, that will do it; also when I look into the roll that I carry in my bosom, that will do it; and when my thoughts wax warm about whither I am going, that will do it."

PRU. "And what is it that makes you so desirous to go to Mount Zion?"

CHR. "Why, there I hope to see him alive, that did hang dead on the cross; and there I hope to be rid of all those things that to this day are in me, an annoyance to me. There they say there is no death, and there I shall dwell with such company as I like best. For to tell you truth, I love him, because I was by him eased of my burden, and I am weary of my inward sickness; I would fain be where I shall die no more, and with the company that shall continually cry, 'Holy, Holy, Holy.' "

Then said Charity to Christian, "Have you a family? Are you a married man?"

CHR. "I have a wife and four small children."

CHA. "And why did you not bring them along with you?"

CHR. Then Christian wept and said, "Oh, how willingly would I have done it, but they were all of them utterly averse to my going on pilgrimage."

CHA. "But you should have talked to them and have endeavoured to have shown them the danger of being behind."

CHR. "So I did, and told them also what God had showed to me of the destruction of our city; but I seemed to them as one that mocked, [Genesis 19:14] and they believed me not."

CHA. "And did you pray to God that he would bless your counsel to them?"

CHR. "Yes, and that with much affection; for you must think that my wife and poor children were very dear unto me."

CHA. "But did you tell them of your own sorrow and fear of destruction? For I suppose that destruction was visible enough to you?"

CHR. "Yes, over and over and over. They might also see my fears in my countenance, in my tears, and also in my trembling under the apprehension of the judgement that did hang over our heads; but all was not sufficient to prevail with them to come with me."

CHA. "But what could they say for themselves why they came not?"

CHR. "Why, my wife was afraid of losing this world, and my children were given to the foolish delights of youth. So what by one thing, and what by another, they left me to wander in this manner alone."

CHA. "But did you not with your vain life damp all that you by words used by way of persuasion to bring them away with you?"

CHR. "Indeed I cannot commend my life, for I am conscious to myself of many failings; therein, I know also that a man by his conversation* may soon overthrow what by argument or persuasion he doth labour to fasten upon others for their good. Yet, this I can say, I was very wary of giving them occasion, by any unseemly action, to make them averse to going on pilgrimage. Yea, for this very thing, they would tell me I was too precise, and that I denied myself of things (for their sakes) in which they saw no evil. Nay, I think I may say that, if what they saw in me did hinder them, it was my great tenderness in sinning against God or of doing any wrong to my neighbour."

CHA. "Indeed Cain hated his brother, because his own works were evil, and his brother's righteous; [I John 3:12] and if thy wife and children have been offended with thee for this, they thereby show themselves to be implacable to good; and thou hast delivered thy soul [Ezekiel 3:19] from their blood."

Now I saw in my dream that thus they sat talking together until supper was ready. So when they had made ready, they sat down to meat. Now the table was furnished with fat† things and with wine that was well refined; and all their talk at the table was about the Lord of the hill, as namely, about what he had done, and wherefore he did what he did, and why he had builded that house. And by what they said, I perceived that he had been a great warrior, and had fought with and slain him that had the power of death, [Hebrews 2:14] but not without great danger to himself, which made me love him the more.

For, as they said, and as I believe (said Christian) he did it with the loss of much blood; but that which puts glory of grace into all he did was that he did it of pure love to his country. And besides, there were some of them of the household that said they had seen and spoke with him since he did die on the cross; and they have attested that they had it from his own lips that he is such a lover of poor pilgrims that the like is not to be found from the east to the west.

---

*Behaviour, conduct in life.

†Rich.

They, moreover, gave an instance of what they affirmed, and that was, he had stripped himself of his glory that he might do this for the poor; and that they heard him say and affirm that he would not dwell in the Mountain of Zion alone. They said, moreover, that he had made many pilgrims princes, though by nature they were beggars born and their original had been the dunghill. [I Samuel 2:8; Psalms 113:7]

Thus they discoursed together till late at night; and after they had committed themselves to their Lord for protection, they betook themselves to rest. The pilgrim they laid in a large upper chamber, whose window opened towards the sun rising; the name of the chamber was Peace, where he slept till break of day; and then he awoke and sang,

Where am I now? Is this the love and care
Of Jesus, for the men that pilgrims are?
Thus to provide! That I should be forgiven!
And dwell already the next door to heaven.

So in the morning they all got up, and after some more discourse, they told him that he should not depart till they had showed him the rarities of that place. And first they had him into the study, where they showed him records of the greatest antiquity; in which, as I remember my dream, they showed him first the pedigree of the Lord of the hill, that he was the son of the Ancient of Days, and came by an eternal generation. Here also was more fully recorded the acts that he had done, and the names of many hundreds that he had taken into his service, and how he had placed them in such habitations that could neither by length of days nor decays of nature be dissolved.

Then they read to him some of the worthy acts that some of his servants had done: as how they had subdued kingdoms, wrought righteousness, obtained promises, stopped the mouths of lions, quenched the violence of fire, escaped the edge of the sword, out of weakness were made strong, waxed valiant in fight, and turned to flight the armies of the aliens. [Hebrews 11:33–34]

Then they read again in another part of the records of the house where it was showed how willing their Lord was to receive into his favour, any, even any, though they in time past had offered great affronts to his person and proceedings. Here also were several other histories of many other famous things, of all which Christian had a view; as of things both ancient and modern, together with prophecies and predictions of things that have their certain accomplishment, both to the dread and amazement of enemies and the comfort and solace of pilgrims.

The next day they took him and had him into the armory, where they showed him all manner of furniture, which their Lord had provided for pilgrims, as sword, shield, helmet, breastplate, all prayer, and shoes that would not wear out. And there was here enough of this to harness out as many men for the service of their Lord as there be stars in the heaven for multitude.

They also showed him some of the engines with which some of his servants had done wonderful things. They showed him Moses' rod; the hammer and nail with which Jael slew Sisera; the pitchers, trumpets, and lamps, too, with which Gideon put to flight the armies of Midian. Then they showed him the ox's goad wherewith Shamger slew six hundred men. They showed him also the jaw bone with which Samson did such mighty feats; they showed him moreover the sling and stone with which David slew Goliath of Gath, and the sword also with which their Lord will kill the man of sin, in the day that he shall rise up to the prey. They showed him besides many excellent things, with which Christian was much delighted. This done, they went to their rest again.

Then I saw in my dream that on the morrow he got up to go forwards, but they desired him to stay till the next day also; and then said they, "We will (if the day be clear), show you the Delectable Mountains," which, they said would yet further add to his comfort, because they were nearer the desired haven than the place where at present he was. So he consented and stayed. When the morning was up, they had him to the top of the house and bid him look south; so he did, and behold at a great distance he saw a most pleasant mountainous country, beautified with woods, vineyards, fruits of all sorts, flowers also, with springs and fountains, very delectable to behold. Then he asked the name of the country; they said it was Immanuel's Land, and it is as common,* said they, as this hill is to and for all the pilgrims. And when thou comest there from thence thou mayest see to the gate of the Celestial City, as the shepherds that live there will make appear.

Now he bethought himself of setting forward and they were willing he should. "But first," said they, "let us go again into the armory." So they did, and when he came there, they harnessed him from head to foot, with what was of proof,† lest perhaps he should meet with assaults in the way. He, being therefore thus accoutred, walketh out with his friends to the gate, and there he asked the Porter if he saw any pilgrims pass by; then the Porter answered, "Yes."

CHR. "Pray did you know him?"

POR. "I asked his name, and he told me it was Faithful."

CHR. "O," said Christian, "I know him; he is my townsman, my near neighbour; he comes from the place where I was born. How far do you think he may be before?"

POR. "He is got by this time below the hill."

CHR. "Well," said Christian, "good Porter, the Lord be with thee, and add

to all thy blessings much increase, for the kindness that thou hast showed to me."

Then he began to go forward, but Discretion, Piety, Charity, and Prudence would accompany him down to the foot of the hill. So they went on together, reiterating their former discourses till they came to go down the hill. Then said Christian, "As it was difficult coming up, so (so far as I can see) it is dangerous going down." "Yes," said Prudence, "so it is; for it is an hard matter for a man to go down into the Valley of Humiliation, as thou art now, and to catch no slip by the way. Therefore," said they, "are we come out to accompany thee down the hill." So he began to go down, but very warily, yet he caught a slip or two.

Then I saw in my dream that these good companions (when Christian was gone down to the bottom of the hill) gave him a loaf of bread, a bottle of wine, and a cluster of raisins; and then he went on his way.

But now in this Valley of Humiliation poor Christian was hard put to it, for he had gone but a little way before he espied a foul fiend coming over the field to meet him; his name is Apollyon. [Revelation 9:11] Then did Christian begin to be afraid and to cast in his mind whether to go back or to stand his ground. But he considered again that he had no armour for his back, and therefore thought that to turn the back to him might give him greater advantage with ease to pierce him with his darts; therefore he resolved to venture and stand his ground. For thought he, had I no more in mine eye, than the saving of my life, 'twould be the best way to stand.

So he went on, and Apollyon met him. Now the monster was hideous to behold; he was clothed with scales like a fish (and

---

*Free to be used by anyone.

†Of tried quality, of tested powers of resistance.

they are his pride); he had wings like a dragon, feet like a bear, and out of his belly came fire and smoke, and his mouth was as the mouth of a lion. When he was come up to Christian, he beheld him with a disdainful countenance, and thus began to question with him.

APOL. "Whence come you, and whither are you bound?"

CHR. "I come from the City of Destruction, which is the place of all evil, and am going to the City of Zion."

APOL. "By this I perceive thou art one of my subjects, for all that country is mine; and I am the prince and god of it. How is it then that thou hast run away from thy king? Were it not that I hope thou mayest do me more service, I would strike thee now at one blow to the ground."

CHR. "I was born indeed in your dominions, but your service was hard, and your wages such as a man could not live on, for the wages of sin is death; [Romans 6:23] therefore when I was come to years, I did as other considerate persons do, look out, if perhaps I might mend myself."

APOL. "There is no prince that will thus lightly lose his subjects; neither will I as yet lose thee. But since thou complainest of thy service and wages, be content to go back; what our country will afford, I do here promise to give thee."

CHR. "But I have let myself to another, even to the King of Princes, and how can I with fairness go back with thee?"

APOL. "Thou hast done in this, according to the proverb, changed a bad for a worse. But it is ordinary for those that have professed themselves his servants after a while to give him the slip, and return again to me. Do thou so too, and all shall be well."

CHR. "I have given him my faith, and sworn my allegiance to him; how then can I go back from this, and not be hanged as a traitor?"

APOL. "Thou didst the same to me, and yet I am willing to pass by all, if now thou wilt yet turn again, and go back."

CHR. "What I promised thee was in my nonage; and besides, I count that the Prince under whose banner now I stand is able to absolve me, yea, and to pardon also what I did as to my compliance with thee. And besides (O thou destroying Apollyon), to speak truth, I like his service, his wages, his servants, his government, his company, and country better than thine; and therefore leave off to persuade me further. I am his servant, and I will follow him."

APOL. "Consider again when thou art in cool blood, what thou art like to meet with in the way that thou goest. Thou knowest that for the most part his servants come to an ill end, because they are transgressors against me and my ways. How many of them have been put to shameful deaths! And besides, thou countest his service better than mine, whereas he never came yet from the place where he is to deliver any that served him out of our hands. But as for me, how many times, as all the world very well knows, have I delivered, either by power or fraud, those that have faithfully served me from him and his though taken by them; and so I will deliver thee."

CHR. "His forbearing at present to deliver them is on purpose to try their love, whether they will cleave to him to the end; and as for the ill end thou sayest they come to, that is most glorious in their account. For, for present deliverance, they do not much expect it; for they stay for their glory, and then they shall have it, when their Prince comes in his and the glory of the angels."

APOL. "Thou hast already been unfaithful in thy service to him, and how dost thou think to receive wages of him?"

CHR. "Wherein, O Apollyon, have I been unfaithful to him?"

APOL. "Thou didst faint at first setting out, when thou wast almost choked in the Gulf of Despond. Thou didst attempt wrong ways to be rid of thy burden, whereas thou shouldest have stayed till thy Prince had taken it off. Thou didst sin-

fully sleep, and lose thy choice thing; thou wast also almost persuaded to go back at the sight of the lions; and when thou talkest of thy journey, and of what thou hast heard, and seen, thou art inwardly desirous of vainglory in all that thou sayest or doest."

CHR. "All this is true, and much more, which thou hast left out; but the Prince whom I serve and honour is merciful, and ready to forgive. But besides, these infirmities possessed me in thy country, for there I sucked them in, and I have groaned under them, been sorry for them, and have obtained pardon of my Prince."

APOL. Then Apollyon broke out into a grievous rage, saying, "I am an enemy to this Prince. I hate his person, his laws, and people. I am come out on purpose to withstand thee."

CHR. "Apollyon, beware what you do, for I am in the King's highway, the way of holiness; therefore take heed to yourself."

APOL. Then Apollyon straddled quite over the whole breadth of the way, and said, "I am void of fear in this matter; prepare thyself to die, for I swear by my infernal den that thou shalt go no further. Here will I spill thy soul." And with that he threw a flaming dart at his breast; but Christian had a shield in his hand, with which he caught it, and so prevented the danger of that. Then did Christian draw, for he saw 'twas time to bestir him; and Apollyon as fast made at him, throwing darts as thick as hail, by the which, notwithstanding all that Christian could do to avoid it, Apollyon wounded him in his head, his hand and foot; this made Christian give a little back. Apollyon therefore followed his work amain, and Christian again took courage and resisted as manfully as he could. This sore combat lasted for above half a day, even till Christian was almost quite spent. For you must know that Christian, by reason of his wounds, must needs grow weaker and weaker.

Then Apollyon, espying his opportunity, began to gather up close to Christian, and wrestling with him, gave him a dreadful fall; and with that Christian's sword flew out of his hand. Then said Apollyon, "I am sure of thee now," and with that, he had almost pressed him to death, so that Christian began to despair of life. But as God would have it, while Apollyon was fetching of his last blow, thereby to make a full end of this good man, Christian nimbly reached out his hand for his sword and caught it, saying, "Rejoice not against me, O mine enemy! When I fall, I shall arise"; [Micah 7:8] and with that, gave him a deadly thrust, which made him give back, as one that had received his mortal wound. Christian, perceiving that, made at him again, saying, "Nay, in all these things we are more than conquerors through him that loved us." [Romans 8:37] And with that, Apollyon spread forth his dragon's wings and sped him away, that Christian saw him no more.

In this combat no man can imagine, unless he had seen and heard as I did, what yelling and hideous roaring Apollyon made all the time of the fight; he spake like a dragon, and on the other side, what sighs and groans brast* from Christian's heart. I never saw him all the while give so much as one pleasant look, till he perceived he had wounded Apollyon with his two-edged sword; then indeed he did smile, and look upward; but 'twas the dreadfulest sight that ever I saw.

So when the battle was over, Christian said, "I will here give thanks to him that hath delivered me out of the mouth of the lion, [2 Timothy 4:17] to him that did help me against Apollyon"; and so he did, saying,

Great Beelzebub, the captain of this fiend,
Designed my ruin; therefore to this end
He sent him harnessed out, and he with rage
That hellish was, did fiercely me engage.
But blessed Michael helped me, and I
By dint of sword did quickly make him fly;

---

*Burst.

418

Therefore to him let me give lasting praise,
And thank and bless his holy name always.

Then there came to him an hand with some of the leaves of the Tree of Life, the which Christian took and applied to the wounds that he had received in the battle and was healed immediately. He also sat down in that place to eat bread and to drink of the bottle that was given him a little before; so being refreshed, he addressed himself to his journey, with his sword drawn in his hand; for he said, "I know not but some other enemy may be at hand." But he met with no other affront from Apollyon quite through this valley.

Now at the end of this valley was another, called the Valley of the Shadow of Death, and Christian must needs go through it, because the way to the Celestial City lay through the midst of it. Now this valley is a very solitary place. The Prophet Jeremiah thus describes it, "A wilderness, a land of deserts and of pits, a land of drought and of the shadow of death, a land that no man (but a Christian) passeth through and where no man dwelt." [Jeremiah 2:6]

Now here Christian was worse put to it than in his fight with Apollyon, as by the sequel you shall see.

I saw then in my dream that when Christian was got to the borders of the Shadow of Death, there met him two men, children of them that brought up an evil report of the good land, [Numbers 13:31] making haste to go back, to whom Christian spoke as follows.

CHR. "Whither are you going?"

MEN. They said, "Back, back; and would have you to do so too, if either life or peace is prized by you."

CHR. "Why? What's the matter?" said Christian.

MEN. "Matter!" said they. "We were going that way as you are going and went as far as we durst; and indeed we were almost past coming back, for had we gone a little further we had not been here to bring the news to thee."

CHR. "But what have you met with?" said Christian.

MEN. "Why we were almost in the Valley of the Shadow of Death, but that by good hap we looked before us and saw the danger before we came to it."

CHR. "But what have you seen?" said Christian.

MEN. "Seen! Why the valley itself, which is as dark as pitch; we also saw there the hobgoblins, satyrs, and dragons of the pit; we heard also in that valley a continual howling and yelling, as of a people under unutterable misery, who there sat bound in affliction and irons; and over that valley hangs the discouraging clouds of confusion; death also doth always spread his wings over it. In a word, it is every whit dreadful, being utterly without order."

CHR. Then said Christian, "I perceive not yet by what you have said, but that this is my way to the desired haven."

MEN. "Be it thy way; we will not choose it for ours." So they parted, and Christian went on his way, but still with his sword drawn in his hand, for fear lest he should be assaulted.

I saw then in my dream so far as this valley reached there was on the right hand a very deep ditch; that ditch is it into which the blind have led the blind in all ages, and have both there miserably perished. Again, behold on the left hand, there was a very dangerous quag, into which, if even a good man falls, he can find no bottom for his foot to stand on. Into that quag King David once did fall, and had no doubt therein been smothered had not he that is able plucked him out.

The pathway was here also exceeding narrow, and therefore good Christian was the more put to it; for when he sought in the dark to shun the ditch on the one hand, he was ready to tip over into the mire on the other; also when he sought to escape the mire, without great carefulness he would be ready to fall into the ditch. Thus he went on, and I heard him here sigh bitterly; for, besides the dangers mentioned above, the pathway was here so dark that ofttimes when he lift up his foot to set forward, he knew not where or upon what he should set it next.

About the midst of this valley, I perceived the mouth of hell to be, and it stood also hard by the wayside. Now thought Christian, "What shall I do?" And ever and anon the flame and smoke would come out in such abundance, with sparks and hideous noises (things that cared not for Christian's sword, as did Apollyon before), that he was forced to put up his sword, and betake himself to another weapon called all prayer. [Ephesians 6:18] So he cried in my hearing, "O Lord, I beseech thee, deliver my soul." [Psalms 116:4] Thus he went on a great while, yet still the flames would be reaching towards him. Also he heard doleful voices and rushings to and fro, so that sometimes he thought he should be torn in pieces, or trodden down like mire in the streets. This frightful sight was seen and these dreadful noises were heard by him for several miles together; and coming to a place, where he thought he heard a company of fiends coming forward to meet him, he stopped, and began to muse what he had best to do. Sometimes he had half a thought to go back. Then again he thought he might be half-way through the valley; he remembered also how he had already vanquished many a danger, and that the danger of going back might be much more than for to go forward; so he resolved to go on. Yet the fiends seemed to come nearer and nearer, but when they were come even almost at him, he cried out with a most vehement voice, "I will walk in the strength of the Lord God"; so they gave back and came no further.

One thing I would not let slip. I took notice that now poor Christian was so confounded that he did not know his own voice, and thus I perceived it; just when he was come over against the mouth of the burning pit, one of the wicked ones got behind him, and stepped up softly to him, and whisperingly suggested many grievous blasphemies to him, which he verily thought had proceeded from his own mind. This put Christian more to it than anything that he met with before, even to think that he should now blaspheme him that he loved so much before; yet, could he have helped it, he would not have done it, but he had not the discretion neither to stop his ears nor to know from whence those blasphemies came.

When Christian had travelled in this disconsolate condition some considerable time, he thought he heard the voice of a man, as going before him, saying, "Though I walk through the valley of the shadow of death, I will fear none ill, for thou are with me."

Then was he glad, and that for these reasons:

First, because he gathered from thence that some who feared God were in this valley as well as himself.

Secondly, for that he perceived God was with them, though in that dark and dismal state; and why not, thought he, with me, though by reason of the impediment that attends this place, I cannot perceive it.

Thirdly, for that he hoped (could he overtake them) to have company by and by. So he went on, and called to him that was before, but he knew not what to answer; for that he also thought himself to be alone. And by and by, the day broke; then said Christian, "He hath turned the shadow of death into the morning." [Amos 5:8]

Now morning being come, he looked back, not of desire to return but to see, by the light of the day, what hazards he had gone through in the dark. So he saw more perfectly the ditch that was on the one hand, and the quag that was on the other, also how narrow the way was which lay betwixt them both; also now he saw the hobgoblins, and satyrs, and dragons of the pit, but all afar off, for after break of day, they came not nigh; yet they were discovered to him, according to that which is written, "He discovereth deep things out of darkness, and bringeth out to light the shadow of death." [Job 12:22]

Now was Christian much affected with his deliverance from all the dangers of his solitary way, which dangers, though he feared them more before, yet he saw them more clearly now, because the light of the day made them conspicuous to him; and about this time the sun was rising, and this was another mercy to Christian. For you must note, that though the first part of the Valley of the Shadow of Death was dangerous, yet this second part which he was yet to go was, if possible, far more dangerous, for from the place where he now stood, even to the end of the valley, the way was all along set so full of snares, traps, gins, and nets here, and so full of pits, pitfalls, deep holes, and shelvings down there, that had it now been dark, as it was when he came the first part of the way, had he had a thousand souls, they had in reason been cast away; but, as I said, just now the sun was rising. Then said he, "His candle shineth on my head, and by his light I go through darkness."*

In this light therefore he came to the end of the valley. Now I saw in my dream that at the end of this valley lay blood, bones, ashes, and mangled bodies of men, even of pilgrims that had gone this way formerly. And while I was musing what should be the reason, I espied a little before me a cave, where two giants, Pope and Pagan, dwelt in old time, by whose power and tyranny the men whose bones, blood, ashes &c. lay there, were cruelly put to death. But by this place Christian went without much danger, whereat I somewhat wondered; but I have learnt since that Pagan has been dead many a day; and as for the other, though he be yet alive, he is by reason of age and also of the many shrewd† brushes that he met with in his younger days grown so crazy and stiff in his joints, that he can now do little more

than sit in his cave's mouth, grinning at pilgrims as they go by, and biting his nails, because he cannot come at them.

So I saw that Christian went on his way, yet at the sight of the Old Man that sat in the mouth of the cave, he could not tell what to think, especially because he spake to him, though he could not go after him, saying, "You will never mend, till more of you be burned." But he held his peace, and set a good face on't, and so went by, and catched no hurt. Then sang Christian,

O world of wonders! (I can say no less.)
That I should be preserved in that distress
That I have met with here! O blessed be
That hand that from it hath delivered me!
Dangers in darkness, devils, hell, and sin,
Did compass me, while I this vale was in.
Yea, snares, and pits, and traps, and nets
*   did lie*
My path about, that worthless silly I
Might have been catched, entangled, and cast
*   down.*
But since I live, let Jesus wear the crown.

Now as Christian went on his way, he came to a little ascent, which was cast up on purpose that pilgrims might see before them. Up there therefore Christian went and looking forward, he saw Faithful before him upon his journey. Then said Christian aloud, "Ho, ho, so-ho; stay, and I will be your companion." At that Faithful looked behind him, to whom Christian cried again, "Stay, stay, till I come up to you." But Faithful answered, "No, I am upon my life, and the avenger of blood is behind me." At this Christian was somewhat moved, and putting to all his strength, he quickly got up with Faithful, and did also overrun him, so the last was first. Then did Christian vaingloriously smile, because he had gotten the start of his brother; but not taking good heed to his feet, he sud-

*Paraphrase of Job 29:3.
†Strong, harsh.

421

denly stumbled and fell, and could not rise again, until Faithful came up to help him.

Then I saw in my dream they went very lovingly on together, and had sweet discourse of all things that had happened to them in their pilgrimage; and thus Christian began.

CHR. "My honoured and well-beloved brother Faithful, I am glad that I have overtaken you, and that God has so tempered our spirits that we can walk as companions in this so pleasant a path."

FAITH. "I had thought, dear friend, to have had your company quite from our town, but you did get the start of me; wherefore I was forced to come thus much of the way alone."

CHR. "How long did you stay in the City of Destruction, before you set out after me on your pilgrimage?"

FAITH. "Till I could stay no longer; for there was great talk presently after you was gone out that our city would in short time with fire from heaven be burned down to the ground."

CHR. "What? Did your neighbours talk so?"

FAITH. "Yes, 'twas for a while in everybody's mouth."

CHR. "What, and did no more of them but you come out to escape the danger?"

FAITH. "Though there was, as I said, a great talk thereabout, yet I do not think they did firmly believe it. For in the heat of the discourse, I heard some of them deridingly speak of you and of your desperate journey (for so they called this your pilgrimage), but I did believe, and do still, that the end of our city will be with fire and brimstone from above; and therefore I have made mine escape."

CHR. "Did you hear no talk of neighbour Pliable?"

FAITH. "Yes, Christian, I heard that he followed you till he came at the Slough of Despond, where, as some said, he fell in; but he would not be known to have so done. But I am sure he was soundly bedabbled with that kind of dirt."

CHR. "And what said the neighbours to him?"

FAITH. "He hath since his going back been had greatly in derision and that among all sorts of people. Some do mock and despise him, and scarce will any set him on work. He is now seven times worse than if he had never gone out of the city."

CHR. "But why should they be so set against him, since they also despise the way that he forsook?"

FAITH. "Oh, they say, 'Hang him; he is a turncoat; he was not true to his profession.' I think God has stirred up even his enemies to hiss at him and make him a proverb, because he hath forsaken the way."

CHR. "Had you no talk with him before you came out?"

FAITH. "I met him once in the streets, but he leered away on the other side, as one ashamed of what he had done; so I spake not to him."

CHR. "Well, at my first setting out, I had hopes of that man; but now I fear he will perish in the overthrow of the city, for it is happened to him according to the true proverb: the dog is turned to his vomit again, and the sow that was washed to her wallowing in the mire." [2 Peter 2:22]

FAITH. "They are my fears of him, too. But who can hinder that which will be?"

CHR. "Well, neighbour Faithful," said Christian, "let us leave him, and talk of things that more immediately concern ourselves. Tell me now, what you have met with in the way as you came; for I know you have met with some things, or else it may be writ for a wonder."

FAITH. "I escaped the slough that I perceive you fell into and got up to the gate without that danger; only I met with one whose name was Wanton that had like to have done me a mischief."

CHR. "'Twas well you escaped her net; Joseph was hard put to it by her, and he escaped her as you did, but it had like to have cost him his life. But what did she do to you?"

FAITH. "You cannot think (but that you

know something) what a flattering tongue she had; she lay at me hard to turn aside with her, promising me all manner of content."

CHR. "Nay, she did not promise you the content of a good conscience."

FAITH. "You know what I mean, all carnal and fleshly content."

CHR. "Thank God you have escaped her. The abhorred of the Lord shall fall into her ditch."

FAITH. "Nay, I know not whether I did wholly escape her or no."

CHR. "Why, I trow* you did not consent to her desires?"

FAITH. "No, not to defile myself, for I remembered an old writing that I had seen, which saith, 'Her steps take hold of hell.' [Proverbs 5:5] So I shut mine eyes, because I would not be bewitched with her looks. Then she railed on me, and I went my way."

CHR. "Did you meet with no other assault as you came?"

FAITH. "When I came to the foot of the hill called Difficulty, I met with a very aged man, who asked me what I was, and whither bound? I told him that I was a pilgrim, going to the Celestial City. Then said the old man, 'Thou lookest like an honest fellow; wilt thou be content to dwell with me, for the wages that I shall give thee?' Then I asked him his name, and where he dwelt? He said his name was Adam the first, and 'I dwell in the town of Deceit.' I asked him then what was his work and what the wages that he would give? He told me that his work was many delights and his wages that I should be his heir at last. I further asked him what house he kept and what other servants he had? So he told me that his house was maintained with all the dainties in the world, and that his servants were those of his own begetting. Then I asked how many children he had. He said that he had but three daughters, 'the lust of the flesh, the lust of the eyes, and the pride of life,' [I John 2:16] and that I should marry them all, if I would. Then

I asked how long time he would have me live with him? And he told me as long as he lived himself."

CHR. "Well, and what conclusion came the old man and you to at last?"

FAITH. "Why, at first I found myself somewhat inclinable to go with the man, for I thought he spake very fair; but looking in his forehead as I talked with him, I saw there written, 'Put off the old man with his deeds.' " [Colossians 3:9]

CHR. "And how then?"

FAITH. "Then it came burning hot into my mind, whatever he said and however he flattered, when he got me home to his house, he would sell me for a slave. So I bid him forbear to talk, for I would not come near the door of his house. Then he reviled me and told me that he would send such a one after me that should make my way bitter to my soul. So I turned to go away from him; but just as I turned myself to go thence, I felt him take hold of my flesh and give me such a deadly twitch back that I thought he had pulled part of me after himself. This made me cry, 'O wretched man!' So I went on my way up the hill.

"Now when I had got about half-way up, I looked behind me and saw one coming after me, swift as the wind; so he overtook me just about the place where the settle stands."

CHR. "Just there," said Christian, "did I sit down to rest me; but being overcome with sleep, I there lost this roll out of my bosom."

FAITH. "But, good brother, hear me out. So soon as the man overtook me, he was but a word and a blow; for down he knocked me and laid me for dead. But when I was a little come to myself again, I asked him wherefore he served me so? He said because of my secret inclining to Adam the first, and with that, he struck me another deadly blow on the breast and beat me down backward; so I lay at his

---

*Suppose.

foot as dead as before. So when I came to myself again, I cried him mercy; but he said, 'I know not how to show mercy,' and with that knocked me down again. He had doubtless made an end of me, but that one came by and bid him forbear."

CHR. "Who was that that bid him forbear?"

FAITH. "I did not know him at first, but as he went by, I perceived the holes in his hands and his side; then I concluded that he was our Lord. So I went up the hill."

CHR. "That man that overtook you was Moses; he spareth none, neither knoweth he how to show mercy to those that transgress his law."

FAITH. "I know it very well; it was not the first time that he has met with me. 'Twas he that came to me when I dwelt securely at home and that told me he would burn my house over my head if I stayed there."

CHR. "But did not you see the house that stood there on the top of that hill on the side of which Moses met you?"

FAITH. "Yes, and the lions, too, before I came at it; but for the lions, I think they were asleep, for it was about noon; and because I had so much of the day before me, I passed by the Porter, and came down the hill."

CHR. "He told me indeed that he saw you go by, but I wish you had called at the house; for they would have showed you so many rarities that you would scarce have forgot them to the day of your death. But pray tell me, did you meet nobody in the Valley of Humility?"

FAITH. "Yes, I met with one Discontent, who would willingly have persuaded me to go back again with him. His reason was for that the valley was altogether without honour; he told me, moreover, that there to go was the way to disobey all my friends, as pride, arrogancy, self-conceit, worldly glory, with others, who he knew, as he said, would be very much offended, if I made such a fool of myself as to wade through this valley."

CHR. "Well, and how did you answer him?"

FAITH. "I told him that although all these that he named might claim kindred of me, and that rightly (for indeed they were my relations, according to the flesh), yet since I became a pilgrim, they have disowned me, as I also have rejected them; and therefore they were to me now no more than if they had never been of my lineage; I told him, moreover, that as to this valley, he had quite misrepresented the thing, for before honour is humility and a haughty spirit before a fall. [Proverbs 18:12, 16:18] Therefore, said I, I had rather go through this valley to the honour that was so accounted by the wisest than choose that which he esteemed most worth our affections."

CHR. "Met you with nothing else in that valley?"

FAITH. "Yes, I met with Shame; but of all the men that I met with in my pilgrimage, he, I think, bears the wrong name. The other would be said nay, after a little argumentation (and somewhat else), but this bold-faced Shame would never have done."

CHR. "Why, what did he say to you?"

FAITH. "What! Why he objected against religion itself; he said it was a pitiful, low, sneaking business for a man to mind religion; he said that a tender conscience was an unmanly thing, and that for man to watch over his words and ways, so as to tie up himself from that hectoring liberty that the brave spirits of the times accustom themselves unto, would make him the ridicule of the times. He objected also that but few of the mighty, rich, or wise were ever of my opinion; nor any of them neither before they were persuaded to be fools and to be of a voluntary fondness* to venture the loss of all, for nobody else knows what. He moreover objected the base and low estate and condition of those that were chiefly the pilgrims, also their ignorance of the times in which they lived

---

*Want of sense or judgment.

and want of understanding in all natural science. Yea, he did hold me to it at that rate, also, about a great many more things than here I relate; as, that it was a shame to sit whining and mourning under a sermon and a shame to come sighing and groaning home, that it was a shame to ask my neighbour forgiveness for petty faults, or to make restitution where I had taken from any. He said, also, that religion made a man grow strange to the great, because of a few vices (which he called by finer names) and made him own and respect the base, because of the same religious fraternity. 'And is not this,' said he, 'a shame?' "

CHR. "And what did you say to him?"

FAITH. "Say! I could not tell what to say at the first. Yea, he put me so to it that my blood came up in my face; even this Shame fetched it up, and had almost beat me quite off. But at last I began to consider that that which is highly esteemed among men is had in abomination with God. [Luke 16:15] And I thought again, this Shame tells me what men are, but it tells me nothing what God or the Word of God is. And I thought, moreover, that at the day of doom, we shall not be doomed to death or life, according to the hectoring spirits of the world, but according to the wisdom and law of the Highest. Therefore, thought I, what God says is best, though all the men in the world are against it. Seeing then that God prefers his religion, seeing God prefers a tender conscience, seeing they that make themselves fools for the Kingdom of Heaven are wisest, and that the poor man that loveth Christ is richer than the greatest man in the world that hates him, Shame depart; thou art an enemy to my salvation. Shall I entertain thee against my sovereign Lord? How then shall I look him in the face at his coming? Should I now be ashamed of his ways and servants, how can I expect the blessing? But indeed this Shame was a bold villain; I could scarce shake him out of my company; yea, he would be haunting of me and continually whispering me in the ear,

with some one or other of the infirmities that attend religion. But at last I told him 'twas but in vain to attempt further in this business; for those things that he disdained in those did I see most glory. And so at last I got past this importunate one.

"And when I had shaken him off, then I began to sing.

The trials that those men do meet withal
That are obedient to the heavenly call
Are manifold and suited to the flesh,
And come, and come, and come again afresh;
That now, or sometime else, we by them may
Be taken, overcome, and cast away.
O let the pilgrims, let the pilgrims then,
Be vigilant, and quit themselves like men.

CHR. "I am glad, my brother, that thou didst withstand this villain so bravely; for of all, as thou sayst, I think he has the wrong name; for he is so bold as to follow us in the streets, and to attempt to put us to shame before all men; that is, to make us ashamed of that which is good. But if he was not himself audacious, he would never attempt to do as he does. But let us still resist him; for notwithstanding all his bravados, he promoteth the fool, and none else. The wise shall inherit glory, said Solomon, but shame shall be the promotion of fools. [Proverbs 3:35]

FAITH. "I think we must cry to him for help against shame that would have us be valiant for truth upon the earth."

CHR. "You say true. But did you meet nobody else in that valley?"

FAITH. "No, not I, for I had sunshine all the rest of the way through that, and also through the Valley of the Shadow of Death."

CHR. " 'Twas well for you; I am sure it fared far otherwise with me. I had for a long season, as soon almost as I entered into that valley, a dreadful combat with that foul fiend Apollyon. Yea, I thought verily he would have killed me; especially when he got me down, and crushed me under him, as if he would have crushed me to pieces. For as he threw me, my sword flew out of my hand; nay, he told me, he was sure of me. But I cried to God, and he heard me, and delivered me out of all my troubles. Then I entered into the Valley of the Shadow of Death and had no light for almost half the way through it. I thought I should have been killed there, over and over; but at last, day broke, and the sun rose, and I went through that which was behind with far more ease and quiet.''

Moreover, I saw in my dream that as they went on, Faithful, as he chanced to look on one side, saw a man whose name is Talkative, walking at a distance besides them (for in this place there was room enough for them all to walk). He was a tall man, and something more comely at a distance than at hand. To this man Faithful addressed himself in this manner.

FAITH. "Friend, whither away? Are you going to the heavenly country?"

TALK. "I am going to that same place."

FAITH. "That is well. Then I hope we may have your good company."

TALK. "With a very good will will I be your companion."

FAITH. "Come on then, and let us go together, and let us spend our time in discoursing of things that are profitable."

TALK. "To talk of things that are good to me is very acceptable, with you or with any other; and I am glad that I have met with those that incline to so good a work. For to speak the truth, there are but few that care thus to spend their time (as they are in their travels) but choose much rather to be speaking of things to no profit, and this hath been a trouble to me."

FAITH. "That is indeed a thing to be lamented; for what things so worthy of the use of the tongue and mouth of men on earth, as are the things of the God of Heaven?"

TALK. "I like you wonderful well, for your saying is full of conviction; and I will add, what thing so pleasant and what so profitable, as to talk of the things of God?

"What things so pleasant (that is, if a man hath any delight in things that are wonderful)? For instance, if a man doth delight to talk of the history or the mystery of things, or if a man doth love to talk of miracles, wonders, or signs, where shall he find things recorded so delightful, and so sweetly penned, as in the Holy Scripture?"

FAITH. "That's true; but to be profited by such things in our talk, should be that which we design."

TALK. "That is it that I said; for to talk of such things is most profitable, for by so doing, a man may get knowledge of many things, as of the vanity of earthly things, and the benefit of things above. Thus in general but more particularly, by this a man may learn the necessity of the new birth, the insufficiency of our works, the need of Christ's righteousness, &c. Besides, by this a man may learn by talk, what it is to repent, to believe, to pray, to suffer, or the like; by this also a man may learn what are the great promises and consolations of the Gospel, to his own comfort. Further, by this a man may learn to refute false opinions, to vindicate the truth, and also to instruct the ignorant."

FAITH. "All this is true, and glad am I to hear these things from you."

TALK. "Alas! The want of this is the cause that so few understand the need of faith and the necessity of a work of grace in their soul in order to eternal life, but ignorantly live in the works of the law, by which a man can by no means obtain the Kingdom of Heaven."

FAITH. "But, by your leave, heavenly knowledge of these is the gift of God; no man attaineth to them by humane industry or only by the talk of them."

TALK. "All this I know very well. For a man can receive nothing except it be given him from Heaven; all is of grace, not of works. I could give you an hundred scriptures for the confirmation of this."

FAITH. "Well then," said Faithful, "what is that one thing that we shall at this time found our discourse upon?"

TALK. "What you will. I will talk of things heavenly or things earthly, things moral or things evangelical, things sacred or things profane, things past or things to come, things foreign or things at home, things more essential or things circumstantial, provided that all be done to our profit."

FAITH. Now did Faithful begin to wonder, and stepping to Christian (for he walked all this while by himself), he said to him (but softly), "What a brave companion have we got! Surely this man will make a very excellent pilgrim."

CHR. At this Christian modestly smiled and said, "This man with whom you are so taken will beguile with this tongue of his twenty of them that know him not."

FAITH. "Do you know him then?"

CHR. "Know him! Yes, better than he knows himself."

FAITH. "Pray what is he?"

CHR. "His name is Talkative. He dwelleth in our town. I wonder that you should be a stranger to him, only I consider that our town is large."

FAITH. "Whose son is he? And whereabout doth he dwell?"

CHR. "He is the son of one Saywell; he dwelt in Prating Row; and he is known of all that are acquainted with him by the name of Talkative in Prating Row, and notwithstanding his fine tongue, he is but a sorry fellow."

FAITH. "Well, he seems to be a very pretty man."

CHR. "That is to them that have not thorough acquaintance with him, for he is best abroad; near home he is ugly enough. Your saying that he is a pretty man brings to my mind what I have observed in the work of the painter whose pictures show best at a distance, but very near more unpleasing."

FAITH. "But I am ready to think you do but jest, because you smiled."

CHR. "God forbid that I should jest (though I smiled) in this matter, or that I should accuse any falsely. I will give you a

further discovery of him: this man is for any company and for any talk; as he talketh now with you, so will he talk when he is on the ale-bench. And the more drink he hath in his crown, the more of these things he hath in his mouth. Religion hath no place in his heart or house or conversation; all he hath lieth in his tongue, and his religion is to make a noise therewith."

FAITH. "Say you so! Then I am in this man greatly deceived."

CHR. "Deceived? You may be sure of it. Remember the proverb, 'They say and do not'; 'but the kingdom of God is not in word, but in power.' [Matthew 23:3, I Corinthians 4:20] He talketh of prayer, of repentance, of faith, and of the new birth; but he knows but only to talk of them. I have been in his family and have observed him both at home and abroad, and I know what I say of him is the truth. His house is as empty of religion as the white of an egg is of savour. There is there neither prayer nor sign of repentance for sin. Yea, the brute in his kind serves God far better than he. He is the very stain, reproach, and shame of religion to all that know him; it can hardly have a good word in all that end of the town where he dwells through him. Thus say the common people that know him, 'a saint abroad, and a devil at home.' His poor family finds it so. He is such a churl, such a railer at, and so unreasonable with his servants that they neither know how to do for or speak to him. Men that have any dealings with him say 'tis better to deal with a Turk than with him, for fairer dealing they shall have at their hands. This Talkative, if it be possible, will go beyond them, defraud, beguile, and over-reach them. Besides, he brings up his sons to follow his steps, and if he findeth in any of them a foolish timorousness (for so he calls the first appearance of a tender conscience), he calls them fools and blockheads and by no means will employ them in much or speak to their commendations before others. For my part I am of opinion that he has, by his wicked life, caused many to stumble and fall and will be, if God prevent not, the ruin of many more."

FAITH. "Well, my brother, I am bound to believe you, not only because you say you know him, but also because like a Christian you make your reports of men. For I cannot think that you speak these things of ill will, but because it is even so as you say."

CHR. "Had I known him no more than you, I might perhaps have thought of him as at the first you did. Yea, had he received this report at their hands only, that are enemies to religion, I should have thought it had been a slander (a lot that often falls from bad men's mouths upon good men's names and professions). But all these things, yea, and a great many more as bad, of my own knowledge I can prove him guilty of. Besides, good men are ashamed of him. They can neither call him brother nor friend; the very naming of him among them makes them blush if they know him."

FAITH. "Well, I see that saying and doing are two things, and hereafter I shall better observe this distinction."

CHR. "They are two things indeed and are as diverse as are the soul and the body. For as the body without the soul is but a dead carcass, so saying, if it be alone, is but a dead carcass also. The soul of religion is the practice part: 'Pure religion and undefiled before God and the Father is this, to visit the fatherless and widows in their affliction, and to keep himself unspotted from the world.' [James 1:27] This Talkative is not aware of; he thinks that hearing and saying will make a good Christian, and thus he deceiveth his own soul. Hearing is but as the sowing of the seed; talking is not sufficient to prove that fruit is indeed in the heart and life, and let us assure ourselves that at the day of doom, men shall be judged according to their fruits. It will not be said then, 'Did you believe?' but, 'Were you doers or talkers only?' And accordingly shall they be judged. The end of the world is compared to our harvest, and you know men at har-

vest regard nothing but fruit, not that anything can be accepted that is not of faith. But I speak this to show you how insignificant the profession of Talkative will be at that day."

FAITH. "This brings to my mind that of Moses, by which he describeth the beast that is clean. He is such an one that parteth the hoof and cheweth the cud, not that parteth the hoof only or that cheweth the cud only. The hare cheweth the cud, but yet is unclean because he parteth not the hoof. And this truly resembleth Talkative; he cheweth the cud, he seeketh knowledge, he cheweth upon the Word, but he divideth not the hoof, he parteth not with the way of sinners; but as the hare he retaineth the foot of a dog, or bear, and therefore he is unclean."

CHR. "You have spoken, for ought I know, the true Gospel sense of those texts; and I will add another thing. Paul calleth some men, yea, and those great talkers, too, 'sounding brass' and 'tinkling cymbals'; that is, as he expounds them in another place, 'things without life, giving sound.' [I Corinthians 13:1, 14:7] Things without life, that is, without the true faith and grace of the Gospel, and consequently, things that shall never be placed in the Kingdom of Heaven among those that are the children of life. Though their sound, by their talk, be as if it were the tongue or voice of an angel."

FAITH. "Well, I was not so fond of his company at first, but I am as sick of it now. What shall we do to be rid of him?"

CHR. "Take my advice and do as I bid you, and you shall find that he will soon be sick of your company, too, except God shall touch his heart and turn it."

FAITH. "What would you have me to do?"

CHR. "Why, go to him, and enter into some serious discourse about the power of religion, and ask him plainly (when he has approved of it, for that he will) whether this thing be set up in his heart, house, or conversation."

FAITH. Then Faithful stepped forward again and said to Talkative, "Come, what cheer? How is it now?"

TALK. "Thank you, well. I thought we should have had a great deal of talk by this time."

FAITH. "Well, if you will, we will fall to it now, and since you left it with me to state the question, let it be this: how doth the saving grace of God discover itself, when it is in the heart of man?"

TALK. "I perceive then that our talk must be about the power of things. Well, 'tis a very good question, and I shall be willing to answer you. And take my answer in brief thus: first, where the grace of God is in the heart, it causeth there a great outcry against sin. Secondly——"

FAITH. "Nay, hold, let us consider of one at once. I think you should rather say it shows itself by inclining the soul to abhor its sin."

TALK. "Why, what difference is there between crying out against, and abhorring of sin?"

FAITH. "Oh! a great deal. A man may cry out against sin of policy, but he cannot abhor it, but by virtue of a godly antipathy against it. I have heard many cry out against sin in the pulpit, who yet can abide it well enough in the heart, and house, and conversation. Joseph's mistress cried out with a loud voice, as if she had been very holy, but she would willingly, notwithstanding that, have committed uncleanness with him. Some cry out against sin, even as the mother cries out against her child in her lap, when she calleth it slut and naughty girl, and then falls to hugging and kissing it."

TALK. "You lie at the catch,* I perceive."

FAITH. "No, not I; I am only for setting things right. But what is the second thing whereby you would prove a discovery of a work of grace in the heart?"

TALK. "Great knowledge of Gospel mysteries."

FAITH. "This sign should have been first, but first or last, it is also false. Knowledge, great knowledge, may be obtained in the mysteries of the Gospel, and yet no work of grace in the soul. Yea, if a man have all knowledge, he may yet be nothing, and so consequently be no child of God. When Christ said, 'Do you know all these things?' and the disciples had answered, 'Yes,' he addeth, 'Blessed are ye if ye do them.' [Matthew 13:51, John 13:17] He doth not lay the blessing in the knowing of them, but in the doing of them. For there is a knowledge that is not attended with doing: He that knoweth his Master's will and doth it not. A man may know like an angel and yet be no Christian; therefore your sign is not true. Indeed to know is a thing that pleaseth talkers and boasters, but to do is that which pleaseth God; not that the heart can be good without knowledge, for without that the heart is naught. There is therefore knowledge and knowledge: knowledge that resteth in the bare speculation of things, and knowledge that is accompanied with the grace of faith and love, which puts a man upon doing even the will of God from the heart. The first of these will serve the talker, but without the other the true Christian is not content. 'Give me understanding, and I shall keep thy law; yea, I shall observe it with my whole heart.' " [Psalms 119:34]

TALK. "You lie at the catch again; this is not for edification."

FAITH. "Well, if you please, propound another sign how this work of grace discovereth itself where it is."

TALK. "Not I, for I see we shall not agree."

FAITH. "Well, if you will not, will you give me leave to do it?"

TALK. "You may use your liberty."

FAITH. "A work of grace in the soul discovereth itself, either to him that hath it or to standers by.

"To him that hath it, thus: it gives him conviction of sin, especially of the defilement of his nature and the sin of unbelief

---

*Lie in wait for a chance to catch out in talk.

429

(for the sake of which he is sure to be damned, if he findeth not mercy at God's hand by faith in Jesus Christ). This sight and sense of things worketh in him sorrow and shame for sin; he findeth, moreover, revealed in him the Saviour of the World, and the absolute necessity of closing with him for life, at the which he findeth hungerings and thirstings after him, to which hungerings, &c. the promise is made. Now according to the strength or weakness of his faith in his Saviour, so is his joy and peace, so is his love to holiness, so are his desires to know him more, and also to serve him in this world. But though I say it discovereth itself thus unto him, yet it is but seldom that he is able to conclude that this is a work of grace, because his corruptions now and his abused reason makes his mind to misjudge in this matter; therefore in him that hath this work there is required a very sound judgement, before he can with steadiness conclude that this is a work of grace.

"To others it is thus discovered:

"1. By an experimental* confession of his faith in Christ. 2. By a life answerable to that confession, to wit, a life of holiness, heart-holiness, family-holiness (if he hath a family) and by coversation-holiness in the world; which in the general teacheth him inwardly to abhor his sin and himself for that in secret, to suppress it in his family, and to promote holiness in the world, not by talk only, as an hypocrite or talkative person may do, but by a practical subjection in faith and love to the power of the word. And now, sir, as to this brief description of the work of grace, and also the discovery of it, if you have ought to object, object. If not, then give me leave to propound to you a second question."

TALK. "Nay, my part is not now to object, but to hear. Let me therefore have your second question."

FAITH. "It is this: do you experience the first part of this description of it? And doth your life and conversation testify the same? Or standeth your religion in word or in tongue, and not in deed and truth. Pray, if you incline to answer me in this, say no more than you know the God above will say 'Amen' to, and also, nothing but what your conscience can justify you in. For, not he that commendeth himself is approved, but whom the Lord commendeth. [2 Corinthians 10:18] Besides, to say I am thus, and thus, when my conversation and all my neighbours tell me I lie is great wickedness."

TALK. Then Talkative at first began to blush, but recovering himself, thus he replied, "You come now to experience, to conscience, and God and to appeals to him for justification of what is spoken. This kind of discourse I did not expect, nor am I disposed to give an answer to such questions, because I count not myself bound thereto, unless you take upon you to be a catechizer; and, though you should so do, yet I may refuse to make you my judge. But I pray will you tell me, why you ask me such questions?"

FAITH. "Because I saw you forward to talk, and because I knew not that you had ought else but notion. Besides, to tell you all the truth, I have heard of you, that you are a man whose religion lies in talk and that your conversation gives this your mouth-profession the lie. They say you are a spot among Christians, and that religion fareth the worse for your ungodly conversation, that some already have stumbled at your wicked ways, and that more are in danger of being destroyed thereby. Your religion, and an ale-house, and covetousness, and uncleanness, and swearing, and lying, and vain company-keeping, &c. will stand together. The proverb is true of you, which is said of a whore, to wit, that she is a shame to all women; so you are a shame to all professors."

TALK. "Since you are ready to take up reports and to judge so rashly as you do, I cannot but conclude you are some peevish

_____

*Based upon or founded in experience.

or melancholy man not fit to be discoursed with, and so adieu."

CHR. Then came up Christian and said to his brother, "I told you how it would happen; your words and his lusts could not agree. He had rather leave your company than reform his life. But he is gone as I said; let him go. The loss is no man's but his own; he has saved us the trouble of going from him, for he continuing, as I suppose he will do, as he is, he would have been but a blot in our company. Besides, the Apostle says, 'From such withdraw thyself.' " [1 Timothy 6:5]

FAITH. "But I am glad we had this little discourse with him; it may happen that he will think of it again. However, I have dealt plainly with him, and so am clear of his blood, if he perisheth."

CHR. "You did well to talk so plainly to him as you did; there is but little of this faithful dealing with men nowadays, and that makes religion so stink in the nostrils of many, as it doth. For they are these talkative fools, whose religion is only in word and are debauched and vain in their conversation, that (being so much admitted into the fellowship of the godly) do stumble the world, blemish Christianity, and grieve the sincere. I wish that all men would deal with such, as you have done; then should they either be made more conformable to religion, or the company of saints would be too hot for them." Then did Faithful say,

How Talkative at first lifts up his plumes!
How bravely doth he speak! How he presumes
To drive down all before him! But so soon
As Faithful talks of heartwork, like the moon
That's past the full, into the wain he goes;
And so will all, but he that heartwork knows.

Thus they went on talking of what they had seen by the way; and so made that way easy, which would otherwise, no doubt, have been tedious to them, for now they went through a wilderness.

Now when they were got almost quite out of this wilderness, Faithful chanced to cast his eye back and espied one coming after them; and he knew him. "Oh!" said Faithful to his brother, "Who comes yonder?" Then Christian looked and said, "It is my good friend Evangelist." "Ay, and my good friend, too," said Faithful, "for 'twas he that set me the way to the gate." Now was Evangelist come up unto them, and thus saluted them.

EVAN. "Peace be with you, dearly beloved, and peace be to your helpers."

CHR. "Welcome, welcome, my good Evangelist; the sight of thy countenance brings to my remembrance they ancient kindness and unwearied labouring for my eternal good."

FAITH. "And, a thousand times welcome," said good Faithful. "Thy company, O sweet Evangelist, how desirable is it to us, poor pilgrims!"

EVAN. Then said Evangelist, "How hath it fared with you, my friends, since the time of our last parting? What have you met with, and how have you behaved yourselves?"

CHR. Then Christian and Faithful told him of all things that had happened to them in the way, and how, and with what difficulty they had arrived to that place.

EVAN. "Right glad am I," said Evangelist, "not that you met with trials, but that you have been victors; and for that you have (notwithstanding many weaknesses) continued in the way to this very day.

"I say, right glad am I of this thing, and that for mine own sake and yours. I have sowed, and you have reaped, and the day is coming when both he that sowed and they that reaped shall rejoice together; [John 4:36] that is, if you hold out, for, in due time ye shall reap, if you faint not. [Galatians 6:9] The crown is before you, and it is an incorruptible one; so run that you may obtain it. [I Corinthians 9:24–27] Some there be that set out for this crown, and after they have gone far for it, another comes in and takes it from them.

Hold fast therefore that you have; let no man take your crown. [Revelation 3:11] You are not yet out of the gunshot of the Devil; you have not resisted unto blood, striving against sin; let the Kingdom be always before you, and believe steadfastly concerning things that are invisible. Let nothing that is on this side the other world get within you; and above all, look well to your own hearts and to the lusts thereof, for they are deceitful above all things and desperately wicked. Set your faces like a flint; you have all power in heaven and earth on your side."

CHR. Then Christian thanked him for his exhortation, but told him withal that they would have him speak farther to them for their help the rest of the way, and the rather, for that they well knew that he was a prophet and could tell them of things that might happen unto them, and also how they might resist and overcome them. To which request Faithful also consented. So Evangelist began as followeth.

EVAN. "My sons, you have heard in the words of the truth of the Gospel that you must through many tribulations enter into the Kingdom of Heaven. And again, that in every city bonds and afflictions abide in you, and therefore you cannot expect that you should go long on your pilgrimage without them, in some sort or other. You have found something of the truth of these testimonies upon you already, and more will immediately follow. For now, as you see, you are almost out of this wilderness, and therefore you will soon come into a town that you will by and by see before you, and in that town you will be hardly beset with enemies, who will strain hard, but they will kill you; and be you sure that one or both of you must seal the testimony which you hold with blood. But be you faithful unto death, and the King will give you a crown of life. He that shall die there, although his death will be unnatural and his pain perhaps great, he will yet have the better of his fellow; not only because he will be arrived at the Celestial City soonest, but because he will escape many miseries that the other will meet with in the rest of his journey. But when you are come to the town, and shall find fulfilled what I have here related, then remember your friend and quit yourselves like men, and commit the keeping of your souls to your God, as unto a faithful Creator."

Then I saw in my dream that when they were got out of the wilderness, they presently saw a town before them, and the name of that Town is Vanity; and at the town there is a fair kept called Vanity Fair. It is kept all the year long; it beareth the name of Vanity Fair, because the town where 'tis kept is lighter than vanity, and also because all that is there sold or that cometh thither is Vanity. As is the saying of the wise, "All that cometh is vanity."

This fair is no new erected business, but a thing of ancient standing; I will show you the original of it.

Almost five thousand years agone, there were pilgrims walking to the Celestial City, as these two honest persons are; and Beelzebub, Apollyon, and Legion, with their companions, perceiving by the path that the pilgrims made that their way to the city lay through this town of Vanity, they contrived here to set up a fair, a fair wherein should be sold of all sorts of vanity and that it should last all the year long. Therefore at this fair are all such merchandise sold, as houses, lands, trades, places, honours, preferments, titles, countries, kingdoms, lusts, pleasures, and delights of all sorts, as whores, bawds, wives, husbands, children, masters, servants, lives, blood, bodies, souls, silver, gold, pearls, precious stones, and what not.

And, moreover, at this fair there is at all times to be seen jugglings, cheats, games, plays, fools, apes, knaves, and rogues, and that of all sorts.

Here are to be seen, too, and that for nothing, thefts, murders, adulteries, false swearers, and that of a blood-red colour.

And as in other fairs of less moment, there are the several rows and streets under their proper names, where such and such wares are vended. So here likewise, you have the proper places, rows, streets (*viz.* countries and kingdoms), where the wares of this fair are soonest to be found. Here is the Britain Row, the French Row, the Italian Row, the Spanish Row, the German Row, where several sorts of vanities are to be sold. But as in other fairs, some one commodity is as the chief of all the fair, so the ware of Rome and her merchandise is greatly promoted in this fair. Only our English nation, with some others, have taken a dislike thereat.

Now, as I said, the way to the Celestial City lies just through this town, where this lusty fair is kept, and he that will go to the city, and yet not go through this town, must needs "go out of the world." [I Corinthians 5:10] The Prince of Princes himself, when here, went through this town to his own country and that upon a fair day, too. Yea, and as I think it was Beelzebub, the chief lord of this fair, that invited him to buy of his vanities; yea, would have made him lord of the fair would he but have done him reverence as he went through the town. Yea, because he was such a person of honour, Beelzebub had him from street to street and showed him all the kingdoms of the world in a little time that he might, if possible, allure that Blessed One to cheapen* and buy some of his vanities. [Matthew 4:8–9; Luke 4:5–7] But he had no mind to the merchandise and therefore left the town, without laying out so much as one farthing upon these vanities. This fair therefore is an ancient thing, of long standing, and a very great fair.

Now these pilgrims, as I said, must needs go through this fair. Well, so they did, but behold, even as they entered into the fair, all the people in the fair were moved and the town itself as it were in a hubbub about them, and that for several reasons; for,

First, the pilgrims were clothed with such kind of raiment as was diverse from the raiment of any that traded in that fair. The people therefore of the fair made a great gazing upon them. Some said they were fools, some they were bedlams, and some they are outlandish men.

Secondly, and as they wondered at their apparel, so they did likewise at their speech, for few could understand what they said. They naturally spoke the language of Canaan, but they that kept the fair were the men of this world. So that from one end of the fair to the other, they seemed barbarians† each to the other.

Thirdly, but that which did not a little amuse‡ the merchandisers was that these pilgrims set very light by all their wares; they cared not so much as to look upon them, and if they called upon them to buy, they would put their fingers in their ears and cry, "Turn away mine eyes from beholding vanity," [Psalms 119:37] and look upwards, signifying that their trade and traffic was in heaven.

One chanced mockingly, beholding the carriages of the men, to say unto them, "What will ye buy?" But they, looking gravely upon him, said, "We buy the truth." [Proverbs 23:23] At that, there was an occasion taken to despise the men the more; some mocking, some taunting, some speaking reproachfully, and some calling upon others to smite them. At last things came to an hubbub, and great stir in the fair, insomuch that all order was confounded. Now was word presently brought to the great one of the fair, who quickly came down and deputed some of his most trusty friends to take these men into examination, about whom the fair was almost overturned. So the men were brought to examination; and they that sat upon them, asked them whence they came, whither they went and what they did there in such an unusual garb? The men told them that they were pilgrims and strangers in the world and that they were going to their own country, which was the heavenly

---

*To barter for, to trade for.

†Foreigners.

‡Cause to gaze in astonishment, wonder.

Jerusalem, and that they had given none occasion to the men of the town, nor yet to the merchandisers, thus to abuse them and to let* them in their journey. Except it was, for that, when one asked them what they would buy, they said they would buy the truth. But they that were appointed to examine them did not believe them to be any other than bedlams and mad, or else such as came to put all things into a confusion in the fair. Therefore they took them and beat them and besmeared them with dirt, and then put them into the cage, that they might be made a spectacle to all the men of the fair. There therefore they lay, for some time, and were made the objects of any man's sport, or malice, or revenge. The great one of the fair laughing still at all that befell them. But the men being patient and not rendering railing for railing, but contrariwise blessing and giving good words for bad and kindness for injuries done, some men in the fair that were more observing and less prejudiced than the rest began to check and blame the baser sort for their continual abuses done by them to the men. They therefore in angry manner let fly at them again, counting them as bad as the men in the cage, and telling them that they seemed confederates, and should be made partakers of their misfortunes. The other replied that for ought they could see, the men were quiet and sober and intended nobody any harm, and that there were many that traded in their fair that were more worthy to be put into the cage, yea, and pillory, too, than were the men that they had abused. Thus, after divers words had passed on both sides (the men behaving themselves all the while very wisely, and soberly before them) they fell to some blows among themselves and did harm one to another. Then were these two poor men brought before their examiners again, and there charged as being guilty of the late hubbub that had been in the fair. So they beat them pitifully, and hanged irons upon them, and led them in chains up and down

the fair, for an example and a terror to others, lest any should further speak in their behalf or join themselves unto them. But Christian and Faithful behaved themselves yet more wisely and received the ignominy and shame that was cast upon them with so much meekness and patience that it won to their side (though but few in comparison of the rest) several of the men in the fair. This put the other party yet into a greater rage, insomuch that they concluded the death of these two men. Wherefore they threatened that the cage nor irons should serve their turn, but that they should die, for the abuse they had done and for deluding the men of the fair.

Then were they remanded to the cage again, until further order should be taken with them. So they put them in and made their feet fast in the stocks.

Here also they called again to mind what they had heard from their faithful friend Evangelist, and was the more confirmed in their way and sufferings by what he told them would happen to them. They also now comforted each other that whose lot it was to suffer, even he should have the best on't; therefore each man secretly wished that he might have that preferment, but committing themselves to the all-wise dispose of him that ruleth all things, with much content they abode in the condition in which they were, until they should be otherwise disposed of.

Then a convenient time being appointed, they brought them forth to their trial in order to their condemnation. When the time was come, they were brought before their enemies and arraigned; the judge's name was Lord Hategood. Their indictment was one and the same in substance, though somewhat varying in form; the contents whereof was this:

"That they were enemies to and disturbers of their trade; that they had made commotions and divisions in the town, and had won a party to their own most dan-

---

*Impede, hinder.

gerous opinions, in contempt of the law of their prince."

Then Faithful began to answer that he had only set himself against that which had set itself against him that is higher than the highest. And, said he, "As for disturbance, I make none, being myself a man of peace; the party that were won to us were won by beholding our truth and innocence, and they are only turned from the worse to the better. And as to the king you talk of, since he is Beelzebub, the enemy of our Lord, I defy him and all his angels."

Then proclamation was made that they that had ought to say for their lord the king against the prisoner at the bar should forthwith appear and give in their evidence. So there came in three witnesses, to wit, Envy, Superstition, and Pickthank. They were then asked if they knew the prisoner at the bar and what they had to say for their lord the king against him.

Then stood forth Envy, and said to this effect, "My Lord, I have known this man a long time and will attest upon my oath before this honourable bench that he is—"

JUDGE. "Hold, give him his oath. So they sware him. Then he said, "My Lord, this man, notwithstanding his plausible name, is one of the vilest men in our country. He neither regardeth prince nor people, law nor custom, but doth all that he can to possess all men with certain of his disloyal notions, which he in the general calls principles of faith and holiness. And in particular, I heard him once myself affirm that Christianity and the customs of our town of Vanity were diametrically opposite and could not be reconciled. By which saying, my Lord, he doth at once not only condemn all our laudable doings, but us in the doing of them."

JUDGE. Then did the judge say to him, "Hast thou any more to say?"

ENVY. "My Lord, I could say much more, only I would not be tedious to the court. Yet if need be, when the other gentlemen have given in their evidence, rather than anything shall be wanting that will dispatch him, I will enlarge my testimony against him." So he was bid stand by. Then they called Superstition and bid him look upon the prisoner; they also asked what he could say for their lord the king against him. Then they sware him; so he began.

SUPER. "My Lord, I have no great acquaintance with this man, nor do I desire to have further knowledge of him. However this I know, that he is a very pestilent fellow, from some discourse that the other day I had with him in this town; for then talking with him, I heard him say that our religion was naught and such by which a man could by no means please God. Which sayings of his, my Lord, your Lordship very well knows what necessarily thence will follow, to wit, that we still do worship in vain, are yet in our sins, and finally shall be damned; and this is that which I have to say."

Then was Pickthank sworn and bid say what he knew, in behalf of their lord the king against the prisoner at the bar.

PICK. "My Lord, and you gentlemen all, this fellow I have known of a long time and have heard him speak things that ought not to be spoke. For he hath railed on our noble Prince Beelzebub and hath spoke contemptibly of his honourable friends, whose names are the Lord Old Man, the Lord Carnal Delight, the Lord Luxurious, the Lord Desire of Vainglory, my old Lord Lechery, Sir Having Greedy, with all the rest of our nobility; and he hath said, moreover, that if all men were of his mind, if possible, there is not one of these noblemen should have any longer a being in this town. Besides, he hath not been afraid to rail on you, my Lord, who are now appointed to be his judge, calling you an ungodly villain, with many other such like vilifying terms, with which he hath bespattered most of the gentry of our town." When this Pickthank had told his tale, the judge directed his speech to the prisoner at the bar, saying, "Thou runagate;* heretic, and traitor, hast thou heard what these honest gentlemen have witnessed against thee."

FAITH. "May I speak a few words in my own defence?"

JUDGE. "Sirrah, sirrah, thou deservest to live no longer, but to be slain immediately upon the place; yet that all men may see our gentleness towards thee, let us hear what thou hast to say."

FAITH. "1. I say then in answer to what Mr. Envy hath spoken, I never said ought but this: that what rule or laws or custom or people were flat against the Word of God are diametrically opposite to Christianity. If I have said amiss in this, convince me of my error, and I am ready here before you to make my recantation.

"2. As to the second, to wit, Mr. Superstition, and his charge against me, I said only this: that in the worship of God there is required a divine faith; but there can be no divine faith without a divine revelation of the will of God. Therefore whatever is thrust into the worship of God that is not agreeable to divine revelation cannot be done but by an humane faith, which faith will not profit to eternal life.

"3. As to what Mr. Pickthank hath said, I say (avoiding terms, as that I am said to rail, and the like) that the prince of this town, with all the rabblement his attendants, by this gentleman named, are more fit for a being in hell than in this town and country. And so the Lord have mercy upon me."

Then the judge called to the jury (who all this while stood by, to hear and observe), "Gentlemen of the jury, you see this man about whom so great an uproar hath been made in this town. You have also heard what these worthy gentlemen have witnessed against him; also you have heard his reply and confession. It lieth now in your breasts to hang him or save his life. But yet I think meet to instruct you into our law.

"There was an act made in the days of Pharaoh the Great, servant to our prince,

that lest those of a contrary religion should multiply and grow too strong for him, their males should be thrown into the river. There was also an act made in the days of Nebuchadnezzar the Great, another of his servants, that whoever would not fall down and worship his golden image should be thrown into a fiery furnace. There was also an act made in the days of Darius that who so, for some time, called upon any god but his should be cast into the lion's den. Now the substance of these laws this rebel has broken, not only in thought (which is not to be borne), but also in word and deed, which must therefore needs be intolerable.

"For that of Pharaoh, his law was made upon a supposition to prevent mischief, no crime being yet apparent; but here is a crime apparent. For the second and third, you see he disputeth against our religion, and for the treason he hath confessed, he deserveth to die the death."

Then went the jury out, whose names were Mr. Blindman, Mr. No-good, Mr. Malice, Mr. Love-lust, Mr. Live-loose, Mr. Heady, Mr. High-mind, Mr. Enmity, Mr. Liar, Mr. Cruelty, Mr. Hate-light, and Mr. Implacable, who everyone gave in his private verdict against him among themselves, and afterwards unanimously concluded to bring him in guilty before the judge. And first Mr. Blind-man, the foreman, said, "I see clearly that this man is an heretic." Then said Mr. No-good, "Away with such a fellow from the earth." "Ay," said Mr. Malice, "for I hate the very looks of him." Then said Mr. Love-lust, "I could never endure him." "Nor I," said Mr. Live-loose, "for he would always be condemning my way." "Hang him, hang him," said Mr. Heady. "A sorry scrub," said Mr. High-mind. "My heart riseth against him," said Mr. Enmity. "He is a rogue," said Mr. Liar. "Hanging is too good for him," said Mr. Cruelty. "Let's dispatch him out of the way," said Mr. Hate-light. Then said Mr. Implacable, "Might I have all the

---

*Apostate or deserter, runaway.

world given me, I could not be reconciled to him; therefore let us forthwith bring him in guilty of death." And so they did; therefore he was presently condemned, to be had from the place where he was to the place from whence he came, and there to be put to the most cruel death that could be invented.

They therefore brought him out to do with him according to their law; and first they scourged him, then they buffeted him, then they lanced his flesh with knives; after that they stoned him with stones, then pricked him with their swords, and last of all they burned him to ashes at the stake. Thus came Faithful to his end. Now, I saw that there stood behind the multitude a chariot and a couple of horses, waiting for Faithful, who (so soon as his adversaries had dispatched him) was taken up into it, and straightway was carried up through the clouds, with sound of trumpet, the nearest way to the Celestial Gate. But as for Christian, he had some respite, and was remanded back to prison; so he there remained for a space. But he that overrules all things, having the power of their rage in his own hand, so wrought it about that Christian for that time escaped them, and went his way.

And as he went he sang:

Well, Faithful, thou hast faithfully professed
Unto thy Lord. With him thou shalt be blest,
When faithless ones, with all their vain
* delights,*
Are crying out under their hellish plights,
Sing, Faithful, sing; and let thy name survive;
For though they killed thee, thou art yet alive.

Now I saw in my dream that Christian went not forth alone, for there was one whose name was Hopeful (being made so by the beholding of Christian and Faithful in their words and behaviour, in their sufferings at the fair) who joined himself unto him, and entering into a brotherly covenant, told him that he would be his

companion. Thus one died to make testimony to the truth, and another rises out of his ashes to be a companion with Christian. This Hopeful also told Christian that there were many more of the men in the fair that would take their time and follow after.

So I saw that quickly after they were got out of the fair, they overtook one that was going before them, whose name was By-ends;* so they said to him, "What countryman, sir? And how far go you this way?" He told them that he came from the town of Fair-speech, and he was going to the Celestial City (but told them not his name).

"From Fair-speech," said Christian, "is there any that be good live there?"

BY-ENDS. "Yes," said By-ends, "I hope."

CHR. "Pray, sir, what may I call you?" said Christian.

BY-ENDS. "I am a stranger to you, and you to me; if you be going this way, I shall be glad of your company; if not, I must be content."

CHR. "This town of Fair-speech," said Christian, "I have heard of it, and, as I remember, they say it's a wealthy place."

BY-ENDS. "Yes, I will assure you that it is, and I have very many rich kindred there."

CHR. "Pray who are your kindred there, if a man may be so bold."

BY-ENDS. "Almost the whole town; and in particular, my Lord Turn-about, my Lord Time-server, my Lord Fair-speech (from whose ancestors that town first took its name). Also Mr. Smooth-man, Mr. Facing-bothways, Mr. Anything, and the parson of our parish, Mr. Two-tongues, was my mother's own brother by father's side. And to tell you the truth, I am become a gentleman of good quality; yet my great grandfather was but a waterman, looking one way, and rowing another; and I got most of my estate by the same occupation."

CHR. "Are you a married man?"

BY-ENDS. "Yes, and my wife is a very

---

*A by-end is an object apart from the principal one.

virtuous woman, the daughter of a virtuous woman. She was my Lady Feigning's daughter; therefore she came of a very honourable family, and is arrived to such a pitch of breeding that she knows how to carry it to all, even to prince and peasant. 'Tis true, we somewhat differ in religion from those of the stricter sort, yet but in two small points: first, we never strive against wind and tide. Secondly, we are always most zealous when religion goes in his silver slippers; we love much to walk with him in the street, if the sun shines and the people applaud it."

Then Christian stepped a little aside to this fellow Hopeful, saying, "It runs in my mind that this is one By-ends, of Fair-speech, and if it be he, we have as very a knave in our company as dwelleth in all these parts." Then said Hopeful, "Ask him; methinks he should not be ashamed of his name." So Christian came up with him again, and said, "Sir, you talk as if you knew something more than all the world doth, and if I take not my mark amiss, I deem I have half a guess of you. Is not your name Mr. By-ends of Fair-speech?"

BY-ENDS. "That is not my name, but indeed it is a nickname that is given me by some that cannot abide me, and I must be content to bear it as a reproach, as other good men have borne theirs before me."

CHR. "But did you never give an occasion to men to call you by this name?"

BY-ENDS. "Never, never! The worst that ever I did to give them an occasion to give me this name was that I had always the luck to jump in my judgement with the present way of the times, whatever it was, and my chance was to get thereby; but if things are thus cast upon me, let me count them a blessing, but let not the malicious load me therefore with reproach."

CHR. "I thought indeed that you was the man that I had heard of, and to tell you what I think, I fear this name belongs to you more properly than you are willing we should think it doth."

BY-ENDS. "Well, if you will thus imagine, I cannot help it. You shall find me a fair company-keeper, if you will still admit me your associate."

CHR. "If you will go with us, you must go against wind and tide, the which, I perceive, is against your opinion. You must also own religion in his rags, as well as when in his silver slippers, and stand by him, too, when bound in irons, as well as when he walketh the streets with applause."

BY-ENDS. "You must not impose, nor lord it over my faith; leave me to my liberty, and let me go with you."

CHR. "Not a step further, unless you will do in what I propound, as we."

Then said By-ends, "I shall never desert my old principles, since they are harmless and profitable. If I may not go with you, I must do as I did before you overtook me, even go by myself, until some overtake me that will be glad of my company."

Now I saw in my dream that Christian and Hopeful forsook him and kept their distance before him, but one of them looking back saw three men following Mr. By-ends, and behold, as they came up with him, he made them a very low congee,* and they also gave him a compliment. The men's names were Mr. Hold-the-world, Mr. Money-love, and Mr. Save-all, men that Mr. By-ends had formerly been acquainted with; for in their minority they were schoolfellows, and were taught by one Mr. Gripe-man, a schoolmaster in Love-gain, which is a market town in the county of Coveting in the north. This schoolmaster taught them the art of getting, either by violence, cozenage, flattery, lying or by putting on a guise of religion, and these four gentlemen had attained much of the art of their master, so that they could each of them have kept such a school themselves.

Well, when they had, as I said, thus saluted each other, Mr. Money-love said to Mr. By-ends, "Who are they upon the

_____
*Or congé, meaning bow.

road before us?" for Christian and Hopeful were yet within view.

BY-ENDS. "They are a couple of far countrymen, that after their mode are going on pilgrimage."

MONEY-LOVE. "Alas, why did they not stay that we might have had their good company, for they and we and you, sir, I hope, are all going on pilgrimage."

BY-ENDS. "We are so indeed, but the men before us are so rigid and love so much their own notions and do also so lightly esteem the opinions of others that let a man be never so godly, yet if he jumps not with them in all things, they thrust him quite out of their company."

MR. SAVE-ALL. "That's bad. But we read of some that are righteous overmuch and such men's rigidness prevails with them to judge and condemn all but themselves. But I pray what and how many were the things wherein you differed?"

BY-ENDS. "Why, they after their headstrong manner conclude that it is duty to rush on their journey all weathers, and I am for waiting for wind and tide. They are for hazarding all for God at a clap, and I am for taking all advantages to secure my life and estate. They are for holding their notions, though all other men are against them, but I am for religion in what, and so far as the times, and my safety will bear it. They are for religion, when in rags and contempt, but I am for him when he walks in his golden slippers in the sunshine and with applause."

MR. HOLD-THE-WORLD. "Ay, and hold you there still, good Mr. By-ends, for, for my part, I can count him but a fool that having the liberty to keep what he has shall be so unwise as to lose it. Let us be wise as serpents; 'tis best to make hay when the sun shines; you see how the bee lieth still all winter and bestirs her then only when she can have profit with pleasure. God sends sometimes rain and sometimes sunshine; if they be such fools to go through the first, yet let us be content to take fair weather along with us. For my part I like that re-

ligion best that will stand with the security of God's good blessings unto us; for who can imagine that is ruled by his reason, since God has bestowed upon us the good things of this life, but that he would have us keep them for his sake. Abraham and Solomon grew rich in religion. And Job says that a good man 'shall lay up gold as dust.' [Job 22:24] He must not be such as the men before us, if they be as you have described them."

MR. SAVE-ALL. "I think that we are all agreed in this matter, and therefore there needs no more words about it."

MR. MONEY-LOVE. "No, there needs no more words about this matter indeed, for he that believes neither Scripture nor reason (and you see we have both on our side) neither knows his own liberty, nor seeks his own safety."

MR. BY-ENDS. "My brethren, we are, as you see, going all on pilgrimage, and for our better diversion from things that are bad, give me leave to propound unto you this question:

"Suppose a man, a minister or a tradesman, &c. should have an advantage lie before him to get the good blessings of this life; yet so as that he can by no means come by them, except, in appearance at least, he becomes extraordinary zealous in some points of religion that he meddled not with before. May he not use this means to attain his end, and yet be a right honest man?"

MR. MONEY-LOVE. "I see the bottom of your question, and with these gentlemen's good leave, I will endeavour to shape you an answer. And first to speak to your question, as it concerns a minister himself: suppose a minister, a worthy man, possessed but of a very small benefice and has in his eye a greater, more fat, and plump by far; he has also now an opportunity of getting of it; yet so as by being more studious, by preaching more frequently, and zealously, and because the temper of the people requires it, by altering of some of his principles. For my part I see no reason but a man may do this (provided he has a call), ay, and more a great deal besides, and yet be an honest man. For why,

"1. His desire of a greater benefice is lawful (this cannot be contradicted), since 'tis set before him by providence; so then, he may get it if he can, making no question for conscience sake.

"2. Besides, his desire after that benefice makes him more studious, a more zealous preacher, &c. and so makes him a better man; yea, makes him better improve his parts, which is according to the mind of God.

"3. Now as for his complying with the temper of his people, by deserting, to serve them, some of his principles, this argueth, 1. That he is of a self-denying temper; 2. Of a sweet and winning deportment; 3. And so more fit for the ministerial function.

"4. I conclude, then, that a minister that changes a small for a great should not for so doing be judged as covetous, but rather, since he is improved in his parts and industry thereby, he counted as one that pursues his call and the opportunity put into his hand to do good.

"And now to the second part of the question which concerns the tradesman you mentioned. Suppose such an one to have but a poor employ in the world, but by becoming religious, he may mend his market, perhaps get a rich wife, or more and far better customers to his shop. For my part I see no reason but that this may be lawfully done. For why,

"1. To become religious is a virtue, by what means soever a man becomes so.

"2. Nor is it unlawful to get a rich wife or more custom to my shop.

"3. Besides the man that gets these by becoming religious gets that which is good, of them that are good, by becoming good himself; so then here is a good wife, and good customers, and a good gain, and all these by becoming religious, which is good. Therefore to become religious to get all these is a good and profitable design."

This answer, thus made by this Mr.

Money-love, to Mr. By-ends' question, was highly applauded by them all; wherefore they concluded upon the whole that it was most wholesome and advantageous. And because, as they thought, no man was able to contradict it, and because Christian and Hopeful was yet within call, they joyfully agreed to assault them with the question as soon as they overtook them, and the rather because they had opposed Mr. By-ends before. So they called after them, and they stopped and stood still till they came up to them, but they concluded as they went that not By-ends, but old Mr. Hold-the-world, should propound the question to them; because, as they supposed, their answer to him would be without the remainder of that heat that was kindled betwixt Mr. By-ends and them at their parting a little before.

So they came up to each other and after a short salutation, Mr. Hold-the-world propounded the question to Christian and his fellow, and bid them to answer it if they could.

CHR. Then said Christian, "Even a babe in religion may answer ten thousand such questions. For if it be unlawful to follow Christ for loaves, as it is, [John 6] how much more abominable is it to make of him and religion a stalking horse to get and enjoy the world. Nor do we find any other than heathens, hypocrites, devils and witches that are of this opinion.

"1. Heathens, for when Hamor and Shechem had a mind to the daughter and cattle of Jacob and saw that there was no ways for them to come at them but by becoming circumcised, they say to their companions, 'If every male of us be circumcised, as they are circumcised, shall not their cattle and their substance and every beast of theirs be ours?' Their daughters and their cattle were that which they sought to obtain, and their religion the stalking horse they made use of to come at them. Read the whole story, Genesis 34:20, 21, 22, 23.

"2. The hypocritical Pharisees were also

of this religion; long prayers were their pretence; but to get widows' houses were their intent, and greater damnation was from God their judgement, Luke 20:46, 47.

"3. Judas the devil was also of this religion; he was religious for the bag that he might be possessed of what was therein; but he was lost, cast away, and the very son of perdition.

"4. Simon the witch was of this religion, too, for he would have had the Holy Ghost that he might have got money therewith, and his sentence from Peter's mouth was according, Act. 8:19, 20, 21, 22.

"5. Neither will it out of my mind, but that that man that takes up religion for the world will throw away religion for the world; for so surely as Judas designed the world in becoming religious, so surely did he also sell religion and his Master for the same. To answer the question therefore affirmatively, as I perceive you have done, and to accept of as authentic such answer is both heathenish, hypocritical and devilish, and your reward will be according to your works." Then they stood staring one upon another, but had not wherewith to answer Christian. Hopeful also approved of the soundness of Christian's answer, so there was a great silence among them. Mr. By-ends and his company also staggered and kept behind, that Christian and Hopeful might outgo them. Then said Christian to his fellow, "If these men cannot stand before the sentence of men, what will they do with the sentence of God? And if they are mute when dealt with by vessels of clay, what will they do when they shall be rebuked by the flames of a devouring fire?"

Then Christian and Hopeful outwent them again and went till they came at a delicate plain called Ease, where they went with much content; but that plain was but narrow, so they were quickly got over it. Now at the further side of that plain was a little hill called Lucre, and in that hill a silver mine, which some of them that had formerly gone that way, because of the rarity of it, had turned aside to see;

but going too near the brink of the pit, the ground, being deceitful under them, broke, and they were slain; some also had been maimed there, and could not to their dying day be their own men again.

Then I saw in my dream that a little off the road, over against the silver mine, stood Demas (gentleman-like) to call to passengers to come and see; who said to Christian and his fellow, "Ho, turn aside hither, and I will show you a thing."

CHR. "What thing so deserving as to turn us out of the way?"

DEM. "Here is a silver mine and some digging in it for treasure; if you will come, with a little pains you may richly provide for yourselves."

HOPE. Then said Hopeful, "Let us go see."

CHR. "Not I," said Christian. "I have heard of this place before now, and how many have there been slain; and besides, that treasure is a snare to those that seek it, for it hindereth them in their pilgrimage." Then Christian called to Demas, saying, "Is not the place dangerous? Hath it not hindered many in their pilgrimage?"

DEM. "Not very dangerous, except to those that are careless." But withal, he blushed as he spake.

CHR. Then said Christian to Hopeful, "Let us not stir a step, but still keep on our way."

HOPE. "I will warrant you, when By-ends comes up, if he hath the same invitation as we, he will turn in thither to see."

CHR. "No doubt thereof, for his principles lead him that way, and a hundred to one but he dies there."

DEM. Then Demas called again, saying, "But will you not come over and see?"

CHR. Then Christian roundly answered, saying, "Demas, thou art an enemy to the right ways of the Lord of this way and hast been already condemned for thine own turning aside by one of his Majesty's judges; and why seekest thou to bring us into the like condemnation? Besides, if we at all turn aside, our Lord the King will certainly hear thereof, and will there put us to shame, where we would stand with boldness before him."

Demas cried again that he also was one of their fraternity, and that if they would tarry a little, he also himself would walk with them.

CHR. Then said Christian, "What is thy name? Is it not the same by the which I have called thee?"

DEM. "Yes, my name is Demas; I am the son of Abraham."

CHR. "I know you. Gehazi was your great-grandfather, and Judas your father, and you have trod their steps. It is but a devilish prank that thou usest. Thy father was hanged for a traitor, and thou deservest no better reward. Assure thyself, that when we come to the King, we will do him word of this thy behaviour." Thus they went their way.

By this time By-ends and his companions was come again within sight, and they at the first beck went over to Demas. Now whether they fell into the pit, by looking over the brink thereof, or whether they went down to dig, or whether they was smothered in the bottom by the damps that commonly arise, of these things I am not certain. But this I observed, that they never was seen again in the way.

Then sang Christian,

By-ends and silver Demas both agree;
One calls, the other runs, that he may be
A sharer in his lucre. So these two
Take up in this world, and no further go.

Now I saw that just on the other side of this plain, the pilgrims came to a place where stood an old monument, hard by the highway side, at the sight of which they were both concerned, because of the strangeness of the form thereof; for it seemed to them as if it had been a woman transformed into the shape of a pillar. Here therefore they stood looking and looking upon it, but could not for a

time tell what they should make thereof. At last Hopeful espied written above upon the head thereof a writing in an unusual hand; but he, being no scholar, called to Christian (for he was learned) to see if he could pick out the meaning. So he came, and after a little laying of letters together, he found the same to be this, "Remember Lot's wife." So he read it to his fellow; after which, they both concluded that that was the pillar of salt into which Lot's wife was turned for her looking back with a covetous heart, when she was going from Sodom for safety. Which sudden and amazing sight gave them occasion of this discourse.

CHR. "Ah, my brother, this is a seasonable sight; it came opportunely to us after the invitation which Demas gave us to come over to view the Hill Lucre. And had we gone over as he desired us, and as thou wast inclining to do, my brother, we had, for ought I know, been made ourselves a spectacle for those that shall come after to behold."

HOPE. "I am sorry that I was so foolish, and am made to wonder that I am not now as Lot's wife; for wherein was the difference 'twixt her sin and mine? She only looked back, and I had a desire to go see; let grace be adored, and let me be ashamed that ever such a thing should be in mine heart."

CHR. "Let us take notice of what we see here, for our help for time to come. This woman escaped one judgement, for she fell not by the destruction of Sodom, yet she was destroyed by another; as we see, she is turned into a pillar of salt."

HOPE. "True, and she may be to us both caution and example: caution that we should shun her sin, or a sign of what judgement will overtake such as shall not be prevented by this caution. So Korah, Dathan, and Abiram, with the two hundred and fifty men that perished in their sin, did also become a sign, or example to others to beware. But above all, I muse at one thing, to wit, how Demas and his fellows can stand so confidently yonder to look for that treasure, which this woman, but for looking behind her, after (for we read not that she stepped one foot out of the way) was turned into a pillar of salt; especially since the judgement which overtook her did make her an example within sight of where they are. For they cannot choose but see her, did they but lift up their eyes."

CHR. "It is a thing to be wondered at, and it argueth that their heart is grown desperate in the case; and I cannot tell who to compare them to so fitly, as to them that pick pockets in the presence of the judge, or that will cut purses under the gallows. It is said of the men of Sodom that they were sinners exceedingly, [Genesis 13:13] because they were sinners before the Lord, that is, in his eyesight, and notwithstanding the kindnesses that he had showed them, for the land of Sodom was now like the Garden of Eden heretofore. This therefore provoked him the more to jealousy and made their plague as hot as the fire of the Lord out of heaven could make it. And it is most rationally to be concluded, that such, even such as these are, that shall sin in the sight, yea, and that too in despite of such examples that are set continually before them to caution them to the contrary, must be partakers of severest judgements."

HOPE. "Doubtless thou hast said the truth, but what a mercy is it, that neither thou, but especially I, am not made, myself, this example. This ministereth occasion to us to thank God, to fear before him, and always to remember Lot's wife."

I saw then that they went on their way to a pleasant river, which David the King called the "river of God" [Psalms 65:9] but John, "The river of the water of life." [Revelation 22:1] Now their way lay just upon the bank of the river. Here therefore Christian and his companion walked with great delight; they drank also of the water of the river, which was pleasant and enlivening to their weary spirits. Besides, on the banks of this river, on either side, were green trees that bore all manner of fruit, and the leaves of the trees were good for medicine; with the fruit of these trees they were also much delighted, and the leaves they eat to prevent surfeits and other diseases that are incident to those that heat their blood by travels. On either side of the river was also a meadow, curiously beautified with lilies. And it was green all the year long. In this meadow they lay down and slept, for here they might lie down safely. When they awoke, they gathered again of the fruit of the trees, and drank again of the water of the river, and then lay down again to sleep. Thus they did several days and nights. Then they sang,

Behold ye how these crystal streams do glide
(To comfort pilgrims) by the highway side;
The meadows green, besides their fragrant
*   smell,*
Yield dainties for them, and he that can tell
What pleasant fruit, yea, leaves, these trees do
*   yield,*
Will soon sell all that he may buy this field.

So when they were disposed to go on (for they were not, as yet, at their journey's end) they ate and drank and departed.

Now I beheld in my dream that they had not journeyed far, but the river and the way, for a time, parted. At which they were not a little sorry, yet they durst not go out of the way. Now the way from the river was rough, and their feet tender by reason of their travels. So the soul of the pilgrims was much discouraged, because of the way. [Numbers 21:4] Wherefore still as they went on, they wished for better way. Now a little before them there was on the left hand of the road a meadow and a stile to go over into it, and that meadow is called By-path Meadow. Then said Christian to his fellow, "If this meadow lieth along by our wayside, let's go over into it." Then he went to the stile to see, and behold a path lay along by the way on the other side of the fence. " 'Tis according to my wish," said Christian. "Here is the easiest going; come, good Hopeful, and let us go over."

HOPE. "But how if this path should lead us out of the way?"

CHR. "That's not like," said the other. "Look, doth it not go along by the wayside?" So Hopeful, being persuaded by his fellow, went after him over the stile. When they were gone over and were got into the path, they found it very easy for their feet; and withal, they, looking before them, espied a man walking as they did (and his name was Vain Confidence. So they called after him, and asked him whither that way led. He said, "To the Celestial Gate." "Look," said Christian, "did not I tell you so? By this you may see we are right." So they followed, and he went before them. But behold the night came on, and it grew very dark; so that they that were behind lost the sight of him that went before.

He therefore that went before (Vain Confidence by name), not seeing the way before him, fell into a deep pit, which was on purpose there made by the prince of those grounds to catch vainglorious fools withal, and was dashed in pieces with his fall.

Now Christian and his fellow heard him fall. So they called to know the matter, but there was none to answer, only they heard a groaning. Then said Hopeful, "Where are we now?" Then was his fellow silent, as mistrusting that he had led him out of the way. And now it began to rain, and thunder, and lighten in a very dreadful manner, and the water rose amain.

Then Hopeful groaned in himself, saying, "Oh that I had kept on my way!"

CHR. "Who could have thought that this path should have led us out of the way?"

HOPE. "I was afraid on't at very first, and therefore gave you that gentle caution. I would have spoke plainer, but that you are older than I."

CHR. "Good brother, be not offended. I am sorry I have brought thee out of the way, and that I have put thee into such

eminent danger; pray, my brother, forgive me; I did not do it of an evil intent."

HOPE. "Be comforted, my brother, for I forgive thee, and believe, too, that this shall be for our good."

CHR. "I am glad I have with me a merciful brother. But we must not stand thus; let's try to go back again."

HOPE. "But, good brother, let me go before."

CHR. "No, if you please let me go first, that if there be any danger, I may be first therein, because by my means we are both gone out of the way."

HOPE. "No," said Hopeful, "you shall not go first, for your mind, being troubled, may lead you out of the way again." Then for their encouragement, they heard the voice of one, saying, "Let thine heart be towards the highway, even the way that thou wentest: turn again." [Jeremiah 31:21] But by this time the waters were greatly risen, by reason of which the way of going back was very dangerous. (Then I thought that it is easier going out of the way when we are in than going in when we are out.) Yet they adventured to go back; but it was so dark, and the flood was so high, that in their going back they had like to have been drowned nine or ten times.

Neither could they, with all the skill they had, get again to the stile that night. Wherefore, at last, lighting under a little shelter, they sat down there till the day brake; but being weary, they fell asleep. Now there was not far from the place where they lay a castle, called Doubting Castle, the owner whereof was Giant Despair, and it was in his grounds they now were sleeping; wherefore he getting up in the morning early, and walking up and down in his fields, caught Christian and Hopeful asleep in his grounds. Then with a grim and surly voice he bid them awake, and asked them whence they were and what they did in his grounds? They told him they were pilgrims and that they had lost their way. Then said the giant, "You have this night trespassed on me, by tram-

pling in and lying on my grounds, and therefore you must go along with me." So they were forced to go, because he was stronger than they. They also had but little to say, for they knew themselves in a fault. The giant therefore drove them before him and put them into his castle, into a very dark dungeon, nasty and stinking to the spirit of these two men. Here then they lay from Wednesday morning till Saturday night, without one bit of bread or drop of drink, or any light, or any to ask how they did. They were therefore here in evil case and were far from friends and acquaintance. Now in this place, Christian had double sorrow, because 'twas through his unadvised haste that they were brought into this distress.

Now Giant Despair had a wife, and her name was Diffidence. So when he was gone to bed, he told his wife what he had done, to wit, that he had taken a couple of prisoners and cast them into his dungeon for trespassing on his grounds. Then he asked her also what he had best to do further to them. So she asked him what they were, whence they came, and whither they were bound. And he told her. Then she counselled him that when he arose in the morning, he should beat them without any mercy. So when he arose, he getteth him a grievous crabtree cudgel and goes down into the dungeon to them; and there, first falls to rating of them as if they were dogs, although they gave him never a word of distaste; then he falls upon them, and beats them fearfully, in such sort, that they were not able to help themselves, or to turn them upon the floor. This done, he withdraws and leaves them, there to condole their misery and to mourn under their distress. So all that day they spent the time in nothing but sighs and bitter lamentations. The next night she talking with her husband about them further, and understanding that they were yet alive, did advise him to counsel them to make away themselves. So when morning was come, he goes to them in a surly manner, as before, and perceiving them to be very sore with the stripes that he had given them the day before, he told them that since they were never like to come out of that place, their only way would be forthwith to make an end of themselves, either with knife, halter or poison. "For why," said he, "should you choose life, seeing it is attended with so much bitterness." But they desired him to let them go; with that he looked ugly upon them, and rushing to them, had doubtless made an end of them himself, but that he fell into one of his fits (for he sometimes in sunshine weather fell into fits) and lost (for a time) the use of his hand. Wherefore he withdrew and left them (as before) to consider what to do. Then did the prisoners consult between themselves, whether 'twas best to take his counsel or no, and thus they began to discourse.

CHR. "Brother," said Christian, "what shall we do? The life that we now live is miserable. For my part, I know not whether is best to live thus or to die out of hand? My soul chooseth strangling rather than life, [Job 7:15] and the grave is more easy for me than this dungeon. Shall we be ruled by the giant?"

HOPE. "Indeed our present condition is dreadful, and death would be far more welcome to me than thus forever to abide. But yet let us consider; the Lord of the country to which we are going hath said thou shalt do no murder, no not to another man's person; much more then are we forbidden to take his counsel to kill ourselves. Besides, he that kills another can but commit murder upon his body; but for one to kill himself is to kill body and soul at once. And moreover, my brother, thou talkest of ease in the grave, but hast thou forgotten the hell whither, for certain, the murderers go? For no murderer hath eternal life, &c. And, let us consider again, that all the law is not in the hand of Giant Despair. Others, so far as I can understand, have been taken by him, as well as we, and yet have escaped out of his hand. Who knows, but that God that made the world may cause that Giant Despair may die, or that, at some time or other, he may forget to lock us in; or, but he may in short time

have another of his fits before us and may lose the use of his limbs, and if ever that should come to pass again, for my part, I am resolved to pluck up the heart of a man and to try my utmost to get from under his hand. I was a fool that I did not try to do it before. But, however, my brother, let's be patient, and endure awhile. The time may come that may give us a happy release, but let us not be our own murderers." With these words, Hopeful at present did moderate the mind of his brother; so they continued together (in the dark) that day, in their sad and doleful condition.

Well, towards evening the giant goes down into the dungeon again to see if his prisoners had taken his counsel; but when he came there, he found them alive, and, truly, alive was all. For now, what for want of bread and water, and by reason of the wounds they received when he beat them, they could do little but breathe. But, I say, he found them alive, at which he fell into a grievous rage and told them that seeing they had disobeyed his counsel, it should be worse with them than if they had never been born.

At this they trembled greatly, and I think that Christian fell into a swound; but coming a little to himself again, they renewed their discourse about the giant's counsel, and whether yet they had best to take it or no. Now Christian again seemed to be for doing it, but Hopeful made his second reply as followeth.

HOPE. "My brother," said he, "rememberest thou not how valiant thou hast been heretofore; Apollyon could not crush thee, nor could all that thou didst hear or see or feel in the Valley of the Shadow of Death; what hardship, terror, and amazement hast thou already gone through, and art thou now nothing but fear? Thou seest that I am in the dungeon with thee, a far weaker man by nature than thou art. Also this giant has wounded me as well as thee, and hath also cut off the bread and water from my mouth, and with thee I mourn without the light. But let's exercise a little more patience. Remember how thou playedst the man at Vanity Fair, and wast neither afraid of the chain nor cage, nor yet of bloody death. Wherefore let us (at least to avoid the shame that becomes not a Christian to be found in) bear up with patience as well as we can."

Now night being come again, and the giant and his wife being in bed, she asked him concerning the prisoners and if they had taken his counsel. To which he replied, "They are sturdy rogues. They choose rather to bear all hardship than to make away themselves." Then said she, "Take them into the castle-yard tomorrow, and show them the bones and skulls of those that thou hast already dispatched; and make them believe, e're a week comes to an end, thou also wilt tear them in pieces as thou hast done their fellows before them."

So when the morning was come, the giant goes to them again, and takes them into the castle-yard, and shows them, as his wife had bidden him. "These," said he, "were pilgrims as you are, once, and they trespassed in my grounds, as you have done; and when I thought fit, I tore them in pieces; and so within ten days I will do you. Go get you down to your den again." And with that he beat them all the way thither. They lay therefore all day on Saturday in a lamentable case, as before. Now when night was come, and when Mrs. Diffidence and her husband, the giant, were got to bed, they began to renew their discourse of their prisoners, and withal, the old giant wondered that he could neither by his blows, nor counsel, bring them to an end. And with that his wife replied, "I fear," said she, "that they live in hope that some will come to relieve them or that they have pick-locks about them, by the means of which they hope to escape." "And sayest thou so, my dear," said the giant, "I will therefore search them in the morning."

Well, on Saturday about midnight they began to pray and continued in prayer till almost break of day.

Now a little before it was day, good Christian, as one half amazed, brake out in this passionate speech, "What a fool," quoth he, "am I, thus to lie in a stinking dungeon, when I may as well walk at liberty? I have a key in my bosom, called Promise, that will (I am persuaded) open any lock in Doubting Castle." Then said Hopeful, "That's good news; good brother, pluck it out of thy bosom and try." Then Christian pulled it out of his bosom, and began to try at the dungeon door, whose bolt (as he turned the key) gave back, and the door flew open with ease, and Christian and Hopeful both came out. Then he went to the outward door that leads into the castle-yard, and with his key opened the door also. After he went to the iron gate, for that must be opened, too, but that lock went damnable hard; yet the key did open it. Then they thrust open the gate to make their escape with speed, but that gate, as it opened, made such a creaking that it waked Giant Despair, who, hastily rising to pursue his prisoners, felt his limbs to fail, for his fits took him again, so that he could by no means go after them. Then they went on and came to the King's highway again, and so were safe, because they were out of his jurisdiction.

Now when they were gone over the stile, they began to contrive with themselves what they should do at that stile to prevent those that should come after from falling into the hands of Giant Despair. So they consented to erect there a pillar and to engrave upon the side thereof, "Over that stile is the way to Doubting Castle, which is kept by Giant Despair, who despiseth the King of the Celestial Country, and seeks to destroy his holy pilgrims." Many therefore that followed after read what was written and escaped the danger. This done, they sang as follows,

Out of the way we went, and then we found
What 'twas to tread upon forbidden ground.
And let them that come after have a care,
Lest heedlessness makes them, as we, to fare;

Lest they, for trespassing, his prisoners are,
Whose Castle's Doubting, and whose name's
  Despair.

They went then till they came to the Delectable Mountains, which mountains belong to the Lord of that hill of which we have spoken before; so they went up to the mountains to behold the gardens and orchards, the vineyards, and fountains of water, where also they drank and washed themselves and did freely eat of the vineyards. Now there was on the tops of these mountains shepherds feeding their flocks, and they stood by the highway side. The pilgrims therefore went to them, and leaning upon their staves (as is common with weary pilgrims, when they stand to talk with any by the way), they asked, "Whose Delectable Mountains are these? And whose be the sheep that feed upon them?"

SHEP. "These mountains are Immanuel's Land, and they are within sight of his city, and the sheep also are his, and he laid down his life for them."

CHR. "Is this the way to the Celestial City?"

SHEP. "You are just in your way."

CHR. "How far is it thither?"

SHEP. "Too far for any, but those that shall get thither indeed."

CHR. "Is the way safe or dangerous?"

SHEP. "Safe for those for whom it is to be safe, 'but transgressors shall fall therein.' " [Hosea 14:9]

CHR. "Is there in this place any relief for pilgrims that are weary and faint in the way?"

SHEP. "The Lord of these mountains hath given us a charge, 'Not to be forgetful to entertain strangers.' [Hebrews 13:2] Therefore the good of the place is before you."

I saw also in my dream that when the shepherds perceived that they were wayfaring men, they also put questions to them (to which they made answer as in other places), as, whence came you, and how got you into the way, and by what means have you so persevered therein? For but few of them that begin to come hither do show their face on these mountains. But when the shepherds heard their answers, being pleased therewith, they looked very lovingly upon them, and said, "Welcome to the Delectable Mountains."

The shepherds, I say, whose names were Knowledge, Experience, Watchful, and Sincere, took them by the hand, and had them to their tents, and made them partake of that which was ready at present. They said moreover, "We would that you should stay here awhile, to acquaint with us and yet more to solace yourselves with the good of these Delectable Mountains." They then told them that they were content to stay, and so they went to their rest that night, because it was very late.

Then I saw in my dream that in the morning, the shepherds called up Christian and Hopeful to walk with them upon the mountains. So they went forth with them and walked awhile, having a pleasant prospect on every side. Then said the shepherds one to another, "Shall we show these pilgrims some wonders?" So when they had concluded to do it, they had them first to the top of an hill, called Error, which was very steep on the furthest side, and bid them look down to the bottom. So Christian and Hopeful looked down and saw at the bottom several men, dashed all to pieces by a fall that they had from the top. Then said Christian, "What meaneth this?" The shepherds answered, "Have you not heard of them that were made to err, by hearkening to Hymeneus and Philetus, as concerning the faith of the resurrection of the body?" They answered, "Yes." Then said the shepherds, "Those that you see lie dashed in pieces at the bottom of this mountain are they; and they have continued to this day unburied (as you see) for an example to others to take heed how they clamber too high, or how they come too near the brink of this mountain."

Then I saw that they had them to the

top of another mountain, and the name of that is Caution, and bid them look afar off. Which when they did, they perceived, as they thought, several men walking up and down among the tombs that were there. And they perceived that the men were blind, because they stumbled sometimes upon the tombs, and because they could not get out from among them. Then said Christian, "What means this?"

The shepherds then answered, "Did you not see a little below these mountains a stile that led into a meadow on the left hand of this way?" They answered, "Yes." Then said the shepherds, "From that stile there goes a path that leads directly to Doubting Castle, which is kept by Giant Despair; and these men (pointing to them among the tombs) came once on pilgrimage, as you do now, even till they came to that stile. And because the right way was rough in that place, they chose to go out of it into that meadow, and there were taken by Giant Despair, and cast into Doubting Castle, where, after they had awhile been kept in the dungeon, he at last did put out their eyes and led them among those tombs, where he has left them to wander to this very day, that the saying of the wise man might be fulfilled, 'He that wandereth out of the way of understanding shall remain in the congregation of the dead.'" [Proverbs 21:16] Then Christian and Hopeful looked one upon another, with tears gushing out, but yet said nothing to the shepherds.

Then I saw in my dream that the shepherds had them to another place, in a bottom, where was a door in the side of an hill; and they opened the door and bid them look in. They looked in therefore and saw that within it was very dark and smoky; they also thought that they heard there a lumbering noise as of fire and a cry of some tormented and that they smelt the scent of brimstone. Then said Christian, "What means this?" The shepherds told them, saying, "This is a by-way to hell, a way that hypocrites go in at; namely, such as sell their birthright, with Esau; such as

sell their Master, with Judas; such as blaspheme the Gospel, with Alexander; and that lie and dissemble, with Ananias and Sapphira his wife."

HOPE. Then said Hopeful to the shepherds, "I perceive that these had on them, even everyone, a show of pilgrimage as we have now. Had they not?"

SHEP. "Yes, and held it a long time, too."

HOPE. "How far might they go on pilgrimage in their day, since they notwithstanding were thus miserably cast away?"

SHEP. "Some further, and some not so far as these mountains."

Then said the pilgrims one to another, "We had need cry to the strong for strength."

SHEP. "Ay, and you will have need to use it when you have it, too."

By this time the pilgrims had a desire to go forwards, and the shepherds a desire they should; so they walked together towards the end of the mountains. Then said the shepherds one to another, "Let us here show to the pilgrims the gates of the Celestial City, if they have skill to look through our perspective glass." The pilgrims then lovingly accepted the motion. So they had them to the top of an high hill called Clear, and gave them their glass to look. Then they essayed to look, but the remembrance of that last thing that the shepherds had showed them made their hands shake; by means of which impediment they could not look steadily through the glass, yet they thought they saw something like the gate and also some of the glory of the place. Then they went away and sang,

Thus by the shepherds secrets are revealed
Which from all other men are kept concealed.
Come to the shepherds, then, if you would see
Things deep, things hid, and that
mysterious be.

When they were about to depart, one of the shepherds gave them a note of the way. Another of them bid them beware of the flatterer. The third bid them take heed that they sleep not upon the Enchanted Ground. And the fourth bid them God-speed. So I awoke from my dream.

And I slept and dreamed again and saw the same two pilgrims going down the mountains along the highway towards the city. Now a little below these mountains, on the left hand, lieth the country of Conceit; from which country there comes into the way in which the pilgrims walked a little crooked lane. Here therefore they met with a very brisk lad that came out of that country; and his name was Ignorance. So Christian asked him from what parts he came and whither he was going.

IGN. "Sir, I was born in the country that lieth off there, a little on the left hand; and I am going to the Celestial City."

CHR. "But how do you think to get in at the gate, for you may find some difficulty there?"

IGN. "As other good people do," said he.

CHR. "But what have you to show at that gate that may cause that the gate should be opened unto you?"

IGN. "I know my Lord's will, and I have been a good liver, I pay every man his own; I pray, fast, pay tithes, and give alms, and have left my country for whither I am going."

CHR. "But thou camest not in at the wicket-gate, that is, at the head of this way. Thou camest in hither through that same crooked lane, and therefore I fear, however thou mayest think of thyself, when the reckoning day shall come, thou wilt have laid to thy charge that thou art a thief and a robber, instead of getting admittance into the city."

IGN. "Gentlemen, ye be utter strangers to me. I know you not. Be content to follow the religion of your country, and I will follow the religion of mine. I hope all will be well. And as for the gate that you talk of, all the world knows that that is a great way off of our country. I cannot think that any man in all our parts doth so much as know the way to it; nor need they matter whether they do or no, since we have, as you see, a fine pleasant, green lane that comes down from our country the next way into it."

When Christian saw that the man was wise in his own conceit, he said to Hopeful, whisperingly, "There is more hope of a fool than of him." [Proverbs 26:12] And said moreover, "When he that is a fool walketh by the way, his wisdom faileth him, and he saith to everyone that he is a fool [Ecclesiastes 10:3] What, shall we talk further with him, or outgo him at present, and so leave him to think of what he hath heard already, and then stop again for him afterwards and see if by degrees we can do any good of him?" Then said Hopeful,

Let Ignorance a little while now muse
On what is said, and let him not refuse
Good counsel to embrace, lest he remain
Still ignorant of what's the chiefest gain.
God saith those that no understanding have
(Although he made them), them he will not
*   save.*

HOPE. He further added, "It is not good, I think, to say all to him at once. Let us pass him by, if you will, and talk to him anon, even as he is able to bear it."

So they both went on, and Ignorance he came after. Now when they had passed him a little way, they entered into a very dark lane, where they met a man whom seven devils had bound with seven strong cords, and were carrying of him back to the door that they saw in the side of the hill. Now good Christian began to tremble, and so did Hopeful his companion. Yet as the devils led away the man, Christian looked to see if he knew him, and he thought it might be one Turnaway that dwelt in the town of Apostasy. But he did not perfectly see his face, for he did hang his head like a thief that is found. But being gone past, Hopeful looked after him, and espied on his back a paper with this inscription, "Wanton professor and damnable apostate." Then said Christian to his fellow, "Now I call to remembrance that which was told me of a thing that happened to a good man hereabout. The name of the man was Little-faith, but a good man, and he dwelt in the town of Sincere. The thing was this: at the entering in of this passage there comes down from Broadway Gate, a lane, called Dead Man's Lane, so called because of the murders that are commonly done there. And this Little-faith going on pilgrimage, as we do now, chanced to sit down there and slept. Now there happened at that time to come down that lane from Broadway Gate three sturdy rogues, and their names were Faint-heart, Mistrust, and Guilt (three brothers), and they, espying Little-faith where he was, came galloping up with speed. Now the good man was just awaked from his sleep, and was getting up to go on his journey. So they came all up to him, and with threatening language bid him stand. At this Little-faith looked as white as a clout, and had neither power to fight nor fly. Then said Faint-heart, 'Deliver thy purse.' But he making no haste to do it (for he was loth to lose his money), Mistrust ran up to him, and thrusting his hand into his pocket, pulled out thence a bag of silver. Then he cried out, 'Thieves, thieves.' With that Guilt, with a great club that was in his hand, struck Little-faith on the head, and with that blow felled him flat to the ground, where he lay bleeding as one that would bleed to death. All this while the thieves stood by. But at last, they hearing that some were upon the road and fearing lest it should be one Great-grace that dwells in the city of Good-confidence, they betook themselves to their heels, and left this good man to shift for himself. Now after a while, Little-faith came to himself, and getting up, made shift to scrabble on his way. This was the story."

HOPE. "But did they take from him all that ever he had?"

CHR. "No. The place where his jewels were they never ransacked, so those he kept still; but, as I was told, the good man was much afflicted for his loss. For the thieves got most of his spending money. That which they got not (as I said) were jewels; also he had a little odd money left, but scarce enough to bring him to his journey's end; nay (if I was not misinformed), he was forced to beg as he went to keep himself alive (for his jewels he might not sell). But beg and do what he could, he went (as we say) with many a hungry belly the most part of the rest of the way."

HOPE. "But is it not a wonder they got not from him his certificate, by which he was to receive his admittance at the Celestial Gate?"

CHR. " 'Tis a wonder but they got not that, though they missed it not through any good cunning of his, for he being dismayed with their coming upon him had neither power nor skill to hide anything; so 'twas more by good providence than by his endeavour that they missed of that good thing." [2 Timothy 1:14]

HOPE. "But it must needs be a comfort to him that they got not this jewel from him."

CHR. "It might have been great comfort to him had he used it as he should; but they that told me the story said that he made but little use of it all the rest of the way; and that because of the dismay that he had in their taking away his money, indeed he forgot it a great part of the rest of the journey; and besides, when at any time, it came into his mind, and he began to be comforted therewith, then would fresh thoughts of his loss come again upon him, and those thoughts would swallow up all."

HOPE. "Alas, poor man! This could not but be a great grief unto him."

CHR. "Grief! Ay, a grief indeed! Would it not a been so to any of us had we been used as he: to be robbed and wounded, too, and that in a strange place, as he was? 'Tis a wonder he did not die with grief, poor heart! I was told that he scattered almost all the rest of the way with nothing but doleful and bitter complaints. Telling also to all that overtook him, or that he overtook in the way as he went, where he was robbed and how, who they were that did it and what he lost, how he was wounded and that he hardly escaped with life."

HOPE. "But 'tis a wonder that his necessities did not put him upon selling or pawning some of his jewels that he might have wherewith to relieve himself in his journey."

CHR. "Thou talkest like one upon whose head is the shell to this very day. For what should he pawn them, or to whom should he sell them? In all that country where he was robbed, his jewels were not accounted of, nor did he want that relief which could from thence be administered to him; besides, had his jewels been missing at the gate of the Celestial City, he had (and that he knew well enough) been excluded from an inheritance there; and that would have been worse to him than the appearance and villainy of ten thousand thieves."

HOPE. "Why art thou so tart, my brother? Esau sold his birthright, and that for a mess of pottage, and that birthright was his greatest jewel. And if he, why might not Little-faith do so too?"

CHR. "Esau did sell his birthright indeed, and so do many besides; and by so doing, exclude themselves from the chief blessing, as also that Caitiff did. But you must put a difference betwixt Esau and Little-faith, and also betwixt their estates. Esau's birthright was typical,* but Little-faith's jewels were not so. Esau's belly was his god, but Little-faith's belly was not so. Esau's want lay in his fleshly appetite, Little-faith's did not so. Besides, Esau could see no further than to the fulfilling of his lusts. 'For I am at the point to die,' said he, 'and what good will this birthright do me?' But Little-faith, though it was his lot to have but a little faith, was by his little faith kept from such extravagancies, and made to see and prize his jewels more than to sell them, as Esau did his birthright. You read not anywhere that Esau had faith, no, not so much as a little. Therefore no marvel, if where the flesh only bears sway (as it will in that

man where no faith is to resist), if he sells his birthright and his soul and all, and that to the Devil of hell; for it is with such as it is with the ass who in her occasions cannot be turned away. When their minds are set upon their [Jeremiah 2:24] lusts, they will have them whatever they cost. But Little-faith was of another temper; his mind was on things divine; his livelihood was upon things that were spiritual and from above. Therefore to what end should he that is of such a temper sell his jewels (had there been any that would have bought them) to fill his mind with empty things? Will a man give a penny to fill his belly with hay? Or can you persuade the turtle-dove to live upon carrion, like the crow? Though faithless ones can for carnal lusts, pawn, or mortgage, or sell what they have, and themselves outright to boot; yet they that have faith, saving faith, though but a little of it, cannot do so. Here therefore, my brother, is thy mistake."

HOPE. "I acknowledge it; but yet your severe reflection had almost made me angry."

CHR. "Why, I did but compare thee to some of the birds that are of the brisker sort, who will run to and fro in untrodden paths with the shell upon their heads. But pass by that, and consider the matter under debate, and all shall be well betwixt thee and me."

HOPE. "But, Christian, these three fellows, I am persuaded in my heart, are but a company of cowards. Would they have run else, think you, as they did, at the noise of one that was coming on the road? Why did not Little-faith pluck up a greater heart? He might, methinks, have stood one brush with them, and have yielded when there had been no remedy."

CHR. "That they are cowards, many have said, but few have found it so in the time of trial. As for a great heart, Little-faith had none; and I perceive by thee, my brother, hadst thou been the man concerned, thou

—————
*Symbolic, emblematic.

art but for a brush and then to yield. And verily, since this is the height of thy stomach,* now they are at a distance from us, should they appear to thee, as they did to him, they might put thee to second thoughts.

"But consider again: they are but journeymen thieves; they serve under the king of the bottomless pit, who, if need be, will come in to their aid himself, and his voice is as the roaring of a lion. [I Peter 5:8] I myself have been engaged as this Little-faith was, and I found it a terrible thing. These three villains set upon me, and I beginning like a Christian to resist, they gave but a call and in came their master. I would, as the saying is, have given my life for a penny, but that, as God would have it, I was clothed with armour of proof. Ay, and yet, though I was so harnessed, I found it hard work to quit myself like a man; no man can tell what in that combat attends us, but he that hath been in the battle himself."

HOPE. "Well, but they ran, you see, when they did but suppose that one Great-grace was in the way."

CHR. "True, they often fled, both they and their master, when Great-grace hath but appeared; and no marvel, for he is the King's champion. But, I trow, you will put some difference between Little-faith and the King's champion. All the King's subjects are not his champions; nor can they, when tried, do such feats of war as he. Is it meet to think that a little child should handle Goliath as David did? Or that there should be the strength of an ox in a wren? Some are strong, some are weak, some have great faith, some have little. This man was one of the weak, and therefore he went to the walls."

HOPE. "I would it had been Great-grace for their sakes."

CHR. "If it had been he, he might have had his hands full. For I must tell you, that though Great-grace is excellent good at his weapons, and has, and can, so long as he keeps them at sword's point, do well enough with them, yet if they get within him, even Faint-heart, Mistrust, or the other, it shall go hard, but they will throw up his heels. And when a man is down, you know, what can he do?

"Who so looks well upon Great-grace's face shall see those scars and cuts there that shall easily give demonstration of what I say. Yet, once I heard he should say† (and that when he was in the combat), "We despaired even of life." [2 Corinthians 1:8] How did these sturdy rogues and their fellows make David groan, mourn, and roar? Yea, Heman and Hezekiah, too, though champions in their day, were forced to bestir them, when by these assaulted, and yet, that notwithstanding, they had their coats soundly brushed by them. Peter upon a time would go try what he could do; but, though some do say of him that he is the prince of the apostles, they handled him so that they made him at last afraid of a sorry girl.‡

"Besides, their king is at their whistle. He is never out of hearing, and if at any time they be put to the worst, he, if possible, comes in to help them. And, of him it is said, 'The sword of him that layeth at him cannot hold: the spear, the dart, nor the habergeon. He esteemeth iron as straw, and brass as rotten wood. The arrow cannot make him flee: slingstones are turned with him into stubble. Darts are counted as stubble: he laugheth at the shaking of a spear.' [Job 41:26–29] What can a man do in this case? 'Tis true, if a man could at every turn have Job's horse, and had skill and courage to ride him, he might do notable things. 'For his neck is clothed with thunder. He will not be afraid as the grasshopper. The glory of his nostrils is terrible. He paweth in the valley, rejoiceth in his strength, and goeth out to meet the

---

*Valor, bravery.
†Once he is reported to have said.
‡Cf. Matthew 26:69–72 and Luke 22:56–57.

armed men. He mocketh at fear, and is not affrighted, neither turneth back from the sword. The quiver rattleth against him, the glittering spear, and the shield. He swalloweth the ground with fierceness and rage, neither believeth he that it is the sound of the trumpet. He saith among the trumpets, 'Ha, ha,' and he smelleth the battle afar off, the thundering of the captains, and the shoutings.' [Job 39:19–25]

"But for such footmen as thee and I are, let us never desire to meet with an enemy, nor vaunt as if we could do better, when we hear of others that they have been foiled, nor be tickled at the thoughts of our own manhood, for such commonly come by the worst when tried. Witness Peter, of whom I made mention before. He would swagger; ay, he would. He would, as his vain mind prompted him to say, do better and stand more for his Master than all men. But who so foiled and run down with these villains as he?

"When therefore we hear that such robberies are done on the King's highway, two things become us to do: first, to go out harnessed, and to be sure to take a shield with us. For it was for want of that that he that laid so lustily at Leviathan could not make him yield. For indeed, if that be wanting, he fears us not at all. Therefore he that had skill hath said, 'Above all take the shield of faith, wherewith ye shall be able to quench all the fiery darts of the wicked.' [Ephesians 6:16]

" 'Tis good also that we desire of the King a convoy, yea, that he will go with us himself. This made David rejoice when in the Valley of the Shadow of Death; and Moses was rather for dying where he stood than to go one step without his God. O, my brother, if he will but go along with us, what need we be afraid of ten thousands that shall set themselves against us? But without him, 'the proud helpers fall under the slain.' [Psalms 3:6, Job 9:13, Isaiah 10:4]

"I, for my part, have been in the fray before now, and though (through the goodness of him that is best) I am, as you see, alive. Yet I cannot boast of my manhood. Glad shall I be, if I meet with no more such brunts, though I fear we are not got beyond all danger. However, since the lion and the bear hath not as yet devoured me, I hope God will also deliver us from the next uncircumcised Philistine." Then sang Christian,

*Poor Little-faith! Hast been among
  the thieves!
Wast robbed! Remember this, who so believes
And gets more faith shall then a victor be
Over ten thousand, else scarce over three.*

So they went on, and Ignorance followed. They went then till they came at a place where they saw a way put itself into their way, and seemed withal to lie as straight as the way which they should go; and here they knew not which of the two to take, for both seemed straight before them. Therefore here they stood still to consider. And as they were thinking about the way, behold, a man black of flesh, but covered with a very light robe, came to them, and asked them why they stood there. They answered they were going to the Celestial City, but knew not which of these ways to take. "Follow me," said the man. "It is thither that I am going." So they followed him in the way that but now came into the road, which by degrees turned and turned them so from the city that they desired to go to that in little time their faces were turned away from it; yet they followed him. But by and by, before they were aware, he led them both within the compass of a net, in which they were both so entangled that they knew not what to do; and with that the white robe fell off the black man's back. Then they saw where they were. Wherefore there they lay crying some time, for they could not get themselves out.

CHR. Then said Christian to his fellow, "Now do I see myself in an error. Did not the shepherds bid us beware of the flatterers? As is the saying of the wise man, so we have found it this day, 'A man that flattereth his neighbour spreadeth a net for his feet.'" [Proverbs 29:5]

HOPE. "They also gave us a note of directions about the way, for our more sure finding thereof. But therein we have also forgotten to read, and have not kept ourselves from the paths of the destroyer. Here David was wiser than we; for saith he, 'Concerning the works of men, by the word of thy lips I have kept me from the paths of the destroyer.'" [Psalms 17:4] Thus they lay bewailing themselves in the net. At last they espied a Shining One coming towards them, with a whip of small cord in his hand. When he was come to the place where they were, he asked them whence they came and what they did there. They told him that they were poor pilgrims, going to Zion, but were led out of their way by a black man, clothed in white, who bid us, said they, follow him, for he was going thither too. Then said he with the whip, "It is Flatterer, a false apostle, that hath transformed himself into an angel of light." So he rent the net and let the men out. Then said he to them, "Follow me, that I may set you in your way again." So he led them back to the way, which they had left to follow the Flatterer. Then he asked them, saying, "Where did you lie the last night?" They said, "With the shepherds upon the Delectable Mountains." He asked them then if they had not of them shepherds a note of direction for the way? They answered, "Yes." "But did you," said he, "when you was at a stand, pluck out and read your note?" They answered, "No." He asked them why. They said they forgot. He asked moreover if the shepherds did not bid them beware of the Flatterer? They answered, "Yes. But we did not imagine," said they, "that this fine-spoken man had been he."

Then I saw in my dream that he commanded them to lie down; which when they did, he chastised them sore, to teach them the good way wherein they should walk. And as he chastised them, he said, "As many as I love, I rebuke and chasten; he zealous therefore, and repent." [Revelation 3:19] This done, he bids them go on their way and take good heed to the other directions of the shepherds. So they thanked him for all his kindness, and went softly along the right way, singing,

Come hither, you that walk along the way;
See how the pilgrims fare that go astray!
They catched are in an entangling net,
'Cause they good counsel lightly did forget.
'Tis true, they rescued were, but yet you see
They're scourged to boot. Let this your
caution be.

Now after a while, they perceived afar off one coming softly and alone all along the highway to meet them. Then said Christian to his fellow, "Yonder is a man with his back toward Zion, and he is coming to meet us."

HOPE. "I see him. Let us take heed to ourselves now, lest he should prove a flatterer also." So he drew nearer and nearer, and at last came up unto them. His name was Atheist, and he asked them whither they were going.

CHR. "We are going to the Mount Zion."

Then Atheist fell into a very great laughter.

CHR. "What is the meaning of your laughter?"

ATHEIST. "I laugh to see what ignorant persons you are, to take upon you so tedious a journey; and yet are like to have nothing but your travel for your pains."

CHR. "Why, man? Do you think we shall not be received?"

ATHEIST. "Received! There is no such place as you dream of in all this world."

CHR. "But there is in the world to come."

ATHEIST. "When I was at home in mine own country, I heard as you now affirm, and from that hearing went out to see, and have been seeking this city this twenty years. But find no more of it than I did the first day I set out."

CHR. "We have both heard and believed that there is such a place to be found."

ATHEIST. "Had not I, when at home, believed, I had not come thus far to seek. But finding none (and yet I should, had there been such a place to be found, for I have gone to seek it further than you), I am going back again, and will seek to refresh myself with the things that I then cast away, for hopes of that which, I now see, is not."

CHR. Then said Christian to Hopeful, his fellow, "Is it true which this man hath said?"

HOPE. "Take heed; he is one of the flatterers; remember what it hath cost us once already for our hearkening to such kind of fellows. What! No Mount Zion? Did we not see from the Delectable Mountains the gate of the city? Also, are we not now to walk by faith? Let us go on," said Hopeful, "lest the man with the whip overtakes us again.

"You should have taught me that lesson, which I will round you in the ears* withal, 'Cease, my son, to hear the instruction that causeth to err from the words of knowledge.' [Proverbs 19:27] I say, my brother, cease to hear him, and let us believe to the saving of the soul." [Hebrews 10:39]

CHR. "My brother, I did not put the question to thee for that I doubted of the truth of our belief myself, but to prove thee, and to fetch from thee a fruit of the honesty of thy heart. As for this man, I know that he is blinded by the god of this world. Let thee and I go on knowing that we have belief of the truth, and no lie is of the truth." [I John 2:21]

HOPE. "Now do I rejoice in hope of the glory of God." So they turned away from the man, and he, laughing at them, went his way.

I saw then in my dream that they went till they came into a certain country, whose air naturally tended to make one drowsy, if he came a stranger into it. And here Hopeful began to be very dull and heavy of sleep, wherefore he said unto Christian, "I do now begin to grow so drowsy, that I can scarcely hold up mine eyes; let us lie down here and take one nap."

CHR. "By no means," said the other, "lest sleeping, we never awake more."

HOPE. "Why, my brother? Sleep is sweet to the labouring man; we may be refreshed if we take a nap."

CHR. "Do you not remember that one of the shepherds bid us beware of the Enchanted Ground? He meant by that that we should beware of sleeping; wherefore let us not sleep as do others, but let us watch and be sober." [I Thessalonians 5:6]

HOPE. "I acknowledge myself in a fault, and had I been here alone, I had by sleeping run the danger of death. I see it is true that the wise man saith, 'Two are better than one.' [Ecclesiastes 4:9] Hitherto hath thy company been my mercy, and thou shalt have a good reward for thy labour."

CHR. "Now then," said Christian, "to prevent drowsiness in this place, let us fall into good discourse."

HOPE. "With all my heart," said the other.

CHR. "Where shall we begin?"

HOPE. "Where God began with us. But do you begin if you please."

*When saints do sleepy grow, let them come
  hither,
And hear how these two pilgrims talk
  together.
Yea, let them learn of them in any wise
Thus to keep ope their drowsy slumbering
  eyes.*

---

*Whisper to you.

Saints' fellowship, if it be managed well,
Keeps them awake, and that in spite of hell.

CHR. Then Christian began and said, "I will ask you a question. How came you to think at first of doing as you do now?"

HOPE. "Do you mean, how came I at first to look after the good of my soul?"

CHR. "Yes, that is my meaning."

HOPE. "I continued a great while in the delight of those things which were seen and sold at our fair; things which, as I believe now, would have (had I continued in them still) drowned me in perdition and destruction."

CHR. "What things were they?"

HOPE. "All the treasures and riches of the world. Also I delighted much in ri-oting, revelling, drinking, swearing, lying, uncleanness, Sabbath-breaking, and what not, that tended to destroy the soul. But I found at last, by hearing and considering of things that are divine, which indeed I heard of you, as also of beloved Faithful that was put to death for his faith and good living in Vanity Fair, 'That the end of these things is death.' [Romans 6:21] And that for these things' sake the wrath of God cometh 'upon the children of dis-obedience.' " [Ephesians 5:6]

CHR. "And did you presently fall under the power of this conviction?"

HOPE. "No, I was not willing presently to know the evil of sin, nor the damnation that follows upon the commission of it, but endeavoured, when my mind at first began to be shaken with the Word, to shut mine eyes against the light thereof."

CHR. "But what was the cause of your carrying of it thus to the first workings of God's blessed Spirit upon you?"

HOPE. "The causes were, 1. I was igno-rant that this was the work of God upon me. I never thought that by awakenings for sin, God at first begins the conversion of a sinner. 2. Sin was yet very sweet to my flesh, and I was loath to leave it. 3. I could not tell how to part with mine

old companions, their presence and actions were so desirable unto me. 4. The hours in which convictions were upon me were such troublesome and such heart-affright-ing hours that I could not bear, no not so much as the remembrance of them upon my heart."

CHR. "Then, as it seems, sometimes you got rid of your trouble."

HOPE. "Yes, verily, but it would come into my mind again; and then I should be as bad, nay worse, than I was before."

CHR. "Why, what was it that brought your sins to mind again?"

HOPE. "Many things, as,

1. If I did but meet a good man in the streets; or,

2. If I have heard any read in the Bible; or,

3. If mine head did begin to ache; or,

4. If I were told that some of my neigh-bours were sick; or,

5. If I heard the bell toll for some that were dead; or,

6. If I thought of dying myself; or,

7. If I heard that sudden death hap-pened to others;

8. But especially, when I thought of myself, that I must quickly come to judge-ment."

CHR. "And could you at any time with ease get off the guilt of sin when by any of these ways it came upon you?"

HOPE. "No, not latterly, for then they got faster hold of my conscience. And then, if I did but think of going back to sin (though my mind was turned against it) it would be double torment to me."

CHR. "And how did you do then?"

HOPE. "I thought I must endeavour to mend my life, for else, thought I, I am sure to be damned."

CHR. "And did you endeavour to mend?"

HOPE. "Yes, and fled from, not only my sins, but sinful company, too, and betook me to religious duties, as praying, read-ing, weeping for sin, speaking truth to my neighbours, &c. These things I did, with many others, too much here to relate."

CHR. "And did you think yourself well then?"

HOPE. "Yes, for a while; but at the last my trouble came tumbling upon me again, and that over the neck of all my reformations."

CHR. "How came that about, since you was now reformed?"

HOPE. "There were several things brought it upon me, especially such sayings as these, 'All our righteousnesses are as filthy rags.' 'By the works of the law no man shall be justified.' 'When you have done all things, say we are unprofitable,' [Isaiah 64:6; Galatians 2:16; Luke 17:10] with many more the like. From whence I began to reason with myself thus: if all my righteousnesses are filthy rags, if by the deeds of the law, no man can be justified, and, if when we have done all, we are yet unprofitable, then 'tis but a folly to think of heaven by the law. I further thought thus: If a man runs an 100 pounds into the shopkeeper's debt, and after that shall pay for all that he shall fetch, yet his old debt stands still in the book uncrossed; for the which the shopkeeper may sue him, and cast him into prison till he shall pay the debt."

CHR. "Well, and how did you apply this to yourself?"

HOPE. "Why, I thought thus with myself. I have by my sins run a great way into God's book, and that my now reforming will not pay off that score; therefore I should think still under all my present amendments. But how shall I be freed from that damnation that I have brought myself in danger of by my former transgressions?"

CHR. "A very good application. But pray go on."

HOPE. "Another thing that hath troubled me, even since my late amendments, is that if I look narrowly into the best of what I do now, I still see sin, new sin, mixing itself with the best of that I do. So that now I am forced to conclude that notwithstanding my former fond conceits of myself and duties, I have committed sin enough in one duty to send me to hell, though my former life had been faultless."

CHR. "And what did you do then?"

HOPE. "Do! I could not tell what to do, till I brake my mind to Faithful, for he and I were well acquainted. And he told me that unless I could obtain the righteousness of a man that never had sinned, neither mine own nor all the righteousness of the world could save me."

CHR. "And did you think he spake true?"

HOPE. "Had he told me so when I was pleased and satisfied with mine own amendments, I had called him fool for his pains: but now, since I see my own infirmity, and the sin that cleaves to my best performance, I have been forced to be of his opinion."

CHR. "But did you think, when at first he suggested it to you, that there was such a man to be found, of whom it might justly be said that he never committed sin?"

HOPE. "I must confess the words at first sounded strangely, but after a little more talk and company with him, I had full conviction about it."

CHR. "And did you ask him what man this was, and how you must be justified by him?"

HOPE. "Yes, and he told me it was the Lord Jesus, that dwelleth on the right hand of the Most High. And thus, said he, you must be justified by him, even by trusting to what he hath done by himself in the days of his flesh, and suffered when he did hang on the tree. I asked him further how that man's righteousness could be of that efficacy, to justify another before God? And he told me he was the mighty God, and did what he did, and died the death also, not for himself, but for me, to whom his doings and the worthiness of them should be imputed, if I believed on him."

CHR. "And what did you do then?"

HOPE. "I made my objections against my believing, for that I thought he was not willing to save me."

CHR. "And what said Faithful to you then?"

HOPE. "He bid me go to him and see. Then I said it was presumption, but he said no, for I was invited to come. Then he gave me a book of Jesus his inditing, to encourage me the more freely to come. And he said concerning that book that every jot and tittle thereof stood firmer than heaven and earth. Then I asked him what I must do when I came. And he told me I must entreat upon my knees with all my heart and soul the Father to reveal him to me. Then I asked him further how I must make my supplication to him. And he said go and thou shalt find him upon a mercy-seat, where he sits all the year long to give pardon and forgiveness to them that come. I told him that I knew not what to say when I came, and he bid me say to this effect, 'God, be merciful to me, a sinner, and make me to know and believe in Jesus Christ; for I see that if his righteousness had not been, or I have not faith in that righteousness, I am utterly cast away. Lord, I have heard that Thou art a merciful God, and hast ordained that Thy Son Jesus Christ should be the Saviour of the world; and, moreover, that Thou art willing to bestow Him upon such a poor sinner as I am (and I am a sinner indeed). Lord, take therefore this opportunity, and magnify Thy grace in the salvation of my soul, through Thy Son Jesus Christ. Amen.' "

CHR. "And did you do as you were bidden?"

HOPE. "Yes, over, and over, and over."

CHR. "And did the Father reveal His Son to you?"

HOPE. "Not at the first, nor second, nor third, nor fourth, nor fifth; no, nor at the sixth time neither."

CHR. "What did you do then?"

HOPE. "What! Why I could not tell what to do."

CHR. "Had you not thoughts of leaving off praying?"

HOPE. "Yes, an hundred times, twice told."

CHR. "And what was the reason you did not?"

HOPE. "I believed that that was true which had been told me, to wit, that without the righteousness of this Christ, all the world could not save me. And therefore thought I with myself, if I leave off, I die; and I can but die at the throne of grace. And withal, this came into my mind, 'If it tarry, wait for it, because it will surely come, and will not tarry.' [Habukkuk 2:3] So I continued praying until the Father showed me His Son."

CHR. "And how was he revealed unto you?"

HOPE. "I did not see him with my bodily eyes, but with the eyes of mine understanding; and thus it was. One day I was very sad, I think sadder than at any one time in my life; and this sadness was through a fresh sight of the greatness and vileness of my sins. And as I was then looking for nothing but hell, and the everlasting damnation of my soul, suddenly, as I thought, I saw the Lord Jesus look down from heaven upon me, and saying, 'Believe on the Lord Jesus Christ, and thou shalt be saved.' " [Acts 16:31]

"But I replied, 'Lord, I am a great, a very great sinner,' and he answered, 'My grace is sufficient for thee.' [2 Corinthians 12:9] Then I said, 'But, Lord, what is believing?' And then I saw from that saying, 'He that cometh to me shall never hunger, and he that believeth on me shall never thirst,' [John 6:35] that believing and coming was all one, and that he that came, that is, run out in his heart and affections after salvation by Christ, he indeed believed in Christ. Then the water stood in mine eyes, and I asked further, 'But Lord, may such a great sinner as I am be indeed accepted of thee, and be saved by thee?' And I heard him say, 'And him that cometh to me, I will in no wise cast out.' [John 6:37] Then I said, 'But how, Lord, must I consider of thee in my coming to thee, that my faith may be placed aright upon thee?' Then he said, 'Christ Jesus came into the world to save sinners. He is the end of the law for righteousness to everyone that believes. He died for our sins, and rose again for our justification. He loved us, and washed us from our sins in his own blood. He is mediator between God and us. He ever liveth to make intercession for us.' [I Timothy 1:15; Romans 10:4, 4:25; Revelation 1:5; I Timothy 2:5; Hebrews 7:25] From all which I gathered that I must look for righteousness in his person and for satisfaction for my sins by his blood; that what he did in obedience to his Father's law and in submitting to the penalty thereof was not for himself, but for him that will accept it for his salvation and be thankful. And now was my heart full of joy, mine eyes full of tears, and mine affections running over with love, to the name, people, and ways of Jesus Christ."

CHR. "This was a revelation of Christ to your soul indeed. But tell me particularly what effect this had upon your spirit?"

HOPE. "It made me see that all the world, notwithstanding all the righteousness thereof, is in a state of condemnation. It made me see that God the Father though he be just, can justly justify the coming sinner. It made me greatly ashamed of the vileness of my former life and confounded me with the sense of mine own ignorance. For there never came thought into mine heart before now that showed me so the beauty of Jesus Christ. It made me love a holy life, and long to do something for the honour and glory of the name of the Lord Jesus. Yea, I thought, that had I now a thousand gallons of blood in my body, I could spill it all for the sake of the Lord Jesus."

I then saw in my dream that Hopeful looked back and saw Ignorance, whom they had left behind, coming after. "Look," said he to Christian, "how far yonder youngster loitereth behind."

CHR. "Ay, ay, I see him; he careth not for our company."

HOPE. "But, I trow, it would not have hurt him, had he kept pace with us hitherto."

CHR. "That's true, but I warrant you he thinketh otherwise."

HOPE. "That I think he doth, but, however, let us tarry for him." So they did.

Then Christian said to him, "Come away, man, why do you stay so behind?"

IGN. "I take my pleasure in walking alone, even more a great deal than in company, unless I like it the better."

Then said Christian to Hopeful (but softly), "Did I not tell you he cared not for our company. But, however, come up and let us talk away the time in this solitary place." Then directing his speech to Ignorance, he said, "Come, how do you? How stands it between God and your soul now?"

IGN. "I hope well, for I am always full of good motions that come into my mind to comfort me as I walk."

CHR. "What good motions? Pray tell us."

IGN. "Why, I think of God and Heaven."

CHR. "So do the devils and damned souls."

IGN. "But I think of them, and desire them."

CHR. "So do many that are never like to come there. The soul of the sluggard desires and hath nothing." [Proverbs 13:4]

IGN. "But I think of them, and leave all for them."

CHR. "That I doubt, for leaving of all is an hard matter, yea, a harder matter than many are aware of. But why, or by what, art thou persuaded that thou hast left all for God and heaven?"

IGN. "My heart tells me so."

CHR. "The wise man says, 'He that trusts his own heart is a fool.' " [Proverbs 28:26]

IGN. "That is spoken of an evil heart, but mine is a good one."

CHR. "But how dost thou prove that?"

IGN. "It comforts me in the hopes of Heaven."

CHR. "That may be through its deceitfulness, for a man's heart may minister comfort to him in the hopes of that thing for which he yet has no ground to hope."

IGN. "But my heart and life agree together, and therefore my hope is well grounded."

CHR. "Who told thee that thy heart and life agrees together?"

IGN. "My heart tells me so."

CHR. "Ask my fellow if I be a thief! Thy heart tells thee so! Except the word of God beareth witness in this matter, other testimony is of no value."

IGN. "But is it not a good heart that has good thoughts? And is not that a good life that is according to God's commandments?"

CHR. "Yes, that is a good heart that hath good thoughts, and that is a good life that is according to God's commandments. But it is one thing indeed to have these, and another thing only to think so."

IGN. "Pray, what count you good thoughts and a life according to God's commandments?"

CHR. "There are good thoughts of divers kinds, some respecting ourselves, some God, some Christ, and some other things."

IGN. "What be good thoughts respecting ourselves?"

CHR. "Such as agree with the Word of God."

IGN. "When does our thoughts of ourselves agree with the Word of God?"

CHR. "When we pass the same judgement upon ourselves which the Word passes. To explain myself: the Word of God saith of persons in a natural condition, 'There is none righteous, there is none that doeth good.' [Romans 3:10,12] It saith also, 'That every imagination of the heart of man is only evil, and that continually.' [Genesis 6:5] And again, 'The imagination of man's heart is evil from his youth.' [Genesis 8:12] Now then, when we think thus of ourselves, having sense thereof, then are our thoughts good ones, because according to the Word of God."

IGN. "I will never believe that my heart is thus bad."

CHR. "Therefore thou never hadst one good thought concerning thyself in thy life. But let me go on. As the Word passeth a judgement upon our heart, so it passeth a judgement upon our ways; and when our thoughts of our hearts and ways agree with the judgement which the Word giveth of both, then are both good, because agreeing thereto."

IGN. "Make out your meaning."

CHR. "Why, the Word of God saith that man's ways are crooked ways, not good, but perverse. It saith they are naturally out of the good way, that they have not known it. Now when a man thus thinketh of his ways, I say when he doth sensibly and with heart-humiliation thus think, then hath he good thoughts of his own ways, because his thoughts now agree with the judgement of the Word of God."

IGN. "What are good thoughts concerning God?"

CHR. "Even (as I have said concerning ourselves) when our thoughts of God do agree with what the Word saith of him. And that is, when we think of his being and attributes as the Word hath taught, of which I cannot now discourse at large. But to speak of him with reference to us, then we have right thoughts of God when we think that he knows us better than we know ourselves and can see sin in us when and where we can see none in ourselves; when we think he knows our inmost thoughts and that our heart, with all its depths, is always open unto his eyes. Also when we think that all our righteousness stinks in his nostrils, and that therefore he cannot abide to see us stand before him in any confidence, even of all our best performances."

IGN. "Do you think that I am such a fool as to think God can see no further than I? Or that I would come to God in the best of my performances?"

CHR. "Why, how dost thou think in this matter?"

IGN. "Why, to be short, I think I must believe in Christ for justification."

CHR. "How! Think thou must believe in Christ, when thou seest not thy need of him! Thou neither seest thy original nor actual infirmities, but hast such an opinion of thyself, and of what thou doest, as plainly renders thee to be one that did never see a necessity of Christ's personal righteousness to justify thee before God. How then dost thou say, 'I believe in Christ?' "

IGN. "I believe well enough for all that."

CHR. "How doest thou believe?"

IGN. "I believe that Christ died for sinners and that I shall be justified before God from the curse through His gracious acceptance of my obedience to his law. Or thus, Christ makes my duties that are religious acceptable to His Father by virtue of his merits; and so shall I be justified."

CHR. "Let me give an answer to this confession of thy faith.

"1. Thou believest with a fantastical faith, for this faith is nowhere described in the Word.

"2. Thou believest with a false faith, because it taketh justification from the personal righteousness of Christ and applies it to thy own.

"3. This faith maketh not Christ a justifier of thy person, but of thy actions, and of thy person for thy actions' sake, which is false.

"4. Therefore this faith is deceitful, even such as will leave thee under wrath in the day of God Almighty. For true justifying faith puts the soul (as sensible of its lost condition by the law) upon flying for refuge unto Christ's righteousness (which righteousness of his is not an act of grace by which he maketh for justification thy obedience accepted with God, but his personal obedience to the law in doing and suffering for us what that required at our hands). This righteousness, I say, true faith accepteth; under the skirt of which the soul being shrouded and by it presented as spotless before God, it is accepted and acquit from condemnation."

IGN. "What! Would you have us trust to what Christ in his own person has done without us? This conceit would loosen the reins of our lust, and tolerate us to live as we list. For what matter how we live if we may be justified by Christ's personal righteousness from all, when we believe it?"

CHR. "Ignorance is thy name, and as thy name is so art thou; even this thy answer demonstrateth what I say. Ignorant thou art of what justifying righteousness is and as ignorant how to secure thy soul through the faith of it from the heavy wrath of God. Yea, thou also art ignorant of the true effects of saving faith in this righteousness of Christ, which is to bow and win over the heart to God in Christ, to love his name, His word, ways and people, and not as thou ignorantly imaginest."

HOPE. "Ask him if ever he had Christ revealed to him from heaven?"

IGN. "What! You are a man for revelations! I believe that what both you, and all the rest of you, say about that matter is but the fruit of distracted brains."

HOPE. "Why, man! Christ is so hid in God from the natural apprehensions of all flesh that he cannot by any man be savingly known, unless God the Father reveals him to them."

IGN. "That is your faith, but not mine. Yet mine, I doubt not, is as good as yours, though I have not in my head so many whimsies as you."

CHR. "Give me leave to put in a word. You ought not so slightly to speak of this matter. For this I will boldly affirm (even as my good companion hath done) that no man can know Jesus Christ but by the revelation of the Father. Yea, and faith, too, by which the soul layeth hold upon Christ (if it be right), must be wrought by the exceeding greatness of his mighty power; the working of which faith, I perceive, poor Ignorance, thou art ignorant of. Be awakened then; see thine own wretchedness, and fly to the Lord Jesus; and by his righteousness, which is the righteousness of God (for he himself is God), thou shalt be delivered from condemnation."

IGN. "You go so fast, I cannot keep pace

with you. Do you go on before. I must stay awhile behind."

Then they said,

Well, Ignorance, wilt thou yet foolish be,
To slight good counsel ten times given thee?
And if thou yet refuse it, thou shalt know
Ere long the evil of thy doing so.
Remember, man, in time, stoop, do not fear,
Good counsel taken well saves; therefore
*   hear.*
But if thou yet shalt slight it, thou wilt be
The loser (Ignorance) I'll warrant thee.

Then Christian addressed thus himself to his fellow.

CHR. "Well, come, my good Hopeful. I perceive that thou and I must walk by ourselves again."

So I saw in my dream that they went on a pace before, and Ignorance he came hobbling after. Then said Christian to his companion, "It pities me much for this poor man; it will certainly go ill with him at last."

HOPE. "Alas, there are abundance in our town in his condition, whole families, yea, whole streets (and that of pilgrims, too). And if there be so many in our parts, how many, think you, must there be in the place where he was born?"

CHR. "Indeed the Word saith, 'He hath blinded their eyes, lest they should see, &c.' [John 12:40] But now we are by ourselves, what do you think of such men? Have they at no time, think you, convictions of sin, and so consequently fears that their state is dangerous?"

HOPE. "Nay, do you answer that question yourself, for you are the elder man."

CHR. "Then, I say, sometimes (as I think) they may, but they, being naturally ignorant, understand not that such convictions tend to their good; and therefore they do desperately seek to stifle them, and presumptuously continue to flatter themselves in the way of their own hearts."

HOPE. "I do believe as you say, that fear tends much to men's good, and to make them right at their beginning to go on pilgrimage."

CHR. "Without all doubt it doth, if it be right. For so says the Word, 'The fear of the Lord is the beginning of wisdom.' " [Psalms 111:10, Proverbs 9:10]

HOPE. "How will you describe right fear?"

CHR. "True, or right, fear is discovered by three things.

"1. By its rise. It is caused by saving convictions for sin.

"2. It driveth the soul to lay fast hold of Christ for salvation.

"3. It begetteth and continueth in the soul a great reverence of God, his word and ways, keeping it tender, and making it afraid to turn from them to the right hand or to the left to anything that may dishonour God, break its peace, grieve the Spirit, or cause the enemy to speak reproachfully."

HOPE. "Well said. I believe you have said the truth. Are we now almost got past the Enchanted Ground?"

CHR. "Why, are you weary of this discourse?"

HOPE. "No, verily, but that I would know where we are."

CHR. "We have not now above two miles further to go thereon. But let us return to our matter. Now the ignorant know not that such convictions that tend to put them in fear are for their good, and therefore they seek to stifle them."

HOPE. "How do they seek to stifle them?"

CHR. "1. They think that those fears are wrought by the Devil (though indeed they are wrought of God) and thinking so, they resist them, as things that directly tend to their overthrow. 2. They also think that these fears tend to the spoiling of their faith (when alas for them, poor men that they are, they have none at all), and therefore they harden their hearts against them. 3. They presume they ought not to fear, and therefore, in despite of them, wax presumptuously confident. 4. They see that these fears tend to take away from them their pitiful old self-holiness, and therefore they resist them with all their might."

HOPE. "I know something of this myself; for before I knew myself, it was so with me."

CHR. "Well, we will leave at this time our neighbour Ignorance by himself, and fall upon another profitable question."

HOPE. "With all my heart, but you shall still begin."

CHR. "Well then, did you not know about ten years ago, one Temporary in your parts, who was a forward man in religion then?"

HOPE. "Know him! Yes, he dwelt in Graceless, a town about two miles off of Honesty, and he dwelt next door to one Turnback.

CHR. "Right, he dwelt under the same roof with him. Well, that man was much awakened once; I believe that then he had some sight of his sins, and of the wages that was due thereto."

HOPE. "I am of your mind, for (my house not being above three miles from him) he would ofttimes come to me, and that with many tears. Truly I pitied the man and was not altogether without hope of him; but, one may see, it is not everyone that cries, 'Lord, Lord.'"

CHR. "He told me once that he was resolved to go on pilgrimage, as we do now; but all of a sudden he grew acquainted with one Save-self, and then he became a stranger to me."

HOPE. "Now since we are talking about him, let us a little inquire into the reason of the sudden back-sliding of him and such others."

CHR. "It may be very profitable, but do you begin."

HOPE. "Well then, there are in my judgement four reasons for it.

"1. Though the consciences of such men are awakened, yet their minds are not changed. Therefore when the power of guilt weareth away, that which provoked them to be religious ceaseth. Wherefore they naturally turn to their own course again; even as we see the dog that is sick of what he hath eaten, so long as his sickness prevails he vomits and casts up all; not that he doth this of a free mind (if we may say a dog has a mind) but because it troubleth his stomach; but now when his sickness is over, and so his stomach eased, his desires being not at all alienate from his vomit, he turns him about, and licks up all. And so it is true which is written, 'The dog is turned to his own vomit again.' [2 Peter 2:22] Thus, I say, being hot for Heaven, by virtue only of the sense and fear of the torments of Hell, as their sense of Hell and the fears of damnation chills and cools, so their desires for Heaven and salvation cool also. So then it comes to pass, that when their guilt and fear is gone, their desires for Heaven and happiness die; and they return to their course again.

"2ly. Another reason is they have slavish fears that do overmaster them. I speak now of the fears that they have of men, 'For the fear of men bringeth a snare.' [Proverbs 29:25] So then, though they seem to be hot for Heaven so long as the flames of Hell are about their ears, yet when that terror is a little over, they betake themselves to second thoughts; namely, that 'tis good to be wise, and not to run (for they know not what) the hazard of losing all, or at least, of bringing themselves into unavoidable and unnecessary troubles. And so they fall in with the world again.

"3ly. The shame that attends religion lies also as a block in their way; they are proud and haughty, and religion in their eye is low and contemptible. Therefore when they have lost their sense of Hell and wrath to come, they return again to their former course.

"4ly. Guilt and to meditate terror are grievous to them. They like not to see their misery before they come into it. Though perhaps the sight of it first, if they loved that sight, might make them fly whither the righteous fly and are safe. But because they do, as I hinted before, even shun the thoughts of guilt and terror, therefore, when once they are rid of their awakenings about the terrors and wrath of God, they harden their hearts gladly, and choose such ways as will harden them more and more."

CHR. "You are pretty near the business, for the bottom of all is for want of a change in their mind and will. And therefore they are but like the felon that standeth before the judge. He quakes and trembles and seems to repent most heartily; but the bottom of all is the fear of the halter, not of any detestation of the offence; as is evident, because, let but this man have his liberty, and he will be a thief, and so a rogue still; whereas, if his mind was changed, he would be otherwise."

HOPE. "Now I have showed you the reasons of their going back, do you show me the manner thereof."

CHR. "So I will willingly.

"1. They draw off their thoughts all that they may from the remembrance of God, death, and judgement to come.

"2. Then they cast off by degrees private duties, as closet-prayer, curbing their lusts, watching, sorrow for sin, and the like.

"3. Then they shun the company of lively and warm Christians.

"4. After that, they grow cold to public duty, as hearing, reading, godly conference, and the like.

"5. Then they begin to pick holes, as we say, in the coats of some of the godly, and that devilishly that they may have a seeming colour to throw religion (for the sake of some infirmity they have spied in them) behind their backs.

"6. Then they begin to adhere to and associate themselves with carnal, loose, and wanton men.

"7. Then they give way to carnal and wanton discourses in secret, and glad are they if they can see such things in any that are counted honest, that they may the more boldly do it through their example.

"8. After this, they begin to play with little sins openly.

"9. And then, being hardened, they show themselves as they are. Thus being launched again into the gulf of misery, unless a miracle of grace prevent it, they everlastingly perish in their own deceivings."

Now I saw in my dream that by this time the pilgrims were got over the Enchanted Ground, and entering into the country of Beulah, whose air was very sweet and pleasant. The way lying directly through it, they solaced themselves there for a season. Yet, here they heard continually the singing of birds, and saw every day the flowers appear in the earth, and heard the voice of the turtle in the land. In this country the sun shineth night and day; wherefore this was beyond the Valley of the Shadow of Death, and also out of the reach of Giant Despair; neither could they from this place so much as see Doubting Castle. Here they were within sight of the city they were going to. Also here met them some of the inhabitants thereof. For in this land the Shining Ones commonly walked, because it was upon the borders of heaven. In this land also the contract between the bride and the bridegroom was renewed. Yea, here, "as the bridegroom rejoiceth over the bride, so did their god rejoice over them." [Isaiah 62:5] Here they had no want of corn and wine; for in this place they met with abundance of what they had sought for in all their pilgrimage. Here they heard voices from out of the city, loud voices, saying, "Say ye to the daughter of Zion, behold thy salvation cometh; behold his reward is with him." [Isaiah 62:11] Here all the inhabitants of the country called them, "The holy people, the redeemed of the Lord, sought out, &c." [Isaiah 62:12]

Now as they walked in this land they had more rejoicing than in parts more remote from the kingdom to which they were bound; and drawing near to the city, they had yet a more perfect view thereof. It was builded of pearls and precious stones. Also the street thereof was paved with gold, so that by reason of the natural glory of the city and the reflection of the sunbeams upon it, Christian with desire fell sick. Hopeful also had a fit or two of the same disease. Wherefore here they lay by it awhile, crying out because of their pangs, "If you see my beloved, tell him that I am sick of love." [Song of Solomon 5–8]

But being a little strengthened and better able to bear their sickness, they walked on their way, and came yet nearer and nearer where were orchards, vineyards, and gardens, and their gates opened into the highway. Now as they came up to these places, behold the gardener stood in the way, to whom the pilgrims said, "Whose goodly vineyards and gardens are these?" He answered, "They are the King's, and are planted here for his own delights and also for the solace of pilgrims." So the gardener had them into the vineyards, and bid them refresh themselves with the dainties. He also showed them there the King's walks and the arbours where he delighted to be. And here they tarried and slept.

Now I beheld in my dream that they talked more in their sleep at this time than ever they did in all their journey; and being in a muse thereabout, the gardener said even to me, "Wherefore musest thou at the matter? It is the nature of the fruit of the grapes of these vineyards to go down so sweetly, as to 'cause the lips of them that are asleep to speak.' " [Song of Solomon 1:9]

So I saw that when they awoke, they addressed themselves to go up to the city. But, as I said, the reflections of the sun upon the city (for 'the city was pure gold') [Revelation 21:18] was so extremely glorious, that they could not, as yet, with open face behold it but through an instrument made for that purpose. So I saw that as they went on, there met them two men in raiment that shone like gold, also their faces shone as the light.

These men asked the pilgrims whence they came, and they told them. They also asked them where they had lodged, what difficulties and dangers, what comforts and pleasures they had met in the way, and they told them. Then said the men that met them, "you have but two difficulties more to meet with, and then you are in the city."

Christian then and his companion asked the men to go along with them. So they told them they would. "But," said they, "you must obtain it by your own faith." So I saw in my dream that they went on together till they came within sight of the gate.

Now I further saw that betwixt them and the gate was a river, but there was no bridge to go over. The river was very deep; at the sight therefore of this river, the pilgrims were much astounded, but the men that went with them said, "You must go through, or you cannot come at the gate."

The pilgrims then began to inquire if there was no other way to the gate. To which they answered, "Yes, but there hath not any, save two, to wit, Enoch and Elijah, been permitted to tread that path since the foundation of the world, nor shall until the last trumpet shall sound." The pilgrims then, especially Christian, began to despond in his mind, and looked this way and that, but no way could be found by them by which they might escape the river. Then they asked the men if the waters were all of a depth. They said no, yet they could not help them in that case; for, said they, "You shall find it deeper or shallower, as you believe in the King of the place."

They then addressed themselves to the water; and entering, Christian began to sink, and crying out to his good friend Hopeful, he said, "I sink in deep waters, the billows go over my head, all his waves go over me, Selah."

Then said the other, "Be of good cheer, my brother. I feel the bottom, and it is good." Then said Christian, "Ah, my friend, the sorrows of death have compassed me about. I shall not see the land that flows with milk and honey." And with that, a great darkness and horror fell upon Christian, so that he could not see before him; also here he in great measure lost his senses, so that he could neither remember nor orderly talk of any of those sweet refreshments that he had met with in the way of his pilgrimage. But all the words that he spake still tended to discover that he had horror of mind and hearty fears that he should die in that river, and never obtain entrance in at the gate. Here also, as they that stood by perceived, he was much in the troublesome thoughts of the sins that he had committed, both since and before he began to be a pilgrim. 'Twas also observed that he was troubled with apparitions of hobgoblins and evil spirits. For ever and anon he would intimate so much by words. Hopeful therefore here had much ado to keep his brother's head above water. Yea, sometimes he would be quite gone down, and then ere a while he would rise up again half dead. Hopeful also would endeavour to comfort him, saying, "Brother, I see the gate, and men standing by it to receive us." But Christian would answer. " 'Tis you, 'tis you they wait for. You have been Hopeful ever since I knew you." "And so have you," said he to Christian. "Ah, brother," said he, "surely if I was right, he would now arise to help me; but for my sins he hath brought me into the snare, and hath left me." Then said Hopeful, "My brother, you have quite forgot the text, where it's said of the wicked, "There is no band in their death, but their strength is firm, they are not troubled as other men, neither are they plagued like other men." [Psalms 73:4–5] These troubles and distresses that you go through in these waters are no sign that God hath forsaken you, but are sent to try you, whether you will call to mind that which heretofore you have received of His goodness, and live upon Him in your distresses."

Then I saw in my dream that Christian was as in a muse a while; to whom also Hopeful added this word, "Be of good cheer. Jesus Christ maketh thee whole." And with that, Christian brake out with a loud voice, "Oh, I see him again! And he tells me, 'When thou passest through the waters, I will be with thee, and through the rivers, they shall not overflow thee.' " [Isaiah 43:2] Then they both took courage, and the enemy was after that as still as a stone, until they were gone over. Christian therefore presently found ground to stand upon; and so it followed that the rest of the river was but shallow. Thus they got over. Now upon the bank of the river, on the other side, they saw the two Shining Men again, who there waited for them. Wherefore being come up out of the river, they saluted them, saying, "We are ministering spirits, sent forth to minister for those that shall be heirs of salvation." Thus they went along towards the gate. Now you must note that the city stood upon a mighty hill, but the pilgrims went up that hill with ease, because they had these two men to lead them up by the arms. Also they had left their mortal garments behind them in the river, for though they went in with them, they came out without them. They therefore went up here with much agility and speed, though the foundation upon which the city was framed was higher than the clouds. They therefore went up through the regions of the air, sweetly talking as they went, being comforted because they safely got over the river and had such glorious companions to attend them.

The talk that they had with the Shining Ones was about the glory of the place, who told them that the beauty and glory of it was inexpressible. "There," said they, "is the Mount Zion, the heavenly Jerusalem, the innumerable company of angels, and the spirits of just men made perfect. You are going now," said they, "to the paradise of God, wherein you shall see the tree of life, and eat of the never-fading fruits thereof. And when you come there, you

shall have white robes given you, and your walk and talk shall be every day with the King, even all the days of eternity. There you shall not see again such things as you saw when you were in the lower region upon the earth, to wit, sorrow, sickness, affliction, and death, 'for the former things are passed away.' [Revelation 21:4] You are going now to Abraham, to Isaac, and Jacob, and to the prophets, men that God hath taken away from the evil to come and that are now resting upon their beds, each one walking in his righteousness." The men then asked, "What must we do in the holy place?" To whom it was answered, "You must there receive the comfort of all your toil, and have joy for all your sorrow; you must reap what you have sown, even the fruit of all your prayers and tears and sufferings for the King by the way. In that place you must wear crowns of gold, and enjoy the perpetual sight and visions of the Holy One, 'for there you shall see him as he is.' [I John 3:2] There also you shall serve him continually with praise, with shouting and thanksgiving, whom you desired to serve in the world, though with much difficulty because of the infirmity of your flesh. There your eyes shall be delighted with seeing, and your ears with hearing, the pleasant voice of the Mighty One. There you shall enjoy your friends again that are got thither before you; and there you shall with joy receive even everyone that follows into the holy place after you. There also you shall be clothed

with glory and majesty, and put into an equipage fit to ride out with the King of Glory. When he shall come with sound of trumpet in the clouds, as upon the wings of the wind, you shall come with him; and when he shall sit upon the throne of judgement, you shall sit by him. Yea, and when he shall pass sentence upon all the workers of iniquity, let them be angels or men, you also shall have a voice in that judgement, because they were his and your enemies. Also when he shall again return to the city, you shall go, too, with sound of trumpet, and be ever with him."

Now while they were thus drawing towards the gate, behold a company of the heavenly host came out to meet them. To whom it was said, by the other two Shining Ones, "These are the men that have loved our Lord when they were in the world and that have left all for his holy name, and he hath sent us to fetch them, and we have brought them thus far on their desired journey that they may go in and look their Redeemer in the face with joy." Then the heavenly host gave a great shout, saying, "Blessed are they that are called to the marriage supper of the Lamb." [Revelation 19:9]

There came out also at this time to meet them several of the King's trumpeters, clothed in white and shining raiment, who with melodious noises and loud made even the heavens to echo with their sound. These trumpeters saluted Christian and his fellow with ten thousand welcomes from the world. And this they did with shouting and sound of trumpet.

This done, they compassed them round on every side; some went before, some behind, and some on the right hand, some on the left (as 'twere to guard them through the upper regions), continually sounding as they went, with melodious noise, in notes on high; so that the very sight was to them that could behold it as if Heaven itself was come down to meet them. Thus therefore they walked on together, and as they walked, ever and anon, these trumpeters even, with joyful sound, would, by mixing their music with looks and gestures, still signify to Christian and his brother how welcome they were into their company, and with what gladness they came to meet them. And now were these two men, as 'twere, in heaven, before they came at it, being swallowed up with the sight of angels and with hearing of their melodious notes. Here also they had the city itself in view, and they thought they heard all the bells therein to ring, to welcome them thereto. But above all, the warm and joyful thoughts that they had about their own dwelling there, with such company, and that forever and ever. Oh! By what tongue or pen can their glorious joy be expressed. And thus they came up to the gate.

Now when they were come up to the gate, there was written over it, in letters of gold, "Blessed are they that do his commandments, that they may have right to the Tree of Life; and may enter in through the gates into the city." [Revelation 22:14]

Then I saw in my dream that the shining men bid them call at the gate, the which when they did. Some from above looked over the gate, to wit, Enoch, Moses, and Elijah, &c. to whom it was said, "These pilgrims are come from the City of Destruction, for the love that they bear to the King of this place." And then the pilgrims gave in unto them each man his certificate, which they had received in the beginning; those therefore were carried into the King, who when he had read them, said, "Where are the men?" To whom it was answered, "They are standing without the gate." The King then commanded to open the gate. "That the righteous nation," said he, "that keepeth truth may enter in." [Isaiah 26:2]

Now I saw in my dream that these two men went in at the gate; and lo, as they entered, they were transfigured, and they had raiment put on that shone like gold. There was also that met them with harps and crowns and gave them to them, the harp to praise withal and the crowns in token of honour. Then I heard in my dream that all the bells in the city rang again for joy, and that it was said unto them, "Enter ye into the joy of our Lord." [Matthew 25:21] I also heard the men themselves that they sang with a loud voice, saying, "Blessing, honour, glory, and power, be to Him that sitteth upon the throne, and to the Lamb forever and ever." [Revelation 5:13]

Now just as the gates were opened to let in the men, I looked in after them; and behold, the city shone like the sun, the streets also were paved with gold, and in them walked many men, with crowns on their heads, palms in their hands, and golden harps to sing praises withal.

There were also of them that had wings, and they answered one another without intermission, saying, "Holy, Holy, Holy, is the Lord." And after that, they shut up the gates. Which when I had seen, I wished myself among them.

Now while I was gazing upon all these things, I turned my head to look back, and saw Ignorance come up to the riverside. But he soon got over, and that without half that difficulty which the other two men met with. For it happened that there was then in that place one Vain-hope, a ferryman, that with his boat helped him over. So he, as the other I saw, did ascend the hill to come up to the gate, only he came alone; neither did any man meet him with the least encouragement. When he was come up to the gate, he looked up to the writing that was above; and then began to knock, supposing that entrance should have been quickly administered to him. But he was asked by the men that looked over the top of the gate, "Whence came you and what would you have?" He answered, "I have eat and drank in the presence of the King, and he has taught in our streets." Then they asked him for his certificate, that they might go in and show it to the King. So he fumbled in his bosom for one, and found none. Then said they, "Have you none?" But the man answered never a word. So they told the King, but he would not come down to see him, but commanded the two Shining Ones that conducted Christian and Hopeful to the city to go out and take Ignorance and bind him hand and foot, and have him away. Then they took him up and carried him through the air to the door that I saw in the side of the hill, and put him in there. Then I saw that there was a way to hell, even from the gates of heaven, as well as from the City of Destruction. So I awoke, and behold it was a dream.

The Conclusion

Now, reader, I have told my dream to thee;
See if thou canst interpret it to me,
Or to thyself, or neighbour. But take heed
Of misinterpreting; for that, instead
Of doing good, will but thyself abuse.
By misinterpreting evil issues.
    Take heed, also, that thou be not extreme,
In playing with the outside of my dream.
Nor let my figure, or similitude,
Put thee into a laughter or a feud;
Leave this for boys and fools; but as for thee,
Do thou the substance of my matter see.
    Put by the curtains; look within my veil;
Turn up my metaphors and do not fail.
There, if thou seekest them, such things to find,
As will be helpful to an honest mind.
What of my dross thou findest there, be bold
To throw away, but yet preserve the gold.
What if my gold be wrapped up in ore?
None throws away the apple for the core.
But if thou shalt cast all away as vain,
I know not but 'twill make me dream again.

PICTURE CREDITS

THE
GREAT IDEAS
Volumes 1 and 2